Part IV   Issues in Social Policy   **285**

Part V   Resources   385

Part VI   Careers in Social Policy   451

Contributors

Waqar Ahmad was Professor and Director, Centre for Research in Primary Care, University of Leeds. He has also worked at Bradford and York Universities. He has served as a member of numerous research commissioning panels and is currently member of the Economic and Social Research Council (ESRC)'s Research Priorities Board. He left academia in 2001 to join the civil service.

Pete Alcock is Professor of Social Policy and Social Administration and Head of the Department of Social Policy and Social Work at the University of Birmingham. His research interests include poverty and social exclusion, and the voluntary sector. He is the author or editor of a number of leading Social Policy texts as well as a range of other publications and is Chair of the Editorial Board of the *Journal of Social Policy*.

Judith Allsop is Professor of Health Policy at De Montfort University and co-director of the Health Policy Research Unit. Her research has included studies of complaints in health care settings, the medical profession and, most recently, health consumer groups and the national policy process and doctors in Russia. She has written extensively on health policy as well as these topics and has acted as an adviser to government.

Melanie Ashford is a Learning and Teaching Adviser for the Learning and Teaching Support Network subject centre for Social Policy and Social Work (SWAFltsn). Her background is in developing flexible learning materials and information management. Her interests include effective use of technology for learning, work-based learning, networking and online tutoring.

John Baldock is Professor of Social Policy at the University of Kent at Canterbury, where he teaches modules on the personal social services and on other aspects of health and social care. He has published widely on social care issues and has carried out research into the provision of care to older people in the United Kingdom and in other parts of the European Union. He is editor of the journal *Social Policy and Administration.*

Fran Bennett is a former director of the Child Poverty Action Group. She is currently working part-time as a research officer and departmental lecturer in the Department of Social Policy and Social Work, University of Oxford; and part-time as a self-employed policy analyst and researcher, working on social policy issues, in particular social security and poverty. With Ken Jones, she is also editor of the Digest in the *Journal of Social Policy.*

Catherine Bochel is a Senior Lecturer in Social Policy at the University of Lincoln, where she teaches a wide range of policy-related courses. Her main research interests are in policy-making processes, local government and gender divisions. She has written extensively on these areas.

Jonathan Bradshaw is Professor of Social Policy at the University of York. His main research interests are in poverty and living standards, family policy, social security policy and comparative social policy. His most recent research has been a comparative study of child benefits and a review of the state of children in the UK.

Edward Brunsdon is a Principal Lecturer in Social Policy at the London Metropolitan University, where he teaches on a wide range of welfare management courses. His main research interests are in commercial and occupational welfare, welfare management and comparative social policy. He has published widely in these areas.

Michael Cahill is Reader in Social Policy at the University of Brighton. He has written about new approaches to the study of Social Policy, and on the environment and social policy.

John Clarke is Professor of Social Policy at the Open University. He has a long-standing interest in the political and ideological conflicts around welfare and the state both in Britain and internationally. He has been studying the conditions and consequences of managerialism in social welfare. He is currently looking at ways in which welfare states are, and are not, being transformed in the context of globalization.

Allan Cochrane is Professor of Public Policy at the Open University where he contributes to a wide range of teaching, particularly in urban and regional policy and the local welfare state. His current research interests include issues of urban policy, local government restructuring and new managerialism, focusing particularly on comparative social policy and the impact of globalization. He has written extensively on these areas and urban/social policy more generally.

Bob Coles is a Senior Lecturer in Social Policy at the University at York and teaches courses on children and young people's issues including an undergraduate course, Applied Social Sciences: Children and Young People. He has written widely on youth policy issues and is research adviser to the Joseph Rowntree Foundation on their research programme on young people.

Dee Cook is Professor of Social Policy and Director of the Regional Research Institute at the University of Wolverhampton. She has researched and published widely on issues centring around the relationships between poverty, crime and punishment, social security fraud, community safety and social inclusion strategies.

Gary Craig is Professor of Social Justice at the University of Hull and President of the International Association for Community Development. He researches in the fields of 'race' and ethnicity, poverty and inequality, community development and empowerment, children and young people, and local governance.

Miriam David is Director of the Graduate School of Social Sciences and Professor of Policy Studies in Education at Keele University. Her research interests include the family, education and social policy. Formerly she was at South Bank University where she was Head of Research for the University.

Alan Deacon is Professor of Social Policy and a member of the ESRC Research Group on Care, Values and the Future of Welfare at the University of Leeds. He has written widely on the welfare reform debates in Britain and the US. He is currently Chair of the Social Policy Association (2001–4).

Bob Deacon is Professor of Social Policy at the University of Sheffield and Director of the Anglo-Finnish Globalism and Social Policy Programme. He researches and writes extensively on supranational social policy issues, global social governance and the role of international organizations. He is currently also acting as a consultant to a number of intergovernmental organizations on the social dimension of globalization and has advised governments on the future of their welfare policies.

Nicholas Deakin is a Visiting Professor at the London School of Economics and previously Professor of Social Policy and Administration at Birmingham University where he taught on a wide range of social policy courses. His research interests include inner city issues, new towns, race relations and voluntary organizations. He has written extensively on these areas and, in 1996, chaired the NCVO's Commission on the Future of the Voluntary Sector.

Hartley Dean lectures at the London School of Economics. Before his academic career he was a welfare rights worker. He has published widely and undertaken a variety of research, including studies of: social security appeals and community-care complaints procedures; the alleged 'dependency culture' and attitudes to dependency; begging; social security benefit fraud; popular discourses of welfare/citizenship and rights/responsibilities; the survival strategies of low-income families; the labour market experiences of people with multiple problems and needs.

Angus Erskine is a Senior Lecturer in Social Policy at the University of Stirling. His research interests are in the fields of social security, poverty and social policies in rural areas. He was Chair of the editorial boards of the *Journal of Social Policy* and *Social Policy and Society* and is currently review editor for the *Journal of Social Policy*.

Tony Fitzpatrick is Senior Lecturer in the School of Sociology and Social Policy at the University of Nottingham. He has published several books and articles dealing with the relevance to social policy of environmentalism, new technologies, the new social democracy and other contemporary social and political theories.

Norman Ginsburg is Professor of Social Policy at the London Metropolitan University. His teaching and research interests include the impact of social policy on class, race and gender divisions, with particular emphasis on housing, social security and family policies and on cross-national analysis of welfare regimes. He has published on capitalism and social policy and comparative welfare.

David Gladstone is Senior Lecturer and Director of Undergraduate Programmes in the School for Policy Studies at the University of Bristol. He is an historian by training, and his teaching and research interests are in aspects of – and the inter-relationship between – British social policy past and present. He has authored and edited several books and is the editor of the *Introducing Social Policy* series for Open University Press.

Howard Glennerster is Professor Emeritus at the London School of Economics where he was previously Professor of Social Administration and contributed to a wide variety of social policy courses. His research has covered most aspects of welfare finance, health service reforms, the finance of education and the history of social policy. He has published extensively in these areas as well as advising governments both in the UK and abroad on social policy.

Ian Gough is Professor of Social Policy at the University of Bath. He has written on the political economy of the welfare state, competition between welfare states and theories of human need. His current research is on well-being and welfare regimes in developing countries. He also edits the *Journal of European Social Policy*.

David G. Green is the Director of Civitas – the Institute for the Study of Civil Society. Previously he was Director of the Health and Welfare Unit of the Institute of Economic Affairs. He has been a Research Fellow at the Australian National University and served as a Labour councillor in Newcastle upon Tyne. He has written books about mutual aid, civil society, the development of the new right and the reform of health care and social security.

Linda Hantrais holds a Chair in the Department of European Studies at Loughborough University and is Director of its European Research Centre. Her main research interests are in cross-national comparative research theory, methodology and practice, with particular reference to socio-economic change, social and family policy in Europe. She has published widely in these areas.

Malcolm Hill is Director of the Centre for the Child and Society at the University of Glasgow. For the last 20 years he has been carrying out research and teaching social work and social policy students at the Universities of Edinburgh and Glasgow. Before that he worked as a social worker in London. His main research interests include children who are adopted or looked after, children's participation and services for children and families.

Michael Hill is Emeritus Professor of Social Policy at the University of Newcastle upon Tyne and a visiting professor at the University of Brighton. He is joint editor of the *Journal of Social Policy* until the end of 2003. He has held academic posts at Reading, Bristol and Oxford and before holding these was a civil servant in social security administration. He was a local councillor in Reading (1966-9) and a member of the Council on Tribunals (1991–7). He has written a number of books on social policy and on the policy-making process.

John Hills is Professor of Social Policy and Director of the ESRC Research Centre for Analysis of Social Exclusion (CASE) at the London School of Economics. His research interests cover issues connected with income distribution and the welfare state, particularly social security, housing and taxation, and he has published extensively in these areas. He was previously Co-director of the LSE's Welfare State Programme and was also Programme Advisor on Income and Wealth to the Joseph Rowntree Foundation and Secretary of its Inquiry Group.

Norman Johnson is Emeritus Professor of Social Policy at the University of Portsmouth, where he taught on a wide range of social policy courses. His main research interests are comparative social policy and mixed economies of welfare. He has published widely in these areas and on social policy more generally. His most recent book was a comparative study of mixed economies of welfare.

Hilary Land is Professor of Family Policy and Child Welfare in the School for Policy Studies at the University of Bristol. Her teaching and research interests include analyses of the relationship between families and the state, particularly from feminist perspectives, the development of social security policies and employment policies in both comparative and historical contexts. Current research includes policies towards lone parents since 1945 and transitions from childhood to adulthood and 'independence'.

Gail Lewis is Senior Lecturer in Social Policy at the Open University. Her research interests focus on the intersection of gender, ethnicity and racialization in social policy and welfare practices.

Jane Lewis is Barnett Professor of Social Policy at the University of Oxford. She is the author of numerous books and articles on gender, family change and family policies, and recently has written on lone motherhood and individualism and intimate relations.

Ruth Lister is Professor of Social Policy at Loughborough University where she teaches on a wide range of social policy courses. Her main research interests are poverty and income maintenance, citizenship, women and social policy and feminist perspectives. She has published widely in these areas and on social policy more generally. She was a member of the Commission on Poverty, Participation and Power and the earlier Commission on Social Justice.

Stephen McKay is a Senior Research Fellow at the Personal Finance Research Centre, University of Bristol. He has conducted research on new tax credits for families with children, and on the links between economic change and family change.

Deborah Mabbett lectures on social policy and political economy at Brunel University. Her research includes the comparative analysis of social policies in the member states of the European Union, along with studies of the development of social policy at the Union level. She has also worked for the World Bank on problems of the economic transition in the former Soviet Union, and has written on the USA, Sweden, Australia and New Zealand.

Tony Maltby is Senior Lecturer in Social Policy at the University of Birmingham. He is Managing Editor of *Social Policy and Society*. He was Honorary Treasurer of the British Society of Gerontology from 1996 to 2002. He has published widely on comparative issues in pensions policy, and ageing and work and is currently completing work with Lorna Warren on a project for the ESRC Growing Older Programme.

Nick Manning is Professor of Social Policy and Sociology, and Director of the Centre for Research in Medical Sociology and Health Policy at the University of Nottingham. His recent research interests include unemployment, poverty, ethnicity and protest in Russia and Eastern Europe, and medical sociology and mental health policy. He has written books on health care, social problems and comparative social policy.

Margaret May is a Principal Lecturer in Social Policy at the London Metropolitan University, where she teaches on a wide range of welfare management courses. Her main research interests are in commercial and occupational welfare, welfare management and comparative social policy. She has published widely in these areas.

Jane Millar is Professor of Social Policy and Director of the Centre for the Analysis of Social Policy at the University of Bath. Her research interests include family policy and the policy implications of family change; income support and labour market policies for unemployed people and lone parents; poverty, inequality and social exclusion; gender and social policy; and comparative social policy. She has recently completed a study comparing employment policies for lone mothers in six countries and a literature review for the Department of Work and Pensions on family poverty and employment.

Alan Murie is Professor of Urban and Regional Studies at the Centre for Urban and Regional Studies at the University of Birmingham. He has been a leading contributor to housing research and policy debates for over twenty years. He was the founder editor of the journal *Housing Studies* and has published widely on housing and related issues.

Janet Newman is Professor of Social Policy at the Open University. She has written widely on the processes of public sector reform and state restructuring, and on gender and organizations. Current research interests include a study of public participation in decision-making and its implications for democratic practice; research into the narratives of leaders and managers involved in the modernization of public services; and into ways in which notions of equality and diversity are incorporated into organizational practice.

Mike Oliver is Professor of Disability Studies at the University of Greenwich and Chair of the Research Sub-Committee of the British Council of Organizations of Disabled People. He is an executive editor of the international journal *Disability and Society* and a recent member of the Social Research Advisory Panel of the National Lottery Charities Board. He remains an active member of the disability movement.

Robert M. Page is Reader in Democratic Socialism and Social Policy at the University of Birmingham. He is the author of books on stigma and altruism and the welfare state, and has been the joint-editor of a number of other texts.

Richard Parry is Senior Lecturer in Social Policy at the University of Edinburgh, where he teaches on Scottish and European social policy and on public policy and management. His recent research projects have been on the role of the Treasury in social policy and on the impact of devolution on the civil service throughout the United Kingdom.

Robert Pinker is Emeritus Professor of Social Administration at the LSE and is a member of the Press Complaints Commission. His teaching and research interests lie in the fields of social welfare theory, military welfare and self-regulatory institutions. He has written on social theory and social policy and the role of social work in an enterprise society.

Martin Powell is Senior Lecturer in Social Policy in the Department of Social and Policy Sciences, University of Bath. His main research interests and publications are in the areas of historical and geographical aspects of social policy, health policy and the new social democracy.

Carol Propper is Professor of Economics of Public Policy at the University of Bristol, where she is Director of the Leverhulme Centre for Markets and Public Organization. She is also a Co-Director of CASE at the LSE, and a Fellow of CEPR. Her research interests include the economics of health care markets, equity in health care, poverty dynamics and the impact of childhood events on adult outcomes. She has written on the economics of social problems and on economics and social policy.

Karen Rowlingson is a Lecturer in Social Research at the University of Bath. She conducts research on social security policy; the financial circumstances of individuals, families and households; and changing family forms.

Duncan Scott is a Research Fellow in the Centre for Applied Social Research at the University of Manchester. His research interests are in the 'third sector' and social policy, social development in transitional societies and qualitative research.

Michael Sullivan is Professor of Social Policy and Director of the National Centre for Public Policy at University of Wales Swansea. His research and teaching interests include the history and politics of social policy and the effect of political devolution on policy development in the UK. He publishes widely in these areas.

Rob Sykes is Principal Lecturer in Social Policy in the School of Social Science and Law at Sheffield Hallam University where he teaches courses in comparative social policy, EU social policy in a global context, comparative social structures, and understanding the city. His research interests are in EU social policy developments and the links between economic and social policy in a global context.

Peter Taylor-Gooby is Professor of Social Policy at the University of Kent and Director of the EU research project on Welfare Reform and the Management of Societal Change. He recently directed the ESRC Programme on Economic Beliefs and Behaviour. His teaching and research interests lie in Social Policy in EU member nations, public opinion and the development of more humane welfare systems. He has written on social change and social welfare, markets and managers, European welfare and the dependency culture.

Clare Ungerson is Professor of Social Policy at the University of Southampton. She has undertaken research on informal care for many years and is now engaged in a cross-national research project looking at the way in which previously unpaid care work is becoming more and more like paid work.

Fran Wasoff is a Reader in Social Policy in the School of Social and Political Studies and Co-Director of the Centre for Research on Families and Relationships at the University of Edinburgh. Her research interests are in the areas of family policy, gender and social policy, family law and social policy and socio-legal studies. She teaches research methods, gender and social policy, and family research and family policy.

Alan Walker is Professor of Social Policy at the University of Sheffield. His research and teaching interests span a wide field in sociology, social policy and social gerontology. He has researched and published extensively on community care, the family care of older people, intergenerational relations, poverty and social exclusion, ageing and the labour market, social planning, disability and European social policy. He is currently Director of the ESRC Growing Older Programme and of the UK National Collaboration on Ageing Research and is Chair of the European Foundation on Social Quality.

Fiona Williams is Professor of Social Policy and Director of the ESRC Research Group for the Study of Care, Values and the Future of Welfare at the University of Leeds. Her current research interests are on the ethics and practices of 'care' and the implications of this for future welfare states. She also teaches and researches in gender, 'race' ethnicity and migration in welfare regimes, and social theory, social change and social policy.

Pat Young is a senior lecturer in Social Policy at the University of the West of England, and a Learning Teaching Advisor in the Learning and Teaching Support Network subject centre for Social Policy and Social Work (SWAPltsn). She has taught Social Policy in further and higher education for many years and is the author of a number of introductory textbooks.

Preface

Social policy has become an increasingly popular subject in recent years. In part this probably reflects the normal growth of what only began to be taught in higher education in the UK as an independent subject in the 1950s and 1960s. But it is also the result of the much increased visibility of the subject as the present and future of the welfare state, its core topic for teaching and research, has become a constant issue of national debate.

The Social Policy Association (SPA) was established over thirty years ago to bring together teachers, researchers, practitioners and students to support the development of the study of social policy and administration. Its object is to encourage teaching, research and scholarship in this broad-based and multi-disciplinary subject, and its contributions include establishing the *Journal of Social Policy* and publishing *Social Policy and Society*. As student resources have become increasingly stretched and the cost of publications greater, the Association has become particularly aware of the need for an up-to date, authoritative and concise handbook which could be made available at a reasonable cost.

The *Student's Companion* is based upon a close, as well as formal, collaboration between the SPA and Blackwell. The Association took the initiative in the production of the book and appointed the editors to act on its behalf to bring it to fruition. The contributors to the volume are members of the SPA and comprise leading academics and researchers in the subject throughout the UK. Their work provides a comprehensive and stimulating insight into the range of ideas and issues in social policy which students will encounter in their studies.

The Social Policy Association is pleased to join with Blackwell in presenting this second edition of the *Student's Companion to Social Policy* and is confident that it will meet the needs and expectations of all those who use it. The whole volume is designed as a handbook and guide to the subject of social policy. We shall be particularly glad to hear from you, its readers, on the use that you have been able to make of it.

Adrian Sinfield
Former President, Social Policy Association

Acknowledgements

The authors and publishers gratefully acknowledge the following for permission to reproduce copyright material:

John Hills for figures II.15.1 and II.15.2;
Manchester University Settlement for figure V.2.2;

Every effort has been made to obtain permission from all copyright holders. The publishers would be grateful for notification of any corrections that should be incorporated in the next edition or reprint of the book.

The publishers apologize for any errors or omissions in the above list and would be grateful to be notified of any corrections that should be incorporated in the next edition or reprint of this book.

The editors would also like to thank Janey Fisher for assisting in compiling the final manuscript and also Sarah Falkus, our Commissioning Editor at Blackwell for her help.

Introduction

This *Students' Companion to Social Policy* is a resource book that will be of practical use to students of Social Policy throughout their undergraduate study. It aims to acquaint students with the study of Social Policy by covering some of the main themes and issues explored in it at undergraduate level in the UK. Readers are introduced to current theoretical and ideological debates, service areas and key social issues and are provided with practical guidance to study and career development. Each chapter includes a short guide to further reading which points to some of the literature that pursues the issues addressed in the chapter in more depth. The *Companion* should be of value to students studying Social Policy on its own, as part of another undergraduate programme (for instance, Sociology, Politics or Applied Social Science) or as part of a professional course in a related field (for instance, Social Work, Nursing and Health Studies, Management or Criminology).

This second edition of the *Companion* has been much expanded and updated from the first. New chapters have been added to take account of new developments in academic debate and policy development; and all existing authors have updated their original contributions. In a very few cases authors from the first edition were not able to provide us with an updated chapter, and in these cases new contributors have been recruited to update the chapters.

All the contributors to this book, both those involved in the first edition and the new contributors included here, are scholars and teachers in the forefront of Social Policy studies in the UK, and were selected on the basis that their expertise in their particular areas would provide readers with an authoritative introduction to a range of thinking and scholarship. Because the book has been prepared as a handbook and guide, rather than as a single text which focuses on one or two main themes, not all readers may want to read it from cover to cover. Indeed most readers are likely to use it as a source of reference for consultation; and so the chapters have been written so that they can be read in any order, separately or in groups.

Since the first edition of the *Companion* was produced the editors have also worked with Blackwell in the production of *The Blackwell Dictionary of Social Policy*. This provides a sister volume to the *Companion*, offering short definitions of all key terms and concepts and longer discussion of major items. We hope that readers will be able to use the two together; and partly for this reason we have excluded from this revised edition the Glossary that appeared in the first edition of this book.

Part I introduces students to the scope and structure of the subject of Social Policy – and its (inter)relationship with other disciplines. These include a brief history of the development of the subject and the ways in which it is studied, together with specific treatment of the importance of time (historical study) and place (comparative dimensions).

Part II provides readers with a guide to the theoretical and ideological context. Key concepts are addressed and explained, and students are introduced to the central themes which provide the intellectual foundations to debates about the focus and aims of the subject. This section then situates the debates about policy development within the changing economic, demographic, international and political structures in which policies are developed and implemented.

Part III focuses on the provision and delivery of social policies. The different providers of welfare are examined by looking at the four main sectors of welfare, setting these in the context of a brief examination of the ways in which welfare is produced and the split between providers, purchasers and consumers. The different geographical organization of welfare within the UK is explained, as well as the role of the supranational agencies, including in particular the European Union. The delivery of welfare is also explored by focusing on how provision is paid for and delivered, with particular emphasis upon the distribution of welfare outcomes and the growing role of procedures to monitor and control welfare providers.

Part IV looks at the way welfare services are organized, and analysed. Welfare is sometimes perceived as being focused upon particular social groups, notably those deemed to be in need of policy intervention or assistance. Some of these groups are examined and the range of services available to them discussed. However, Social Policy analysts do not generally conceive of welfare as being organized around client groups, but rather as providing a range of services for the population at large - from which a wide range of needs, from all social groups, will be met. These main services are covered in separate chapters, each

updated to take account of recent policy developments.

Part V serves a more practical function for students of Social Policy. It focuses upon the resources that can be drawn upon while studying. There is a general over-view and guide to published material in the Social Policy field and summaries of the main sources of statistical and research data which students of Social Policy may use. Different modes of teaching and learning are examined, drawing attention in particular to the role of new forms of learning and assessment, and to the central place now occupied by the use of electronically stored and managed data, including the internet.

Part VI focuses on the opportunities for the further study of the Social Policy beyond undergraduate level and the use of Social Policy in the pursuit of a range of both specialist and non-specialist careers.

The editors wanted to ensure that the *Companion* would provide an accessible guide to the subject, covering a wide range of material within a manageable size. We therefore asked contributors not to refer to additional sources in their text, but rather to provide a brief annotated guide to further reading at the end of their chapter. This is not the referencing style required by most programmes of study for undergraduate students in their essays; and readers should refer to the referencing used in chapter V.3, by Robert M. Page, where the normal academic conventions have been followed, for a model that should more usually be adopted in the preparation of assignments.

As editors we are very grateful for the work put into this volume by the contributors. We set out to produce a collection written by some of the most distinguished teachers and lecturers in social policy, and in this second edition we have followed this with an expanded range of contributions. We asked all our contributors to write in as accessible a way as possible while introducing complex issues in a short space. Authors in social policy are no different from other authors: some write sharply and clearly, others are more difficult to follow and pack difficult ideas together. This collection reflects the range of styles of writing and the range of ideological and political positions students of social policy are likely to encounter. We hope that it will encourage readers to investigate further and read more widely.

We were successful in persuading our authors to contribute to both editions of the *Companion* because it was prepared with the support and backing of the Social Policy Association (SPA) – the professional association for academics in Social Policy. While we, as editors, made the difficult and contentious decisions about what should be left out, what should be included and who should be asked to write, the SPA's support was essential in persuading many of our contributors to take part. We hope that what we have produced is worthy of the backing of the SPA and will be of value to the Social Policy community as a whole. Any shortcomings in the collection as a whole are, however, our responsibility.

Part I
What is social policy?

I.1
The subject of social policy

Pete Alcock

What Do We Study?

The study of social policy is a one of the academic social sciences. It is different to other areas of social science such as sociology, economics and politics, however, because it is based upon a distinct empirical focus – support for the well-being of citizens provided through social action, as discussed in more detail by Angus Erskine in chapter I.2. Nevertheless, as Erskine also discusses, social policy draws on the methods used and the understanding developed within these other areas of social science. Thus, although on the one hand we can see social policy as a discrete academic *discipline*, which is studied and developed in its own right; on the other we can recognize that it is also an interdisciplinary *field*, drawing on and developing links with other cognate disciplines at every stage and overlapping at times with these in terms of both empirical foci and methods of analysis. To put this another way, the boundaries between social policy and other social science subjects are porous, and shifting; and students and practitioners of social policy may also be working within or alongside these other areas or cooperating closely with others who do.

The term 'social policy' is not only used to refer to academic study, however; it is also used to refer to the social actions taken by policy-makers in the real world. So social policy refers both to the activity of policy-making to promote well-being and to the academic study of such actions. This may seem a bit confusing at first – whereas sociology students study *society*, social policy students study *social policy* – but it is a confusion that we all soon learn to live with.

This confusion is also true of the discipline versus interdisciplinary field debate referred to above. The subject of social policy has the core features of an academic discipline, with its own theoretical debates and empirical foci, and it is recognized as such in the management and planning of higher education in the UK. At the same time, however, the study of social policy is developed and extended through interdisciplinary collaboration. This may seem odd in principle; but it is not a problem in practice. Thus students studying social policy may well find themselves in the same departments, or on the same degree programmes, as others studying different subjects such as sociology; or they may be studying social policy as part of professional education and training, for instance in social work. This variety and collaboration are to be welcomed, and students on these different courses will learn much from each other through learning together; but this does not mean that social policy can be subsumed within sociology or social work. Similarly, those engaged in social policy research often work alongside others such as economists, or statisticians; but the focus of their concern is distinct – on investigating the development or delivery of policy, rather than on economic modeling (as economists) or data analysis (as statisticians).

Some of these links and overlaps with cognate areas of study and some of the implications of these for the study of social policy are explored in more detail in Part II, where we examine the values and the perspectives which underlie social policy. And, as May discusses in chapter I.3, although social policy is studied as a discrete subject within the UK, this is not the case in all other advanced welfare capitalist countries, where significant differences in both the practice and the study of social policy can be found. However, we will not discuss these more general issues any further here, rather we will move on to look at the development of social policy as an academic subject in the UK, for it has a particularly interesting history, involving even a change of name from *social administration* to *social policy*.

The Development of Social Policy

The development of social policy can be traced back a hundred years or so to the end of the nineteenth century. This is because it is closely linked to the development of the *Fabian Society* and to the influence of Fabian politics on policy development in Britain. The Fabian Society was established in 1884, and was strongly influenced by the work of Sidney Webb, a civil servant who later became a Labour MP. It developed critical analysis of the social and economic problems found in late-nineteenth-century British capitalism and campaigned for the introduction of social protection through the state to combat these. Fabian politics were closely linked to the establishment and growth of the Labour Party in Britain, which Webb and others saw as the political vehicle through which policy innovation and reform could be achieved. The early development of Fabian social policy thinking also drew on new research evidence emerging from some of the earliest empirical studies of social problems in the country by people like Booth and Rowntree, whose research revealed that the extent and depth of poverty in Britain at the end of the nineteenth century was both serious and widespread. Booth and Rowntree's work challenged conservative political assumptions that economic markets could meet the welfare needs of all. The Fabians used this to argue that policy intervention through the state was needed to provide those forms of support and protection which markets could not; and in the new Labour Party they saw a potential base for securing the political power to implement these changes.

In fact, of course, it was some time before the Labour Party did achieve political power in Britain, and important reforms were introduced before this by the Liberal governments of the early twentieth century. The context for these reforms was influenced significantly by a review of the *Poor Laws*, the mainstay of nineteenth-century welfare policy, by a Royal Commission established in 1905. The work of the commission was an important step in the development of debate about social policy reform in Britain, in part because the commissioners themselves could not agree on the right way forward and so produced two separate reports:

- a *Minority* Report, which was largely the work of Beatrice Webb, married to Sidney and herself a prominent Fabian;
- a *Majority* Report, which was largely the work of Helen Bosanquet, who with her husband Bernard were leading figures in the Charity Organisation Society (COS), a body which coordinated voluntary action to relieve poverty.

Interestingly both reports stressed the need for policy reform to improve welfare provision; but, whilst the minority Fabian report saw the public provision of state services as the means of achieving this, the majority COS report envisaged a continuing central role for voluntary philanthropic activity. This debate about the balance between state and non-state provision of welfare continued to influence the development of social policy throughout the rest of the twentieth century, as the chapters in Part III of this book reveal; and the concern to secure the appropriate mix between public and voluntary provision remains a key element in social policy planning at the beginning of the twenty-first century.

What is particularly significant for our purposes about the policy debate between the Webbs and the Bosanquets, however, is that this did not only influence the development of social policy reform, but extended also into the study and evaluation of policy as it developed. Despite their political differences both the Webbs and the Bosanquets were concerned to promote the study of social policy as well as the development of welfare reform. And this took concrete form with the establishment by the Webbs of the London School of Economics (LSE) and the incorporation within it of the COS's School of Sociology to form a new Department of Social Sciences and Administration in 1912. This was the first, and most important, base for the study of social policy. Its first new lecturer was Clement Attlee (later Prime Minister in the reforming Labour government after the Second World War); and later members included Beveridge (architect of the modern social security system), Tawney (who developed theoretical analysis of poverty and inequality) and T. H. Marshall (whose idea of 'social citizenship' has been used by many as a theoretical basis for understanding the development of social policy in modern society).

The LSE has continued since then to provide the leading base for the study and evaluation of social policy. In 1950 they appointed Richard Titmuss as the first Professor of Social Administration in the UK. Titmuss's appointment was significant. Although he himself had no formal academic qualifications he had already established a reputation for his detailed analysis of social services in wartime Britain, and during his 23 years at the LSE he became a leading figure in the academic study of social policy throughout the developed world. Titmuss's major contributions to the development of the study of social policy have now been collected together

in a single volume (see further reading), and his writing remains at the centre of academic debates about theory and practice today.

However, Titmuss also attracted to the LSE a range of other major social policy scholars, including Brian Abel-Smith and Peter Townsend (who revitalized research into poverty and inequality in the 1960s) and Tony Atkinson (who developed the economic analysis of social policy). Some of the contributors to this *Companion* come from the LSE's current Department of Social Policy and Administration or from its research centres; but the study of social policy has now extended much further than this. In the 1950s a Chair was also created at Birmingham and over the last fifty years social policy teaching and research has spread to most other universities in Britain, and has been taken up much more widely in schools and colleges too. There are also major research centres in a number of universities, and other independent agencies and think-tanks providing specialist research and consultancy in particular fields or from different perspectives.

What is more, as we shall see shortly, this wider development of teaching and research has promoted debate and controversy over the aims and methods of study and over the direction of, and priorities for, research and policy reform – and this has provided a challenge to the Fabianism which dominated debate within social policy until the 1970s.

- Much of the early teaching of social policy was geared to the training of social workers and others to act as providers within existing welfare services – it was focused upon how to administer welfare, rather than upon what welfare should be administered.

- Much of the early research work concentrated on measuring poverty and other social problems in order to provide evidence of the need for policy intervention – it was focused upon measurement of social need, rather than upon definitions of need or debate about the appropriateness of seeking to respond to it.

These broader questions became much more important as social policy expanded and developed in the latter quarter of the twentieth century. However, in the middle of the century such questions seemed to a large extent to be answered by the introduction of a 'welfare state' by the Labour government of 1945–51. At this stage the debate about the direction of reform appeared to have been won conclusively by the Fabian supporters of state welfare, and the focus of academic study upon the training of state welfare workers and the empirical measurement of new welfare needs appeared to have been established as the orthodoxy for all.

The Welfare State and the Welfare Consensus

The most important development in social policy during the twentieth century, and the most important feature of it for academic study, was the creation of what has come to be called the welfare state in the years immediately following the Second World War. In fact, of course, the depiction of these reforms as a welfare state is to some extent a controversial and contested analysis. It begs questions about what we mean by this and why these particular reforms should be seen as achieving it; and these questions are matters of significant debate and disagreement. Nevertheless, the post-war welfare state thesis has been widely promulgated – and for important and obvious reasons.

Part of the reason for the electoral success of the Labour government in 1945 was its manifesto commitment to introduce state provision to meet major welfare needs – and to do this on a comprehensive basis, replacing the piecemeal and partial provision which had been developed in the earlier part of the century. This message had been prefigured in Beveridge's famous report on the need for comprehensive social security reform, published in 1942 and included in Labour's manifesto promises. Beveridge had

written about the *Five Giant Social Evils* which had undermined British society before the war: ignorance, disease, idleness, squalor and want. He argued that it was in the interests of all citizens to remove these evils from British society, and it was the duty of the state, as the representative body of all citizens, to act to do this.

In the years following the war, comprehensive state provision to combat each was introduced:

- free education up to age 15 (later 16), to combat ignorance;
- a national health service (NHS) free at the point of use, to combat disease;
- state commitment to securing full employment, to combat idleness;
- public housing for all citizens to rent, to combat squalor;
- national insurance benefits for all in need, to combat want.

All of these required the development of major state services for citizens and they resulted in a major extension of state responsibility – and state expenditure. Many of the reforms were enacted by the post-war Labour government; but despite their Fabian roots they were not supported only by Labour. Indeed, the state education plans had been introduced by a Conservative member of the coalition government (R. A. Butler) in 1944, and the Conservative governments of the 1950s supported the spirit of the reforms and maintained their basic structure. This cross-party consensus on state welfare was so strong that it even acquired an acronym – *Butskellism* – comprised of the names of the Labour Chancellor (Gaitskell) and his Conservative successor (Butler).

For Fabian social policy, therefore, the post-war welfare state could be seen as the culmination of academic and political influence on government, and after this analysis and debate focused more on the problems of how to administer and improve existing state welfare than on the question of whether these were appropriate mechanisms for the social promotion of well-being. However, this narrow Fabian focus within post-war social policy did not last for long. It was soon under challenge from other perspectives which queried both the success and the desirability of state welfare.

Theoretical Pluralism

From the 1970s onwards the focus of social policy began to move beyond the narrow confines of Fabian welfare statism. This was symbolized most dramatically by a change in the name of the academic subject from social administration to social policy. In fact both terms had been used to some extent interchangeably before then (most notably by Titmuss himself) and the difference between the two has never been a hard and fast one. However at its 1987 annual meeting the professional association (then the Social Administration Association) agreed to change its name, primarily because it was felt that *social administration* was associated too closely with a focus largely upon analysis of the operation of existing welfare services, whereas *social policy* encompassed also a more general concern with analysis of the political and ideological bases of welfare provision. And to some extent this change was representative of more general trends within academic and political debate to embrace a wider range of conflicting perspectives challenging the orthodoxy of Fabianism, and to move academic study towards a more open theoretical pluralism in which questions of *whether* or *why* to pursue state welfare became more important than questions of *how* or *when*.

The New Left

The predominant focus of Fabianism on the success and desirability of state welfare was challenged in the 1960s and 1970s by critics on the left. Drawing on Marxist analysis of capitalist society, they argued that welfare services had not replaced the exploitative relationships of the labour market; and that, although they had provided some benefits for the poor and the working class, these services had also helped to support future capitalist development by providing a secure base for the market economy to operate. Unlike the Fabian socialists of the early twentieth century, these New Left critics did not necessarily see the further expansion of the existing state welfare base of social policy as resolving this dilemma; rather they argued that changes would be needed in the economic structure of capital and labour if well-being was to be promoted successfully for all. For the New Left, therefore, state welfare was in a constant state of contradiction, or conflict, between the pressure to meet the welfare needs of citizens and the pressure to support the growth of capitalist economic markets.

The New Right

In the 1970s and 1980s rather different criticisms of state welfare began to appear from the right of the political spectrum. Right-wing proponents of free market capitalism, most notably Hayek, had been critical of the creation of the welfare state in the 1940s, but at the time these had been marginal voices in academic and political debate (see chapter II.6). In the 1970s, as the advent of economic recession revealed some of the limitations of state welfare, these voices became both more vocal and more widely supported – especially after the move to the right of the Conservative Party following the election of Margaret Thatcher as leader in 1975. The essence of the New Right critique is that the development of extensive state welfare services is incompatible with the maintenance of a successful market economy, and that this problem will get worse as welfare expands to meet more and more social needs. Therefore, social needs must be met in other ways and state welfare withdrawn or removed – as was attempted to some extent by the Thatcherite governments of the 1980s through their policies of privatization and marketisation. For the New Right, therefore, the desirability of state welfare itself is called into question.

New social movements

The failings and limitations of state welfare also came under challenge in the late twentieth century from perspectives outside the traditional left/right political spectrum (see chapter II.14). Most significant here was the challenge of feminism and its analysis of the unequal treatment of men and women in the development and delivery of welfare services. As feminists point out, the provision of welfare is 'gendered'. Other critical perspectives have also challenged traditional analysis of state welfare and have suggested that the study of social policy should address a range of social divisions and social issues which are generally ignored in debates which focus only on the extent and desirability of public welfare provision. Anti-racists have pointed out that some welfare services can be discriminatory and exclusive and can act to reinforce social divisions within society; disability campaigners have suggested that the needs of certain social groups can be systematically ignored; and environmentalists have argued that existing service provision is in any case predicated upon trends in economic development which cannot be sustained over the longer term.

The new pragmatism

The new radical voices which began to influence social policy towards the end of the twentieth century have widely varying, and sometimes mutually conflicting, implications. They challenge state welfare and the orthodoxy of Fabianism, but they are also critical of the New Left and the New Right, as can be seen in more detail in some of the chapters in Part II. And at the beginning of the twenty-first century these differing perspectives have resulted in a theoretical pluralism which has not only transformed academic study but has also shifted the focus of policy-making itself. The Labour governments of the new century have openly eschewed the policy programmes of the Fabian left and the New Right, and have appealed instead for a 'third way' for social policy – between the state and the market. There is much debate about what is meant by this new third way politics (see chapter II.10); but its embrace of the legacy of theoretical pluralism has meant that, in seeking to recognize and respond to differing demands and perspectives, it has invoked a more pragmatic approach to policy planning – captured in the phrase 'what counts is what works'.

This new pragmatism is more concerned with the process and outcome of policy planning than with the principles upon which different forms of provision are based (private and public welfare are openly combined), and it has led to an emphasis on regulation and evaluation which is reminiscent in some ways of the heyday of social administration. However it has not displaced a concern with principle, as well as practice, within the academic study of social policy; and this has been fuelled too by other developments which have broadened the base of study and analysis.

Geographical Boundaries

Another challenge to the focus on state welfare in social policy has come from critics who have argued that a concentration on the national services of the early post-war period has ignored the importance of the local base of much welfare provision in Britain, and the impact of international and supranational pressures on policy development within this country and others.

The central/local divide in the development and delivery of social policy has always been a feature of the policy agenda, and even in reforms of the 1940s responsibility for major welfare services such as education, social care and housing remained largely in local hands. More recently, however, the appropriate balance between central and local control of services has become an important focus of research and analysis – and has also become a site of political debate and conflict, as discussed in chapter III.6. This is a conflict which cannot easily be resolved and there are arguments on both sides of the central/local debate; but it is a debate which must be addressed by all serious students of social policy.

The impact of international forces on policy development and debate in Britain is also not really a new development. Titmuss was a leading promoter, and practitioner, of international and comparative policy analysis. However, the increasingly globalised nature of economic and political activity has placed ever greater pressure on national policy planning, and analysis, as discussed in chapter II.18; and this is accentuated by the increasingly powerful influence which major international agencies now wield over policy debate, as we see in chapter III.9. Moreover the international context of British social policy has been altered significantly over the past three decades by Britain's membership of the European Union (EU); and, as discussed in chapter III.8, the supranational powers of the EU now mean that policy planning in Brussels can directly affect policy practice within Britain. The study of social policy can thus no longer be contained within the geographical and political confines of one state. This means that the study of social policy must recognize and respond to this international policy order too, and it is for these reasons, among others, that comparative analysis has become an essential feature of both study and research, as May explains in chapter I.3.

The Future of Social Policy

At the beginning of the twenty-first century, therefore, social policy has developed from its Fabian roots at the LSE and its support for the welfare state reforms of the early post-war years to embrace a wide range of diverse – and conflicting – theoretical debates about both the value and the success of public welfare provision and a wider conceptualization of the policy context as the product of local and global action as well as national politics. Social policy is now characterized by theoretical and geographical pluralism. It is also characterized by 'welfare pluralism': the recognition, as discussed in the chapters in Part III, that state provision is only one feature of a broader mixture of differing forms and levels of welfare service.

We could perhaps capture these new pluralisms within social policy as the product of a shift in the focus of study from the *welfare state* to the *welfare mix* – and this is a shift which is likely to develop further in the early years of this century. As all social scientists know social forces, and hence social policies too, are dynamic. The legacy of the past will continue to structure the agenda for study in the future; but change is always taking place. And in social policy trends for future change are already being set:

- We are moving beyond state-based welfare, to focus not only upon public services but also upon partnerships between the state and other providers of welfare and well-being and on the role of the state as a subsidizer and a regulator of the actions of others;
- We are moving beyond the provider culture, to focus not only upon questions of who provides welfare services but also on examination of who uses and benefits from these and how access to such benefits is determined, or prevented;
- We are moving beyond provision through redistribution, to focus not only upon the consumption of welfare services but also upon how policy interventions can influence investment and production, and the initial distribution of wealth and power within society.

These changes will accentuate further the overlap and the collaboration between social policy and the study of other cognate subjects such as sociology, economics, politics and law. However, it is just such interdisciplinary flexibility which has always been a central feature of the study of social policy – that this is likely to develop and to grow is a sign of continuing academic vitality and strength.

Guide To Further Reading

There are no textbooks dealing with the history and development of the discipline of social policy – perhaps it is too boring a topic for a whole book. However, M. Bulmer, J. Lewis and D. Piachaud (eds) *The Goals of Social Policy* (London: Unwin Hyman, 1989) is an interesting review and history of the work of the leading department at the London School of Economics (LSE). The major work of Titmuss, undoubtedly the founding father of the subject, is now gathered together, with commentaries, in P. Alcock, H. Glennerster, A. Oakley and A. Sinfield *Welfare and Wellbeing* (Bristol: Policy Press, 2001).

More recently, however, a number of authors have sought to provide introductory guides to the discipline. The most well established is M. Hill *Understanding Social Policy*, 6th edn (Oxford: Blackwell, 2000), which provides a service-based review of welfare policy. P. Alcock *Social Policy in Britain: Themes and Issues* (Basingstoke: Macmillan Press, 1996), takes a broader approach identifying key questions of structure, context and issues – 2nd edn. due from Palgrave in 2003. J. Baldock, N. Manning, S. Miller and S. Vickerstaff (eds) *Social Policy* (Oxford: Oxford University Press, 1999) is a collection which covers both contextual issues and service areas and is also being updated. K. Blakemore *Social Policy: An Introduction* (Buckingham: Open University Press, 1998), uses key social policy questions to provide a different perspective on provision in different service areas. F. Williams, *Social Policy: A Critical Introduction* (Cambridge: Polity Press, 1989), provides an alternative critical introduction which points out the way in which much traditional writing within the discipline has underemphasized the important issues of gender and 'race'. A collection of topical essays on UK policy issues is provided by N. Ellison and C. Pearson *Developments in British Social Policy* (Basingstoke: Macmillan Press, 1998), to be updated in 2003. Finally the Social Policy Association also produce an annual collection of topical essays, *Social Policy Review* (Bristol: Policy Press).

I.2
The Approaches and Methods of Social Policy

Angus Erskine

Introduction

Social policy is studied and taught in universities and colleges as an academic subject, as well as being an area of practice. This is to point to a distinction, which is frequently confusing for students of social policy, between social policy as a field of study and social policy as a set of policies adopted by government, local authorities and other organizations to achieve social purposes.

The connection between academic study and practice is central to social policy, but that can create a further difficulty for students when they first come across the subject. Social policy analysts direct their attention to improving conditions. The problem with this is that there is no one way of agreeing what is 'better'. The answer relies upon a value judgment. For example, some people argue that it is better for children to be brought up by biological parents who are married. Others argue that it is better for a child to be loved by his or her parent(s) than to live in a household in which the parents are fighting. Despite the attempts to 'measure' the outcomes of these alternatives, by looking at school performance, truancy or juvenile delinquency, neither case can be proved or disproved in a scientific way. The dispute is really about what a 'good' family and upbringing is, and this is a normative view. Ultimately the debate cannot be resolved because it is based upon values, not upon facts.

In social policy, there is another tension, that between analysis and practice. To an extent, they involve different skills and approaches. Analysis requires scepticism, while practice requires conviction. Those who study social policies have to ask questions about evidence. While social policy cannot claim to be a science, it draws its legitimacy as a subject on its ability to draw upon the methods of a number of social sciences and apply these in a rigorous and disciplined way to understand the field in which we are interested. But social policy also involves beliefs and taking sides about issues which social science cannot resolve. As chapters II.1 to II.14 illustrate, social policy involves understanding a range of philosophical and political perspectives.

Some people see social policy as a sub-branch of sociology. Sociology is interested in the relationships between social groups and individuals and in understanding how they work; and in many universities social policy is taught in the same department as sociology. But social policy makes a claim to be more than just a branch of sociology. Social policy is different, because while there is a set of areas which all social policy analysts would agree that they find of common interest, there is no one discipline to which they turn in examining them. Social policy analysts share a common concern with a particular field of study – social well-being. Within the subject, there are a diversity of approaches and methods. It is this, which makes it difficult to understand what social policy is. Social policy draws upon methods and theories used in sociology, statistics, management science, history, law, economics, political science, philosophy, geography and social psychology to help to explore well-being. It does not make a claim to having any unique set of methods, concepts, theories or insights. I would describe it as a multidisciplinary field of study rather than a discipline.

Social Issues

Within social policy there are a number of different starting points which authors and researchers take in developing the subject. One starting point to the study of social policy is exploring current social issues. For example, the demographic structure (the age profile) of the population is changing. People are living longer in most advanced capitalist countries and they are having fewer children. This rise in life expectancy, accompanied by a lower birth rate, is also taking place while the structure of households and families is changing. More people are living on their own, particularly young people and single elderly people; the former as a result of increasing affluence and the latter as people outlive their spouses for more years. At the same time, there is a growth in the number of people living together whilst not being married and an increasing number of lone parent households. These trends in demography and in the social structure of the family are a starting point to consider the future consequences for social policies. These trends are social, in that while they are experienced by individuals as personal, they are shared between groups of individuals. Longevity is not just a consequence of personal good health but of societal changes in diet, living and working conditions, and health care. Divorce is not just a consequence of the breakdown of a relationship between two individuals, but takes place within a socially determined context of norms and laws. These trends are social is-

sues. For example, social policy cannot ignore that future health care planning requires paying attention to the growing number of elderly people in the population. Housing policy (see chapter IV.11) needs to respond to the different housing needs which come about as a result of the different size and form of households which are developing.

These issues interact with developing social policies. For example, the quality and quantity of care for people in the community (as opposed to care in institutions like hospitals, which was the predominant model in the post-war years) is affected by the social trends which are taking place. An issues based approach to social policy requires an assessment of the relative future importance of these social trends. For example, many commentators argue that there will be a crisis in the funding of the state pension in the early part of the next century, whereas others point out that this is not necessarily the case (see chapter III.12). An issues based approach seeks to identify the central, relevant trends and examine their consequences for social policies.

To explore the impact of these social issues, we can draw upon a range of methods from other disciplines: demography, public sector economics, social psychology and law. Demography, the study of patterns of births and deaths, provides us with the context. Statistics may provide us with techniques that can help us to predict. Public sector economics helps to analyse the likely pressure points on government finances. Social psychology and sociology provide an understanding of the structure and content of care and needs. A knowledge of law helps to analyse the legislative framework within which policy is implemented.

Social Problems

Another related approach is a 'social problem' focus on social policy. Many students are attracted to social policy because they hope it will help to resolve social problems.

They want to study social policy, so that decisions can be made on a rational basis which will improve policies and overcome the difficulties that people face in their life. This is part of a long tradition in social policy research (although it has been criticized because it fails to question how far problems are constructed by dominant groups rather than being externally existing facts). A social problem approach looks for solutions. The work of early social policy analysts like Seebohm Rowntree was devoted to studying the problem of poverty and the measures necessary to overcome poverty. More recently, social policy has become interested in exploring other social problems, such as homelessness, long term unemployment, AIDS, juvenile crime or the growth in lone parenthood.

In all Western European countries, unemployment has been an issue of growing concern. This problem has been explained in a variety of ways.

- Some suggest it is a result of the development of new technologies, particularly those associated with new information technologies such as computing and telecommunication.
- Others identify the problem as having its roots in the characteristics of the people who are unemployed for a long period of time: either they lack enterprise because they have been brought up to expect that they will be employed by one employer for life or they do not have skills which can be transferred into other jobs.
- Others explain the problem in terms of economics. As a result of the speed of communication across the globe, the world is being drawn together into a single economic entity and long-term unemployment reflects the inability of the economies of Western Europe to compete effectively with the developing and growing economies in other parts of the world.
- Others explain the problem as a result of the institutional structures that sur-

round unemployment, which make people unwilling or unable to accept the changes that are taking place in a post-industrial society in which paid work has a different role in people's life course. Therefore people who are unemployed should be encouraged to think about their lives in different ways.
- Another set of institutional explanations focuses upon the ways in which the structure of the benefits system interacts with paid employment, creating an unemployment trap for those who are unemployed, in which they are better off unemployed and living off state unemployment benefits than they are taking a low-paid job.

These sorts of explanations all derive from a focus on unemployment as a social problem. Investigation of social policies to deal with unemployment, for instance, can draw on a range of methods. We might want to know about how unemployment has been tackled in the past, and this would involve investigating historical documents. A knowledge of labour markets and their analysis and the market for particular skills could be brought to bear to help understand the reasons for the trends, and would involve methods drawn from economics. We might investigate who are the unemployed, their employment history, how they became unemployed and their attitudes towards paid work. The problem of unemployment can be approached from a number of different angles. Each provides part of an understanding of the nature of the problem.

Social Groups

Another approach to social policy is that which focuses upon the needs of particular social groups, such as elderly people, children, homeless people or unemployed people. For example, while unemployment may be approached as a social problem, equally it might be approached by looking at the needs of people who are unemployed.

A needs-based approach starts by looking at what happens to those who become unemployed and how unemployment affects their lives. Social policy analysts want to know how unemployed people's lives are changed by unemployment, how people who are unemployed experience it and what they identify as their needs and the impact of unemployment upon their lives. They would also be interested in the extent to which policies directed towards the unemployed in different countries meet their needs (or do not meet them): for example, whether the unemployed are socially isolated, facing financial hardship or being reintegrated into new employment more in one country than another.

Social Services

In Britain, however, the traditional approach to social policy was concentrated upon the 'big five' social services. Education, health care, housing, personal social services and social security are the starting point of this approach to social policy. Social policy is concerned with how these services are organized and administered, how they perform and whom they benefit. This original approach taken by social administration reflected the importance of state institutions in the development of social provision in Britain over the past century. The focus of study was upon what governments do and how the policies pursued in the broad areas of social services affect the social divisions of class, and (more recently) gender and ethnicity, and the contribution they make in promoting the well-being of different social groups. To analyse these social policies requires knowledge of legislation, organization and politics. It brings to its analysis methods developed in a range of other disciplines.

Social Policies in People's Lives

In contrast to this traditional social administration approach, a new approach to social policy is developing which argues that social policy should be understood differently. Instead of looking at the range of ways in which social services (in their widest definition) are produced, we should be looking at how people live, experience and consume a range of goods and services that together contribute to their welfare. What this approach contributes to the debate about the nature of social policy is a view of the subject in terms of how it connects to people's lives. It adds to our understanding of the nature of social policy because whereas most of the previously discussed approaches are to an extent detached from people's experiences and lives, this approach fosters awareness of the way social policies are integrated in the lived experience of individuals and groups.

In the past, social policy authors have tended to look at what happens to 'them', because, social policy has not been studied by those who are in a position to experience the conditions which people face. Therefore the questions are posed differently from the way in which they would be if they were informed by experience. A new concern with identity, users and experience has been developing in social policy which suggests that those who have direct experience have a crucial understanding of what is happening. Therefore women provide the basic understanding of the position of women in relation to social policies. Disabled people provide an essential insight into the study of policies for disabled people. Unemployment cannot be understood without listening to the voice of the unemployed. This view has an important political message for social policy analysts – the importance of listening to direct experience.

All students of social policy have important experiences which can help to illuminate their studies. We are all users of services which promote or detract from our welfare and these experiences should be reflected upon in a systematic way. The immediate, intimate or experiential has to be structured in such a way as to provide an account which contains elements of the general and which can illuminate events for those who have no similar experience.

What Is Social Policy?

Explanations of what social policy is frequently focus upon its breadth and diversity and illustrate how wide an area of study it is and the range of disciplines upon which it calls in its analysis. This can lead a student to wonder whether social policy is not about everything and about nothing. There are a number of different starting points for studying social policy: social issues, social problems, social groups, social services and the experience of users. Social policy uses methods of inquiry drawn from a range of disciplines and it is more than the sum of the part of a number of different approaches taken in social policy and administration. But what holds it all together?

- First, there is an interest in the welfare of individuals and social groups. But 'welfare' is an essentially contested concept and one lesson from the history of social policy is that there is not any one agreed view of what constitutes it. Traditional Fabian approaches, the New Right, Greens and the diversity of feminist approaches are all concerned with the same issue, but the major differences between them lie in what they identify as being the constituents of 'welfare' and the appropriate routes towards it.
- Second, there is an interest in not just a philosophy or theory of welfare but an analysis of policies and their impact. Evaluating social policies according to specific criteria is the business of social policy academics, but different views of welfare give rise to assessments and analyses based upon different criteria,

such as effectiveness, efficiency, equity, opportunity, liberation, autonomy or sustainability.
- Third, there is a concern with how policies are institutionally organized and implemented. This is because any evaluative analysis requires an understanding of the structures of organizations and the way in which those structures impinge both upon those who work within them and upon the consumers of their services. This involves examining not only state services but also personal and informal care and private providers of welfare services.
- Fourth, there is an examination of the components which construct 'welfare'. That is why social policy is concerned with looking at new areas and expanding its range of interests away from a focus just on state welfare services.

The study of social policy is concerned with those aspects of public policies, market operations, personal consumption and interpersonal relationships which contribute to, or detract from, the well-being or welfare of individuals or groups. Social policy explores the social, political, ideological and institutional context within which welfare is produced, distributed and consumed. It seeks to provide an account of the processes which contribute to or detract from welfare, and it does this within a normative framework which involves debating moral and political issues about the nature of the desired outcomes. This definition of social policy has two important components: a concern with welfare, and a recognition of the normative and contested nature of social policy. It is the latter which distinguishes social policy from other social science subjects and makes it exciting.

Guide to further reading

Much of the reading suggested for the previous chapter provides a useful starting point to looking at some of the different approaches to the subject of social policy. There are a number of good examples of the approaches that I have outlined above, for example

J. Hills, *The Future of Welfare* (York: Joseph Rowntree Foundation, 1997) looks at some of the issues which the welfare state faces. M. May, R. Page and E. Brunsdon *Understanding Social Problems* (Oxford: Blackwell, 2001) takes a social problems approach. G. Payne *Social Divisions* (Basingstoke: Macmillan Press, 2000) examines a range of social groups in society. H. Glennerster and J. Hills *The State of Welfare* (Oxford: Oxford University Press, 1998) approaches the subject from a service-based perspective and takes an economic analysis. J. Morris *Independent Lives?* (Basingstoke: Macmillan Press, 1993) looks at the experience of disability and caring.

I.3
The Role of Comparative Study

Margaret May

The study of welfare provision inevitably involves some form of comparison between current practice and past or alternative ways of meeting need or improving existing policies. Such comparisons may not always be explicit, and the value bases may vary, but they are central to a discipline geared to evaluating welfare arrangements. This chapter focuses on the ways in which policy analysts have attempted to compare and contrast provision between different societies. It considers the aims of comparative study, the types of questions most commonly asked, the special demands such inquiry places on students and researchers, and the key areas of current debate.

It is important to recognize, however, that comparative cross-national study is a relatively recent development, especially in the UK, where it was for long impeded by a widespread belief in the superiority of the Beveridge settlement (see chapters I.1 and I.4). It has also been constrained by the locus of social policy as an academic discipline. In the United States and Canada, for instance, social policy is based primarily in social work departments, with a corresponding emphasis on professional practice. Elsewhere, apart from some separate provision in Australia, New Zealand, Hong Kong and the Republic of Ireland, it is located in political science, economics, sociology, public administration, law, management studies or combinations of these. This diverse base has oriented comparative research in particular ways in different institutions, adding to the complexity of cross-national analysis.

But whatever the setting, early studies tended to focus on advanced industrialized societies and within these on statutory welfare. Though these preoccupations still frame comparative enquiry, a number of factors have inspired a growing interest both in non-statutory forms of welfare and provision in other parts of the world. These developments have in turn opened up new questions and stimulated reconsideration of earlier theorizing, with analysts contributing to and drawing on research initiated elsewhere. Seeing provision through 'outside' eyes has, moreover, given an added twist to national debates about the direction and outcomes of current welfare reforms.

Why Comparative Social Policy?

Historically the starting point for comparative analysis was the observation that in the decades after the Second World War many countries, especially those of the industrialized West, experienced a massive expansion in publicly financed and delivered welfare. This was underpinned, as the reports by Marsh in Canada, Van Rhijn in the Netherlands, Laroque in France and Beveridge in Britain showed, by a widespread belief in the state's duty and capacity to care for its citizens. Funding methods and forms of provision, however, varied considerably, as did the scale of state involvement. One stimulus to comparative analysis then was that of charting and explaining common trends and accounting for national differences.

A more pragmatic impetus came from reformers anxious to expand or improve provision and 'learn' from the experience (and 'mistakes') of others. Indeed, the fact that countries develop different responses to ostensibly similar problems was projected as offering a sort of natural experimental basis on which to build. Given the potential political and economic costs of innovation, governments too have long recognized the benefits of considering programmes developed elsewhere. As will be seen, however, policy importation tends to be highly selective, often serving simply to legitimate desired change, with reformers from across the political spectrum deploying comparative ammunition to substantiate or disprove their particular prescriptions.

Policy 'borrowing' along these lines has a long pedigree. But in the late twentieth century it gained a new resonance as advanced industrial capitalist societies became aware of the manifold implications of an increasingly globalized economy. The extent to which economic change is undermining the autonomy of nation states and exerting a downward pressure on public welfare spending is hotly debated (see chapter II.18). It is clear, though, that national social policies were subject to several common pressures. During the 1980s and 1990s in many countries, the combination of economic recession, high unemployment and changing work and family patterns with new political formations, rising consumer expectations and demographic fears inspired a reassessment of the welfare settlements of the 1940s. While the pace and nature of restructuring varied, there was considerable commonality in the policies adopted and it is clear that many governments engaged in some form of comparative exercise, if only to leaven domestic debate.

Within Europe, including the UK, interest in comparative study was further fuelled by awareness of the extent to which policy was increasingly being shaped not only by the operation of global markets but by the activities of various international agencies. This was most visible in the expanding social policy remit of the European Union (discussed in chapter III.8) and the parallel growth in cross-European lobbying and networking by voluntary agencies and other pressure groups. It was manifest too in the growing involvement of other supranational agencies (such as the World Bank and the International Monetary Fund) in policy formation and delivery. Though their interventions applied particularly to Eastern Europe and the countries of the 'South' they also impacted on policy development elsewhere (see chapter III. 9).

While the role of such external agencies looks set to increase over the next decade, welfare provision is also internationalizing in other ways. The deregulation of national markets in financial services means pensions, health insurance and mortgages in many advanced industrial societies may well be provided by local subsidiaries of multinational conglomerates. Similar trends can be discerned in health, social care and housing as well as in 'support' areas such as welfare data-processing, service and facilities management. The liberalization of trading in services upheld by the World Trade Organization in the current round of GATT negotiations is likely to accelerate. Higher education, for instance, is gearing up for a global market, whilst British social insurers are already trading in Europe, and European and American companies in Asia and the new Chinese welfare markets. Overseas companies not only own many ex-public utilities in the UK, but also manage housing, leisure and other public services. Meanwhile global communication systems are bringing welfare advertising to a wider audience and enabling individuals to make their own policy comparisons. Such benchmarking is becoming more overt, not least in the UK where the Blair government has pledged to raise NHS provision to 'European levels', partly by commissioning hospital facilities in, and medical personnel from, other EU countries.

Supranational agencies and cross-national activities are therefore a key focus for policy analysis, producing a welter of statistics and proposals to transplant provisions from one society to another. Welfare restructuring in North America, Australia, New Zealand and much of Europe, East and West, during the 1980s and 1990s involved remarkably similar shifts in the forms and role of state of welfare. Different countries appeared to experience a resurgence of 'neo-liberal' policies and a weakening of the forms of class solidarity and social concerns which underpinned post-war welfare state building. This raised questions not only about the nature and processes of policy diffusion, but the extent to which national policy-making is structured by broad global processes, as against more localized factors, and the sustainability of inherited welfare formations. With welfare arrangements in many countries apparently shifting again, particularly around the axes of active labour market and work-oriented policies, these issues have taken on an added imperative.

Approaches to Comparative Social Policy

Comparative social policy thus centres on the complex task of examining the welfare order in different countries, identifying commonalties and differences, explaining these and considering possible future developments. More pragmatically it is concerned with improving provision in one country through drawing on the experience of others and assessing the implications of different systems for individuals and the wider society.

In addressing these overarching concerns, analysts have tended to operate at different levels of abstraction. Some have undertaken the necessary groundwork of providing country-specific studies, detailing the range and type of policies and delivery systems but tending to leave direct comparative assessments to the reader. Others, while adopting a more strictly comparative approach, vary in the specificity of their focus. Many – especially those who are undertaking government-sponsored studies or are concerned to inform policy-making – concentrate on comparing programmes, usually in countries with broadly similar socio-economic and political structures. While adopting a similar 'micro' or 'single issue' approach, a second group start from other points on the social policy compass, exploring provisions for specific users, responses to particular 'problems' or policy processes. Whatever the starting point, these 'micro' studies potentially involve comparing a number of inter-related elements:

- the extent and nature of the 'need'/ 'problem';
- the range of provision;
- the overall welfare context;
- policy-making processes;
- the aims of a particular programme(s)/ service(s)/benefit(s);
- its origins and development over time;
- entitlement criteria;
- the provider structure (statutory/non-statutory);
- the resource structure;
- the administrative structure;
- delivery/allocation processes;
- the regulatory structure;
- the 'efficacy' of current provision;
- pressures for change;
- policy proposals.

A further group of analysts follow a more 'macro' approach, attempting to characterize and compare 'whole systems' across a range of societies and often over time as well. This involves capturing the essence of a country's response to social need through considering:

- the general welfare milieu;
- policy-making 'styles';
- key forms of welfare 'input' or 'effort';
- predominant processes of welfare allocation;
- predominant patterns of welfare production;
- the main welfare output(s);
- the major welfare outcome(s).

Research Dilemmas

As later chapters show, exploring these issues within one's home country is far from straightforward. Cross-national study is even more problematic and presents major challenges in terms of ensuring that 'like is being compared with like' both conceptually and functionally. 'Social needs', for instance, are highly contested. Benefit systems and welfare services may have several, possibly conflicting, aims, not all explicated in legislation or government statements, and which have to be 'read' from other sources. The purpose of one scheme may only be clear in the context of the overall patterning of welfare in a particular country. Providers may be governmental, non-statutory or 'mixed'. Establishing the resource structure involves analysing not only funding arrangements (national or local taxation, compulsory or private insurance, charging schemes or combinations of these), but staffing profiles and, in many instances, the role of non-paid carers or other helpers. Comparing administrative structures entails not only mapping formal organizational arrangements but comprehending management cultures and the more informal processes of service delivery. Evaluating the efficacy of provision, whether in terms of take-up relative to 'need', enhanced individual well-being, decreased inequality, cost-effectiveness or other possible criteria, is a highly value-laden and difficult process.

Such problems are even more pronounced when comparing 'whole systems'. In many ways the methods used are no different from those deployed in intra-national studies and demand similar methodological sensitivity. But comparative study confronts additional issues. The well-documented limitations of official statistics, for instance, are compounded by differing national conventions which may pre-empt direct comparison. The sources, categories and format may vary; records for some programmes may not have been kept; there may be gaps in coverage, changes in definitions (as with unemployment statistics in Britain) or in methods of collecting and classifying data. Considerable effort has been invested in constructing harmonized cross-national data-sets (discussed in chapter V.6); but these still reflect governmental priorities rather than those of other stakeholders, and may conceal different conceptions of need or provision. Nevertheless, the availability of such data combined with the manifold difficulties and cost of conducting alternative quantitative or more qualitative studies has made comparative study particularly reliant on official sources.

The issues, however, are not only a matter of accessing valid sources but of research reliability and the difficulties of a researcher of whatever nationality being able to undertake research according to the same investigative rules as a researcher from another country. Social policy analysts are not 'culture-free' in either their interpretations or their research remits. Indeed, one salutary feature of comparative research is the discovery that burning issues in one country may not be so significant elsewhere and that to a large extent, as social constructionists have long argued, 'social problems' may be differently perceived in different places. Superficially similar terms can carry very different meanings and informal customs are easily misread. Traversing such cultural and linguistic frontiers demands considerable methodological caution, especially in the contested arena of social policy. But the intrinsic difficulties of comparative inquiry should not mask the many policy insights gleaned through cross-national study and debate.

Studying Welfare Regimes

One major contribution has been the development of classificatory frameworks specifying the key features of different kinds of welfare systems. Although differing typologies can be found in the literature, until recently the most influential were variants on that advanced by the American writers Wilenski and Lebeaux in *Industrial Society and Social Welfare*. Writing in the wake of the post-war settlements (1958), they distinguished two 'models of welfare': the 'residual', based on the principles of economic individualism and free enterprise, and the 'institutional', based on the notions of security, equality and humanitarianism.

These two 'models' characterized both the historical development of social policy (which they saw as a gradual evolution from residualism) and the patterning of welfare in particular countries. In the first 'needs' were met primarily through the market or the family. The state provided an emergency 'safety net' when these 'normal' supports broke down. Public welfare was, accordingly, highly selective, with low means-tested benefits, and was widely perceived as stigmatizing. In contrast, the institutional model embraced universal, rights-based, non-stigmatizing state welfare as a 'normal' function of industrial society. In the UK, Titmuss similarly distinguished a 'residual' from an 'institutional-redistributive model', exemplified by the Unites States and Scandinavia respectively. To these he added a third ideal type, the 'industrial-achievement' model typified by West Germany, in which state welfare functions as an adjunct to the economy and needs are correspondingly met on the basis of work performance and status.

These and similar ideal-type taxonomies formed the implicit template for other forms of macro analysis, especially in English-speaking countries. They involved developing ways of plotting a country's welfare prowess, comparing quantitative aggregate data relating to the timing and coverage of national legislation and welfare expenditures. Equating high social spending with extensive welfarism, many studies similarly distinguished the welfare commitment exhibited in Scandinavia with that of the United States and fed into attempts to identify the pressures leading to increased welfare spending in Western states and variations between them.

Initially, purposive or teleological explanations tended to prevail, with state welfare perceived as safeguarding individuals against the shocks of industrial change and the vagaries of the market. From this evolutionary perspective welfare-statism appeared as the indispensable concomitant of industrial urbanization and demographic change. Such theorizing was increasingly contested by Marxist-inspired analysts who highlighted its role in maintaining labour discipline, productivity and social stability, and, from the 1970s, by researchers drawing on other perspectives and focusing more on theorizing cross-national variations. Many emphasized the correspondence between the spread of universal public welfare and the strength of social democratic or labour movements. Some, however, highlighted the role of other political groupings and controversy was furthered by research on the input of state bureaucracies and related institutional arrangements.

From the 1980s this intense cross-national debate shifted again, stimulated by the restructuring of state welfare in many countries and growing concern about its future. In trying to make sense of the changing pattern of welfare both within and between countries, a number of writers devised new classificatory schemes, the most powerful being that of the Danish analyst G. Esping-Andersen. His seminal work, *The Three Worlds of Welfare Capitalism* (1990), developed a welfare state taxonomy based not only on differences in the scale, scope and entitlements of public provision in capitalist countries, but on differences in policy-making styles and processes and underlying patterns of class formation and political structures. It rested on a conception of state welfare as sustaining social citizenship along two related dimensions:

- *'decommodification'* – the extent to which the state frees individuals from the operation of market forces and enables its citizens to lead a socially acceptable life independent of the labour market;
- *'stratification'* - the extent to which state welfare differentiates between social groups and promotes equality and social integration.

Recognizing that the traditional gauge of welfare commitment, high social expenditure, often obscured these distributional issues, Esping-Andersen devised 'decommodification' indices to measure the accessibility, coverage and performance of social security schemes in 18 OECD states. His analysis led him to distinguish three ideal type 'welfare regimes':

- *Social Democratic Regimes*, typified by Scandinavian countries, where the pressure of a broad coalition of left-wing labour organizations and small farmers secured a state committed to full employment and generous, redistributive universalist welfare benefits, incorporating both middle and working class interests;
- *Conservative/Corporatist Regimes*, typified by Germany, France and Austria, where occupationally segregated benefits were introduced by conservative-dominated governments to secure both working class adherence and middle class support;
- *Liberal Welfare Regimes*, typified by the United States and Anglo-Saxon countries, where in the absence of stable cross-class alliances, state welfare mainly operated on selective lines as a residual safety net for the poor.

As with any ideal-type framework, some societies fitted these constructs more easily than others. But Esping-Andersen concluded that the welfare systems of developed countries could be incorporated within this schema, which also had a predictive value indicating that different regimes appeared to be moving along different trajectories.

New Directions

While contributing significantly to our understanding of differences between welfare states, Esping-Andersen's work also attracted considerable criticism, reinvigorating debate on the gestation of welfare systems and their potential for change. Equally salient for this chapter is the extent to which his study heightened awareness of crucial lacunae in comparative research generally and inspired a new wave of cross-national analysis.

Like most of its predecessors, Esping-Andersen's typology had a narrow geographical and statist focus. To its critics it also neglected other variants in welfare provision both within and between countries. For some the way forward lay in modifying or extending his analysis to allow for further 'regimes' such as the 'fourth world' of Australasian labourism and the welfare systems of the Mediterranean Rim, Eastern Europe or the Pacific Rim. For others it posed more fundamental questions about whether taxonomies based on democratic welfare capitalism could (or should) be modified to include welfare systems in other parts of the world or whether different approaches with different explanatory models are needed.

This on-going debate highlighted other weaknesses in traditional comparative study, particularly its preoccupation with statutory welfare and the marginalization of social divisions other than class. As comparative analysts were well aware, these limitations partly stemmed from their reliance on aggregate statistical information produced by governments and international agencies and the resultant use of income transfer schemes as the proxy for a state's 'welfarism'. Yet, as recent research has revealed, a different international picture emerges if services such as health, social care, housing or education are used as a measure of welfare activity. If non-statutory provision or the state's varying fiscal and regulatory role as well as its provider one are factored in, it can shift again.

The picture can change further if other neglected dimensions of welfare activity are also added in. Traditionally welfare programmes were predominantly assessed in terms of their impact on social class differences, with minimal reference to cross-national variations in terms of gender, ethnicity or other divisions. As feminist-inspired studies in particular have shown, the concentration on statutory welfare masked the extent to which, irrespective of 'regime type', it was contingent on private, gendered provision. For some this again meant adapting Esping-Andersen's typology to incorporate both the notion of 'mixed economies of welfare' and gender issues; for others it involved a radical re-theorizing of comparative analysis. This debate is still on-going. But it has generated a wealth of studies, bringing new insights into cross-national variations in women's welfare status and the gendering and re-gendering of welfare arrangements.

Related concern over the ageing of advanced industrial societies also prompted comparative analyses of provisions for the elderly. Far less headway has been made, however, in comparing the welfare experiences of other groups, particularly those of ethnic minorities. Cross-national inquiry is bedevilled by the lack of reliable, compatible national data. But qualitative research is now beginning to track the dynamics and impact of different welfare systems, pointing to possible 'race regimes' (Castles and Miller, 1998) and approaches to both economic migrants and asylum-seekers. In highlighting the varying role of migrants' welfare networks in this process it has also stimulated interest in the welfare cultures of Muslim and other 'non-Western' societies. Concerns over the 'internationalization' of labour mean that such studies are likely to feature more prominently in cross-national research. In

the long run this may redress another much criticized aspect of comparative social policy, the 'false segregation' between 'North' and 'South' and the often ineffective uni-directional nature of policy prescriptions (Kennett, 2001).

Expanding the comparative canvas, however, involves more than 'adding in' or refocusing on the role of the state within different welfare 'mixes'. As we have seen some analysts now look to make programme-specific comparisons and others use the notion of regimes to make country-based comparisons. The challenge for comparative study remains that of understanding the nature and direction of change in current national welfare arrangements, assessing whether this indicates convergence or divergence, and adumbrating the influence of exogenous as distinct from endogenous factors. It means exploring their differential exposure to common pressures and the ways these are mediated by internal political processes and circumstances; looking at the 'path dependencies' created by existing structures and funding mechanisms as against the systemic shifts that may flow from new political alignments; and, equally critically, addressing the interconnections between welfare systems, the patterning of social divisions and the changing constructions of citizenship (see too chapters II.6 and III.11).

Such research is already feeding into national and international policy debates. It is supported both by more sophisticated use of large-scale data sets and new techniques such as user profiling, expert panel studies, attitudinal surveys and, increasingly, the direct involvement of user groups. Against the backcloth of yet another reordering of welfare edifices in the 'North' and signs of a repositioning of social policy in development strategies in the 'South', comparative analysts are also re-emphasizing the role of collective provision. The growth of public spending in 'less mature' welfare systems within Europe and 'middle income' countries such as South Korea or Mexico points to the multiple pressures sustaining rather than curtailing state welfare. Though re-shaped the 'classic' welfare states too have proved highly resilient. It may be then that, alongside assessing its redistributive impacts, analysing the 'piggy-bank' function of state welfare (Barr, 2001) and the role of social protection in increasingly volatile world markets will constitute a key element in future comparative analysis.

Guide to further reading

Stimulating review of current issues in comparative analysis along with surveys of developments in a variety of societies are provided by P. Alcock and C. Craig (eds) *International Social Policy* (Basingstoke: Palgrave, 2001) and, within Europe, by A. Cochrane, J. Clarke and S. Gewirtz (eds.) *Comparing Welfare States* (London: Sage, 2001). P. Kennett *Comparative Social Policy* (Buckingham: Open University Press, 2001) looks more broadly at theoretical and methodical issues including those posed by the 'North/South divide'. Some of these are also pursued by N. Barr *The Welfare State as Piggy Bank* (Oxford: Oxford University Press, 2001). H. Dean and Z. Khan 'Muslim perspectives on welfare', *Journal of Social Policy* 26, 2 (1997) offers a different route into comparative study.

D. Sainsbury, (ed.) *Gender, Equality and Welfare States* 2nd edn (Cambridge: Cambridge University Press, 1999) considers variations in women's experiences; S. Castles and M. Miller *The Age of Migration* (Basingstoke: Macmillan, 1998) those of different ethnic minorities, issues also addressed in J. Fink, G. Lewis and J. Clarke (eds) *Rethinking European Welfare* (London: Sage, 2001).

The many methodological issues faced in comparative study are considered in L. Hantrais and S. Mangen, (eds) *Cross-National Research Methods in the Social Sciences* (London/New York: Pinter, 1996) and J. Clasen (ed.), *Comparative Social Policy* (Oxford: Blackwell, 1999). The value of W. Arts and J. Gelissen, 'Three worlds of welfare capitalism or more? A state of the art report' *Journal of European Social Policy* 12, 2 (2002), is self-explanatory.

I.4
History and social policy

David Gladstone

Those who study social policy are often more concerned with the present and the future than with the past. They engage with current issues about the supply and distribution of welfare. They discuss how social policies might be improved and made more effective and efficient in the future. Why, then, study the past? What can an historical perspective contribute to social policy as an academic subject and as a programme for action? Those themes are central to this chapter.

What is History?

The Shorter Oxford English Dictionary defines history as the study of past events. That definition suggests that history is both an academic study or discipline and a narrative or chronology of past events. As an academic discipline, history's origins are comparatively recent and are usually attributed to a nineteenth century German scholar Leopold von Ranke. Ranke's contribution lay, first of all, in emphasizing that the task of the historian was to understand the past and to provide a narrative of past events. His second contribution was methodological. For Ranke, understanding the past meant uncovering as many documents as could be found and using them as evidence from which to create or construct a narrative history of change.

Documentary or written materials remain an important source of historical evi-dence. But the range of sources which historians use in their attempts to re-create the past has widened immeasurably since the time of Ranke. They now include interviews (often tape-recorded) in which individuals recall experiences and events in their own past, as well as a whole variety of visual and material artefacts from which the past can also be re-created. Jordanova (2000) lists a wide range of examples: seals, maps, photographs, drawings, prints, paintings, jewellery, costume, tools and machines, archaeological remains, buildings, town plans, films: many of them, in her phrase, 'transparent windows onto past times'. For those interested especially in the history of welfare, children's toys, the legacy of the large barrack-like buildings in which the poor, the mad and the criminal were incarcerated, and the class-segregated housing developments of towns and cities are just such transparent windows. The past, in other words, is not confined to the written records of previous centuries or generations. It is, in a variety of ways, all around us as a component of our present.

The increasing diversity of sources is, in part at least, a reflection of the growing specialization that has taken place within academic history itself. Whereas history used to be the study of kings and queens, battles, wars and great national events, it is now a much more multi-faceted view of the past. One of the most significant developments over the past half century has been the growth of social history. Once crudely defined as 'history with the politics left out', social history provides a distinctive perspective on the past. As Harold Perkin, one of its foremost protagonists expressed it: 'We want to know not only what laws were made or battles fought or even how men (sic) got their living, but what it felt like to be alive, how men in history – not merely kings and popes, statesmen and tycoons – lived and worked and thought and behaved towards each other' (*The Structured Crowd*, Sussex: Harvester Press, 1981, p.24). In that quest, the history of welfare is an important ingredient: for it addresses issues of risk and responsibility as part of the way in which state and citizen, men and women, parents and children, people of different social classes, ethnic origin and economic and political power, behaved towards each other in past time.

Specialization in research – whether by period or theme – has created the diversity of history as an academic subject. But it is also necessary to acknowledge that there are a variety of perspectives on the past: not one history but many histories. As Jordanova (2000) notes, there is 'a diffused awareness of the past that varies from person to person, group to group, country to country.' In part, this is the result of the ideological and experiential baggage which individual scholars bring to their historical inquiry and investigation. That represents a challenge to Ranke's notion that there could be an agreed narrative of events because the widest possible selection of relevant documents had been examined. As Dorothy Porter has noted: 'History writing is no longer dominated by one ideological vantage point even within Western societies where a new multi-cultural mix ensures that a huge variety of historical perspectives has been able to gain legitimate authority' (*Health, Civilisation and the State*, London: Routledge, 1999, p.4).

Furthermore, we are now much more aware that the documentary evidence that has survived from the past was generally written and recorded by those in powerful positions of authority. As such, it is official history. Thus, for example, while much documentary evidence exists concerning the Poor Law, one of the key agencies of British social welfare in the past, there is comparatively little recording the experiences and reactions of those who were on the receiving end of its policies as paupers, whether living at home or in a workhouse. The sources of historical evidence, that is to say, are more often 'top down' records of policy makers and administrators rather than 'bottom up' accounts of the impact of their decisions on the lives of ordinary people.

At the beginning of the twenty-first century the historian's task is thus much more specialist and diverse than it was in the Germany of Ranke two centuries ago; and postmodernism is simply the latest challenge to attempts to reconstruct the past of human experience. Yet the past remains a central feature of the way in which we understand and make sense of the present, not least in welfare and social policy. Present-day ideological and political debates about rights and responsibilities, organizational and administrative arrangements and demarcations between service sectors, as well as the language and terminology of welfare, all resonate with echoes of the past. The past may be, in H.E. Bates' phrase, 'a foreign country', but the historical perspective is one which no present-day explorer can afford to ignore. Those who are ignorant of history, as Santayana observed, are doomed to repeat it.

Themes in Welfare History

It is possible to identify three distinct yet inter-related themes in the historical approach to welfare - *risk, resources* and *responsibility*. These themes also link past and present in the study of social policy.

Risk

What were the risks or threats to their well-being to which individuals were exposed in the past? How similar or different are present-day 'diswelfares'? The historian Paul Johnson (1996) defines social risk as 'the probability weighted uncertainty that derives from the changing and dynamic world in which people live.' In other words, it constitutes what the social policy tradition tends to define as social problems. Johnson's analysis highlights four categories of risk. Each will now be examined in turn.

Health

It is now well established by demographic historians that death rates only began to fall significantly from the beginning of the twentieth century. In the preceding century there was a high level of infant deaths (until 1900 about 150 in every 1000 children died in their first year), an average life expectancy of 40 years, and a much greater risk of premature death for those living in the expanding industrial towns and cities. The contrast with present-day statistics suggests a considerable improvement or reduction of risk measured by nineteenth century standards, an improvement which historians explain in different ways. Some see it as the consequence of a general improvement in the financial and material conditions of the population; others as the result of more comprehensive and accessible health services, in the sense of both public and environmental health improvements and the wider range of medical and clinical treatments that are now available.

Life course

In this category Johnson highlights the vulnerability of large families with several dependent children and the poverty of old age consequent on declining physical powers and enforced withdrawal from the labour market. Both of these categories of risk were identified by Rowntree, one of the early social investigators at the beginning of the twentieth century, in his discussion of the life cycle of poverty based on his research in York. With the high infant mortality of the nineteenth century, a large number of children represented an insurance for care of their parents in old age; while as life expectancy improved so too did the poverty that invariably accompanied the final phase of the life course. The abolition of child and family poverty has been identified as one of the priorities of the present New Labour government, and it is now generally recognized that there are two nations in old age: those who have the benefit of occupational pensions and those who are dependent on the state retirement pension.

Economic and occupational risk

Economic risks are very much determined by the availability and remuneration of paid employment. In the second half of the nineteenth century, on average some 4.5 per cent of male workers were unemployed, but of greater significance at that time was underemployment. Workers in many trades and industries were hired and paid by the day on a casual basis. Such irregularity of employment had considerable effects on household finances which became more precarious when the main wage-earner was ill, became disabled or died. Though presently at its lowest level for forty years, the experience of unemployment still impacts on individual self-worth, as well as the economic and social well-being of the household unit.

Environmental risk

The final type of risk in Johnson's analysis is that which results from living in a physically hazardous world. This category ranges, therefore, from all types of accidents to industrial pollution and environmental hazard on a grander scale such as that occasioned by global warming. It has been observed that 'it is those near the bottom of the social scale who are most exposed to hazards at work': something which accords very closely with the historical evidence on the nineteenth century. One study of coal mining, for example, notes that between 1869 and 1919 one miner was killed every six hours, one seriously injured every two hours and one injured badly every two or three minutes.

Resources

Historians have not only researched the risks and threats to welfare in the past: they have also mapped the strategies of survival and sources of available support. That evidence shows the existence of a mixed-economy welfare system in the nineteenth century in which a developing diversity of agencies – formal and informal – played an often overlapping role.

Household strategies, often initiated by women who deprived themselves in the interests of their husbands and children, were an important resource, as were the earnings of children even after the introduction of compulsory elementary schooling in 1880. Mutual support networks existed in working class communities and faith-based organizations also provided support for some. Self-help organizations, such as savings banks and commercial insurance, provided a means for those with a regular and reliable income to save against the eventuality of hazards and risks. This was especially important at a time when most medical treatment required payment and when the accident or death of the principal wage earner could create considerable financial difficulties for the household unit. The trade union movement and the Friendly Societies, controlled by the working class themselves, provided a range of benefits for their members and their dependents at times of unemployment, ill health or death which were based on the payment of weekly subscriptions - although the benefits of membership were limited to those who were able to pay the weekly dues. Membership of such organizations thus became one of the defining characteristics of the so-called *respectable* working class.

Philanthropic charity expanded dramatically during the nineteenth century, coordinated to some extent by the Charity Organisation Society (see chapter I.1). Philanthropy encompassed housing schemes, schools and specialist hospitals (such as Great Ormond Street Hospital for Sick Children), as well as many of the voluntary societies which still exist today (such as the children's charity Barnardo's). At the time some critics deplored the unorganized spread of philanthropic endeavour, seeing it as an encouragement to dependency and pauperization; although more recent criticism has stressed the intrusions made into working-class households by the middle class 'lady' visitors of many local charitable associations.

The state – both centrally and locally – became more proactively involved in aspects of welfare during the course of the nineteenth century. The long-established system of state-provided financial assistance – the Poor Law – was reformed in the interests of the emerging industrial society in 1834, and parliamentary legislation was also introduced in relation both to public health and elementary education. But despite the activity of the encroaching state, the level of intervention and public spending remained small and much welfare provision remained largely localized and amateur.

By contrast the twentieth century was characterized by more extensive state-provided welfare and a growing professionalization of welfare activities. A variety of social legislation passed by the Liberal government between 1906 and 1914 encompassed the provision of school meals, school medical inspection and Old Age Pensions, as well as the creation of a National Insurance scheme of sickness and unemployment insurance which was progressively expanded during the inter-war years. But it was the classic welfare state, developed between 1944 and 1948 in legislation passed by the wartime coalition and post-war Labour government, that provided a more comprehensive coverage of risks – from the cradle to the grave – of the British population. The 5th July 1948 was the appointed day for the introduction of the National Health Service and the schemes of post-war social security and financial assistance. It was described by the prime minister Clement Attlee as 'a day which makes history'.

The introduction of a more comprehensive system of state-provided welfare meant something of a readjustment in the roles of other suppliers in the mixed economy of welfare. But, though their roles may have been redefined over the past fifty years in relation to changing state activity, each of the sources of formal and informal assistance and support continue to operate; and Britain's welfare system today is made up of a diversity of responses to risk, just as in the past.

Responsibility

Historians do not only describe change, they also seek to explain it. In that task, Britain's welfare system is a fertile area for investigation both of particular policy changes and more general and significant transformations. At the general level is the comparative historical study which locates the development of welfare states in Europe and America in the context of political mobilization (the voter motive in the conditions of mass democracy) and specific levels of economic development (i.e. when sufficient resources are available to yield the tax revenues necessary to fund public welfare services). In contrast more detailed studies of particular policy changes indicate a wide range of change agents. In the middle are theories drawn from a number of historical case studies which explain change in more conceptual terms such as:

- *legitimacy* – is this an area in which government is legitimately involved?
- *feasibility* – is the proposed change feasible in terms, for example, of resources?
- *support* – is the change in question likely to enhance rather than diminish government support?

Such a framework indicates the inevitably political and value-laden nature of welfare-state change and takes the historian into the history of ideas and political debate. What an historical perspective suggests is that current discourse around the respective welfare responsibilities of state and citizen is in fact by no means new. Political discussion has been around for the past century and more, and over that time a number of distinct ideological positions have been developed, many of which still influence policy debates today, see chapters II.6-14. These different ideological positions raise important questions for the historian about the changing role of the state in welfare and the factors which can explain the greater comprehensiveness of the classic welfare state of the 1940s, the much-discussed 'crisis' of the welfare state in the 1970s which provided the springboard for the Thatcherite agenda of 'rolling back the frontiers of the state', and the 'third way' between state and market promoted by Labour at the turn of the twenty-first century.

One final issue which needs to be considered in the context of responsibility is the objective of state welfare. Whereas earlier writers on Britain's welfare past tended to portray it as an essentially beneficent activity, more recent critical commentators have emphasized the functional necessity of public welfare in a capitalist economy, and its role in regulating the poor.

The Historiography of the Welfare State

Early studies written in the aftermath of the creation of Britain's classic welfare state in the mid-twentieth century, with titles such as *The Coming of the Welfare State* tended to be *Whiggish* in character - that is they characterized the emergence of comprehensive state welfare as a unilinear progression from the 'darkness' of the nineteenth century Poor Law to the 'light' of the Beveridge Plan of 1942 and the post-war welfare state. These Whiggish accounts saw comprehensive public welfare as part of a generally beneficent process, although, as mentioned earlier, more modern commentators would dispute that welfare provision has been an unqualified benefit for all.

Such a 'welfare state escalator' view of history has therefore largely been replaced in more recent accounts by the mixed-economy approach. This recognizes the continuance of the diversity of welfare suppliers, the growth of state intervention and the changing role of the state (from direct service provider to financier and regulator of other agencies) and the moving frontier between providers that has characterized both the present and the past of welfare. It is this dynamic that has made these historical studies of social policy, drawing on a wider range of sources, more stimulating than previous teleological accounts.

Increasingly too more recent studies of welfare have pushed its history back beyond the nineteenth and twentieth centuries. The Poor Law, it is true, has a long history dating from the sixteenth century and historical studies of welfare have ranged over its total time-frame. But much more attention is now being given to a wider range of risk and resources in earlier historical periods which encompasses households and families, philanthropy, community and informal networks.

Furthermore, the British experience is now increasingly set within a wider geographical context of comparative study. Such research has challenged both the notion of the primacy of Britain's welfare state (itself a German term of the 1920s) and located the British experience within a broader discussion of welfare-state regimes. It is appropriate, therefore, to end with Jane Lewis's observation that:

> Rather than seeing the story of the modern welfare state as a simple movement from individualism to collectivism and ever increasing amounts of (benevolent) state intervention, it is more accurate to see European countries as having had mixed economies of welfare in which the state, the voluntary sector, employers, the family and the market have played different parts at different points in time.
>
> Jane Lewis 'The voluntary sector in the mixed economy of welfare' in David Gladstone (ed.) *Before Beveridge: Welfare Before the Welfare State* (I.E.A. Health and Welfare Unit, 1999), p.11

Guide to further reading

Gladstone, David, 1999. *The Twentieth Century Welfare State* (Basingstoke: Macmillan Press). A review of twentieth-century welfare from the mixed-economy perspective.

Glennerster, Howard, 1999. *British Social Policy since 1945* (Oxford: Blackwell). An authoritative account. The second edition includes a chapter on New Labour.

Johnson, Paul, 1996. 'Risk, redistribution and social welfare in Britain from the poor law to Beveridge' in Martin Daunton (ed.) *Charity, Self Interest and Welfare in the English Past* (London: UCL Press) examines how a variety of welfare instruments were used to reduce the incidence of social risk between the late nineteenth century and the Second World War.

Jordanova, Ludmilla, 2000. *History in Practice* (London: Arnold). A stimulating and wide ranging study of recent historical scholarship and what is involved in studying history.

Lowe, Rodney, 2000. *The Welfare State in Britain since 1945* (Basingstoke: Palgrave). A detailed study of the period of the classic welfare state set within a useful theoretical perspective.

Page, Robert M and Silburn, Richard, 1999. *British Social Welfare in the Twentieth Century* (Basingstoke: Macmillan Press). A well-selected series of essays reviewing political ideas, sectors of the welfare state and welfare outside the state.

Tosh, John, 2001. *The Pursuit of History* (Harlow: Longman). Now in its third edition, this is a comprehensive and thoughtful guide to historians and their work.

Part II
Values and Perspectives

Key Concepts

II.1
Social Needs, Social Problems and Social Welfare

Nick Manning

The study of social policy focuses on the way in which social welfare is organized to meet the needs of individuals and groups, for health care, for shelter, food, clothing and so on. It is also concerned with the way in which social problems are recognized and dealt with. In this chapter I will examine the growth and structure of social welfare provision; introduce some basic definitions of need; review the debates that have developed about this concept; and examine the way it is used in practice. I will also discuss ideas about social problems; the way these are related to needs and to social welfare provision; and the considerable debates about this.

What is Social Welfare?

Social welfare refers to the various social arrangements that exist to meet the needs of individuals and groups in society and to tackle social problems. Our use of the term social policy in modern times implies that social welfare means government welfare. This is not at all the case. Welfare for most people is still provided through other social mechanisms than the state. There are three main types: family and friends; the market; and non-governmental organizations (NGOs) such as voluntary organizations, mutual associations and charities. Social policy as an area of study is concerned with the way in which all these institutions affect the welfare of individuals

> **Box II.1.1 Types of social welfare institution**
>
> - Family
> - Market
> - NGOs (non-governmental organizations)
> - The welfare state

and groups and is taken up in more detail in some of the chapters in part III.

Social policy is a branch of social science. From this point of view, the basic conditions for the existence and survival of individual people are necessarily social. No individual, however resourceful, could survive for long in isolation. Human beings, in contrast to many other animals, are not capable of mediating directly with nature without mechanisms of cooperation and a division of labour between individuals. This is illustrated well by the long period of dependence that children need for them to become adults. The family, then, may be taken as the archetypal social welfare institution, both in fact and as an ideal. Markets, governments and NGOs are by comparison modern developments.

Families not only meet a whole variety of social needs at various stages of our lives, but they are at the same time the object themselves of government and academic concern. Of course families come in different shapes and sizes as is discussed in chapter II.17. With the lengthening of life expectancy, the steady rise in the rate of marriage dissolution and the consequent growth of sole parenthood, the classic family form of two parents and dependent children has now become a minority structure within the overall mix of households. Nevertheless over time the majority of people will at some point experience this pattern as children and in turn as parents themselves.

Taking a historical view, however, the modern family provides less welfare than it did two hundred years ago. Hospitals, schools, shops, workplaces, transport and leisure facilities have developed to fulfil a variety of functions that mean that social welfare provision has become a more complex and mixed system than it used to be. Much of this change occurred in the nineteenth century, when hospitals, schools, shops and factories came to prominence. Two rival mechanisms underlay these changes: the market and NGOs. The market developed in two senses relevant to social welfare. The first sense is the market in labour as individual workers shifted increasingly from agriculture towards industrial wage labour. The vicissitudes of this means of livelihood threw up new insecurities whenever the availability of, or ability to, work stopped. The second sense is the market in goods and services, such as food, clothes and medical care, that accompanied these changes and through which families increasingly met their various needs rather than through self-provisioning. Inability to pay could have disastrous consequences for a range of needs of family members.

Alongside the market and very often in response to its failures to provide either adequately waged work, or adequately priced goods and services, NGOs developed. However this was not always for humanitarian reasons. On the one hand, for example, mutual associations such as Friendly Societies were indeed designed for the mutual benefit of members when social needs arose. On the other hand, however,

the settlement house movement for the 'improvement' of working class lives, was also motivated by fear that upper middle class organizers had about the consequences of poverty life styles, such as the spread of disease, for all social classes. In addition there were also concerns about the costs of market failure, not to individual victims, but to those who might have to 'pick up the pieces'. For example in the later part of the nineteenth century the provision of education was motivated by the employment needs of industrialists and the provision of agreed compensation for industrial accidents was designed to avoid more expensive court proceedings.

For a while the market and NGOs enjoyed considerable independence from the attentions of government, but there was a growing concern by the end of the nineteenth century to regulate their activities. In the twentieth century regulation led on to the provision of financial support and eventually to state provision of welfare services. Motives for this were again mixed. Genuine humanitarian concern for the meeting of social needs coexisted with the fear of social problems threatening the wider social order and the realization that the costs of social reproduction (both the biological production of children for the future workforce and the daily replenishment of the capacity for work) might be better organized by the state. The climax of this process was the establishment of the British welfare state by the Labour government of the 1940s.

All of these institutions of social welfare, family, market, state and NGO continue to coexist, but with regular changes in their functions and scope, most recently under the impact of five years of 'modernization' by the 'New Labour' government. State regulation has been strengthened in these recent years, while privatization and market mechanisms have been encouraged to the point where social welfare can increasingly be thought of as a consumption good. Nevertheless the level of state expenditure on social welfare has remained at about 25 per cent of gross national product (GNP), albeit covering a steadily changing mix in favour of social security and health services and away from education and housing.

What Are Social Needs?

While I have suggested that there were mixed motives for organizing social welfare institutions, the meeting of social needs remains their central concern. We must therefore review the definition of this crucial concept. A useful starting point is to distinguish needs from two related notions: wants and preferences. There are two important senses in which wants and needs differ. First, wants are more inclusive: we may want things that we do not need; indeed marketing experts make great efforts to persuade us to do so. Second, we may need things which we do not want, either through ignorance or our dislike of them. Medical intervention can often be of this type. Both of these distinctions suggest that needs are more basic or essential to us than wants.

Preferences, a concept frequently used in economic analyses, differ from needs and wants in the sense that they are revealed only when we make choices, usually in the act of buying goods or services as consumers. The argument here is that it is difficult to really know what people need or want unless they act in some way to try to secure for themselves the things in question. This action component however has its limits, for of course wants cannot be revealed in the market if we do not have the money to pay for things and needs cannot be revealed by individuals where they are not aware of them, or there are no services to meet them. Needs, then, may well have to be discovered by those other than the individual concerned.

We should also make a distinction between needs and social needs. Needs (and problems and welfare) are 'social' in the sense that they are not merely concerned with, for example, individual causes and

---

Box II.1.2 Needs, wants and preferences

- Needs
  - felt need
  - expertly defined need
  - comparative need
- Wants
- Preferences

---

experiences of illness and poverty, but also with the amount and distribution of illness and poverty in different social groups; the reasons for this that arise out of the shared conditions of life for those social groups; and the social structures and processes through which they might be ameliorated. For example, it is only necessary to vaccinate a proportion of the population to stop the spread of infectious disease. In this case, the population can be seen to have a need, but any specific individual may not necessarily feel, or be defined by others as, in need. Waiting in line for an injection, we may have all felt this way as children!

These considerations enable us to make some simple classification of types of need. First are those needs which we are aware of ourselves, felt needs. These are obvious when we feel ill, or have an accident. The second type of needs are those defined for us by others, usually experts or professionals, such as doctors or teachers, but also importantly by family and friends. The third type of need is partly an extension of the second, to focus on needs as revealed, perhaps in surveys, in comparison with other people in the same social group. Here an individual can be said to be in comparative need because others have something that they do not.

An important aspect of needs, shared by all three types, has given rise to many debates in social policy. This is the question of how needs can be measured, particularly when we move away from the obvious examples such as major medical emergencies. The classic case is that of poverty. How much income do we need? One approach, drawing on the second type of need as defined by experts, is to think about the basic essentials, such as food, clothing and shelter, and to work out the amount of money needed to buy the cheapest minimal provision of these and to define anyone with less as poor, or in need. However any close study of the way in which poor people live reveals that the notion of 'basic essentials' or 'cheapest minimal provision' varies with the way of life of the particular family and community in which an individual lives. Is television an essential? Is meat-eating essential? What cultural prescriptions about dress codes are essential?

An alternative approach is to use the first type of need and merely to ask poor people what they feel they need. However where this has been done, it seems that poor people often adjust to their circumstances and feel less in need than they 'ought' to, especially if they are older people; while others can feel poor where they 'ought' not to. Finally we could merely define as poor those people with less than others as in the third type of need, comparative need, for example by ranking incomes and identifying, say, the bottom 10 per cent as poor.

This problem of measurement has resulted in an oscillation in social policy debates between those who favour an objective interpretation of what is 'basic' or 'essential', for example in terms of the ability of an individual to remain alive and to retain the capacity to act as a 'person' in society (Doyal and Gough, 1985); and those who argue that needs are really more subjectively defined by individuals themselves, experts, and government agencies and others who provide services designed to meet needs (Piachaud, 1981).

What Is a Social Problem?

Social welfare institutions are also concerned with social problems, which are related to, but not the same as social needs. For example, as C. Wright Mills famously observed, one person suffering from unemployment may be in acute need, but it is only when unemployment becomes a more widely shared experience in a community that there may be said to be a social problem. Social problems then are to be distinguished from individual need.

A further distinction should be made between the mere existence of a shared set of social misfortunes in a community, whether or not they have been defined as needs and three further elements of a social problem: the extent to which they are perceived; the judgements made about them and the values they threaten; and the actions recommended to deal with them. Needs can exist whether or not they are known about by anyone. Social problems cannot. They exist within the public domain rather than private experience. The perceptions, judgements and recommended actions are in the broadest sense of the term part of the political process of a society or community.

Perceptions of social problems can occur through the eyes of experts or the general public. In the case of experts, social problems are typically defined in relatively objective terms such as the incidence of divorce, where the rate of change is a crucial issue (usually upwards!). However since many social issues are less amenable to objective measurement, for example the effects of family neglect on children, experts can differ widely in their claims about the objective state of a social problem. In these cases the general public, community groups, pressure groups and so on may have widely varied views, such that a so-

---

Box II.1.3   Elements and types of social problems

- Elements of social problems
  - social conditions
  - perceptions
  - judgements
  - solutions
- Types of social problems
  - open/contested
  - closed/uncontested

cial problem is more subjectively defined. Social problems, in the extreme version of this view, become merely 'what people think they are'. Since most of our experience of and knowledge about social issues is indirect, the mass media are an important influence not only on our knowledge of social issues, but also the way in which they are framed, judged and dealt with.

Perceptions are heavily influenced by judgements about the kinds of values felt to be under threat. This brings us to the heart of defining a social problem, since it is the sense that something is wrong that motivates any attempt to put things right. There are two aspects of this that we have to consider. First is the issue of whose values are threatened. Some issues command widespread consensus, for example that threats to life are unacceptable. The judgement that the spread of disease such as HIV-AIDS is a social problem from this point of view is relatively uncontested. Other issues however may be the site of sharp value conflict, for example the relevance of people's sexuality to family life in various ways.

However, a second important aspect of value judgements in definitions of social problems can sharply modify the effects of these value concerns. This is the issue of who is to blame for the problem. In the case of HIV-AIDS, what might have been an ordinary medical issue was transformed in this regard by very sharp dissensus over the judgements of blame made about gay men and therefore about the nature, status and solution to the problem. Where problems are the site of value conflict, or blame is attributed, we can speak of contested or open social problems, the solutions to which are far from clear. Where consensus and lack of blame are typical we can think of social problems as closed or uncontested.

The solutions proffered to social problems have an intimate connection to perceptions and judgements made about them. Indeed, it has been argued that often the solution may indeed tend to determine these other aspects. An example of this process was the development in the 1970s of a social problem of hyperactivity amongst children, at a time when a drug treatment to calm them down became available. Certainly the ways in which a problem is perceived and judged strongly affect the kind of solution suggested. The running battle between the former Conservative government and the poverty lobby over the level and distribution of poverty illustrates this clearly. Both used conventional statistical analysis to try to demonstrate the presence or absence of poverty and the two sides took very different positions over who should take the moral responsibility for the problem. The government's solution, to create jobs through the enforced flexibilization of employment conditions, was the very cause of the problem from the point of view of the poverty lobby.

A related example has been the current government's attitude to the problem of income poverty in the case of lone parents, discussed in detail in chapter IV.5. While benefits have been increased, the main solution was felt to be the strong encouragement for lone parents to take up paid employment. The government has here been borrowing ideas from the USA, particularly ex-President Clinton. Benefits have been statutorily limited to a total of five years in the USA and there is evidence that the number of lone parents claiming support has declined. Such a 'solution' to this perceived social problem may not actually increase the welfare of lone parents.

The current government's approach to solving social problems illustrates the subjective nature of the perception and definition of social problems, which in earlier years was used by progressive commentators to attack official or expert opinions (for example patriarchal elements of medical opinion). However such a strategy can be turned round by a government to deny the existence of a problem, or to argue that only certain kinds of solutions are reasonable. Thus the claim that globalization demands low rates of taxation, or flexible labour markets, or the use of private finance to fund health care infrastructure development, has helped to obscure alternative solutions.

Conclusion

Social welfare institutions have evolved in their current form alongside the development of industrial society. As industrial societies change, so do their welfare institutions. This is most clearly observed in the countries of Russia and Eastern Europe, where a variety of neo-liberal social policy innovations have been developed and already modified in response to economic and political forces. Western societies have not been immune to such influences, with the ubiquitous assumption of globalization used to justify significant debates and changes in the trajectory of social policies for the twenty-first century. While they are chiefly oriented to meeting social needs and tackling social problems, this has not been the only motive. Both the nineteenth-century German chancellor, Bismarck, and Winston Churchill argued in favour of social welfare institutions as a buttress against the attractions of socialist ideas.

Social needs and social problems are subject to contested definitions. In both cases a major debate concerns the relative weight to be given to objective or subjective definitions. Can needs and problems be scientifically measured in some absolute sense, or are they inescapably subject to the relative social circumstances of both those in need and the particular interests of the definers? The genomic revolution, which seems to offer so many tantalizing health benefits and yet to raise an even larger number of ethical uncertainties, illustrates well the interaction between industrial and scientific developments and public concerns. Public debate has never been more wide ranging, buttressed through public opinion surveys, focus groups and the development of professional committees and academic departments of ethics.

These points lead us back to the nature of social policy as a subject. The word 'policy' implies that it is a part of the political processes and institutions of modern society and that social needs, social problems and social welfare are similarly political. While some observers have come to anticipate the decline of the nation state in the wake of an increasingly globalized world, discussed further in chapter II.18, social policy issues have in reality grown in importance in regional affairs, whether at a sub-national level, or more widely in multi-country regional welfare 'blocs', most noticeably in the development of a European social model, alongside the distinctive American or Asian patterns of welfare development.

Guide to further reading

On social welfare institutions:
Thane, P. (ed.), 1978. *The Origins of British Social Policy* (London: Croom Helm). This book provides a left wing account of the struggle between different social welfare institutions to influence social policy in the late nineteenth and early twentieth centuries.
Hay, J. R., 1975. *The Origins of the Liberal Welfare Reforms 1906–1914* (London: Macmillan). This short book gives a very clear account of the variety of different reasons for the rapid development of state welfare in the early twentieth century.
Green, D. G., 1993. *Reinventing Civil Society* (London: Institute of Economic Affairs). This book argues from a right-wing perspective that the state has eroded other effective forms of social welfare institution.
On social needs:
Bradshaw, J., 1972. 'The concept of social need', *New Society*, 30 March. This article was a milestone statement about different types of social need.

Piachaud, D., 1981. 'Peter Townsend and the Holy Grail', *New Society*, 10 September. This article presents a strong argument for the impossibility of finding an objective definition of need.

Doyal, L. and Gough, I., 1985. 'A theory of human needs', *Critical Social Policy*, 10, 6–38. This work represents a cogent argument for returning to an objective basis for the definition of needs.

On social problems:

Manning, N. (ed.), 1985. *Social Problems and Welfare Ideology* (Aldershot: Gower). This book offers a detailed review of the theory of social problems, together with a range of case studies.

May, M., Page, R. M. amd Brunsdon, E. (eds), 2001 *Understanding Social Problems* (Oxford: Blackwell). This book provides a more recent set of analyses of social problems.

Rubington, E. and Weinberg, M. S., 1995. *The Study of Social Problems*, 5th edn (New York: Oxford University Press). This book presents a detailed analysis of six different models of social problems.

II.2
Equality, Rights and Social Justice

Peter Taylor-Gooby

'Equality', 'rights' and 'social justice' have been prominent among the rallying cries of those who call for radical reform in social policy, whether in terms of a Hayekian condemnation of the shameful perversion of a tax and spend policy based on an appeal to social justice (George and Page, 1995, p. 22), or the expansionary claims of those who link social justice to social investment (Commission on Social Justice, 1994, pp. 17–22). Since the concepts have been interpreted in different ways and used as ideological slogans by different groups at different times, we are faced with two main tasks in this chapter: understanding the root meanings attached to these terms, and tracing changes in the way in which they are used over time.

Meanings and Definitions

Equality

In mathematics, equality refers to a relationship whereby two distinguishable elements have equal value. Note that claims about equality for elements that are the same in every respect are uninteresting – if they are completely identical you cannot distinguish them. Similarly, no serious reformers who use a language of equality have argued for social uniformity, although detractors sometimes wish to treat them as if they do. The egalitarian claim of welfare reformers has been that different groups should be treated as of equal value in social policy. In practice this has led to demands for equality in entitlement to benefits and services, in treatment by welfare authorities and in participation in decision-making.

The main issues arise in two areas. First there is a problem in setting limits to the range of egalitarianism. Views on the scope of equality will depend on theories about what influences people's behaviour. The view, associated with neo-classical economic theory, that people are inclined to maximize their individual utility implies that egalitarianism may undermine work incentives and kill the goose that lays the golden egg. If being a victim of inequality gets you welfare benefits, why bother to be anything else? The view that individuals are more influenced by their social relations and by norms of behaviour suggests that the impact of equalizing policies will depend much more on the social framework within which they operate (Dean and Taylor-Gooby, 1992, chapter 3).

The second point concerns the practical rather than the moral scope of inequality. Many policy-makers have distinguished between 'equality of outcome' and 'equality of opportunity'. Policies directed at the former must aim to put people in positions of equal value, while those seeking the latter are more modest. The objective is simply to give individuals an equal starting point in an unequal society. Egalitarianism in this sense is entirely compatible with wide divergences in people's life-chances. Since few would describe the capitalist societies in which welfare states have flourished as equal in outcome, the main practical application of egalitarianism has been in the area of equal opportunities. The notion is immediately relevant to education and training, and to policies in relation to the acknowledged social divisions of sex, disability and ethnicity. It has been particularly influential in the rhetoric surrounding New Labour (Blair, 1998).

Different groups have struggled to ensure that particular divisions are recognized as meriting equal opportunity intervention. Issues of sexuality, of age, of disability, of region, of linguistic facility and sometimes even of social class are discussed as areas where equal opportunities policies should apply, and these struggles are traced elsewhere in this book (see George and Page, 1995, chapters 8, 9 and 18).

Rights

'Right' is essentially a juristic concept referring to the legitimacy of an individual's claims. In the context of social policy the question is whether claims to social benefits and services should be backed by state force, so that social rights become an element in citizenship in the modern state. In a celebrated analysis, T. H. Marshall distinguished civil, political and social rights originating at different periods and based on individual status in relation to the legal, political and social system (George and Page, 1995, chapter 6; see also Taylor-Gooby, 1991, pp. 190–200). Many commentators have pointed out that different patterns of rights have evolved at different speeds in different countries, as the chapter on comparative social policy shows. Developments in the UK indicate a gradual shift from residence-based rights towards an exclusionary notion of citizenship based on hereditary rights.

Weber, the prominent social theorist, pointed out that the development of the modern state and its framework of social individuation and categorization made possible the establishment of a precise and formal structure of social rights. This is one of the achievements of modern civilization. At the same time, the process of categorization also subordinates the individual to a structure of authority that enforces obligations as a member of society – the individual becomes a 'mere cog in the machine', victim of the 'iron cage of bureaucracy'.

The conflict between individual rights and state authority has been one of the central themes of modern literature from Kafka to the *X-Files*. In relation to welfare, governments have sought to impose obligations to pay taxes and to conform to particular norms in relation to work, sexuality, household and family transfers of income, child care, retirement and residence. The welfare components of the modern state apparatus can be particularly powerful in enforcing desired patterns of behaviour. In the UK, child support policies have been designed to enforce transfers between separated parents, recent changes to social security are intended to regulate job-seeking behaviour and in some cases area of residence, and employers are required to administer sick pay at a minimal level. Social rights, far from being a simple reflection of social progress, are two-edged.

Claims in the welfare area can be legitimated as rights in a number of ways. In practice, ideas about need and ideas about desert are most important. *Need-based* arguments tend to maintain that a class of human needs can be identified, which provides the justification for an obligation on government to ensure that these are met, at least as well as the society at its current stage of development is able to meet them. Although there are a number of problems in this approach, not least in establishing a bedrock of human needs that is secure against relativist reduction (a position recently defended vigorously by Doyal and Gough, 1991, chapters 1 to 3), the human needs approach has offered some of the most profound bases for the legitimation of welfare as an ineluctable duty of government (see, for example, Plant, 1991, chapter 5).

Desert-based claims are essentially founded on the view that some quality or activity of a particular group imposes a requirement on society to provide them with certain services as a matter of obligation. Examples of such arguments are claims that motherhood or contribution through work or in war are deserving of social support, and that the obligation to provide it should come home to the state. Such claims are typically linked to functional or reciprocal arguments or are part and parcel of a normative system.

Functional arguments suggest that some activity is essential for the maintenance of society and that therefore the obligation is owed to those who carry it out. It is difficult to specify such activities in a society subject to rapid change in the way ours is. Social theorists such as the American writer Parsons tend to identify them at the highest abstract level ('authority', 'production', 'reproduction', 'communication'; see Doyal and Gough, 1991, chapter 5). The disadvantage with such generality is that abstract categories can be applied to a very wide range of activities. These arguments tend to parallel at a social level the issues raised in earlier discussions of individual obligation.

One result is that arguments about 'desert' are typically linked to normative systems. In our society the principal ethics involved are the family ethic, with its attendant claims about the gender division of labour, the spheres of childhood and adulthood, appropriate forms of sexuality and the work ethic, and the implied legitimacy of the market (Taylor-Gooby, 1991, chapter 8). These ethics are subject to modification. Traditional norms of family childcare seem detachable from a strict gender division of spheres of home and paid employment. In relation to work, the boundaries between the life stage where maintenance should depend on work or property and periods appropriate to retire-ment and education/training appear to have a certain malleability. Ideas about the desert of particular groups are of considerable importance in relation to social rights and the way in which they are put into practice: for example:

- entitlement to social insurance benefits based on work records is more secure and less subject to official harassment than entitlement to means-tested benefit based on need;
- support services designed to help those caring for frail elderly people are sometimes rationed by status and access to employment of the carer and receipt of them is influenced by gender and age;
- allocation of social housing of particular quality may involve the grading of tenants as appropriate to particular estates.

Social justice

Social justice is concerned with who ought to get what. Resource allocation in most welfare states is dominated by market systems which rest on the idea that goods are property to be owned, valued, bought and sold, and on normative systems of distribution closely linked to kin relationship. Arguments about rights and about equality have provided a basis for claims about justice which often cross-cut market and kin allocation. The most important arguments developed in recent years have been those of Nozick and Rawls, and these illustrate the way in which individualistic and social approaches to social justice may be developed.

- **Nozick** essentially argues that the core of just claims is labour – people have a right to what they have 'mixed their labour with', i.e. improved by their work. As a matter of strict justice, it is a violation of individuals' autonomy to appropriate or redistribute the goods that people have gained through their work, although individuals may as a matter of charity choose to surrender property

EQUALITY, RIGHTS AND SOCIAL JUSTICE **45**

to those they view as needy and deserving (Plant, 1991, pp. 210–13).

- **Rawls**'s approach rests on the notion of a 'veil of ignorance'. The central idea is that just arrangements are those which people would agree on if they did not know what position in society they themselves would come to occupy, if they had no vested interests themselves (Plant, 1991, pp. 99–107). He goes on to argue that it is in principle possible to 'second guess' the kinds of choices about the allocation of goods (and bads) that individuals would arrive at under these circumstances. Unable to be certain that they would not end up in the worst possible position in an unequal and exploited society, they would tend to legislate for a social order in which only those inequalities existed which improved the position of the worst off; for example, by raising living standards throughout the community.

Both approaches have been extensively discussed and criticized. The first rests on a particular individualism in relation to labour which is not compelling. Production in modern society involves the interlinked labour of many people. The correct allocation of credit for work is highly controversial and is carried out in practice mainly through market institutions. The impact of a Nozickian approach, linking just distribution to work, may be to legitimate the market and to undermine any justification for welfare interventions. The Rawlsian approach is attractive in that it rests on negotiation free from the biases that social position – class, gender, tenure, age, employment opportunities, state of health and so on – in the welfare sphere generates in the real politics of social policy. However, there are severe problems in deciding *a priori* what allocation of benefits and services people who were abstracted from their social circumstances would agree. There is nothing irrational in favouring a grossly unequal world and hoping to come out as a winner; or, if one felt more charitable, in

supporting the highest average standard of living, providing the worst off are not too hard hit. It is difficult to devise approaches to social justice which both take seriously the autonomy of individual citizens and lay down the definitive policies a society must follow if it is to be labelled just – to put the seal of social justice on particular welfare arrangements.

The Concepts as Ideology

Equality

In the post-war decades of confident welfare expansion the advancement of equality – in the sense of equality of opportunity – was often used to justify policy, particularly in relation to educational reform. Crosland's influential book *The Future of Socialism* (see George and Page, 1995, pp. 131–2, 144) argued that technical and economic change squared the circle. Meritocracy was both rational and just. Harold Wilson as Labour leader succeeded in developing a political ideology based on this approach, which united traditionalists and modernizers among party supporters by arguing that both class struggle and class privilege were outdated by the requirement to get the best people in the Right positions. Equality of outcome has never been seriously advanced as a dominant policy goal by the main left currents in British politics.

The remaking of Conservative policy associated with the charismatic leadership of Mrs Thatcher from the mid-1970s resulted in a vigorous commitment to free market principles and to a traditional family ethic. Egalitarianism had no place in this doctrine. Equal opportunity policies become a corrupt and unfashionable 'political correctness'. Reappraisal on the Left after four successive election defeats led first to the programme of the Commission on Social Justice (1994, p. 1), which deprecated egalitarians as backward-looking 'levellers' and defined justice in terms of 'the need to spread opportunities and life chances as widely as possible', and more recently to the conception of a 'Stakeholders' Britain' in which equality of opportunity again plays a clear role but in which there is also a strong emphasis on individual responsibility to contribute to society. This has been vigorously developed in New Labour policies.

In short, the Right in politics prioritizes rights, derived from market and family, over claims based on considerations of equality. The Left has regarded equality as important, but as only one policy objective among several. The commitment is increasingly to equality of opportunity (with an obligation to group opportunities) and to the linking of welfare to social contribution.

Rights

Individual rights are closely linked to notions of social justice. Equality has been one of the principal foundations of rights claims in social policy debate, so that citizenship in itself is seen to justify rights to welfare. The other major foundation has been the notion of desert. In policy debate, ideas about desert, linked to work and family ethics, have become increasingly important, so that rules of entitlement to benefit are drawn more stringently, the mechanisms for ensuring that able-bodied people are pursuing employment have been strengthened and obligations to maintain children after the breakdown of a relationship have been codified (Dean and Taylor-Gooby, 1992, chapter 3). Much of this policy reform has also been concerned to reduce state spending, in line with the general emphasis on property rights which requires collective spending decisions to be justified against a stricter criterion than is applied to individual spending.

The emphasis on desert is a central pillar of right-wing approaches to welfare. However, recent arguments about stakeholding on the Left have also been concerned to emphasize individual contributions as part of a move towards more active policies. These are characterized by concern to expand opportunity and also to give due weight to individual responsibility for outcomes, rather than simply provide maintenance as in the passive receipt of benefits.

Social justice

Developments in relation to social justice follow largely from the above. The key shift is towards a more active notion of how social entitlements should be structured, in keeping with the move away from an egalitarian approach and towards one influenced by meritocracy or by ideas about property- and family-linked desert.

The impact of the New Labour approach has been to shift debate on the Left from rights justified by equal citizenship to rights justified by desert. Most unemployed people, for example, can only get benefits provided they demonstrate appropriate behaviour as 'job-seekers' or by taking part in New Deal programmes. Similar ideas are being applied to groups such as single parents or some categories of sick and disabled people.

Conclusion

Debates about equality, rights and social justice have become both broader and narrower. On the one hand, struggles for the recognition of the Rights of a wider range of groups, based on evidence of unjustified inequalities, have extended the range of social policy intervention. On the other, ideological pressure justifying allocation on market and family-ethic principles is stronger than it has been for half a century. Such an approach requires the state to step back a pace. Welfare interventionism is spread thin.

Social policy in the new millennium is overshadowed by concerns about the impact of population ageing, technological un- or sub-employment, growing international competition, tax revolt, the weakening of kinship care networks, general distrust of big government and the future sustainability of Western welfare states. The climate of policy-making is one of retrenchment. Under these circumstances it is hardly surprising that conceptual debates turn away from a highly interventionist concern with the promotion of equality of outcome to an interest in the nourishment of more equal opportunities or the use of policy to promote greater economic competitiveness or to tackle social exclusion.

It is striking that these new directions are widely understood as more active policies in contrast with a previous regime of passivity, on the grounds that they expect and require individuals to act, whereas traditional welfare states allocated benefits and services to groups in need of them. It is as if the retreat of government and the imposition of extra responsibilities on the individual is to be understood as greater activity and involvement on the part of the state. Citizenship is increasingly what you do – not what you get.

Guide to further reading

The best (and most clearly written) guide to the main currents in contemporary political philosophy in relation to the issues discussed above is Plant (1991), especially chapters 3 to 7. Goodin (1998) covers similar ground in more detail. Doyal and Gough (1991) provide an analysis of need as a basis for rights in chapters 4 to 7. Dean and Taylor-Gooby (1992) review the political debate about work, family ethic and welfare entitlement. George and Page (1995) provide succinct accounts of the views of major policy commentators and critics. Taylor-Gooby (1991), chapters 7 and 8, discusses competing notions of citizenship and develops the argument that any desert-based view must include assumptions about social context. Fitzpatrick (2001, chapters 1 to 4) provides an introductory review of the main concepts. The Commission on Social Justice (1994) devised a policy framework designed to be feasible in twenty-first century Britain on the basis of a left-leaning meritocratic theory of social justice. Blair (1998) sets out his vision of a welfare system based on equal opportunities rather than equal outcome, and this has been extensively discussed – see the Nexus webpages, http://www.netnexus.org/library/papers/3way.html, and the *New Statesman* special edition: http://www.newstatesman.co.uk/thirdway.htm.

Blair, T., 1998. *The Third Way*. Fabian Pamphlet 588, London: Fabian Society.

Commission on Social Justice, 1994. *Social Justice: Strategies for National Renewal*. London: Vintage.

Dean, H. and Taylor-Gooby, P., 1992 *Dependency Culture: The Explosion of a Myth*, Hemel Hempstead: Harvester Wheatsheaf.

Doyal, L. and Gough, I., 1991. *A Theory of Human Need*, Basingstoke: Macmillan Press.

Fitzpatrick, T., 2001. *Welfare Theory: An Introduction*, Basingstoke: Palgrave.

George, V. and Page, R. (eds), 1995. *Modern Thinkers on Welfare*, Hemel Hempstead: Prentice Hall/Harvester Wheatsheaf.

Goodin, R., 1998. *Reasons for Welfare*, Princeton NJ: Princeton University Press.

Plant, R., 1991. *Modern Political Thought*, Oxford: Blackwell.

Spicker, P., 1988. *Principles of Social Welfare*, London: Routledge.

Taylor-Gooby, P., 1991. *Social Change, Social Welfare and Social Science*, Hemel Hempstead: Harvester Wheatsheaf.

II.3
Efficiency, Equity and Choice

Carol Propper

Economic ideas and concepts are widely used in public policy. The domain of social policy is no exception: 'effective' and 'efficient' are adjectives frequently cited by politicians and policy-makers as goals for the welfare state and those responsible for delivering such services. Yet the ideas of economics are considerably more than current buzz words. Economic analysis provides a framework which can be – and is – used to analyse questions about behaviour as diverse as worker participation in unions, the relative welfare of nations, the tendency of bureaucracies to grow or the behaviour of politicians. In addition, terms such as efficiency and effectiveness have rather more precise meaning within economics than when used by politicians or policy-makers. Economists see efficiency, equity and (sometimes) choice as ends: and ends which may be achieved through a number of possible means. These means include the market, the state and a mixed economy. This chapter presents these key economic concepts and illustrates their applicability to social policy (see also chapter III.10 on Paying for Welfare).

Scarcity and Choice

Economic analysis begins from a single fact: we cannot have everything we want. We live in a world of scarcity. One way of seeing this scarcity is to notice that no one can afford all the things he or she would really like. This is obvious in the case of the homeless, but it applies equally to the carer who works part time and would like to have more time to devote either to her work or to the person she cares for, or to the wealthy rock star who goes on giving concerts in order to buy yet one more Caribbean island. It equally applies to governments who have a larger budget than an individual but can never spend as much on health services or education as the voters would wish.

Faced with scarcity, be it of money or time, people must make choices. To make a choice, we balance the benefits of having more of something against the costs of having less of something else. Because resources are finite, in making choices we face costs. Whatever we choose to do, we could have done something else. So, for example, the carer with limited time can choose between working more or spending more time looking after the person she cares for. Or a society which invests in building roads uses up time and material that could be devoted to providing hospital facilities. Economists use the term 'opportunity cost' to emphasize that making choices in the face of scarcity implies a cost. The opportunity cost of any action is the best alternative forgone. So if building a hospital is viewed by society as the next best thing to building a road, the cost of building a hospital is the opportunity cost of building a road.

In many situations the price paid for the

use of a resource is the opportunity cost. So if a road costs £1 million to build, then if the materials and labour used in road construction would be paid the same amount were they used in construction of something else, £1 million is its opportunity cost. But market prices do not always measure opportunity costs and nor are all opportunity costs faced by an individual the result of their own choices. For example, when you can't get on to a bus in the rush hour, you bear the cost of the choices made by all the other people on the bus. This is not a price that is quoted by the market and nor it is one that the others on the bus take into account when choosing to get on the bus.

Efficiency

Efficiency has a specific meaning within economics and in this section I will outline what this meaning is and how it relates to the behaviour of individuals. When deciding how much of a good or service should be produced we need to take into account that having the good or service gives rise to both benefits and costs, and how the benefits and the costs vary with the amount that is produced. In general, benefits are desirable and costs are to be avoided. Given this, it would seem sensible to choose that amount of the good at which the gap between benefits and costs is largest. When society has selected this amount of the good and allocated resources of production accordingly, economists say that this is the efficient level of output of this good, or alternatively that there is an efficient allocation of resources in production of this good.

In determining the level of output which is efficient, we need to take into account both the benefits from the good and the opportunity costs of producing it. As an example I consider the consumption and production of something simple – a foodstuff: ice cream. But the analytical framework can be equally applied to hospitals, schools, social work services and nuclear submarines.

Benefits of consumption

We would expect the benefits from eating ice cream to vary according to the amount eaten. In general, for someone who likes ice cream we would expect the total benefit to rise the more is eaten. However, this total benefit may not rise proportionately with each mouthful consumed. Let us consider the first spoonful. If the eater is really hungry the first spoonful will give considerable satisfaction. But as the amount eaten is increased the satisfaction derived from each additional spoonful will begin to fall. By and large, we would expect to find that the benefit derived from each additional spoonful falls the more has been consumed. If we define the last spoonful as the marginal spoonful, we can say that the marginal benefit falls as the quantity of ice cream eaten increases. Either you become full, or because variety is nice, you would rather eat something else.

This analysis can be applied to society as a whole. Defining society's benefits as the sum of the benefits received by all individuals from ice cream, we can add up across all individuals to get the total social benefit. Similarly, we can add up each person's marginal benefit at each amount of ice cream eaten to get the marginal social benefit. This is the increase in total social benefit as we increase society's consumption by one unit. We assume that we can add up the benefits received by different people. Often we can do this easily because benefits are measured in a single unit, say pounds. But in some cases there may be measurement problems: for example, when it is hard to value a good, or when £1 is worth much more to one person than another.

Both the total social benefit and the marginal social benefit can be drawn on a graph. Figure II.3.1 shows the total social benefit from ice cream consumption. The amount of ice cream consumed is on the horizontal axis and the benefit from this in pounds is on the vertical axis. Total social benefit rises as consumption increases, but

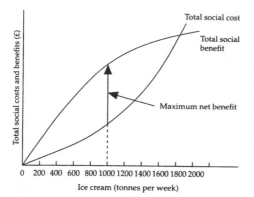

Figure II.3.1 Total benefits and costs of ice cream consumption

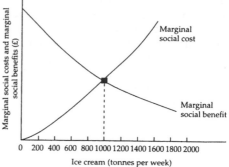

Figure II.3.2 Marginal benefits and costs of ice cream consumption

it rises at a falling rate. It rises at a falling rate precisely because the marginal social benefit of consumption falls as more ice cream is eaten.

Figure II.3.2 shows this marginal social benefit of ice cream consumption. The total amount consumed is on the horizontal axis and is measured in the same units as in figure II.3.1. On the vertical axis we show the value in pounds of the marginal benefit. The marginal benefit curve slopes downwards from left to right, showing that the marginal social benefit falls as consumption of ice cream increases.

Costs of production

To determine the efficient level of production and consumption of ice cream we also need to consider the costs of production. Typically, the more of a good that is produced the more costly it is to produce. So total costs increase with production. However, what is required to establish efficiency is the cost of producing an extra unit of output, known as the marginal cost. Studies of production generally show that there is a level of production beyond which it becomes increasingly costly to expand output. This could be for all sorts of reasons: firms may have to pay overtime or use less

productive machinery, or the costs of coordinating production or delivery rise as the amount of good produced rises. In other words, the marginal cost of production increases as output increases.

Assuming that ice cream production has the same pattern, we can add up the total costs of production across all producers. This will be the total social cost. We can also add up all the marginal costs to obtain the marginal social cost for each unit of output. The total social cost of figure II.3.1 shows the way that total social cost rises with output of ice cream. The corresponding marginal social cost of production is shown in figure II.3.2.

The efficient level of output

We can use the information on how social benefits and social costs of ice cream consumption and production vary with output to identify that level of output at which the difference between total social benefits and total social costs (net social benefit) is at a maximum. This is the efficient level of output. From figure II.3.1 we can identify this as at 1000 tonnes per week. Looking at figure II.3.2 we can see that this is the point at which marginal social benefits equal marginal social costs. This is no coincidence. As long as the marginal social cost is below the marginal social benefit, society will gain by producing and consuming more ice cream. Conversely, if the marginal social benefit is below the marginal social cost, society would do better by putting its resources to other uses and consuming and producing less ice cream. Only when the marginal social benefit is equal to the marginal social cost will it be impossible to increase net social benefits.

The analysis of the efficient amount of ice cream output is relevant to all goods and services. So we can define the socially efficient output of hospitals, home helps, education or cars in exactly the same way. We may have more problem in measuring the benefits and costs, but the principle remains the same: the socially efficient amount of the good or service is produced at the point where the marginal cost and benefit are equal. An efficient level of production is thus a desirable end: if all goods are produced in their efficient quantities then net social benefit cannot be increased by reallocating resources. Conversely, if the level of production is not efficient, then net social benefits can be increased by producing more (or less) of one good and less (or more) of at least one other. Given that resources are always finite, efficiency is thus an important social objective.

Efficiency and effectiveness

Although efficiency and effectiveness are often used synonymously by policy makers, they are different. Effectiveness means producing something in the best possible way technically, and is sometimes called technical efficiency. We can check whether a production is technically efficient by seeing whether, given the current technology, more output could be produced from the present inputs. As an example consider the delivery of meals on wheels by one person with one van. One service might visit houses by order of number. If all the even houses are on one side of the street and all the odd numbers on the other, this will mean crossing the road between each delivery. This is likely to be less technically efficient than delivering meals to all the odd numbered houses and then to all the even ones.

Efficiency goes further than (and encompasses) effectiveness. To know whether a production process is efficient we must first check that it is effective. Then we have to see whether its current technology produces the output in a cheaper way than the alternatives. This requires looking at the prices of inputs, whereas effectiveness does not. So in our example it may be that once costs are taken into account, it might be found that it is better to change the amount spent, and so to employ two people and one van. Then we must check that consumers cannot make themselves better off by choosing to buy other goods. Finally, we must check that all the costs and benefits involved have been taken into account. (Technically, this is known as checking that there are no external costs and benefits. In the bus example given above, there were external costs – those imposed by bus users on others.)

So before we can say that something is efficient we must first ensure that it is effective; hence the drive toward effectiveness in the use of scarce medical resources, for example. However, just because a production method is effective, it does not mean it is efficient. We need to know the costs and the benefits of the service and of alternatives to know that. At present, for many areas of social policy, we are only at the stage of establishing effectiveness and not efficiency.

Efficiency versus Other Goals

Equity

Even though efficiency is a desirable end it is not the only one. An efficient outcome is not necessarily a fair or equitable one. An efficient output is one for which the sum of all individuals' marginal valuations equals the marginal social costs of production.

But each individual's valuation of a good or service – and so the sum of these valuations – will depend on the resources he or she has. So the efficient level of production will be defined in relation to the existing distribution of resources. If initial resources are distributed in a way that is judged as unfair, there is no reason why an efficient allocation of those resources should be fair.

An example may make this clearer. Suppose there are only two members of society, Ms A and Ms B. Given their initial resources, their likes and dislikes and the production methods available to them, the efficient level of production of ice cream is four tubs per week. These tubs could all go to Ms A, or all to Ms B, or they could share them equally. Each of these divisions of the total production is possible, but not all will be judged as fair or equitable. On the other hand, if each received only one tub, this allocation might be judged as fair, but it is not efficient. It is not efficient because we know that the efficient level of production is four tubs. If only two tubs were produced, net social benefit would be increased by producing more and in so doing we could make both Ms A and Ms B better off.

There are many possible definitions of equity or fairness – for example, minimum standards or equal distribution for all – which we do not discuss here. The points to note are: first, that efficiency is not the same as fairness; second, that there is often a trade-off between the two (a fair allocation may be one which is not efficient); third, that efficiency embodies a value judgement just as definitions of fairness do. The value judgement underlying the definition of efficiency is that some distribution of income (often the existing one) is legitimate.

Choice

Choice is often seen as an important goal by economists. By making choices, individuals can indicate their valuations of goods and services. If valuations are known

then the production of those services which have greater net (marginal) value will be increased and the production of others decreased, and so the outcome will be more efficient. Choice is often linked to competition: competition is one means by which individuals can exercise choices. To see this, consider the case where there is no competition in the supply of goods and services because there is only one supplier. In this case individuals cannot choose the good they prefer as there is only one on offer.

Of course, there are costs to making choices – individuals have to decide which product they prefer and this will mean finding out about each possible option. In some circumstances it could be the case that very small differences between goods do not merit the costs of trying to choose between them. However, in general, more choice is judged to be better than less.

In the field of social policy, where choice has often been limited, increasing choice – and the allied goal of increasing responsiveness of suppliers to users' wishes – is viewed as an important goal. From an economics perspective this is viewed as a move in the right direction. However, this does not mean that the benefits of increasing choice necessarily outweigh the costs. This will depend on the particular service.

The Means of Delivering Efficiency and Choice

All societies have had methods of trying to get the most out of limited resources. In large-scale societies, two dominant mechanisms of allocation have been used. These are allocation by the government and allocation by the market. Under the former system (often called command economies), planning and administration are used to decide what and how goods should be produced, and to whom they should be allocated. Under the latter, allocation decisions are made by the ostensibly uncoordinated decisions of large numbers of individuals and private firms.

Markets are seen as desirable by economists since – in the absence of market failure – they will lead to an efficient allocation of resources without the need for coordination mechanisms and the costs of planning. In practice, of course, not all decisions in a market system are made by individuals, and not all ownership is private. Government has a large role in all market economies. However, the market mechanism currently has dominance. In social welfare the ideas of choice and competition have been introduced into systems where previously allocation was by means of administrative decision. In health care, education, social care and social rented housing in the UK (and elsewhere), competition in supply has been introduced as a means of increasing choice, responsiveness and efficiency. Services which were previously delivered by government monopoly have been opened up to competition – some of which comes from within the public sector, and some from without. So now private firms collect garbage, build houses for low-income tenants and run prisons. Private suppliers compete to provide care for the mentally handicapped, and not-for-profit public education providers compete for contracts to provide education. Twenty-five years ago these arrangements would have been seen as the wrong way to provide services: today, some of them go without comment. On the other hand, in health, education and transport (amongst other services) there is considerable debate about the role for the private sector and for competition. It still remains to be seen whether the precise institutional arrangements that have emerged bring the promised gains. Nevertheless, if choice and efficiency are important goals, market mechanisms have their uses in welfare services as in other parts of the economy.

Summary

The key points of this chapter are:

- Economics provides a framework to analyse the production and use of welfare services.
- Economic analysis begins from the assumption of scarcity – we cannot have everything we want. So people and society must make choices.
- The appropriate cost of these choices to society is the opportunity cost – the resources forgone if the choice is made.
- Economic efficiency means making the most of scarce resources. Economic efficiency occurs when the opportunity cost of using resources in a particular activity is equal to the sum of everyone's marginal benefits from that activity.
- Efficiency is not the only goal. Other goals include fairness and choice. These goals may clash with efficiency.
- Economists see markets as one way of delivering efficiency and choice in social and welfare services.

Guide to further reading

Le Grand, J., Propper, C. and Robinson, R. *The Economics of Social Problems*, 3rd edn (Basingstoke: Macmillan Press, 1992), provides an economic analysis of social policy concerns and assumes no previous knowledge of economics. A more advanced textbook, designed for those already studying economics, is Barr, N. *The Economics of the Welfare State*, 3rd edn (London: Weidenfeld and Nicholson; Oxford: Oxford University Press, 1998). Barr, N. and Whynes, D. (eds) *Current Issues in the Economics of Welfare* (Basingstoke: Macmillan Press, 1993), contains essays useful for the study of social policy, but requires some knowledge of economics. For a review of whether market-orientated reforms have worked in the British NHS, see Le Grand, J., Mays, N. and Mulligan, J-A. (eds) *Learning from the NHS Internal Market* (London: Kings Fund, 1992).

Note

The first two sections of this chapter draw heavily on Le Grand et al. (1992). I am grateful to both my two co-authors for use of this material.

II.4
Altruism, Reciprocity and Obligation

Hilary Land

Human Nature

Resources in societies, whether in the form of cash, kind or services, are claimed by and distributed to individuals and households within a variety of institutions. The family, broadly or narrowly defined, is important in all societies as a system for allocating resources between the young and old as well as between men and women. In market economies, in addition to the market itself, there may be state welfare systems alongside voluntary societies, charities and churches. The relative importance of each of these systems varies over time and between countries. For example, in England charities and voluntary societies play a much smaller role now than they did in the nineteenth century or than they do today in Italy or the Netherlands. The principles underlying the distribution of resources in each of these systems are often different because some claims are based on 'desert', others on 'need' – both highly contested concepts (see chapter II.3). Some principles are enshrined in law as obligations, which one person owes another and which the courts can enforce and punish those who fail to honour them – for example, the obligation that parents maintain their children. These also change over time and differ between countries. In the UK, for example, until 1948 grandparents could be obliged in law to maintain their grandchildren. That is still the case in Germany. Others are less well defined and are in part the product of

a society's history and culture, or what the sociologist O'Neill (1994) calls 'rituals of reciprocity that celebrate exchanges between society, nature and God, involving a covenant between them as a model of all other civic reciprocities between individuals, neighbours, families, communities and the state'.

The assumptions about human nature on which these principles and practices are based also differ. Some assume that individuals are motivated primarily by self-interest and selfishness, others by altruism and concern for others. Adam Smith, one of the founding fathers of political economy in the early nineteenth century, recognized both but is more often quoted in support of the former view, particularly by those on the right of the political spectrum. He wrote:

It is not from the benevolence of the butcher, the brewer or the baker that we expect our dinner, but from their regard to their own interest. We address ourselves, not to their humanity but to their self-love, and never talk to them of our necessities but of their advantage.
An Inquiry into the Nature and Causes of the Wealth of Nations, cited in Collard (1978)

However, he did recognize that not all human activity could be interpreted in this way. In a less well-known quote he wrote: 'How selfish so-ever man may be supposed, there are evidently some principles in his nature, which interest him to the fortune of others, and render their happiness necessary to him, though he derives nothing from it except the pleasure of seeing it.' In the words of a twentieth-century economist, Collard (1978) this means that:

> altruism implies externalities in consumption. The happiness of one individual is a function not only of the volume of goods and services consumed by himself but also of certain goods and services consumed by others. Thus many people would be distressed to know that the sick were, for financial reasons, receiving very inadequate attention.

Adam Smith also recognized altruism to be particularly important within the family, for 'they are naturally and usually the persons upon whose happiness or misery his conduct must have the greatest influence'. However, by and large, political economy placed the family outside of its domain (it is no accident that the male pronoun is used in the above quotes) and concentrated instead on developing models of human society comprising solitary and independent individuals acting rationally and freely making contracts in pursuit of their own self-interest. As the philosopher Midgley (1985) has pointed out, this model derives from seventeenth-century physics, in which the ultimate building blocks of matter were conceptualized as hard, impenetrable atoms. It is a model, she writes, in which 'all significant moral relations between individuals are the symmetrical ones expressed by contract'.

However, there are other ways of thinking about human behaviour and human relationships. If, on the other hand, we use a biological or 'organic' model, we can talk also of a variety of asymmetrical relations found within a whole. Leaves relate not only to other leaves but to fruit, twigs, branches and the whole tree. People appear not only as individuals, but as members of their groups, families, tribes, species, ecosystems and biospheres and have moral relations, as parts, to these various wholes. In this model people are not independent but interdependent, and relationships cannot be specified with reference to a contract.

Family Relations

Family relationships have always been perceived to be different from those of the market place and not subject in the same way to rational calculation. Reciprocity between men and women or between parents and children is informed by love or altruism rather than narrow self-interest. Many economists treat the family or household as a 'black box' and have developed models which assume a household can be treated as if it were an individual – a male individual – with identifiable interests or 'joint utilities', to use the jargon. Becker is one of a minority of economists who has shown an interest in the family and in altruism, arguing that:

> families in all societies, including modern market oriented societies, have been responsible for a sizeable part of economic activity – half or more – for they have produced much of the consumption, education, health and other human capital of the members. If I am correct that altruism dominates family behaviour, perhaps to the same extent as selfishness dominates market transactions, then altruism is much more important in economic life than is commonly understood.
>
> Becker, G. *A Treatise on the Family*, Cambridge, MA: Harvard University Press, 1981

However, he accepts women's willingness to invest in the 'human capital' of their husbands and children rather than in their own, using a rather circular argument, namely that since on average they enter marriage with less education, training and marketable experience (i.e. less human capital) than their partners, it is rational from the point of view of maximizing the family's interest for them to use their time and effort in this way. Families invest less in the human capital of their daughters than their sons because they are expected to devote at least part of their adulthood to marriage and children and so the cycle is repeated. This changes, however, with improved opportunities for girls or if marriage becomes more risky. As Folbre, a feminist economist, has recently argued (1994):

> As long as male individualism is counter-balanced by female altruism, as long as rational economic man is taken care of by irrational altruistic women, families play a particularly important (and unfair) role. But when women gain the freedom to act more like men, pursuing their rational self interest, the price of caring labour goes up.

Hilary Rose and I argued (Land and Rose, 1985) that because many social policies are still based on taken-for-granted assumptions about women's willingness and availability to care for other members of their families – so much so that it is only remarkable when it does not happen – women's altruism within the family is more accurately described as 'compulsory'. Women who do not care for their children, their partners or other relatives needing care may well find their access to resources such as housing substantially reduced. Moreover, it is argued that, in contrast to commodities sold in the market, payment for care within the family destroys the value of the care itself. For example, foster parents receive expenses, not a salary, unless the child they are looking after is especially difficult in some way. The caring professions, such as nursing, have historically been badly paid because nurses, it was argued, should be attracted by a sense of vocation rather than by the size of the salary. The same argument has never been applied to doctors.

Some of the assumptions about women's availability to care have been examined since the 1990s because of the demise of the male breadwinner-female housewife model. This has been replaced, at least in the rhetoric by the individual worker model in the government's plans for the British welfare state in the twenty-first century. As Tony Blair explained in 1998: 'We want to rebuild the system around work and security. Work for those who can; security for those who cannot.' Beveridge's post-war social security scheme was also built around the centrality of 'work' but unlike Blair he included unpaid as well as paid work, although both were gendered concepts. Women, once married, had no obligation to undertake paid work, unlike their husbands and unmarried sisters. They belonged primarily in the home in which they were, or should have been, engaged in unpaid work i.e. care. In contrast in 1998, the Labour government developed a national childcare strategy with the objective of developing the formal childcare market so that mothers could take up paid employment outside the home while other paid workers (almost entirely female) cared for their children.

Nevertheless distinctions between the formal labour market and the informal care system remain. The childcare strategy only supports care in the formal sector: care provided within the family, by a friend or by a paid worker in the child's own home attracts no subsidy. While free half-time education has been expanded for pre-school children, childcare services must be paid for. Similarly, the government rejected recommendations of the Royal Commission on Long Term Care in 1999 that care of older people should be provided free on the same basis as health care. In England and Wales (but not in Scotland) social care attracts charges. The assumption that care provided among family members is, and should be free is still strongly held despite the evidence that payments are made, particularly among poorer families. As the minority of the Royal Commission, who supported charging for social care, wrote:

> Informal care is a term which hides a rich variety of human relationships between spouses, between children and parents; between kith and kin, friends and neighbours. Most care without giving a thought to the financial cost of caring – it somehow demeans them to reduce their dedication to cash amounts.
>
> Royal Commission on Long Term Care, *With Respect to Old Age. A Note of Dissent* (London: Stationery Office, Cm.4192, 1999)

Family Obligations

Finch and Mason's (1995) research on family obligations has looked at how the meaning of responsibility or obligation is understood and put into practice in families. They challenge the concept of 'fixed obligations' associated with a genealogical link and argue that 'in reality the responsibilities which people feel and acknowledge towards their relatives have more complex and more individual roots'. Obligations between spouses may be more fixed in character (although we know less about obligations cohabitors feel towards each other), but those between parents and adult children can be very variable. They argue for seeing responsibilities as commitments which are built up between specific individuals over time, perhaps over many years. This is done

> through contact, shared activities and particularly through each giving the other help as it is needed. This process of reciprocity – accepting help and then giving something in return – is the engine which drives the process of developing commitments. Although people do not work with a simplistic balance sheet, reciprocal help given and received over time is a crucial factor in understanding how family relationships operate.

These commitments between the generations can survive divorce. They warn policy-makers against defining and attempting to enforce obligations which are not consistent with the ways in which families practise and understand these obligations. The controversy surrounding the implementation of the Child Support Act 1991 is a good example of how, by shifting the obligation to maintain children and their mothers from the legitimate or social father to the biological father, the government is ignoring deeply held beliefs about family responsibilities. As a result it is not working as well as the government intended, and absent fathers have not paid as much maintenance as was hoped.

Collective Obligations

The relationship of state welfare policies to both the market and the family has always been the subject of debate. Some have argued that the development of market economies has damaged the family and the capacity to support its members. As Alva Myrdal wrote in an influential book over fifty years ago, when many Western industrialized nations were debating the future of their state welfare systems: 'Changes in the economic structure of society weakens the family as an institution. Unproductive age groups have no assured place in the new economic order of individualistic money making in nationwide competitive markets' (*Nation and Family*, London: Kegan Paul, 1945). Social welfare provision, or what she calls 'collective devices', were therefore necessary to substitute for the security once provided by families. Titmuss, writing in the 1950s and 1960s, had a similar view of social welfare as a mechanism for compensating individuals and families who were damaged by economic growth. Those who benefited from a thriving and expanding economy had an obligation to share those benefits with the less fortunate. For him, state welfare policies were also mechanisms for extending altruism beyond the family (1971):

> The ways in which society organizes and structures its social institutions – and particularly its health and welfare systems – can encourage or discourage the altruism in man; such systems can foster integration or alienation, they can allow for 'the theme of the gift' – of generosity towards strangers to spread among and between social groups and generations.

Titmuss studied blood donors in the NHS as an example of a willingness to give to strangers – moreover, strangers never encountered. However, he found that their willingness to give did stem from a sense of obligation to a wider society and confidence in the behaviour of future unknown strangers, who in their turn would give their blood should others, including themselves, ever need it. (It is interesting that the recent NHS practice of selling blood products abroad has reduced the willingness of some to donate their blood.)

Beveridge, regarded as one of the principal architects of the British post-war welfare state, proposed a social insurance system which was based on a clear contract between employers, employees and the state. He was also very clear about the pattern of obligations between husbands and wives, and between parents and children. Embedded in his social insurance and social assistance scheme were rules to ensure that men's obligations to take paid work in order to support their families and women's obligations to provide domestic services for their husband and children were carried over from earlier social security systems. In the last resort prison faced men who refused work and failed to support their families. However, he too wanted to encourage altruism within the wider society. This he called 'a sense of Divine Vocation' (although he was careful to point out that he had not been brought up in any particular faith). By this he meant 'that in the daily life of each of us there should be something done, not by instinct, but more and more consciously without thought of reward, whether it is part of our paid work or not. There should be something that is spending ourselves, not getting anything' (Beveridge, W. *Pillars of Society*, London: Allen and Unwin, 1943). Unlike many social policy analysts at the time – or since – he noticed that 'serving, exhausting oneself without thought of personal reward – isn't that what most women do most of their lives in peace or war?'

Others have been rather more sceptical of developing what Pinker (1971) subsequently called 'the altruistic potentialities of ordinary citizens'; he took a harder look at the evidence for this. He concluded that:

The welfare institutions of a society symbolize an unstable compromise between compassion and indifference, between altruism and self-interest. If men were predominantly altruistic, compulsory forms of social service would not be necessary; and if men were exclusively self-regarding such compulsion would be impossible. The spirit of altruism, far from being a natural flowering of human nature, must be seen as the product of the rigorous discipline of injunction to self-denial and the repression of the grosser form of self-love.

Jose Harris, Beveridge's biographer, has also more recently urged historians to investigate 'if, for good or ill, particular welfare policies do encourage particular types of economic, moral or civic behaviour'.

Baldwin has posed the question the other way around in his examination of the social bases of the welfare state in five European countries. He asks why and how solidaristic social policies ever occur: 'Why have the fortunate ever agreed to institutionalize aid for the worse off except to the degree necessary to prevent unrest or still the naggings of conscience?' He rejects the economists' explanation derived from their ability 'to reduce even apparently genuine altruism to rationally motivated self interest . . . [so that] . . . much of what appears to be redistribution is in fact merely insurance'. True, there are economic efficiencies to be won from altruistic behaviour; but, that being so, why then would anyone oppose mutually beneficial arrangements? In any case, 'individuals may be economically rational, but groups and classes – the actors in politics – must recognise and develop their stake in reciprocal exchanges before they can be realised'. He also rejects a simple appeal to altruistic sentiments so that social policy is understood as an expression of altruism generalized to wider society. Rather, he concludes that:

Solidarity – the group's decision to allocate resource by need – is only misleadingly analogous to altruism. An individual sentiment, altruism is generally confined to narrow circles of like-minded. Solidarity, in those few instances where it has been realised, has been the outcome of a generalized and reciprocal self-interest. Not ethics, but politics explain it.

> Baldwin, P., *The Politics of Social Solidarity: Class Bases of the European Welfare State* (New York: Cambridge University Press, 1990)

His meticulous examination of the development of social insurance systems led him to the conclusion that an analysis of the role played by the middle classes is essential for understanding Western European welfare states.

Self-reliance and Self-protection

The debates about social welfare in the UK during the 1980s and 1990s have been dominated by those who believe that state welfare provision undermines both the efficient working of the economic market and obligations within the family. This was coupled with a view that only the poor need state welfare provision – the middle classes and the wealthy can look after themselves. Baldwin's analysis of the history of state welfare provision seems correct, for the role of state welfare systems in distributing resources in society has been eroded in the past twenty years as the middle classes seek more services in the private sector. Before she became prime minister, Margaret Thatcher had written: 'The sense of being self-reliant, of playing a role within the family, or owning one's property, of paying one's way, are all part of the spiritual ballast which maintains responsible citizenship and a solid foundation from which people look round to see what more they can do for others and for themselves.' Taxation was seen to be not only damaging to enterprise but also a way of 'buying your way out of your obligations to society', to use the words of a Home Secretary, and therefore undesirable. Margaret Thatcher herself asserted that 'there is no such thing as society'. So, by definition, state welfare policies could neither foster, nor be fostered by, altruism and reciprocity beyond the family.

This view of society comprising self-seeking, individualistic people has been strengthened by the rise of sociobiology. Eugenics, which underpinned the belief in the naturalness of inequalities and hierarchies in the first half of this century, was influential in the social policy debates of the time in Britain and the United States. Sociobiology is now providing a similar ideological basis for undermining the arguments for a universalistic welfare state. From the early 1970s its proponents have been arguing that prime among the traits inherent in our nature is selfishness. Dawkins claims that everything organisms do is done out of self-interest, because 'selfish genes' exist only to replenish themselves: 'They are in you and me; they created us, body and mind, and their preservation is the ultimate rationale for our existence.' In this model women's greater commitment to child rearing follows from the belief that women and men must adopt different strategies to maximize opportunities to spread their genes into future generations. Altruism is explained away.

> What passes for co-operation turns out to be a mixture of opportunism and exploitation. The impulses that lead one animal to sacrifice himself for another turn out to have their ultimate rationale in gaining advantage over a third, and acts for the good of the 'society' turn out to be performed for the detriment of the rest . . . Scratch an 'altruist' and watch a 'hypocrite' bleed.
>
> Dawkins, R., *The Selfish Gene* (Oxford: Oxford University Press, 1976)

wrote a more extreme advocate of this position. Sociobiology is being challenged within the biological sciences but genetic determinism and genetic reductionism do serve to turn attention away from the environmental and structural causes of inequalities, fail to recognize the inter dependence of individuals within society or of societies across the globe and so support the view that a minimal welfare state is not only desirable but all that is possible. There are parallels here with nineteenth-century political economy and debates about the role of the national state in relation to the market economy.

At the beginning of the twenty-first century, these debates are taking place in the context of the global dominance of neo-liberalism. Beck and Beck-Gernsheim (2001) in their analysis of the changing relationship of individuals to each other and to wider society, have developed the concept of individualization. This is different from individualism and the concept of the self-sufficient individual embedded in neo-liberal economic theory. Individualization can be thought of as 'institutionalized individualism', which does not breed a 'me-first' society. On the contrary, those who want to have a life of their own have to be very sensitive to others' needs and wants as well as able to negotiate the terms of living together. Traditional family relationships and class divisions can no longer be taken for granted as they were earlier in the twentieth century. They argue that:

> The individual creativity which [institutionalised individualism] releases is seen as creating space for the renewal of society under conditions of radical change. In developed modernity...human mutuality and community rest no longer on solidly established traditions, but, rather, on a paradoxical collectivity of reciprocal individualization.

This 'daily culture' of freedom is happening in the context of growing social and economic inequalities intensified by what they call 'the global victory of neoliberalism'. However, these new inequalities which are forming worldwide are also a collective experience. 'The key question, therefore . . . is how the bubbling, contradictory process of individualization and denationalization can be cast into new democratic forms of organization'.

Pinker (1971) described the study of social welfare as 'a study of human nature in a political context'. Central to this are the concepts of altruism, reciprocity and obligation. To understand their full meaning, students of social policy have to draw on economics, philosophy, history and biology as well as politics, sociology and social policy.

Guide to further reading

Beck, U. and Beck-Gernsheim, E., 2001. *Individualization* (London: Sage) explores the meaning and consequences of individualism.

Collard, D., 1978. *Altruism and the Economy* (Oxford: Oxford University Press) discusses altruism and its relevance to economic and social analysis from an economist's point of view.

Finch, J. and Mason, J., 1995. *Negotiating Family Responsibilities* (London: Routledge) reports on a study which researched the processes by which family members actually meet – or do not meet – the obligations between them.

Folbre, N., 1994. *Who Pays for the Kids?* (London: Routledge) gives an economist's perspectives on the costs – in time and care as well as in money – of bringing up children and examines the very different distribution of the obligations to meet these costs between men and women.

Land, H., 2002. 'Spheres of care in the UK: Separate and unequal', *Critical Social Policy* Jan/Feb., reviews the distinctions made between formal and informal care by users of care as well as the policy-makers.

Land, H. and Rose, H., 1985. 'Compulsory altruism for some or an altruistic society for all?', in P. Bean, J. Ferris and D. Whynes (eds), *In Defence of Welfare* (London: Tavistock) reviews a number of social policies and exposes the extent to which women's altruism underpins the policies' analytic.

Midgley, M., 1985. *Evolution as Religion* (London: Methuen) gives a philosopher's perspective on these concepts and provides an excellent critique of sociobiology.

O'Neill, J., 1994. *The Missing Child in Liberal Theory* (Toronto: University of Toronto Press) argues for a renewal of the social contract between the generations and criticizes a political economy which emphasizes individualism and ignores social responsibility.

Pinker, R., 1971. *Social Theory and Social Policy* (London: Heinemann) reviews some of the key concepts used in social policy analysis and has also stood the test of time.

Titmuss R. M., 1971. *The Gift Relationship* (London: Allen & Unwin) has remained an important contribution to the social policy literature on altruism and reciprocity and includes his empirical study of blood donors.

II.5
Divisions, Difference and Exclusion

Pete Alcock and Angus Erskine

Divisions

A key feature of all societies is that they are socially divided. Different social groups have access to different amounts of power, wealth and influence. This results in unequal outcomes in terms of welfare: for example, life expectancy differs between social groups - the more affluent tend to live longer. Thus societies are divided by inequalities between different social groups and these determine the life chances and well-being of individuals. As a result of this the welfare which is provided through social policy to promote well-being, may mean different things for one group compared to another. Indeed the welfare interests of one group may even conflict with the welfare interests of another. For example, the provision of care may enhance the welfare of the recipient at the expense of the person providing it.

The main consequence of recognizing that we live in such a divided society is the realization that we can understand better the structure and workings of that society if seek to identify and analyse the different social divisions that exist and to explore the implications of these for policy planning and practice. Sociologists have written extensively about social divisions, indeed these are one of the key foci of sociological research (see Payne, 2000). However, although they all agree about the importance of social divisions within modern societies, they are far from agreed about how these

divisions should be defined and measured, and this dissensus spills over into social policy too.

It is important to be clear also about the contrast between social divisions and some related concepts (and structures) which are also used by sociologists and policy analysts. In particular social divisions are not the same as social *inequalities*. Divisions may be unequal, indeed most generally are; but it is not inequality which determines them. Nor do divisions capture all inequalities, indeed there may be massive inequalities within particular social divisions (some women are much richer than others). The study of social divisions is also not the same as the study of social *stratification*. Stratification focuses upon hierarchies and the extent to which in any society (in fact in all societies) hierarchies of power, resources and influence exist. Again social divisions are not all hierarchically distributed; and power and influence may be stratified within social divisions. Social divisions rather focuses attention upon social groups, upon the different ways in which societies may be grouped, and, most critically, upon the relations between these different social groups. In summary then study of social divisions is the study of social *relations* at the macro level of social groups.

The most significant social division in British society, at least in terms of the academic research and debate that it has generated, is that of social *class*. For over a century much sociological analysis has focused upon questions of social class, both how to define and measure class structures and what the implications of these are for social relations. Class analysis can be traced back to the work of two of the leading social theorists Marx and Weber. Marx's view was that the exploitative relations between the capitalist and the working classes created a conflict at the heart of capitalist society that would drive social change through struggle between the two. Weber's approach was based on a broader and more descriptive conception, linked to occupational position, but one in which class would similarly be the key determinant of social status and life chances.

More recently there have been a number of attempts to define and measure social class (see Crompton, 1998). The leading sociological approaches are those of Goldthorpe, who produced a hierarchy of class divisions ranging from professionals and managers at the top to agricultural workers at the bottom; and Wright, who drew on Marx's notion of the ownership and control of property to produce a list of classes which would take different forms in different societies over time. However, the notion of class division as a means of categorizing social structure has also been taken up by bureaucrats and policy-makers to develop 'official' definitions and measurements of class. In the UK two such official classifications are particularly important. The first is the Registrar General's scheme used in official statistics which divides people into six numbered groups by occupation:

I   Professional and managerial
II   Intermediate middle-class
III(N) Skilled non-manual
III(M) Skilled manual
IV   Partly skilled
V   Unskilled

The other is the socio-economic group (SEG) scheme which contains a broader and more sophisticated range of categories.

What is clear from these various classifi-cation schemes is that different definitions can lead to different measures, with different implications for understanding and analysis. All, however, draw heavily upon occupational status. This raises questions about how to deal with divisions outside of, or unaffected by, labour market structure – a point to which we shall return shortly. It also means that relatively static pictures emerge of what is in essence, of course, very much a dynamic process.

There is dynamism within classes. During the course of their lives people can move from one class to another, for instance by gaining or losing a job. This is generally referred to as *social mobility*. There is also dynamism between classes. Marx's original notion of classes as struggling for power and resources is still of critical importance for understanding class relations in modern society; and this is particularly important for an understanding of the social policy implications of class analysis.

To some extent we can see that social policy development is the outcome of class struggle – for instance, improved social security protection, health care and housing conditions have been the focus of political campaigning, and their introduction has helped to improve the circumstances of most members of the working class(es). However, it is also true that social class differences continue to affect policy development and policy delivery – for instance, much private welfare provision has been developed by and is restricted to the wealthy middle class, and there is also evidence that middle-class people benefit most from some public provision, such as higher education and some forms of health care. However we define and measure social class therefore it remains of central importance in determining our position in, and prospects in, society and the way in which welfare policies are designed and delivered within this.

However, all social scientists now recognize that class is not the only such social division. There are other social groupings which are just as important in structuring our experiences and our prospects, and in influencing the way social policy is developed. As we have seen most class divisions are based upon occupational status; what about those differences which do not flow from labour market position? Most obvious here is *gender* difference. The experiences, and circumstances, of men and women are very different, and can lead to conflicts in relations between them; but these differences and conflicts are only in small part due to labour market status. The importance of gender divisions within society has been taken up in particular by feminist academics and campaigners, and the implications of this for social policy are discussed in more detail in chapter II.11. Some feminists have argued that there is a fundamental conflict between the genders, similar in some ways to Marx's notion of class conflict, in which women are unequal and oppressed – sometimes referred to as *patriarchy*. But, as with class, there are differences of both theory and practice within gender analysis too.

Gender relations are, of course, at least as longstanding as those of class. However, widespread analysis of them within social policy is a relatively recent phenomenon. This is also true of some other social divisions, which like gender and class are in practice deep-seated and longstanding ones. Because of the recent attention they have been given these are sometimes referred to as 'new social movements'. As Fitzpatrick mentions in chapter II.14, however, another 'new' feature of these divisions, at least within the context of social policy, is the fact that the differences they experience are in part a product of the differential operation of welfare services themselves – for instance, in the case of divisions over ability and disability, the way in which welfare services have (or have not) addressed the circumstances of disabled people.

There are a number of distinct divisions within the new social movement umbrella. Payne's (2000) book on social divisions focuses upon eight divisions other than class

and gender. Williams' (1989) critical introduction to social policy focuses upon gender and race. Most lists would include ethnicity and race (see chapter II.12), age, (chapters IV.2 and IV.3) and disability (chapter IV.4). Others of importance are sexuality, nationality and religion. The latter two in particular have been the immediate source of bitter struggles in various parts of the world in recent times, including Northern Ireland. This highlights one of the major implications of social divisions for social policy analysis – that it leads to differences in experiences and outcomes; and it is to this that we now turn.

Difference

The divisions that we have discussed give rise to very different needs, different experiences and different outcomes in relation to welfare. Take for example health care and gender. Women and men have different health care needs: women live longer, men are more likely to have accidents when they are young, and obviously only women give birth to children. These different needs mean that men and women are likely to have contact with health care services at different times in their lives, for different reasons and thus have a different experience of health care.

The provision of health services like other services is also both horizontally and vertically stratified by gender - certain jobs tend to be more usually performed by women (nurses) and men tend to be more often in senior positions (consultants). So men and women are likely to be using the services for different reasons and have a different relationship to the service when they do so. But there also different outcomes: men and women suffer from different forms of ill-health.

This illustration has used gender and the health service as the example, but similar points could be made in relation to other social divisions such as ethnicity and to other welfare services such as education, social security or housing. For example the needs of some minority ethnic groups for particular diets or the costs of religious observance are not recognized in the social security system.

That different groups of people have different needs may be incontestable, but what is important to consider is the ways in which these differences lead to better or worse experiences of welfare provision and also to unequal outcomes in terms of quality of life and life chances. At times, attempts have been made to explain away these unequal experiences and outcomes in terms of differences in needs and nature. However, these arguments have been countered by emphasizing the sameness of people, thus leading to arguments that to treat people equally we must treat them the same.

Recognizing that people and social groups are different presents challenges for social policy. How to avoid, on the one hand, treating people as if they are all the same and therefore not respecting the different experiences of welfare provision that people will have according to their different biographies, life styles and social groupings; and on the other hand using 'difference' as an excuse to allow inequalities and social divisions to be perpetuated by treating people differently.

This presents a challenge to the usual divide between selectivism and universalism. Selectivism aims to target services and goods on those who are most in need whilst universalist approaches seek to provide services and goods for everyone. Universalist approaches may fail to recognize different needs and different experiences, thus failing to meet some particular needs. On the other hand selectivist approaches can be stigmatizing. They involve the recipient making a claim to a negative social status – for example , poor ; and, they may involve intrusive questions about the personal cricumstances of the recipient. Also, by attempting to target particular groups, they fail to hit this target. For example Child Benefit, which is a universal payment, hits nearly 100 per cent of its target – everyone entitled claims. Yet means-tested Jobseeker's Allowance for families with children which is a selective benefit hits only about 85–95 per cent of its target.

The challenge that social policy then faces is how to respect differences without reinforcing and institutionalizing the social divisions which are constructed on the basis of these differences.

Social Exclusion

The importance of social divisions and differentiation for the analysis of social policy is that these help us to understand and explain differences, and inequalities, in the development and delivery of welfare policy. These inequalities are an intrinsic feature of modern society, and they flow from the structural divisions which characterize social relations. However, social relations are not just the product of structural forces. Social relations are determined by social structures; but they are also carried out by social agents. It is individual people, within particular social institutions, who engage in social relations and perpetuate the inequalities and differences that result from these. In social scientific terms social relations are the product of both *structure* and *agency*.

One of the most extreme consequences of social divisions and differences, and a situation in which the role of agency is clearly of central importance, is the problem of social exclusion. Social exclusion has become a major feature of recent policy analysis and policy planning within social policy, both within the UK and within the European Union, although like social divisions more generally it is not in fact a new problem. The concern with social exclusion takes a number of forms. In part it is an extension of concern about poverty and deprivation to include the social and relational aspects of such inequality. In part, however, it is about a more general breakdown of social relations and the process by which this can lead some people to be more or less excluded from social intercourse, and even perhaps within a separate class location.

The explicit focus on social exclusion at the beginning of the twenty-first century extends both to policy-makers and social policy academics. In 1998 the government set up a new Social Exclusion Unit (SEU) to coordinate the work of public, and other, agencies in combating key targets associated with exclusion – their coordinating role was referred to by the prime minister as providing 'joined-up solutions to joined-up problems'. A year earlier an academic Centre for the Analysis of Social Exclusion (CASE) had been established at the LSE to carry out a ten year programme of research in the area. The concern to understand, and to combat, social exclusion is thus a core social policy issue. However, as with social divisions, there is also much debate about what social exclusion is, and how we might best seek to challenge it.

The CASE researchers at the LSE have produced a summary of some of the main definitional issues surrounding social exclusion (see Hills, Le Grand and Piachaud).

In earlier papers they had identified three key features:

- *Relativity* – social exclusion is manifest in social relations, not individual circumstances,
- *Agency* – social exclusion is the result of actions taken by those who exclude others,
- *Dynamics* – social exclusion is the result of experience over time and can be transmitted across generations.

These help to distinguish social exclusion from poverty, which is associated more with the low (or no) income status of individuals. However, they also make clear the extent to which social exclusion is a feature of social relations, and a product of the role of agency within these.

Another way of looking at social exclusion is to examine the extent to which our circumstances are determined by our participation in social networks. In practice social relations are largely experienced through various networks within which we interact. Of particular importance here are employment networks and family and community networks; but equally significant are access to and use of public and private services and 'voluntary' activity in clubs and local organizations. Non-participation in any or all of these key networks can contribute to social exclusion – for instance, the exclusion from work contacts experienced by the unemployed.

Social exclusion is therefore the product of the breakdown, or failure, of social networks; and hence, therefore, to some extent the breakdown of society itself. The concern of many analysts and policy-makers is that social exclusion can lead to social disruption, and it is in part for this reason that it has become for some a core feature of social policy planning in recent years. Many measures exist to combat exclusion, or rather to promote inclusion, focused in particular at promoting and supporting social networks at local or neighbourhood level. This is sometimes now referred to as investment in *social capital*, with networks being seen as a kind of capital, which, like investment in physical capital, could lead to improved social and economic development.

As we have seen, however, the process of social exclusion is one which highlights the role of agency in social relations. This leads to a concern with the activities of agents who exclude some from networks and services; but it also leads to a concern with the activities (or lack of them) of those who are excluded. People can exclude themselves from social networks, both intentionally and unintentionally; and this can contribute to a more general experience of social exclusion. Indeed some commentators have argued that it is the actions, and intentions, of the excluded that are the primary cause of their separation from social networks – for instance, unemployed people who do not seek paid employment but remain instead on social security benefits.

This, often morally loaded, understanding of social exclusion as a process of voluntary withdrawal from social relations is particularly associated with the work of an

American academic, Charles Murray, who argued that it led to those so excluded becoming in effect a separate social class division 'below' the rest of society, referred to as the *underclass*. Actually there is much debate amongst social scientists about the extent to which social exclusion can be equated with the creation of new class structures (see Morris, 1994), and in general sociologists do not find evidence that the unemployed and other deprived groups do exhibit characteristics which might distinguish them from other sections of society.

However, the notion of an underclass of the socially excluded is a longstanding one – Marx referred to them as the *'lumpenproletariat'*. And this view of social exclusion as the product of the failure, of refusal, of some sections of society to engage in effective social relations – referred to by some critics as 'blaming the victim' – is a quite extensive feature of the way in which social exclusion is conceived by policy-makers. Much policy action to combat social exclusion is targeted on particular social groups or local areas, with the implicit expectation that it is through changes in attitudes and actions within these that inclusion can be promoted. As a broader understanding of divisions and differences reminds us, however, our divided society is a product of structural forces (for example the economic changes leading to high unemployment in some areas) as well as the actions of agents; and agency too involves the actions of those who exclude as well as those who are excluded. Social policies in this field will only be effective if they embrace all aspects of such processes.

Guide to further reading

There are a number of sociological texts on social divisions; Payne's collection of essays – Payne, G. (ed.) *Social Divisions* (Basingstoke: Palgrave, 2000) – is a recent addition and includes chapters on a wide range of groups. Crompton's book on class – Crompton, R. *Class and Stratification*, 2nd edn (Cambridge: Polity Press, 1998) – provides a good summary of the key debates about definition and measurement of this core concept.

Issues concerning difference are well covered in Saraga, E. (ed.) *Embodying the Social: Constructions of Difference* (London:Routledge, 1998). Williams, F. *Social Policy: A Critical Introduction* (Cambridge: Polity Press, 1989) provides an alternative critical introduction which points out the way in which much traditional writing within the discipline has under-emphasized the important issues of gender and 'race'.

Some of the best research and writing on social exclusion has come from work promoted by the EU, for instance, Room, G. (ed.) *Beyond the Threshold: The Measurement and Analysis of Social Exclusion* (Bristol: Policy Press, 1995); but the LSE CASE group have now produced a good summary of theoretical issues and UK material: Hills, J., Le Grand, J. and Piachaud, D. (eds) *Understanding Social Exclusion* (Oxford: Oxford University Press, 2002). Morris's book on the underclass - Morris, L. *Dangerous Classes: The Underclass and Social Citizenship* (London: Routledge, 1994) – reviews the historical legacy of this notion and covers the more recent work of Murray and others.

Key Perspectives

II.6
The Neo-Liberal Perspective

David G. Green

The task of this chapter is to explain neo-liberalism as an intellectual tradition as distinct from the public policies pursued by the Thatcher, Reagan and subsequent governments. These policies reflected a variety of intellectual influences, of which neo-liberalism was only one.

The Neo-liberal Understanding of History

Let me begin with a rather brisk survey of the interpretation of history to which neo-liberals typically subscribe. They see themselves as the heirs of a long historical struggle for freedom. For much of human history, rulers were able to do more or less whatever they wished, but in Europe during the Middle Ages limits were gradually placed on royal power. Acton (1907, p. 39) assesses the achievement of the Middle Ages in these terms: 'the principle that no tax was lawful that was not granted by the class that paid it . . . was recognized . . . Slavery was almost everywhere extinct; and absolute power was deemed more intolerable and more criminal than slavery. The right of insurrection was not only admitted but defined, as a duty sanctioned by religion.'

Despite its inclination to favour absolute authority, leaders of the medieval Catholic Church commonly bestowed religious legitimacy on secular rulers only on condition that they acknowledged a force superior to their own, usually by means of an oath of fidelity which gave them limited authority, to be enjoyed only during good behaviour and in accordance with the law of the land. Consequently, during the Middle Ages, rivalry between church and state had helped to limit the power of governments. However, under the impact of the Reformation in the sixteenth and seventeenth centuries, the clergy, having fought slavery and despotism, began to side with absolute monarchy to keep Protestantism at bay. As Acton (1907, p. 44) remarked, instead of emancipating nations, religion 'had become an excuse for the criminal art of despots'. Campaigns for what today might be called 'religious cleansing' were conducted. In 1685 Louis XIV (1643–1715) had ordered all French Protestants to renounce their religion on pain of death. He enjoyed the right of arbitrary arrest and exile and openly asserted that kings were 'no more bound by the terms of a treaty than by the words of a compliment; and that there is nothing in the possession of their subjects which they may not lawfully take from them' (Acton, 1907, p. 48.) Protestant monarchs were equally quick to use force to achieve their ends.

In France tyranny was to survive until the nineteenth century, but in England the efforts of Charles I to emulate French kings led to bloody revolution in the 1640s, as ordinary people sought freedom of worship without fear of persecution and the opportunity to improve their lives without the imposition of arbitrary taxes or controls. It was in this age, when the cause of liberty had suffered reverses at the hands of tyrants, that modern liberalism had its origins. Seventeenth-century liberals felt that they were restoring liberties stolen by absolutist rulers and turned their minds to discovery of the shared laws and morals under which Catholic and Protestant alike could live in peace, despite disagreement. They sought a common core of laws conceived for the most part as the pure word of God, unadulterated by the all-too human interpretations of any given religion.

William Blackstone, whose *Commentaries on the Laws of England* (1765) became the most influential legal guide on both sides of the Atlantic, believed that law was based on the will of God who had provided us with two kinds of law: 'revealed law' and the 'law of nature'. Revealed law, as expressed in the scriptures, was of 'infinitely more authority' because it was 'expressly declared so to be by God himself', whereas the law of nature was 'only what, by the assistance of human reason, we imagine that law to be' (vol. 1, p. 42).

Liberty was understood as living under the protection of the law, not at the mercy of arbitrary rulers. The purpose of law, said Blackstone (1765, vol. 1, p. 53), was to ensure: that every man may know what to look upon as his own, what as another's; what absolute and what relative duties are required at his hands; what is to be esteemed honest, dishonest, or indifferent; what degree every man retains of his natural liberty; what he has given up as the price of the benefits of society.' After the reverses of the sixteenth and seventeenth centuries, the eighteenth and nineteenth centuries brought further progress towards liberty and wherever freedom reigned it brought extension of the franchise and unparalleled prosperity.

Then, the twentieth century saw the rise of new tyrannies in the extreme form of German and Italian fascism and Russian communism, accompanied in Western countries by a renewed faith in the capacity of rulers to govern the lives of subjects for their own good. Western socialists often expressed their ultimate aims in terms that Stalin could have accepted, but they renounced terror and were democratic, displaying a willingness to be voted out of office and refrain from violence against liberal opponents. During the first half of the twentieth century, liberals were slow to see the dangers of creeping collectivism, but during and just after the Second World War they began to warn that Western countries were slowly surrendering their liberties without noticing. It is no coincidence that the most active in warning of the dangers of burgeoning state power had experienced fascism at first hand. Popper had left Nazi-dominated Austria in 1937 before writing *The Open Society and Its Enemies*, and Hayek had encountered the rise of fascism in Austria before leaving for the London School of Economics in 1931. In 1947 Hayek and others had founded an international academic society, the Mont Pelerin Society, to improve understanding of liberty through public discussion. In Britain, Hayek's initiative led eventually to the foundation of the Institute of Economic Affairs in the mid-1950s.

The Ideal of Liberty: A Restatement

Against the backdrop of this all-too-hasty survey of the ebbing and flowing of freedom since the Middle Ages, let me try to restate the ideal of liberty in modern terms. Michael Oakeshott (1975) distinguished between two rival models of modern society: 'corporate association' and 'civil association'. Each represents a different approach to understanding the relationship between the individual and the collectivity. There are three questions:

- What are people like?
- How are people united?
- What should the government do?

Initially, I will consider the answers typically given to these questions by collectivists, or adherents of 'corporate association'. A common strategy is to state the collectivist approach positively and then to employ a false contrast to caricature the opposing view.

1   *What are people like?* The corporatist view is that human nature is moulded by outside forces, including environmental and social influences, and the economic structure. They often deploy a false contrast. The only alternative view, they say, is that individuals are autonomous bundles of wants or preferences not 'social' at all.
2   *How are people united?* The corporatist view is that we are united in pursuit of a common purpose, part of a team under leadership. The false contrast they make is to claim that the only alternative is 'isolated individualism' that people have no concern for others, and no sense of unity.
3   *What should the government do?* According to corporatists, it should give leadership by managing and directing lives. Again, a false contrast is deployed: the only alternative aspiration is said to be 'no government', or *laissez-faire.*

The civil associate answers each question in a different way.

1   *What are people like?* They are not the product of outside forces. They are bearers of responsibility, carriers of a moral compass, capable of facing moral dilemmas, self-management, learning from mistakes and self-improvement.
2   *How are we united?* A society should not be conceived as a collectivity of followers under leadership, but the alternative is not isolated individualism. There is a sense of community, but not that of leaders and followers. Individuals are united by their free acceptance of the obligation not to exempt themselves from the rules, their willingness to do their bit to uphold a mutually respect-

ful moral framework and acknowledgement that everyone has a chance to succeed.
3   *What should the government do?* The government's task is not to direct and manage people, but to create and uphold the framework of law that allows the exercise of responsibility, and to provide some services. *Laissez-faire* is not the ideal. The government has important duties, but they are limited.

Civil association is the tradition of liberty embodied in Locke, Smith, Hume, Burke, Tocqueville, Acton and Hayek. It is not *laissez-faire*, isolated individualism, or naked market forces. Nor is it 'negative freedom'. On the contrary, classical liberals were concerned not only to limit government, but also to devise and uphold a constitution that made it possible for people to put their talents to positive use. But how does this claim square with the common perception that neo-liberals celebrate the naked pursuit of self-interest?

Adam Smith and Selfishness

Some critics (such as Haworth, 1994, p. 6) identify Adam Smith as the arch-exponent of a society based on the pursuit of self-interest, in which the invisible hand will 'magically' sort everything out. To understand Smith's theory of the human condition it is necessary to know *The Theory of Moral Sentiments* (1759) as well as *The Wealth of Nations* (1776). The most important human quality, in Smith's view, was the inclination to seek the approval of others, which meant that the greatest happiness came from acting in a manner that brought praise and the greatest misery from that which brought blame. This tendency rested on 'sympathy', an emotion described in the opening sentence of *The Theory of Moral Sentiments:* 'How selfish soever man may be supposed, there are evidently some principles in his nature, which interest him in the fortune of others, and render their happiness necessary to him, though he derives nothing from it, except the pleasure of seeing it' (Smith, 1976, p. 48).

Smith believed that we can achieve much by pursuing our legitimate self-interest through mutual adjustment to others, but that we should also seek to do right according to our sense of duty. According to Christian teaching, he said, the sense of duty should be the 'ruling and the governing' principle of our conduct: 'to feel much for others, and little for ourselves, that to restrain our selfish, and to indulge our benevolent, affections, constitutes the perfection of human nature; and can alone produce among mankind that harmony of sentiments and passions in which consists their whole grace and propriety' (Smith, 1976, pp. 71–2). Thus, Smith did emphasize the importance of harnessing self-interest, but for him self-interest was not enough. We have a duty to pursue our objectives unselfishly.

Modern Neo-liberals

Some core beliefs are shared by all neo-liberals.

1   Neo-liberals favour a competitive market economy and oppose an economic system planned and directed by the state.
2   They contend that a market economy is an essential bulwark of democracy because, by dispersing property ownership, it prevents the concentration of power in the hands of the few.
3   Neo-liberals subscribe to the rule of law, that is the doctrine that the powers of governments should be limited by a higher constitutional law and that the exercise of power should be based on predictable laws rather than discretionary commands.
4   Implicit in the third, they contend that there is a higher morality to which governments are subject and which in extreme cases may justify rebellion against tyrannical rulers.

However, as acceptance of the value of a competitive market economy has spread, so neo-liberals have turned their attention to other elements of a free society, not least the moral underpinnings. This departure has highlighted some differences of view. Two traditions may be discerned: 'hard-boiled economism' and 'liberty rightly understood'. There are two fundamental philosophical disputes. The first is about how best to understand human nature: on the one hand are those neo-liberals (mostly economists) who see people as 'rational utility maximizers', and on the other are those who find this approach too narrow, insisting that people are, above all, moral agents who constantly face the burden of choice between right and wrong, good and bad. This dispute is closely related to a second, namely about how best to understand the community to which we belong. One view is that it is a unity brought about by bargainers seeking mutually acceptable arrangements, a state of affairs considered to be in the common good because such bargaining leads to outcomes beneficial for all. This claim is also challenged as too narrow, despite containing much truth. The rival view asserts that the bond of unity essential to a free society is not the 'accidental' outcome of bargaining, but rests upon a conscious effort to uphold a liberal way of living a culture across the generations.

The tradition of 'hard-boiled economism' sees an economy as a self-balancing system which ensures the efficient allocation of resources. One of the weaknesses of this view, exemplified in the work of Becker (1976), is that economic investigators see themselves as 'outside the society looking in'. But such methods of understanding tend to see people as reacting to stimuli, and to play down their inner motivations and perceptions. When applied to public policy, this behaviourist approach can have serious limitations, not least because it is a mentality that appeals to centralizers of all parties who want to use economic incentives to achieve their objectives. This 'system design' approach led, for instance, to the introduction of an 'internal market' within the National Health Service during the early 1990s, but the mere introduction of prices and tendering does not provide what a fully competitive market can offer, let alone restore the institutions necessary for liberty.

As Hayek taught, competition is valuable as a 'discovery procedure' and can only be understood as part of a wider philosophy which acknowledges how the free use of personal initiative under law helps to overcome human fallibility and to encourage progress. Competition and free entry into the market allow consumers to discover who can do a better job in three senses. First, prices tend to settle at that point which cannot be beaten by anyone else, at least for the time being. Second, products or services tend to be developed only if consumers want them. Many people are free to try their hand at predicting what consumers will want and from their efforts we learn who produces the best ideas. It is not obvious in advance. Third, the people and organizations offering their services depend on consumers' decisions. At any given moment, some suppliers may be advancing their case despite a lack of customers but, in time, the competitive process filters out the unwanted producers.

From the standpoint of 'liberty rightly understood', the NHS reforms also lacked a moral dimension which should have led to the privatization of hospitals. The rational utility maximizers also advocate privatization of hospitals, but in the form of for-profit corporations in order to maximize 'efficient allocation'. The alternative tradition urges privatization in the form of voluntary hospitals, to restore civil society and encourage the rebuilding of an ethos of mutual service. Before their nationalization in 1948, the voluntary hospitals were the backbone of the acute hospital service and relied entirely on private finance. Above all, they were focal points for local people of goodwill, providing means whereby people could show their mutual concern by donating blood, visiting lonely patients and giving money.

'Liberty rightly understood' emphasizes that each person is a custodian of his or her character and a custodian of the culture which shapes personal virtues. People are not seen as having 'given' preferences which they seek to fulfil, but as leading lives of thinking, learning and choosing. It is exemplified in Martin Luther King's 'I have a dream' speech, delivered in August 1963 in Washington, DC: 'I have a dream that my four little children will one day live in a nation where they will not be judged by the color of their skin but by the content of their character. I have a dream today!' He did not say, they will live in a nation where they will be able to fulfil themselves, or achieve as much as their talent allows, let alone to maximize their return on capital. He referred only to character, their moral achievement. The task of each person is to use his or her talents for the greater good, to uphold the values worth preserving and to pass them on from generation to generation.

The conflict between rational utility maximizers and adherents of 'liberty rightly understood' can also be found in social security. The former tend to favour the 'treat 'em mean and keep 'em keen' approach to social security reform, based on low benefits and avoidance of moral judgement. Friedman and Friedman's (1980) negative income tax is an example of such a scheme: they advocate a single payment to simplify an over-complex tax-benefit system and avoid administrative discretion.

The counter-view concentrates on the character of the person being helped, with the intention of trying to enhance the chances of each person for making the most of his or her abilities. Its focus is on helping individuals to acquire the skills and virtues they need for self-support. Instead of relying on material incentives alone, it urges a combination of a state minimum with the additional support of charities and mutual aid associations because they attend also to character and are better able to appeal to people's strengths, not their weaknesses, by devising personalized schemes to help them back on their feet.

Neo-liberalism in the Twenty-First Century

The advent of a Labour Government in 1997 may superficially seem to have signalled the end of the neo-liberal revival, but in reality New Labour embraced much that the Labour party had earlier denounced as Thatcherism. It pursued a policy of sound money earlier attacked as hard-line monetarism; it followed a responsible policy of taxation and public spending earlier seen as an excuse for 'cuts'; it kept the most significant Thatcher trade union reforms; it spoke enthusiastically of 'labor markets' previously denounced as 'slave labour'; and it was committed to the kind of market economy despised by earlier socialists as 'exploitation'.

Neo-liberal thinkers increasingly focus on the new world order that followed the collapse of communism. Now that there is no longer a battle between two economic blocs, the emphasis has shifted to a comparison between the West and alternative civilizations, especially Islam. It came as something of a shock to liberal thinkers who had spent their lives defending the free world against totalitarianism to be denounced as apologists for the 'Great Satan' by Muslim fundamentalists. Such critics drew attention to declining Western morals, reflected in a high level of crime, the prevalence of narcotic drug-taking, alcoholism, family breakdown and welfare dependency. Writers such as Francis Fukuyama in *The Great Disruption* and Samuel Huntington in *The Clash of Civilizations* were typical of scholars who called the attention of Western intellectuals to the potential consequences of neglecting fundamental beliefs and practices that historically made free societies worthy of admiration.

Conclusion

During the 1970s and 1980s the collectivist economic planning of the post-war years was abandoned in favour of competitive markets. Few wish to exhume economic planning, but a market economy is only one element in a free society.

Neo-liberals historically did not make a sharp distinction between economic questions and other issues. They sought a society based on a democratic political system that recognized the value of open discussion and accountability; the rule of law (rules for living that applied equally to all and were not subject to arbitrary interpretation); and recognition that government had important but limited duties.

Underlying these beliefs was mistrust of unfettered authority and confidence in the potential for progress through learning and experience. Classical liberals pictured a society, not comprising individuals with established preferences, but made up of people learning as they went along, discovering new things about themselves, measuring up to the expectations of others, doing good and being of service.

Participants in a market economy may be guided by a narrow, self-centred materialism or they may be influenced by a more generous ethos based on strong family life and a commitment to serving others. Adam Smith understood that self-interest, enlightened or otherwise, was not enough and that justice and benevolence were no less indispensable elements of a free society. For this reason, many of the free-market intellectuals who in the 1980s were concerned about monetary policy, fiscal constraint and privatization have moved on to talk of civil society, mediating structures and social capital.

Guide to further reading

Lord Acton's two short essays 'The history of freedom in antiquity' and 'The history of freedom in Christianity' (1907) continue to be excellent introductions. F.A. von Hayek's *The Constitution of Liberty* (London: Routledge and Kegan Paul, 1976) provides clear statements of the essential principles of a free society and the implications for social policy. Jerry Z. Muller's *Adam Smith in His Time and Ours* (New York: Free Press, 1993) is a very readable appraisal of Adam Smith. Jonathan Sacks in *The Politics of Hope* (London: Vintage, 2000), Melanie Phillips in *All Must Have Prizes* (London: Little Brown, 1996), and Francis Fukuyama in *Trust* (London: Hamish Hamilton, 1995) and *The Great Disruption* (London: Profile, 1999) offer good insights into the changing moral concerns of liberal thinkers; and Samuel Huntington in *The Clash of Civilizations and the Remaking of World Order* (London: Simon and Schuster, 1996) reflects the impact of the new international order that followed the end of the Cold War.

Acton, J., 1907. 'The history of freedom in Christianity', in *The History of Freedom and Other Essays*. London: Macmillan, pp. 30–60.

Becker, G. S., 1976. *The Economic Approach to Human Behavior*. Chicago: University of Chicago Press.

Blackstone, W., 1765. *Commentaries on the Laws of England*. 4 volume facsimile, Chicago: University of Chicago Press, 1979.

Friedman, M. and Friedman, R., 1980. *Free to Choose*. London: Secker & Warburg, p. 119.

Haworth, A., 1994. *Anti-libertarianism: Markets, Philosophy and Myth*. London: Routledge.

Oakeshott, M., 1975. *On Human Conduct*. Oxford: Clarendon Press.

Smith, A., 1976. *The Theory of Moral Sentiments*. Indianapolis: Liberty Fund.

The Conservative Tradition of Social Welfare

Robert Pinker

Conservatism and the Enlightenment

Conservatism is as much an attitude of mind as the doctrine of a political party. It is a generic way of looking at the world, of conceptualizing society and responding to social change. True conservatives know in their hearts that all political and economic theories are subject to a law of diminishing marginal utility. They are as sceptical of the free play of market forces as they are of state regulation, which sets them apart from both neo-liberals on the one hand and socialists on the other. They look on compromise as the invisible hand that reconciles equally important but frequently conflicting imperatives. Extreme reluctance to compromise turns conservatives into reactionaries, just as an excessive disposition to temporize destroys the delicate balance between scepticism and conviction that made them conservatives in the first place.

The scholars of the Enlightenment laid the foundations of the modern social sciences and opened a new era in the application of scientific methods to the analysis and solution of social problems. They challenged the traditional institutions of political and religious authority and delineated new kinds of relationship between the state, civil society and individuals in a spirit of optimism regarding the possibilities of social progress. Enlightenment scholarship was characterized by a belief in the powers of human reason to enhance human well-being and in the abstract principle of natural law individualism. The guiding tenets of the French Revolution – liberty, equality and fraternity – were inspired by some of the most powerful traditions of Enlightenment thought.

By the start of the nineteenth century, however, an intellectual reaction against Enlightenment thought was becoming more overt, widespread and influential. This development was inspired by a number of conservative thinkers who were opposed to the ideals and objectives of the French Revolution, and wished to restore the old, pre-revolutionary order. There were also a number of early socialists who had supported many of the revolutionary ideals, but were deeply disillusioned with the political, social and economic outcomes. Although these intellectual movements were separated by fundamental political differences, their leading thinkers shared a common belief in the virtues of an organic model of society and an aversion to what they saw as the rampant individualism of the new social orders which were emerging in Western Europe and North America.

Throughout the eighteenth century, most of the help given to the poor and needy had always been provided through the informal networks of social care based on the family, local community, church and workplace, and these networks were to survive the Industrial Revolution, the triumph of political economy and the rise of the modern administrative state. In the structure and functioning of these informal networks we can identify two major traditions of welfare, the first of which had always derived its authority and effectiveness from the paternalistic values of a hierarchical social order in which the high-born and wealthy discharged their welfare responsibilities to the low-born and poor. The second tradition of welfare took its character from the egalitarian and fraternal values which held together the countless forms of mutual aid through which the poor discharged their responsibilities to each other, as kinsfolk, neighbours and fellow workers. The dictates of rationality and reason played little part in the moral dynamics of either of these informal traditions of welfare, and the idea of the state as an involved and benevolent partner was looked on with general suspicion and doubt.

The Conservative approach to social welfare starts not from the formulation of abstract principles, but from the reality of established social institutions such as the family, community, class, religion, private property and government. It expresses a preference for order and continuity and a spirit of deference to the past rather than an assumption that change is necessary because existing institutions are deficient or that progress has more to offer than does the status quo. A second characteristic of Conservative political and social thought is its veneration for society as such, and its organic view of social institutions. When Mrs Thatcher remarked that there was no such thing as society, she was expressing a profoundly un-Conservative sentiment.

In essence, we can say that the central tenets of traditional English Conservative thought were the commitment to an organic model of society and a respect for responsibilities, rights and liberties grounded not in abstract notions of natural rights or contract, but in the traditions and moralities embedded in established institutions. Allied to these beliefs was a hostility towards the encroachments of the central government into local affairs and a natural suspicion of free-market liberalism. While believing in minimal government, Conservatives rejected the distinctions drawn in Enlightenment thought and liberal political economy between the state and civil society.

The Evolution of Modern Conservatism

Historically, the British Conservative, or Tory, political tradition dates from the Restoration of 1660. The term 'Tory' was first used in the Exclusion crisis of 1679-81 but, after the Hanoverian succession of 1714, the Tories were left in more or less permanent opposition to the Whigs, upholding the established church, opposing high taxes and foreign wars and defending rural interests. The Whigs grew from the political factions which opposed James II's succession to the throne, and supported the Glorious Revolution of 1688–9 and the establishment of the supremacy of parliament. Yet there were throughout the eighteenth century many Conservatives who came to accept and defend the Glorious Revolution and to see it as a restoration and reaffirmation of 'ancient rights'.

Edmund Burke is generally considered to be the founding father of modern Conservatism, although for the greater part of his life he was a leading Whig politician. 'Politics', Burke argued, 'ought to be adjusted, not to human reasoning, but to human nature; of which the reason is but a part and by no means the greatest part' (*Reflections on the Revolution in France*, London: Penguin Books, p.106). Certainly there was a place for reason in politics but it should be exercised under the guidance of precedent and what Burke called 'prejudice'; that is, opinions which have stood the test of time. He thought that in political life, the arts of government and reform should not 'be taught *a priori*' (p.135) because abstract principles took insufficient account of the complexities of human nature and society.

The pretended rights of these theorists are all extremes; and in proportion as they are metaphysically true, they are morally and politically false. The rights of men are in a sort of *middle*, incapable of definition, but not impossible to be discerned . . . Political reason is a computing principle, adding, subtracting, multiplying and dividing, morally and not metaphysically, or mathematically, true moral dimensions.

(Burke, Reflections on the Revolution in France, p.153)

I give this quotation in full because it seems to me that it summarizes the essence of Conservative political philosophy.

Burke was not opposed to constitutional and social reform, arguing that 'A state without the means of some change is without the means of its conservation. In the interests of order and continuity it was, however, vitally important to strike the right balance between 'the two principles of conservation and correction'. He described the sentiments which create the moral framework of a nation in developmental terms: 'To be attached to the subdivision, to love the little platoon we belong to in society, is the first principle (the germ, as it were) of public affections. It is the first link in the series by which we proceed towards a love to our country and to mankind.'

From the early nineteenth century onwards close normative affinities developed between the doctrines of political economy, utilitarianism and British liberal thought. By contrast, Conservative political philosophy remained closely identified with an organic ideal of social organization and the defence of traditional institutions against the attacks of social critics and innovators. Romantic Conservatives such as Samuel Coleridge, Tory radicals such as Richard Oastler and William Wilberforce and maverick populists such as William Cobbett shared a common detestation of the theories propounded by Bentham, Ricardo and Malthus.

These Conservatives acknowledged that the old traditions of paternalist concern had been eroded in many parts of the country. They denounced the new Poor Law because they believed that its introduction would further undermine the traditional framework of obligations and entitlements on which British society had always been based. In their opinion the transition from status to contract as the basis of political obligations in the newly emergent market economy was destroying the organic bonds of social life and degrading the poor to the status of either rootless wage-earners or paupers.

Much of the subsequent history of Victorian Conservatism can be seen as a gradual process of coming to terms with the realities of industrial and urban change and reconciling as far as possible the old values of order, hierarchy and paternalism with the new values of competition and possessive individualism. Under Peel's administration the Corn Laws were finally repealed, and a long overdue start was made on fiscal and administrative reform. Disraeli's vision of 'one nation' sought to reaffirm the ideal of an organic model of society held together by traditional bonds of patriotic sentiment but strengthened by new solidaristic doctrines and objectives, including the extension of representative democracy through the enfranchisement of the respectable working class, a programme of popular welfare reforms and the inculcation of a sense of imperial mission in the British people.

In brief, some important changes were taking place within the Conservative political tradition. The party that had once opposed the growth of empire became the party of empire, and the old values of patriotism became overlaid with a new doctrine of imperialism. In the 1890s Joseph Chamberlain set out to make the Conservatives the leading party of social reform. In his Tariff Reform League he tried to link the objectives of imperial preference and social reform together in one programme. Chamberlain hoped that the revenue raised from tariffs on non-imperial imports could be used to finance a radical programme of free education and universal old-age pensions. The League was founded in 1903 but it did not long survive the Liberal election victory of 1905.

Conservatism and Social Reform

By the end of the nineteenth century, British Conservatism had come to terms with market capitalism. Its own paternalist tradition of collectivism lived on but it was now complemented by a defence of industrialism *and* a limited measure of state intervention in social welfare. It had become a tradition of thought that was as much opposed to liberal individualism as it was to socialist collectivism. Writing in 1947, the young Quintin Hogg, a leading Conservative thinker later to become Lord Hailsham, indicted liberalism as the 'body of doctrine aimed at reducing the authority of the state to a minimum'. It was, he went on to argue, 'the Tory Party which took its stand in the nineteenth century against the principles of *laissez-faire* liberalism' and supported the idea of state regulation in some spheres of economic activity. ('An open letter to the Tory Party' in Tom Hopkinson, ed., *Picture Post, 1938-50*, Harmondsworth: Penguin Books, 1970, p.134). Conservatism, he argued, stood for the ideals of economic democracy, the extension of property ownership and the diffusion of political power.

Nevertheless, the Conservative Party spent most of the first two decades of the twentieth century in standing against the rise of liberal collectivism. It opposed most of the social reforms introduced by the liberals from 1905 to the outbreak of the First World War. It should, however, be noted that when the Conservatives were in office during the inter-war years they left the basic structure of these new provisions intact. In some sectors of social service they imposed cuts and in others they introduced new benefits, notably with regard to widows, orphans and old age pensions. It was a Conservative administration that replaced the Poor Law with Public Assistance in 1929 and opened the way for local authorities to

develop their own hospital services. In many respects the Conservatives were more successful than the liberals in reconciling the conflicts between individualism and collectivism that beset both parties during the inter-war years.

It was, however, during this period that a minority of Conservative politicians began to campaign for more radical collectivist policies. In 1938 Harold Macmillan – then a young and dissident backbencher- published his classic exposition of the case for Tory collectivism, *The Middle Way*. Ritschel describes this work as 'essentially a conservative vision of a business commonwealth, nominally subservient to parliamentary authority, but in practice free to determine the course of economic development'. *The Middle Way* set out 'a spirited defence of private enterprise and a corporatist style economy' managed on Keynesian lines. It commended a substantial degree of subsidy for state-owned public utilities, policies of full employment with minimum wage legislation, and a major extension of the statutory social services.

If a Labour backbencher were to publish such a book today it would cause almost as much embarrassment and shock to the Labour Party leadership as it caused to the Conservative establishment in the late 1930s. At the time, Macmillan and his supporters were largely ignored. Like the neo-liberal Conservatives of the 1950s and 1960s, they had to wait for nearly two decades before their policy proposals were to be taken seriously and implemented.

During the Second World War the Conservative Party was both collectivist and anti-collectivist in its approach to social reform. It committed itself to supporting policies of full employment, educational reform and the introduction of family allowances. It opposed many of the key proposals of the Beveridge Report and went on to suffer a humiliating electoral defeat in 1945 as a consequence. Quintin Hogg had anticipated this defeat in 1943 when he wrote an 'open letter' to his party. He asked his colleagues: 'are we being progressive enough in our attitude to reform . . . are we being quite true to our traditions as a national party?' He went on to argue that if the Conservatives continued to oppose the Beveridge plan they would end up not only 'dead but damned'.

In the event the Conservatives were damned but not left for dead. During their years in opposition they began a radical reappraisal of their approach to social policy issues. Some of the younger Conservatives, notably Enoch Powell, Iain MacLeod and Angus Maude, were invited by the Conservative Political Centre to write a monograph on the future of the social services. Their proposals were published in 1950 under the title *One Nation* and were endorsed at the party's annual conference of that year.

Although the *One Nation* group were critical of some aspects of the newly established post-war welfare state, notably with regard to what they considered to be its undue reliance on universalism, they recommended a higher rate of public sector home-building, support for the National Health Service, the maintenance of full employment and closer cooperation with the trade unions.

Much has been written about the extent to which the years between 1951 and 1979 can be described as a period of post-war consensus between the major political parties regarding the future of the welfare state. When the Conservatives were returned to office in 1951 they did not dismantle the institutional framework of the post-war settlement. In many respects they extended it. Harold Macmillan himself played a major role, first as Minister of Housing and later as prime minister, in defending and extending the institutions of the British welfare state. Yet it was during this period that neo-liberal Conservative scholars and politicians started to mount their critique of collectivist welfare and to extend their influence throughout the rank-and-file as well as the top echelons of the Conservative Party.

Conservatism and the Challenge of Neo-liberalism

When Edward Heath took office in 1970 he dallied briefly with some of the free-market policies of the neo-liberal 'new right', but soon abandoned these approaches in the face of rising unemployment. After Margaret Thatcher became leader of the Conservatives in 1976, the tide of influential opinion in the party turned sharply against all forms of collectivism and the neo-liberal theories of the 'new right' moved into their ascendancy. The ensuing battle for the 'soul of the Conservative Party' is described in retrospect by Ian Gilmour, who was to become one of its first casualties. Only two years before Margaret Thatcher became Prime Minister in 1979, Gilmour felt able to claim in his book *Inside Right* (1977) that the Conservatives supported both private enterprise and private property but that first and foremost they were a party of national unity. As such the party abjured all forms of ideology because all ideologies support particular class interests and as such are 'a threat to national unity' (p.132).

Up to that point, at least, it can be said that the ideals of an organic society and a unitary welfare state still enjoyed support in some sections of the Conservative Party. In his most recent work, *Dancing with Dogma* (1992), Gilmour reflects on the subsequent triumph of 'new right' ideology and the demise of traditional Conservatism during the Thatcher years.

There may still be dimensions of normative consensus between the neo-liberals and the traditionalists within the Conservative Party. It is, however, the doctrinal divisions between the 'drys' and the 'wets' that are currently most in evidence. At the present time it is the collectivistically minded 'wets' who are most strongly pro-Europe. Nevertheless, it remains to be seen whether these pro-European Conservatives can reconcile the new ideal of 'one Europe' with the older ideal of 'one nation'. Over time, the Conservative Party ceased to be more or less exclusively identified with landed interests and came to terms with the political, social and economic changes that followed the Industrial Revolution. The party faces challenges of similar magnitude in the immediate future, notably with regard to Europe.

Traditional Conservatives like Macmillan, Butler and Macleod – were they alive today – would have taken the euro in their stride. The paradox at the heart of British Conservatism is the manner in which it balances an attachment to tradition with the unrivalled ability to adapt retrospectively to radical change and make conventional virtues out of brute necessity. A landslide referendum vote in favour of monetary union would test that adaptive ability to its limits. A close call either way would strengthen the position of the Euro-sceptics and enhance the party's electoral prospects.

The next general election, however, will be fought over a wide range of issues, one of which will undoubtedly be the future of the British welfare state. The Conservative Party, under Iain Duncan Smith, has launched a review of its whole approach to public and social policy issues, with three main objectives – raising standards of public sector service, reducing the role of government and cutting taxes. This has strong affinities with the policy objectives that the New Right consistently advocated during the years between 1979 and 1997.

At a strategic level, the New Right mission failed to achieve its objectives. By 1997, the broad infrastructure of statutory social services had survived. Levels of taxation and social expenditure had been held down but not significantly reduced. At a tactical level, however, much had been achieved, notably with regard to the introduction of internal markets and the promotion of new kinds of public-private sector partnerships, as Green argues in chapter II.6. Over a period of 18 years, the Conservatives had successfully grafted a new model of welfare pluralism onto the old collectivist structures and ethos of the British welfare state.

The outcome of these policy changes could be seen as reassuring evidence that a viable welfare state could function effectively without significant increases in taxation. It could also be construed as no more than a staging post on the way to further privatization. The first of these interpretations is consistent with the values of traditional Conservatism. The second reflects the neo-liberal aspirations of the New Right.

Since 1997, however, public confidence in the viability of the British welfare state has declined. Government and opposition parties alike are now confronted by widespread and growing dissatisfaction with the quality of the services provided by all the major public sector agencies. In the field of social policy, successive governments have struggled to meet current welfare needs while holding down tax levels to the detriment of longer-term investment requirements. The renewal of the welfare infrastructure and the training of skilled staff has not kept pace with the rising levels of demand and social expectations. Voters, for their part, have been unwilling to accept the fact that their rising expectations can only be met by paying more tax, paying more from their own pockets or by a combination of both options. A newly elected Conservative Government committed to raising public service standards, reducing the role of government and cutting taxes would have to sponsor a massive expansion of private sector funding and service provision.

Whether or not such a policy change would mark the final demise of the Conservative tradition of welfare would depend on the outcome of the next general election. In the meantime, Conservatives will have to maintain a united front on Europe and accommodate the policy aspirations of a social liberal wing. In today's uncertain world, governments and oppositions parties alike are hostages to events that they can neither anticipate nor control. If, however, the Conservatives suffer a bad electoral defeat they may belatedly decide that returning to the traditional middle ground and opting for a pro-European future is better than opting for no future at all.

Conclusion

Paul Johnson recounts ('All Odd Cons', *Spectator*, 18 May 1996, pp.15–20) how he was 'once present when a journalist asked Harold Macmillan what was the biggest single factor in shaping his policies as Prime Minister. "Events dear boy, events," said Macmillan cheerfully.' It is this quality of opportunism, combined with an attachment to custom, that makes Conservatism and its approach to social welfare issues such a baffling subject for so many students of social policy, imbued as they are with a belief in the powers of reason and the virtues of rational planning.

Traditional Conservatives have no difficulty in conceptualizing statutory social services as practical and effective expressions of an organic model of society. They also accept the need for policy change, as long as it is gradual and evolutionary in character and rests on the broadest possible consensus. In this respect it can be argued that Conservatism in Britain has become a political tradition without a political party. Whether this state of affairs proves to be permanent or temporary remains to be seen. True Conservatives will put their faith in their ability to turn unexpected events to their own best advantage.

Guide to further reading

Robert Nisbet's essay *Conservatism* (Milton Keynes: Open University Press, 1986) provides a lucid and wide-ranging analysis of the origins of Conservative thought and its impact on the development of european sociology. Roger Scruton's *The Meaning of Conservatism* (London: Macmillan, 1984) explores its diverse philosophical qualities in comparison with those of liberalism, socialism and Marxism. Ian Gilmour's *Inside Right: A Study of Conservatism* (London: Quartet, 1978) contains clear and useful chapters on some key conservative thinkers and various constitutional themes and issues. Frank O'Gorman's *British Conservatism* (Harlow: Longman, 1986) combines extracts from key texts and commentaries.

Part III of W. H. Greenleaf's second volume of *The British Political Tradition* (London: Routledge, 1988) explores the conservative response to the rise of collectivist ideologies over the past 150 years. Harold Macmillan's *The Middle Way* (London: Macmillan, 1938) sets out a new agenda for modern Conservatism as a social-democratic response to the problems of reforming capitalism and defeating socialism. Gilmour's *Dancing with Dogma: Britain Under Thatcherism* (London: Simon & Schuster, 1992) offers a riveting account of the politics of change in the Conservative Party under Mrs Thatcher's leadership.

Robert Blake's two volumes (*The Conservative Party from Peel to Thatcher*. London: Fontana, 1985) are still, when taken together, the definitive study of the development of the modern Conservative Party. Two recent publications also merit consideration: a lively collection of essays on current policy issues entitled *Conservative Realism*, edited by Kenneth Minogue (London: HarperCollins, 1996); and John Charmley's engaging and perceptive *History of Conservative Politics, 1900–1996* (Basingstoke: Macmillan Press, 1996).

Chapter 8 of Rodney Barker's *Political Ideas in Modern Britain* (London: Routledge, 1997) and chapter 10 of John Dearlove's and Peta Saunders' *Introduction to British Politics* (Cambridge: Polity Press, 2000) provide concise and balanced overviews of recent trends in the development of Conservative ideas on social policy.

The Social Democratic Perspective

Michael Sullivan

Fabianism, Ethical Socialism and Social Democracy

Social democracy (or democratic socialism, as its British practitioners sometimes prefer to call it) is often seen as the political fount from which welfare statism sprung. This chapter attempts:

- to define the nature of early twentieth-century social democracy, which, it argues, gave rise not only to the rise of the Labour Party but also to the specific nature of the welfare state;
- to describe the nature of post-war social democratic thought and its impact on the development and scope of social policy; and
- to map out the effect of changing conceptions of social democracy on social policy.

In the UK context, twentieth-century social democracy can be seen as heavily influenced by the development of two strands of thought: Fabianism and ethical socialism. Both of these influenced the Labour Party in the first half of the century and were significant in providing the ethical and administrative bases for the UK post-war welfare state.

Fabianism's contribution to social democracy

Fabianism's major contributions in the pre-war period were as follows. First, and in contrast to earlier and later Marxists, Fabians argued that socialism was entirely compatible with political institutions and modes of behaviour which were peculiarly British. Socialism could be and should be achieved through a parliamentary route and, once this had been realized, a politically neutral civil service could be left to administer it. Marx and Marxists had called for the abolition of the capitalist state if socialism was to be achieved. Fabians, on the other hand, saw in socialism an extension of the existing British state (including parliament, the armed forces and the monarch). Socialism for the Fabians was a sort of collectivism, the rules of which would be guaranteed, and if necessary enforced, by a set of neutral umpires, who would include state functionaries, the law and the royal family. In Shaw's words, 'the socialism advocated by the Fabian Society is state socialism exclusively'. Fabian political thought diverged fundamentally from orthodox Marxism in this respect. For Fabians, unlike their Marxist counterparts, the capitalist state was not, in itself, a hindrance to the achievement of socialism. Early Fabians saw it as controlled temporarily by the bourgeoisie but as capable of transformation. The state was, in other words, essentially neutral.

Second, and importantly, Fabianism's faith in the expert administrator as the guarantor of British socialism became a touchstone for British social democracy. The civil service was to be the guiding hand of socialism, with the elected parliament acting as a check on its activities. If the parliament could also be well endowed with experts, then so much the better: 'a body of expert representatives is the only way of coping with expert administrators. The only way to choose expert representatives is popular election, but that is just the worst way to obtain expert administrators' (Fabian Society).

The contribution of Fabianism considered that Fabian thinking, then, might be summarized in the following way. Socialism, or more accurately social democracy, required not that the state be smashed but that it be fashioned into an instrument of social change. This would be possible because the state *per se* was not the creature of any particular social class but the politically neutral administrative arm of government. None the less, the expertise possessed by state personnel made them ideally placed to be guarantors of a socialism won through the ballot box. As we shall see later, Fabian political theory had a not insignificant effect on the Labour Party in the 1940s and 1950s and on its creation and stewardship of welfare statism.

Ethical Socialism: The Heart of Social Reformism

If Fabianism was the *head* of social democracy during this period, then ethical socialism was its *heart*. Ethical socialism is here defined as that strand of political thinking for which the social deprivation experienced by large sections of the working class before the Second World War was seen as reason enough to support a movement for social reform. At the centre of this reform coalition was the Independent Labour Party (ILP; formed in 1893 and later to affiliate to the Labour Party), but its adherents included many individuals driven by a sense of Christian obligation or moral outrage at the appalling conditions of many citizens' lives. Though many so-called ethical socialists were committed, like the ILP,

to the collective ownership of the means of production, distribution and exchange, that commitment was often fired by a non-conformist notion of social morality rather than a Marxist passion for class conflict. Thinkers like Tawney, author of the now famous *Religion and the Rise of Capitalism* (London: George Allen & Unwin, 1977, first published in 1922), belonged to this grouping. He, like other ethical socialists, was clear that the *raison d'être* of socialism was the achievement of a more equal society. Like many social democrats who followed him, Tawney was concerned not only with the achievement of greater equality but also with the development of a philosophy to underpin this egalitarian drive. For him, as for many social reformers, socialism was also the expression of a Christian or quasi-Christian morality.

In *The Acquisitive Society* (London: George Allen & Unwin, 1921), Tawney located the sources of poverty and inequality in the capitalist emphasis on individual rights to the exclusion of individual obligation. Such an emphasis allowed the wealthy to exercise rights under law in order to accrue wealth. Its corollary was that it understressed the responsibility persons should feel to act in ways which ensured that the acquisition of wealth for some did not lead to the immiseration of others. Capitalist societies like Britain in the 1920s 'may be called *acquisitive societies* because their whole tendency and interest and pre-occupation is to promote the acquisition of wealth'. Driven by the development of an ethical socialist morality which saw the justification for social reform as the abolition of the mean-mindedness of capitalism, Tawney looked for vehicles capable of carrying this morality forward into practical politics. One of these vehicles was Fabian political economy and especially the Webbian formulation of the relationship between the individual and the collective.

The marriage of an ethical socialist morality with Fabian political theory led Tawney to call for a functional society based on the performance of duties rather than the maintenance of rights. This is particularly clear in his *Equality* (London: George Allen & Unwin, 1952, originally published in 1931). This book, rightly seen as presenting a philosophy for Labour socialism, mounted a blistering attack on the inequalities seemingly inherent in an unbridled capitalist system, including criticism of the British upper classes for practising a form of class war by their determination to amass wealth through the exploitation of a labouring class. Rather than regard such inequalities as natural or inevitable, Tawney believed them to be grotesque and barbarous. This led him to promote a notion of equality which emphasized equality of esteem and dignity based on common humanity, a definition of equality which allowed for disparities in income and wealth which were not the result of crude exploitation and which placed him at the head of a tradition of thought later expanded by the Labour politician Crosland and the sociologist Marshall.

Labour Social Democracy: Social Reformism Comes of Age?

By 1945, when Labour gained a landslide general election victory, the hostility of the labour movement to state social welfare appears to have evaporated. In part, this appears to have been the result of workers' experience of the protracted slump in the twenties and thirties. During that period, privilege and privation appeared to exist side by side – on the one hand the continued drive for profit by entrepreneurial and corporate capitalists, on the other the crushing poverty for the many of the inter-war years – and as a result the hostility of ordinary people to state intervention to improve living conditions understandably diminished. Trade union opposition to the imposition of a social wage became less strident as many trade union members found themselves without a real wage to be increased by trade union activity. In these circumstances Labour plans such as those for a national health service, originating from the

Socialist Medical Association in 1930 but becoming party policy by 1934, looked increasingly attractive (see Sullivan, 1992). The call by Keynes, Beveridge and others for a full-employment policy and a welfare state were similarly attractive. Labour's plans during the 1930s to administer a planned economy should it be returned to government and its emerging championing of a welfare state package made it identifiable with the crucial social issues of the day and was responsible, according to one commentator, for its reaching its zenith as a working-class party. It was, however, undoubtedly the experience of war which set the seal on Labour as a social reformist party and on social reformism as an electoral advantage.

The influence of social democracy was also no doubt aided by the emphasis placed during the Second World War on policies, often introduced by Labour ministers in the coalition government, aimed at a rough and ready egalitarianism (for fuller treatment of this see Sullivan, 1992, chapter 2). What seems incontestable is that the Labour Party had, by the end of the Second World War, come of age as a social reformist party wedded to the practical politics of Fabianism and the political philosophy and morality of ethical socialism.

Citizenship and Social Policy

Following the establishment of a UK welfare state which was rooted, or so I would argue, in the marriage of inter-war Fabianism and ethical socialism, one might have seen social democracy's influence on social policy as then at its zenith. However, social democracy was to be refined and renewed by the contributions of the academic Marshall and the academic-*cum*-politician Crosland. The contributions of these to the redefinition of the citizen marked both a development of social democracy and a set of principles to guide the role of government and state in relation to its role in social policy.

In a seminal article entitled 'Citizenship

and social class', first published as his Cambridge inaugural lecture in the late 1940s (in *Sociology at the Crossroads*, London: Heinemann), Professor T. H. Marshall outlined a model of social policy development, rooted in social rights, which has had considerable influence. The model owes much to Tawney and to the nineteenth-century economist Alfred Marshall's hypothesis that there is a kind of human equality associated with the concept of full membership of a community. Full membership of a community, or society, is – according to the later Marshall – contingent on possession of three sets of citizen rights: civil rights, political rights and social rights. In contemporary society such rights may be defined in the following way:

- *Citizen rights* are those rights concerned with individual liberty and include freedom of speech and thought, the right to own private property and the right to justice;
- *Political rights* are primarily those rights of participation in the political process of government, either as an elector or as an elected member of an assembly;
- *Social rights* cover a whole range of rights, from the right to a modicum of economic security through to the right to share in the heritage and living standards of a civilized society.

State provision of social welfare was perceived by Marshall as part of the package of social rights which are one component of the citizenship rights. The development of a complete bundle of rights which is the property of all social classes is relatively recent. In approximate terms, the formative period for the development of each set of rights can be set in one of the three last centuries. In the eighteenth century, civil rights, especially those of equality before the law, were extended to wider sections of the population than had hitherto been the case. In the nineteenth and early twentieth centuries, political rights, previously limited to the aristocracy, were extended first to the middle classes, then to working-class men

and finally to women. In the twentieth century, social rights, previously available only to the destitute (and then on unfavourable conditions through the operation of the Poor Law), were extended to working people – in the form of selective social welfare provisions – and then, through the creation of a universalist welfare state, to the whole population.

Thus, this approach might be understood as presenting the development of state social welfare as a unilinear and inevitable process. Such an interpretation, however, does this approach less than justice. The roots of citizenship rights are traced back through history and the extension of these rights seen as extensions in the British (social) democratic tradition. However, social rights – including state welfare provision – are seen as having emerged out of a democratic process, which led ultimately to consensus over social and political affairs but which included conflict between classes and genders.

Marshall argues that the movement for equality of political rights, including Chartism in the nineteenth century and suffragism in the early twentieth century, developed from a determination to extend the rights of all citizens beyond equality of civil rights. Similarly, the establishment of universal political rights and enfranchisement, contributing, for example, to the election of working people's representatives to parliament, aided the struggle for equality of social rights. These social rights, enshrined in welfare state policies, included the right to a modicum of economic security (through the income maintenance system), the right to share in the living standards of a civilized society (through policies of full employment and the health system) and the right to share a common cultural heritage (through the education system).

Although the extension of rights at each stage has been accompanied by political struggle to achieve those rights, the effect has been, at every stage, to mould a new consensus on rights reaching its climax in the extension of social rights. This having been achieved, social rights (education, health and income maintenance rights, for example) advanced the individual's ability to utilize fully his or her civil and political rights. This citizenship-democracy model was given further substance by the Labour intellectual Anthony Crosland. In his path-breaking work, *The Future of Socialism* (London: Cape, 1952), he argued for a refinement of British social democracy which put a greater emphasis on the rights of citizens. Eschewing the class-war socialism of inter-war social democracy, he promoted instead the idea of socialism as the guarantor of equality of esteem. In a speech reproduced in a collection of essays published towards the end of his attenuated life, he located the movement for comprehensive secondary education within Marshall's citizenship model. 'I believe . . . this represents a strong and irresistible pressure on British society to extend the right of citizenship. Over the past three hundred years these rights have been extended first to personal liberty then to political democracy and later to social welfare. Now they must be further extended to educational equality.'

Social democratic views of the state and government are overt in Crosland's analysis. The consensus on rights has roots in a democratic tradition. It may, at times, have been forged out of struggle and conflict but once that consensus had emerged governments inevitably responded to an irresistible groundswell of opinion and the state machinery aided the expansion and implementation of social rights.

Citizenship theory's emphasis on the creation of equality of rights did not, however, imply the creation of material equality through redistributive social and economic policies. On the contrary, Marshall's analysis saw equality of social status as legitimizing economic inequalities. It is, for Marshall, no accident that the growth of citizen rights coincided with the growth of capitalism as an economic system. For economic rights are indispensable in a market economy. This is so because they permit individuals to engage in economic struggle for the maximization of profit through the right to buy, own and sell. Political rights may have redressed some of the power imbalance between the social classes in capitalist society but social rights – by peripherally modifying the pattern of social inequality – had the paradoxical, but utilitarian, effect of making the social class system less vulnerable to change. Social rights accorded community membership to all – and thus made all citizens stakeholders in capitalist society – without effecting any fundamental redistribution in income or wealth. Social welfare raised the level of the lowest (through income maintenance schemes, education, healthcare systems and the like), but redistribution of resources, where it occurred, was horizontal rather than vertical. In the British welfare state, inequality persisted but the possession by all citizens of a package of social rights created a society in which no *a priori* valuations were made on the basis of social class or social status. For Marshall, then, the aims of social policy and service provision include: the incorporation of all as members of the societal community; the modification of the most excessive and debilitating inequalities of British society; but the legitimization of wider and more fundamental inequalities through this process of incorporation.

Similarly for Crosland, the aims and objectives of welfare state policy were not primarily those of equality through redistribution. For him, social equality, even if desirable, could not be held to be the ultimate purpose of the social services. Rather, the aims were to provide relief of social distress and the correction of social needs. Inequalities would, he believed, be lessened as a result, but the creation of equality was, at most, a subsidiary objective of social democratic social policy. Indeed, in an earlier contribution to the debate on welfare, Crosland made his views on welfare state aims even more explicit:

The object of social services is to provide a cushion of security . . . Once that security has been provided further advances in the national income should normally go to citizens in the form of free income to be spent as they wish and not to be taxed away and then returned in the form of some free service determined by the fiat of the state.

The creation of a welfare state in the 1940s had, in Crosland's view, substantially, if not completely, satisfied the need for universal and full membership of the societal community. The objects of state welfare provision were to cushion insecurity and to ameliorate excessive inequality rather than to promote equality. The idea of state welfare as the shock absorber of inequalities in capitalist society is one which is also found in some of the Marxist views on welfare. The difference is that – while Marshall, Crosland and others see this function as an appropriate one – it formed part of the Marxist critique.

What springs from the pre- and post-war social democratic literature, then, is a set of theoretical perspectives and a practice that served well enough for much of the post-war period. The emergence of a rational/moral consensus led to the development of state social welfare and to the creation of a welfare state. That welfare state aimed at, and to some extent succeeded in, ameliorating social dis-welfares and dulling the edges of inequality. It did so by making available hitherto unprovided services and by according a form of non-material equality to citizens. It emerged from a capitalist system which supported – and was supported by – welfare. Social democratic welfare created, in other words, a 'hyphenated society', part capitalist, part socialist, or in Harold Macmillan's words, a *middle way* (see chapter II.6). Social democratic, mixed-economy, welfare capitalism appeared to work well enough for thirty or so years (see Sullivan, 1992). But even during this fair-weather period storm clouds were gathering for social democracy.

Social Democracy in a Cold Climate

The oil-shock economic crises of the 1970s, together with the consequent renewal of neo-liberalism (discussed in chapter II.5), consigned social democracy and the Labour Party as its political representative, to the back seat for almost two decades (see Sullivan, 1992). During this period Labour moved some way towards a new centre of political gravity which has emerged during and owed much to the Thatcherite policies of the 1980s and 1990s, and this process was completed by the definition of social democracy offered by the Labour leader of the late 1990s, Tony Blair. In the 1990s it seems that Labour has abandoned the ethical socialism of Tawney, the principles of Fabianism and the inclusiveness of citizenship theory.

Social democracy, then, formed the common-sense politics of policy development in social and economic policy for much of the twentieth century. Its heyday was the extended period between the establishment of the welfare state and the global economic crises of the 1970s. Since the late 1970s, aided by the Thatcherite project and Labour's response to it, social democracy has waned in influence. As Labour has moved further towards the centre of UK politics, the philosophies of Fabianism and ethical socialism seem to have been translated into insubstantial icons. The extent to which New Labour has, in office, thought about and refined the social democratic mantra of Old Labour and, with it conceptions of citizen rights, is addressed by Powell in this volume (see chapter II.10) and elsewhere. He leaves open the possibility that what is emerging – conceptually and practically – is a new form of social democracy, though not 'social democracy as we know it' to misquote Mr Spock! This writer, however, inclines to the conclusion that social democratic principles – and particularly the rights-based entitlements that stem from them – are in free fall in the UK and elsewhere.

Guide to further reading

Addison, P., 1975. *The Road to 1945* (London: Quartet). A social and political history of the period and the influences leading to the establishment of the welfare state, including the growth and influence of social democracy.

Addison, P., 1992. *Churchill on the Home Front* (London: Cape). An account of the efforts of the wartime coalition government in relation to social and economic policy which highlights the contribution of Labour ministers and social democratic ideas to the rough and ready egalitarianism of the war years.

Crossman, R. H. S. (ed.), 1952. *New Fabian Essays* (London: Turnstile Press). A collection of essays by post-war Fabians devoted to domestic policy. Many of the essays assume that the establishment of a welfare state had tackled the problem of inequality successfully and that social and economic policy should concentrate on increasing opportunity.

Glennerster, H., 1995. *British Social Policy since 1945* (Oxford: Blackwell). A critical history of the welfare state written from a Fabian perspective.

Hennessy, P., 1992. *Never Again* (London: Jonathan Cape). A history of the post-war period in relation to public policy.

Powell, M., 1999. *New Labour, New Welfare State: Social Policy and the Third Way* (Bristol: Policy Press). A collection of papers exploring the New Labour policy agenda.

Sullivan, M., 1992. *The Politics of Social Policy* (Hemel Hempstead: Harvester Wheatsheaf). A study of consensus politics and social democracy in the post-war period.

Timmins, N., 1995. *The Five Giants: A Biography of the Welfare State* (London: HarperCollins). An extremely well-written account of post-war social policy.

The Socialist Perspective

Norman Ginsburg

Essentials

The socialist perspective embraces two assumptions about capitalism or at least the forms of capitalism witnessed hitherto. First, it suggests that capitalist societies do not or cannot meet adequately basic human welfare needs for all their people. Only public services and effective welfare rights, or possibly strictly regulated private services, can provide universal access and democratic accountability. Second, socialists believe that capitalism sustains fundamental social inequalities and divisions, which are both morally unacceptable and economically debilitating. These divisions, particularly class divisions, serve to underpin competitive, socially corrosive individualism, and to weaken popular anti-capitalist pressures and movements.

Socialism therefore offers three core principles for the transformation of capitalism:

1 the development of collective social welfare measures and organizations to meet fundamental needs and to achieve substantial amelioration if not elimination of social inequality;

2 a radical democratization of the state and civil society, developing social solidarity and popular power through accountable political and social organizations;

3 popular planning and control of the economy to restrict, if not eliminate exploitation, unemployment and private profit, and to develop community ownership and industrial democracy.

The last is certainly the most controversial principle for socialists and non-socialists alike, raising the thorny question of public ownership of business. For economic fundamentalists the socialization of the economy is the wherewithal for subsequent creation of a socialist welfare state. Many other socialists would see all three principles as intertwined. Socialists also differ fundamentally on the extent to which socialism is delivered through the national state or, for example, through self-help organizations like cooperatives. The origins of modern socialism in the nineteenth century coincide with the development of the modern nation state. Statism and anti-statism, nationalism and internationalism are huge fault lines within the socialist perspective. Socialists are, however, consistent in their scepticism, if not outright opposition to private provision of welfare, especially where it is for profit or marketized.

Socialism has the goal of either a radical transformation of capitalism or its transcendence into a quite different form of economy and society. There are widely differing views among socialists about the degree of radical transformation of capitalism required to achieve socialism.

• *Gradualists* or *revisionists* believe that socialism can emerge from the consolidation and radical development of social democracy. Capitalism can be transformed by deepening and extending both the welfare state and democratic institutions, for example through collective or cooperative forms of ownership, enterprise and public service. One of the most widely recognized examples of gradualism in social welfare is the achievement of Swedish social democracy over the past seventy years. Closer to home, most gradualists would see the post-1945 construction of the welfare state in Britain, particularly the National Health Service, as developing socialist institutions and egalitarian outcomes.

• *Revolutionaries* or *radicals* envisage recurrent politico-economic crises of capitalism brought about by its self-destructive ultra-competitiveness, as originally conceived by Karl Marx. These crises create the opportunity to construct a socialist state and society, or perhaps even a new global order if socialism in one country is a contradiction in terms. The revolutionary moment would initiate a radical break from the capitalist economy and competitive individualism. There are parallels with the anti-capitalist revolutionary processes witnessed, for example, in Russia (1917), China (1948) and Cuba (1958), though few Western socialists today see these revolutions as establishing acceptable forms of socialism.

It will be readily apparent that the very use of the word 'socialism' is extremely problematic for at least two reasons.

1 'Socialism' is most commonly associated with the Stalinist and Maoist regimes in Eastern Europe, China and beyond. These regimes unquestionably achieved considerable amelioration of social inequalities and improvement in the meeting of basic needs, compared with their predecessors. Indeed, their welfare states lent them a certain amount of legitimacy and popular support. The Cuban health service continues to be widely acclaimed as the best in Latin America. These state collectivist regimes established public ownership of big business and government control of the labour market, though this hardly amounted to popular control thereof. In any event the state collectivist economies proved to be very inefficient and environmentally destructive – the notion that economic activity can be rigidly planned and controlled by a government bureaucracy proved unworkable in practice. The state collectivist regimes were held in place not by a democratic mandate, but by terror and authoritarianism. Hence although they described themselves as socialist welfare states and were so described by most outsiders, in fact they embodied forms of authoritarian welfare collectivism which were either very deformed models of socialism or not worthy of the description 'socialist' at all. There are many on the left, particularly in Eastern Europe, who believe that the Stalinist and Maoist experiences have rendered the word socialism valueless. Nevertheless, the idea of socialism remains alive and inspirational for many in the West and beyond.

2 In Britain the Labour Party has always proclaimed itself as socialist and has been so described by its opponents. Historically it has embraced many elements of a gradualist socialist programme for social policy. However, in government at both local and national levels it has generally sought a moderate and pragmatic accommodation with capitalism, very much in the post-war continental social democratic tradition. This position was modernized and strengthened with the emergence of New Labour in the 1990s. In contemporary Britain socialists have been marginalized by the electoral triumphs of New Labour, and similar processes are occurring across Western Europe. Nevertheless socialist political activism remains significant, particularly in the new regional politics of Scotland and Wales, while socialist

and Marxist perspectives continue to form an important element within the discourses of the academic social sciences including social policy.

Key Ideas and Concepts

The first key component of the socialist approach to human welfare is its universalism in two particular senses. Socialists believe that there are *universal human welfare needs* and a *universal societal responsibility* for seeing that those basic needs are met. When and where those needs are not met fully, humanity is devalued, human potential is unfulfilled and social conflict is likely to be endemic. Universalism, however, by no means necessarily implies that every individual's needs are the same or that the implementation of the social responsibility for welfare should take the same form for all needs and in all contexts. Universalism does not mean uniformity. In historical reality the specification of universal welfare needs has been shaped by particular struggles of social and political movements. Hence during the nineteenth century workers' movements began to demand and become involved in the organization of social insurance against loss of wages due to industrial accidents, old age and sickness. In the twentieth century this was extended to insurance against unemployment, healthcare costs and other welfare risks. The right to universal, publicly provided education has always been a fundamental socialist principle. Gough (2000) has rigorously analysed the concept of welfare need from a socialist perspective, reinvigorating the notion that there are indeed basic and universal human needs.

Many non-socialists would agree with these universalist sentiments, but the second aspect of socialist universalism is the goal of achieving *social equality* of outcome in meeting these welfare needs, not just achieving a basic minimum level or developing equal opportunities. The meaning and application of the idea of equality has been widely debated among socialists but, as discussed in chapter II.2, it is rarely taken to mean an absolute uniformity of outcome. For socialists the poverty, unemployment, discrimination and maldistribution of wealth, income, health status and educational resources endemic to capitalism are fundamentally unjust, and fuel social conflict and crime as well as undermining the economy, not least by the under-utilization of human resources. The contribution of social policies to the dramatic growth in poverty and inequality in Britain since 1979 has of course been witnessed with horror by socialists.

Class is the key parameter of social inequality for socialists. Capitalist society is inherently divided into classes and the utopian goal of socialism is the achievement of a classless society. Ethical and libertarian gradualists are as forthright on this as Marxist socialists. As discussed in chapter II.5, class status is determined by position in the labour market. In traditional social democratic terms this is linked to occupational status, the working class being blue-collar workers and their families. In Marxian terms class is determined by relations in the workplace, the working class being those dependent on selling their labour power for subsistence. In practice, socialist analysts sometimes use both concepts of class almost interchangeably, since those in less privileged occupations tend to be those who are most dependent on wages. The core of the working class, skilled and semi-skilled workers organized in trade unions, are the natural constituency for socialism. The class structure has of course never been as clear-cut as socialist theory would suggest, and intra-class divisions have often seemed even more politically and socially significant. The class positions of poor people, unemployed people, unpaid carers, professionals and managers, for example, are keenly debated. Socialists are nevertheless united in seeking to overcome structural class inequalities in meeting basic needs either by radical social policy reform or by agitating for revolutionary change, or perhaps both.

The historical development of the welfare state, whether it is embryonically socialist or not, is attributed by socialists to *class struggles*, both those of the labour movement and myriad other forms of working-class pressure. Hence the beginning of the modern welfare state in Germany in the late 1880s was the response of an authoritarian, undemocratic state to acute socialist pressure from below. The modern Swedish welfare state is widely attributed to more than a century of socialist pressure emanating principally from the labour movement.

Another key element in a socialist approach to social policy is that there must be a firm *public and democratically accountable responsibility* for meeting needs and combating class inequality with the fullest participation of both users and providers. In effect this normally means guaranteeing welfare rights through legislation and underwriting the costs of welfare provision through redistributive taxation. It should also mean that the delivery of services is subject to regulation and scrutiny by elected representatives of the community served and/or, more directly, by users themselves. The providers of services, welfare workers, should also be able to participate actively in shaping delivery. For some socialists democratic accountability and universalism can only be assured if welfare benefits and services are delivered by agencies of the state nationally or locally. For others a more pluralist approach to delivery is possible provided adequate welfare outcomes are guaranteed by legislation and regulatory supervision of non-statutory providers. These issues are amply illustrated by the history of social housing in Britain.

Council housing developed and managed directly by elected local authorities has been seen by many socialists and non-socialists alike as a socialist or proto-socialist form of delivery. Over the twentieth century council housing delivered low-cost rented housing to millions of working class households, much of it built to reasonable standards and allocated according to need under local democratic supervision. On the other hand, it also delivered much poor quality accommodation, frequently allocated and managed to reflect prevailing prejudices on class, ethnic, gender and other grounds. Council tenants themselves have had few effective legal powers to challenge their landlord or to participate in management. Over the past twenty years, the role of providing social rented housing has been increasingly transferred to housing associations. The latter are not-for-profit organizations regulated by a government agency and financed through a mix of public and private funds. Housing associations come in diverse forms, including some charities with specialist clienteles, and housing cooperatives developing a particular strand of socialist practice. Apart from more generous public funding and enforced access to private funding, housing associations have had advantages of greater flexibility and less bureaucratism precisely because they are not democratically accountable to their local communities. Housing associations may be more sensitive to their tenants, but formal local accountability is often minimal. There are profound differences among socialists about which forms of delivery can best develop socialist outcomes – council housing reflected a collectivist tradition, housing associations a more pluralistic tradition including cooperation. Both traditions are now in sharp decline under New Labour, as councils are prevented from investing in new housing, while housing associations are increasingly shackled by business plans agreed with their now predominantly private bankers.

Diversity of Socialisms

In discussing key concepts for socialist analysis of social policy here, an attempt has been made to lay out the ideas which are shared across the range of socialist schools of thought. In British discourse, however, it has become the norm to make a clear distinction between 'democratic socialism' (the gradualist tradition) and 'Marxism' (the revolutionary tradition). The juxtaposition of these is in some ways an unfortunate distortion because it suggests that Marxists cannot be democratic socialists and implicitly associates Marxism entirely with anti-democratic, Stalinist ideas. The juxtaposition of gradualism with revolutionism is further problematic because it is possible to combine the two in the belief that a gradual consolidation of socialist forces within capitalism can eventually achieve a wholesale transformation. There is in any event much diversity within socialist thinking which is relevant for social policy, including eco-socialism, communitarian socialism, Christian socialism, libertarian socialism and market socialism. Here there is only room to discuss very briefly three strands of socialist thought which have been particularly influential within academic social policy in contemporary Britain, namely neo-Marxism, feminist socialism and Fabian socialism.

- Neo-Marxism emphasizes the contradictory unity of social welfare under capitalism. On the one hand, it is a response to working-class pressures and in some cases hard-fought class struggle. The welfare state relieves some of the pressures and risks borne by the working class in selling their labour power as a commodity, which is their sole access to the means of subsistence. The welfare state therefore brings about the 'decommodification' of the working class, which is a very positive achievement. On the other hand, the welfare state functions in various ways to bolster and renew capitalism. First, its very existence makes capitalism seem more humane and acceptable, disguising its underlying brutality. This has been described as the function of legitimation or the reproduction of class relations. Second, the welfare state (in theory at least) ensures that a sufficiently educated, healthy and securely housed

working population is available in the labour market. This is described as the function of reproduction of labour power. Third, the welfare state contributes directly to capital accumulation through its investment in infrastructure – buildings and equipment for schools, hospitals, universities, social housing etc. This is described as the function of reproduction of capital. The period since the early/mid-1970s in the West is seen by neo-Marxists as one in which the working class has been in retreat as capital has rolled back the achievements of the post-war class compromise. For capital, the costs of the welfare state have outweighed the functional benefits in terms of reproduction and legitimation, and the coercive power of the commodification of labour in the labour market has been reasserted in the form of mass unemployment and a general widening of class inequalities.

- Contemporary socialist feminism sees patriarchy and capitalism as mutually reinforcing systems of oppression (see also chapter II.11). The post-war welfare state was underpinned by the ideological assumption that people would live in patriarchal families, in which the male breadwinner would earn a 'family wage' to support a female partner as a dependent unpaid domestic carer and service provider. Women's unpaid work fulfilled the vital functions of the day-to-day reproduction of workers and the unpaid care of children and elderly dependants. The undervaluation, dependence and isolation of women's role in the family contributed to their inferior psychological, cultural and political status. Women also formed part of the reserve army of labour brought into the paid labour force on a temporary or casualized basis when required. Women were thus dependent on their husbands' pensions contributions and were denied access to other benefits in their own right. Strong vestiges from the post-war era remain today, but in recent decades capital has recruited women permanently into paid employment, albeit often still on a casualized or part-time basis. Hence women have increasingly shouldered the dual burden of paid employment while carrying on with the domestic caring role. Further, as pressures on the patriarchal family have intensified, women are increasingly bringing up children unsupported. Socialist feminists have pressed for the development of welfare rights and benefits to relieve women of some of this burden by sharing it with men and the state, thus to enfranchise them fully as citizens. At the core of the socialist feminist tradition are expectations and demands of the welfare state, particularly in the form of affordable childcare facilities, reproductive rights, parental leave, protection from male violence and support for lone mothers. The pace and extent of reform in these areas has varied enormously among Western European nations over the past twenty years, often reflecting variations in socialist influence.

- Fabian socialism can be distinguished from social democracy by its emphasis on a conception of social justice which looks towards the achievement of social equality and the abolition of poverty. Fabians take the firm view that these goals can be fulfilled within capitalism because the social policy measures required to attain them underpin the long-term survival and prosperity of capitalist society. Such measures contribute to economic growth by preventing the wastage of human resources and making efficient use of them; they also underpin social cohesion and foster positive social values of altruism and collective responsibility for human welfare. Fabian socialists, traditionally, have been very sceptical about the ability of private organizations, particularly profit-making ones, to provide fair universal access to welfare benefits and

services. For them the welfare state is built around redistributive taxation and universal benefits in partnership with municipal services delivered by competent professionals and administrators, regulated and financed to ensure an acceptable uniformity across the country. In recent decades, particularly in response to the rise of the New Right, Fabians have put much more emphasis on a fairer distribution of liberty as well as of resources, with consequently less emphasis on equalizing welfare outcomes. Hence in contemporary Fabian discussion there is much more emphasis on the empowerment of users and the development of choice through regulated markets or quasi-markets, alongside renewed emphasis on welfare citizenship and legal rights.

Prospects for Socialism

There is a widespread view that the epoch of socialism is either dead or drawing to a close. Certainly socialist political and labour movements have been in retreat across most of the world over recent decades with the seemingly global triumphs of capitalism and neo-liberalism. This has been accompanied by apparent retrenchment and privatization within the welfare state, alongside increased poverty, inequality and unemployment. Yet the aspirations of socialism – social equality, radical democracy and a socially responsible economy – have a natural, common sense appeal as people constantly come up against the risks and the adverse, sometimes catastrophic consequences of free markets and possessive individualism. Examples abound in post-Thatcherite Britain, including railway privatization, mortgage arrears and repossessions, homelessness, university student funding, failures of private pensions and endowments, the private costs of infirm elderly care. Struggles towards socialist aspirations, mostly unrecognized as such, go on as witnessed constantly almost wherever we look.

One example from contemporary British social policy illustrates this well. The National Health Service (NHS) (see chapter IV.9) was inspired, in part, by gradualist socialism and a very limited espousal of the principles of equality, democratic accountability and social economy. Equality boiled down to universal and equal access at no direct cost to the patient; democracy equated to parliamentary accountability and participation of local politicians in NHS administrative structures; social economy came in the forms of funding almost entirely through taxation and of a decentralized, sprawling nationalized industry. The NHS has encountered huge problems on each of these fronts. Equality of access has always been limited by the so-called postcode lottery and by queue-jumping private patients; accountability has been ineffective in the face of physicians' clinical power and bureaucratism; and financial dependence on taxation has delivered chronic underinvestment. Yet both the principles and the realities of the NHS remain very popular. Universal and equal access at no direct cost is seen as a fundamental human right, which is not fulfilled in many other capitalist welfare states. Parliamentary accountability at least ensures that NHS issues are kept constantly on the political agenda. Taxation funding and public expenditure scrutiny have forced the NHS into comparative economic 'efficiency' in the use of its resources, through, for example, low pay for its staff and fast patient throughput. There is a culture of public service and altruism about the NHS, which

is widely appreciated. The survival of the NHS for over fifty years suggests that popular aspirations in healthcare share much in common with the socialist perspective, even though the reality of the NHS is very far from being a truly socialist institution. New Labour, like the Conservatives, has tinkered with the NHS, introducing more private capital finance and contracts with private providers, which almost inevitably undermine its socialist elements. The coming years will see a continuing struggle between, on the one hand, the protection and development of the NHS's socialist aspirations, and further elements of privatization and continued underfunding which will undermine those aspirations.

Conclusion

Movements espousing socialist aspirations may no longer be called socialist in the future, because socialism may in the end be irrevocably tainted by its association with the evident failings of state collectivism and nationalization, whether in the form of the Soviet model or the NHS. Nevertheless, the pursuit of reasonable social equality, popular democracy and popular control of economic resources are goals which will always inspire political movements, social struggles and progressive social policy. At this stage in human history it would be premature to abandon the word socialism to describe these ever-present aspirations, especially in the absence of an appropriately modern alternative.

Guide to further reading

Bryson, V., 1992. *Feminist Political Theory* (Basingstoke: Macmillan Press). Still in print, an outstanding history of feminist thought with a strong emphasis on both the socialist contributions and social policy issues.

Ferguson, I., Lavalette, M. and Mooney, G., 2002. *Rethinking Social Welfare: A Critical Perspective* (London: Sage). An accessible attempt to apply a class struggle perspective to contemporary social policy issues including the family, neo-liberalism, globalization and New Labour.

Gough, I., 2000. *Global Capital, Human Needs and Social Policies* (Basingstoke: Palgrave). A clear and thoughtful collection of essays, which revisit and update the neo-Marxist perspective, demonstrating its relevance for the twenty-first century.

Mooney, G. and Lavalette, M., 2000. *Class Struggle and Social Welfare* (London: Routledge). An edited collection which describes and analyses some of the key welfare struggles in Britain over the past two centuries from the anti-Poor Law movements to the poll tax rebellion.

Sassoon, D., 1997. *One Hundred Years of Socialism: The West European Left in the Twentieth Century* (London: Fontana). A thorough, reflective and accessible survey of ideas and movements, including, for example, Swedish social democracy, feminism and environmentalism.

Wright, A., 1996. *Socialisms: Old and New* (London: Routledge). A lucid account of the diversity of socialist ideas and debates from their origins to the present day, focusing on the divergences between Marxism and the Fabian, ethical tradition espoused by the author.

Among a host of web sites dealing with socialist perspectives, the following may be particularly useful for British social policy students:

www.marxists.org/ A very comprehensive site covering Marx, Marxists and Marxism.

www.redpepper.org.uk/ Site of a lively, non-sectarian, radical socialist magazine, concentrating on economic, green and globalization issues.

www.chartist.org.uk/ Site of a group on Labour's democratic socialist left, with useful discussion on social policy issues and good links.

www.fabian-society.org.uk/ Site of a celebrated founding organization of the Labour Party, which continues to promote discussion of socialist social policy.

www.catalyst-trust.co.uk/ Site of a relatively new democratic socialist think-tank with lots of downloadable documents of interest to social policy students.

II.10
The Third Way

Martin Powell

Unlike some of the political perspectives covered in the other chapters in this section, the Third Way has a short history. There have been a number of previous third or middle ways associated with such diverse individuals as David Lloyd George and Harold Macmillan (see chapter II.7), and movements as different as Swedish social democracy and Italian fascism. However, the recent use of the term is generally associated with the writings of Anthony Giddens and the policies of the Democrat Administrations of Bill Clinton in the USA and of the New Labour Governments of Tony Blair in the UK.

Giddens' (1998) book *The Third Way* is very influential. It was an (academic) bestseller, and has been translated into many languages. Proponents of the 'third way' claimed that it is new and distinct from both traditional social democracy and neo-liberalism, but stress that it is a renewed or modernized social democracy: a left-of-centre project. In this sense, the 'Third Way' is simply a convenient label that may be used interchangeably with new social democracy or progressive governance. Any search for a third way must begin with a trichotomous framework, differentiating the Third Way from the Old Left and the New Right. However, some critics find a dichotomy, arguing that the Third Way is essentially neo-liberalism (see chapter II.6). Blair and Giddens have also claimed that the Third Way represents a combination of the best features of the USA and Continental Europe, bringing together American economic dynamism with European social inclusion.

There are continuing debates about the definition of the term, and whether governments can be termed 'Third Way'. Clinton and Blair have claimed the label for their administrations. Others use a different label. For example, the German social democratic party (SPD) under Gerhard Schröder uses the slogan of *Die Neue Mitte* (the new middle). Social Democratic and Labour parties in countries such as Belgium, Denmark and the Netherlands have introduced different policies from 'old' social democracy. Like the British Labour party, they generally claim that their values have not changed, but that economic and social changes mean that new policies must replace old policies that no longer work in today's world, as we discuss below. Even former French prime minister Lionel Jospin, who rejects the Third Way, argues for what he calls modern socialism with new policies reflecting traditional values.

This chapter aims to provide a brief introduction to these large and complex debates. The first part examines the dimensions of the Third Way, arguing that it is useful to unpack the concept with a focus on discourse, values, policy goals and policy mechanisms. The second part discusses the broad features of the Third Way in practice, concentrating on the social policies of New Labour in Britain, but also introducing examples from other countries.

The Essence of the Third Way

Much has been written about the Third Way, but its essence or main 'dependent variable' remains unclear. Many critics dismiss it as vague and amorphous. This view has considerable validity, but does not apply solely to the Third Way. Despite much effort, similar attempts to pin down the essence of socialism, social democracy or democratic socialism have not resulted in a clear consensus (see chapters II.8, II.9).

The problem in examining the Third Way is that the term is used in very different senses. A number of commentators have suggested broad characteristics or themes of the Third Way or new social democracy. These include social inclusion, civil society, active government, investment in human and social capital, redistributing opportunities or assets rather than income, positive welfare, prevention, an active approach to employment and rights and responsibilities. However, this conflates different elements such as means and ends. As a heuristic device, it is useful to distil these out into separate discussions of discourse, values, policy goals and policy mechanisms.

The Third Way has generated a new discourse or a new political language. Clinton and Blair share a number of key slogans or mantras such as being 'tough on crime; tough on the causes of crime'; 'a hand up, not a hand out'; 'hard working families that play by the rules', and 'work is the best route out of poverty'. In addition to new phrases, there is a redefined language where old words have new meaning. For example, the Third Way vocabulary or *NewLabourSpeak* includes terms such as full employment and equality, but they have very different meanings from their traditional usage. The term 'welfare' itself is a good example of how discourse is central to 'winning the welfare debate': there have been some attempts to view 'welfare' in its more negative meaning as held in the USA. Conversely, terms such as active and modern are regarded as unambiguously good.

The new discourse does not simply consist of new terms, but also emphasizes the relationship between them. The Third Way is a political discourse built out of elements from other political discourses. For example, enterprise belongs to the Right, while social justice belongs to the Left. The language of the Third Way is a rhetoric of reconciliation such as 'economic dynamism as well as social justice', 'enterprise as well as fairness'. They are not deemed antagonistic: while neo-liberals pursue the former and traditional social democrats the latter, the Third Way delivers both. The more radical claim is of 'going beyond' or transcending such themes: it is not simply about managing the tension between the promotion of enterprise and the attack on poverty, but claiming that they are no longer in conflict. However, it does seem difficult to achieve a reconciliation of some terms such as inclusion and responsibility. The carrot of inclusion can be dangled in front of all, but there must be some stick with which to beat the 'irresponsible'.

Some commentators have suggested a number of core values for the Third Way. These include CORA (community, opportunity, responsibility and accountability) and RIO (responsibility, inclusion, opportunity). However, the values of the Third Way remain problematic. This is mainly for two reasons.

1. An adequate understanding of values requires more than one-word treatments (see chapter II.2). Terms such as equality are essentially contestable concepts, meaning different things to different people. It follows that values must be more clearly defined and linked with goals (see below).

2. Second, and linked, it is not clear whether the Third Way is concerned with 'old' values, new or redefined meanings of old values, or new values. The best known accounts argue the first

position. For example, Tony Blair has claimed that the Third Way is concerned with the traditional values of social democracy. However, critics dispute that Blair's values – equal worth, opportunity for all, responsibility and community – adequately sum up traditional socialism in Britain. Moreover, some terms have been redefined. For example, the old concern with equality of outcome and redistribution has been diluted. A few new values also appear to have been smuggled in. Positive mentions of terms such as entrepreneurship were rarely part of the vocabulary of traditional social democracy.

Blair has claimed that policies flow from values. In this sense, goals or objectives may be seen as a more specific operationalization of values. For example, equality is often referred to as a value, but this may result in very different policy objectives such as equality of opportunity or equality of outcomes. It follows that advocates of equality might desire very different goals such as a reduction of inequalities of income, wealth, health status and educational qualifications or merely that there must be an equal opportunity to enter a race with a large gap between rich prizes for the winners and nothing for the losers.

It is claimed that traditional values and goals must be achieved by new means. In some ways this has parallels with Croslandite revisionism (see chapter II.8). Crosland separated the means and ends of socialism, suggesting that the Labour means of nationalization was not the best way of achieving the end of equality. Similarly the Third Way claims that new times call for new policies. The world has changed and so the welfare state must change. However, new solutions will not be based on outdated, dogmatic ideology. There is a new emphasis on evidence-based policy-making. Research, experiments and trials will find the best ways of working that will be mainstreamed throughout govern-

ment. A key phrase of this new pragmatism is 'what works is what counts'. The Third Way is more receptive to solutions based on the market and civil society than traditional social democracy. This results in a more eclectic policy mix. For example, the market is no longer regarded as automatically bad. New Labour selectively and pragmatically embraces the market. There are no textbook, ideological solutions, but each case will be examined on its merits, and what works in one area may not work in another. Table II.10.1 presents a necessarily rather stylized account of the Third Way that has been distilled from a variety of sources. It does run the risk of some rewriting of history, caricaturing the Old Left, the New Right and the Third Way that has been a feature of both advocates and critics.

The Third Way in Practice

This section develops some of the themes of policy goals and means from Table II.10.1. While most of the examples are taken from perhaps the clearest exemplar of the Third Way, the UK (more details on individual policy areas may be found in chapters IV.6–14), a few from other countries are included.

New Labour emerged during the long period of opposition to the 1979–97 Conservative government. In opposition the Labour Party carefully studied the electoral success of Clinton's 'New Democrats' in the USA. Clinton's Third Way stressed the themes of work, conditionality and responsibility, and promised to 'end welfare as we know it'. One result of Labour's desire to copy Clinton's success in modernizing the party and broadening its electoral appeal was to set up the Commission on Social Justice. Many elements of the Third Way were flagged up in its report of 1994. It rejected the approaches to social and economic policy of the *Levellers* – the Old Left – and the *Deregulators* – the New Right and advocated the middle way of *Investors'* Britain. This approach features much of the discourse which was to become central to New Labour – economic efficiency and so-

Table II.10.1   Dimensions of the Third Way in social policy

Dimension	Old Social Democracy	Third Way	Neo-Liberal
Discourse	Rights	Rights and responsibilities	Responsibilities
	Equity	Equity and efficiency	Efficiency
	Market failure	Market and state failure	State failure
Values	Equality	Inclusion	Inequality
	Security	Positive welfare	Insecurity
Policy goals	Equality of outcome	Minimum opportunities	Equality of opportunity
	Full employment	Employability	Low inflation
Policy means	Rights	Conditionality	Responsibilities
	State	Civil society/market	Market/civil society
	State finance and delivery	State/private finance and delivery	Private/state finance and delivery
	Security	Flexicurity	Insecurity
	Hierarchy	Network	Market
	High tax and spend	Pragmatic tax to invest	Low tax and spend
	High services and benefits	High services and low benefits	Low services and benefits
	High cash redistribution	High asset redistribution	Low redistribution
	Universalism	Both	Selectivity
	High wages	Minimum wage/tax credits	Low wages

cial justice are different sides of the same coin; redistributing opportunities rather than just redistributing income; transforming the welfare state from a safety net in times of trouble to a springboard for economic opportunity; welfare should offer a hand-up not a hand-out; an active, preventive welfare state; paid work for a fair wage as the most secure and sustainable way out of poverty; and the balancing of rights and responsibilities. An Investors' welfare state is proactive, emphasizing prevention, and stressing causes rather than effects: attacking the causes of poverty rather than its symptoms, preventing poverty through education and training rather than simply compensating people in poverty.

New Labour has probably set itself more targets than any previous British government. In addition to initial five key pledges on the 1997 pledge card, it has since outlined a 'contract' or 'covenant' of 10 pledges and 177 manifesto commitments that are monitored in the government's Annual Reports. It has established public service agreements and performance assessment frameworks throughout government departments. However, despite the claim of SMART (specific, measurable, accurate, relevant, timed) targets, many are vague and difficult to put into operation. In broad terms, it has set targets on increasing educational qualifications, reducing child poverty and health inequality but not, crucially for old Labour critics, income equality. New Labour rejects a simple, fiscal equality to be achieved through the tax and benefit system. It claims that it seeks a more ambitious and dynamic redistribution of assets or endowments. In short, instead of compensating people for their poverty with transfer payments, it aims to increase opportunities by increasing poor people's levels of health and education. Critics who argue that *all* New Labour's aims are less radical than Old Labour's are wide of the mark. Old Labour would be proud of the child poverty and health inequality targets. However, they are long term, and there is no certainty that they will be met. There have been similar but generally less marked retreats from fiscal redistribution and equality of outcome in countries such as France, Germany and Sweden.

In terms of policy instruments, New Labour emphasizes conditional or contractarian welfare. Rights are not dutiless but tend to be given to those who have fulfilled their obligations. The main obligations are connected with work, but others are concerned with public housing (for example evictions for anti-social behaviour) and health (checking a baby's progress with a health professional). At the extreme, this can be seen as a change from a patterned to a process-driven distribution. In other words, benefits and services may no longer be delivered simply on the basis of a criterion such as need, but might be varied to accord with behaviour. For example, an individual may be in need, but may have benefits reduced if he or she is deemed not to have fulfilled conditions such as accepting a job. This fits with changes in other countries. The most extreme examples are found in the USA. Welfare is now time-limited, indicating that it is seen as a temporary 'hand-up' not a permanent 'hand-out'. This means that there is a large incentive to find work, even in low-paid McJobs (temporary and insecure service work, such as offered by the McDonalds restaurant chain). In some US states single mothers on welfare are not given additional benefits for any subsequent children, and single mothers with young children are forced to find paid work. However, in many countries there are less extreme moves to conditionality through active labour market policies that aim to move people from welfare to work. For example, Denmark stresses activation and reciprocity. Individuals on social assistance have an obligation to find work, but local government must enable them to fulfil their obligations. Although the right to benefit is no longer automatic, the obligations of government mean that is not generally regarded as a US-style workfare scheme.

Services are largely financed by the state, but may be delivered by private or voluntary bodies in a purchaser/ provider split. Rather than hierarchies or markets, coordination and collaboration through partnerships or networks is stressed. New Labour has ended the old class war with private education and health providers, and now wishes to work with them through agreements or concordats. This is one area in which many countries were already on the Third Way. Britain tended to be exceptional in the state owning most of the hospitals and a relatively high percentage of housing, while elsewhere there was a more pluralist ownership of facilities. In some cases, there is encouragement to supplement basic state services with a private or voluntary extension ladder (such as in the area of pensions). The state will expect people to provide more of their own resources towards contingencies such as old age, but in return the government will assist low-income savers and provide regulation of the financial market. Tax and service levels will be pragmatic rather than dogmatic. There is a general tendency to prioritize services such as health and education that can be preventive in nature and increase human capital over reactive, passive, 'relief' cash benefits. Redistribution will be for a purpose and based more on endowments rather than in terms of transfer payments, although there has been some silent or backdoor fiscal redistribution especially to families with children.

Work is central to the Third Way. Key policy goals may be seen in the slogans of 'work for those who can; security for those who cannot' and 'making work pay'. There will be full employment, but this is to be achieved in terms of employability through the supply-side than by old-style Keynesian demand management (see chapter II.15). It is claimed that in a globalized world, no government can deliver old-style full employment as the days of 40 hours a week for 40 years working for one firm, leading to the gold watch on retirement, are gone. Work is now more flexible, with an increase in part-time and temporary employment. All governments can do is to equip workers with the skills to meet these new challenges and to add some element of security to this flexibility to produce *flexicurity*. The balance between security and flexibility varies. Countries such as the Netherlands appear to have stressed a genuine mix, while the UK and the USA seem to tend more towards the neo-liberal concept of a lightly regulated labour market. Similarly, the Third Way's work-centred social policy may have a different mix of 'carrots' and 'sticks'. On the one hand, it may emphasize carrots in the form of advice from case workers and investment in human capital. The slogan of making work pay includes a national minimum wage, in-work benefits of tax credits (or fiscal welfare) and making high quality affordable childcare available. On the other hand, although noting the carrot of tax credits, some critics have argued that the Third Way in the USA tends to starve the poor back into work through low or time-limited benefits.

Debates about universalism versus selectivity will not be dogmatic. On the one hand, inclusion through universal services or civic welfare is stressed. On the other hand, there may be increasing selectivity in cash benefits such as targeting the poorest pensioners and new area-based policies.

Conclusion

It is as yet difficult to judge the success of the Third Way in principle and in practice. Part of the difficulty is due to the relatively short period in office of 'Third Way' governments, but a greater part is perhaps associated with the diverse nature of the Third Way project. Defining the Third Way, and deciding which governments and policies are 'third way' remains problematic. Different commentators argue there is a single third way, that there are different third ways, or that the Third Way is simply neo-liberalism. Similarly, it has been claimed that the Third Way is largely confined to the USA and the UK, or that most countries in Europe are Third Way.

Overall, however, we might conclude a number of countries are pursuing policies that have some new and distinctive elements. These developments require a new label, as they are not 'old' social democracy, neither (more arguably) are they simply neo-liberalism. Policies vary between countries due to different social and economic circumstances and different political institutions and traditions. The extent to which they are sufficiently close to be seen in terms of a third way (or new social democracy) or third ways is less clear. The more important question, perhaps, is whether the Third Way can produce better social policies. Here, again, there are a range of views, associated with different political views and expectations. But, whatever the positive achievements, two final caveats should be noted. First, particularly in the UK, many targets such as reducing child poverty and health inequalities are long term. Second, it is not clear how the Third Way social policies pursued in the UK, the USA and some other European nations might fare in a recession.

Guide to further reading

As Third Way social policy represents work in progress, the most up-to-date details will be found in newspapers, articles in academic journals and new books and new editions of existing books on the area. However, the list below gives a selection of some of the existing sources.

Blair, T., 1998. *The Third Way* (London: Fabian Society). This brief pamphlet gives the political equivalent of Giddens' book.

Commission on Social Justice, 1994. *Social Justice: Strategies for National Renewal* (London: Vintage). The report of the Commission set up by John Smith, the late Labour leader, to provide some material that would inform debate to changes in Labour policies. Many of the ideas that underpin New Labour are clearly present, but there are also some important differences.

Department of Social Security, 1998. *New Ambitions for our Country* (London: Stationery Office). An early attempt by the Labour Government to set out a broad policy route map of the Third Way.

Giddens, A., 1998. *The Third Way* (Cambridge: Polity Press). The influential original source written by the leading academic proponent of the Third Way.

Giddens, A., (ed.), 2001. *The Global Third Way Reader* (Cambridge: Polity Press). In this edited collection, Giddens responds to his critics, and presents a series of largely friendly international commentaries on the Third Way.

Powell, M. (ed.), 2002. *Evaluating New Labour's Welfare Reforms* (Bristol: Policy Press). This examines New Labour's successes and failures in social policy in its first term.

Powell, M. and Hewitt, M., 2002. *Welfare State and Welfare Change* (Buckingham: Open University Press). Takes a broader approach, examining the changes between New Labour's modern welfare state and earlier social policies, and providing some explanation for these changes.

White, S. (ed.), 2001. *New Labour: the Progressive Future?* (Basingstoke: Palgrave). Contains chapters on aspects on New Labour's policies, together with material on policies in other countries.

Feminist Perspectives

Jane Lewis

Feminist Approaches

Post-war writing on the welfare state made very little mention of women. Richard Titmuss's classic essay on the divisions of social welfare (*Essays on the Welfare State*, London: Allen & Unwin, 1958) stressed the importance of occupational and fiscal welfare in addition to that provided by the state, but omitted analysis of provision by the voluntary sector and the family, both vital providers of welfare and both historically dominated by women providers. Titmuss, like other post-war commentators, also focused on social class as the most significant variable in the analysis of social welfare, missing gender (as well as race). Yet the post-war settlement in respect of social provision made huge assumptions regarding the roles and behaviour of men and women in society. Policy-makers followed Beveridge in assuming that adult men would be fully employed, that women would be primarily homemakers and carers, and that marriages would be stable. However, the most significant post-war social trends have been the vast increases in married women's labour market participation, in the divorce rate and in the extra-marital birth rate, all of which have had a disproportionate effect on women.

The first post-war feminist analyses of social policies began to appear in the 1970s. Emanating mainly from socialist feminists, they tended to be critical of the post-war settlement. For example, Wilson's (1977) pioneering study of women and welfare argued that 'social welfare policies amount to no less than the state organization of domestic life' (p. 9). This view was similar to that adopted by some Scandinavian feminists at the time and stressed the patriarchal nature of the post-war welfare state. The Scandinavians stressed the way in which women had become the employees of the welfare state on a huge scale, but found themselves for the most part doing the same kind of jobs that they had traditionally done at home; for example, childcare. These jobs remained low paid and low status in the public sector; hence the charge that state patriarchy had replaced private patriarchy. In Britain, it was also stressed that many of the assumptions of the social security system, for example, were traditional. Thus if a woman drawing benefit cohabited with a man it was assumed that he would be supporting her and her benefit was withdrawn. This early feminist analysis attacked the family as the main site of female oppression and also attacked the welfare state for upholding traditional ideas about the roles of men and women within the family.

In some important respects early feminist analysis of the welfare state had much in common with the analysis of the new right that emerged in the early 1980s. Mount, Mrs Thatcher's family policy adviser during the early 1980s, wrote a book praising the family for resisting unwelcome incursions by the state (*The Subversive Family*, London: Allen & Unwin, 1983). Mount sought to argue that the family should be left entirely free of state intervention, unless of course it had demonstrably failed in some significant measure, such as child abuse, whereas early feminists had sought more appropriate forms of state intervention. Nevertheless, the analysis of state welfare in terms of social control was similar.

More recent feminist analysis has focused less on whether state intervention is good or bad, and rather more on unpacking the complicated relationships between women and welfare systems, and the significance of gender in the analysis of social policies. For it is not possible to reach any easy conclusion as to the effects of social welfare policies on women. If we return briefly to the example of cohabiting women, while state policies enforced traditional assumptions about men's obligation to maintain as soon as a man appears in a household, social security benefits have nevertheless played a significant part in permitting non-traditional, lone mother households to exist autonomously and have thus played a part in permitting the transformation of traditional family forms.

The more recent feminist analysis of social policy has stressed the extent to which gender – the social construction of masculinity and femininity – is important as a variable in the analysis of policies, particularly in respect of their outcomes, and as an explanatory tool in understanding social policies and welfare regimes. Feminist analysis has insisted that the whole fabric of society is gendered. Thus access to income and resources of all kinds – for example, education – is gendered, as are the concepts that are crucial to the study of social policy: need, inequality, dependence, citizenship. Once the persistence of gender divisions is understood, it becomes easier to appreciate the persistence of inequalities. For example, while the occupational structure has changed enormously over the past century, there are still men's jobs and women's jobs. A man's job may become a woman's job, as in the case of librarian or bank clerk, but the gender divisions remain and with them status and pay differentials.

However, it would be a mistake to think that it is possible to identify a single feminist approach to social policy. Feminists have differed both in their theoretical approaches and in the issues they have focused on. Thus liberal feminists have tended to emphasize the importance of rights and equal opportunities and treatment, radical feminists have focused more on male power and on issues such as reproductive technology and domestic violence, and socialist feminists on the relationship between state welfare and capital and its implications for women's position. However, these boxes worked better for the 1970s and 1980s than for the 1990s, and were always much too neat and tidy. More important has been the recent emphasis on 'difference' within feminism and the realization that the interests of women carers may be different from those of women being cared for, as will black women's interests differ from those of white women. In other words, the politics of contested need will be present between different groups of women as well as between women and men. Nevertheless, feminist social policy analysts have evolved their own questions and vocabulary and it is to these that we now turn.

Feminist Challenges

Feminists began by challenging mainstream sociological and economic literature that purported to explain women's position, particularly in the family and in employment, the central argument being over the reasons for gendered inequalities in society. Mainstream analysis considered these to be the product of a combination of biology and choice, which in turn rendered them inappropriate targets for social reform. Functional sociologists and neoclassical economists agreed that, given that women wanted children, biology and differential earning power made it rational for husbands and wives to maximize their utilities by husbands becoming the primary earners and wives the primary carers. If they did go out to work, women would therefore choose local part-time work that suited them. The traditional male breadwinner model was thus portrayed as the most efficient and as an essentially harmonious family form.

Feminist questioning of these models focused on both the family and the workplace. Rethinking the family involved first stressing that there was no such thing as *the* family, either in terms of a single family form or in terms of a single experience and understanding on the part of the different family members. As Bernard pointed out (*The Future of Marriage*, 1976), there were in fact two marriages, his and hers. Male and female interpretations of their position could differ fundamentally. In regard to the economics of the family, Eleanor Rathbone raised the crucial question about the purpose of the wage as early as the 1920s (*The Disinherited Family*, 1924). If the wage was and is a reward for individual effort and merit, how was and is it supposed to provide for dependent wives and children? Feminists have continued to ask awkward questions about the maintenance of family members. Both social investigation and policy-makers assumed that money entering the family was shared equally between family members, but feminist investigation has shown unequivocally that this is not the case and that where conflict between the partners becomes violent, women often find themselves better off drawing benefits than relying on their male providers. Thus feminists have questioned both the harmonious working and the efficiency of the male breadwinner model.

They have also questioned whether women's role in reproduction is sufficient to explain their position in the labour force. Such a view minimizes the role played by discrimination. It also ignores conflicting evidence in terms of women's aspirations revealed by the post-1960s dramatic rise in female educational achievement, and the structural constraints experienced by women. Women may choose to have children, but mainstream models also assume that they must necessarily rear them. Questions as to who should care for and maintain children have therefore been central to the feminist analysis of social policies, in particular how far there should be collective provision for children in the form of cash (typically in modern welfare states in the form of child benefits) and care (via day care and nurseries), and how far individual mothers and fathers should assume responsibility for both cash and care.

Analysing Women's Relationship to the Welfare State

In so far as women have entered the traditional social administration texts, they have tended to do so as clients of the welfare state. Feminist analysis has emphasized that women's position in relation to modern welfare states is far more complicated than this. In brief, they should be considered as clients, paid and unpaid providers, and agents.

Those who have made the charge that women have done disproportionately well out of the welfare state have pointed to the fact that they more often become clients, whether in terms of the number of visits they make to general practitioners, or the amount of benefit they draw, especially as lone mothers and elderly women. But women have also been the main providers of welfare. The vast majority of the increase in post-war employment for married women has been in the service of the welfare state (for example, as health workers and teachers), and women have always provided most of the informal, unpaid welfare within the family.

Women's position as both clients and providers is complicated and is directly related to the unequal gender division of paid and unpaid work in society. Analyses of entitlements to welfare, such as Esping-

Andersen's (*The Three Worlds of Welfare Capitalism*, Cambridge: Polity Press, 1990), which examine the conditions under which people are permitted to withdraw from the labour market and thus depend on a strict distinction between work and non-work, cannot encompass the reality of women's existence. The woman who withdraws from the labour market often does so in order to care for children or a dependent adult. She therefore withdraws from paid work in order to engage in unpaid work. So women who are clients of the welfare state are quite likely also to be acting at the same time as unpaid providers of welfare. Similarly, analyses of welfare outcomes that do not take into account women's contribution as unpaid providers will inevitably over-estimate what women take out of the system as opposed to what they put in.

Women's agency is also problematic. Seemingly women have had little say in the making of modern welfare states. Recent historical literature has suggested that women may have had more influence when the mixed economy of welfare was tipped more firmly in favour of voluntary and family provision at the turn of the century. Thus in the United States, for example, women's voluntary organizations lobbied successfully for mothers' pensions (an early form of child benefit), protective labour legislation for women workers and maternal and child welfare legislation. Skocpol has suggested that at the beginning of this century the United States set out on the road to becoming a 'maternalist' welfare state in contrast to the 'paternalism' of the European states, which were built up around the concept of social insurance and which in turn relied heavily on the male breadwinner model (*Protecting Soldiers and Mothers. The Political Origins of Social Policy in the United States*, 1992).

Certainly the relationship between social provision and women's political participation is difficult. T. H. Marshall's idea that states proceeded from the granting of civil rights in the eighteenth century, to the granting of political rights in the nineteenth and to social rights in the twentieth ('Citizenship and Social Class' in T. H. Marshall, *Sociology at the Crossroads and Other Essays*, 1963), breaks down completely when women are introduced into the analysis. Women in most Western countries were granted social protection before they were granted the vote, usually in the form of protective labour legislation, which was in turn often designed to reinforce the gender division of labour and to exclude women from certain kinds of employment. The major programmes of modern Western European welfare states were legislated by men and, in the case of social insurance, working as it does through the labour market, primarily for men. However, women have historically played an important role in local politics and in local campaigns around welfare rights and tenants groups, for example. In addition, the fact that women played very little part in the establishment of the programmes of the modern welfare state does not mean that the development of social provision is unimportant in securing women's participation. In the Scandinavian countries, which are acknowledged to have developed the most generous citizenship-based welfare entitlements, women have also succeeded in gaining the greatest formal political representation in parliament.

The Concept of Dependence

Because of the gendered division of income and work in society and of women's complicated relationship to both work and welfare, the feminist analysis of dependency has been central in exposing the assumptions underlying policy formation. From the policy-making point of view, in both Britain and the United States during the past decade there has been increasing concern about female 'welfare dependency', especially in respect of the growing numbers of lone mother families.

There are three main sources of income

for women in modern industrial societies: men, the labour market and the state; although in some countries charity may still play an important part (for example, Italian unmarried mothers must still resort to charity if there is no family support forthcoming). Over the past century, single women without children and married women with children have become increasingly dependent on wages, and single women with children have become dependent on the state, rather than on male relatives. But because of the gendered division of work, whereby women do a disproportionate amount of the unpaid work, over the life cycle women will tend to rely on more than one source of income. The woman caring for an elderly relative may become more dependent on state benefits in order to render the person she is caring for more independent. The way in which women package income is therefore likely to be more complicated than it is for men, reflecting the different pattern of their dependencies on the labour market, wages and men.

The assumptions that governments have made about female dependency have historically been simple and in accordance with the male breadwinner model: that adult married women will be dependent on men. However, rapid family and labour market change over the past quarter of a century, resulting in a large increase in the numbers of lone mother families and in women's labour market participation, has served to erode the assumptions of stable families and full male employment that underpinned post-war social policies. Nevertheless, different countries have varied in the speed with which they moved away from the male breadwinner model as a basis for policy-making. Sweden and Denmark moved furthest and fastest. At the end of the twentieth century, it was assumed in these countries that all adults, male and female, would participate in the labour market, making the dual-earner family the norm. This changed assumption regarding the behaviour of adult women

was accompanied by strengthened collective provision in respect of childcare, in the form of day care and parental leave insurance. France attempted to make parallel provision for adult women as mothers and as paid workers, while Germany and Britain retained relatively strong male breadwinner models. Until the late 1990s, British Governments remained at best neutral, making the division of paid and unpaid work a private matter for individual men and women, whereas the French and Scandinavian governments attempted in different ways to reconcile paid and unpaid work. Most recently the trend in most Western European countries has been towards an adult worker model family, the assumption being that men and women will be in the labour market, and in the UK this has been accompanied by the first steps in introducing a national childcare policy. However, in many Western European countries, the UK included, women tend to be employed part-time. Thus they are not fully individualized or economically autonomous, which raises the possibility that policies based on the new adult worker model assumptions may be as far removed from the social reality as the old model of dependence.

The difficulty and the importance of the ways in which governments have tended to identify adult women as primarily either mothers or workers is shown clearly in the case of lone mothers. In Britain since the Second World War, lone mothers with children under 16 have not been required to make themselves available for employment, whereas in France this applies only to lone mothers with children under three. In the 1990s, the pendulum has been swinging back towards treating lone mothers more as workers, and in Britain, an attempt was made to force men to maintain their biological children. The point is that within the traditional assumptions regarding female dependence on men, if there is no male breadwinner present, the state has to decide under what conditions it will step in to maintain the woman and her children, or whether it prefers to encourage her to be dependent on wages. Recent policies have treated this group of women as 'citizen workers' rather than as 'citizen mothers', which has raised difficult questions about the value that is placed on the unpaid work of caring for children, and about the extent to which such policy initiatives may be at odds with what women themselves regard as their most important 'job'.

Traditional assumptions regarding female dependence on men, which has been the pattern of dependence preferred by government, have meant that women's substantial contributions to welfare, both informal and formal, have tended to be ignored, together with the entitlements that would have been their due. In addition, there has been a tendency to define women's needs in terms of motherhood as a social function rather than an effort to meet need on an individual basis.

Women's Claims: Equality or Difference?

Feminist analysis of women's structural position in society and the particulars of their relationship to modern welfare regimes has shown why it is that equal opportunities legislation that focuses heavily on the public world of employment is bound to have at best only moderate success. The gendered divisions of paid and unpaid work and the gendered inequalities that result require much more sophisticated policies. Aiming to treat women the same as men will not do. On the other hand, acknowledging female difference within social policies is likely to reinforce it, as was the case with post-war social security policy which, recognizing the degree to which married women were dependent on men, served to perpetuate it. Feminist analysis has shown that the problem of same or different treatment is a central one for modern social policies.

Guide to further reading

There is now a range of texts that provide an introduction to feminist approaches to social policy, beginning with Elizabeth Wilson *Women and the Welfare State* (London: Tavistock, 1977). Gillian Pascall's 1986 contribution *Social Policy: A Feminist Analysis* has recently been updated (London: Routledge, 2nd edition, 1999). Fiona Williams *Social Policy: A Critical Introduction* (Cambridge: Polity Press, 1989) provides an interesting introduction to feminist theory as it relates to social policy. There are many books of essays that treat particular themes of importance to the study of women and social policy, e.g. Clare Ungerson (ed.) *Women and Social Policy. A Reader* (Basingstoke: Macmillan Press, 2nd edition, 1997). Most recently there have been a number of important books of essays that take a comparative perspective: my own *Women and Social Policies in Europe* (Aldershot: Edward Elgar, 1993); and Diane Sainsbury (ed.) *Gender, Equality and Welfare States*, 2nd edition (Cambridge: Cambridge University Press, 1999) are starting places. Work that has served to gender crucial concepts and approaches to the study of social policy is also important, see especially Ruth Lister, *Citizenship: Feminist Perspectives* (Basingstoke: Macmillan Press, 1998).

'Race' and Social Welfare

Waqar Ahmad and Gary Craig

This chapter summarizes some major conceptual and policy issues in 'race' and social welfare before discussing three specific areas of social policy. Racism in state welfare has a long history. For example, Queen Elizabeth I ordered compulsory repatriation of black people from Britain so that state welfare would be accessed only by white citizens. Williams (1996, and see also chapter II.16) identifies three important recent historical moments in the relationship between racism and state welfare. These were:

- the importance of the construction of notions of nation, welfare state and citizenship, in the early twentieth century, characterized by increasing exclusion of certain categories of people;
- the significance of the eugenics movement, which constructed certain groups as pathological and to be contained to ensure the greater good of the wider society. She argues that 'discourses involved in this [eugenics] movement were racialized, and overlapped with notions of class, gender, disability and sexuality';
- the post-war period of black immigration encouraged by the state to meet labour shortages, and during which the 'historical legacy of racism reconstituted itself, especially in relation to the pathologization of black family life'. Indeed, the emergence of the welfare state

itself was based on fears of the degeneration of the 'British race' and the loss of the empire.

That the state's relationship to racialized minorities remains ambivalent today is therefore not surprising, and this ambivalence is reflected in the policies of successive governments to immigration, refugees and asylum-seekers (see chapter IV.6).

This ambivalence is not confined to social policy as *practice*; it is shared by the academic discipline of social policy, where it is still not uncommon for mainstream social policy texts to ignore 'race' and racism. This is an odd omission considering that social policy as a discipline is concerned centrally with issues of citizenship rights, welfare, equality, poverty alleviation and social engineering.

Racism: Definitions and Their Implications

'Racism' is a messy concept, as it encompasses attitudes, behaviour and outcomes and has been conceptualized in a variety of ways. 'Scientific racism', based on notions of the inherent superiority of certain 'races' over others, is now largely discredited by biologists and social scientists alike. However, versions of it continue to have some popularity. A belief in the natural superiority of some 'races' over others was used to justify slavery and imperialism, and is now being used to argue for the abolition of anti-poverty policies. A particularly popular definition of 'racism' rested on psychological assumptions about an individual being racially prejudiced and having the power to exercise this prejudice to discriminate against people from a different racial group. This psychological approach had great salience in British social policy in the shape of 'multiculturalism' which has strongly shaped discourses in major areas of social policy. This conception locates racism in cultural difference: in terms of policy, it can only articulate arguments for tolerance of difference rather than for equality of treatment, resources or outcomes.

An important point in British 'race relations' literature was the publication of *The Empire Strikes Back* (CCCS, 1982), which provided a powerful critique of multiculturalism and psychological approaches to racism. In this the contributors argued for a conceptualization of racism in terms of institutional structures, organizational and professional ideologies and the routine workings of a racist society in which an understanding of imperialism, contemporary relationships between developed and under-developed worlds, and intersections of 'race' and class were vital. Racism is practised by ordinary people in a racist society, and not solely by evil people; combating racism is thus an issue not of changing attitudes or preaching tolerance but of changes in legal and institutional structures, practices and ideologies. Institutions built on white British, Judaeo-Christian values and a racist ideology may well discriminate against individuals and groups of minority ethnic background through the application of routine procedures (residence requirements, ability to speak English, etc.), without the individual functionaries (clerks, administrators etc.) themselves necessarily being racially prejudiced. Anti-racism, the approach to combating inequities built on this notion of racism, emphasized the need to challenge and change structures and procedures – institutional racism rather than individual prejudice was thus the fo-

cus of anti-racist strategies (Bulmer and Solomos, 1999).

In this approach, what was important for minority ethnic communities was their shared experience of racial marginalization and discrimination – leading to the popular adoption of the description 'black' to signify this unity of experience – rather than the discreteness of individual cultures, ethnicities and religions. Anti-racism, in the 1980s, was espoused by a number of 'left' local authorities, including the Greater London Council (GLC), and had salience in social policy areas such as social work and housing. The late 1980s was notable for a backlash against anti-racism, from both within and without the movement. The Right criticized it for being politically dangerous and divisive – the tabloid press routinely published stories about the 'excesses' of 'loony left boroughs' as well as of individual activists. Some on the Left were concerned about the hardening orthodoxy of the anti-racist movement, which no longer acknowledged difference, or the value of culture, while others questioned its relevance to certain sections of the political black alliance, namely Asian communities. In the late 1980s, questions were also raised about the relevance of anti-racism to struggles centred not on colour-based racism, but on racism articulated increasingly around notions of culture and religion (e.g. in increasing anti-Muslim sentiments). The Runnymede Trust established a Commission on the Future of Multi-Ethnic Britain which reported in 2000, arguing that, in a context of the equal worth of all citizens, regardless of colour, gender, ethnicity and so on, that Britain could move towards becoming 'a society in which all citizens and communities feel valued' (Parekh, 2000, p. x).

Controlling the 'Race Relations Problem'

A central plank of British social policy concerns the containment of the 'race relations problem', an important facet of it being repressive and increasingly restrictive immigration control. Punitive immigration control has been justified by both Conservative and Labour governments in terms not just of its importance to the state, but of it being in the interest of minority ethnic communities themselves. Progressively restrictive immigration controls, from the 1960s onwards, have been employed through formal legislation as well as administrative techniques such as understaffing British High Commissions in countries of the 'New Commonwealth', which creates long queues of potential entrants and delay applications for entry.

The state response to the welfare needs of minority communities has been characteristically ambivalent: increasingly restrictive access to state welfare alongside specific funding to local authorities. The 'twin-track' state response, involving both improved integration, including measures to make racial discrimination illegal, and restrictions on immigration, is evident in the way immigration and race relations legislation has developed in tandem. For example, the 1965 and 1976 Race Relations Acts were each preceded and then followed by Immigration Acts. Divided families are one consequence of such policies. Even those who possess formal citizenship (characterized by a British passport, voting rights etc.) do not enjoy equality of substantive citizenship (characterized by access to the array of state-funded social welfare) (Ahmad and Husband, 1993), as is discussed in the case studies below. Access to state welfare is also conditioned by continued expectations that minority ethnic communities should prove their deservingness, both literally (see Craig, 1999) and symbolically (for example, Home Secretary David Blunkett's suggestion that new immigrants should swear an oath of allegiance to 'the Queen, her heirs and successors', Home Office, 2002).

More recently attention has focused more sharply on the growing numbers of refugees and asylum-seekers entering – or attempting to enter – Britain. Successive governments have introduced a variety of immigration regimes for these groups which have been increasingly restrictive and harsh. At the same time, most 'developed' countries, including the UK, have recognized the need to allow increased immigration of skilled workers – such as doctors and computer engineers – to fill niches within the labour market where there are labour shortages. More recent events which have heightened the political salience of debates about race relations have included the murder of Stephen Lawrence, leading to the Macpherson Inquiry into his death (charging the Metropolitan Police with institutional racism) and to the Race Relations (Amendment) Act 2000, which placed a duty on public bodies to introduce anti-racist policies; and a series of disturbances involving black and Asian young men in several northern cities in the summer of 2001. The Act also enhanced the Commission for Racial Equality's powers to monitor progress against race equality targets, and impose a 'specific duty' of race equality against failing authorities. Whilst the need to incorporate issues of race equality within the wider goal of social inclusion is increasingly recognized in many recent government initiatives, the government faces the considerable challenge of turning words into action.

Case Studies

Below, we provide case studies of three important policy areas (social security, housing and education) which illustrate some of the ways in which institutional racism limits the access of minority ethnic communities to state welfare. It is important to note that different minority ethnic groups have shown different trajectories in many areas of social and economic life and there is a growing recognition of the importance of exploring differences within the minority population as well as between minorities as a whole, and the white British population. Thus, in terms of income and housing and employment status,

Indian, Chinese and African populations are doing rather better than other minority groups.

Social security

What is the problem?
Minority ethnic communities are more likely to experience poverty than the UK population as a whole. This is due to:

- higher than average unemployment levels (minority ethnic communities are concentrated in inner cities where recession and industrial restructuring have weakened older industrial sectors);
- for many, poor prospects of decent education with resultant poor job related skills;
- racism in the selection of people for jobs or redundancy;
- the greater likelihood of low-paid work;
- inadequate health and housing provision;
- increasingly harsh restrictions on state financial help for refugees and asylum-seekers.

The social security system should maintain adequate income levels, and be a means for identifying minority ethnic communities at greatest risk. In addition, we cannot assume that the minority ethnic community experience of poverty can be extrapolated from that of the population at large. For example, household and age structures of different minority ethnic groups are diverse, and the UK minority ethnic population as a whole is considerably 'younger' than the white population. Given the lower level of educational qualifications achieved by older members of minority ethnic communities while in the labour market, their shorter UK employment careers and their greater experience of unemployment and low pay, minority ethnic community pensioners are more likely to have both reduced access to occupational pensions and reduced state pensions and other contributory benefit provision. Minority ethnic elders' income is thus generally more dependent on income-replacement (usually means-tested) social security benefits and therefore lower than that of their white counterparts.

Independent research has suggested that the social security system creates further problems for minority ethnic communities. For example, the National Association of Citizens Advice Bureaux (NACAB) monitoring of minority ethnic users' experience indicated that direct and indirect racism were common, that 'black clients and clients who speak or write no or little English are not receiving full entitlement to benefit, and their encounters with the social security system are often distressing and humiliating'. Other studies highlighted low benefits take-up among minority ethnic communities, resultant on language difficulties, lack of specialist advisers, insufficient awareness and information about sources of help, and cultural and religious factors among the minority ethnic communities themselves.

The policy response
The social security system cannot identify minority ethnic communities at risk with any degree of precision because it has no effective ethnic monitoring system. Targeted research aimed at exploring the experience of minority ethnic communities is thus difficult to execute and the relevant department, Department for Work and Pensions (DWP), provides only a very limited 'race'-based analysis of data, through, for example, the small-scale Family Resources Survey. Other structural factors which undermine the ability of the social security system to maintain adequate income levels among minority ethnic communities include:

- an emphasis in contributory schemes on non-interruption of contributions, discriminating against those with short or irregular UK working lives;
- their consequent over-reliance on means-tested benefits, notorious for low take-up;

- direct and indirect discrimination against 'people from abroad'.

Following publication of a series of critical research reports during the 1980s and 1990s, the Department for Social Security (now Department of Work and Pensions) has begun slowly to respond to the need to provide services more sensitive to minorities, including publishing key leaflets and offering helplines in minority languages, better training for staff, and limited interpretation/translation services. In response specifically to NACAB's report, the Department commissioned a small-scale investigation into the information needs of minority ethnic communities. Most large-scale research into the social security system still has no adequate 'race' dimension although some small-scale projects have begun to be commissioned including explorations of the situations of minority lone parents and elders.

Housing

What is the problem?
Minority ethnic communities are residentially segregated, in terms of regional distribution (being concentrated mainly in South East and North West England and the West Midlands), between urban and rural areas and within urban areas, where the vast majority of minority ethnic communities live. Most white people live in areas with very small minority ethnic populations and about 10 per cent of whites live in urban enumeration districts containing about three-quarters of all minority ethnic communities. Explanations for regional segregation focus particularly on the demand for workers in occupations where there were labour shortages and, within defined urban areas, on the impact of cultural preferences in shaping the concentration of particular minority ethnic communities. This explanation, however, does not clarify why 'they should pursue this in the more run-down segments of the housing stock, rather than in areas where

they could secure the symbolic and economic benefits associated with suburban life' (Smith, 1996, p. 37). Minority ethnic communities are most likely to be found in areas which are deprived on many indicators, where housing is older and of poorer quality and where other services such as education are inadequate. This phenomenon derives from the way the labour market interacts with the housing market.

Because members of minority ethnic communities are more likely to have been working in low-paid, insecure occupations, they have generally had to resort to the poorest forms of housing. A further structural reason for these concentrations, however, lies in the existence of direct individual and indirect structural discrimination in both public and private housing sectors. This has been reflected in policies of direct exclusion, the manipulation of information and opportunities by key housing gatekeepers such as local authority housing managers and private sector estate agents, racist public housing allocation policies and differential access to private housing finance.

The policy response
Addressing racism in housing provision has been complicated by major changes in the housing market, consequent on government policy shifts over the past 20 years, particularly towards the growth of owner-occupation and (to a lesser extent) of private rented and housing association sectors, and away from direct local authority housing provision. Growth in the small Housing Association movement offered opportunities for specialist housing provision for minority ethnic communities and in 1986 the Housing Corporation adopted a formal housing strategy for minority ethnic communities. This has led to a larger number of independent associations controlled by minority ethnic communities, but some of the more successful of these are losing their identity as they are absorbed within mainstream housing providers.

Minority ethnic communities have fared

less well in other housing sectors, however. For example, low-income minority ethnic owner-occupiers in disadvantaged urban areas found that a combination of higher repair and maintenance bills, overcrowding and higher loan repayments hindered a general enhancement of their housing status. At the same time, 'right to buy' policies have differentially affected those minority ethnic communities in poorer quality public sector housing to which they had originally been directed on racist grounds. The private rented sector remains a disproportionately significant source of housing for minority ethnic communities but racism in access and allocation continue to be extensive in what is becoming an increasingly deregulated sector. The process of housing segregation of ethnic groups within urban areas continues to prompt concern about ghettoization of some, particularly more economically marginalized groups, concern which was heightened in the wake of the 'northern disturbances' involving minority communities in late 2001.

Education

What is the problem?
Discussion about 'race' and education focuses, as with education more generally, on attempts to identify the factors which affect educational achievement. These have been heightened by claims in some quarters that educational achievement is genetically determined. The minority ethnic community population has a 'younger' demographic profile than the population at large: thus the school population contains proportionately half as many again ethnic minority children as might be expected from the UK population as a whole, and this proportion is continuing to grow. Until 1989, the only source of data on ethnicity and educational attainment was from labour market statistics. These focus on the achievement of formal qualifications but do not 'reflect the educational 'value-added' to pupils over the course of their education through

a combination of school input and pupil effort' (Law, 1996, p. 171).

Analysis of data suggests that underachievement is variable between different minority ethnic communities and that this is affected by several factors, including religious, cultural, social or political motivation, broader socio-economic factors, differences in the general quality of schools (including, particularly, the quality of teaching and of school facilities) and racial harassment. Although these factors are not in themselves determined by 'race', there is a strong correlation between low socio-economic status, poor educational provision and 'race', as a result of the kind of structural factors described earlier. The interaction of these factors can be complex: for example, many minority ethnic communities have a higher rate of participation in post-16 education than white communities; here, parental motivation appears to be reinforced by a reluctance to enter what may be seen as a racist labour market. However, the rate of minority ethnic communities' admissions to higher education, while again variable between different groups, do not reflect the high level of post-compulsory schooling. Studies suggest that the discretion inherent in admissions procedures often operates in a racist way. Racist assumptions often also underpin the assessment of special needs or the selection of children for exclusion from school; for example, rates of exclusion for young African-Caribbean males are particularly high (SEU, 1998).

The policy response
The collection of data from ethnic monitoring has improved at both school and higher education levels since the late 1980s and shows that the gap between minority ethnic pupils and white pupils is narrowing in terms of qualifications, as result of antiracist policies in a number of policy areas, including housing, health, the labour market and education itself.

However, educational policy developments since 1980 – for example, the growth of local management of schools with de-volved (but tight) budgets and the weak-ened influence of local authority 'race' polices (because of both local management and financial constraints on local govern-ment) – mean that there is little impetus for the further enhancement of anti-racist prac-tice within schools. As with housing, mi-nority ethnic groups have reacted in part by developing 'complementary' forms of educational provision such as Saturday schools and autonomous adult education provision. Although local proposals for the development of separate educational pro-vision for Muslim children have generally been opposed on the grounds that 'special' provision should not be needed, (a particu larly ironic response to racism in the gen-eral educational system) and that separate provision might undermine the process of inter-cultural trust and understanding, a few Muslim-only schools have now

emerged as a defensive response to this rac-ism and government is beginning to sup-port this development.

The population of Britain's minorities is growing relative to the population of the UK as a whole and 'minorities' (representa-tives of which can now be found in every local authority area within the UK) now predominate in some areas of urban Brit-ain. Their position within the life of Britain remains marked by economic and social disadvantage as a whole, although some minorities (e.g. those of Indian and Chinese origin) are achieving in educational, social and economic life ahead of the majority population. In the next few years, if tensions are not to mount between communities, policy and politics will have to address both this overall picture of disadvantage and the implications of growing numbers of minori-ties for a multicultural society built on re-spect for difference and diversity.

Guide to further reading

Ahmad, W. I. U. and Husband, C., 1993. 'Religious identity, citizenship and welfare: the case of Muslims in Britain', *American Journal of Islamic Social Science*, 10, 2, discusses issues of formal and substantive citizenship with a particular focus on Britain's Mus-lim communities.

Bulmer, M. and Solomos, J. (eds), 1999. *Racism* (Oxford: Oxford University Press). A reader which provides a very wide variety of historical and contemporary perspectives on racism, anti-racism and the state.

Centre for Contemporary Cultural Studies (CCCS), 1982. *The Empire Strikes Back: Race and Racism in 70s Britain* (London: Hutchinson). An important critique of multicultural approaches in ethnic relations and state policy.

Craig, G., 1999. '"Race", poverty and social security' in J. Ditch (ed.) *An Introduction to Social Security* (London: Routledge) reviews poverty and income maintenance research, pointing both to racism in benefit administration and delivery, and to weaknesses in research methodology.

Home Office, 2002. *Secure Borders, Safe Haven*, White Paper on Immigration (London: Stationery Office). Official response to growing debates about both refugees and asy-lum-seekers, and the more general social and economic position of minorities within the UK.

Law, I., 1996. *Racism, Ethnicity and Social Policy* (Englewood Cliffs, NJ: Prentice Hall) ex-plores questions of racial equality and ethnicity in relation to most major areas of social welfare provision, in context of review of theoretical and conceptual debates.

Parekh, B., 2000. *Commission on the Future of Multi-Ethnic Britain* (London: Profile Books) reviews the current position of 'race relations' within the UK, identifies barriers to progress towards a multi-cultural Britain and suggests strategies for change.

Social Exclusion Unit (SEU), 1998. *Truancy and school exclusions* (London: Cabinet Office). One of the few SEU reports to have a clear analysis in terms of 'race', pointing to the racialized nature of the process of school exclusion in particular.

Smith, S. J., 1996. *The Politics of 'Race' and Residence* (Cambridge: Polity Press) examines racial segregation in Britain, with particular reference to housing, urban and immigration policies: argues for combating racial inequality within a broader strategy for dealing with socio-economic disadvantage.

Williams, F., 1996. '"Race", welfare and community care: A historical perspective', in W. Ahmad and K. Atkin (eds), *'Race' and Community Care* (Buckingham: Open University Press), pp. 15–28, provides a useful overview of racism in welfare provision.

II.13
The Green Perspective

Michael Cahill

The environmental damage produced by our economic system is all too plain to see in oil spills, greenhouse gases, the loss of the rain forests, traffic pollution and many other consequences of the industrial way of life. Over the last quarter of the twentieth century concern for the environment has moved from the province of small, uninfluential pressure groups on to the agenda of the world's leading nations. There are many varieties of green thought but they are all united in their belief that the environment should take priority in social and political discussion. Social policy may seem a long way from these concerns but there is now a growing recognition that environmental issues and social policy are connected.

The Development of Environmentalism

Widespread interest in the environment can be traced back to the publication of the *Limits to Growth* report in 1972 (D. H. Meadows et al., *The Limits to Growth: A Report for the Club of Rome's Project on the Predicament of Mankind*). The authors used various computer models to see how long the world's stocks of basic non-renewables would last given population increases and continuing economic growth. In the same year Friends of the Earth and Greenpeace were formed and began to popularize the environmental message with imaginative and persist-

ent campaigning. Shortly afterwards, in 1973, the oil price hike made by the Middle East oil producers led to widespread energy saving measures in the Western world, although this was not to endure. An environmental movement began to emerge with a growth in the membership of environmental pressure groups.

However, green (ecology) parties were in their infancy in the 1970s. Green parties gained some electoral success in the 1980s, particularly in Germany, with Die Grünen gaining seats in parliament, taking power in local government and by the late 1990s forming part of the national government. The German greens popularized green policies throughout Europe. But it was not so much political parties or pressure groups which spread green ideas but rather the impact of what was happening to nature. In the late 1980s two extremely serious environmental problems were acknowledged: global warming and the discovery of holes in the ozone layer. In the 1990s the quickening pace of environmental crisis – particularly the onset of climate change – pushed the issue of the environment on to the agenda of the leading industrial countries. This was symbolized by the attention given to the United Nations Earth Summit held in Rio de Janeiro in 1992 which committed the international community to a programme of sustainable development.

Greens are united in their recognition of the fact that there are natural and social limits to material progress. These have now been reached: the planet is over-populated, the emissions from industrial and transport activity are damaging the biosphere and there is insufficient food to feed the population, while species extinction proceeds apace. The green response is to call for a reduction in the burden of human activity on the planet which could have important implications for social policy. How the reduction of humankind's burden on the planet can occur is at the heart of green arguments and debate. Obviously it is of paramount importance that environmental policies do not damage the welfare of the poorer sections of the population.

There are a great many ways to classify green thinking. It is possible to characterize light and dark green thinking.

- *Dark greens* see the survival of nature and the planet as all-important. Human activity particularly in the past two hundred years since the emergence of industrialism has despoiled the planet and now threatens the existence of other life forms and even the planet itself. This leads some greens to call for severe curbs on population. Dark ecologists believe that humans, in order to reduce their burden on the planet, need to reduce their consumption patterns. They are at one with supporters of animal rights in calling for an end to the second-class treatment of other sentient creatures on the planet. Rather than people from the poor world looking to the rich West for a model, 'dark' greens would have the rich world try to imitate the poor world. Lifestyle change is key to this with people changing their way of life in order to reduce the damage they cause to the planet earth. In reply to the charge that this is not terribly attractive to generations reared on consumer products they answer that if people were to give up some of the consumerist lifestyle then they would gain immeasurably. Yet this seems to ignore the fact that many people do gain a sense of their own identity from material possessions. It is important to note that this is a message for the here and now. A sustainable way of life involves reducing one's impact on the environment straight away, not waiting for some future government to legislate. It can be seen that 'dark' greens integrate a set of ethical beliefs with their political and social views.

- *Light greens* are reformists: they want to work with the grain of advanced industrial societies and adopt a pragmatic approach. For them, the environmental problems of the world are not too grave or too large to be beyond the problem solving capacity of science and technology. They believe that it is possible to have continued economic growth yet solve environmental problems. Many think that it is possible to use market mechanisms to correct the environmental imbalances which abound. Various techniques can be used to weigh the claims of the environment against other factors. Forms of cost-benefit analysis, assigning a monetary value to natural resources, can be used to decide on the degree of environmental protection required. Equally, it is possible for modern industry to clean up its act and, indeed, the production of technologies to do this will be a highly profitable investment. 'Light green' thinking is not a distinctive ideological position: it prioritizes green issues within existing modes of thinking about the world's political and economic problems. It is frequently described as environmental (or ecological) modernization.

Varieties of Green Thought

Many writers dispute the claim that there can be a distinctive green ideology arguing that many of its key propositions are taken from other traditions of political and social thought. Clearly this is an important and contentious issue, for its resolution will bear upon the viability or otherwise of separate green parties. Let us now summarize some of the positions whose adherents have added the prefix 'eco' to their belief.

- *Eco-socialism* is really only as old as the green movement, although it has to be admitted that many of its decentralist arguments were anticipated by the early socialists a hundred years ago. Eco-socialists link the damage wrought to the biosphere to the organization of economic life under capitalism. They are of the belief that the replacement of this economic system will lead to a society where the profit imperative will not lead to ceaseless encroachment on nature. They do not believe that large-scale production processes must disappear, only that they should be planned and controlled to prevent pollution and waste. Clearly there is a real question mark as to whether the international capitalist system would permit such a transformation to occur.

- *Eco-feminism* attributes the environmental problems of our time to the triumph of 'male' values – ambition, struggle for control and independence – over 'feminine' values – nurturing, caring and tending. Naturally there is some considerable doubt as to whether these values can be seen as specifically male or female. All we can say with certainty is that in the history of the modern world one set has been more widespread among men than women and vice versa. Eco-feminists argue that men must become more caring and nurturing and this should be reflected in the world of work, with unpaid, caring work being given a much higher priority by men. Women, for their part, need to take from masculinity the idea of being strong and assertive. In practical terms this might mean much more sharing of the care of children and more sharing of domestic work. In paid work eco-feminists would call for a retreat from a masculine ambience which devalues the emotional life. At the same time it is critical of those feminisms which exalt individual autonomy and self-determination for women for they are merely the female embodiment of consumerist capitalism. There is within eco-feminism a quasi-spiritual dimension exalting 'female' values but there is also a more practically based eco-feminism in the poor world which points to the importance of women's resistance in some countries to the environmental destruction wrought by industralism.

- *Green conservatism.* At first sight it might appear that greens and conservatives were at opposite ends of the political spectrum. But then remember that traditional conservatism in England emphasized the small community and the rural village, and was, on the whole, opposed to urban life. In some ways this made it akin to the programme of greens today. Dark greens might be said to have some affinities with conservatism. The system of market liberalism is a powerful force which, in moulding and expressing many people's desires for greater wealth, has released enormous energies which endanger the environment. There are many ways in which a politics of 'limits' and restraints on the use of economic and technological power would be close to traditional conservative position.

What eco-socialism, eco-feminism and green conservatism have in common is that they emphasize certain aspects of their 'parent' ideology in order to reformulate it as a response to the environmental crisis.

The Welfare State

The welfare state divides green thinkers and reveals the strands of thought which are present in green movements. Many greens are opposed to the welfare state. Not that they are against the goods which it delivers – free education, free healthcare, a national minimum income – rather that they object to the *state* delivering these services. However, for some greens this is tempered by the acknowledgement that inequalities in access to services and inequities in distribution are capable of being ameliorated by a state apparatus. Welfare states are welfare bureaucracies and as such become organizations which have the ability to control people's lives, and greens believe that this tendency has to be resisted. They believe that a decentralized welfare system would mean less need for welfare, as citizens would be providing these services for themselves and each other. There is a high degree of emphasis on the advantages and positive benefits of mutuality – organizations of like-minded citizens providing services for themselves.

The welfare state, in most green accounts, would be a local and decentralized welfare state with a high degree of citizen participation and an important role for voluntary organizations. In discussing the future of the welfare state under a green regime one must remain sensitive to the differing green positions. Welfare does not have to be provided by the state; indeed, it will be more spontaneous and appropriate if it is not provided by the state. The neighbourhood, the voluntary organization and whatever form of local administration is then organized will attend to the welfare needs of the local population. One of the key problems with this line of argument is that it plays down the role of social justice and disparities in income. Admittedly, structures of welfare can be oppressive, but they are also routine and accessible. This is an important consideration for the weak, vulnerable and isolated who rely on the local welfare state for regular support and assistance. It might also be added that there are some who will find it difficult, whatever the society, to find ready acceptance and help – they might be mentally ill or they might have a disability of some kind – and state services through their employment of professionals aim to integrate such people into the community. The role of the professional is central to the discussion of the place of welfare in a green society. Many greens are unenthusiastic about welfare state professionals, believing that they have usurped the caring and nurturing which individuals and communities ought to be doing themselves. They feel that they tend to turn their clients into passive consumers of welfare when they should be self-determining individuals.

Green Social Policies

Greens argue that the overvaluation of paid work has had destructive consequences for both society and the individual. They were among the early proponents of a basic income (BI) – or citizen's income as it has come to be called – which gives, as a right to all, a weekly income. The intention here is that this will provide some recognition of the worth of unpaid work. There are many variations but the essential thrust is that it would replace all National Insurance benefits, tax allowances and as many means-tested benefits as possible. Such an income has the attraction for greens that it can begin the process of revaluing unpaid work, for those who do unpaid caring work will receive the BI in their own right. It fits in with the green idea that there should and could be more opportunities for local employment, such as workers' cooperatives, and removes some of the disadvantage associated with the low rates of pay often attached to such work. Equally, the income would be paid to those who do voluntary work. Critics of such a scheme point out that it could bear very heavily on the taxpayers who have to fund it, especially the full blown scheme outlined here, although it is crucial of course at what rate the income is paid. The BI has also received a fair amount of criticism for possibly removing the incentive to work, although this is a problem common to all social security provision of a safety net income and is not peculiar to BI. Another telling criticism is that it would require a great deal more centralized and bureaucratic state machinery than is currently available in most accounts of a green society.

In the green society the local economy

and society is restored to its place as the centre of people's lives. Another way, therefore, in which greens believe that the volume of unpaid work can be recognized is through the spread of local employment transfer schemes (LETS). These are token economies where people trade their skills with one another and are usually computed on the basis of so many hours worked. The tokens earned, however, remain a local currency and this ensures that the local community benefits from this activity. The advantages of LETS are obvious. They enable a great deal of 'economic' activity to go on without the need for conventional employment. They enable those who are poor (that is, without cash income) to obtain goods and services outside of the cash economy.

At the national level environmental modernizers argue for a taxation regime which moves away from taxes on individual income towards taxes on pollution. These eco-taxes would need to take many forms in order to deal with the various unsustainable activities prevalent in an advanced economy. For example, a resource depletion tax would try to ensure that a certain resource was only extracted to an agreed level. Pollution taxes could be levied on goods which have deleterious consequences for the environment in order to promote the sale of benign products. In like manner benign goods can be zero rated for some taxes in order to encourage their consumption.

Sustainable Development

Following the United Nations Earth Summit in 1992, which pledged the world's leading nations to a programme of sustainable development, the UK government committed itself to sustainable action across all policy sectors. Sustainable development is defined as development that meets the needs of the present without compromising the ability of future generations to meet their own needs. With the advent of the Labour government in 1997 sustainable development has been linked to issues of

social policy. Its sustainable development strategy, *A Better Quality of Life* published in 1999, outlined sustainable development objectives across government and contained indicators upon which its progress can be judged. These indicators are a mix of social, economic and environmental: including air pollution levels, populations of wild birds, river water quality; but also unfit homes, crime levels and educational levels amongst many others. Ever since someone coined the slogan 'think global, act local' the locality has been central to green and environmental thinking. The recognition that one's local environment was important has been seen in the Local Agenda 21 projects sponsored by local authorities throughout the UK following the 1992 Rio Summit and now part of the community strategy in local government. Most people will not have heard of the word sustainability but they will be concerned about their local environment: the dog dirt on the pavement, graffiti, lack of safe play space for their children and so on. All sections of the population can relate to issues around their local government and will have views on what needs to be done. The future of Brazilian rainforests or the holes in the ozone layer are literally more remote and less easy to understand.

Evidence is accumulating that poor people tend to suffer disproportionately from the effects of pollution. To give some examples, the bulk of vehicle exhaust pollution generated by commuter motorists driving into and out of urban centres might be said to fall on those in low-income areas living adjacent to major roads. While children in social class 5 are five times more likely than children in social class 1 to be killed in road accidents. The major polluting factories tend to be sited close to low-income areas. The focus of the government on social exclusion has revealed the ways in which those on low incomes are often coping with a poor environment and inferior facilities.

The days when social policy and environmental policy were distinct and seemingly unrelated areas of public policy are now over. There is a challenging agenda ahead to ensure that social priorities and environmental policy are both given due weight as the UK responds to the environmental crisis. An inclusive social and environmental policy would produce a society where all citizens had a safe and healthy environment and this has to be the goal for a sustainable social policy.

Guide to further reading

There are a number of texts which explicitly examine the links between the environment and social policy. Meg Huby *Social Policy and the Environment* (Buckingham: Open University Press, 1998) is essential reading. Michael Cahill *The Environment and Social Policy* (London: Routledge, 2002) is an introductory text. For more extended discussion see the essays in Michael Cahill and Tony Fitzpatrick (eds) *Environmental Issues and Social Welfare* (Oxford: Blackwell, 2002) and Tony Fitzpatrick and Michael Cahill (eds) *Greening the Welfare State* (London: Palgrave Macmillan, 2002).

There are some excellent introductions to green ideologies. Andrew Dobson *Green Political Thought*, 3rd edn (London: Routledge, 2000) is a good starting point, as he covers issues of sustainability and discusses policy implications. Equally useful is John Barry *Environment and Social Theory* (London: Routledge, 1999), which examines the various ways in which the environment is explored in social theory. For a brief guide to the politics of environmentalism in the broadest sense – policy-making, ideologies, parties, pressure groups – consult Robert Garner *Environmental Politics,* 2nd edn (Basingstoke: Macmillan Press, 2000). A longer and more detailed account is to be found in J. Connelly and G. Smith *Politics and the Environment* (London: Routledge, 1999).

Postmodernism and New Directions

Tony Fitzpatrick

Postmodernism was *the* intellectual fashion of the 1980s and like all fashions it attracted zealous supporters and equally zealous critics. Yet postmodernism's legacy has somehow confounded both sides. It did not sweep away traditional schools of thought, as its supporters had anticipated, yet nor has it proved to be an empty, transitional fad, as its critics had hoped. This is because postmodernism's roots reach far into the history of ideas, reinventing some old themes within new social, political and cultural contexts. The fact that social policy did not engage with postmodern ideas until the 1990s was a belated recognition that, whatever its weaknesses, postmodernism had contributed to our understanding of those contexts.

Theories of the Postmodern

The turn towards postmodernism was largely inspired by disillusionment with traditional forms of politics and social philosophy. The 'rediscovery' of Marxism in the 1960s inspired the Left to believe that alternatives to consumer capitalism were both imaginable and achievable. By the 1970s, however, many activists and intellectuals had become disenchanted with Marxism and began to rethink the meaning of emancipation and progress.

One key author, Jean-Francois Lyotard, contended that we can no longer cling to 'meta-narratives'. A meta-narrative is a system of thought that attempts to understand the social world within a single, all-encompassing critique. Marxism is one such 'grand narrative' in that it seeks to explain all aspects of society in terms of material production and class struggle. This is like trying to understand the world from the outside. But Lyotard, like Wittgenstein before him, insisted that there is no 'outside' to which we can aspire; since we are enmeshed within language there is no space beyond language that would enable us to map the world in its entirety. Therefore, knowledge must proceed from 'the inside', from within our language-using communities: knowledge is always local and particular rather than universal. Lyotard defines postmodernism as an "incredulity towards metanarratives" and so a rejection of the view that emancipatory politics can be based upon a single system of thought (see box II.14.1).

Another author, Jean Baudrillard, goes even further. Marxism may have been appropriate in an age of production but we now live in societies of signs and codes. Indeed, so ubiquitous are these signs and codes that they no longer symbolically represent reality; instead, the philosophical distinction between reality and representation has collapsed into a 'hyper-reality'. Whereas we could once distinguish between original objects and their copies, hyper-reality implies that only copies exist and no originating source for those copies

Box II.14.1

In contemporary society and culture –
post-industrial society, postmodern
culture – the question of legitimation
of knowledge is formulated in different terms. The grand narrative has lost
its credibility…regardless of whether
it is a speculative narrative or a narrative of emancipation.

Jean-Francois Lyotard,
The Postmodern Condition
(Manchester: Manchester University
Press, 1984) p. 37.

is identifiable. Ours, then, is an age of
simulations that endlessly refer only to
other simulations. The infinite circularity of
these self-references is what Baudrillard
calls the *simulacra*: everything is a reproduction of other reproductions. Society im-
plodes in on itself and we cannot liberate
ourselves from the simulacra: ideologies of
progress are just a form of seduction to the
system of codes.

These ideas came under considerable attack from other social theorists. Habermas
alleges that postmodernism is a philosophical justification of conservatism. For if
progress is now taken to be impossible, or
at least very improbable, then this resembles a conservative defence of the capitalist
status quo. Habermas charges postmodernist theorists with depending upon
the very philosophical premises and assumptions that they claim to have dispelled.

However, there are other theorists who,
while not supporting postmodernism *per se*,
insist that its emergence and popularity reveal something very important about recent
social change. Jameson describes postmodernism as 'the cultural logic of late capitalism' in that it accurately describes the
fragmentation and heterogeneity of contemporary life. This is because of developments within capitalist production and
consumption. Our cultures are pervaded by
surfaces, hybrids, repackaging, parody,

pastiche and spectacle because this is now
the most effective way in which commodities can be circulated and exchanged. Capitalism dominates by seeming not to
dominate, by fragmenting both itself and
the objects of domination. So Jameson is
insisting that postmodernism *can* be utilized by those committed to a progressive
politics of the Left.

What, then, are the basic tenets of
postmodernism (see box II.14.2)?

Postmodernists reject the idea that certain values, judgements and propositions
apply universally across space and time.
For critics of postmodernism such as
Christopher Norris this leads inevitably to
relativism, the idea that there are *no* universal standards of morality and truth. This,
he argues, tempts postmodernists into intellectual absurdity, such as Baudrillard's
1991 claim that the Gulf War had not happened. However, as a defender of postmodernism, Richard Rorty argues that it is
the futile search for absolute truth which
creates relativism, so if we stop searching
for that which is unobtainable then we can
transcend the sterile distinction between
universalism and relativism.

This does not leave us unable to speak
about truth, it means that truth is contextual, i.e. dependent upon the environment
within which truth-claims are made. As
Mouffe observes, ideas are rooted within
particular traditions and there is no 'God's
eye view' which is external to all traditions.
Postmodernists define liberalism not as a
universal doctrine but as a tradition that

Box II.14.2

Postmodernists:

- Reject universalism
- Believe truth to be contextual
- Reject foundationalism and essen-
  tialism
- Avoid binary distinctions
- Support identity politics
- Celebrate irony and difference

must engage equally with other traditions and perspectives. The world resembles a text and so we can only speak about it from within the text itself.

Postmodernists also reject foundationalism and essentialism. Foundationalism is the notion that knowledge and belief are based upon self-evident foundations that are in no need of further proof or justification, e.g. murder is immoral. Postmodernists argue that there are no such foundations since *all* knowledge- and belief-claims require justification. Essentialism is the idea that objects have essences which, once identified, enable us to explain the object in question, e.g. human nature is essentially good. For postmodernists, though, all objects are social constructs, as are the very essences that some claim to have discovered.

Postmodernists insist that we should avoid thinking in terms of binary distinctions, hierarchies and structures, e.g. nature vs. culture. Postmodern feminists such as Judith Butler argue that this way of thinking reflects masculinist assumptions about the world, i.e. that the world is divisible into parts and that these parts relate to one another in relations of higher and lower, superior and inferior. Postmodernist architecture is not organized around a centre: there are no edges and peripheries or, rather, everywhere is an edge and a periphery! Instead, postmodernists prefer to emphasize the importance of centreless flows, fluidity, networks and webs.

Postmodernism is often taken to prefer a form of identity politics based around culture and the self. Oppression and discrimination is not just about a lack of resources but also about a lack of recognition and status, an exclusion from certain norms. Yet identity – of individuals, groups, societies – is never fixed but is in a state of indeterminate flux, being constantly renegotiated and redefined. Identity implies not only 'resemblance to' but also 'difference from'.

Finally, postmodernism embodies a playful, ironic stance: postmodernists often refuse to take anything seriously, including postmodernism! Yet rather than being self-indulgent this playfulness is meant to be a celebration of diversity, hybridity, difference and pluralism. For Rorty, philosophy is not the 'mirror of nature' but a means of devising new vocabularies and descriptions. Rather than debating which description is real our job is to assist each other in endlessly deconstructing and reconstructing our understanding of the social world. Solidarity, rather than truth, is the proper object of inquiry.

Postmodernism and Social Policy

The initial reluctance of the social policy community to engage with these ideas is understandable. Postmodernism challenges some of the fondest assumptions of those working in the field of social policy. In order to defend those assumptions it is the *weaknesses* of the postmodern critique that social policy theorists have often chosen to highlight.

For instance, if social policy is concerned with welfare then we must be able to distinguish between higher and lower forms of well-being in making interpersonal, historical, cross-national and cross-cultural comparisons. Yet it is precisely these judgements that postmodernism might disallow. By embracing relativism, contextualism, anti-foundationalism and anti-essentialism, postmodernists seem to undermine notions of truth and social progress and so undermine efforts to create greater freedom and equality. But if those notions should *not* be dismissed – as their enduring popularity might suggest – then perhaps we should reject postmodern ideas because their political and social consequences are likely to be damaging.

To take one example, social policy is arguably based upon the view that there is such a thing as human nature consisting of certain basic needs. The job of welfare systems is to enable those needs to be fulfilled. But if human nature is a humanist fiction, as postmodernists claim, and if needs are constructed through language rather than being natural, then the rationale of state welfare may be reduced. This is one of the reasons why some social policy commentators are very suspicious of postmodernism, accusing it of providing an intellectual justification of anti-welfare state politics.

Others, though, insist that postmodernism and social policy need not be so hostile. Traditionally, social policy has been concerned with class, i.e. income and occupation. Yet although our identities are undoubtedly constructed in terms of class relations there may be other forms of relations and divisions that are also important: gender, ethnicity, sexuality, religion, disability, nationality, age. Therefore, social policy must take account of these additional categories and perhaps postmodernism might assist the subject in doing so. Yet this is where disagreement kicks in, for how should we weigh class against non-class divisions? For some, class is still of central importance and postmodernism is therefore an unwelcome distraction. For others, there has to be a more equitable balancing of class and non-class relations. Nancy Fraser suggests that social justice requires both redistribution and recognition, so not only material questions of distribution but also cultural questions of status and respect for different groups.

Another form of rapprochement between postmodern themes and social policy is outlined by Zygmunt Bauman. Bauman believes that we now live in a postmodern world, one which has been individualized, fragmented and, through the flows of globalization, speeded up. Yet in their rush to celebrate this postmodernists themselves often neglect the role of deregulated, global capitalism in bringing that state of affairs about. Postmodern capitalism, says Bauman, empowers the wealthy by disempowering the poor. Collective systems of welfare – though also the victims of global capitalism – are the means by which we recognize our interdependency and reassert the importance of common

---

> **Box II.14.3**
>
> One measures the carrying capacity of a bridge by the strength of its weakest pillar. The human quality of a society ought to be measured by the quality of life of its weakest members. . . . This is, I propose, the only measure the welfare state can afford, but also the only one it needs . . . this is also the sole measure which resolutely and unambiguously speaks in the welfare state's favour.
>
> Zygmunt Bauman, *The Individualized Society* (Cambridge: Polity Press, 2001), p.79

---

values and needs (see box II.14.3).

The influence of postmodernism may also extend to the delivery of services. Social policy has been characterized by a debate between universalists and selectivists, with the former resisting the means-testing advocated by the latter. A postmodern slant on this debate suggests the provision should be universal but that, within this framework, there must be a greater sensitivity to the particular needs and demands of certain groups. This could, for example, require changes in employment policy so that all are able to flourish in the labour market and not just the traditional, full-time male worker.

So although some believe postmodernism and social policy to be irreconcilable opposites, others think that both contribute to our understanding of self and society.

Post-structuralism

Post-structuralism agrees with postmodernism that we cannot transcend the traditions in which we are embedded, but post-structuralists are perhaps less willing to compromise with traditional social science. For post-structuralists, what we call reality is no more than an effect of discourse and signification: for something to be real it has to be named, as there is no reality beyond the play of language. Truth is also discursive, i.e. there is no such thing as 'Truth', merely a series of truth-claims that have to be understood in terms of the interests of the person making them. What we call truth is just another form of power and there are no structures of reality lying beneath the social surface. The aim of post-structuralism, then, is to unmask power.

Michel Foucault focuses upon the conditions (the discourses) through which knowledge and ideas are generated. He sets out to understand discursive practices through a 'genealogical' approach which closely traces the history and operation of power within a number of institutional settings, e.g. prisons, asylums, clinics. For instance, in the nineteenth and twentieth centuries madness was medicalized, i.e. redefined as mental illnesses that require specialized treatment rather than imprisonment. Foucault analyses the extent to which medicalization is just another form of incarceration. The rest of us define ourselves as normal and reasonable through this categorization of madness as the 'other' of normality and rationality (see box II.14 4).

So Foucault identifies the 'panopticon' as the essential metaphor for all modern forms of discipline and normalization. The panopticon was a design for a prison that would use the least number of prison officers to survey as many prisoners as possible. The prisoners would not know when they were being observed and so would need to act as if they were under constant surveillance. Using these ideas we can understand welfare systems as discourses that do not necessarily create well-being and liberation. So post-structuralism does not offer easy prescriptions for welfare reform. Instead, it is a kind of 'spring-cleaning' exercise, a way of undermining our commonly held assumptions.

Many within the social policy community reject these ideas, however. If universal accounts of the good or of welfare are impossible then what reason do we have to prefer one truth-claim over another?

> ## Box II.14.4
>
> The judges of normality are present everywhere. We are in the society of the teacher-judge, the doctor-judge, the educator-judge, the 'social worker'-judge; it is on them that the universal reign of the normative is based; and each individual, wherever he may find himself, subjects to it his body, his gestures, his behaviour, his aptitudes, his achievements.
>
> Michel Foucault, *Discipline and Punish* (Harmondsworth: Penguin), p.304

What happens to the struggle for universal emancipation, progress and justice? Ironically, just as some Marxists interpret everyone as a representative of their class, so post-structuralists reduce all propositions to the interests of the speaker. As a white, Western, middle-class male, I may believe in progress and rationality, but that does not mean I hold those beliefs *because* I am a white, Western, middle-class male. Perhaps truth is not simply another face of power.

Risk Society

There are other theorists who, while believing that modernity has changed, do not imagine that the modern period is over. Ulrich Beck argues that we have reached the beginning of a *second* modernity. The first modernity was an age of industrial progress and all political and social institutions were designed to generate 'goods' (welfare, economic growth) in a world that was taken to be stable, knowable and scientifically calculable. By contrast, the second modernity is a risk society characterized by the attempt to limit, manage and negotiate a way through a series of 'bads' and hazards. For instance, nuclear and industrial pollution undermines the simple class hierarchies of the industrial order, affecting the ghettoes of the rich as well as

Box II.14.5

... risk societies are *not* exactly class societies; their risk positions cannot be understood as class positions, or their conflicts as class conflicts.

Ulrich Beck, *Risk Society* (London: Sage), p.36

those of the poor (see box II.14 5).

One implication is that whereas state welfare was once thought of as a protection against collective risks, e.g. through social insurance provision, the welfare state has now become a principal source of risk. Giddens agrees with much of Beck's thesis and insists that welfare reform must be based upon a notion of 'positive welfare' in which people are equipped with the skills needed to find their way through the new social environments of risk and insecurity.

The risk society idea has proved to be very influential but has attracted many criticisms. Some reject the sociological assumptions upon which it is based. The contrast between the first and second modernities may be too crude and the suggestion that class structures have become less important has been condemned as naïve. Also, Beck may neglect the extent to which risks have been produced politically by those opposed to welfare state capitalism.

Social Movements

Nevertheless, the idea that class is less salient now than in the past has also appeared in other schools of thought. Some have argued that society is best understood as consisting of social movements. A social movement is a process of collective action, a network of inter-related actors who share similar values, identities and objectives in a given socio-historical context.

Social movement theories emerged in the 1960s when those such as the civil rights, the feminist, the peace and the gay/lesbian movements arose to challenge specific

forms of injustice. Those theories do not necessarily replace a class analysis, e.g. the capital/labour distinction is an enduring feature of modern society, but they certainly demand that class analyses be re-thought.

In terms of social policy we can identify the 'new' social movements, listed above, partly as a product of the welfare state. With rising prosperity, increased educational opportunities and the growth of the public sector, new social movements emerged as traditional distributional conflicts begin to decline. For instance, as the middle class expands in size and influence, conflicts related to culture and lifestyle appear and lead to new conceptions of politics and social organization (see box II.14 6).

This means that new social movements may also bear implications for the welfare policies of the future. They offer new perspectives on what it means to be a citizen and a client of the welfare state. So as well as providing for basic needs and aiming at the goal of social justice, perhaps social policy should also try to fulfil other needs, ones that are less material in nature and related more to quality of life. This is the point that Fraser seems to be making (see above, page 130). Some, though, resist these ideas, arguing that society should not be thought of in terms of social movements or that the existence of the latter should not distract us from the fundamental questions of distributive justice.

Box II.14.6

By drawing on forms of action that relate to daily life and individual identity, some forms of contemporary collective action detach themselves from the traditional model of political organisation and increasingly distance themselves from political systems.

Alberto Melucci, 'The New Social Movements Revisited', in L. Maheu (ed.) *Social Movements and Social Classes* (London: Sage), p.117

Conclusions

All of the ideas reviewed above deal with three main themes: first, whether we should describe ourselves as still living in a period of modernity; second, whether class is the main organising principle of contemporary society; finally, how we should try to understand society and judge the best means of reforming it and its welfare institutions. Social policy debates in the twenty-first century are likely to revolve around these themes and these new directions.

Guide to further reading

Bertens, Hans and Natoli, Joseph, 2002. *Postmodernism* (Oxford: Blackwell). A comprehensive survey of the key figures in postmodernism, also providing an effective introduction to contemporary social theory.

Best, Steve and Kellner, Douglas, 1991. *Postmodern Theory* (New York: Guilford Publications). Although getting on in years, this book still provides one of the best introductions to the philosophy of postmodernism.

Carter, John (ed.), 1998. *Postmodernity and the Fragmentation of Welfare* (London: Routledge). A useful collection of essays reviewing the initial impact of postmodernism on social policy.

Leonard, Peter, 1997. *Postmodern Welfare* (London: Sage). A well-written and accessible book that provides an incisive overview into the relevant debates.

Rodgers, John, 2000. *From a Welfare State to a Welfare Society* (Basingstoke: Macmillan Press). A wide-ranging analysis that places postmodernism within a broader theoretical and policy-related context.

Sim, Stuart (ed.) , 2001. *The Routledge Companion to Postmodernism* (London: Routledge). A comprehensive guide with articles on philosophy, politics and culture, as well as some of the key figures of postmodernism.

The Social Policy Context

II.15
Social Policy and Economic Policy

Ian Gough

Introduction

Economic policy and the performance of the economy are obviously of tremendous importance for social policy. In recent years the two have become more and more inter-related. But there is still a difference – and social policy continues to play second fiddle. There is much debate about the dividing line between economic and social policy. For some the distinction is one of policy goals; for example, efficiency (economic policy) versus distribution (social policy). For others, it concerns policy area; for example, financial policy versus housing policy. Yet none of these dividing lines is clear. Some social policies, like housing, have implications for the efficiency of the productive economy and almost all economic policies affect the distribution of resources between different groups. Some policy areas, like employment policy, straddle the dividing line between the economic and the social and many commentators regard full employment as an integral part of the post-war welfare state.

Economic policy affects such things as:

- the overall growth of economic output and hence the resources potentially available to pursue social goals;
- the scale of unemployment in society and hence the need for income support;
- the degree of income inequality and the extent of poverty;

- rates of interest and hence the cost of buying a house or of building a hospital;
- the extent of inward and outward investment and hence job opportunities for younger people.

So it affects both the scale of social problems and the ability of social policies to meet them.

On the other hand, social policy impacts on economic policy and performance:

- direct government spending on the main welfare services lays claim to almost two-thirds of total public expenditure and about one quarter of total national output or gross domestic product (GDP) (see box II.15.1);
- taxes and national insurance contributions add to overall labour costs and thus affect firms' ability to compete;
- social benefits like income support and housing benefit can discourage people from seeking work in the formal economy, or from saving;
- on the other hand, education, training and nursery places improve productivity and the ability of the economy to compete in high value-added areas of production.

So social policy reacts back on to the economy in both negative and positive ways.

The rest of this chapter looks at:

Box II.15.1   Social spending and taxing

- Total government spending grew rapidly in the post-war period as a share of GDP, but then abruptly levelled out from the mid-1970s. Figure II.15.1 shows this total fluctuating around a *downward* trend since the early 1980s. Since total tax revenues have been more constant, the amount the government has to borrow has been cut. Figure II.15.2 shows that public *social* expenditure has remained roughly constant at around one-fifth of total national output for the last quarter of a century. Its share of public spending has therefore risen (counterbalanced by a collapse in public investment and falls in defence spending among other items). Yet government social spending in Britain claims a lower share of national income than in most other industrialized countries, including all other members of the EU except Portugal.

---

1. changes in economic policies, mainly in Britain;
2. the impact of economic changes and policies on social policy;
3. the impact of social policies on the economy.

However, it does not discuss the economics of social policy or the application of economic theory to social problems.

What Is Economic Policy?

Economics is a theory-driven discipline, so that conflicts between economic paradigms are intense, none more so than between Keynesians and monetarists (or 'neoclassicals' or 'supply-siders' or 'rational expectationists'). These disputes matter a great deal for actual policy-making, and we can speak of two eras of economic

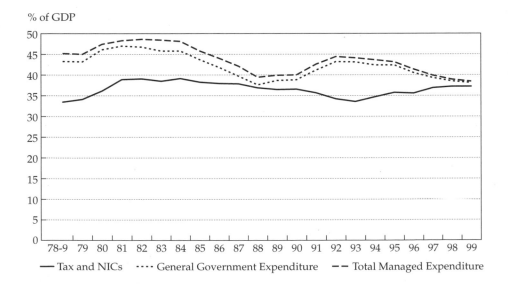

% of GDP

—— Tax and NICs   ···· General Government Expenditure   –– Total Managed Expenditure

Figure II.15.1   Tax and public spending 1978/9–1999/2000 (Hills, 2000, Figure 3)

% of GDP

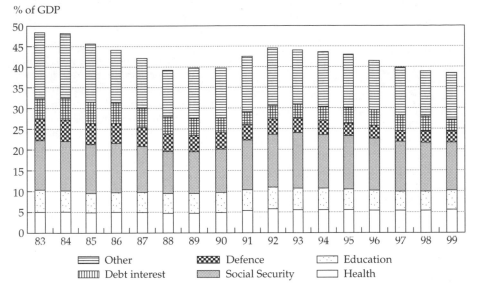

Figure II.15.2   Government spending as percent of GDP 1983/4–1998/9 (Hills, 2000, Figure 4)

policy up to the early 1990s: Keynesian from the end of the Second World War to the later 1970s, and monetarist in the 1980s. With the election to power of New Labour in 1997, and the appointment of Gordon Brown as Chancellor of the Exchequer, a new and unified system of economic management has been introduced. The jury is still out on whether this marks a radical break with the 1980s and a shift to a third distinct paradigm of macro-economic policy.

In the first period the classic *goals* of economic policy were usually described as:

- the maintenance of full employment;
- price stability (a low level of inflation);
- equilibrium in the balance of payments;
- a reasonable rate of economic growth.

These objectives are not very precise (what is 'full', 'low', 'reasonable'?) and they have been specified in various ways. Moreover, they frequently conflict and priorities must be made, but none would or could be ignored for long.

The main *instruments* of economic policy were traditionally divided into three.

- *Monetary policy.* The government (in the UK, the Chancellor of the Exchequer and the Treasury) and the central bank (the Bank of England) try to control either the supply of money and credit or its price – the rate of interest.
- *Fiscal policy.* This involves the management of taxation and public expenditure in order to manage aggregate demand in the economy.
- *Regulation and other direct controls.* A mix of instruments comprising such things as nationalization, labour and product market regulation and incomes policies.

There was some link between economic and social policy in this period, though they frequently conflicted, as when the sterling crisis of 1976 led to IMF-dictated cuts in spending programmes. In other European countries the mesh between the two has been closer, as in Sweden's active labour market policies or Germany's vocational training policies.

In the 1970s this older system of economic management began to break down. Partly this was due to a series of major changes in the global economy.

1. The rise of information technology and the service economy was transforming technologies, jobs and skills.
2. The globalization of markets and the end of fixed exchange rates ushered in greater freedom of capital movements; individual governments, like the French in 1981, found that they could not buck the global capital markets.
3. New competitors emerged, particularly the 'tiger economies' of East Asia such as Singapore, Hong Kong, Taiwan and Korea, which undercut many traditional Western industries.

In Britain these shifts coincided with the election of the Thatcher government in 1979, which brought about a sea-change in the goals and instruments of economic policy in the direction of monetarism. The major shifts in *goals* were:

- giving priority to the fight against inflation and maintaining sound public finance, while rejecting any government responsibility for tackling unemployment;
- a new concern with 'competitiveness' rather than the balance of payments and growth ('No one owes us a living. We must stand on our own two feet').

The new economic policy *instruments* were:

- *'Monetarism'*. Originally this meant the pursuit of targets for government borrowing and the money supply; after the Lawson boom and bust the goal has become a stable macroeconomic environment based on low inflation and sound public finance.
- *Cutting back the public sector.* Spending cuts, privatization and tax cuts became an instrument of economic policy in their own right. The thinking here was that these would boost the 'supply side' of the economy, encouraging flexibility in the labour market and elsewhere. The government failed to reduce the share

of state welfare in the economy, but it did prevent it rising at a time of acute unemployment and economic restructuring (see box II.15.1, page 138).

- *Deregulation.* Removing government controls over labour markets and other markets also became an explicit method to enhance economic performance. This has included weakening trades unions and wages councils, privatizing public utilities, contracting out local authority services and so on.

Some argue that the change in British economic policy in the 1980s and early 1990s was a rational response to the 'globalization' trends noted above (see chapter II.18). However, the USA and New Zealand apart, it is clear that most Western countries did not pursue such policies to anything like the extent that Britain did. It is more likely that they reflected a distinct ideological and political attack on the old system of political economy – including the old welfare state.

Since 1997 the New Labour government, under the economic leadership of Gordon Brown, the Chancellor of the Exchequer, has undertaken a radical rethink of economic policy and management.

In terms of goals, the prime importance of a low and stable rate of inflation and of sustainable public finances have been confirmed. These are seen as essential to win the trust of international financial markets in the new globalized economy. However, these goals are now seen more explicitly as means to enable rising private and public consumption. To this end, the government has committed itself to some important social policy targets, such as a 'New Deal' for the unemployed, the 1999 commitment to 'end child poverty' within 20 years, and the pledge in 2000 to raise the share of health spending to the European average. Every budget since 1997 has also entailed progressive redistribution, with significant gains at the bottom and small losses at the top. However, at the same time market inequalities have continued to widen (a result of the relative lack of change in the regulatory environment?), so the net effect on poverty is difficult to estimate.

A range of new policy instruments have been introduced. The incoming Chancellor made the Bank of England independent, creating an independent Monetary Policy Committee responsible for setting interest rates. The changes in the fiscal policy framework have been as far-reaching, and only some can be considered here.

1. A Code of Fiscal Stability and associated measures creates a tight framework around decisions on taxation and public spending. For example, the 'Golden Rule' commits the government, over the economic cycle, to a level of net borrowing no greater than net capital spending. This rule has so far been met. It is designed to ensure that later generations are not forced to pay higher taxes than now without the benefit of higher standards of public services.
2. The budgetary process explicitly focuses on outputs not inputs. New public service agreements have been set up for each main department in Whitehall and for cross-departmental programmes. These set out aims and objectives for three years ahead (a longer-term planning horizon than previously) and below them 'specific, quantified and measurable performance targets against which progress can be judged'. To some this marks a significant shift towards a more socially rational management of the public finances. To others, this obsession with targets undermines professional and managerial autonomy in the public services and extends the power of the Treasury over spending departments.
3. The government has pledged not to raise income tax rates, which entails a greater reliance on other sources of taxation. A further change has been the development of various tax credits e.g. the Working Families Tax Credit: this marks a closer integration of tax and social policies. Taxation is seen not simply as a means to finance social policies but as an integral measure to redistribute incomes and achieve other goals such as providing incentives to work.

The Impact of Economic Policy on the Social Policy Environment

These shifts in economic policy have had a profound impact on the environment of social policy. In the 1980s the use of taxes to achieve a more equitable distribution of income was replaced with the pursuit of tax cuts to improve competitiveness. The government, because it rejected Keynes's theories, simply washed its hands of any responsibility to pursue the goal of full employment – unemployment became a 'price worth paying' to get inflation down and to boost British industry. Economic policy became more detached from social policy and in some cases diametrically opposed to it. In the later 1990s, however, the New Labour government began to refashion the link between the two.

To illustrate this let us trace through the ways that developments in just one part of the economic environment – the labour market – have impinged on social policy in the past two decades (Gregg et al, 2001). In the 1980s and early 1990s, these changes included:

*   The rise of mass unemployment, from 1 million unemployed in 1975 to over 3 million.
*   Within this total long-term unemployment soared: from 0.1 million in 1975 to over 1 million in 1993.
*   Increasing part-time work: by 1991, 23 per cent of all employees worked part-time (44 per cent in the case of women).
*   The decline of the traditional one-worker family, and the rise of two-worker and no-worker families. By 1993, 19 per cent per cent of households (among the population of working age) had no workers. Jobs and unemploy-

ment clustered in families, leading to a growing inequality between 'work-rich' and 'work-poor' households.

- At the same time earnings have become more unequal and low pay more prevalent.
- Lastly, more people worked in insecure employment on temporary or casual contracts, or were self-employed.

Taken together, these changes transformed the environment of social policy. The modern social security system was fashioned in the years following the Second World War, when unemployment was low and stable and when the majority of working-age families had one male breadwinner in a full-time job. Social policy in the 1980s responded only fitfully to these transformations in working life – the real agenda was a different one as we have seen. As a result, poverty and social exclusion escalated, heaping more burdens on a stretched and retrenched welfare state.

Since the mid-1990s, and especially since the 1997 election, the Labour government has steered a different course in response to different economic trends (partly resulting from its changes in economic policy). Emerging labour market trends include the following:

- a rapid fall in unemployment to 1.3m in 2000, a rate of 5.0 per cent;
- a rise in the numbers in employment, but not back to 1970s levels. Large numbers of men and women without a job say they would like one but still don't search for one (and therefore don't appear in the unemployment figures);
- a sharp fall in the numbers of long-term unemployed – down to one third of the 1993 level;
- a fall in the number of jobless households, to 16.7 per cent by 2000, especially those with children;
- a similar rise in pay across the spectrum (apart from the rich) that is stabilizing pay disparities, albeit at the high levels of inequality bequeathed by the earlier regime.

This is a more benign economic environment for social policy, though we should not forget that rates of poverty in general and child poverty in particular, in the UK, remain among the highest in the EU. The government has partly contributed to this by refashioning the link between economic and social policy to 'make work pay'. The New Deals for Youth have made a modest contribution to reducing youth unemployment; the minimum wage provides a floor to low wages and the Working Families Tax Credit has contributed to falling child poverty.

The jury is still out on whether this new economic-social policy mix is sustainable and robust in a globalizing world economy. Some have argued that the labour market changes are so far-reaching that a quite different principle must inform future social security: an unconditional 'basic income' or 'citizen's income' paid to all. But all agree that changes in the labour market have transformed the environment of social policy-making.

The Impact of Social Policy on the Economy

What of the reverse relationship – the impact of social policy on economic performance? There has been no shortage of disagreement here ever since the Thatcher government claimed that the traditional welfare state was one of the central causes of Britain's economic problems. The Blair government, in addition to the above changes, accepts that public investment in education and some services is a precondition for economic success in the modern world, yet attacks the European 'social model' and urges the EU to deregulate more.

Let me conclude by disentangling some of the issues here, beginning with the anti-welfare state view.

- *Disincentives.* The OECD has stated: 'unemployment insurance and related benefit systems . . . have drifted towards quasi-permanent income support in many countries, lowering work incentives' (*The Jobs Study*, 1994). According to economic theory, high benefit levels will reduce the cost of being without a job and thus prolong periods of unemployment. Minimum wages for particular trades will drive up the wage that people will regard as acceptable and price them out of work. This would suggest that countries with high benefit replacement rates will have higher rates of unemployment, but different studies come to different conclusions. If the alternative is to replace insurance benefits with means-tested ones, a different disincentive effect appears. Nevertheless, concern over the economic impact of Europe's 'passive' unemployment benefits is fostering a shift to workfare or 'activation' measures across the continent.

- *Ageing, state pensions and saving.* Most state pension programmes, like Britain's basic pension and SERPS (the State Earnings-Related Pension Scheme), are pay-as-you-go; that is, contributions paid in today finance today's pensions. The World Bank and others argue that this reduces the savings rate, since people have less incentive to save for their old age, and this in turn weakens investment and thus growth rates. It is better, therefore, to switch to privately funded schemes and confine the state's role to providing a basic pension, possibly means-tested. Others argue that reality does not bear out the theory. Higher savings do not necessarily translate into higher investment (nor higher investment into higher growth). Private pension funds may pursue short-term profit-maximizing strategies which weaken firms' investment. And a means-tested pensions guarantee will weaken savings still more: why save for your old age if those who do not will receive a pension anyway?

- *Taxation and disincentives to work and invest.* In box II.15.1 (page 138) we have noted the large claims made by the welfare state on GDP. All this spending has to be paid for and a principal argument is that the resulting tax levels discourage both work and capital investment. The view that high marginal rates of income tax discourage people from working longer or harder lay behind the continuing commitment of British Chancellors not to raise income tax. If this is the case, high tax countries should experience lower rates of growth and competitiveness than lower tax ones (like Britain), but the studies undertaken to test this have failed to find a consistent relationship between the two. More important perhaps is the effect of high non-wage labour costs on firms' investment decisions. German firms, it is argued, are forced by these costs to locate new factories over the border in Poland or the Czech Republic, or, if they want to stay in the EU, in Ireland or Britain.

Turning now to pro-welfare state arguments:

- *Social protection and economic flexibility.* Parts of the social security system can enhance flexibility in the labour market and overall economic performance. Unemployment assistance enables people to take longer looking for a new job, which in turn may lead to more effective matching of available skills and jobs. Protection in sickness and maternity assists workers in maintaining links with the workforce. Employment protection may promote commitment to work and raise the productivity of employees. Inadequate social benefits may mean that the unemployed run down their savings and therefore become more dependent and costly to the welfare system when they retire. In these and other ways a well funded income maintenance system can pay for itself in the form of greater productivity.

- *Investing in people.* Much attention has been paid recently to the effects on productivity of an educated workforce.

Education and training can teach skills and foster flexible attitudes which encourage individual and collective productivity. Most studies show that public investment in post-school education yields not only a private return in the form of higher earnings but also a social pay-off in the form of faster growth. Britain performs poorly in educating the lower half of the ability range both during and after school, and for some economists this has trapped the country in a 'low skills equilibrium'. Investing in nurseries can also help the economy by enabling women (or men) childminders to return to work. All this remains a big challenge for Britain's government.

- *Inequality, crime and the economy.* Countries with weak welfare states, such as the USA, exhibit high rates of poverty and crime, and the two features appear to be linked. A rational individual living in a no-hope ghetto may well decide that the benefit-cost ratio of illegal activities exceeds that of legal alternatives. It has been suggested, though there is no hard evidence, that high crime discourages investment. Insurance costs more or is unobtainable, firms must employ large numbers of security personnel and higher grade employees move from the area. In some states of

the USA, higher prison and law enforcement costs are directly eating into education budgets. The rapid rise in the British prison population is also expensive to the Treasury. At some stage the 'carceral state' will conflict with the 'welfare state'.

In conclusion, we find arguments for and against the view that social policy harms economic policy. Some policies are clearly harmful, like means-tested benefits with high withdrawal rates or final salary, high-replacement, pay-as-you-go pension systems. Others, like education, training and some welfare to work and income security measures, are clearly helpful. Cross-national studies have found no consistent relationship between high levels of state welfare spending and poor economic performance. Yet there is evidence that countries with less inequality enjoy higher rates of growth.

The task in the years ahead is to design social policies which, while meeting individual needs and pursuing other welfare goals (discussed in earlier chapters in this section), do not harm our ability to compete in an increasingly global capitalist economy. Better still is to develop those welfare policies which, through investing in people and communities, positively help their economies to develop in a sustainable way.

Guide to further reading

Balls, E. and G. O'Donnell (eds), 2002. *Reforming Britain's Economic and Social Policy* (Basingstoke: Palgrave). An up-to-date insider account by the Treasury team of New Labour's macroeconomic policy framework.

Glennerster, H., 1992. *Paying for Welfare: The 1990s* (Hemel Hempstead: Harvester Wheatsheaf). Comprehensive introduction to the financing and planning of social services in modern Britain.

Gough, I., 2000. 'Social welfare and competitiveness', in Ian Gough, *Global Capital, Human Needs and Social Policies* (Basingstoke: Palgrave).

Gregg, P. and J. Wadsworth (eds), 2001. *The State of Working Britain*, 2nd edn (Manchester: Manchester University Press). An essential handbook on all aspects of the British labour market and the main events and policies shaping it.

Hills, J., 1993. *The Future of Welfare: a Guide to the Debate* (York: Joseph Rowntree Foundation). Concise and well illustrated guide incorporating material on economic aspects.

Hills, J., 2000. *Taxation for the Enabling State* (LSE: Centre for Analysis of Social Exclusion: CASE paper 41). Up-to-date discussion of taxation, spending, fiscal policies and redistributive outcomes.

Hutton, W., 1995. *The State We're In* (London: Jonathan Cape). Wide-ranging and provocative argument linking the British economic system to the decline in our social fabric.

Two journals provide excellent yet readable coverage of economic issues useful to social policy students: the *Economist* (weekly) and *New Economy* (published four times a year by the Institute for Public Policy Research).

II.16
Social Policy: Culture and Nationhood

Fiona Williams

Introduction

An examination of the relationship between social policy and notions of nationhood and nationality involves a critical understanding of the development of welfare in relation to the nation state. In the case of British social policy it requires us to unpack the ideological and material dimensions of 'Britishness' in welfare policy and practice, and how these have changed over time as the meanings and conditions attached to British nationality and culture have themselves changed. In terms of welfare states in general, a range of processes contribute to this relationship (Williams, 1995, pp. 146–7):

- the formation and changing organization and conditions of the nation state, systems of indentured labour, systems of migration, colonialism and imperialism;
- the social relations of power engendered by these processes;
- the legacy of ethnic/cultural/religious conflict and relations of domination and subordination (e.g. anti-Semitism);
- the articulation of nation with 'race', ethnicity and culture;
- processes of inclusion and exclusion from the nation state (e.g. citizenship rules of eligibility);
- discourses around nation, 'race', ethnicity, culture and religion (e.g. scientific racism, eugenics, cultural assimilation, anti-racism);

- discursive practices (e.g. state, institutional, personal racism);
- forms of mobilization and resistance (e.g. around racism and nationalism)

This chapter develops the discussion from two key aspects of these processes. The first is the role of social policy in the process of *nation-building* and the development of *national unity*. The second is the relationship between the development of the nation state and the social rights associated with *citizenship*, in particular the processes of inclusion in and exclusion from citizenship. This also involves a reference to the *cultural norms* underpinning welfare practice. It should be noted that processes of inclusion and exclusion from citizenship, nation-building, and cultural normativity, also affect 'others', such as lone mothers, gays and lesbians and disabled people (the Eugenics movement, discussed below, is a case in point). The final section looks briefly at some of the current challenges to traditional notions of culture and nationhood within welfare, including the acknowledgement of *cultural diversity*, the development of *supranational social policy* and the increases in *migration*. First, we look at the significance of the nation in a historical analysis of the development of welfare states.

The Historical Context

The period from the 1870s to the 1920s was when most Western industrialized welfare states were established. It is commonly accepted that the context in which the first forms of state collectivism took place was the development of industrial capitalism, combined with a sharpening of class-capital relations; that is, an increasingly organized and enfranchized labour movement. It was also a period that saw the removal of women, children and older people from the paid labour force, the ideological and material drawing of boundaries between the public sphere of paid work and political life and the private sphere of domestic life, along with the mobilization of women's organizations to challenge these processes and to protect their interests within them (see chapter II.11). However, in order to acknowledge the significance of *nation* we need to add a third important process that was taking place at this time as part of the development of the modern nation state: that is, the greater emphasis being placed upon national unity and national identity by the setting of a geographic boundary around an imagined homogeneous cultural, ethnic, racial and linguistic community. This was a period of an increasing '*nation*alization' of society, when the boundaries of nationhood were being given greater economic, social, legal, political and ideological meaning. In other words, the introduction of social rights through social policy reforms took place within a context in which the boundaries of citizenship were becoming more circumscribed (for example, by nationality) and its constituency more complexly differentiated (by class, gender, disability, age and sexuality). The consolidation of national unity and the national ideal was achieved partly through state social reforms around the first forms of collectivism: education, public health, social insurance and, later, maternity provisions. At the same time, the rights and benefits attached to these provisions marked the different degrees of exclusion from, and inclusion in, the 'nation-welfare state' – a process that has itself been challenged over the century.

Some social policy writers have identified this relationship between nation and welfare as equally central to an analysis of social policy development as that between the state, the market and the family. Williams (1995, and see also Lewis, 1998) argues that over the twentieth century, in different industrialized countries, a variety of welfare settlements emerged from the state's attempt to consolidate changes in the social relations of power caught up in three interconnected spheres.

- *Work*: the organization and conditions of production.
- *Family*: the organization and conditions of social reproduction.
- *Nation*: the organization and conditions of the nation state.

Citizenship and nationality

One of the ways in which exclusion from the social rights associated with citizenship operated was through the tying of eligibility to those rights to the condition of nationality. So, for example, anyone who had not been both a resident and a British subject for twenty years was not eligible for a pension under the 1908 Pensions Act, and non-British residents who had been living in Britain for less than five years received a lower rate of benefit under the health insurance policies of the 1911 National Insurance Act, even though they paid full contributions. Just as significant was the fact that the context in which these Acts were passed was one which fed easily into the racialization of nationality; that is, that an assumed ethnic or racial difference marked out an individual as alien or non-British. The 1905 Aliens Act marked the introduction of the first immigration controls and, with it, the institutionalization of the 'no recourse to public funds' rule – that any person entering the country who could not support herself or himself without recourse to public funds or welfare provision, or who was homeless within the first twelve months, should be deported – a rule which still exists today and has been tightened up for refugees (see chapter II.12).

Campaigns at this time were aimed at Jewish refugees and were supported by all political parties and most labour organizations. They gave rise to and legitimated virulent anti-Semitism and imperialist chauvinism. Moral panic about foreigners provided a stepping-stone to link the politics of welfare and nationality to the practices of racism. It became common for people who were assumed to be 'aliens' (that is, who were not white, English-speaking and Christian) to be threatened with deportation if they applied, legitimately, for public funds, or for welfare agencies to be used to police illegal immigrants, or for racialized groups to be treated as scroungers irrespective of their social rights. For example, during a time of growing unemployment in 1919 the Ministry of Labour sent secret instructions to labour exchange managers that black seamen who were eligible for the 'out-of-work-donation' – a relatively generous, non-contributory, non-means-tested benefit – should not be informed of their rights (Fryer, 1984). In these ways the formalized condition of nationality was translated into the racialized conditions of eligibility and into a fear of 'aliens' as the bearers of inferior cultures and as welfare 'scroungers'. The use of welfare agencies as internal immigration controls and the perception of racialized groups as scroungers were carried in different ways into the post-war welfare state (see Williams, 1989).

The subsequent history of Commonwealth migration to Britain from the 1950s is an ironic twist in the relationship between citizenship, race, nationality and welfare. In the debates in the late 1940s on the shortage of labour, the recruitment of labour from the Commonwealth (especially the Caribbean and later the Indian subcontinent) was perceived by the government as administratively more straightforward compared with recruitment from Southern Europe precisely because, by virtue of Britain's imperial model of citizenship, these colonized workers were British citizens. However, as British citizens they had access to more than work and residence rights: they had, formally at least, rights to welfare benefits and services. In effect, many of these were denied through the processes of direct or indirect racism. For example, new migrant workers were unable to fulfil residency qualifications for low-cost public housing and were forced into the private sector and into further forms of discrimination. At the same time, the very universalism of the welfare state depended upon a restricted notion of the norms of eligibility and need. At its heart was the image of the white male-breadwinner family. Where black migrant workers and their families deviated from this norm, then cultural and material differences were cast in pathological terms. An example of this dynamic was the recruitment of Afro-Caribbean women to work in low-paid jobs with unsocial hours (often in the newly developing welfare services). This meant that children were left behind with relatives until it was possible to bring them over, or if they did migrate, they stepped into a situation where there was little formal provision for the children of working mothers. Either way, their actions challenged the dominant familial ideology of the day, which emphasized the role of women in the home as wives and mothers and warned against the disastrous consequences of mother-child separation. Because of the entrance conditions imposed upon them as migrant workers Afro-Caribbean women were seen to be failing as mothers, especially by welfare professionals. Evidence that emerged by the 1980s showed that disproportionately higher numbers of black children had been taken into care.

It should be noted that the formation of the relationship between the nation state, citizenship and the rights of minority groups took place in different ways with different policy effects in different countries. For example, the German concept of nationhood is based on a restrictive notion of common ethnic descent (*Volk*), whereas in France the concept is more extensive, but assimilationist, based on the acceptance of a common French culture (Brubaker, 1990).

Nation-building, National Unity and Welfare

Richard Titmuss identified war as a spur to social policy reform. Not only, in his view, did war lead to post-war reconstruction ('homes for heroes' was the slogan for public housing development after the First World War) and to improvements in the quality and quantity of the population (the poor state of recruits for the Boer War led to nutritional and health reforms for children), but he also saw the experience of wartime in Britain in the 1940s as providing a national identity and solidarity which overruled existing social divisions and produced 'an enlargement of obligations – an extension of social discipline – to attend to the primary needs of all citizens' (Titmuss, 1963). In other words, the egalitarian and solidaristic impulse of wartime was an important generator of a welfare society.

While acknowledging these positive outcomes, it is important to examine a little more critically these meanings of national responsibility and identity and the material and discursive influences upon Britain's role in its foreign and domestic politics. War, in effect, represents only one end of the continuum of an intensified opportunity for a nationalism which operates on different terrain in peacetime. War was not so directly influential, in the 1930s, in the generation of Sweden's welfare state, yet a particular national identity was central to the People's Home in Sweden, as it was called. In Britain there have been a number of shifts in this relationship between nation-building, national unity and welfare over the twentieth century.

The first was in the role of *social imperialism* in the welfare reforms at the beginning of the century. From the 1880s the certainties of the old *laissez-faire* regime were rocked by a number of developments, including the increase in competition challenging Britain's industrial supremacy abroad, the militant 'new unionism' of workers, the successive slumps and booms of the economy and the international growth of socialist and feminist movements. State collective reform was one way of stabilizing these threats. In the British imperialist context this collectivism was heavily tied to social imperialism. Social imperialism aimed to subordinate class interests to those of nation and empire by suggesting a necessary interdependence between the power and profits of imperialism, national supremacy and welfare reforms, and this was supported by all the main political parties. Thus many trade unionists pressing for welfare reforms did so in the belief that such reforms were the fruits of imperial policy and were necessary to create the national efficiency upon which imperial power depended.

Social imperialist aims were influenced by the scientific and social discourses of Darwinism and the eugenics movement. Darwinism posited the theory of the survival of the fittest, which, when transposed to imperialist social relations, could justify the conquest and domination of the 'uncivilized races' by those at the top of the evolutionary tree – the Anglo-Saxon 'civilized race'. Eugenics was the belief in heredity as the cause of social problems, including physical and mental disabilities, 'feeble-mindedness', pauperism, prostitution and alcoholism, which could be eradicated by policies aimed at encouraging the 'fit' to breed and discouraging the 'unfit'. These two theories tied an imperialism abroad to a social imperialism at home. For the working class and others fighting for social reforms there was thus some apparent material and ideological basis for a belief in imperialism and racial supremacy and the jealous guarding of social rights being restricted to British workers.

Two examples of social policies illustrate the complex ways in which improvements for the working class were cast in ways which superimposed the national interest over class or gender interests. They also show an elision between the notions of 'the British' (or, more specifically, 'the English'), the 'nation', and the white 'race'. One example is policies geared to the regulation and supervision of motherhood which were introduced in the first two decades of the century, e.g. school meals for the needy (1906) and the Maternity and Child Welfare Act (1918). The latter established clinics and health visitors and was accompanied by the emergence of voluntary organizations working to promote and supervise child welfare and domestic hygiene. While these services met women's needs, they also served to consolidate women's place in the home and to tie women's role in the family to the development of 'race' and nation (see Davin, 1978; Williams, 1989). These policies were aimed at increasing the quality of the 'race' to maintain national efficiency and to prevent 'racial decay', and the quantity to sustain imperial defences. A propaganda film made in 1917 to mark National Baby Week started with the slogan 'the Race marches forward on the feet of the children'. Women, as bearers of children and reproducers of culture, formed a real and symbolic link between the racialized ideals of nationhood and nation-building by unifying the nation, populating it and servicing it.

Other policies, however, aimed to deter certain groups from breeding. The 1913 Mental Deficiency Act followed eugenic thinking by implementing the grading and segregating of 'mental defectives' – a category broad enough to encompass unmarried mothers, epileptics, people with mental health problems, petty criminals and people with physical, speech and hearing impairments. These groups were institutionalized in what were called 'colonies', away from both the outside world and the opposite sex.

These ideas about the role of welfare in sustaining Britain's imperial role and racial supremacy shifted after the Second World War. On the one hand, the 1942 Beveridge Report captured once again the white woman's duty: 'housewives as wives and mothers have vital work to do in ensuring the adequate continuance of the British race and British ideals in the world'. On the other hand, the main doctrines of the empire began to fall away. Of power, profits and civilization only civilization remained. The welfare state in Britain became central to the reconstruction of post-war Britain and represented Britain's civilizing mission brought home. This was a civilization of a new order – of social justice and egalitarianism – an order that could replace the old imperial ideal in sustaining cohesion. If national unity and egalitarianism provided the bricks and mortar of the new welfare state, it was migrant workers from the former colonies who also helped to build and service it. Even more ironically, as we have seen, it was these workers and their families who over the post-war period found themselves excluded from these same institutions and began, in response, to challenge the boundaries of citizenship and the cultural norms of policies which had been moulded in earlier decades.

Contemporary Shifts in Nation and Welfare

Up until the Second World War, national unity and British cultural supremacy tied the development of social policy to imperialism abroad. By the Second World War the welfare state became central to post-war national reconstruction. British culture and national unity were used to justify state intervention. By the 1980s the notions of national unity (as well as the traditional family) were used to justify *less* state intervention, but with more central state control. Emphasis was placed upon the family as the transmitter of 'decent' British values and responsible for the morality and discipline of its members. The 1988 Education Act sought to reduce the impact of anti-discriminatory practice in favour of traditional morality and British cultural values. The Act also provided for parents to choose education for their children appropriate to their children's culture. While this could be seen as a shift towards the acknowledgement of cultural diversity, it also represented a form of cultural essentialism where cultures are seen as fixed and unchanging in both form and attachment. In addition, nationality and immigration laws were further tightened. The attempts by the New Right to reassert and protect the supremacy of British culture were, primarily, a form of defensive resistance to challenges to the viability of a sovereign, culturally homogeneous nation state. These challenges included, from within Britain, the reality of a multi-ethnic population, greater visibility in the diversity in family forms and sexual partnerships, and pressure for devolution. Outside Britain, the breaking up and shifting of national boundaries, the growing significance of supranational political bodies, such as the European Union, the rise in transnational identities and movements, increases in migration and asylum-seeking across the globe, and economic and cultural globalization worked to undermine national identity and sovereignty.

Where the New Right sought to resist many of these changes, New Labour from 1997 attempted to accommodate and manage them, albeit in contradictory ways. New Labour emphasized the need to tolerate cultural diversity within civil society, yet it also strove to present an image of a 'one nation' Britain based upon 'strong families' and 'strong communities' and bound by a common set of moral values attached to the rights and responsibilities of citizenship. In this, nation and citizenship are tied together through the responsibility of men and women to be in paid work, for paid work is seen as the defence against social exclusion, the passport to tax credits and benefits, as well as the basis for Britain's prosperity in the global economy.

The report of the Macpherson inquiry in 1999, set up by New Labour, challenged this consensual image by revealing the extent of institutional racism in the police force. It recommended anti-racist strategies and monitoring, not only within the police force, but also in all public institutions (Race Relations Amendment Act 2001). At the same time, however, New Labour's practice in relation to asylum-seekers contradicted this anti-discriminatory commitment. The 1999 Immigration and Asylum Act eroded the rights of asylum-seekers by withdrawing their eligibility to social security assistance and a work permit. A new 'racialized subject' was re-born: claims of 'bogus asylum-seekers' from both media and government gave substance to the idea of Britain as part of an emerging 'Fortress Europe', rather than the possibility for some sort of 'post-national citizenship'.

A dynamic yet cautionary vision of 'Britishness' was provided by the Parekh Report on *The Future of Multi-Ethnic Britain* (Parekh, 2000). It talked of a 'community of communities', of finding ways of nurturing, not simply tolerating, diversity 'whilst fostering a common sense of belonging'. The report was vilified by the media for what was seen as an attack on Britishness, and few of its recommendations saw the light of day. Yet, within months, these overlapping issues of belonging, identity and racism were vividly demonstrated in disturbances in Northern towns following provocation by the National Front. The riots drew attention to the experiences of young Asian people of racial harassment, segregation, and lack of employment and training opportunities. While recognizing this, the Home Secretary, David Blunkett, called for minority ethnic groups to take greater responsibility to become integrated into 'British norms' and assume a 'British identity', proposing also a requirement on migrants to pass an English-speaking test of citizenship. This exemplifies New Labour's contradictory approach: to recognize the dynamics of racism but to disconnect them from the discourses of nation, and to reiterate instead a fixed idea of 'Britishness'. How far it will be able to ride these two horses remains to be seen.

Guide to further reading

To pursue this subject you need to go beyond the discipline of social policy to work on nation states, nationality and 'race'. However, two works which do look at the historical significance of nation both in itself and in relation to family and work in the development of the modern welfare state are F. Williams *Social Policy: A Critical Introduction. Issues of Race, Gender and Class* (Cambridge: Polity Press, 1989); and F. Williams 'Race/ethnicity, gender and class in welfare states: A framework for comparative analysis', *International Studies in Gender, State and Society*, 2, 2 (1995), 127–59. An interesting set of case-studies on the relationship between nation and welfare are to be found in G. Lewis (ed.) *Forming Nation, Framing Welfare* (London: Routledge, 1998). There is also the classic essay on the relationship between war and welfare in R. Titmuss *Essays on 'the Welfare State'* (London: Unwin University Books, 1963).

Detailed historical work can be found in A. Davin 'Imperialism and motherhood', *History Workshop Journal*, 5 (1978), 9–65; P. Fryer *Staying Power: The History of Black People in Britain* (London: Pluto Press, 1984); and W. R. Brubaker 'Immigration, citizenship and the nation state in France and Germany: A comparative historical analysis', *International Sociology*, 5, 4 (1990), 379–407. The three titles are self-explanatory; these works cover the historical background to the issues raised in the chapter. Finally, for contemporary issues on Britishness, see B. Parekh *The Report of the Commission on the Future of Multi-ethnic Britain* (London: Runnymede Trust, 2000), and for a collection of articles on asylum-seeking and refugees, see the *Critical Social Policy Special Issue*, 22, 3 (2002).

II.17
Social Policy and Family Policy

Jane Millar

Families are very much at the centre of contemporary political and policy debate in Britain. Both major political parties claim to have policies that support families, media attention on issues such as working mothers, divorce and teenage motherhood is intense and academic interest in the relationship between family and state has made this a growing area of research and publication. Yet, at the same time, it is also possible to argue that Britain has no family policy at all – if 'family policy' is taken to mean a defined set of goals, pursued by a coherent set of policies, and implemented through an institutional framework of a designated government department. We have no 'Department of the Family'; policies are sometimes contradictory and certainly uncoordinated; there is little agreement over what goals we should be seeking to achieve. On the other hand, however, almost every action that government takes or does not take – whether it be in the fields of social security, taxation, health, education, housing, employment or whatever – has an impact on families and on family life. Family policy, it seems, is nothing and everything at the same time.

This chapter covers three areas. In the first section I consider the family as *context* for social policy. Family change, it is often argued, has upset the assumptions on which the welfare state was built and created new needs that require different policy responses. This section summarizes some of the recent key trends in family formation and structure. The second section considers the question of how far family change can be seen as a *consequence* of social policy and examines the different views as to what should or could be done about this. The third section examines the different ways in which *family policy*, as a specific area of government activity, has been defined and discusses how the approach in Britain compares with that of other countries.

The Family as a Context for Policy

Much social policy is concerned with families and family life, and in the making of policy certain assumptions must be made about families and family roles. It has often been argued, for example, that the provisions of the post-war British welfare state rested on a very clear model of family life, in which men were full-time workers and women were full-time carers. Men were responsible for supporting their families and they therefore acted as the main point of contact between the family and state financial support. They received tax allowance for their wives and children and most social security benefits were paid to the man, on behalf of the family as a whole. Women were responsible for family care and therefore acted as the main point of contact between the family and state services such as health care, education and social care services.

These services provided a back-up to wom-en's caring work, just as benefits provided a back-up to men's earnings. Families were assumed to be stable and long lasting, and the family roles of men and women were seen as being quite distinct.

It is debatable how far real families ever conformed to this idealized model, even in the 1950s, a decade in which family struc-tures were unusually stable and homoge-neous. Families today, however, are much more volatile and heterogeneous. Although the 1960s are often characterized as the 'per-missive decade', it was really in the 1970s that patterns of family life in Britain began to change very rapidly. The 1969 Divorce Reform Act, implemented in 1971, made divorce possible for a much wider range of people. Cohabitation also began to rise, as did rates of extra-marital births. Married women started to move into the labour market in significant numbers, usually into part-time jobs. Table II.17.1 summarizes some key features of family formation and structure in the early 1990s and at the start of the 1970s. As can be seen, there have been some very significant changes over this period. More children are born outside marriage, more couples live together before they marry, first marriage is later, women have fewer children, abortion is more com-mon and there is a higher risk of divorce. As a consequence there are more lone-par-ent families, more people live alone and the average household size is smaller. Moth-ers are now more likely to be employed than not, although much still depends on the age of their children.

Thus, at the turn of the century, British families take a variety of diverse and chang-ing forms. People live alone, have children alone, live with partners, marry, divorce, remarry, have more children – and then they may do it all again. Family patterns also vary by social class, by region, by eth-nic group, by income level and so on. Thus to talk about 'the family' is to fail to reflect the range of 'families' that people actually live in. Such diversity, however, poses par-ticular problems for social policy: provid-ing the appropriate support for one type of family may disadvantage another. Or, of more concern to some people, providing support for some types of family may en-courage people to behave in particular, and not necessarily welcome, ways.

Table II.17.1   Family formation and family structure in Britain over 30 years

	Early 1970s	Late 1990s
Percentage children born outside marriage	8	38
Percentage single women cohabiting	8 (1979)	25
Median age at first marriage for women/men	21/24	27/29
Number of abortions	111,000	178,000
Abortion rate per 1000 women aged 16–19	2.5 (1968)	26.5
Fertility rate (live births per 1000 women)	84	59
Number of divorces	79,000	158,000
Divorce rate per 1000 married population	5.9	13.0
Percentage families headed by lone parents	8	24
Percentage one-person households	18	29
Average household size	3.1	2.4
Percentage mothers employed	49	69

Sources: *Social Trends 30, the 2000 edition* (London: Stationery Office, 2000), *Population Trends no 105* (London: Stationery Office, autumn 2001).

What Is to Be Done About the Family?

Reactions to family change vary enormously, but can be summarized under three broad headings.

1. the *'family reactionaries'*, who think the family is disintegrating and who would like to see policy directed towards restoring 'traditional' family patterns;
2. the *'family pragmatists'*, who feel that these changes are part of wider trends that cannot be reversed, and therefore policy must adapt and support new family forms;
3. the *'family libertarians'*, who positively welcome these changes as a sign of increasing freedom and autonomy for people to live in ways that they choose.

The right-leaning think-tank, the Institute of Economic Affairs, has been assiduous in putting forward a 'family reactionary' position. Patricia Morgan's (1995) monograph *Farewell to the Family* brings together all the various threads that make up this argument. She argues that 'since the 1970s, a climate of hostility to the family has provided the general context in which its legal and economic foundations have been easily undermined' (p. 1). Two factors in particular are singled out as the causes of family decline: state welfare policies that have created disincentives to marriage and incentives to lone parenthood; and feminist influences that have marginalized men in the family and encouraged women to seek gratification through paid employment rather than through family life. For Morgan the consequences are already visible and worrying but, she predicts, these will get much worse. Without the traditional family to socialize children, and in particular to provide role models and discipline for young men, delinquency and crime will escalate and society as a whole will be at risk. To avoid this, social policy should seek positively to support marriage and promote traditional gender roles for men and women.

The pragmatic family view can be found in a variety of accounts, but is well represented through the publications of the left-leaning think-tank, the Institute for Public Policy Research. Its 1990 publication *The Family Way*, by Anna Coote, Harriet Harman and Patricia Hewitt, sets this out clearly: 'Long term cross-national trends in the patterns of family life cannot be halted, let alone reversed, by any efforts of government . . . the aim should be to ensure that policies are adapted to suit changing practice' (p. 33). The types of policies they propose centre on the goal that men and women should have equal opportunities to be both parents and workers, to be both breadwinners and carers. Ways to reconcile work and family life – schemes of parental leave, state childcare provisions or subsidies, equal access to benefits for part-time workers and so on – are at the heart of this. This is also the sort of policy agenda being taken on board in the European Union, where the relationship between employment and family is attracting increasing attention.

The pragmatic approach does welcome family change to some extent, particularly in respect of greater equality between men and women. However, the 'libertarian family' view, in which family change is viewed as positive rather than negative, is most particularly associated with feminism. Many feminist writers have pointed to the 'family' as a site of gender inequality and have analysed the way in which the definition of family as 'private' has obscured, and even legitimated, these inequalities. Changes in the family which have reduced the dependency of women on men have therefore been valued as increasing autonomy and choice for women. However, in this highly politicized debate, 'feminism' is often depicted as 'anti-family' and vice versa: those who are seen as 'anti-family' are labelled 'feminist'. This takes little account of the more complex debates within feminism about the relationship between family and state.

Positive views of family change have

been increasingly crowded out of political and policy debates. For example, the report of the Finer Commission on One-Parent Families published in the mid-1970s (1974), could welcome changing family patterns as a sign of greater freedom of choice. It is difficult to imagine such views gaining a voice in official publications today. The difficulties that recent governments have faced over the reform of divorce law illustrate the way in which more recent debate focuses almost entirely on the negative aspects of family change. One of the aims of the 1996 Family Law Act was to reduce the conflict surrounding divorce but much of the debate focused on the extent to which it made divorce 'easier', which, for many opponents of the legislation, was self-evidently a bad thing.

One of the most important issues dividing these three points of view is the question of causality, and in particular the extent to which state provisions of welfare have affected family behaviour.

- Do we have more lone parents than most of our European neighbours because state welfare provides them with social security benefits and homes?
- Do we care less about, and less for, our family members because the state will provide for them?
- Do we choose not to marry because there is little financial advantage in doing so?

These are difficult questions to answer. Understanding the *outcomes* of welfare provisions on family circumstances and well-being is complicated but not impossible. We can, for example, examine relative poverty rates, or calculate the level of financial support offered to one family type as compared with another, as in the recent study by Bradshaw et al. (1993) of support for children in different countries. Millar and Ridge (2001), in their report for the Department for Work and Pensions, provide a comprehensive review of recent literature on poverty and families, including an examination of the outcomes of welfare-to-work and other employment policies.

But understanding the *consequences* of policy for family behaviour is much more difficult. There are so many factors involved and our theoretical understanding of the relationship between policy, attitudes and behaviour is very under-developed. However, many of the family trends we see here in Britain are found to a greater or lesser extent throughout the Western industrialized world, despite differences in type, level and nature of welfare provisions. This suggests that our social welfare provisions are unlikely to be the main cause of family change and, if so, changing policy will not reverse these trends.

Family Policy

As already pointed out, there is no simple way to define family policy. Maximalist definitions include everything that affects families, whether intended or not. Minimalist definitions include only those policies directly targeted on families, with particular goals in mind. The difficulties of defining family policy are discussed by Sheila Kamerman and Alfred Kahn in the introduction to their 1978 collection, *Family Policy: Government and Families in Fourteen Countries*. They start by making a distinction between 'implicit' and 'explicit' family policies.

- Implicit are policies which have consequences for families, although these are not their main target or goal. Their examples are 'industrial locations, decisions about road building, trade and tariff regulations, immigration policy' (p. 3).
- Explicit are areas where families are the object of policy and where particular goals are usually, although not always, specified in advance. Their examples are 'day care, child welfare, family counseling, family planning, income maintenance, some tax benefits, some housing policies' (p. 3).

The terminology of 'explicit' and 'implicit' is perhaps a little misleading, since the notion of implicit can carry with it a suggestion of 'covert' or 'hidden', i.e. that there is a policy agenda that is deliberately being obscured. The terms 'direct' and 'indirect' would express more clearly the notion that families are affected both by policies in particular and by policies in general. Using this terminology, then, three main areas of policy seem to fit under the 'direct family policy' heading.

1 The legal regulation of family behaviour: laws relating to marriage and divorce, to sexual behaviour, to contraception and abortion, to parental rights and duties, to child protection.
2 Policies to support family income: tax allowances, family and child benefits, parental leaves and benefits, enforcement of child support.
3 The provision of services for families: childcare provisions, subsidized housing, social services, community care.

In all these areas families are the target of policy and family functioning and well-being will be affected by the nature of the provisions made. And within and across these areas policy goals may overlap, change over time, be articulated more or less clearly and be more or less complementary or contradictory. Different countries also approach family policy in very different ways. At the end of her historical review of the development of family policy in 22 industrialized countries, Gauthier (1996) identifies four main approaches to family policy.

1 *Pro-family/pro-natalist.* Low fertility is a major concern and policies are aimed at encouraging people to have children. This includes policies to help mothers reconcile work and family life, so that employment does not act as a barrier to childbearing. France is the main example here.
2 *Pro-traditional.* The preservation of 'the family' is the main concern. Government takes some responsibility for supporting families, but the most important sources of support are seen as the fami-

lies themselves, the communities in which they live, and voluntary and charitable, including church, organizations. Policies support women to stay at home rather than go out to work. Germany is the main example here.
3 *Pro-egalitarian.* The promotion of gender equality is the main concern. Men and women are treated as equal breadwinners and equal carers and policy aims to support dual parent/worker roles. Liberal policies on marriage, divorce and abortion mean that there are few restrictions on how people can choose to organize their family life. Sweden and Denmark are the examples given.
4 *Pro-family but non interventionist.* The main concern is with families in need. Families are viewed as basically self-sufficient and able to meet their own needs through the private market, with only limited help from the state. There is little by way of support for working parents because it is believed that the market will meet any needs that emerge, as long as it is not hindered by government regulation. The UK and the USA are the examples given of this approach.

Models such as these are, of course, idealized accounts of the rather messier reality in which policies reflect a mixture of objectives and values. Furthermore, policy goals and provisions change over time. The placing of the UK in the 'pro-family but non-interventionist' category seems to have become less appropriate since the election of the Labour government in 1997. Millar and Ridge (2002), reviewing Labour's family policy between 1997 and 2002, argue that policy in areas such as childcare (the introduction of a 'national childcare strategy'), child poverty (the pledge to end child poverty within twenty years), lone parents and employment (the target of 70 per cent employment rates for lone parents within a decade), and measures to help parents reconcile employment and family life (parental leave and improved maternity leave and pay) represent significant changes in the nature of family policy in Britain. Family policy in Britain has become more explicit, with new goals and new sorts of measures and provisions. However, Millar and Ridge also point to an ongoing tension between supporting 'traditional' families, and in particular marriage, and being responsive to, and supportive of, family diversity and change.

Many of the measures introduced are aimed at promoting employment, and this is a central goal of Labour government policy. Family policy is thus closely bound up with wider policy goals and with approaches to social policy more generally. Family change, alongside employment change, has already put considerable pressure on welfare provisions. If current trends continue, the whole question of the boundaries between family and state is likely to become an even more central issue on the future policy agenda.

Guide to further reading

For statistical data on family trends: *Social Trends* (published annually by the Stationery Office, London) and *Population Trends* (published quarterly by the Stationery Office, London).

Bradshaw, J., Ditch, J., Holmes, H. and Whiteford, P., 1993. *Support for Children: a Comparison of Arrangements in Twenty Countries* (London: HMSO). Interesting both for the methodology used to compare across different countries and for the wealth of information about different systems of support.

Coote, A., Harman, H. and Hewitt, P., 1990. *The Family Way: A New Approach to Policy Making* (London: Institute for Public Policy Research). Sets out a policy agenda that seeks to accommodate to family change.

Gauthier, A. H., 1996. *The State and the Family: A Comparative Analysis of Family Policies in Industrialized Countries* (Oxford: Clarendon Press). Wide-ranging over both time and place, and argues that demographic change has been a major factor influencing policy development.

Kamerman, S. B. and Kahn, A. J. (eds), 1978. *Family Policy: Government and Families in Fourteen Countries* (New York: Columbia University Press). Something of a classic. The country case studies are perhaps of more historical than contemporary interest, although Hilary Land and Roy Parker provide an excellent analysis of the gendered basis of UK social security and housing policy. The introduction discusses definitions of family policy.

Millar, J. and Ridge T., 2001. *Families, Poverty, Work and Care: A review of the literature on lone parents and low-income couples with children* (DWP Research Report 153, Leeds: Corporate Document Services) provides a comprehensive review of the literature on poor families, mainly focused on the 1990s and including some comparisons with other countries.

Millar, J. and Ridge, T., 2002. 'Parents, children and new Labour: developing family policy', in Powell, M. (ed.) *Evaluating New Labour's Welfare Reforms* (Bristol: Policy Press). The book examines the record of the Labour government since 1997, with this chapter specifically examining family policy.

Morgan, P., 1995. *Farewell to the Family: Public Policy and Family Breakdown in Britain and the UK* (London: Institute for Economic Affairs). Argues that government activity is destroying the family and promotes a policy agenda to support marriage.

Websites:
The National Children's Bureau http://www.ncb.org.uk/

One Plus One http://www.oneplusone.org.uk/
National Council for One-Parent Families http://www.oneparentfamilies.org.uk/
European Observatory on National Family Policies http://europa.eu.int/comm/employment_social/family/observatory/home.html

Social Policy and Globalization

Rob Sykes

Today we hear a lot about globalization and the ways in which it is, supposedly, changing our world. Yet on closer inspection the various writers, politicians and political activists who talk about globalization and who express concern about its negative effects do not usually provide any clear definition of what they mean when they use the term, nor, very often, do they provide much evidence of how and why globalization is causing the problems they talk about. In short, debates about globalization might be said to have generated more political 'heat' than analytical 'light'. If we want to understand what the connections are between globalization and social policy we need to cut through some of this 'hype' and try to answer two related questions:

- What is globalization and how should we think about it?
- What is the evidence of the relationship between globalization and social policy thinking and practice?

What Is Globalization ?

The term globalization has been applied to a wide range of phenomena. Most commonly 'globalization' has been used as a generic term to refer to a variety of economic processes such as: an increasing internationalization of the production and exchange of goods and services; the deregulation of financial transactions; the spread of free trade on a world-wide scale; and the restructuring and relocation of productive activities between different regions of the world. Globalization has also been implicated in a number of political processes such as: the weakening of nation states and their loss of social and political autonomy in the face of global economic processes; a decentralization process within national states; and attempts to create new international political institutions to manage the new 'global politics'. In the field of social and cultural analysis, globalization has been associated with a massive increase in the availability and circulation of information especially through the spread of the internet; a greater interconnectedness between societies so that distances in both space and time seem to be shrunk through telephonic communication, real-time television broadcasts etc.; a threat to traditional cultures and social cohesion coupled with cultural homogenization, or so-called 'Macdonaldization', via the spread of global brands and products.

At a more general level it has been argued that the spread of globalization has meant that the economic links between nation states in the world market have become increasingly systemic, competitive and essentially corrosive of pre-existing political and economic relations. Globalization is increasingly seen as an intrinsic feature of the development of world capitalism leading inevitably, unless resisted and checked, to the demise of autonomous, nationally managed economies, to the collapse of nation states as sovereign bodies able to make effective policy decisions in the face of global economic forces, and, ultimately, to a loss of democratic control by ordinary citizens over their lives. This 'apocalyptic' version of the globalization thesis has now been largely discredited by more recent analysts. This has not stopped a growing number of 'anti-globalizers', loosely organized members of a variety of social movements, from protesting in strikingly similar terms about the essentially negative effects of the spread of global capitalism, led, as these protesters see it, by bodies such as the World Trade Organization, the International Monetary Fund, and even the European Union. Their concern is that the inhabitants of the poorer parts of the world, and the poorer and excluded of the richer countries, are and will continue to be consigned to poverty and exploitation if the forces of globalization are left unchecked. In short, in this view the welfare of all citizens is under threat except for those with the ability to pay for it.

Somewhat less dramatically, others have argued that globalization has changed the general economic context in which social policies are implemented. Welfare transfers and services are seen as comprising an element of rigidity in the economy, and as a burden for the companies (labour cost) and states (budget deficits) that try to compete in new, global markets. Recognition and response to this new context is said to require a radical adaptation of welfare states. This adaptation implies policies of retrenchment in social policy, and the general change of welfare states in order to render them more market- and employment-friendly.

To sum up, the nature of globalization and its connections with social policy are highly contested. There is no space here to examine globalization's many dimensions with the hope of establishing what, definitively, globalization is (but see the Guide

to further reading on page 66). Instead, accepting that globalization is bound to be contested both theoretically and empirically, this chapter summarizes three different theoretical perspectives on globalization and social policy, then moves on to assess these perspectives in the light of what actually appears to be happening to social policy around the world.

Theoretical Perspectives on Globalization and Social Policy

Three major perspectives on globalization and social policy are summarized as in boxes II.18.1– II.18.3.

An example of each of these perspectives will make their different implications for the analysis of social policy more apparent. Mishra (1999) provides an example of the first perspective. He argues that the major effect of globalization is the decline of the nation state in terms of its freedom to make policy, and in particular to pursue full employment and economic growth policies. These economic pressures tend to generate an increasing inequality in wages and working conditions both within countries and between countries, and increasing competition tends to exert a downward pressure on systems of social protection and social expenditure. Increasingly, as a result of these economic pressures from the globalized capitalist system, the ideological support for social protection systems becomes weakened, social democratic governments find their scope for welfare policy more and more limited and, indeed, democratic national political control tends to lose out to the forces of global economic powers. In short, Mishra argues that globalization has empowered and privileged neo-liberal economics as a transnational force beyond the control of nation states and governments.

Pierson (2001) provides an example of the second perspective. He asserts that the welfare state, rather than facing fundamental retrenchment and decline, is likely to be

Box II.18.1: Globalization causes welfare retrenchment through capitalism's dominance

- Internationalization of the world economy implies the demise of nation state autonomy, a reduction of national governments' policy options and a weakening of labour movements – i.e. main foundations of the national welfare state are fundamentally weakened
- Development of global capitalism responsible for unemployment and rising inequality, creating worsening problems for the welfare states
- Both international trade and technological change create a significant decline in demand for unskilled, semi-skilled and traditionally skilled workers
- Need for national economies to compete in world market exerts pressure for reduction in social expenditure by governments and private firms
- All the above create pressures to shift from social-democratic and collectivist to neo-liberal and individualist welfare ideologies – overall retrenchment and decline of welfare states

Box II.18.2: Globalization has little effect upon welfare states

- Changes in the world economy are less widespread, smaller and more gradual than the full-blown globalization thesis suggests
- Even if globalization has occurred, welfare states remain compatible with this process - globalized economies need to provide some sort of social welfare and political counterbalance to the effects of economic change
- 'Threat of globalization' more an ideological ploy of national governments wishing to restructure welfare than an unchallengeable economic force
- Welfare states are changing, but due to factors other than globalization (e.g. population ageing; technology, changes in family structures, new risks)

Box II.18.3: Globalization's effects on welfare states are mediated by national politics

- External global forces are impacting upon national welfare state changes
- Certain types of welfare state are more compatible with economic competitiveness than others, and can adapt better than others to the new environment
- World-wide competitive economic environment means that high wage national economies will lose jobs to low(er)-wage countries unless checked
- Particular character of the previous political and institutional arrangements (i.e. form of welfare state) in different countries will heavily affect responses to global challenges
- Thus, *different welfare states will change in different ways* in responding to globalization – not simple welfare retrenchment or decline – and the support of different constituencies (unions, politicians, voters etc.) will ensure continuation of welfare state in some form

sustained in almost all countries in the future. This is not to say that there are not pressures on welfare states. These are likely to lead to renegotiation, restructuring and modernization, but not to dismantling of welfare states. What Pierson calls the 'irresistible forces' playing upon welfare states are *domestic* forces, in particular the changed economies of advanced societies, the consequences of the 'maturation' of welfare states, and demographic change such as the ageing of populations especially in the Western capitalist economies. Globalization as an *exogenous* set of forces is, at best, of secondary significance.

Esping-Andersen (1996) and his associates provide a good example of the third perspective. They argue that a nation's economic growth now appears to require economic openness, involving greater competition and vulnerability to international trade, finance and capital movements. Consequently, national governments are more constrained in their economic and other related policies. So far this perspective sounds similar to that of Mishra and others, but Esping-Andersen et al. come to quite different conclusions. Esping-Andersen's key point is that in responding to the dilemmas created by globalization, *different* national systems can and do respond in *different* ways, and also survive rather than decline. One only has to look at the differences, for example, in Sweden, the UK and the Netherlands, all of which have recently developed their welfare sytems in quite different ways. Summing up, far from foreseeing a system of 'competitive austerity', Esping-Andersen concludes that the welfare state is here to stay. Within the advanced economies, though perhaps less so in the embryonic welfare states, existing political alignments of clients, welfare state workers, trades unions, political parties etc. in support of existing welfare arrangements imply that welfare state change will be limited and slow, even in the face of global economic changes and challenges.

From Theorizing to Analysing

Having considered these three perspectives, how would each of them suggest we should expect to find globalization having an impact upon social policy? Let us look at each in turn then look at the evidence to see which appears to offer the best guide to analysis.

- *Perspective 1: Globalization causes welfare retrenchment through the increasing dominance of capitalism in the world's economy.* For this view to be upheld, we would expect the direct impact of economic globalization to have led to various countries experiencing substantial, and essentially similar, welfare state changes
- *Perspective 2. Globalization has had little effect upon welfare states, though other social and economic processes have.* In this case, we would expect globalization to have had little or no clear or direct impact on welfare state changes in individual countries. Changes that occur are likely, in this view, to be slow and incremental with a high degree of continuity with the past. Furthermore, any similarities in trends in welfare state policies between countries are, in this view, related to the choice of similar policy solutions by governments, rather than to the external constraints of globalization.
- *Perspective 3: Globalization affects welfare states but its effects and roles are mediated by national politics and policies.* According to this view, we would expect to see policy changes that are path-dependent, but that may be quite significant. The nature of change will depend on the pre-existing national welfare ideology and the institutional framework of the welfare state in each country, but with similarities in trends within the same broad type of welfare state system.

In relation to the first perspective, there is actually little evidence from recent research of a direct and essentially similar impact by globalization on all welfare states. Changes which have occurred, though they may have been indirectly related to globalization, have been mediated through national governmental policies and institutions, a process that has led to quite different outcomes, as we shall see below. Even in Central and Eastern European countries, where the situation after the collapse of the communist system may have seemed ripe for the neo-liberal characteristics of globalization to make the strongest impact, the evidence is not of unfettered forces of global capitalism causing welfare changes. Certainly, changes there have been as these countries have re-entered the capitalist fold, but the policies for change have emanated from the ideological and practical policy prescriptions of the major actors promoting the 'Washington Consensus' – international organizations, such as the World Bank, backed by the dominant world governments. Though the rhetoric of globalization has been used by national governments in the Central and Eastern European states to legitimate the introduction of sometimes harsh social policies, their own role as policy-makers was crucial in terms of the interpretation of the welfare changes to be made and the decision to accept the general ideological thrust of the international organizations.

There are similar problems with the second perspective, which links changes in welfare states primarily to domestic factors. The significance of factors mentioned by Pierson, such as population ageing, the increasing costs of and demands for even bigger welfare systems, and the shift to service sector economies with in-built productivity problems in the advanced economies with the biggest welfare states should not be undervalued. However, it is clear that factors in the international economy, some or which might be regarded as part of the globalization process, have also been part of the reason for changes in welfare states. In fact part of the problem here is the separation of factors causing change as either

'internal' such as population ageing and its effects, and 'external' such as changes in international labour markets – the two sets of factors are in practice related. Globalization is not a monolithic 'exogenous' force that impacts directly and with equal impact on nation states from outside. Rather it is a complex set of ideological and practical processes, some of which are accepted, internalized and acted on by national governments in the light of these and other 'internal' pressures. In this broader view it is possible to argue that welfare state change is due more to the ideological projects of governments seeking to restructure, who use the 'pressures of globalization' argument to explain their policies, rather than to the unmediated impact of economic globalization processes themselves.

This takes us to the approach of Esping-Andersen and others which suggests that globalization does indeed affect welfare states but that its effects and roles are mediated by national politics and policies. In short, 'national politics matter'. The evidence which has been recently accumulated (see Guide to further reading) seems to support their view that existing welfare institutional arrangements and commitments in different countries significantly constrain the amount of change which can be and has been made in various countries around the globe as governments seek to respond to the pressures of economic globalization. Thus we see how different welfare states and different groupings of welfare states have responded in what have been dubbed 'path-dependent' ways – i.e. in ways which reflect pre-existing ways of delivering welfare and different sorts of welfare ideologies. These arrangements and commitments, and the constituencies they created of welfare users and welfare providers, coupled with the need for governments to sustain political support, mean that welfare state responses and adaptations to globalization will tend to be slow and piecemeal.

Globalization and Social Policy as a Dynamic Process

So where does this brief review of theoretical perspectives and comparing them with the evidence take us? It has been suggested that behind the hype about globalization causing welfare state collapse, or at best retrenchment, as usual a rather more complicated 'reality' presents itself. It would certainly seem that *economic* globalization is presenting various welfare states with pressures upon their capacity to fund and sustain their welfare provisions, let alone expand them. On the political front, however, the picture of increasingly powerless governments whose autonomy is being significantly reduced by globalization appears exaggerated – governments around the globe are responding to globalization, albeit within a more heavily constrained range of policy options, in supporting, restructuring or retrenching their welfare states. In addition, in Europe the role of the European Union is increasingly important as a supra-national body which could, simultaneously, be seen as promoting *and* resisting the pressures of globalization depending upon which area of its activities one looks at. Similarly, we need to consider carefully how other international organizations such as the World Bank, the International Monetary Fund, the World Trade Organization, the International Labour Organisation and others are actually implicated in the interplay of pressures between globalization and national welfare state policy making rather than simply accepting the these bodies represent and promote the unmitigated 'evils' of world capitalist globalization (see chapter III.9).

Dispassionate consideration of both the theories and evidence about globalization and social policy suggest that a more 'reciprocal' view of the links may offer a fruitful way forward, rather than thinking only in terms of how far and in what ways globalization causes social policy change. Research suggests that the character of globalization is being constructed and interpreted differently in different national systems, or types of welfare system. Different types of welfare state (or rather governments running welfare states) have different perceptions of globalization and the problems and opportunities it presents, connected to the ways in which these different types of national welfare system are themselves constructed and their pre-existing welfare ideas and practices. So, the social-democratic welfare state of, say, Sweden brings to its perception and range of possible responses to globalization a quite different legacy than that of, say, the more market-focused USA or the post-Communist Hungary. It could be argued then that at the national level, there are *different globalization processes* since there are *different welfare state contexts*. National welfare systems have not only been developed to counter market failure, but are a reflection and a reinforcement of the specific social structural and labour market characteristics of a given country. Welfare systems constitute specific normative, ideological and cultural legacies in each country. Therefore, welfare states should be seen as important parts of the socio-economic and politico-cultural structures of countries which themselves shape the way that globalization influences these countries. Welfare state reforms apparently 'caused by globalization' could alternatively be understood as having either anticipated or even developed so-called globalization trends. For example, moves by national governments to reduce welfare costs as a major part of a rising public debt have themselves contributed to the austerity which globalization is supposed to be generating. The attempt to improve labour market flexibility as well as to reduce overall labour costs through reforms to the system of financing social policy are also reinforcing international competition between workers.

Guide to further reading

Probably the best single-volume introduction to the variety of perspectives on globalization from a social science perspective is M. Waters *Globalization*, 2nd edn (London: Routledge, 2000). Try J. A. Scholte, *Globalization: A Critical Introduction* (Basingstoke: Macmillan Press, 2000) for something more advanced.

Exemplars of the three theoretical perspectives outlined in the chapter can be found in the following three texts: G. Esping-Andersen,(ed.) *Welfare States In Transition: National Adaptations in Global Economies* (London: Sage, 1996); R. Mishra, *Globalization and the Welfare State* (Cheltenham: Edward Elgar, 1999); and P. Pierson,(ed.) *The New Politics of the Welfare State* (Oxford: Oxford University Press, 2001).

Finally, for texts which try to bring together theories and evidence about globalization and social policy try: F. Scharpf,and V. Schmidt (eds) *Welfare And Work In The Open Economy*, 2 vols (Oxford: Oxford University Press, 2000); and R. Sykes, B. Palier and P. M. Prior (eds) *Globalization And European Welfare States: Challenges And Change* (Basingstoke: Palgrave, 2001).

For those of you interested in reading what the major international organizations are saying and doing here are some key websites:

European Union (EU) Europa website: http://europa.eu.int
World Trade Organization (WTO): http://www.wto.org
World Bank: http://www.worldbank.org
International Monetary Fund (IMF): http://www.imf.org
International Labour Organisation (ILO): http://www.ilo.org
Organisation for Economic Co-operation and Development (OECD): http://www.oecd.org
Also, here are some of the anti-globalization/protest sites:
 http://www.protest.net
 http://www.flora.org
 http://www.indymedia.org

II.19
Social Policy and the Political Process

Michael Hill

There are two popular images of the politics of social policy, extensively taught in the past, and still implicit in much talk and journalistic writing. One sees our 'governors' (however defined) as essentially benign problem-solvers, trying to do their best to solve social problems and meet people's (or society's, or the economy's) needs. The other sees those same people as responding to our desires and wishes, and tends to talk about social policy-making as if 'we' are governing ourselves. Clearly there are good reasons why popular and media conceptions of government evolved into a form which assumes that 'democracy' works, and that the things done by our rulers are done either in our best interests or in response to our demands (or both). In mocking this view, here, moreover, I am not trying to attack it as an ideal or aspiration. I am merely suggesting that this is not a very realistic way to explore the politics of social policy.

Instead, I want to offer four alternative models for the analysis of the politics of social policy, all of which make claims to be more realistic, and one of which, furthermore, retains within it some kinds of assertions that the democratic model works. The best simple labels for these models are:

- pluralism;
- elitism;
- economic determinism;
- institutionalism.

These four labels have been chosen to embrace a range of related theories. Alternative labels are on offer. This taxonomy, for instance, does not include Marxism – which may be seen as the major form of economic determinism but also appears in forms very close to elitism. The same may be said of some forms of feminist theory. Another body of theory, used in 'new right' analyses of social policy, is 'public choice'. However, this is a combination of a version of pluralism which stresses the capacity of special interests to make demands for government expenditure with a version of institutionalism which emphasizes public bureaucrats' power as monopoly providers of services. Clearly, realistic models for the examination of the politics of social policy will want to combine the basic approaches discussed here into mixed forms like that. This is a point to which we will return. Meanwhile, let us examine each model in turn.

Pluralism

Pluralism sees decision-making within the state as a product of competition between interests. The simplest way in which that competition may be manifested is through the efforts of the electorate to influence parliamentary decision processes. It has been recognized that this simple model is seldom realized: first, because the process is inevitably mediated through political parties and individual politicians (this is what is described as 'representative government'); second, because much political competition is not direct and does not simply involve parliamentary processes, but is mediated in a variety of ways through pressure groups. Some who have emphasized the latter point talk of 'post-parliamentary democracy'.

Pluralism is seen as offering the nearest we can get to true democracy. Public choice theory sees it providing a distorted political 'market place' in which unrealistic individual demands are made of the kind which would not be made in a true market. Radical critiques suggest that the ideal is undermined by inequalities; we do not compete equally; some interests are much stronger than others.

Elitism

Elitist theory is in many respects the alternative picture of the political process offered by radical critics of pluralism: it asserts that 'the heavenly choir sings with a distinctly upper class voice'. The problem about elitist theory lies in its simplicity. Merely to say that political decision processes are inherently biased and that power is concentrated in the hands of a few does not offer any explanation of why this is the case. This label tends to bring together under a general umbrella a variety of theories about why power is unevenly distributed. Conflicting explanations are on offer, from, at one extreme, psychological or even genetic theories stressing the superiority of elites, to theories which stress the importance of economic inequalities at the other (which come very close to the Marxist theory to be discussed in the next section). Important perspectives which share much in common with elitism are feminist theories about the way male domination is maintained, and theories which explore the mechanisms racial or national groups use to exercise power. There is also an important vein in elitist theory which stresses the way in which state institutions facilitate concentration of power.

Economic Determinism

Quite the most important form of economic determinist theory is Marxism, which is discussed in some more detail in chapter II.9. In its main forms this theory is not merely saying that power is concentrated in the hands of economic elites but that the logic of the system of production makes this domination inevitable. Social policy decision-making is then seen as subordinate to the requirements of capitalism. Social policy is inevitably limited to a role supporting or helping to legitimize the capitalist order. Modern Marxist theorists have extensively explored the nature and extent of this determinism, sometimes moving a long way from Marx's original position. But determinism also crops up in non-Marxist forms. One such has been comparative theory, which stresses the commonalities in the forms of social policy development, seeing them as explained by industrialization or urbanization, for example. These have been widely attacked by scholars who have shown how specific political forces seem to have produced varied national responses. However, new forms of determinism keep emerging. To some extent politicians and thinkers on the 'Right' who stress the limits to social policy growth in the capitalist economy take very similar stances to those of Marxist determinists. Some of the theory on the global economy similarly tends to treat the logic of evolving capitalist production processes worldwide as relatively determinist for issues like social policy, stressing in this case the constraints 'globalism' imposes upon individual state decision making.

Institutionalism

The last of the models also takes many forms. All of the three previous theoretical approaches tend to take stances on the importance of state institutions themselves. The pluralists tend to treat the state as a neutral body to be influenced. The elitists are interested in the way power outside and inside the state interlocks. The economic determinists see the state as inevitably having limited autonomy. The question is: how much do we need to look inside the state institutions themselves – at how they are structured and organized, at their rule systems (including even constitutions) and standard operating procedures, at the interests of state officials – in order to explain the role of the state in social policy? Such questions are self-evidently pertinent in a society like the United Kingdom, where state expenditure is nearly 40 per cent of gross domestic product and where many are either direct or indirect employees of the state.

All the other theoretical approaches have had to come to terms with this issue; hence, instead of arguing that 'institutionalism' offers a distinctive perspective on its own, it is suggested that the other three theoretical approaches have tended to undergo modification in the way indicated in table II.19.1. Essentially we see here the various approaches accepting the importance of exploration of interactions and links between state and society. Two approaches of particular importance for social policy, and not fully brought out in table II.19.1, are:

- work on policy communities (seeing, for example, health policy as very influenced by cohesive professional communities running across the conventional state/society boundary);

- work which stresses the way past decisions create structures of constraints and opportunities for future ones (seeing, for example, a social insurance system which gave new advantages to white working class males as a source of blockages to the advancement of the concerns of other groups).

The Policy Process

The model of the political process, outlined at the beginning and most closely approximated in the propositions associated with pluralism, sees social policy as *made* by elected representatives, responding to democratic demands, and *implemented* by publicly employed officials who have a duty to translate the general aspirations embodied in policy into detailed practice. The other theories suggest doubts about the extent to which this is the case. Thus they tend to direct attention to interventions which may occur outside the democratic arena. Implicit in their approaches, and particularly in 'institutionalist' theory, is a view that the so-called implementation process may in many respects create policy. Hence it is appropriate to speak of policy-making processes as comprising both policy formation and policy implementation.

For traditional democratic theory, creative activity during the implementation phase of

Table II.19.1   Theoretical models of the politics of social policy

Original theory	Development
Pluralism	Consideration of policy networks in and outside the state
Public choice pluralism	Economic theory of bureaucracy
Elitism	Analysis of bureaucratic power
Economic determinism, Marxist version	Exploration of 'relative autonomy of the state'
Other determinist theory	Acceptance of structural constraints within the state, and the distinctiveness of the responses of specific states to global pressure

the policy process represents a threat. It engenders a range of 'top-down' control issues – about the ways in which doctors, teachers, social workers, social security benefit clerks etc. may be made democratically accountable. But the alternative perspectives offered by other theories suggest that it is in many respects more realistic to expect policy to be created within the implementation process and for there to be a complex interaction between the more overt politics of legislation and the more covert politics which follow it. This does not mean that democratic control issues are regarded as irrelevant (though of course that is in many respects the position taken by economic determinism), but that they are more subtle than those embodied in the traditional theory of representative government. This seems particularly important in social policy, where policy goals and policy systems are complex and a great deal of the real politics (in the broadest sense of that term) which influences 'who gets what, when and how' occurs far away from public parliamentary debates.

Clearly here, as throughout any discussion of the politics of social policy, there is a distinction to be made between a realistic analysis of what actually happens and a prescriptive stance on what should happen. A great deal of political activity is directed towards trying to exercise control over a complex process, and legitimized by philosophical propositions about the way the policy system *should* work. The alternative to the theory of representative democracy offered by those who stress the importance of public participation close to the point at which services are delivered is partly grounded upon a recognition of the importance of policy processes occurring at or near to the 'street level'.

The Political Process in The United Kingdom

Until 1998 any account of the politics of social policy in the United Kingdom (UK) was comparatively simple because of the existence of a unitary system of govern-

ment. The main forum of party political conflict was in parliament at Westminster, and the main focus of legislative activity was in ministries located in Whitehall (this reference to the geography of central London emphasizes the point about the centralization of system). However, even then there was some administrative devolution to Scotland, Wales and Northern Ireland. In 1998, however, much more far reaching political devolution began to occur, particularly to the new government of Scotland. Policy divergence is beginning to occur – for health, social services, education and housing policy but not for social security – between what applies in England and what applies in the other countries of the UK. A significant new politics is beginning to emerge where there is disagreement between that adminstration in London and that in Edinburgh (or perhaps in Cardiff or Belfast, see chapter III.7). Two early issues of this kind concerned fees for higher education and payments for residential care. The European Union has social policies, too, which may also challenge UK autonomy (discussed in chapter III.8).

As far as the still-dominant politics at Westminster and Whitehall are concerned there has been an increasing tendency for the executive to dominate over the legislature. The very large Labour majorities resulting from the elections of 1997 and 2001 have tended to exacerbate this process. The Labour government has been dominated by two powerful figures – the prime minister Tony Blair and the Chancellor of the Exchequer Gordon Brown. There has been little consultation of the Cabinet. Hence it is increasingly being argued that the United Kingdom has a presidential system without the checks and balances of an independent legislature as in the United States.

The British system of local government is important for social policy – since much social policy comes wholly or partly within its remit (education, personal social services and housing). However, the dominant model is very much one in which local government's powers derive from central government. Its politics mimic those of central government (so much so that the media treat local elections as if they were merely opinion polls for the parliament). The period of Conservative government from 1979 saw a very extensive tightening of central powers over local government – above all through the assertion of absolute dominance over finance but also through attacks upon rights to make choices about how services are delivered. The new Labour government continued this process in a rather different way, legislating to require performance indices from local government and giving itself powers to replace all or parts of underperforming authorities. It has also legislated to regulate how local authorities manage their own business.

What is being described here is a very centralized system of government for England (with closely parallel arrangements in the other parts of the UK). The centralization of the political processes apply to party politics and to the creation and design of legislation. But this chapter has suggested that the politics of social policy needs to be conceptualized more widely to take into account what is often called implementation. When we do this the British system is seen to be very much more complex, with its complexity increasing. The central-local relationship described in the last paragraph is one aspect of this complexity. There obviously remain many areas where local politicians and officials can play creative roles in putting central policies in practice.

Rather similar things can be said about the social policy systems over which central government has more obviously direct political control. For example, as discussed in chapter IV.9, the health service is organized through a partially decentralized system of primary care team or trust service 'purchasers' and health service trust or direct practitioner 'providers'. The politics of this area of policy is essentially inter-organizational. The purchaser-provider split is rather more a set of arrangements structuring inter-organizational relationships, generating an intense politics of their own,

than the quasi-market system it was claimed to be when it was first created. Furthermore, health politics, in the UK as elsewhere, is dominated by a series of issues about professional rights, prerogatives and duties, in which bodies like the British Medical Association are key actors.

Until the late 1980s, social security policy in the UK could have been described as very largely policy delivery through a large and complex organization, with its inevitable internal politics (see chapter IV.7). Then the government transformed the system into one in which implementation became the responsibility of a group of agencies, each with a separate contract with the central Department for Work and Pensions. This adds a new complexity to implementation, highlighted by the unhappy history of the Child Support Agency, charged with responsibility to collect financial contributions from absent parents and set goals which it found impossible to achieve. In some respects in this situation a new politics of implementation developed – very like some aspects of central-local government relations – in which an allegedly quasi-independent organization was forced to take the blame for unrealistic politically set goals.

In all sectors policy delivery is becoming more complex. This is a consequence of the view that social policy implementation should involve many new relationships and partnerships – between central department and agencies, between purchasers and providers – with the implementers being actually (as in social care or social housing) or potentially (in all areas) independent, even profit-making, organizations. In the rhetoric of the Blair government there is a great emphasis upon joined-up government, looking to various kinds of partnerships and overarching bodies to try to avoid compartmentalized approaches to social problems. Accountability to service users is also stressed. But often these measures are accompanied by ever stronger efforts by central government to impose its will and secure accountability. Hence those with responsibility for policy implementation have to cope with contradictory pressures (see Newman, 2001).

Inasmuch as this chapter has distinguished two kinds of policy process – one up front and parliamentary while the other is much more 'below stage' – we end up having to have regard to two very different political process stories. In the UK the former is much simpler than the other, but given much more attention. The latter is complex and often not readily open to public scrutiny.

However, these two kinds of 'politics' should not be seen as ultimately separate. There are many issues to consider about how much the former sets the ideological context and the main parameters for the other. Conversely, the latter feeds back issues into the party political and parliamentary system.

The extent to which this is the case varies very much from issue to issue – in relation to levels of controversy and the extent to which party politicians choose to make issues their own. The theories outlined in the earlier part of this chapter offer alternative perspectives on the extent to which these linkages can be seen to be democratic, in the pluralist sense, and the extent to which policy agendas are really open to influence. The analysis of centralization in this section suggests that perhaps elitist theories are more pertinent for the analysis of policy processes in the United Kingdom. But then complexity in the implementation process offers opportunities for more pluralist forms of influence whilst institutional arrangements continue to have a strong impact.

Guide to further reading

It is difficult to make wide reading recommendations without taking students deep into the political science literature. On the theoretical models, J. Schwartzmantel *The State in Contemporary Society* (Hemel Hempstead: Harvester Wheatsheaf, 1994), offers a good introduction. A rather more difficult book on the same lines is P. Dunleavy and B. O'Leary *Theories of the State* (Basingstoke: Macmillan Press,1987). The use of the institutional approach is best exemplified by T. Skocpol *Social Policy in the United States* (Princeton, NJ: Princeton University Press, 1995), and D. E. Ashford *The Emergence of the Welfare States* (Oxford: Blackwell, 1986).

M. Hill *The Policy Process in the Modern State* (Hemel Hempstead: Harvester Wheatsheaf, 1997) offers a theoretical exploration of the policy process as a whole. A recent case study of British policy for the care of children under five, S.Liu *The Autonomous State of Child Care* (Aldershot: Ashgate, 2001), provides a good exploration of the use of policy theory to explain policy processes.

The importance of relationships between professions and the state has been emphasized. Still the best general work on this is P. Wilding's now dated *Professional Power and Social Welfare* (London: Routledge, 1982), but there is a considerable literature on the significance of this for health services. M. Moran and B. Wood *States, Regulation and the Medical Profession* (Buckingham: Open University Press, 1993), offers a comparative account.

J. Newman *Modernising Governance* (London: Sage, 2001) is cited above as a good analysis of the conflicts arising within the Blair government's efforts to control policy processes.

On the United Kingdom it is difficult to identify anything very specific on the legislative 'politics of policy' other than either general British government textbooks or books like H. Glennerster *British Social Policy since 1945* (Oxford: Blackwell, 1995), which are concerned to offer up-to-date accounts of the political controversies around social policy. On the other hand, T. Butcher *Delivering Welfare* (Buckingham: Open University Press, 2nd edition 2002), offers a good account of the more complex aspects of the policy implementation process.

Part III
The Production, Organization and Consumption of Welfare

The Production Of Welfare

III.1

State Welfare

Norman Johnson

Defining Terms

Before we look in more detail at the role of the state in the production of welfare, some consideration must be given to what the term means. There are numerous theories of the state. Schwarzmantel, for example, identifies four different approaches: pluralism, elite theory, Marxism and feminism. He also considers some alternatives to the social democratic state: communist and fascist states and those based on particular forms of nationalism. It would not serve the interests of this chapter to describe and evaluate these competing perspectives, but Schwarzmantel (1994, p.8) offers the following definition: 'The state . . . can be described as a set of institutions constituting a specialized apparatus of domination. Not only is the modern state in this sense distinct from the society over which it rules, but it is also a centralized apparatus of power, which . . . possesses a monopoly of rulemaking'. The varying and changing interrelationships between state and society is the subject of this and the next three chapters.

The state is an abstraction; there is nothing one can point to that can be said to constitute the state, and the simplest strategy in considering its role in the production of welfare is to focus on the most obvious manifestations of the state: government and its agencies. Government is defined widely and includes:

- *Ministers and the Cabinet*. Central government departments (notably the Department of Health, the Department for Work and Pensions, the Department for Education and Skills, the Department for Environment, Food and Rural Affairs, the Department for Transport, Local Government and the Regions and the Home Office).
- *Local authorities*. A variety of agencies within the National Health Service (NHS): health authorities, hospital, community and primary care trusts, the National Institute for Clinical Excellence and the Commission for Health Improvement.
- A very large number of semi-autonomous executive agencies, which may be known as *non-departmental public bodies* (NDPBs), next steps agencies, quasi-autonomous non-governmental organizations (quangos) or extra-governmental organizations (EGOs): the Benefits Agency, the Child Support Agency, Jobcentre Plus, the Environment Agency, the Highways Agency, the Countryside Agency, the Prison Service Agency, Regional Development Agencies, Urban Regeneration Companies, Local Strategic Partnerships, Learning and Skills Councils, the Housing Corporation, police authorities and many more.

Some of the above have regulatory functions. Other regulatory bodies include: the

Office for Standards in Education, the Commission for Social Care Inspection, the Commission for Healthcare Audit and Inspection and the Financial Services Authority (see chapter III.13).

This wide range of institutions indicates that the state is diffuse and fragmented. The creation of a vast number of executive and regulatory agencies is one aspect of what has been termed new public management which, among other things, attempts to import the principles and practices of the private sector into the management of public services (Clarke and Newman, 1997; Horton and Farnham, 1999). But even the list above does not give a complete picture. The term 'governance' has been used to describe a much wider concept than the more conventional term 'government'. Rhodes (1997) claims that governance calls attention to the differing permutations of government and the private and voluntary sectors in service provision and policy formulation. The key notion in this analysis is a series of self-organizing networks. In this formulation, the boundaries between the public, private and voluntary sectors become increasingly blurred. Rhodes says that 'the unitary state is a multiform maze of interdependencies' (1997, p.16).

The United Kingdom after the Second World War introduced a massive programme of social legislation covering education, housing, family allowances, national insurance and assistance, children, services for older and disabled people and the NHS (see chapters I.1, I.4). This legislation represented an acceptance by the state of a responsibility to protect and promote the welfare of all citizens. It is fair to say, however, that it was designed to provide a national minimum rather than reduce inequalities. One consequence of this legislative activity was a substantial increase in state power and in its pervasiveness in people's lives. During the same period two other developments conspired to increase the role of the state: nationalization of public utilities, and policies designed to maintain high levels of employment (Timmins, 1996).

This chapter is concerned with the state's role in the production of welfare, but this has to be seen in the context of the state's other roles and the ideologies underpinning them. Although the issues are discussed mainly in the context of the UK, the role of the state in welfare is a matter of significance internationally (see chapter I.3), and there is much to be gained from a comparative approach (Hill, 1996).

The Main Forms of State Involvement in Welfare

There are several ways in which the state can influence welfare provision. First, the government has the capacity to determine overall policy and policies specific to individual services. Crucially, the national government controls expenditure. Second, the state may engage in direct provision of benefits and services. Indeed, this was the usual mode of provision until the 1980s, and even after the changes made in the delivery of welfare, central and local government are still heavily involved in the social security benefits system, the NHS, education and personal social services. Policy changes in the 1980s and 1990s have reduced, but by no means extinguished, direct service provision by the state.

Third, statutory authorities have important planning and supervisory roles in relation to the delivery of welfare. For example, although local authority social services departments are required to make the maximum feasible use of independent providers, they have a responsibility to assess the needs of the local population and to ensure that these are met. They are also required to produce community care plans. In the NHS, parallel functions are performed by health authorities and the hospital, community and primary care trusts. There are, however, some problems in producing realistic and workable plans which accurately reflect need if responsibility for planning is divorced from direct provision.

Fourth, statutory responsibility for

planning implies some obligation to try to ensure that the plans are implemented. This directs attention to the regulatory role of the state in welfare provision. Regulation may be divided into:

- *input regulation* (deciding who should be allowed to act as providers and what qualifications will be required of the staff they employ);
- *process regulation* (specifying how a service should be provided);
- *output regulation* (evaluating the quantity and quality of provision).

Regulation may be strengthened by a formal system of audit or inspection (see chapter III.13). The system in which statutory purchasers enter into contracts with independent providers involves all three forms of regulation backed up by a variety of inspectorates.

The fifth role for the state is in the area of direct financial assistance, fiscal support and subsidies (discussed in more detail in chapter III.10). Direct financial assistance to providers may take the form of grants (to voluntary agencies, for example) or payment to independent providers for contracted services. Fiscal support takes the form of granting tax relief for certain categories of expenditure or to certain groups of people. The relief granted on occupational and private pensions is one example: the tax relief on mortgage interest payments, once very generous, has gradually been whittled away. Tax relief is clearly a form of subsidy, but more direct subsidies are also used. Housing benefit is a good example of a subsidy. Free prescriptions is another.

Globalization, Privatization and the Changing Role of the State

Globalization (see also chapter II.18) is given considerable prominence in current political and economic debate (Hutton and Giddens, 2000). I will refer briefly to four aspects of the globalization thesis. The first relates to the global economy and the need to compete successfully in terms of selling a country's products and attracting inward investment; paradoxically, globalization also implies increased interdependence. The second aspect relates to the enormous power of multi-national corporations which have the power to switch production from one country to another (see chapter III.9). The third aspect relates to the power of international financial institutions such as the International Monetary Fund (IMF), The World Bank and the Organisation for Economic Co-operation and Development (OECD). Typically, any aid given by the IMF and the World Bank has conditions attached to it (e.g. reducing social expenditure, introducing greater selectivity). Fourth, although not strictly speaking globalization, there is the increasing influence of transnational governmental institutions; the most significant for Britain and the other members is the European Union (see chapter III.8). It is frequently claimed that each of these aspects of globalization erodes the capacity of governments to design discrete social policies. It is, however, possible to exaggerate the nation state's loss of autonomy.

Privatization in the context of social welfare means a reduction in the role of the state and the transfer of some of its functions to private institutions. The private institutions may be commercial undertakings, voluntary associations or informal networks of families, friends and neighbours. As already noted, after the war the UK experienced an increase in government intervention on a number of fronts. The welfare mix that emerged was one dominated by the state, which was responsible for policy-making in a national framework and the setting of priorities. In many instances, however, the state was also virtually a monopoly provider. Some of the virtues claimed for state provision stemmed from the perceived weaknesses of other sources of welfare. It was argued, for example, that the state's superiority over both markets and voluntary organizations lay in its ability to guarantee rights of access and use and to protect and enforce procedural and sub-stantive rights. Furthermore, the state's power to levy tax meant that statutory services enjoyed a greater degree of certainty and continuity than either voluntary or commercial services.

The state could more easily secure equality and equity than the market, because it responded to need rather than demand backed up by the ability to pay (see chapter II.1). As sources of welfare, markets were hampered by imperfect knowledge on the part of consumers, and the consumption of health and welfare services was characterized by uncertainty and unpredictability. Furthermore, many consumers did not have sufficient mobility to take advantage of more suitable or cheaper provision elsewhere.

Another set of arguments compared the state and the voluntary sector as potential sources of welfare. Coverage by the state was national, implying more equitable distribution, whereas voluntary sector coverage was uneven. This wider coverage had two further advantages:

- It facilitated planning over a broad area.
- It allowed for economies of scale and the achievement of greater uniformity of provision in mass-produced services such as social security.

Moreover, the voluntary sector was characterized by unclear and multiple accountabilities: the political accountability typical of public service organizations was absent.

It is not suggested, however, that all of these potential advantages of the state have been realized: that is clearly not the case. Critics of state provision argue that it is too centralized, too bureaucratic and too much dominated by professionals and administrators. These characteristics, it is claimed, make statutory services unresponsive to different individual needs and to changing needs. Furthermore, critics argue, after decades of state-dominated provision, Beveridge's five giants of want, disease, ignorance, squalor and idleness have not been overcome.

These anti-state sentiments have been in the ascendancy since the late 1970s, leading to demands for the creation of a mixed economy of welfare in which the state ceased to be a major direct provider of health and welfare services, with greater reliance upon commercial and voluntary sector providers. The basis of the new system is the separation of the purchasing or commissioning of welfare from its provision. The clearest expression of this is to be found in the community care provisions of the National Health Service and Community Care Act of 1990, which took effect in 1993. The local authorities are responsible for assessing the needs of the local population and for drawing up plans to see that needs are met by purchasing services, wherever possible, from independent providers. Contracts are drawn up under which commercial and voluntary sector agencies agree to provide a specified quantity of a particular service for a particular group of clients, meeting certain criteria with regard to mode of delivery and quality. It should be noted that local authorities, while losing their dominant position in direct provision of services, retain, and possibly enlarge, their role in the planning, finance and regulation of provision. The state moves from being a providing state and becomes an enabling or a contracting state. The main advantages claimed for this change were the introduction of competition for contracts among providers and the enlargement of choice for service users. The personal social services have been taken as an example of the changes, but similar developments are to be found in health, education and social housing.

These changes are not restricted to the UK: to different degrees and at different speeds, they are occurring throughout the world. Mixed economies of welfare have become the new orthodoxy, seeming to offer the prospect of a reduced role for the state and the curtailment of public expenditure.

The use of contracts and the introduction of what are known as quasi-markets is an attempt to overcome some of the perceived shortcomings of state-provided welfare, especially its alleged bureaucratic rigidities and lack of responsiveness. It may, however, be possible to realize these benefits by improving state provision: two such developments would be greater decentralization and the introduction of more participatory services designed to empower users. Decentralization and user empowerment are key issues in state welfare, and are considered in a little more detail below.

Key Issues and Debates

It may be helpful to identify some of the key issues and debates surrounding the role of the state which will recur at various points in the course of your studies. The issues selected are restricted to those having a significance which goes beyond individual services. It is also important to remember that social policy is never static and that new issues will arise from time to time.

Issue 1: The balance in the welfare mix

The overriding issue is the changing balance in the mixed economy of welfare, and the role of the state within this. At present in most welfare states there are attempts to reduce the state's role in provision and to rely more heavily on the commercial, voluntary and informal sectors. This raises questions about the relationship of the state to each of these providers. It is clear that the state will retain responsibility for planning and regulation, and that it will have a major role in finance. At present, one of the words which occurs with great frequency in social policy discourse is 'partnership', indicating the need for public, private and voluntary and community sectors to work together. The benefits of partnership has been a central feature of social policy discussion for many years, but the Labour government has made partnership a key element of its approach to welfare provision. Nearly every document it produces in relation to social policy mentions partnership; the 1998 White Paper,

Modernising Social Services, for example, devotes a chapter to the notion. In 1998 the government also issued a compact outlining the principles on which government/ voluntary and community sector relationships were to be based. More controversially, the second Labour government has been emphasizing what it perceives as the need for public-private sector partnerships in the provision of public services – especially in health and education.

Issue 2: Rights

One of the features of the state is its ability to coerce. This can lead to tyranny and totalitarianism. As we have seen, however, the state's power to coerce also makes it the only body that can guarantee civil, political and social rights. Rights to a basic standard of living, education and health care are sometimes described as citizenship rights because they derive from people's status as citizens. Citizenship and social rights are, however, contested concepts, and it is clear that citizenship rights are not available to all citizens without regard to race, gender, social class or disability.

Issue 3: Empowerment

One of the criticisms of state welfare is the predominance within it of professionals and bureaucrats, which, it is claimed, renders the services unresponsive to people's expressed needs (see chapter III.5). These features of state welfare have given the impetus, as we have seen, to new non-state forms of service production and delivery. The challenge, irrespective of which sector provides the services, however, is how to ensure that users have a say, going beyond mere consultation, in stating their needs, in deciding what kinds and levels of service best meet those needs and in determining how the services shall be provided and by whom. The involvement of users in policy-making, service provision and even the management of facilities and services all need to be carefully considered, and there is increasing evidence that both central and local government are taking the issue seriously and attempting to do something about it. The Carers (Recognition and Services) Act was passed under the previous government in 1995 and this has been considerably expanded under the Carers and Disabled Children Act, 2000.

There has, without doubt, been an extension and strengthening of users' rights since 1997: the rights of children and older people, for example, are much more clearly stated than they were. User and carer empowerment has certainly received much publicity in recent years. A variety of service-user organizations have kept the issue at the forefront of the welfare debate. Importantly, the Joseph Rowntree Foundation Shaping Futures Programme has made user and carer involvement central to its deliberations. It consulted an organization called 'Shaping Our Lives' (SOL), the main focus of which is user-defined outcomes. SOL responded by launching a new project under the title of 'Our Voice in Our Future' (OVIOF). The publications stemming from this project were produced by The National Institute for Social Work, which itself has given considerable attention to user and carer empowerment.

Issue 4: Regulation

The different forms of regulation (input, process, output and outcome) have already been identified. The most appropriate form of regulation by statutory purchasers/commissioners is a matter for discussion. There has to be some balance between the need for regulation and the need for experimentation and innovation, which requires a degree of independence. What are sometimes forgotten are the financial costs of regulation. To ensure that regulations are complied with requires the providers to furnish documentary evidence, and the scrutiny of this evidence by purchasers. Monitoring may be continuous but is much more likely to be intermittent. It cannot be assumed that government agencies have both the resources and the skill for effec-

tive monitoring. As services become increasingly fragmented, with a multiplicity of providers, the task of regulating provision becomes more difficult. Decentralization also makes regulation more complex.

Issue 5: Decentralization

Despite the rhetoric of decentralization and rolling back the state, power in the UK became more highly centralized during the 1980s, and with one major exception, there have been few reversals in the 1990s. The major exception was the devolution of power to representative assemblies in Scotland, Wales and Northern Ireland in the late 1990s. Other countries have also pursued decentralization strategies. France, traditionally the most highly centralized country in Europe, began a programme of decentralization in 1982; in Germany the principle of subsidiarity guarantees more power at sub-central levels; and a similar situation prevails in the Netherlands. Decentralization to more local units has also been a major theme in Denmark, Italy, Norway, Sweden and the USA.

Issue 6: Equity and equality

Left to themselves, markets and the voluntary sector will not produce equitable outcomes: voluntary organizations are unevenly distributed and markets are little concerned with equity and equality. Furthermore, each individual provider sees only a small segment of the total picture and is concerned only with its own contribution. The state in its role of planner and enabler has greater opportunity to promote equality and equity, particularly because it controls resources. Whether the opportunity is taken will depend on the government's views about the proper pursuits and aims of the welfare state. Is the aim of the welfare state simply to pick up the social casualties, with public services performing a residual role? Or is the welfare state essential to social integration and a society based on justice? If the latter, then decent public services available to all without reference to social class, race, gender or disability have an important role to play.

Issue 7: Globalization and the European Union

To what extent do global pressures and membership of the EU limit the autonomy of states and diminish their capacity for making independent, discrete decisions in social and economic policy? Certainly, states have to comply with EU law, and they cannot afford to ignore global pressures. Nevertheless, states are not powerless in the face of relentless global pressures: there may be considerable room for manœuvre, choices will have to be made among several possible alternative responses and they can broker deals and enter into international agreements. As far as the EU is concerned, it embraces the principle of subsidiarity, and individual states participate in decision-making.

Conclusion

Until comparatively recently, most social policy courses were predominantly concerned with *state* welfare. The worldwide reassessment of the role of the state has meant that more attention is now given to the part played by families, voluntary agencies and commercial enterprises in welfare provision, and this is reflected in the next three chapters. The state, however, remains a major concern in social policy. Although the state's role as a direct provider of welfare may have diminished, its role in policy-making, planning, regulation and finance means that it determines the direction of policy and it fundamentally influences the scale and mode of provision. The environment in which the other sectors operate is an environment created and sustained primarily, though not exclusively, by the state.

Guide to further reading

A good introductory book on the state is J. Schwartzmantel *The State in Contemporary Society: An Introduction* (Hemel Hempstead: Harvester Wheatsheaf, 1994), which examines and evaluates different theories of the state. N. Charles *Feminism, the State and Social Policy* (Basingstoke: Macmillan Press, 2000) also reviews theories of the state, but the value of the book is in its distinctly feminist perspective. Chapter 2 of my own book, N. Johnson *Mixed Economies of Welfare: A Comparative Perspective* (Hemel Hempstead: Prentice Hall, 1999), looks in rather more detail at most of the issues raised in this chapter. There are several books dealing with social policy from 1945 to the present day. N. Timmins *The Five Giants: A Biography of the Welfare State* (London: Fontana, 1996), is admirably clear and readable, dealing with both personalities and policies. It is particularly strong on the Beveridge Report and its continuing relevance. The best book on governance and policy networks is R.A.W. Rhodes *Understanding Governance: Policy Networks, Governance, Reflexivity and Accountability* (Buckingham: Open University Press, 1997). There are two interesting books dealing with the management of public services: J. Clarke and J. Newman *The Managerial State* (London: Sage, 1997) and S. Horton and D. Farnham (eds) *Public Management in Britain* (Basingstoke: Macmillan Press, 1999). A good example of a comparative approach is M. Hill *Social Policy: A Comparative Analysis* (Hemel Hempstead: Prentice Hall/Harvester Wheatsheaf, 1996). There is a rapidly growing literature on globalization. A noteworthy example is: W. Hutton and A. Giddens (eds) *On the Edge: Living With Global Capitalism* (London: Jonathan Cape, 2000).

Students might find it useful to consult the various websites detailed in chapters V.4, V.5 and V.6.

III.2
Private Welfare

Edward Brunsdon

For centuries private welfare has been a feature of the mixed economy of care in the UK. While its magnitude and scope have fluctuated, it has been and remains an important element of provision in health, housing, social security, education and social care. In spite of this, however, it has until recently received scant attention from social policy analysts.

This oversight can be explained by the confluence of two key factors: the academic interests of policy analysts and the politics of the post-war period. As discussed in chapter I.1, social policy developed primarily under the guidance of Fabian socialist academics (such as Tawney, Marshall, Titmuss and Townsend) whose main focus was state welfare. Although often critical of provision for particular client groups, in general terms they sought to justify or defend the existence of state-produced, state-delivered, provision as a politically and morally superior way of organizing welfare.

In these same post-war decades, successive Labour and Conservative governments operated with broadly similar Keynesian strategies for managing the economy, which included an acceptance of state welfare as the major means of providing accessible services for all the population. Together with the discipline's own concerns, this political agenda pushed private welfare to the periphery. For the majority of academics and politicians there was little interest in its functioning and development. When analysts did address it, it was primarily as a negative point of reference in comparisons with state provision.

All this changed in the 1980s and early 1990s. Political interest emerged as successive Conservative governments drew up welfare agendas in which more efficient and effective services were sought through the development of welfare markets. Private provision grew as these governments:

- cut services (e.g. free eye checks and free dental examinations for adults);
- reduced subsidies (e.g. for prescriptions and council housing);
- offered financial inducements to encourage people to purchase welfare services and benefits (as in the case of personal pensions, medical insurance and council houses);
- transferred responsibility for a range of services from the state to employers (e.g. short-term sickness and maternity benefits); and, in the early 1990s;
- directed local authorities to spend 85 per cent of their community care budgets on the purchase of non-statutory services.

New Labour extended the opportunities for commercial providers when it came to office in 1997. Sharing the concern of its Conservative predecessors about the potential costs of an ageing population, it advocated 'self-provisioning' against life cycle contingencies through tax-discounted individual savings accounts (ISAs) and a revamped pensions system. The new government also encouraged local authorities to increase the use of voluntary and commercial providers in the delivery of social care services. It enhanced commercial provision in nursery education; proposed closer liaison between state and commercial schools providers and, by 2000, was supporting the NHS purchase of elective surgical procedures and theatre space in UK and international private hospitals as a way of reducing waiting lists.

It was primarily through such government-led initiatives that private welfare expanded rapidly in the last two decades of the twentieth century. People were made more aware of the need for self-provisioning and businesses responded accordingly. A range of new and existing organizations, including banks and high street chain stores, developed strategies and business arms to meet these product and service needs.

The response to these developments from social policy analysts was slow and focused initially on the nature and impact of privatization (discussed in chapter III.1). By the beginning of the new millenium, however, their remit had widened. Research had been undertaken on why people chose to purchase private welfare. There were detailed analyses of specific services such as health and long-term care as well as more general surveys of commercial and occupational welfare both in the UK and elsewhere.

This awakening of interest is important. Its significance however does not simply rest with the investigation of a previously under-researched area. It also resides in the fact that without an understanding of the funding, operations and services of private welfare organizations, it is difficult to have either a clear conception of past welfare arrangements or a comprehensive picture of the welfare mix engineered over the past two decades. A first stage in that understanding is a consideration of the general nature of private welfare and the issues it generates. The rest of this chapter is devoted to these tasks.

Private Welfare Markets: The Key Constituents

Private welfare is best understood as *a range of markets trading in welfare products and services* in diverse institutional conditions. These markets are of two main types:

1. those trading in direct service and product provision (e.g. childcare, schooling, further and higher education, long-term care, hospital provision, community health, dental and eye care and housing); and
2. those trading in financial products (e.g. mortgages, pensions, health and social care insurances and education plans).

The suppliers to the financial products markets are commercial carriers that are either provident associations or proprietary businesses. Provident associations are organizations (such as Western Provident Association and British United Provident Association – BUPA) that are limited by guarantee and do not distribute profits. They are exempt from corporation tax and their surpluses over costs become part of the companies' reserves. In contrast, proprietary businesses (such as Legal & General Assurance, Private Patients' Plan (PPP) Healthcare and Norwich Union) can distribute profits to owners or shareholders and are subject to corporation tax. They, however, find it much easier than the provident associations to raise equity and attract external investment. Both types of supplier sell directly to the public but can also use intermediaries such as brokers or link with high street retailers and banks to sell their products.

Few organizations operate in both the direct service and financial products markets (BUPA is an exception, selling both private medical insurance and health care services). For the most part, the markets have different mixes of suppliers. Whereas insurance companies and banks supply welfare finance, a more disparate group of suppliers offer direct services. These range from multi-nationals and national companies (as in the housing and health care markets), small businesses (as in the long-term care and education markets) and single traders (as in domiciliary and childcare). It can also extend to voluntary and statutory agencies competing for custom with their commercial counterparts.

Purchasers within each of these markets are either:

- individuals buying financial products and health or care services for their own present or future consumption; or
- 'proxy' buyers (or 'principal agents') purchasing on behalf of present or future 'end-users'.

Traditionally, this second grouping comprised of individuals buying for their parents, parents purchasing for their children, companies buying for their employees, and trade unions and professional associations buying for their members. Government legislation in the early 1990s (notably the NHS and Community Care Act 1990) and subsequent strategy statements added NHS trusts and local authorities purchasing services for different user groups from non-statutory providers. The market for health screening services is an illustration of the diversity of purchaser that can occur. Here companies, trade unions, professional associations and individuals are among those buying services from proprietary and provident health care providers and NHS trusts.

Both buyers and suppliers enter these markets to make gains from their trading. Commercial suppliers, whether individuals or multinational companies, *typically* seek financial gains. Indeed, this has led some policy analysts to characterize private welfare as the 'for profit sector'. Such a representation, however, is both inflexible and misleading. To begin with it cannot be assumed that commercial suppliers always seek profits in the market place. There may well be occasions when, with sufficient financial reserves, they are prepared to trade at a loss in order, say, to capture or secure a section of the market. Again, statutory and voluntary agencies might also seek 'profits' in order to invest in the future development of the services they sell – think here of NHS 'pay beds' and the voluntary agencies providing residential psychiatric care for local health and social care authorities. A further, more conceptual, argument is that the notion 'for profit' is simply a supply-side view of private welfare. It ignores other important market characteristics such as their many institutional features as well as the buyers and the various gains they might anticipate from trading.

Buyers and proxy buyers have numerous different grounds for purchasing. For instance, in buying personal pensions people are aiming to develop their disposable income in retirement. In buying private schooling, parents typically seek to enhance their children's life chances. Employers – as the main 'proxy buyer' – have tended to purchase health insurance and health and social care services to attract, retain or motivate staff although they have also used such purchases to reduce absenteeism and, more generally, to maintain employee discipline. Underwriting these very varied calculations, however, is the anticipation of making gains (financial or otherwise) and getting a return on their financial 'investments'.

Beyond the sellers and buyers and their calculations are the more general institutional market constituents of size, structure, degrees of competition, modes of regulation and forms of state intervention. These are best construed as *processes* rather than static features, and processes that can interact in different ways in the socio-economic organization of different markets. They variously shape and are shaped by trading and have the potential to operate as both precursors and products of the activity. As such, they are central to understanding the ways in which markets operate and change – a point illustrated in the following case study of the health insurance market.

The Health Insurance Market: A Case Study

This market is one in which banks, building societies and insurance companies compete to supply a range of insurance products to corporate and individual purchasers. The products are then employed to meet the full (or partial) cost of diagnosis and treatment in private hospitals, clinics or NHS pay beds, or to compensate for the loss of income resulting from illness and disability.

The products traded

The products traded in health insurance are varied and inherently complex in both medical and insurance terms. It is possible, however, to identify a number of key commodities:

- *Private medical insurance (PMI)* pays for care in private hospitals or NHS pay-bed units should the policy-holder suffer from one or more of a specified list of medical conditions. Although typically limited to elective surgery, some policies also cover outpatient treatment and home nursing. It is by far the most popular form of private health insurance among both corporate and individual purchasers.
- *Permanent health insurance (PHI)* is an income replacement plan designed to replace some or all of the income lost by an individual who is unable to work due to sickness or disability.
- *Critical illness insurance (CII)* provides a lump sum payment in the event of a serious illness such as a heart attack, a stroke or cancer (the illnesses covered vary).
- *Long-term care insurance (LTCI)* is designed to pay for long-term domiciliary or institutional care through either a fixed lump sum or annual payments. LTCI is a recent initiative and currently has a low take-up but may well expand, particularly in the light of the ageing population and the on-going debate about ways of funding long-term care.
- *Dental Plans* provide for the expenses of private dental treatment. They are offered either as independent products or as part of a composite PMI package. Cutbacks in NHS adult dental care have made these increasingly popular.

Market size

Measured in terms of subscriber numbers, the health insurance market grew from 1.3 million subscriptions (covering 2.8 million people) in 1979 to 3.5 million subscriptions (covering 6.4 million people) by 2000 (Laing, 2000). Within the two decades, the last significant period of strong growth was 1987 to 1990 when subscription levels increased by 25 per cent. Industry analysts suggest that the primary driver in this period was increased demand from corporate businesses buying insurance cover for their employees, itself the product of a buoyant economy and expanding company profits. Growth in the 1990s was much flatter with the total subscriber base rising by just 500,000 between 1990 and 1999. In the early 1990s this was attributed to the economic recession of that time combined with a sharp rise in insurance premiums. The economic recovery that began in 1994 and the subsequent benign conditions (high employment levels, low inflation and GDP growth) did not however stimulate demand at rates equivalent to those of the late 1980s or in equal measure amongst the different types of buyer. Whilst corporate business did increase, the continued rise in premium costs led to an eventual decline in the number of individual subscribers. In spite of such disparities between the different types of buyer, the market did continue its upward growth in subscription income into the new millenium and was valued in 2000 at £2.3 billion (Laing, 2000).

Competition and market composition

The market saw major changes in composition and competition during this time period. Throughout the 1980s, provident associations were dominant collectively earning 92 per cent of subscription income in 1989 with their leading player – BUPA – holding some 52 per cent. All this was to change in the 1990s with the market entrance of a number of small proprietaries and two key general insurers – Norwich Union and Guardian Royal Exchange (GRE) – both seeking to extend into a potentially lucrative area. Norwich Union came to the market in 1991 with the declared aim of creating new health insurance business. Its rapid growth, to third largest operator, however, was largely gained at the expense of other insurers – particularly that of the provident associations. GRE entered the market through the takeover of Orion Healthcare in 1994. The new company – Guardian Healthcare – also enjoyed sustained growth, again by drawing business away from the providents. Their joint impact along with the smaller companies was to increase the proprietaries' market share to 22 per cent by 1997. By 1999, their share had risen to 50 per cent, a further increase that was largely the result of the second largest provident operator PPP Healthcare (with 28 per cent of subscription income) crossing the divide to become a proprietary provider in 1997. Its business was acquired by GRE in 1998 with the parent company transferring its own health care insurance to the PPP Healthcare brand. In 1999, GRE was itself taken over by the French-based composite insurer AXA which also merged its pre-existing health insurance into PPP Healthcare at the beginning of 2000.

At that time, there were 14 proprietary companies and eight provident associations selling private health insurance with PPP (29 per cent market share) and BUPA (by then reduced to 40 per cent) the main market players. The flat market is likely to lead to increased competitiveness between the two in the ensuing decade and their cost-containment initiatives will lead to additional pressure on other providers and the strong possibility of further supply consolidation. The threat of new entrants, at least under current market conditions, has diminished. For the future, much will depend on the state of the economy and the prevailing political climate, as well as corporate and individual buyer calculations.

The purchasers

Given that the National Health Service offers medical care free at the point of consumption, it is clear that buyers of private health care cover must see a difference between NHS services and those of private medical establishments. Research into the individual purchase of private health care suggests that people calculate in terms of the perceived quality of medical care and 'hotel' facilities, the individualized nature of care, the speed of access to services and the privacy provided. Employers, the main 'proxy' buyer, purchase some 60 per cent of health insurance subscriptions and do so primarily as a means of attracting, retaining and motivating key staff. Market research regularly suggests that among large companies private [health] insurance ranks along with pensions and company cars as a highly valued employee benefit.

Regulation and government intervention

Until the mid-1990s, health insurance providers operated under a liberal regulatory regime subject only to the same sales and insolvency requirements as other insurers. The general ethos was one of self-regulation by the industry, an approach to finance upheld by the neo-liberal policies of the Thatcher and Major administrations. Within such parameters, there was some attempt at input and process regulation (i.e. who supplied and their sales practices), there was much less concern with regulating output. This was to change however in the latter half of the decade following a number of critical reports from consumer groups and government bodies. The industry became subject to more stringent controls over what was sold and how it was sold. Under pressure from the health insurance providers, these additional controls initially took the form of more rigorous self-regulation but, under Labour's Financial Services and Markets Act 2000, they are set to give way in 2004 to a more direct regulatory framework operated by the Financial Services Authority.

Alongside this tightening regulatory framework, Labour also intervened to change the fiscal environment in which the market operated. It abolished tax relief on health insurance for the over-60s (introduced by its Conservative predecessors), increased the rate of Insurance Premium Tax and closed the loophole whereby health insurance policies written in a long-term fund had escaped the tax altogether. In addition it extended employers' national insurance contributions to cover health insurance and other 'benefits in kind'. Whilst these measures clearly contributed to harsher trading conditions at the beginning of the new century, long-term change is more likely to be shaped by Labour's overall health policy and the extent to which projected increases in public spending increase the efficiency and effectiveness of NHS provision.

Private Welfare in a Changing Welfare Mix: Issues and Implications

The different influences on health insurance can also be seen in other markets, many of which offer expanding opportunities for commercial provision. Policy statements and planned initiatives from the current Labour administration suggest that private welfare is set to feature more prominently in the welfare mix of the future and in ways that are unlikely to be undermined by a government of a different political hue. In

the areas of private education and hospital care, for instance, Labour has rejected its longstanding hostility in favour of 'partnership' arrangements embodied in a series of 'concordats'. Private hospitals in particular are seen as having a continuing role in easing pressures on the NHS and Labour is also promoting private provision of intermediate care. Its social care policies are predicated on an expanding 'mixed economy', as are those for early-years and post-compulsory education. Its vision for social security also rests on increased individual self-provisioning both for retirement and other life-cycle contingencies. To secure the necessary consumer confidence for these developments, it is investing heavily in the regulation of both the direct and financial products markets.

The increasing significance of private welfare in both funding and delivery poses a number of questions for policy analysts. Some of these are derived from the discipline's Fabian socialist beginnings, others stem from the organization of private welfare itself. In the former grouping are concerns emanating from the Fabian conceptions of social justice and universalism (and therein issues about equality and equity). Can, for instance, the development of private welfare be justified? Will private provision contribute to the continuance or will it undermine the welfare state? More specifically, will it lead to growing inequities in the finance and consumption of welfare services? Will those who can afford private welfare opt out of the state system? Does private welfare complement the state welfare system or does it provide an alternative and conflicting basis? Is the needs-led system subjugated by issues of affordability?

What should be clear from this chapter is that any attempt to respond to such questions must involve the initial disaggregation of private welfare into different markets (and a comparable disaggregation of state funding and provision for different services). Neither private welfare nor state welfare are homogeneous entities; such questions therefore demand both an appreciation of the diverse nature of services and markets and the recognition that the questions *may* generate different responses in different markets for different products and services. As the case study of the health insurance market indicates, welfare markets are complex. They differ in size, product, the nature and range of purchasers and suppliers, levels of competition, and forms of regulation and government intervention. They also change in different ways and at different rates. It is this, above all else, that signifies the intricacy of their formation. Any analysis of private welfare must therefore address each market independently while recognizing that they are part of a wider realm and an ever-changing mix of welfare production and consumption.

The second cluster of issues concern private welfare *per se*. One of the more general questions here relates to the explanation of welfare market changes. For example, how can the uneven development of welfare markets be explained? How much is it due to shifts in government policies, as against the changing calculations of provider organizations and both proxy buyers and end-users? Is there consumer pressure for new or different services and

benefits and how much of this is stimulated by a perceived decline in statutory provision? There are also issues that should be raised concerning the operation of welfare markets. In a number of observers' eyes, markets are extremely weak at self-regulating and have very little tendency to stability (other than through oligopolistic and monopolistic arrangements). Given this, questions can be asked about *who* is to regulate the markets, *how* are they to be regulated, and the effectiveness of the approaches adopted. This in turn involves complex assessments of the trade-off between compliance costs and consumer protection.

Again, what if markets fail? Where there is no statutory responsibility, who is going to protect the consumers and how? Will the government subsidize private welfare in order to limit damaging outcomes, require in-built compensation systems, devolve financial responsibilities to local health and social care authorities, or rely on increased consumer education and media coverage to ensure individuals make informed choices (and pay the price for their 'mistakes')? It is these clusters of concerns that students are likely to encounter in their studies of private welfare in the future.

Guide to further reading

The following provide complementary analyses of the issues raised in this chapter:

Brunsdon, E. and May, M., 2002. 'Evaluating New Labour's approach to independent welfare provision' in M. Powell (ed.), *Evaluating New Labour's Welfare Reforms*. Bristol: Policy Press.

Johnson, N. (ed.), 1995. *Private Markets in Health and Welfare: An International Perspective*. Oxford/Providence, RI: Berg.

Laing W., 2000. *Laing's Healthcare Market Review 2000–2001*. London: Laing & Buisson.

May, M. and Brunsdon, E., 1994. 'Workplace care in the mixed economy of welfare' in R. Page and J. Baldock (eds), *Social Policy Review 6*. Canterbury: Social Policy Association.

May, M. and Brunsdon, E., 1999. 'Commercial and occupational welfare' in R.M. Page and R. Silburn (eds), *British Social Welfare in the Twentieth Century*. Basingstoke: Macmillan Press.

III.3
The Voluntary Sector

Nicholas Deakin

Over the past decade, there has been a marked revival of interest in the voluntary sector in the UK, what it is, what it does and its relationship with other sectors – the state, the market and the world of informal care. As a result of this renewed interest there has been substantial debate about:

- the *definition* of the voluntary sector and its activities;
- the *functions* with which it should be entrusted;
- the *terms* on which it should engage with the other sectors, especially the state sector.

The progress of this debate can be traced through a series of reports and inquiries on the role of the sector. These extend from the Wolfenden Report of 1978 to the inquiries made by the Labour Party in the 1990s. These in turn led to the negotiations that produced the signing of compacts between the voluntary sectors in England and Scotland and the government in 1998; now, further inquiries are being undertaken by central government's Performance and Innovation Unit (PIU) (2001/2).

In the course of these discussions the politicians have frequently 'rediscovered' the sector and its potential. There have been many references by successive ministers to the unique qualities of the sector and the various roles that it might perform in future. Public consciousness of the significance of voluntary action has also been greatly heightened through the promotion of a number of fund-raising events designed to raise money for charities operating in the Third World and the UK, such as telethons, concerts, sponsored marathons and 'red nose' days.

Finally, the introduction of the National Lottery in 1995, with its emphasis on raising funds for 'good causes', has greatly enhanced the profile of the sector but also exposed its activities to closer public scrutiny through the media.

Background

Until recently, there was a widespread view that the leading role of the voluntary sector in the provision of social welfare had come to an end with the establishment of the welfare state at the end of the Second World War. 'Charity' and 'philanthropy', terms which acquired strong negative associations for many of those at the receiving end of voluntary provision in the Victorian period, could be relegated to the history books, along with the Poor Law that the welfare state displaced.

In fact, the position is more complex. After 1945, voluntary bodies continued to perform a wide variety of functions. Several senior figures in the Labour government of 1945–51 (for example the prime minister Clement Attlee, and Herbert Morrison) were strong supporters of voluntary action. Nevertheless, voluntary organizations were seen very much as junior partners in the new structure. As we saw in chapters I.4 and III.1, these reforms transferred and consolidated many functions in health, education and social services under state control.

The steady expansion of the role of the state under both Labour and Conservative governments eventually brought with it disillusionment about the quality and responsiveness of services provided by state bureaucracies (see chapter III.5). New developments on the broader scene – the rise of the women's movement, the impact of immigration from the 'New Commonwealth', a revived interest in community development – began to change the character and composition of the voluntary sector.

During the 1960s and 1970s new organizations appeared (and existing ones were revitalized), concerned with issues like:

- Third World poverty;
- environmental questions;
- local community action;
- provision for excluded groups.

Bodies like MIND, Mencap, Greenpeace, Shelter and the Child Poverty Action Group (CPAG) were founded or refounded during this period.

These changes in the voluntary sector also generated a new style of operation. This meant: more open and democratic internal management; pressure groups using up-to-date campaigning techniques; concern for rights of service users and their involvement as partners. Such developments helped to produce what is sometimes called the *new voluntary sector*. Outside the field of welfare, voluntary action has continued to be the main stay of a whole range of activities: for example, in sports and recreation, the arts and education.

Over the post-Second World War period as a whole, these developments have helped to produce a voluntary sector which is diverse in its range of activities, complex in its internal relations and constantly evolving, both internally and in its relations with users and other providers of welfare.

The Present State of the Voluntary Sector

Definitions

The term 'voluntary sector', which is currently the standard term in general use, is generally not much liked. It is of comparatively recent origin (twenty years) and not employed outside the UK. It tends to be used very loosely. The task of definition is usually approached negatively: thus, the 'sector' covers formally constituted organizations, managed by unpaid committees, that are not part of the state, the market or the informal world of spontaneous or unstructured action (which is discussed in chapter III.4). The term includes organizations with paid staff; they can trade, but not distribute profits. Their objectives are generally taken as being to enhance public benefit. The situation is further complicated by the simultaneous employment of three other terms, which overlap with the notion of a 'voluntary sector' and which are often used in the same context, sometimes even jointly, to describe similar activities. Thus it is becoming common in government to refer to a 'voluntary and community sector'. The three terms are *charities, community sector* and *volunteers*.

Charities

The term *charity* has deep roots in English history. The four heads of charity were defined in legislation in 1601: religion, education, the relief of poverty and other purposes beneficial to the whole community. This definition has evolved since then through case law; the terms on which charities operate were most recently reformed by the Charities Act of 1993. Charitable status confers benefits (for example, tax reliefs); it also imposes strict obligations on the trustees of charities.

Charities are regulated by a non-ministerial department, the Charity Commission. The definition of charities encompasses a substantial number of bodies (mostly in the education sector, like the 'public' schools) not customarily thought of as operating in the general public interest, and excludes many that are. The legislation only applies to England and Wales: Scots law is different and the Charity Commission's writ does not run there. A recent report prepared for the Scottish Executive suggests that a new regulatory body, Charity-Scotland, should be set up there. Nevertheless, the term 'charities' is frequently employed as a description in debates and discussions as if it covered the British voluntary sector as a whole, on similar terms.

Community sector

This term has come into general use to refer to small groups which operate on a local scale and which are not necessarily formally constituted. These can be distinguished from voluntary organizations by their size and informality, as in the case of village hall committees and tenants' associations. The government's increasing interest in these activities has been shown in a number of neighbourhood renewal programmes that have been introduced and by the 'rebranding' of the coordinating unit in the Home Office as the 'Active Communities Unit'.

Volunteers

Much discussion about the voluntary sector is conducted on the assumption that those involved in its operations are volunteers. This is not by any means always the case. Volunteers play a very significant part in the operation of a wide range of bodies, including some statutory agencies; but although the sum total of their efforts is substantial it does not by any means encompass the whole of the sector's activities. However, the distinction is often blurred and politicians, in particular, often appear to have difficulty with the distinction between volunteering (by individuals) and voluntary action (by organizations).

Finally, different terms are employed outside the UK to describe the world of voluntary action. In the United States the preferred term is 'third sector', and this is now also sometimes used in the UK. Elsewhere in Europe the term 'associations' is used; this may be significant in future because of moves to evolve a common legal definition identifying the rights and responsibilities of organizations across the European Union as a whole.

Size of the sector

The best recent estimate of the size of the voluntary and community sectors is between 300,000 and 500,000 organizations (Passey et al., 2002). The Charity Commission maintains a register of charitable bodies; in 2000 there were 185,000 organizations on this register. However, this register only covers England and Wales. General charities benefit from the contribution of over three million unpaid workers; just over half this contribution relates to fundraising, and 750,000 people contribute to the management of organizations through acting as trustees. If the extent of voluntary action is taken to include the informal *community organizations,* one recent study concluded that there are probably around 1.3 million organizations in the UK. *Volunteering* takes place on a very substantial scale in this country. The National Centre for Volunteering (NCVO)'s most recent review of activity (1997) shows that the numbers of those involved in some kind of voluntary activity could be as high as 21 million.

Main areas of activity

The range of activity covered by the voluntary sector is very great. An international study of the sector, conducted from Johns Hopkins University in the USA, found that the UK voluntary sector's main areas of action were to be found in the following 'industries': education, social services, culture and recreation, and development and housing. This pattern contrasts quite sharply with the distribution in other countries examined as part of this study. For example, the health sector in the UK is much smaller, mainly as a result of the dominant role played up to now by the NHS in the UK, and the housing section considerably larger (Kendall and Almond, 1998).

Categories of organization

Another way of distinguishing different parts of the sector is to divide organizations by type (Knight, 1993). They can be split between:

- service providers;
- campaigners;
- 'intermediaries';
- cooperatives and 'mutuals';
- self-help bodies.

Examples of 'service providers' are organizations providing residential care (such as homes for old people); 'campaigners' include organizations like Greenpeace and Friends of the Earth; 'intermediaries' are organizations which exist to provide services for other bodies in the sector, such as the NCVO; 'self-help bodies' consist of groups of people in similar situations who come together to help each other – the Spastics Society (now Scope) started in this way.

The resourcing of the voluntary sector

The resources which support the voluntary sector come mainly from the following sources:

- individual giving;
- grants from charitable trusts and foundations;
- donations from the corporate sector;
- support from the state (central and local);
- income generated by voluntary organizations themselves (through investments, trading, charity shops).

In the last financial year for which we have full data (2000–1), the total gross income of the sector was estimated by the NCVO as being £15.6 billion. One third of this income is concentrated in the 150 or so largest organizations. This total represents an increase of almost one third over the decade of the 1990s. But expenditure has also risen and is now estimated to be around £15 billion. Alongside these financial resources, we also need to take into account gifts in kind, including time, in the form of volunteer labour. Estimates have valued this contribution at over £7 billion (Passey et al., 2002).

The pattern of individual giving has not changed very much over the past decade, despite the stimulus of the new types of fund-raising events referred to earlier and the introduction of new means of giving, such as direct deduction from payrolls, 'affinity cards' which automatically assign a small proportion of sums spent to a specific charity and the 'CAFcard', which facilitates tax-efficient individual giving to charities. More recently, additional measures to provide tax relief on donations were introduced in 2000 by the Chancellor, Gordon Brown as part of the Labour government's attempt to promote a 'giving culture'. Despite these efforts, the level of individual donations per capita remains quite low compared with some other countries, notably the USA (Wright, 2001). The proportion of those giving is static at just over two-thirds of the population and the average monthly donation is only just over £10 (CAFD/NCVO, 2001) and, as yet, the government's attempts to raise the level of donations through an officially sponsored giving campaign have not shown signs of substantial success.

State funding, on the other hand, has expanded substantially. Both local and central government fund activities by the voluntary sector: the Home Office, the government department principally concerned, provides substantial block grants for a number of key national organizations through its Active Communities Unit. Other government departments support bodies which operate within their departmental area of interest. Most local authorities have a long tradition of supporting their own local voluntary bodies, both by grants to specific organizations to perform particular tasks and by providing support for local coordinating bodies – known as Councils of Voluntary Service (CVSs), or Rural Community Councils (RCCs) in country areas. Latterly, state funding has increasingly come to be provided on different terms, not in the form of grants but through contracts. This development and the reasons for it are explored below.

A major new source of funding for the sector in the 1990s has been the National Lottery. After the shares of the profits assigned to the operators (Camelot) and taken by the Treasury are deducted the Lottery has generated substantial additional income which is distributed by five appointed boards, covering arts, sports, heritage, the millennium and 'charities'. Voluntary organizations have benefited from grants made by all these boards; but the main source of funding has been the National Lottery Charities Board (NLCB), now known as the Community Fund.

A breakdown of the funding from different sources is shown in table III.3.1. developments over the recent past suggest that the share of income generated from sale of goods and services is likely to increase, while the proportion raised through grants and donations is on a downward path (Passey et al., 2002). One striking feature of the UK scene is the very low level of corporate donation, when compared with the United States.

Commentary

The complex problems of defining the voluntary sector and the wide range of activities that it encompasses make it difficult to provide a realistic estimate of the scope of voluntary activity in this society and its impact. However, the importance of voluntary action can be seen in two contrasting ways. First, the growth of activity and increased political visibility of the sector can be emphasized. Attention can be drawn to such factors as:

- the amount of employment generated in the sector;
- the extent of contribution of additional resources;
- the size of membership of voluntary organizations;
- new areas of activity pioneered and an open and 'user-friendly' approach.

The latest statistics from the government's Labour Force Survey indicates that the numbers employed in voluntary sector organizations of all kind is over half a million and that this represents over 2 per centof the national workforce. The economic contribution to GDP is estimated to be £4.8bn, without taking into account any costing of voluntary effort (NCVO *Almanac*, 2000). Membership of large organizations

Table III.3.1   Percentage of voluntary sector funding received from different sources

Source	Percentage
General public	35
Other charities	10
Corporate sector	5
State (central and local)	29
Internally generated	22

Source: adapted from NCVO *Voluntary Sector Almanac* (2000).

such as the National Trust now vastly out-numbers that of the political parties, and many important areas of new activity, such as action on the environment, the hospice movement or provision for those with HIV/AIDS, have been developed within the voluntary sector. In addition, claims are made for the significance of voluntary action in underpinning the health of civil society through participation in activities that fall between state and market; and re-inforcing democracy by encouraging 'active citizenship'.

However, it is important to be wary of indiscriminate 'boosterism'. Analysts point to such problematic issues as:

- the uneven spread of voluntary act-ivity, both geographically and in class terms;
- the difficulty of focusing voluntary ac-tion (diversity precludes a 'master plan' and their concern with their independ-ence makes organizations wary of col-laboration – hence there is much duplication);
- the problems associated with relying on voluntary action to support minority or unpopular causes.

Some commentators also argue that many of the functions that voluntary organizations are now carrying out can be and are discharged with equal efficiency in the market or even by the state; and many important innovations in policy and prac-tice are not the outcome of voluntary sec-tor initiatives. Furthermore, where voluntary organizations do discharge their tasks efficiently and effectively, they often only do so (it is suggested) by ceasing to operate as traditional voluntary bodies and imitating the style and practice of either statutory bodies or commercial organiza-tions.

Relations with the State

The range of activities for which the state is responsible has begun to diminish – a proc-ess that began in the middle 1970s and is still continuing. As a result, the boundaries between statutory and voluntary action have shifted and territory once conceded by voluntary organizations is being repos-sessed. In some ways, this process can be read as a straightforward reversal of past trends; but in other respects the relation-ship between the two sectors is taking new forms and has a different dynamic. Either way, it is important to set events in the vol-untary sector in the context of the wider changes involving the state and the mar-ket, considered in chapters III.1 and III.2. The character of the tasks which voluntary organizations are now being expected to take on derive at least in part from the per-ception outside the sector of its main strengths. Those most often cited include:

- innovation;
- flexibility;
- lack of bureaucracy.

The voluntary sector is also often seen as possessing particularly important sets of specialist skills and experience. One key example of this is in the personal social services. Here, there has been movement over the course of the period from the 1980s towards a 'mixed economy of wel-fare', in which the local authorities that had previously taken responsibility for all aspects of these services were expected to withdraw to an 'enabling' role. (Similar de-velopments have taken place in other serv-ices discussed elsewhere in this book.) The voluntary organizations and for profit agencies which are increasingly expected to perform the function of service deliv-ery do so on the basis of contracts entered into with local authorities. The resulting set of arrangements have become gener-ally known as the 'contract culture', in which the two parties to the contract are the customer (the authority) and the con-tractor (the agency).

Involvement in the contract culture has been a mixed blessing for voluntary organi-zations. On the positive side, contracts of-ten provide greater security than the previous pattern of annual grants, which were often not renewed until near (or even after) their date of expiry. Contracts also specify the nature of the task that has to be performed and set up explicit standards by which performance can be judged; this is, potentially at least, helpful to the contracting agency. On the other side, contracting often involves much detailed paper work and requires production of large quantities of information in a form prescribed by the customer. Perhaps more importantly, specifying the nature of the work and ways in which it is to be carried out may sometimes appear to threaten the contracting agency's independence or even compromise its values.

The election of a Labour government in 1997 opened a new phase in relations between the state and service providing voluntary bodies – the new model of relationships was generally referred to as 'partnership'. These arrangements, at both local and national level, cover a wide variety of activities and offer voluntary bodies the opportunity of being involved in the design of policies as well as their execution. Although the introduction of partnerships was generally welcomed, critics have highlighted the risks of too close engagement and the development of 'partnership fatigue' as demands for partnership have intensified.

All these concerns have been crystallized by the introduction of compacts between the government and the voluntary sector, referred to at the beginning of this essay. Such compacts now exist in all the countries of the United Kingdom and in many local authority areas. They seek to lay down the terms on which the relationship between the authorities and the sector should be conducted: the terms on which funding should be provided and the rights and responsibilities of both parties, including the acceptance of the right for voluntary and community groups to campaign. Critics have argued that by entering into such relationships voluntary organizations have curtailed their independence and limited their effectiveness as advocates and their capacity to act spontaneously. Advocates point to the importance of security over the longer term in funding arrangements; the opportunity to participate in policy making and the right of review built into the compact structure (Plowden et al., 2001).

These developments have also thrown a spotlight on the issue of the management and the efficiency of voluntary organizations in an environment in which they have to compete for contracts with bodies from other sectors. Some of the important issues arising in this area are shown in box III.3.1: they have been systematically addressed by the Quality Standards Task Force set up by the NCVO. This checklist illustrates the competing pressures under which voluntary bodies now have to work. It is important that the quality of what is being provided by the organizations should not be compromised; but there is also a pressing issue of how to maintain the distinctive character of the voluntary sector.

A further issue is the question of the advocacy role of voluntary organizations and the part this plays in the democratic culture, locally and nationally. It is important that voluntary bodies should be able to make the case on behalf of their particular group or interest; but funding bodies also have the right to expect that criticism remains within legitimate limits. If it does not, they may come to wonder why they should continue to fund their critics. (The Charity Commission provides helpful guidance to

---

Box III.3.1

Issues in the management and efficiency of voluntary organizations:

- Governance
- The situation of users
- Standards
- Accountability
- Regulation
- Internal management and staff relations

Source: NCVO (1996)

organizations which have charitable status and may be concerned about the implications of 'political' campaigning.) As for democracy, it is reasonable for voluntary organizations to present their activities as an intrinsic part of the democratic process; but if they do so, it is important that they should measure up to democratic standards in their own procedures.

A number of these issues are now being addressed by central government in the review of the regulatory context within which voluntary and community organizations function. It has for some time been commonly asserted that the law of charity is overdue for reform; the Scottish inquiry referred to above and a further investigation by the NCVO both endorsed the view that a stricter test of public benefit was needed in order to justify the privileges associated with charitable status. The inquiry being conducted at the time of writing by the Performance and Innovation Unit (2001/2) reflects the government's desire to provide a regulatory context within which a strong 'civic society' can be constructed (Brown, 2001). This also led the Treasury to undertake, as part of its review of public spending, an examination of the role of voluntary and community organizations in the delivery of services.

Key Issues and Debates

The revival of voluntary action and the growth of interest in what it can or should achieve has set off a continuing debate among academics and politicians. Among the main issues now being discussed are:

- What is the exact nature of the distinctive contribution made by the voluntary sector to civil society as a whole?
- What form of legal framework would be appropriate for such a diverse sector?
- How many of the tasks until recently performed by the state can the voluntary sector takes on without risking forfeiting its independence?
- Is there a limit to the amount of structuring of its contribution that can take place –as for example, through the compacts – without damaging the spontaneity and innovation that should characterize the sector's activities?
- How can the voluntary sector best respond to the pressure for users' rights?
- How can voluntary organizations best contribute towards helping black and ethnic minorities and their own organizations?
- How can the sector equip itself to make an effective contribution to providing services without becoming over-professional?

Many of these questions have not yet been convincingly answered. But the increased attention that the sector is attracting means that it will need to able to demonstrate convincingly its competence and commitment, often in the face of increased scepticism on the part of the media and the general public.

Guide to further reading

The best current account of the sector is J. Kendall and M. Knapp *The Voluntary Sector in the UK* (Manchester: Manchester University Press, 1996). The volumes edited by C. Rochester and M. Harris *Voluntary Organisations and Social Policy in Britain* (Basingstoke: Palgrave, 2001) and B. Knight *Voluntary Action* (London: Centris,1993), are also helpful. The statistical profile of the sector is covered in the *UK Voluntary Sector Almanac* produced every two years by the NCVO (latest edition: A. Passey et al., (eds) 2002). The Community Fund (formerly National Lottery Charities Board) produces regular information about the grants it awards. Useful reviews of funding issues can also be found in the CAFD/NCVO *Charity Tax Review Research Briefing* (2001) and K. Wright *Britain's*

Culture of Giving (London: Centre for Civil Society, 2001). G. Brown *Civic Society in Modern Britain* (London: Smith Institute, 2001) provides a useful starting point for exploring the Labour government's approach to the sector.

Much important comparative information is contained in L. Salaman and S. Anheier *The Emerging Nonprofit Sector* (Baltimore/London: Johns Hopkins Press, 1995) and J. Kendall and S. Almond *The UK Voluntary Sector in Comparative Perspective: Exceptional Transformation and Growth* (Kent: PSSRU, 1998). Future policy for the sector is examined in the review commissioned by NCVO of developments in the five years since their report *Meeting the Challenge of Change* was published: W. Plowden, J. P. Kearney, A. P. Williamson, E. Burt, J. Taylor, C. Green and M.Drakeford. NCVO *Next steps in Voluntary Action* (London: NCVO/CCS, 2001) sets out developments in all the countries of the United Kingdom.

For up-to-date coverage of developments in the sector the following web sites are particularly useful: cafonline.org.uk and ncvo-vol.org.uk.

III.4
Informal Welfare

Clare Ungerson

Defining Terms

The term 'informal sector' has become common currency in social policy discussion only over the past two to three decades. The phrase is used to describe an important source of services for people with dependencies. It is often used in conjunction with the idea of 'welfare mix' or the 'mixed economy of welfare': this is taken to mean the combined sources of the state, the voluntary sector, the private for-profit sector and the 'informal sector', all of which provide services for people with dependencies living in their own homes, or, as it is often put, in 'the community'. The term 'informal sector' is best understood in contrast to the 'formal sector'. The *formal sector* consists of paid professionals and para-professionals, such as social workers, care managers, district nurses and home carers. Their task is to assess people's needs, using professional and resource-driven criteria, and then provide those people directly with services, or else ensure that they are getting what they 'need' from some other source, such as the private, voluntary or informal sectors. (This formal sector is usually called the 'personal social services', which are part of the state sector, but it can also include the voluntary and private for-profit sectors.)

In contrast, the *informal sector* is the term used to describe the essentially unpaid provision of services to people with dependencies living in the 'community'. These services are provided by family (or kin), friends and neighbours. Note that the lack of pay could, in theory, mean that volunteers are included in the informal sector, because they also provide services for free. But the term does *not* normally include volunteers, and this is because the other central feature of the informal sector is that the people who provide the services normally have had a relationship of some kind with the person they are providing services for. It is precisely because of this relationship that they are willing to look after the dependent person. Thus members of the same family may feel they want to look after someone because they love him or her, or they feel that being part of the same family means they are subject to a particular set of moral obligations to care for him or her. Similarly, friends and neighbours may feel they should look after someone because they are fond of him or her, or in return for kindnesses and services that were once provided by the person who needs them now. In short, the informal sector is based on motivation to provide services based on non-monetary 'ties that bind', such as love, duty, shared biography and reciprocity (Finch, 1989).

Claiming and Naming the Informal Sector

The 'informal sector' has only been named as such since the 1970s. Previously, this sector of service provision was widely referred to as 'the family' or 'the community', without any attempt, by policy-makers or policy analysts, to unwrap the constituent parts of those families or communities that provide care, let alone to begin to understand why some people care and others do not. The claiming and naming of the informal sector arose out of 'second wave feminism' – that is, the feminism of the late 1960s and early 1970s – which took as one of its central features the problematization of women's position in the home, and critiqued women's expected role as housewives and servicers of their men and their children (see chapter II.9). It was a short step from the feminist analysis of housework and other forms of domestic labour to an analysis of what feminist policy analysts called 'caring'. Much of the early feminist work on 'care' criticized the British government for encouraging the closure of residential institutions without having regard to who would actually provide the care in the 'community'. As the authors of a classic early article put it: 'Care in the community equals care by the family equals care by women' (Finch and Groves, 1980).

This view of the sexed and gendered assumptions built into policies for community care, and the claiming of what increasingly came to be called 'informal care' as women's work, became very powerful in the 1980s. Not only did it generate feminist-led analysis of the sexism embedded in government policies (Finch and Groves, 1983) and a considerable literature on the sociology of informal care (Ungerson, 1987; Lewis and Meredith, 1988; Qureshi and Walker, 1989), but it also formed the basis for a politics of community care and the development of various carers' lobbies, including, and most particularly, the Carers National Association – now renamed Carers UK. Feminists argued that community care and care by families were intrinsically exploitative of women. Janet Finch, arguing from an essentially pessimistic perspective about the likelihood of men entering informal care, argued that the only

way out was to reintroduce a policy of institutional care, while Gillian Dalley (1988), arguing from a more optimistic perspective and within a utopian tradition, argued that family care should be rejected in favour of new forms of collective and communal care based on libertarian and reciprocal principles.

The Convincing of Government and the Generation of National Research

Policy-makers increasingly listened to these critiques, and, at the same time, became more and more concerned that, faced with an ageing population and with the majority of women of working age active in the labour market, they would find that the informal sector was simply no longer able to cope with the demands for care. Policy documents began to refer to the need to provide social service support for carers. Government-funded research was also influential. In 1985, and again in 1990 and 1995, the government annual sample survey of British households (the General Household Survey) decided to count the number of carers nationwide, to find out who they were, what they did and how many hours a week they spent caring. When the results of the 1985 survey were published in 1988, there was some amazement at two features. First, the survey indicated that there were six million carers in Britain, thus demonstrating the enormous importance of the informal sector in sheer numbers. Second, it appeared that there were almost as many men carers as there were women carers: 11 per cent of men were carers, compared to 15 per cent of women. (The two later surveys in 1990 and 1995 found little variation in these proportions – for example the 1995 General Household Survey found 11 per cent of men and 14 per cent of women were carers.)

Immediately researchers began to re-analyse the data, and ferret about within it to find out if, given the apparent number of men carers, the feminists had got it all wrong. Some commentators suggested that the survey questions used to identify 'carers' were likely to underestimate the number of women carers in relation to men because men would more easily identify themselves as doing something special for someone with particular needs, whereas women would simply assume that what they did for others was part of being a 'woman'. Others found, after re-analysing the data, that men and women carers were caring for different kinds of people: men were much more likely to be caring for their wives than for other people, whereas women were almost as likely to be caring for people of a different generation (disabled children or frail elderly people) as they were to be caring for their husbands. As a result, men carers, who were caring for their chronically ill wives, were likely to be older than many women carers. Moreover, when the tasks of caring were re-analysed, it emerged that men and women undertook different kinds of care, with women, much more than men, undertaking the messy and more urgent tasks of care.

Finally, the figure of six million carers came to be refined downwards. While that figure is still frequently used, particularly by organizations wishing to speak up for carers and make claims that their work should be recognized by the politicians, it is now generally acknowledged that the number of people undertaking the really hard and stressful types of care within the British population is currently within the region of 1.3 million. Nevertheless, as the population ages, as residential care becomes increasingly rationed by price and by care managers, and hospitals discharge earlier and earlier, that number is likely to increase – slowly but steadily.

From Feminism to the Mainstream

It is probably the case that second wave feminism's greatest triumph, as far as British social policy is concerned, is the successful identification of informal care as a legitimate issue for public discussion and as part of the policy agenda. Perhaps the most concrete example of this is the recent history of the payment of a benefit paid to carers of working age – the Invalid Care Allowance – which, when first introduced in 1977, was not available to married women, who, it was argued by the policymakers, would 'be at home anyway'. This benefit has, since 1987 and a decision of the European Court of Justice, been available to married women carers such that 380,000 people now receive it, of whom 75 per cent are women (although it is not known how many of these women are actually married). The rhetoric of policy documents has become much more sensitive, at least in theory, to carers' needs. In particular the 1988 Griffiths report *Community Care: Agenda for Action*, which laid the basis for the National Health Service and Community Care Act 1990, referred to the need to support informal carers, and the need to integrate them in the 'welfare mix'. The Department of Health has funded much research into carers' needs and their integration in the welfare mix (for example, Twigg and Atkin, 1994). Carers were first legislatively recognized in 1995: the Carers (Recognition and Services) Act 1995 was introduced as Private Member's legislation but received all-party support as it went through parliament. As a result, carers were given the right to an assessment of their needs when the person they are caring for is assessed by care managers, although this legislation does not give carers any rights to services as such.

Since the advent of a Labour administration in 1997, there has been a strong emphasis, coming from central government, exhorting and, to some extent, financing local government to ensure that carers' needs are more than recognized, and are actually met. Two years after the implementation of the 1995 Act a report from the Department of Health Social Services Inspectorate entitled, significantly, *A Matter of Chance for Carers?*, had suggested that 'support [for carers] depends far more on where carers live and who they are in contact with in social services than on what they need' (Social Care Group, Department of Health, 1998). In response to this report, and other pressures coming from well-established lobbying groups from the voluntary sector that look after the interests of carers (such as the Princess Royal Trust for Carers, and Carers UK), the new Labour government published *Caring about Carers: A National Strategy for Carers* in 1999. The main thrust of this national strategy was to give local authorities additional funding (£140 million over three years) earmarked specifically for carer support, and in particular to finance schemes that allow carers to 'take a break' from care. As well as this, the Department of Health set up a special web site for carers – www.carers.gov.uk – which is an excellent resource for all those, including students, who are interested in (and/or providing) informal care. A further piece of legislation – the Carers and Disabled Children Act 2000 – has taken the original 1995 Act a step further by making it possible for carers to have an assessment of their needs even if the person they care for has refused an assessment. Moreover, local authorities are empowered to offer carers cash, called a 'direct payment', which is specifically to fund help which the *carer* needs – for example to 'take a break' or employ someone to help them with the housework or the garden while they provide personal care (or vice versa).

The Critique of the Feminist Perspective on Informal Care

While feminism has been relatively successful in bringing an issue on to the policy agenda even though it took a considerable time to do so, it would be mistaken to think that feminist analysis has now ceased to develop (see too chapter II.11). Indeed, as one would expect, given what has happened to feminism in relation to all other disciplines, feminist analysis of the informal sector has begun to point up 'difference and diversity' in relation to our understanding of the way in which the informal sector works. Thus Hilary Graham, one of the early writers on informal care from a feminist perspective, has more recently argued that the understanding of the social relations of care should include an analysis of race, disability and sexuality as well as gender. In particular, she suggests that not all care in the home is unpaid, and traditionally it has been undertaken by paid domestic servants, many of whom have been, and continue to be, ethnically distinct from their employers. Sara Arber and Jay Ginn have also argued that the early feminist analysis ignored the fact that many recipients of care are themselves elderly women, and that the feminist analysis overemphasized the dependency and burdensome nature particularly of elderly people. Thus research on the informal sector is increasingly concerned with differences between carers, and work on informal care among ethnic minorities and on the care undertaken by young carers of school age is developing quickly.

Apart from this expansion of a gendered perspective on the informal sector to a perspective that takes account of the diversity of carers, the most important critique of the feminist analysis has come from disabled people. Commentators like Jenny Morris (1993), who is herself disabled, have argued that the treatment by feminists of the so-called 'cared for' or 'care-recipients' as an undifferentiated, uncharacterized, homogeneous burden is profoundly demeaning to disabled people. Other disabled people, such as Lois Keith, have argued that it is wrong to think of all disabled people as in need of care, and that many are carers themselves – of their own children and, if they are heterosexual women, of their men. This literature, coming from the 'disabled lobbies', is gaining a considerable legitimacy, both in government circles, where their views fit well with the current ideas about the need to empower consumers of the 'welfare mix', and with research funders, who have long sought ways of involving 'the researched' (who, in social policy, are often people with special needs) in research projects (see chapter IV.4). The politics of the informal sector in general, and informal care in particular, have, as a result, become increasingly awkward, with both carers' and disabled lobbies often in opposition to each other, both in terms of debates about the nature and origins of 'dependency' and in terms of arguing about where scarce public resources should best be spent – whether emphasis should be put on ena- bling disabled people to lead independent lives by providing them with suitable and affordable housing and paid-for personal assistants, or on supporting their informal carers through social security benefits and social service support designed specifically for those who care.

Current Policy Issues for the Informal Sector

As policy-makers and analysts would now be the first to acknowledge, the informal sector is the linch pin of the community care reforms put in place under the National Health Service and Community Care Act 1990. Moreover, a recent policy decision, at least in England and Wales – as opposed to Scotland – means that the demand for in- formal care can only increase. In the late 1990s a Royal Commission on Long Term Care recommended that personal care for the long-term sick elderly should be funded entirely through general taxation, which would have made the residential care op- tion for elderly people much cheaper since they would only have had to pay for the so-called 'hotel' costs of their care – the costs of their accommodation, their food, etc. However, the Labour government turned this recommendation down and private sector residential care remains expensive, except for the very poor who are eligible to have their fees paid by their local authori- ties. In Scotland, the Scottish parliament decided to go it alone, and accept the Royal Commission's recommendation, which means that residential care will be relatively cheap for Scots as opposed to residents of

England and Wales. Whether, as a result, the size of the informal care sector in Scot- land will increase more slowly than in Eng- land and Wales remains to be seen, as does the possibility of different policy develop- ments in Wales. But in all these nations, it remains clear that policy has to be con- cerned with the maintenance of the infor- mal care sector, and research has to be funded to discover the conditions under which informal care works best. The cen- tral questions are concerned, first, with the supply of informal carers, and, second, with the appropriate forms of support for those carers who have come forward to under- take the tasks of care.

As far as supply is concerned, there are good reasons for concern. The increasing 'dependency ratio', the high proportion of women of working age entering paid work, the breakdown of the 'traditional' family which might mean that family obligations to care become far more fluid and negoti- able than they have been in the past (who should care for an ex-mother-in-law who is the grandmother of your children; do you have a responsibility to care for your ex- wife?) all mean that the traditional sources of supply may falter.

Methods of persuading people to become and *remain* informal carers have moved rap- idly on to the agenda. Indeed, the National Carers' Strategy (mentioned above) can be seen as one of the ways in which govern- ment has set out to make informal caring more palatable and manageable such that informal carers continue to come forward in large numbers and keep going when life gets tough. Support services for carers, par- ticularly respite care which allows them to 'take a break', are likely to remain a prior- ity. This is especially the case at a time when the National Health Service is under enor- mous pressure to discharge people quickly from hospital, and, at the same time, the numbers of places in residential care – to which chronically ill elderly people could be discharged – may well be in decline as private sector residential homes become less profitable (a particular feature of the private residential care sector at the time of writing, in 2002). However, research on carers often indicates that some of them are reluctant to accept support in the form of respite care in particular, partly because they feel that they themselves know best what the person they care for needs and partly because the care user, especially if they are elderly and possibly confused, may be upset by change. Thus the innovation, under the Carers and Disabled Children Act 2000, of cash payments to carers which they can use as they want, may well be a harbinger of stronger policy initiatives, backed up by funding, that devolve all decision-making about appropriate forms of support directly to carers themselves.

The Labour government has adopted a model of citizenship which assumes that every citizen of working age will engage in paid work. This assumption is promoted through a whole raft of measures that very closely link social rights to participation in the labour market. Such policies pose a particular problem of 'care', both of children, and of people with disabilities, for it is not at all clear how, if everyone of working age is at work, children (when they are not at school) and long-term disabled people (when they are not in residential care) will be cared for by their relatives and friends of working age. As far as combining paid work with informal care is concerned, this government has pursued a policy of exhorting businesses to introduce so-called 'family friendly' employment practices such that paid workers find it easy to take time off from work and/or work a flexible day so that they can care informally at home (see chapter II.17). However, so far, there is no material support to businesses that adopt such practices, and those family-friendly policies that have emerged in large companies such as banks only allow their employees *unpaid* leave in special circumstances. It is noticeable that even central government itself only offers unpaid leave for family emergencies to its own employees. It is likely, then, that pressure for the acquisi-

tion of rights to paid leave to take care of sick and dying relatives, funded from taxation, will develop. Such systems already exist in the countries of Scandinavia, where participation in the labour market is the necessary condition to the acquisition of social rights to paid leave of many different kinds, ranging from lengthy parental leave for mothers and fathers, to rights to take paid time off to care for a dying relative in their home.

Finally, it is now possible, under the Community Care (Direct Payments) Act 1996, for care users to opt to receive cash rather than services, and use that cash to employ personal assistants. In Britain it is forbidden to use this money to pay relatives to care (or indeed anyone living in the same household). However, there are other countries in Europe (such as Austria, Italy, the Netherlands) where it is possible for care users to be given cash by the state and then they are allowed to pay their relatives to care for them. In these countries then, 'informal care' as we in Britain now understand the term is no longer necessarily unpaid. It may be the case that eventually, if pressure from carers' associations is strong enough, and the poverty and lack of social rights of informal carers emerges as a major problem in the recruitment of informal carers, that the British policy on direct payments will bend, so that care users can use direct payments to pay their relatives to care. If this were to happen, then a fundamental shift will take place in our understanding of what informal care is. It would no longer be defined as essentially unpaid work, but rather would become a form of paid work, taking place in the home and between family members. However, if policy-makers can continue, with confidence, to believe that the supply of informal carers is guaranteed through the operation of the powerful twin emotions of love and guilt, then such a policy shift in Britain is located in the dim and distant future.

Guide to further reading

An excellent collection of readings on community care brings together excerpts from the work of many of the authors mentioned in this article: J. Bornat et al. (eds) *Community Care – a Reader* (Basingstoke: Macmillan Press/Open University, 1994/1997).

For the early feminist perspective, the following publications are essential reading: J. Finch and D. Groves 'Community care and the family: a case for equal opportunities?' *Journal of Social Policy*, 9, 4 (1980); J. Finch and D. Groves (eds) *A Labour of Love: Women, Work and Caring* (London: Routledge and Kegan Paul, 1983); J. Lewis and B. Meredith *Daughters Who Care: Daughters Caring for Their Mothers at Home* (London: Tavistock, 1988); C. Ungerson *Policy is Personal: Sex, Gender and Informal Care* (London: Tavistock, 1987).

On the caring relationship, and the reasons why carers come forward, see J. Finch *Family Obligations and Social Change* (Cambridge: Polity Press, 1989); H. Qureshi and A.Walker *The Caring Relationship: Elderly People and Their Families* (Basingstoke: Macmillan Press, 1989); M. Nolan, G. Grant and J. Keady *Understanding Family Care: A Multidimensional Model of Caring and Coping* (Buckingham: Open University Press, 1996).

For an insight into the early feminist argument about the need to return to collective provision, see G. Dalley *Ideologies of Caring: Rethinking Community and Collectivism* (Basingstoke: Macmillan Press, 1988).

More recent work that looks at the way carers are integrated (or not) into the welfare mix, is contained in J. Twigg and K. Atkin *Carers Perceived: Policy and Practice in Informal Care* (Buckingham: Open University Press, 1994), and the perspective on care developed by disabled people is outlined by J. Morris *Independent Lives? Community Care and Disabled People* (Basingstoke: Macmillan Press, 1993).

As already mentioned, the best web-based starting point is: www.carers.gov.uk

The Organization Of Welfare

III.5
Managing and Delivering Welfare

John Clarke

This chapter looks at changing systems of welfare delivery in Britain. It traces a shift away from a system dominated by integrated professional-bureaucracies of the state. These two principles of bureaucratic administration and professional expertise were at the heart of this system between the 1940s and 1980s. By the late 1990s, two distinctive changes were visible. The first, discussed in chapters III.1 to III.4, was a move away from service provision by the state to a more complex set of arrangements involving a greater role for other providers – particularly those in the voluntary and private sectors. The second was an associated shift to structuring welfare provision around market and managerial principles rather than bureaucracy or professionalism.

These changes were incomplete, partial and contested. They emerged in the context of widespread political and public debate about the 'costs of welfare' following the downturn of capitalist economies in the 1970s. They were given extra impetus in the English-speaking world, at least, by the rise of 'New Right' politics which were both anti-welfarist and anti-statist (Clarke and Newman, 1997). In the process, not only were the purposes and desirability of the 'welfare state' brought into question, but the organization of welfare provision and delivery also became 'politicized'. New Right governments sought to break up the institutions of the welfare state, create welfare markets and introduce ways of 'becom-

ing businesslike' through new management approaches derived from the private sector.

Although 'markets' and 'management' are claimed to be outside politics – they are merely technical ways of coordinating services – they have proved to be profoundly controversial. Arguments about how to improve, reform or modernize welfare have echoed around the end of the twentieth century and the beginning of the twenty-first. Such arguments range across whether welfare is being – or should be – 'privatized'; through controversies about the balance between competition and collaboration in service provision; to arguments about how to involve citizens, users and/or consumers in policy, planning and provision (see chapters III.11 and III.13). Although the welfare state has been unsettled, retrenched, partially dismantled and partially 'reformed' – what has replaced it is both less clear and more argued over. It seems likely that arguments about how best to organize welfare, how to protect and promote the 'public interest' and how to manage organizations, staff and users will continue to occupy the public imagination.

Welfare and Bureaucracy

Bureaucratic administration was central to the development of the welfare state. It was an organizational system which was 'rule bound' in that the delivery of welfare services was governed by sets of rules and regulations that could be applied to individual cases. Although bureaucratic administration has been heavily attacked in recent years, its centrality to welfare systems was the result of a number of perceived organizational and social advantages. Organizationally, bureaucratic administration was a highly rationalized system, with the capacity to handle high volumes of demands for welfare benefits and services with efficiency (Cousins, 1987). Its hierarchical structure was intended to ensure that each employee knew their task and could refer more complex issues or demands upwards to more senior staff. Accountability also flowed upwards to senior levels of the system and, ultimately, to politicians (see also chapter III.13). Socially, bureaucracies promised impartiality and neutrality in the administration of social welfare. Cases would be dealt with according to the rules, rather than being subject to irrelevant social judgements (of moral desert or worth) or to the personal whims or enthusiasms of the individual dealing with the case. Given the earlier history of social welfare in Britain, this promise of impartial administration was of considerable social significance.

Bureaucratic administration was the organizational form that predominated in both central and local government in departments with specialized functions (health, education, housing, etc.), each with its administrative hierarchy responsible for the implementation of government policies, rules and regulations. Power in bureaucratic systems was attached to particular places in the hierarchy and was legitimated by reference to administrative policies and the competence needed to apply them.

Welfare and Professionalism

Nevertheless, not all social welfare was delivered according to these principles. Particularly in areas where needs were seen as complex, the welfare state was built upon the exercise of professional judgement. This was most obviously the case in relation to

health in which medical professionals and other groups of health workers used expert knowledge to identify symptoms and appropriate treatments. Medical knowledge and power were thus central to the organization of the post-war National Health Service in both hospital settings and in General Practice. Other areas of welfare provision also rested on professional expertise – education centred on teachers and lecturers; personal social services on social workers and so on. Such groups were both less powerful and more dependent on the state than the medical profession, leading to discussions about whether they were 'real' professions or semi-professions or quasi-professions or mediating professions (Cousins, 1987). These different qualifying terms try to indicate the distinctive character of welfare professionalism in contrast to the model of the traditional or independent professions, such as medicine and the law.

Like bureaucracy, professionalism organizes power in a particular way. Professions stand in a relation of power to users of welfare services (who are dependent on the professional for treatment, access to resources or other forms of intervention). This power is legitimated by reference to the professional's possession of expert knowledge (gained through training and a qualifying process) which enables them to make judgements that lay knowledge cannot. So we submit ourselves to professional intervention in the belief (or hope) that 'professionals know best'. Professionalism also structures power within organizations, since it involves a demand for autonomy – the space in which professional judgement can be exercised without interference, for example, the right for doctors to make clinical decisions; or teachers to control the curriculum (Cousins, 1987).

Managerialism and the Crisis of Bureau-Professionalism

Most state welfare organizations in the post-war period combined bureaucratic administration and welfare professional-ism, although with different sorts of bal-ances of power between the two axes. The NHS, for example, involved much higher levels of professional power and discretion than social work or teaching which were more confined by bureaucratic frameworks. In general, though, the welfare state can be seen as having the organizational form of bureau-professionalism (Clarke and Newman, 1997).

By the 1980s, however, this system of or-ganizing welfare was under attack on a number of fronts. First, there was a series of challenges to the 'neutrality' of bureau-professionalism. As chapters II.11, II.12 and IV.4 show, social movements taking shape around inequalities of gender, 'race', dis-ability and sexuality challenged not just social policies but also the systems through which these policies were implemented. For example, women's groups challenged the (male) medical control of childbirth; while black groups challenged definitions of edu-cational failure, the practices of discrimina-tory policing, and the inappropriate judgements of social workers. Disabled people's movements organized to combat the 'disabling' effects of the medical model of disability and the exercise of professional power that went with it.

Secondly, from the mid-1970s bureau-professional systems were accused of fail-ing to manage the growing costs of public spending. The accounting, budgetary and resource control capacity of these systems appeared to give little control over the costs of providing welfare and even seemed to be designed to encourage incremental growth in such costs. Administrators and professionals could always find some new activity or project that needed more re-sources. This was linked to a more system-atic critique of bureau-professionalism in 'public choice theory'. This suggested that administrators and professionals had vested interests in maintaining and expand-ing their 'empires', rather than being disin-terested public servants. In addition, the 'monopoly provider' status of state agen-cies meant that they were insulated from competitive pressures to become more ef-ficient and more responsive to the demands of consumers. Public choice theory asserted the superiority of the market over the state as a mechanism for distributing goods and services.

This was closely associated with New Right attacks on the welfare state and shaped many of the reforms of social wel-fare provision in the late 1980s and 1990s. In particular, it influenced reforms intended to introduce market-like relationships into social welfare (through competition, con-tracting and a focus on consumer rights). Such changes, it was argued, would simul-taneously increase efficiency, create greater choice for service users, and break up the old monopoly provider power bases of bu-reau-professional systems of welfare (Clarke and Newman, 1997, see also chap-ter II.6).

These changes were connected to the shift to managerial forms of organizing welfare provision. The demand for 'new and better management' was seen as a way of making social welfare organizations more 'busi-ness-like' – managers would carry the drive for greater efficiency and better resource control. They would make welfare organi-zations more customer-centred and would be a check on the 'empire-building' self-in-terest of bureaucrats and professionals. Such arguments presented management as a set of techniques and technologies which were the best way of running any organi-zation, whether in the private, public or voluntary sectors. This linked to a wide-spread set of initiatives, sometimes identi-fied as the 'New Public Management' (Flynn 2002; Pollitt and Bouckaert, 2000). However, this 'techniques and technolo-gies' view of management neglects issues about *managerialism* as an ideology and a form of social and organizational power (Pollitt, 1993). Managerialism involves a claim to organizational power that chal-lenges the discretion of other groups (whether workers, professionals or bureau-crats) in the name of managers needing the 'freedom to manage'. The result was a series of complex power struggles within welfare organizations for control of resources, decision-making and agenda-setting power (Clarke and Newman, 1997).

Contracts, Competition and Cooperation

So many changes have taken place in the systems of delivering welfare that accounts of them differ widely in what they identify as the main features. Here I will suggest that two different sets of tensions mark out the main trends. On the one hand, an emphasis on decentralization, devolution and delegation to front-line organizations has produced a tension between centralization and decentralization. On the other, a commitment to the greater use of market-like mechanisms to coordinate welfare systems has produced a tension between competition and collaboration. At different times, and in different services, these tensions have been resolved in different ways – sometimes emphasizing decentralization or competition, at others emphasizing centralization or collaboration. In this section, I set out some of the main shifts in the organization of welfare from the 1980s.

The New Right belief in the superiority of the market over the state as the mechanism for dealing with the distribution of goods and services affected the organization of welfare in a wide range of ways. Most obviously, Conservative governments of the 1980s and 1990s promoted 'private' or 'market' solutions to welfare matters – encouraging home ownership (through the sale of council/public housing), health care and pensions, for example. Secondly, they created processes of 'externalization' or 'contracting out', requiring competitive tendering for the provision of services ranging from social care to ancillary services in the NHS. Thirdly, they encouraged the development of more 'mixed' economies of welfare by fostering multiple and competing providers (particularly in the private and voluntary sectors)who could displace existing public sector provision. Fourthly, where 'external' markets could not be created, they created competitive 'quasi-markets' (Le Grand and Bartlett, 1993) within services – so, schools were put into competition with one another for pupils and parents. Fifthly, there was a general shift towards using forms of contracting, purchasing, and service agreements as the favoured mode of coordinating activities between and within organizations, typically embodying a distinction between 'purchasers' and 'providers'(Walsh, 1995).

These 'marketizing' trends, promoting greater competition, went alongside decentralizing and devolving processes aimed at giving service-providing organizations the 'freedom to manage their own business'. Schools, health trusts and GP practices, for example, were 'empowered' to manage themselves. Welfare organizations – whether in the public, private or voluntary sector – were encouraged to see themselves as small or medium-size enterprises, and were expected to turn themselves into 'well managed businesses' (Clarke and Newman, 1997). However, such decentralizing processes took place within new forms of centralization – of funding and resources; of targets and performance measurement; and of service control (e.g., in the creation of a 'national curriculum' for education). The centralization-decentralization axis became a consistent source of tension between government and service-providing agencies and organizations, particularly when government wished to control the results of services but blame 'local management' for service or policy failures.

The effects of these changes have been much debated. For enthusiasts, they introduced a much-needed dose of 'market discipline' into over-inflated and inert public bureaucracies. Competition promoted efficiency, driving down the costs of services and promoting innovation. Market mechanisms induced a 'customer orientation' in place of the paternalism of public services, leading to more responsive, flexible services – an orientation enshrined in the proliferation of service 'charters' that followed the creation of the Citizen's Charter in 1991. For many on the neo-liberal wing of the New Right, the moves towards markets failed to go far enough – and constant pressure was maintained from think-tanks and intellectuals for the creation of more 'real' markets in welfare services. But there has also been a wide range of criticisms. Public arguments have been dominated by concerns about the 'privatization' of public services, and whether private sector providers form a safe, reliable and appropriate alternative to public sector provision. This argument was given new weight at the beginning of the twenty-first century by the growing number of closures of private residential and nursing homes serving older people. Others argued that the market mechanism was not the most effective means for coordinating public services – suggesting that contracting tended to be cost- rather than quality-driven; and that the management and transaction costs of marketized processes took resources away from service delivery. At the same time, there were fears that the costs of welfare were being 'externalized' (e.g. through employing cheaper labour in contracted provider organizations, or by pushing costs out onto families and households expected to fill the gaps left by diminished services).

Other critics pointed to the structural and cultural problems resulting from the marketizing and decentralizing trends. Some pointed to the erosion of forms of accountability at national and local levels, as the 'freedom to manage' by-passed or subverted traditional political arrangements (see chapter III.6). Others emphasized the erosion of the 'public service ethos' as organizations strove to create competitive advantages, withdrew from collaborative arrangements, and treated staff as a 'resource to be managed'. Finally, many critics pointed to the ways in which decentralization and competition combined to create an unpredictable, ill-coordinated and fragmentary pattern of service provision (Clarke and Newman, 1997). All of these

trends – and the problems associated with them – have been partial and uneven ones, occurring in different forms in different services and different places.

Much was expected of the incoming 'New Labour' government of 1997, not least that they might restore or revive welfare, and public services more generally. However, it and its successors have had a profoundly ambivalent, even contradictory, relationship with the New Right's reforms of welfare organization. Many of the reforms have been kept in place, and even intensified (particularly the centralization of resource control, service specification and performance management). During the 1997–2001 government, strict public spending controls were also kept in place, leading to a deepening set of 'underfunding' problems for service organizations. At the same time, 'New Labour' committed itself to remedying some of the problems resulting from Conservative reforms (in the pursuit of a 'third way' politics between Old Left and New Right – see chapter II.10). They attempted to address some of the problems of fragmentation through a commitment to more 'joined-up government', linking significant policy issues (such as social exclusion and health improvement) across departments at national level. At the same time they promoted more collaborative forms of working at local level, requiring partnerships and other forms of cross-organization working between different agencies, sectors and interests. At local level as well, they have been making demands for greater participation and consultation of local communities in relation to service provision and planning (see Newman, 2001, on New Labour and the governance of public services).

New Labour's commitment to 'modernizing' and 'reforming' the welfare state was the continuous focus of controversy. Two areas stand out in particular. Its view of those working in public services oscillated between celebrating their contribution to public well-being and a more hostile view of them as 'small c conservatives' and 'wreckers' who block the reform of services. In these latter moments, the government represented itself as on the side of the 'citizen-consumer' against intransigent producer interests. One aspect of this tension is the continuing controversy about how best to organize and deliver welfare services, since public service workers have been critical of plans to 'privatize' welfare provision. New Labour proclaimed itself 'agnostic' about the merit of different sectors – claiming that 'what counts is what works' and where private sector providers or methods work better, they will be used for the delivery or management of services. For many, including those working in welfare services, this agnosticism has looked more like an enthusiasm for the private sector. Its role has increased in a range of settings: in public-private partnerships, in the identification of the 'business community' as an active participant in local partnerships, in the greater involvement of private sector management in running public services and so on. This set of conflicts about the organization and management of public services looks likely to continue. However, it is worth drawing explicit attention to another aspect of managing welfare where New Labour not only continued Conservative approaches, but enthusiastically and systematically developed them – the use of 'evaluative' agencies to scrutinize service delivery (see also chapter III.13).

Keeping Control: Inspection, Regulation and Audit

Given the greater complexity created by decentralization, competition, contracting and collaboration, questions of how the new system of welfare provision is to be integrated and controlled has taken on greater importance. The old hierarchical systems of bureaucratic administration with their principles of instructions being passed downwards while reports and information flows back to the top are no longer appropriate. They have been re-placed by a number of different forms of control.

The decentralization of managerial autonomy to individual organizations (and thus the responsibility for delivering welfare services) has been tempered by a high level of centralization of power in central government. This power focuses most obviously on policy formation and resource control, particularly financial resources. Within such limits, organizations are (at least nominally) 'set free' to 'go about their business'. However, this mixture of centralization and decentralization has been supplemented by the development of an array of evaluative systems. These originally centred around issues of financial management – whether organizations could prove that they were being responsible in the management of public funds. The Audit Commission was created in 1983 to monitor the financial processes and controls of local authorities and the NHS with the purpose of ensuring that they delivered the 'three E's': economy, efficiency and effectiveness. Subsequently, evaluation has expanded to a wider concern with organizational performance – assessing the effectiveness, quality, and standards of welfare organization. In many areas, this has led inspectorates, the Audit Commission and other 'quangos' into the business of organizational design – advising or telling organizations how to manage themselves.

The New Labour governments of 1997 and 2001 intensified this trend towards external scrutiny and evaluation, contributing to what Power has called the 'audit explosion' (Power, 1997). Two distinctive features of New Labour's integration of evaluation into the modernization of welfare stand out. The first is the rhetorical commitment to agnosticism – the view that 'what counts is what works' – and to 'evidence-based' policy and practice. Such a view placed a premium on the collection of data to inform government policy-making, encourage or enforce 'continuous improvement' by service organization, and to aid choices by the consumers of welfare services. So much of the data took the form of comparative (and competitive) evaluations – so-called 'league tables' (of hospitals, police services and schools). Secondly, external (and nominally independent) evaluation provided a machinery for ensuring compliance not just with the policy goals of central government but with the prescribed models of organizational design and management. Such evaluative processes remained controversial in a number of ways. They incurred extra costs in an under-resourced system (and therefore diverted resources from immediate service delivery activities). They raised expectations about the possibility and ease of service improvement; and they trod an uneasy line between 'neutral evaluation' and politicized interventions (nowhere more than in the Office for Standards in Education – OFSTED – during the 1990s).

Dispersed Welfare Provision and Managerialism

It is difficult to know what all these changes in the delivery of welfare add up to. This problem can be indicated by the diversity of terms used to describe these new forms. Have we arrived at a new mixed economy of care characterized by a reduction in the state's role and the growth of other 'sectors'? Has welfare become marketized or even quasi-marketized'? Has the welfare state been 'privatized'? Do we now have an 'ena-

bling state' whose role is to set free individuals, families, communities and diverse provider organizations to create social welfare? Is this a contracting state – both shrinking and resorting to contractual mechanisms to secure services for welfare users? Is it an evaluative state developing new processes to scrutinize the performance of agencies and organizations involved in delivering welfare? This diversity of terms indicates the scale of the problem of defining the new welfare order. In my view, the new arrangements are best understood as a 'managerial state' (Clarke and Newman, 1997). Managerialism is central to both the ideology and practice of the new arrangements. It provides the organizing principle that attempts to hold together the dispersal of power, responsibilities, resources and tasks between organizations. It promises that 'better management' will ensure efficient running, effective coordination, greater customer satisfaction and the delivery of more or less in the battle to control public spending on welfare in the face of rising public demand. Despite those promises, conflicts about the organization and management of welfare continue – ranging from scandals about hospital failures through to the funding crisis of old people's care. The purposes, resourcing and organization of welfare are not easily separable. The ways in which they intersect seem likely to keep 'welfare delivery' in the centre of public arguments for some time to come.

Guide to further reading

Clarke, J. and Newman, J., 1997. *The Managerial State* (London: Sage) extends some of the arguments of Clarke, Cochrane and McLaughlin in examining the role and consequences of managerialism in the restructuring of the British welfare state.
Cousins, C., 1987. *Controlling Welfare* (Hemel Hempstead: Harvester Wheatsheaf) provides a sociological analysis of the organizing principles of social welfare, focusing on bureaucracy and professions and their changing place in the welfare state.
Flynn, N., 2002. *Public Sector Management*, 4th edn (Hemel Hempstead: Prentice Hall/ Harvester Wheatsheaf) is a lucid – and regularly updated – introduction to the conditions and problems of managing in the public sector.
Le Grand, J. and Bartlett, W. (eds), 1993. *Quasi-Markets and Social Policy* (Basingstoke: Macmillan Press) explores the theory and practice of market relations in social welfare.

Newman, J., 2001. *Modernising Governance* (London: Sage) addresses the ways in which policy is being reshaped and public management realigned under 'New Labour' and the consequences for governance in the UK.

Pollitt, C., 1993. *Managerialism and the Public Services* (Oxford: Blackwell) is a pioneering study of the application of managerial ideology and practice to the public sector in the USA and the UK.

Pollitt, C. and Bouckaert, G., 2000. *Public Management Reform: A Comparative Analysis* (Oxford, Oxford University Press) is a thorough exploration of changes in the management of public services across countries.

Power, M., 1997. *The Audit Society* (Oxford: Oxford Unversity Press) provides a thoughtful critique of the rise of audit and other evaluative practices in modern society.

Walsh, K., 1995. *Public Services and Market Mechanisms* (London: Macmillan) examines the impact of contracting on the organization and delivery of public services.

Useful 'starter' internet sources from which to explore the on-going changes in service managment and delivery are:

www.cabinet-office.gov.uk
and
www.audit-commission.gov.uk.

III.6
The Governance of Local Welfare

Allan Cochrane

As other chapters make clear, the state has never been the sole (or even the most important) provider of welfare for most people. Although this chapter focuses on aspects of welfare which are directly associated with the state, it highlights the internally differentiated nature of that state. The British welfare state is not a homogeneous entity. This chapter explores the relationships between some of its different elements and is specifically concerned with the relationships between local and central government – the position of the local welfare state within the wider state system.

For much of the last twenty-five years the British state seems to have been subject to a relentless process of centralization. Not only has local government faced a series of reorganizations imposed from above, but (following the poll tax debâcle of the late 1980s) councils have found their capacity to raise tax income on their own account substantially reduced. As chapter III.10 notes, over 80 per cent of local authority income is now derived from central government grant of one sort or another. At the same time rules and regulations about how councils may operate have become tighter. A wide range of activities, previously handled in-house, are now dealt with through the issuing of contracts to private sector agencies. Any possibility of significant investment in new social housing has been removed, while council houses have been offered for sale to sitting tenants. A national

curriculum has been introduced in England and Wales and some schools have been given the right to opt out of local authority control. Social services departments are increasingly constrained by a plethora of guidelines and the requirement to work in partnership with other agencies, such as health authorities and the police, as well as voluntary sector and private providers.

In some respects, however, the centralized authority of the unitary UK state appears to have been eroded in recent years with the creation of new political authorities in Scotland, Wales and Northern Ireland. Since 1999 the map of the UK state has become more complex. There were always differences between the operations of local welfare states in the component countries of the United Kingdom. But devolution of responsibility for some key policy areas (including most of those handled in practice by local government), to assemblies in Wales and Northern Ireland and to the Scottish parliament, has made things still more complicated (see chapter III.7). It is less clear that it has significantly changed the position of local government – instead of dealing with a centre in London, local authorities in those countries now have their own (increasingly active) centres in Cardiff, Belfast and Edinburgh with which to deal. The new devolved centres have retained much the same position within their own realms as the UK state from which they formally derive their powers.

All this, it seems, simply confirms the subsidiary position of local government within the British political system. Unlike many other European countries, there are no constitutional guarantees of autonomy for local authorities in Britain. In principle, all political power is delegated from above, usually through parliamentary legislation. So, it might be concluded, central-local relations don't really matter. Whatever the centre or now the multiple centres want, they can get. In practice, however, such a conclusion would be misleading. Central initiatives can rarely be imposed by edict from above, and local authorities continue to develop their own policy initiatives in unexpected ways (see, e.g., Atkinson and Wilks-Heeg, 2000). An understanding of central-local relations makes it easier to interpret social policy as it is practised, rather than the way it appears in White Papers, guidance notes or the policy statements of government departments.

Divisions of Labour

The British welfare state is divided along functional lines. Different central government departments have responsibilities for its different elements. Despite their changing names over time, mergers and demergers between them, and differences between the structures in the UK's component nations, responsibility for social security, education and training, housing, urban policy, health, community care and children's services is shared between a number of departments. Increasingly, too, a number of specialist (semi-autonomous) agencies have been allocated responsibility for specific aspects of provision (see also chapter III.1). These currently include the National Health Service, the Northern Ireland Housing Executive, the Benefits Agency and the Child Support Agency, as well as a range of regulatory agencies such as OFSTED (Office for Standards in Education) in England and educational inspectorates in the other nations of the UK, the Social Services Inspectorates (of England and Wales) and

Social Work Services Inspectorate (in Scotland) and even the Audit Commission (in England and Wales) and Audit Scotland. It will already be apparent, therefore, that the relations between these bodies are likely to be important in influencing social policy outcomes. Questions are bound to arise about the extent to which they follow similar approaches to the tasks that they have been set. It is not always clear that they do. The resources which each is allocated may vary according to their success (or the success of the ministers who speak for them) in the internal battles over budgets. Even if the overall ethos of a government is one that stresses financial prudence, like that of the Labour government after 1997 (or the 'rolling back of the state' which was said to characterize the Thatcher governments of the 1980s), each agency and department is likely to find itself arguing that its own budget deserves to be protected.

These spatial divisions of labour, however, find their strongest expression in the allocation of responsibility for delivering (or ensuring the delivery of) many welfare services to local authorities of one sort or another. In principle it is relatively easy to identify which council is responsible for overseeing the delivery of which service. Each local government textbook has a chart showing who does what at the time of its publication, although there is always a danger that as soon as they have been pinned down the precise allocation will change again. Currently, Northern Ireland has its own quite distinctive arrangements, which allocate little responsibility to elected councils, but instead largely work through appointed boards. By contrast, Scotland and Wales have one principal layer of local government in the form of district councils, which have responsibility for most of the traditional functions of local government, including social services, housing, planning and education. In England matters are rather more complicated, with five distinct types of local government (in addition to parishes). There are metropolitan councils in the big urban agglomerations (West Midlands, Greater Manchester, South and West Yorkshire, Merseyside, Tyne and Wear), while Greater London is divided into a series of London boroughs (such as Lambeth, Richmond upon Thames, Tower Hamlets and Westminster), and some urban areas in other parts of the country (including Milton Keynes, Luton and Southampton) are governed by unitary district councils. The creation of these councils followed a review of local government in England's counties outside the metropolitan areas in the early 1990s. Only some councils in the counties were given unitary status, and the changes were introduced on a piecemeal and gradual basis. These unitary district councils have similar responsibilities to the districts in Scotland and Wales. Elsewhere, and outside these areas, county councils (such as Buckinghamshire, Derbyshire and Northamptonshire) share responsibility with district councils. The counties look after education and social services, while the districts within them are responsible for housing and development control. In England, the nature of your local government will depend on where you live. In addition to the local boroughs, there is now (since 2000) a city-wide Greater London Authority with an elected mayor and assembly and broad responsibility for economic and social development, transport, aspects of planning and policing.

Alongside elected local government there is also an extensive array of unelected local agencies which have responsibility for specific aspects of welfare provision (and are increasingly helping to define what is meant by welfare in the UK). So, for example, within the National Health Service local hospital trusts and health authorities, as well as primary care trusts, all have some role in determining what is available; in the field of education, further education colleges are now run as independent agencies, being formally overseen by specialist agencies in most of the UK's nations (the Learning and Skills Council in England, the Education and Learning Wales Agency

(ELWA) in Wales, the Scottish Further Education Funding Council in Scotland), and the local management of schools has become more important, even for those which are not 'foundation' schools or their equivalent; in England regional Learning and Skills Councils have been given the responsibility for managing the government's training budgets. Ad hoc agencies associated with specific government initiatives have also been important, whether in the form of urban development corporations or partnerships associated with a range of urban regeneration schemes (including Social Inclusion Partnerships in Scotland and the Single Regeneration Budget in England).

Dual State or Unitary State?

There have been many attempts to explain the division of labour that has emerged between levels of government. One approach (e.g. Saunders, in Boddy and Fudge,1994) has suggested that there is a 'dual state'. This argument contrasts national and local politics and identifies functional divisions between different levels of the state. The national level is said to be mainly concerned with issues relating to production and the economy, with any bargaining taking place between major interests, such as the representatives of capital and labour. By contrast, it is argued, the local state concerns itself principally with issues of social consumption (that is, largely welfare issues), and is more open, more pluralist and less corporatist than the national state. Because the local state is not responsible for the issues which are of central concern to business (and which are dealt with at national level), there is said to be space for initiative which can be utilized by locally based groups. The approach implies that at national level structural factors effectively determine political decision-making, while at local level diverse political interest groups have a more or less direct influence on policy-making, through a sort of 'imperfect pluralism'.

The dual state thesis helpfully highlights

some of the divisions that exist, and identifies some of the roots of conflict between central and local government. The central state is responsible for the overall management of public spending, but decisions on the levels and nature of that spending are often made at local level. The tensions between central and local government can be seen as part of a battle for control over state expenditure. They can also be seen as a continuing battle over political direction, since the greater openness of local government may sometimes allow councils directly to challenge unpopular governments over key issues of their policy. In the mid-1980s councils such as the Greater London Council saw themselves as developing high-profile alternatives to the policies of the Thatcher government, which had a very strong national agenda of its own. Not surprisingly, perhaps, one consequence of the local challenge was that the Greater London Council and the other metropolitan councils were simply abolished in 1986.

Although it is useful in highlighting some of the pressures and tensions, however, the dual state thesis cannot be used as a universal template. It takes aspects of the existing division of labour for granted and assumes that there is some functional reason for them. Unfortunately, the actual division of labour is rather more complex than the theory seems to allow (e.g. Dunleavy, 1994). Some key aspects of social consumption, such as the National Health Service, have been handled through national agencies through most of the period since 1945, while others (such as education) have been handled quite differently in other European countries (for example, as a regional responsibility in Germany and a national responsibility in France). Other key aspects of welfare are barely considered by dual state theorists because they fit uneasily with the argument. So, for example, over the past fifty years, the prime responsibility for income maintenance through social security payments has been handled through a national system, al-

though before that the operation of the Poor Law was a local responsibility.

The importance of the politics of production at local level also fits uneasily with the model. The reshaping of Britain's main urban centres in the 1950s and 1960s (with new road networks, city centre redevelopment and the building of industrial estates) was in large part the product of local rather than central government initiative. The increased profile of local economic development on the local government agenda since the early 1980s has been widely noted, and has been accompanied by the emergence of new corporate style public-private partnerships and agencies at local level. Since 1997 (with the election of the Blair government) the blurring of any notional division between welfare and economic policy has been still more marked, to the extent that it is now expected that councils will produce plans that explicitly consider issues of economic well-being and will work alongside other agencies and business representatives in Local Strategic Partnerships. As indicated above, the introduction of devolved political authority to Scotland, Wales and Northern Ireland also implies a more complex structure, as does the emergence in England of a plethora of regional institutions with a primary but not exclusive focus on economic development and competitiveness.

In other words, any belief that there is some straightforward structural basis for the division of labour between central and local government is mistaken.

Networks and Relations

It is increasingly apparent that what are rather misleadingly called central-local relations are instead characterized by complex cross-cutting networks, which help to constitute the welfare state as a set of relationships rather than a unitary and undifferentiated entity, in what Bob Jessop (*State Theory Putting Capitalist States in Their Place*, Cambridge: Polity, 1980) calls an 'institutional ensemble'. One problem with the assumptions underpinning popular conceptions of central-local relations is (as Rhodes, 1988, argues) that there is no unified 'central' government, at least in the sense that some agency at the centre can pull a decision-making lever and expect its ambitions to be realized throughout the system. Central government is, as suggested above, itself divided on functional lines. And within the different departments there are likely to be further divisions (in the case of the Department of Health in England, for example, between those concerned principally with the health service and those concerned with the personal social services, as well as between those concerned with community care and those concerned with children's services). Each of these 'multiple centres' will be part of its own 'policy network' which brings together those working in the field: politicians, professionals and civil servants, those operating in unelected agencies, as well as those working for local government. There is, Rhodes suggests, little coordination between these policy networks, even if there is coordination within them.

This makes the imagery of central control difficult to sustain, despite the emergence of the array of new controls discussed in chapter III.13. Policy networks are service based and cut across hierarchies (being represented at different levels of government) within what Rhodes calls a 'differentiated polity' (see also chapter III.5). Each side of the network is dependent on the other: at local level officers are dependent for finance from the centre, and at national level civil servants (and ministers) are dependent on local officers for implementation. In the case of community care following the National Health Service and Community Care Act 1990, for example, the implementation of the policy was highly dependent on local initiative, as social services departments attempted to redefine their roles in the new context. The term 'governance' (rather than 'government', which implies a top-down model) is increasingly being used to describe the working of this 'differentiated polity' (see, e.g., Rhodes, 1997).

At central level, departments (or parts of departments) may also act as representatives of those they manage. So, for example, the government may be arguing strongly for reductions in spending as part of an overall economic programme or for a shift in patterns of spending, while at the same time, civil servants within the Department for Education and Skills, or the Department of Health, are arguing with their counterparts at local level for increased spending on particular schemes. In England, the department responsible for local government is in a particularly uncertain position. In arguments with the Treasury, it is likely to support more spending in the areas for which it is responsible through local government, yet in its relations with local government it acts as the policer of budgets – indeed, it effectively plays the Treasury role. And matters are made still more complex because, even in this context of departmental pressure for retrenchment, some parts of the department – those responsible for housing, planning and other spending areas – may also be encouraging increased spending.

If one important aspect of this is the acknowledgement that the centre cannot be seen as a homogeneous category, a second is that the same applies to local government. At one level that may not be very surprising – after all, one of the claims made by the defenders of local government is precisely that there may be significant variation in the policies adopted by different councils. And, of course, the emergence of more locally based agencies might also be expected to encourage policy variation between places. Perhaps what is more surprising – given the variation one might expect – is how similar councils are in the ways in which they operate. The point being made here, therefore, is not so much that there is variation between places, but rather that there are significant divisions between professional and other groups *within* local authorities. These reflect the extent to which those groups and the institutional arrangements that follow from them fit into wider national (and sometimes even international) networks.

Conclusion

Historically, one of the tensions within central-local relations in Britain seems to have been that those at the 'centre' appeared to believe that they could simply direct a system which is highly differentiated and characterized by extensive negotiation through networks of professional and bureaucratic politics. But this tension is exacerbated by the way in which apparently functional divisions of labour are mapped on to democratic structures, which have a clear territorial dimension. Although many local political institutions are now run by unelected boards, it is the existence of elected local government which gives councillors and officers their own locally based political legitimacy. The local welfare state is not just the product of devolved administrative responsibility from the centre. On the contrary, it has emerged from a historical process of claim and counter-claim, of continuing contestation. The particular division of labour between different levels of government in the UK reflects the ways in which the welfare state has developed since the middle of the nineteenth century. Most of the activities which we currently understand as constituting the welfare state began as locally based initiatives. The Poor Law was operated through local boards, as was education. Public health provision emerged from local networks linking state, charities and private interests. Through the first half of the twentieth century, local governments took the initiative in developing welfare services across the board, from housing to education, health to children's services.

Only after 1945 was it taken for granted that some activities and services would best be handled at national level. But the nationalization of some activities was accompanied by a massive expansion of others, as local budgets increased and a local welfare state emerged with responsibilities for a massively expanded programme of social housing, a growing personal social services sector and a major commitment to state education. The incorporation of this local welfare state into the existing democratic structures of local government has helped to guarantee a continuing process of conflict as attempts have been made to control and restructure the welfare state since the mid-1970s. But the survival of local forms of political legitimacy has been an important element in ensuring that conflicts between central and local government are not always resolved in favour of the centre, even if the presumption is that they often will be.

This helps to explain some of the difficulties which central government had in reducing spending dramatically through the 1980s and early 1990s. Certainly there were cuts and pressures to cut back further, but the scale was less significant than the political rhetoric suggested. The dramatic failure to impose a new system of local taxation in the form of the community charge or poll tax at the end of the 1980s (which brought in its wake a change of prime minister, if not of government) is only the highest profile example of the difficulties that were involved. Even where the overall direction of change can be identified with some confidence, the differentiated nature of the welfare state, with its overlapping policy networks cutting across levels of responsibility, means that the outcomes of specific policy initiatives are likely to be unpredictable. This helps to explain the ever more complex funding regimes that were developed, with their arcane and often incomprehensible formulae for determining what each council was allocated. And it also explains the massive expansion in ring-fenced allocations for particular initiatives that characterized the first term of the Blair government as they tried to guarantee that spending took place on what the centre wanted.

However new approaches to the direction of local welfare from above do seem to be emerging that reflect a fuller understanding of the nature of the local welfare state and local government, in particular. In part, of course, this reflects the realization that local government has changed – elected local authorities no longer have the monopoly on most public service provision within their boundaries. But there is a wider recognition that both central and local government have to operate within complex systems of governance which have to be managed rather carefully. It is no longer possible to operate on the assumption that a decision taken at the top (whether by a minister or by a Council Committee) will simply be implemented by subordinates.

In this context there has been first a shift in attention towards changing the management structures of local government (for example through a move towards mayoral and cabinet systems of government and away from committee-based systems). At the same time, there has been a renewed emphasis on the need for partnerships to build legitimacy and link aspects of governance at local level (e.g. through Local Strategic Partnerships and the preparation of community plans). In Scotland, for example, the Local Government Act gives councils the power to promote the well-being of their areas; introduces a requirement for councils to produce community plans in collaboration with a range of partners; and introduces a duty of best value, alongside a more developed audit system to oversee it.

This is being followed both by promises of more autonomy and fewer direct restrictions, and also by new forms of regulation. In England a White Paper published in 2002 on *Strong Local Leadership – Quality Public Services* promises a new performance assessment system which will allow councils to be positioned on a four point scale – high performing, striving, coasting, or poor-performing. Depending on their position on the scale, councils will be treated differently and allowed more or less scope for autonomous action, with the expectation of direct central government intervention for those identified as poor-performing. A reduction in the number of ring-fenced grants is also promised. In other words, there is less of an emphasis on direct control, although it might be wise to retain some scepticism about the extent to which civil servants and politicians can resist the temptation, but instead what is being pursued is a form of self-management through targets coupled with a more developed scrutiny system. The expectation seems to be that by changing the environment within which councils operate, they will effectively police themselves, but where they fail there will still be the scope for direct intervention.

Guide to further reading

This chapter has concentrated largely on debates around the issue of central-local relations. It has not looked specifically at the operation of local government. There are several books that provide useful introductions to the local government system in the UK, although most of them in practice principally draw on examples from England. These include T. Byrne *Local Government in Britain* (Harmondsworth: Penguin, 2000), which is regularly updated, and D. Wilson and C. Game *Local Government in the United Kingdom*, 2nd edn (Basingstoke: Macmillan Press, 1998). A stimulating exploration of the changing position of local government in the UK is provided by H. Atkinson and S. Wilks-Heeg *Local Government from Thatcher to Blair. The Politics of Creative Autonomy* (Cambridge: Polity, 2000), which also explores the ways in which local authorities are able to develop innovative policy approaches without reliance on the centre.

Books tend to focus either on local government or on particular policy areas, such as housing, education or health. But there are exceptions. In her stimulating book on *Urban Policy and Politics in Britain* (Basingstoke: Macmillan Press, 2000), D. Hill explores the linkages between New Labour's emergent urban policy and the changing face of urban politics and government. The title of M. Hill and F. Tolan's *Local Authority Social Services* (Oxford: Blackwell, 2000), is self-explanatory.

The dual state thesis is well summarized in P. Saunders and P. Dunleavy's contributions to M. Boddy and C. Fudge (eds) *Local Socialism? Labour Councils and New Left Alternatives.* (Basingstoke: Macmillan Press, 1994). Although the particular examples may by now seem very dated, the most comprehensive discussion of central-local relations in Britain remains R. A. W. Rhodes *Beyond Westminster and Whitehall: Sub-central Governments of Britain* (London: Unwin Hyman, 1988). His more recent study, *Understanding Governance* (Buckingham: Open University Press, 1997), takes some of these issues further, looking at the complex networks of governance that connect local, central and European levels. R. Leach and J. Percy-Smith *Local Governance in Britain* (Basingstoke: Palgrave, 2001) and G. Stoker (ed.) *The New Politics of British Local Governance* (London: Macmillan Press, 2000) provides a useful starting point for exploring the notion of governance.

A guide to the wide range of web-based information on current developments and debates on local government across the UK can be found in chapter V.4.

Social Policy within the United Kingdom

Richard Parry

The United Kingdom is a strongly unitary state and lacks a clear concept of regional differences in social policy in terms of formation, implementation and content. The main source of difference is the status of Scotland, Wales and Northern Ireland within the United Kingdom, enjoying nationhood but not statehood and, since 1999, having their own devolved elected administrations with extensive powers over social policy. This chapter seeks to provide a guide to the range and type of country-specific social policy legislation in England, Scotland, Wales and Northern Ireland; the powers and responsibilities of the devolved systems and their separate social policy agencies in the latter three nations and the English regions; and the major policy initiatives at sub-national level.

The Problem of English Dominance

The starting point is the dominance of England in the United Kingdom. It accounts for nearly 85 per cent of the population and London, its capital, is the centre of political, governmental, cultural and media activity. This dominance, so taken for granted in Britain, is not inevitable. Many countries, most notably Germany, have a spread of regional centres. In the United States the levels of unemployment and health benefits vary among the states. In Germany all of education is run at the *Land* level and so-

cial care services vary according to municipality. Italy, Spain and to some extent France have been developing regional government in recent years. There is a general uniformity of social security benefits in these countries, but the systems have a less concentrated administration than does Britain's. Only Britain carries through the concept of uniformity and standardization so far (for example, there are no official figures on inflation at below the United Kingdom level, partly to avoid debates about differential upratings of benefit). Britain has a lesser sense of federal political structure, with a uniform structure of sub-national government, than any country of comparable size.

Scotland, Wales and Northern Ireland have each long had a separate historical tradition and political profile. Scotland was independent until 1707 and the Act of Union preserved its legal system, Presbyterian Church and local government. It had stronger traditions in education and medicine than did England, and became a United Kingdom leader in these fields. Wales was never a defined independent state but its linguistic and religious pattern was clearly different. Ireland had a separate parliament until 1801, then united with Great Britain but split in 1922 into an independent country (later the Republic of Ireland) and the six counties of Northern Ireland, which remained in the United Kingdom but were given a local parliament. This was suspended in 1972 and attempts to resuscitate it in some form in 1973, 1982 and 1996 all failed; it was only with the IRA ceasefires of 1994 and 1997 that the peace process led to the Belfast, or Good Friday, Agreement of April 1998 which specified a lawmaking assembly and an executive with members of all political parties. In the autumn of 2002 the assembly was suspended again, and at the time of writing Northern Ireland was being ruled from Westminster.

In a host of cultural and social forms, the patriotic identity of the non-English nations has been asserted and cherished but this did not reach the political sphere until the election of the Labour government in 1997. Pressure from the Scottish and Welsh Labour Parties during the Conservative years had led to a political commitment by Labour to transfer the existing powers of the Scottish and Welsh Offices to a Scottish parliament able to pass primary legislation in those areas, and a National Assembly for Wales administering and financing them within a framework of Westminster legislation. Both were to be elected under a reform of proportional system that included a minority of regional seats allocated from party lists to make the overall seat distribution (including the first-past-the-post contests for constituencies identical to those at Westminster) as proportional as possible. Referendums in September 1997 approved the proposals by a strong majority in Scotland (74 per cent) but a bare 50 per cent in Wales. Scotland also voted by 63 per cent to give the parliament limited powers to raise income tax, but this has not so far been used. Elections were held in May 1999 and the new administrations assumed their powers on 1 July 1999. Labour fell short of overall majorities and (in Scotland from the start and in Wales from October 2000) formed a coalition government with the Liberal Democrats. In Northern Ireland the new ministers took office in December 1999, but the devolved institutions were suspended from February to May 2000 and there were further technical suspensions in 2001 connected to disputes over arms

decommissioning.

Devolution does not mean that social policy is no longer developed at the UK level. If separate systems at sub-national level are less good than the norm they will not be politically attractive, and if they are better and more expensive national governments may not be happy to finance them. Politically, the need for separate political management of Scotland, Wales and Northern Ireland is now decisively conceded, but rather than take different directions on the welfare state the devolved administrations have been seeking to operate it in the traditional British way, but at a more generous level. With Westminster still the fiscal underwriter of devolution, there is a tension in United Kingdom social policy between tolerating and resisting differences.

Nation-specific Social Policy Legislation

The legislative framework for social policy is generally the same for social security throughout the United Kingdom (Northern Ireland has different original legislation but has had strict parity of structure and rates, and devolution has not altered this). Pre-devolution, education and housing legislation was largely the same in England and Wales but different in Scotland and Northern Ireland (especially in the structure of school examinations in Scotland and denominational education in Northern Ireland). These latter two nations also had a distinct tradition in health, but Scotland especially has converged with the English norm. While Scotland had a separate Act in 1946 to found the National Health Service (actually passed before the English one), it was included in the National Health Service and Community Care Act 1990. Under Labour, the NHS in Scotland was reorganized separately from England in April 1999: Scotland's Primary Care Trusts go further than England in removing all vestiges of GP fundholding.

Since devolution, the Scottish parliament has been free to legislate in non-reserved areas, and in addition the 'Sewel Convention' allows it to ask Westminster to make technical changes in statutes in devolved areas as a consequence of UK legislation. Actual legislation in social policy has been relatively undramatic. The Scottish parliament passed a Standards in Scotland's Schools etc. Act 2000 that reformed the governance of education on lines set out in a pre-devolution White Paper; an Education (Graduate Endowment and Student Support) (Scotland) Act 2001 to give effect to a fees and grants policy; the Housing (Scotland) Act 2001 which created a single kind of social tenancy and new policies on homelessness and came before legislation on similar matters for England; and a Community Care and Health (Scotland) Act 2002 to set a framework for non-means tested personal care.

The National Assembly for Wales does not have powers to make primary legislation and so has to request the Westminster parliament to make any changes it wants. The single Wales-only post-devolution act has been one to establish a Children's Commissioner for Wales, but there have been major Wales-only provisions in legislation like the Learning and Skills Act 2000. There are Welsh sections in the Education Bill and NHS Reform and Health Care Professions Bill published by the UK Government in November 2001 that will give the Assembly the framework to carry through reforms in these areas. The potential constraints on the Welsh system are clearly greater than in Scotland, but there is scope for significant change through secondary legislation and administrative action.

The Northern Ireland Assembly has been slow to pass any distinctive social policy legislation. A Health and Social Services Act 2001 was about professional regulation, and social security legislation on matters like child support and fraud paralleled British policy as it is in practice required to do. The 2001–2 programme included some more substantial legislation on Best Value in local government and payment to carers. Social policy debate in Northern Ireland is less

on the policy framework than on the allocation of resources within it. Abolition of post-primary educational selection is likely to be the first contentious social policy issue the Assembly will have to confront.

The Operation of the Devolved Administrations

The Scottish and Welsh administrations (which call themselves the Scottish Executive and the Welsh Assembly Government) are descendants of the 'joined-up' former Scottish and Welsh Offices. Scotland has non-statutory departments in social policy areas: Education, Health, Justice and Development (which serves the Minister for Social Justice and covers housing and social inclusion). Wales has groups serving ministers for Education, Health, and Local Government. In Northern Ireland social policy departments are Education, Employment and Learning (including post-16 education), Health and Public Safety (both with Sinn Fein ministers) and Social Development (including housing and social security, with a Democratic Unionist Party minister). In practice, the office of First Minister and Deputy First Minister (run by the Ulster Unionists and the nationalist Social Democratic and Labour Party) provides strategic control and controls funds in cross-cutting areas.

The role of committees of elected members is an essential part of the systems, as part of a general philosophy of openness and participation. All three have permanent committees in the subject-area of each minister which combine the functions of legislative scrutiny and policy investigation. In Scotland the committees have the power to initiate legislation; there is also a Public Petitions Committee to consider petitions from citizens on an issue or grievance, which has sometimes led to the investigation of a local health problem by a single member of the Health Committee. In Wales, the assembly and administration form a single legal and corporate entity, the National Assembly for Wales; assembly clerks are civil servants and ministers sit on committees. The adoption of the (non-statutory) brand name 'Welsh Assembly Government' in 2002 expressed a general wish for a clearer separation of the ministers and the Assembly Members in the public mind.

In Northern Ireland the Committees have a part to play in the policy process: they are chaired by Members of the Legislative Assembly (MLAs) of an opposing political party to the minister as lobbyers for funding bids in their areas. Concurrent membership of local authorities by many members, and the running of most social policy through province-wide central government bodies, mean that the Assembly's work is much more issue- and locality-based than external impressions of political divisions might suggest. Northern Ireland's previous social devolved government which operated from Stormont between 1921 and 1972 maintained religiously discriminatory features in education and housing while seeking parity with mainland standards in health and social security. Later policies emphasized equal opportunities (with explicit legislation against religious discrimination, and Catholic schools now funded equally) and left a relatively benign and well-resourced climate for social policy, with minimal direct political input. The economic and security context of policy left politicians disinclined to attack the welfare state. School education retains selectivity on academic grounds in a way not found in the rest of the United Kingdom (although a review of post-primary education in 2001 recommended that it should be ended). The Northern Ireland Civil Service is separate and is not bound by all the various policies on civil service reform emerging from Whitehall since 1999.

The residual Whitehall arms remain. The Northern Ireland Office still has responsibility for police, prisons and criminal justice but these are intended for devolution to the Assembly at a later stage. The Welsh Office has a role in facililtating Welsh legislation within the UK government's programme, but the Scottish Office has no such function and its official role of monitoring Scottish interests in the UK Cabinet system is of dubious necessity. Where liaison is really important – as in the interface between social security and health and social work support for the elderly – the Executive will deal directly with the Whitehall department.

The administration of social policy in the four nations of the United Kingdom is summarized in table III.7.1. Local government in the three nations is much more neatly organized than it is in England (see chapter III.6), reflecting the strength of the pre-devolution territorial departments in moulding the systems. In 1996, local government in Scotland and Wales was reorganized from two-tier (regions or counties and districts) to single-tier (32 and 22 authorities). Wales is reorganising the NHS into bodies coterminous with local authorities, and Scotland has absorbed NHS Trust boards into Health Boards. Northern Ireland has had 26 districts since 1973 but with all important social functions administered by appointed bodies (Education and Libraries Boards, Health and Social Services Boards (uniquely in the United Kingdom uniting health and social work) and the Northern Ireland Housing Executive). Other functions – roads, water, social security – are administered by agencies of the Northern Ireland Civil Service. England, by contrast, has a patchwork quilt of two-tier county and districts in most areas, broken up by most-purpose metropolitan councils and single-tier unitary authorities in major urban centres (from 1997) and former counties judged not to have built a strong local identity. Management of local expenditure outside England is easier because of the smaller number of local authorities, their closer relations to central government departments and the higher level of central financial support.

Territorial Organization of Social Policy in England

It is impossible to run the social policies of 50 million people from a central department, but government in England sometimes gives a good impression of trying. Social security and employment services are run by civil service agencies (from April 2002 'Jobcentre Plus') on an all-Britain basis; Northern Ireland has a separate Social Security Agency. Local offices are linked to a computer network and have lost most discretion on benefit payments; pensions are run Britain-wide by the Pension Service. Central government outposts have been consolidated into 'Government Offices for the Regions' (responsible for industry, employment, training, agriculture, transport and the environment), which have a potentially higher profile and advocacy role. Health, in contrast, has been deregionalized. In 1996 the former regional health authorities were merged into the former NHS Management Executive to form the NHS Executive, based in Leeds, whose staff are civil servants, with eight regional offices. Higher and further education have separate England-wide funding bodies. Outside the formal public sector altogether are Learning and Skills Councils and housing associations, again with long lines of control. Labour has also shown a weakness for centrally-run local 'challenge' projects such as Health and Education Action Zones and Employment Zones that provide money in return for cooperative working by local agencies.

Pressures for elected regional government in England are weak, with Labour failing to act on previous promises to take it forward in its first term; a long-delayed White Paper on English regional government was due to emerge in 2002. Instead, we have a pattern of smaller than ever operating entities on the ground tied by long lines of control to Whitehall. This is an expression of the conviction of both the Conservative and the Labour governments that once the right answer is found it is the right answer for everywhere and is not to be denied by the intervention of local politicians. In Scotland, Wales and Northern Ireland the national institutions provide a pause for adaptation; in England there is no such provision.

Needs and Resources at Sub-national Level

The United Kingdom's social policy has been underwritten by an implicit northwest to south-east gradient – that Scotland, Wales, Northern Ireland and Northern England were relatively deprived and so could claim additional resources to deal with their problems. The spending relativities remain (table III.7.2) but the justification for them is less certain since the recession of the early 1990s, which undermined the prosperity of the Midlands and South of England. Scotland is only 5 per cent behind England in disposable household income (but Wales is 10 per cent and Northern Ireland 15 per cent behind). On some measures, there are points of weakness: large parts of Scotland and Wales qualify for help from European Union Structural Funds because of the decline in smokestack industries such as coal and steel, urban multiple deprivation or rural deprivation. An opportunistic redrawing of the map in 1999 allowed West Wales and the Valleys to Northern Ireland to qualify for 'Objective 1' status because of their low income per head. Unemployment in Scotland and Wales, nearly equal to the English level in the mid-1990s, has subsequently fallen less fast. But because house prices are lower and public sector health and education better serviced, the non-English nations may feel better off and rank high in subjective quality-of-life indices.

This provides the backdrop to the position on relative public spending (table III.7.2). Figures for 1999-2000 reveal that Northern Ireland, Scotland and Wales (in that order) receive more social expenditure per head than does any region of England: 24, 16 and 11 per cent more than the average. Social security does not have different policies. Public housing expenditure is now so small (3 per cent of the total in table III.7.2) that the wide variations, attributable to different tenure structures, are no longer of great significance; 25 per cent of Scottish dwellings are still owned by local authori-

Table III.7.1 Who runs United Kingdom social policy?

Health	Scottish Executive Department	Welsh Assembly Government NHS Directorate	Department of Health and Public Safety	Department of Health
	NHS Management Executive for Scotland	22 local health groups	4 Health and Social Services Boards	NHS Executive and 8 regional offices
	15 Health Boards		15 Health and Social Services Trusts	99 Health Authorities
	28 NHS Trusts			377 NHS Trusts
Education	Scottish Executive Education Department/ Enterprise and Lifelong Learning Department	Welsh Assembly Government (Education Group)	Department of Education/ Department of Employment and Learning	Department for Education and Skills
		22 local authorities		Local authorities
			5 Education and Library Boards	Higher Education Funding Council for England
	32 local authorities	Education and Learning Wales (ELWA)		Further Education Funding Council
	Scottish Higher Education Funding Council/Scottish Further Education Council (joint secretariat)			
Housing	Communities Scotland (agency within Scottish Executive Development Department)	Housing for Wales (Tai Cymru) (within Welsh Assembly Government)	Department of Social Development'	Local authorities
			Northern Ireland Housing Executive	Housing Corporation
	32 local authorities	22 local authorities		Housing Associations
	Registered Social Landlords (including Housing Associations)	Housing Associations	Housing Associations	
Training	Scottish Enterprise, Highlands & Islands Enterprise	Education and Learning Wales	Training and Employment Agency (within Department of Employment and Learning)	47 Learning and Skills Councils
	22 areas of the local enterprise network			

Source: Compiled mainly from *Departmental Reports* (Cm 5101–20), London: Stationery Office, 2001.

Table III.7.2   Spending per head on social policy 1999–2000 (pounds sterling)

Index: UK = 100	Total social	Social Security	Health and Personal Social Services	Education	Housing
Northern Ireland	124	120	111	136	325
Scotland	116	108	119	126	176
Wales	111	115	110	100	145
London	109	97	121	108	304
North-East	109	119	102	100	57
North-West	106	112	100	101	90
Yorkshire & Humberside	100	103	98	96	71
West Midlands	96	99	92	101	37
South-West	94	97	91	92	35
East Midlands	91	94	88	93	35
East	90	89	92	96	4
South-East	83	84	85	82	25
UK average	3532	1724	1072	685	51

Source: Calculated from HM Treasury, *Public Expenditure Statistical Analyses 2001-02* (Cm 5101 2001), London: Stationery Office, tables 8.6b and 8.12.

tics against 15 per cent in England and Wales, but general rent subsidies have been nearly eliminated in recent years. More important is the advantage in health and education, especially in Scotland, which is more structural in nature and does raise issues for expenditure management; a comparable issue of health expenditure per head in London, which is the highest in the UK. A Needs Assessment Study in 1979 confirmed that provision to Scotland ran ahead of need, and there has been post-devolution pressure for a new exercise. For long, statistics of regional English differences were unavailable, but they now show a range from 83 to 109 per cent of the United Kingdom average, with the North-East and North-West gaining in social security but not other services and London leading on health and education.

The formula used for apportioning expenditure to the territories (the Barnett Formula) remains after devolution: put simply, the budget changes in relation to changes in corresponding English expenditure and is made available as a block to the devolved administrations who can alter priorities within the block without reference to the Treasury. This avoids constant haggling over items and is meant to converge expenditure over time. In practice the differentials are not moving much and they are no longer underwritten by palpable economic disadvantage.

Flexible Initiatives at Sub-national Level

An important justification for devolution is that it allows for flexibility and experimentation. Centralization of policy change, with its massive reorganizations (health, education, local government structure and finance) proceeding in one step throughout the country, risks a centralization of error.

Devolution has enabled Wales to match

some of Scotland's long standing capacity to innovate and experiment in social policy. In 1968 the Scottish system of children's hearings (non-judicial disposals of the cases of children in trouble) had been implemented, in contrast to England, defining the policy area as social work rather than law and order. Scottish school examinations remain quite different, with broadly based highers rather than more specialized A-levels. From 1998 the 'Higher Still' proposals integrated post-16 academic and vocational qualifications. The Welsh language is promoted in Welsh schools more than ever before, even in nearly exclusively English-speaking areas, and post-devolution Wales has moved further towards a distinctive educational policy through the abolition of school tests for seven-year olds, the elimination of league tables for school examination results, and pilot work on a 'Welsh baccalaureate' to replace A-levels. A new funding body, Education and Learning Wales, is responsible for further and higher education and training.

Since devolution, policy initiatives have tended to greater generosity in Scotland and Wales. The main developments are that Scotland has abolished student tuition fees and partially reinstated grants; Wales has made prescriptions and check-ups free for the under-25s and over-60s, and introduced a 'Learning Grant' to provide variable financial support to students in both higher and further education. Scotland has agreed a three-year pay deal with its teachers regarded as generous. Scotland, and to a lesser extent Wales, is moving towards free personal care for the elderly in assessed need in response to the Royal Commission on Long Term Care of 1999 (see also chapters III.4 and IV.3). All of these have been pursued under pressure from the Liberal Democrats and many Labour ministers have been uncomfortable at moving in different policy directions from New Labour in London.

On the administrative side, much depends on the scale of the problems and the personal interest of ministers and officials.

Wales had pioneered de-institutionalization in the mental health area. The speed and nature of response to drug addiction and AIDS in Scotland has been facilitated by local responsibility. Housing has national bodies (Communities Scotland, formerly Scottish Homes, and Tai Cymru) able to mobilize housing associations and now absorbed into the civil service. Industrial development and training has had a much stronger and better resourced administrative impetus in the territories than in England. The distinctiveness of policy in the territories should not be exaggerated, but the existence of their administrative apparatus both before and after devolution is a clear advantage when compared to the English regions.

Conclusion: The Stability and Acceptability of Variations

Devolution to Scotland, Wales and Northern Ireland has emphasized two themes of British social policy of much longer standing: the uniformity of social security rules (and of Treasury-based policies like the New Deal and tax credits), and the ability of the three non-English nations to do things their own way through policies that may be different in substance rather than necessary to take account of local circumstances. Before devolution, the relatively kind treatment of Scotland and Northern Ireland (less so of Wales) on policy and expenditure was not much of an issue: now, it is coming under closer scrutiny, especially in some English regions. Paradoxically, devolution policies that were meant to leave the territories to take local decisions have highlighted the occasions where the logic of their policy-making differs from that of the UK Government. Free personal care for the elderly, and to a lesser extent student support, have been the issues defining the extent of universality in the British welfare state, on which the devolved administrations have taken a position closer to the traditional approach of British social policy.

A sense of instability is evident in the

current devolution settlement. It seeks to respond in a non-uniform way to political pressures around the United Kingdom without any overall concept of what the policy and financial responsibilities of the various level of government should be. The budgetary arrangements are over 20 years old and have not yet been redesigned to accommodate any moves to English regional government. Even under Labour-led administrations and an unusually free flow of additional spending power there have been enough signs of challenge to the view from Whitehall to suggest the kind of difficulties that may arise in future years should

Labour's position weaken. Devolved administrations want to deliver social policy better but their aspirations usually require money; so far there has not been full fiscal responsibility on them to fix tax levels in accordance with their spending decisions. The principal opposition parties in Scotland and Wales (the Scottish National Party and Plaid Cymru – the Party of Wales) are to the left of Labour on social policy but favour full self-government for their nations. This advocacy of both more generous social provision and further constitutional change is the likely future challenge to Westminster.

Guide to further reading

Keeping up with post-devolution developments is not always easy: the best work is that of the of the Constitution Unit, which publishes quarterly monitoring reports on each of the devolved nations and the English regions, available online at ucl.ac.uk/constitution-unit, and annual volumes. R. Hazell (ed.) *The State and the Nations* (London: Imprint Academic, 2000) and A. Trench (ed.) *The State of the Nations 200* (London: Imprint Academic, 2001). A special issue of *Public Policy and Administration* 15, 2 (2000) on 'Devolution and Decentralisation in the UK' has much useful material. Journals like the quarterly *Scottish Affairs* and the annual *Contemporary Wales* are also worth consulting. D. Wilson and C. Game *Local Government in the United Kingdom*, 2nd edn (Basingstoke: Macmillan Press, 1998) is a very useful handbook, which takes account of the variations in Scotland, Wales and Northern Ireland. There is wealth of statistical data in *Regional Trends*, published annually by the Stationery Office for the Office for National Statistics.

Publications of the devolved administrations are available on their websites: scotland.gov.uk, wales.gov.uk and nics.gov.uk. In Scotland, parliamentary reports are on scottish.parliament.uk (with full evidence and an immediate verbatim record of all committee proceedings) and Northern Ireland Assembly debates and reports are on ni-assembly.gov.uk. The websites (especially the Scottish ones) compare favourably with their London equivalents.

III.8
Social Policy and the European Union

Linda Hantrais

Britain was not one of the six founding member states of the European Economic Community (EEC) when it was established in 1957 with the signing of the Treaty of Rome. Following accession in 1973, the United Kingdom opposed Community action in the social policy area and was the only member state not to sign the 1989 Community Charter of the Fundamental Social Rights of Workers. Its opposition led to the chapter on social affairs being relegated to a Protocol and Agreement on Social Policy, which were appended to the Maastricht Treaty on European Union when it came into force in 1993. The UK also sought to impede the progress of legislation on workers' rights, including proposals for improving part-time working conditions and introducing parental leave, on the grounds that they would impinge on national sovereignty and adversely affect employment. The election of the New Labour government in Britain in 1997 marked a turning point in the country's relations with Europe. The government signed up to the Agreement on Social Policy, which meant that the social chapter could be incorporated into the Treaty of Amsterdam in the same year, thus lending social policy a stronger legal base. Employment moved up the European agenda, and its priority was endorsed by both the Treaty and the Luxembourg summit, also held in 1997, when the first employment guidelines were adopted. At the turn of the century, as the Union prepared for enlargement, a European social model was emerging, embodying the core values that all member states were committed to pursue.

This chapter looks at the way in which the social policy remit of the European Union (EU) has emerged and developed both prior to and in the period of British membership. The European social policy formation and implementation processes are examined in an overview of the main policy-making bodies, the instruments available to them and the areas of intervention in which they have been most active. The chapter goes on to identify some of the key debates surrounding the European social dimension, before commenting briefly on the linkages between national and European institutions engaged in social policy formation.

The Development of the EU's Social Policy Remit

Although, as its name implied, the EEC was essentially an economic community, from the outset it was attributed a social policy remit. Articles 117–28 of the Treaty of Rome, which dealt with social policy, advocated close cooperation between member states, particularly in matters relating to training, employment, working conditions, social security and collective bargaining. They also stated the need to observe the equal pay principle and make provision for the harmonization of social security measures to accommodate migrant workers. Specific arrangements were to be made for operating a European Social Fund (ESF) to assist in the employment and re-employment of workers and to encourage geographical and occupational mobility.

In the post-war context of rapid economic growth, the underlying objectives of European social policy were to avoid any distortion of competition and to promote free movement of labour within the Community. Since the welfare systems of the founder member states (Belgium, France, the Federal Republic of Germany, Italy, Luxembourg and the Netherlands) were based largely on the insurance principle, which depended on contributions from employers and employees, it was feared that unfair competition might arise if some countries levied higher social charges on employment, leading to social dumping as companies relocated to areas with lower labour costs. The expectation was that the functioning of the common market, in conjunction with the Treaty's rules preventing unfair competition, would automatically result in social development, so that the Community would not need to interfere directly with redistributive benefits. By the mid-1970s, economic growth was slowing down following the oil crises, and the belief in automatic social harmonization was being called into question. A more active approach to social reform was therefore required. A 1974 resolution from the Council of Ministers on a social action programme proposed that the Community should work to develop objectives for national social policies but without seeking to standardize solutions to social problems and without removing responsibility for social policy from member states.

Despite attempts to give a higher profile to social policy in the 1980s, the principle established in the social action programme set the tone for social legislation in subsequent years. The 1980s were marked by pressures to develop a 'social space', which the Commission President, Jacques Delors, saw as the natural complement to the completion of the internal market. Delors advocated a social dialogue between trade unions and employers (the social partners) as a means of reaching agreement over objectives and establishing a minimum platform of guaranteed social (implying workers' employment related) rights, which could then be applied by individual member states with a view to stimulating convergence.

The problem of agreeing even a minimum level of protection for workers was apparent in the negotiations leading up to the Community Charter of the Fundamental Social Rights of Workers, which did not have force of law and was couched in non-specific terms. The action programmes for implementing the Charter continued to recognize the importance of observing national diversity, and the Maastricht Treaty formalized the principle of subsidiarity, which means that the Union is empowered to act only if its aims can be more effectively achieved at European than at national level. Since decisions about social policy frequently concern individuals or families, it can be argued that they are best taken at a local level remote from European institutions. Accordingly, opportunities for concerted action among nations are minimal.

EC membership has taken place in four successive waves, each making harmonization, or even convergence, of social policy provisions more difficult to achieve. As mentioned above, the social protection systems of the six original EEC member states can be considered as variants of what has come to be known as the Bismarckian or continental model of welfare, based on the employment-insurance principle. The new members (the United Kingdom, Denmark and Ireland), which joined the Community in the 1970s, subscribed to social protection systems funded from taxation and aimed at universal flat-rate coverage. The southern states (Greece, Portugal and Spain), which became members in the early 1980s, had less developed welfare systems, whereas the Nordic states (Finland and

Sweden), which took up membership in 1995, shared features with Denmark, and Austria was closer to the German pattern. While the goal of harmonizing social protection would seem to have become more pressing with the move towards the Single European Market (SEM) and economic and monetary union, doubts have increasingly been expressed about the feasibility and desirability of attempts at European level to harmonize such different welfare systems. There was, however, evidence to suggest that some convergence occurred in the 1990s as a result of the common trend towards retrenchment of welfare, made necessary by economic recession, the shift towards mixed systems of welfare and progress towards economic and monetary union.

Social Policy-making Processes in the EU

Despite the relatively limited social policy remit in the founding treaty, after fifty years of operation, the European Union has developed what can be described as a multi-tiered system of governance. The decision-making, legislative and implementation procedures of the Union depend upon a number of institutions, with their own functions and operating mechanisms, but often in competition with one another. The Nice Treaty adopted at the European Council meeting in December 2000 set out to revise these decision-making procedures to pave the way for enlargement.

The Council of Ministers remains the main governing body representing national interests and responsible for taking decisions on laws to be applied throughout the Union. All the heads of government meet twice a year to determine policy directions. The presidency of the Council rotates between member states every six months, providing the opportunity for national governments to set the policy agenda, with each member state having a fixed number of votes. The Nice Treaty proposed a re-weighting of votes to ensure that the influ-

ence of the smaller countries would not become disproportionate to their size: ranging from twenty-nine votes for France, Germany, Italy and the UK to four for Luxembourg and three for Malta. The Single European Act (SEA) of 1986 introduced qualified majority voting (QMV) in the areas of health and safety at work, working conditions, information and consultation of workers, equality between men and women and the integration of persons excluded from the labour market, with the aim of facilitating the passage of contentious legislation. QMV was extended to active employment measures when they were introduced into the Amsterdam Treaty, and provision was made in the Nice Treaty to apply QMV to anti-discrimination measures, mobility and specific action for economic and social cohesion.

The Commission formally initiates, implements and monitors European legislation. Commissioners are political appointments but are expected to act independently of national interests. The UK has two members, as do the other larger member states, but from 2005, each member states will have one commissioner. The directorates general (DGs) are responsible for preparing proposals and working documents for consideration by the Council of Ministers and, therefore, play an important part in setting the EU's policy agenda. For example, the 1995 White Paper on European Social Policy, drafted by the DG for Employment and Social Affairs, established a framework for EU action through to the twenty-first century. The Nice Treaty reinforced this role by providing for the Commission to establish a Social Protection Committee to monitor the social situation, promote exchange of information and prepare reports and opinions.

The European Court of Justice (ECJ), which sits in Luxembourg, is the Union's legal voice and the guardian of treaties and implementing legislation. Its judges are appointed by the governments of member states for six-year terms of office. Its main tasks are to ensure that legal instruments adopted at European and national level are compatible with European law. Through its interpretation of legislation, it has built up a substantial and influential body of case law in the social area. The Amsterdam Treaty extended the ECJ's jurisdiction further by giving it powers to ensure that the article on fundamental rights is observed by EU institutions.

The European parliament is directly elected by citizens of member states. The parliament has budgetary and supervisory powers. It cannot initiate bills, but it can decline to take up a position on a Commission proposal and require the Commission to answer its questions. MEPs form political rather than national blocks. Their powers were increased by the SEA, and then by the Amsterdam Treaty, which extended the parliament's involvement in decision making in the social policy area. The Nice Treaty applied the co-decision procedure to the same social areas as for QMV.

The EU's legal sources include primary legislation in the form of treaties and secondary legislation ranging from regulations, directives and decisions, which are its most binding instruments, to recommendations, resolutions and opinions, which are advisory, or communications and memoranda, which are used to signal initial thinking on an issue. Relatively few regulations have been introduced in the social field, with the exception of freedom of movement of workers and the Structural Funds. Directives, which lay down objectives for legislation but leave individual states to select the most suitable form of implementation, have been used to considerable effect in the areas of equal treatment and health and safety at work. Recommendations have played an important role in developing a framework for concerted action and convergence in the social policy field.

The EU has established a broad array of multi-layered and fragmented policy-making institutions and instruments, which are often in competition with national systems. European policy-making is, therefore, sub-

ject to a complex process of negotiation and compromise, involving vested interests and trade-offs. While the progress of the social dimension has undoubtedly been slowed down by internal wrangling, the Union has gradually extended its area of competence and authority.

EU Social Policy Intervention

From the 1970s, Community programmes were initiated in the areas of education and training, health and safety at work, workers' and women's rights and poverty; many of them funded by the ESF. The Commission also set up a number of networks and observatories to stimulate action and monitor progress in the social field.

Rather than seeking to change national systems, action in the area of education and training focused initially on comparing the content and level of qualifications across the Community in an attempt to reach agreement over transferability from one member state to another. General directives were issued on the mutual recognition of the equivalence of diplomas. From the mid-1970s, initiatives were taken at European level, through a series of action programmes, to develop vocational training, encourage mobility among students and young workers and stimulate cooperation between education and industry. At the turn of the century, the Commission was advocating investment in human resources through quality education as an important component in the European social model and European identity.

Several articles in the EEC Treaty were devoted to the improvement of living and working conditions as a means of equalizing opportunities and promoting mobility. Particular attention has been paid to health and safety at work, resulting in a large body of binding legislation. The introduction of QMV in this area has meant that the health and safety banner has been used to initiate directives designed not only to ensure the protection of workers against dangerous products and other industrial hazards but also to control the organization of working time, to protect pregnant women and to take forward wider issues concerning public health. In response to the public health scares of the 1990s, an article on public health was introduced into the Amsterdam Treaty, making reference to the importance of achieving high standards of safety.

In line with the priority given to employment policy and working conditions at European level, the Commission has been concerned to legislate and set up action programmes to protect women as workers rather than as citizens. Directives on equal opportunities in respect of equal pay for work of equal value, equal treatment and employment-related social insurance rights have sought to redress the balance for economically active women. Increasingly, attention has been paid to measures designed to help reconcile occupational and family life. Legislation in this area was, for many years, opposed by some member states – notably the UK and Denmark – who were wary of the possible impact on employment practices and equal opportunities. The British opt-in to the social chapter in 1997 resulted in the UK signing up to the parental leave directive. It also meant that the directive on part-time work could finally be adopted.

In a context where greater life expectancy has been accompanied by heavy demands on health and care services, member states have become increasingly concerned, individually and collectively, about the effects of population ageing on social protection systems. The Commission has monitored provision for older and disabled people, particularly with regard to maintenance and caring, arrangements for transferring the rights of mobile workers and pensioners and the overall impact of policy on living standards. In a communication published in 1999, 'Towards a Europe for all ages', it proposed a strategy for strengthening solidarity and equity between the generations.

In the 1970s, the impact of economic recession, rising unemployment and demo-graphic ageing moved on to the policy agenda, while the prospect of greater freedom of movement heightened concern about welfare tourism and the exporting of poverty from one member state to another, on the grounds that unemployed workers and their families might seek to move to states with more generous provision. From the 1970s, the Commission funded a series of action programmes to combat poverty and social exclusion, and the Structural Funds have been deployed to underpin regional policy by tackling the sources of economic disparities. At the Berlin summit in 1999, the Council agreed to set up a Cohesion Fund to help the pre-accession states to meet the criteria for membership. The employment guidelines, introduced by the Amsterdam treaty, served as a major plank in the EU's strategy to combat exclusion from the labour market by improving employability through active policy measures.

The Commission's objective of removing barriers to the free movement of labour has served to justify policies for coordinating social protection systems, mutual recognition of qualifications, the general improvement of living and working conditions and directives on equality of access to social benefits and measures to combat poverty. Despite the considerable body of legislation in this area, information about intra-European mobility suggests that migration between member states has remained relatively low. Progressively, more attention has been paid to the problems arising from third-country migration and the challenges it poses not only for coordinating national policies but also for issues concerning refugees and asylum seekers. This progression was recognized when the fundamental right to equality of opportunity and treatment, without distinction of race, colour, ethnicity, national origin, culture or religion was written into the Amsterdam Treaty.

While doubts may be expressed about the coherence of the EU's social policy remit, these examples illustrate how the Union's institutions have developed a wide-ranging competence in social affairs, with the result that they have become a major, if disputed, social policy actor.

Key Issues in European Social Policy Analysis

By the mid-1990s, the Commission had formally recognized that member states should remain responsible for their own systems of social protection, but, as in the original Treaty of Rome, it was again advocating closer cooperation with a view to identifying possible common objectives and solutions. The debates of the 1970s and 1980s over such fundamental issues as whether or not the Community should have a social dimension seemed to have lost their salience in the face of pressing social problems requiring a common response.

Although EU member states have generally failed to agree about the extent of the involvement of the Union in the social policy area or the form it should take, they did seem able to reach a broad consensus about the major social problems they were confronting as they prepared for the twenty-first century (see also chapter I.3). Demographic trends in combination with technological and structural change, the prospects for further enlargement of the Union to the countries of Central and Eastern Europe, and the extension of its sphere of influence were creating new pressures on welfare systems. Member states were seeking innovative ways of dealing with persistently high levels of unemployment, the inadequate supply of skilled labour, long-term dependency of older people and the changing structure of households and gender relations, while struggling to contain the costs of providing high-quality services.

These changes were calling into question the principles on which national social security systems were founded. EU member states were concerned to ensure the financial viability of social protection, while safeguarding employment and avoiding the development of a dependency culture. Population ageing had raised questions about the conditions governing retirement age and pension rights, while also exacerbating the problems of making provision for health and caring. Different mixes of solutions were being tried: from greater targeting of benefits, the tightening of eligibility criteria and emphasis on active measures to get people into work and off benefits, to the introduction of new social insurance schemes to cover long-term care and the privatization of services. At the turn of the century, the prospect of enlargement to the East focused attention on the sustainability of social protection systems. The Commission had identified as a major challenge the need to modernize social protection systems in response to socio-economic change and enlargement, while at the same time consolidating the European social model.

Sharing European and National Competence

Despite the blocking tactics of some member states, a considerable body of legislation and practice – *acquis communautaire* – has been put in place, requiring compliance from national governments and constraining their domain of action. However, the changes brought about by the SEA, Maastricht, Amsterdam and Nice Treaties, the British opt-in to the social chapter and the shift towards less binding forms of legislation in the social field have tended to result in standards being set that can realistically be achieved by the least advanced countries – the lowest common denominator – and have left individual member states with greater discretion in the way they implement policy.

The examples used in this chapter to illustrate the EU's social policy competence suggest that the policy-making process is dependent upon the ability of a plurality of national and supranational actors to cooperate in setting objectives, initiating, enacting and implementing legislation. The sharing of responsibility distinguishes European structures from those of most international organizations. As in federal states, the Union has to steer a difficult path in acting for the greater good of its member states, which is itself not easy to identify, while not encroaching too far into national sovereignty or infringing the principle of subsidiarity. A delicate balance has to be struck in accommodating the interests of the different tiers of the Union's institutions, some of which are protecting and promoting national causes (Council of Ministers and parliament, national governments), while others are expected to act independently of governments (Commission and ECJ). Consequently, the EU has still not secured full legitimacy as a supranational authority in the social policy field, whereas the competence of member states has undoubtedly been eroded.

Guide to further reading

The European Commission's annual reports on *The Social Situation in the European Union* and *Employment in Europe*, and its biennial report on *Social Protection in Europe* (Luxembourg: Office for Official Publications of the European Communities) provide commentary on social and employment trends, and the progress made towards achieving common objectives for national systems of social protection.

Websites:
The website of the Directorate General for Employment and Social Affairs contains a wealth of material on all aspects of social policy in the European Union, its member and applicant states, which can be accessed at the following address: http://europa.eu.int/comm/dgs/employment_social/index_en.htm

The SCADPlus web site for Employment and Social Affairs provides links to information about the legal framework for social policy as well as updates on the social action programmes at: http://europa.eu.int/scadplus/leg/en/s02000.htm

Detailed information about the operation of national social security arrangements is contained in the annual reports produced for the Commission by the Mutual Information System on Social protection in the EU Member States and the EEA, available on-line at: http://europa.eu.int/comm/employment_social/missoc2001/index_en.htm (the date refers to the most recent edition available).

The development of the social dimension of the European Union, its role in setting a European-wide social policy agenda and the impact of its policies at national level are examined by L. Hantrais *Social Policy in the European Union*, 2nd edn (Basingstoke and New York: Palgrave, 2000). The author analyses the central concepts associated with European social policy-making, covering education and training, the improvement of living and working conditions, provision for families and women, older and disabled people, and policies to combat social exclusion and encourage mobility. The text by T. Hervey *European Social Law and Policy* (Harlow: Addison Wesley Longman, 1998), and the edited collection by J. Shaw *Social Law and Policy in an Evolving European Union* (Oxford and Portland, OR: Hart, 2000) documents changing social law and practice in selected policy areas. R. Geyer *Exploring European Social Policy* (Oxford: Polity Press, 2000), examines social policy as a central issue in EU politics and in theories of European integration, concentrating on labour policy and workers' rights, gender policy, the structural funds, socially excluded groups and public health.

III.9

Supranational Agencies and Social Policy

Bob Deacon

As we have seen in chapters I.3 and II.18 globalization is impacting upon social policy in several ways. Not only is it setting welfare states in competition with each other and facilitating the growth of global welfare markets, it is also bringing new actors at supranational level into the picture. These are increasingly important in influencing both national developments and in making supranational social policy. This chapter looks at some of these organizations and the extent to which they constitute an effective mechanism of global social governance. Some ideas for thinking about global social governance reform are suggested. The chapter also looks at some of the ways the debate and contest within and between these organizations has influenced not only an emerging supranational social policy but also impacted upon national social policies.

Though this is a relatively new field of enquiry within social policy and one that is still developing, its central concerns are already clear. They centre on what I have called the supranationalization or globalization of social policy instruments, policy and provision. This supranationalization takes three forms each of which raises a number of interrelated questions for policy analysts:

- *Supranational regulation* embraces those mechanisms, instruments and policies at a supranational and global level that seek to regulate the terms of trade and

the operation of firms in the interests of social protection and welfare objectives. At a global level such instruments and policies are at a primitive level of development. The key issue here is whether the social regulation of capitalism practised by the European Union can and will be elevated to the global playing field.

- *Supranational redistribution* operates between countries. At a subglobal level this operates effectively already within the European Union through the structural and associated funds that ensure a degree of support for poorer regions by richer ones. As the much valued United Nations Human Development Report for 1996 suggested 'human society is increasingly taking on a global dimension. Sooner or later it will have to develop the global institutions to match' and 'a system of progressive income tax [from rich to poor nations]'.

- *Supranational provision* occurs at a level above that of national government. This refers to the embryonic measures so far almost exclusively developed only at the subglobal, especially European, level, whereby people gain an entitlement to a service or are empowered in the field of social citizenship rights by an agency acting at a supranational level. The European Court of Justice in Luxembourg hears cases brought by EU citizens against countries that are perceived as breaking EU law in the social (and other) spheres. The Council of Europe empowers the citizens of member states to take their government to the Strasbourg Court of Human Rights if they believe their rights have been circumscribed. At a global level the only court that exists is the International Court of Justice in the Hague, which is exclusively concerned with war crimes, and not yet accessed by individuals. The United Nations High Commission for Refugees acts in the welfare interests of stateless persons and refugees.

Social Policy Concepts in a Global Context

Supranational citizenship

Thinking about the concept of social needs and the concept of social citizenship entitlement in a globalizing world only serves to highlight the double-sidedness of the concept of citizenship (see too chapter III.11). On the one hand, citizenship within the context of democratic capitalist society is about securing rights and entitlements for all within a state. On the other hand, it is about excluding from the benefits of citizenship those outside the state. The last years of the twentieth century saw a simultaneous deepening and strengthening of citizenship rights and entitlements within some states and the tightening of restrictions on migrants to gain access to the citizenship rights of many of those same Northern and Eastern countries.

This process looks set to continue. But, while these citizenship rights and associated duties were developed historically within capitalist societies within one state, the globalization process is at the same time generating the emergence of supranational citizenship entitlements. This has developed furthest in the European context. The thirty-odd member states of the Council of Europe provide for their citizens the right to equal treatment before the Court of Human Rights in Strasbourg with regard to

human rights issues. No supranational political and social rights are guaranteed for the citizens of the member states of the Council of Europe, but states are encouraged to ratify the Council's Social Charter, which lays down a range of minimum social rights and entitlements. For the smaller number of states of the EU a plethora of political, civil and social rights now exist and are enshrined in the supranational law of the community. At a global level, the UN Declaration of Human Rights embraces social questions but as yet there is no legal enforcement of these rights in member states of the UN and no individual rights of petition. At the same time there are other ways in which the social aspects of citizenship are, in a piecemeal way, developing an international dimension. Numerous bilateral agreements exist between states regarding the reciprocal recognition of social security and other social rights. At a global level the UN High Commission for Refugees assumes responsibility for the livelihood of stateless persons.

Justice between states

At one level the transposition of the concepts of equality, rights and social justice from the interpersonal or inter-group to the inter-state provides no major conceptual problems. Social policy analysts, thinking globally, would simply join forces with development studies specialists and analyse the extent to which the world was a 'fair' place. Data concerning social inequalities within and between nations are now much more available. We can describe the extent to which the welfare needs of the world's population are increasingly being met but also the extent to which they are being met inequitably both within and across borders.

At another level, however, the issue of transnational justice raises difficult analytical and political questions. The Rawlsian conception of justice appropriate to a capitalist state (whereby that inequality is justified that raises the level of the poorest) becomes problematic at a global level. Equally, the political processes of democratic class struggle within small relatively homogeneous states, which have secured in parts of the North and West a degree of social justice, are not easily replicable on a global terrain. Put simply, how can an alliance be constructed between the poor of the South and the better off poor of the North to struggle to achieve an improvement in the conditions of the poor of the South, without unacceptably undermining the relatively better off poor of the North, and in ways which are economically and ecologically sustainable? By what social and political processes will the uncertain global alliances from below translate into the construction of global political institutions that seek to secure an acceptable measure of global justice? Daunting as this prospect might seem, it is part of the argument here that we are already witnessing this process and the progress it is making is central to an understanding of social policy.

Global Governance and Social Policy

One way of examining this is through the global social governance reform debate. This is likely to be an issue on the international agenda for some time. In 2002 the International Labour Organisation (ILO) established a World Commission on the Social Dimension of Globalization. It reports in 2003. Later in 2003 the United Nations (UN) General Assembly will consider any emerging reform ideas. At one level the global reformist project might be simply expressed as the further development of those systems of *redistribution, regulation* and *provision* just described. A global progressive taxation policy that levied disproportionally from the richer countries to fund social security schemes in the poorer would be an example of the first. An extension of the European social regulation of capitalism project to all of the globe would be an example of the second. The increasing of the powers of supra-

national courts and the greater empowerment of citizens to use these against governments would be an example of the third.

One way to think about radical global social governance reform therefore is to compare governance arrangements at the national, European and global level. Tables III.9.1 and III.9.2 summarize the social functions of governance at these levels and the reforms to global institutions that might be needed to emulate what is done at lower levels.

This idealized (utopian?) set of global social governance reforms is clearly not capable of realization in the short term, even if all of them were considered desirable. It is, however, creeping up both the global agenda and that of a number of key international bodies. For instance, the World Commission on the Social Dimension of Globalization has been charged by the ILO Secretary General with 'examining ways in which all the international organizations can contribute to a more inclusive globalization process that is fair to all' (www.ilo.org). One of its members, Nayyar (forthcoming), has advocated three specific reforms: full or partial independent UN financing; the establishment of a Global People's Assembly along the lines of the EU parliament; and the creation of an Economic Security Council to ensure the UN provides an institutional mechanism for consultations on global economic policies and, wherever necessary, becomes the international regulatory authority.

The considerable support building up for some form of global social governance should not, however, blind us to the formidable obstacles to change. As with the debate over the enlargement of the EU these involve both the practical issues of designing appropriate structures and more principled concerns over the types of policy these should promote. The scale of these issues, which may serve as smokescreens for countries/organizations with conflicting interests, are indicated below.

Table III.9.1 The social functions of governance at national, regional and global level

Function/ policy field	National government	EU regional government	Current global arrangements
Economic stability	Central Banks	Central Bank in EURO zone	IMF/ Bank of International Settlements?
Revenue raising	National taxation	Customs revenues plus government 'donations' (talk of tax harmony and regional tax)	None but mix of UN appeals, *ad hoc* global funds, bi and multilateral ODA
Redistribution	Tax and income transfers policy plus regional funds	Structural funds on social criteria	None but *ad hoc* humanitarian relief, special global funds, debt relief and differential pricing (drugs)
Social regulation (labour and social standards)	State laws and directives	EU laws and directives	Soft ILO, WHO etc. conventions. UN Conventions Voluntary codes
Social rights (citizenship empowerment)	Court redress Consumer charters Tripartite governance	EU Luxembourg Court Redress Tripartite governance (note also C of E Strasbourg Social Charter)	UN Commission For Human Rights but no legal redress Civil society monitoring

Global Social Governance Issues

Institutional fragmentation and competition

Currently international social governance is characterized by fragmentation, overlap and competition between a plethora of international agencies and the proliferation of poorly coordinated meetings where agendas are set, policies debated and opinions formed. Among the most obvious overlap and competition issues are those between:

- The World Bank/IMF/WTO and the rest of the UN system;

- The UN secretariat in New York and UN social agencies (such as the ILO, World Health Organization (WHO), and UNICEF);
- Differing, though overlapping, self-appointed groupings of countries (such as the G8, G20, G16, G77);
- Other global and regional level bodies (such as the EU, MERCOSUR, ASEAN);
- The OECD (particularly its recent activities on tax havens, globalization and development and its series of regional global forums);
- Global think tanks and development networks (such as the 'Davos' World Economic Forum, the 'Porte Allegro'

Table III.9.2   The institutions of social governance at national, regional and global level

Constituent interests	National institutions	EU regional institutions	Potential reformed global institutions
The electorate	Parliament	EU parliament with fewer powers	World People's Assembly?
Government ministers	Cabinet etc.	Councils of Ministers	Reformed UN ECOSOC?
Civil service	Ministries	EU Commission	Combination and rationalization of overlapping sector functions of UNDESA, UNDP, ILO, WHO, UNESCO, World Bank, WTO, OECD, and NEW tax authority
Judiciary	Courts	Luxembourg Court (and C of E Strasbourg Court of Human Rights)	New International Court with human rights mandate
Capital	Central Bank	Central Bank	Central Bank
Labour (civil society)	Trade unions and statutory consultations	TUs on Economic and Social Committee and consultations	Enhanced TU and civil society consultation mechanisms

World Social Forum, the State of the World Forum's Commission on Globalization, and the Global Development Net (GDN) sponsored by the World Bank);
- International philanthropic foundations (including the Ford, Rockefeller, Soros, Turner, and Gates foundations);
- International NGOs and civil society organizations (including Oxfam, ICSW, TNI, ICFTU, and Southern equivalents such as TWN, Focus on the Global South etc.);
- International scholarly gatherings and processes;
- International political alliances (such as the Second International).

Reconfiguring these into a common schema is clearly a marathon task! More fundamentally inter-agency differences are compounded by divisions between those, primarily in the North, who wish to bring more order into this situation by, for example, empowering the UN in global economic and social affairs and by empowering the South to be more effective actors in the international game, and some, primarily in the South, who uphold decentred globalization with a plurality of institutions especially at regional level offsetting the major (Northern) players.

Global social redistribution and international finance for global public goods

An equally important question is how existing or new/reformed international organizations might access funds to provide for any agreed international social policy. Here too there are deep fissures among the key agencies/ countries. Whilst some EU countries are sympathetic to the notion of international taxation for international public goods, the USA generally speaking opposes such proposals. A major strategic issue then is whether and how the American position can be confronted.

Global social regulation

Here debate centres on how the global economy might be subject to regulations that protect social well-being, particularly through:

- preserving and improving labour standards in a global economy;
- establishing a global set of social policy principles;
- maintaining and improving international health standards;
- regulating the emerging international markets in private health, education and social protection;
- establishing voluntary or mandatory guidelines for corporate social responsibility.

These hinge on whether EU policy and practice that tries to ensure minimum cross-border common standards within the EU is regarded by the South as an example to be followed or an obstacle to global regulation serving only EU protectionist interests.

Global social rights

Globalization has given enormous rights to capital to flow freely from one country to another. An issue for social policy analysts is whether this economic globalization can be matched by the globalization of social rights. Among the aspects of this problematic are:

- moves to strengthen the attention given to social rights within the UN's international rights agenda and procedures;
- tension between this trajectory of reform and the increased attention being given to cultural and regional diversity;
- the implications of international labour mobility (both legal and illegal) for the social rights of migrants;
- the calls for dual citizenship rights among migrant workers;
- the decentring of national claims to social citizenship rights in favour of both ethnic/religious claims and of international citizenship claims;
- moves to establish an international social security and social assistance regime.

Global Social Governance Prospects: The Influence of International Organizations on National Social Policy

Assessing the extent to which these developments are likely to reinforce or undermine pressure for more integrated, sustainable forms of international governance capable of delivering redistributive provision presents a major challenge for the future. The prospects for global social governance, however, are also contingent on the stance taken by the key international agencies whose activities set the framework, directly and indirectly, for national as well as supranational social policies. Their influence is most visible where, for example, funding is conditional on the adoption of certain social policies or certain programmes are followed in preference to others. But the discourse within and between international organizations on desirable policy also influences national policy-making in other ways as it constitutes a background climate of international opinion about best practice.

These processes are most visible in the

countries of the South and Eastern Europe. But they are also conditioning developments elsewhere. To make this point is to draw attention to the politics of globalization and in particular the 'hidden' politics of international organizations such as the World Bank, the International Monetary Fund (IMF), World Trade Organization (WTO), UN social agencies and the OECD. Many of these, it has been argued, have been major players in encouraging a particular neo-liberal form of globalization and hence a neo-liberal or residual form of national social policy. (Deacon et al., 1997; Mishra, 1999). While encouraging economic globalization they were engaged in prescribing a set of social policies that they regard as appropriate in a globalizing context.

This is not to say that all international organizations spoke with one voice. There was and continues to be extensive controversy within and between them as to how far the neo-liberal form of globalization and associated social policies should be pursued which in some ways parallel many of the 'regime' distinctions made in comparative social policy (see chapter III.3). Thus the IMF regarded welfare expenditure as a burden on the economy and upheld an American *workfare* safety net approach to social policy. The World Bank's focus on poverty alleviation led it too to a residualist approach. Within the ILO and some other UN agencies, on the other hand, were to be found supporters of the view that social expenditures were a means of securing social cohesion. The ILO in particular supported a conservative-corporatist Bismarckian type of social protection. The OECD favoured the notion that certain state welfare expenditures should be regarded as a necessary investment. But no international organization, save possibly UNICEF, could be said to uphold the redistributive approach to social policy characteristic of the Scandinavian countries (Deacon et al., 1997)

Though these conclusions still broadly stand interesting shifts have taken and are taking place in the position of particular players and these are beginning to filter into national policy debates as well as the activities of the key players. First it appears there are signs that some agencies are beginning to modify their earlier neo-liberal prescriptions. For instance, the OECD, whose 1981 report on the welfare state crisis epitomized the belief that public welfare impeded economic growth, appears to have undergone a paradigm shift. It is now warning that globalization may require more not less social protection and that social expenditure may contribute to growth. The IMF too has begun to modify its approach, most notably in recent papers and conferences considering whether some degree of equity facilitates economic expansion.

There are also indications of shifts in the stance taken by the World Bank, evidenced in some of the 'sector strategies' produced by its Human Development Network set up in 1996. In line with past thinking its proposals for social protection uphold risk management and the individual's responsibility to self-insure against old age and other contingencies, supported only by a basic state scheme. That for health, however, views statutory involvement as the best means of securing universal access, equity and efficiency by correcting market failure, especially where there are significant externalities or serious information asymmetries.

Paradoxically, meanwhile, some within the ILO, the organization most committed to universalism, have begun to show signs of conceding to the World Bank's pensions' policy, whilst its attempts to establish common global labour and social standards have been bedevilled by Southern governments' mistrust of the motives of Northern states. The resultant impasse within the ILO has not, however, prevented support for what have come to be known as core labour standards concerning the prohibition of forced and child labour, freedom of association and the right to organize and bargain collectively, equal remuneration for men and women for work of equal value, and non-discrimination in employment.

Developments of this kind stand in sharp contrast to those promoted by other agencies with different remits and policy 'messages' that have gained a new prominence in the global discourse about social policy. The WTO in particular has emerged as an important player. Within the framework of its General Agreement on Trades and Services (GATS) it is actively attempting to increase the global trade in services, including health, education and personal insurance (see chapter I.3). For many observers its proposals threaten core public services to the detriment of users across the world, particularly in the North. They also portend a further, more intense round of global economic restructuring of the kind experienced in the wake of the liberalizations of the 1970s and 1980s.

Whether these fears will be realized, or offset by the movement for global social reformism remains to be seen. Either way it is clear that in considering the future of welfare systems social policy analysts need to take cognisance of the role and influence of supranational and global actors. This means looking not only at the traditional welfare hubs of the North and West but developments in the South. It also means looking both at the agencies themselves and the issues posed by the emergence of international social policy.

Guide to further reading

As yet there are few texts that deal with issues addressed in this chapter, but useful starting points are provided by: H. O. Bergensen and L. Lund *Dinosaurs or Dynamos: The UN and the World Bank at the Turn of the Century* (London, Earthscan, 1999); B. Deacon et al. *Global Social Policy: International Organisations and the Future of Welfare* (London, Sage, 1997).; I. Kaul, I. Grunberg and M. Stern, (eds) *Global Public Goods.* (New York: Oxford University Press, 1999).; D. Nayyar *The Governance of Globalisation* (forthcoming; unconfirmed title – prior to publication consult www.wider.unu.edu); R. O'Brien et al. *Contesting Global Governance* (Cambridge, CUP, 2000).

The journal to keep up to date with is *Global Social Policy*. It contains a regular digest which can be accessed electronically from the web pages of the Globalism and Social Policy Programme (GASPP) at www.stakes.fi/gaspp.

You should also keep a regular eye on the web pages of the international organizations mentioned in the text (see chapter V.6) and on those web pages that provide critical opinion about the activities of the international organizations. Of these the following are particularly useful for tracking international social policy development:

Bretton Woods project: A group of UK NGOs monitoring IMF and World Bank:
    www.brettonwoodsproject.org
CROP – the Comparative Research Programme on Poverty established by the International Social Science Council:
    www.crop.org
Global Policy Forum. A UN watching organization. A very extensive archive of materials:
    http://www.globalpolicy.org/socecon
ICSW – The International Council on Social Welfare:
    www.icsw.org
TNI – Transnational Institute – an international network of activist-scholars concerned to analyse and find viable solutions to global problems:
    www.tni.org

World Forum (State of the World Forum) with its associated Commission on Globalization:
  www.worldforum.org
World Social Forum –The Porte Allegro Annual Social Summit:
  http://www.forumsocialmundial.org.br/eng
WTO Watch:
  http://www.wtowatch.org
World Economic Forum– The Annual Davos Event:
  http://www.weforum.org

The Consumption of Welfare

III.10
Paying for Welfare

Howard Glennerster

Who Pays Matters

None of the ideals discussed by earlier contributors to this volume are attainable unless the means to achieve them are paid for by someone. Meeting socially defined needs, through some kind of welfare state, or providing for the care and education of those in one's own family, have to be paid for. One of the reasons why the state has continued to play a large role in providing services like education and health, despite concerns about taxation, is the sheer cost to families of meeting school or hospital bills at those times in their lives when these burdens are greatest and incomes are low. So, despite the high-minded ideals of all the various advocates of change, the hard realities of how you pay for them drive much of practical social policy.

This was perfectly illustrated at the beginning of Tony Blair's second term. The Labour government had won the general election in 2001 promising to improve Britain's public services. It had not promised it would raise taxes to pay for these improvements. An enquiry was set in train to decide how much should be spent on the NHS in the longer term and how it should be paid for (Wanless Report, 2001). A Royal Commission on Long Term Care had reported in 1999 (Cm4912, London: Stationery Office). A review of university funding was underway in 2002. The same was true of public transport. Wherever you looked the question – how do we pay for it? – seemed to dominate politics.

Moreover, if you, as a graduate of social policy, go to work in a human service agency, the first thing you will become aware of is the budget limit and the means by which that agency is funded. It is crucial to be able to put these facts into a wider context. How do schools get their cash, or hospitals or social service organizations? Your working life will not make much sense unless you can answer these questions.

What Are We Paying For?

Previous authors have discussed what social policy means in general terms. For our purposes we define it as the allocation of scarce resources necessary to human existence. We are not concerned with the economics of video recorders – at least not yet! The notion of what is a basic necessity changes over time and between societies. We are concerned with minimum food requirements, shelter, education, health care and the care of those who can no longer look after themselves because of old age or infirmity. There is no intrinsic reason why any of these services should not be purchased by individuals for themselves, if they have the money. All are purchased privately by the rich. Many economists argue that the state should confine itself to giving poor people enough money to exist and should cease to provide services. That case was made in a highly influential book many years ago by Milton Friedman (1962). There are, however, some basic characteristics of many human services that mean that they are not well suited to individual purchases in the market place. A clean and healthy environment cannot be bought across the counter. We cannot buy clean air in bottles and consume it as a private product. If the air is clean it will be enjoyed by the whole population of our own and other countries. This 'non-excludability' is a characteristic of what economists call a public or a social good. Where goods and services are like this we say that markets fail. Nevertheless, such goods are not free. We pay for the cost of clean air regulations in the prices of the goods produced in factories that have to install filters and burn smokeless fuels.

While some aspects of social policy concern the production of social goods such as clean air, others do not. We may be able to buy medical care or education yet we may tend to make inefficient choices as private consumers. The information we need to buy our own medical care efficiently is not read-

ily available to most of us. There is an imbalance of information between seller and buyer. We may have to rely on a doctor to advise our buying. Economists call this a problem of information failure. Market failure and information failure between them explain why, in most of the world, many human services are provided and paid for, not through ordinary private markets but through collective means of funding – taxes, insurance contributions and the like.

Paying for them is a problem for other reasons. The things we need, such as education for our children, a new home for the family, health care and pensions, cannot be financed very readily at exactly the time we want them. When we are ill we have little, or possibly no, income to pay high health care fees. Education and housing are very expensive and demand payment early in a family's existence before it has had time to amass sufficient savings. Only if the family has very rich parents or a secure inheritance will banks lend you the money to pay the bills now and let you repay later. So the market may make it possible for some families to borrow now to pay later for expen-

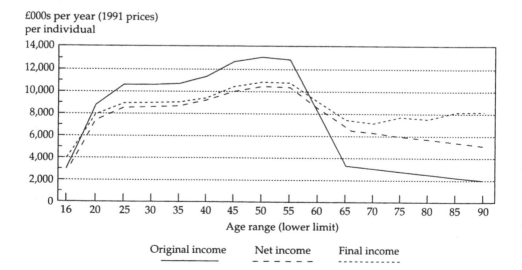

£000s per year (1991 prices) per individual

Age range (lower limit)

Original income   Net income   Final income

Figure III.10.1 Incomes by age as affected by 1991 tax and social security systems in Great Britain (Hills, 1993)

sive necessities but will not do so for most people. Part of what social policy is doing, therefore, is to shift the time at which people pay for the services they need from periods when they cannot pay to times when they can. Social policy is acting like a lifetime savings bank. This is illustrated in figure III.10.1.

The unbroken line shows the average incomes individuals would earn at each age through their lives assuming the world were frozen in 1991 terms. Net income is the income of individuals after income taxes are taken off. The final income line includes all individuals' income after tax and the value of benefits received from the state, not just in cash but including the value of services in kind like health and personal social services. We can see very clearly from this figure how taxes are creamed off during working life to pay for the heavy costs of old age. In addition, those of us with higher lifetime incomes are paying for the services given to the lifetime poor, but it turns out that this is far less important than the life-

time redistribution from us when young to us when old (Falkingham and Hills, 1995).

There is another way of looking at the question of what we are paying for. The total social policy budget funded by taxation is spent in ways you can see in figure III.10.2. Pensions and other social security payments constitute nearly half of the total. The share taken by social security was much lower fifty years ago when there was less unemployment and fewer old people. Then housing was a more important cost to the state. Now most people are buying their own houses. Education and health take a fifth and a quarter of the total respectively. Housing and the personal social services make up the remainder.

Who Pays?

Despite the natural focus on public tax-financed social services in this volume, many of the human services included in social policy's remit are, as discussed in chapter III.2, paid for directly out of individuals'

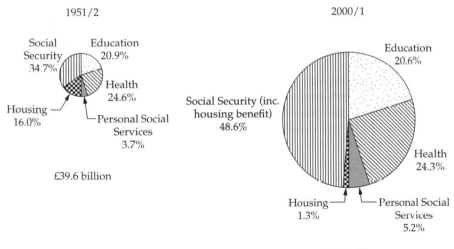

1951/2

Social Security 34.7%
Education 20.9%
Health 24.6%
Housing 16.0%
Personal Social Services 3.7%

£39.6 billion

2000/1

Education 20.6%
Social Security (inc. housing benefit) 48.6%
Health 24.3%
Housing 1.3%
Personal Social Services 5.2%

£216.4 billion

The sums are in billions of pounds expressed in 2000/1 prices and on a UK basis

Figure III.10.2   The size of the welfare state 1951–2001 (H. Glennerster, *British Social Policy Since 1945*, Oxford: Blackwell, 2000)

own earnings now or by private borrowing or through private insurance policies. In addition to this form of private welfare, firms may provide their employees with pension schemes or health care. Titmuss called this occupational welfare. A study by CASE at the LSE recently calculated how much of the total costs of welfare were paid for in these different ways (Burchardt, Hills and Propper, 1999). It was the first time since Titmuss's early work that the national accounts had been recalculated to cover this range of funding sources. It turns out that roughly half of all the nation's income is spent on the broad purposes of providing human services – the long-term care of dependent elderly, health, education, pensions and housing. Even this does not cover items not included in the nation's accounts: the care provided by the family for its own members discussed in chapter III.4, for example. Of that vast total spent on human services, 40 per cent is paid for through the private market. That figure varies enormously between services. Roughly three-quarters of the costs of housing are paid directly by individuals for themselves, but only 20 per cent of education and 13 per cent of health costs (Burchardt et al 1999 updated).

This leaves a very large sum – well over £200 billion in 2001– to be paid for out of taxes of one kind or another. Unusually among advanced industrialized countries, the United Kingdom relies overwhelmingly on taxes raised by the national government to pay for its social services. Less than 5 per cent is paid for out of taxes raised by local government – the council tax. Health and social security are directly provided by central government agencies in one form or another. But housing, education and the personal social services are not and there therefore has to be a complex system of grants that rechannels the taxes raised by central government to pay local councils to provide them.

A diagrammatic representation of this flow of money is to be found in figure III.10.3. On the far left of the figure are the originators of income and wealth – households and firms. Central government taxes these individuals either directly by taking a proportion of their incomes in income tax and corporation tax or through indirect taxes on goods and services. Value added tax is an example. In addition, government may tax some individuals less heavily to encourage a particular form of saving for retirement, house purchase or giving to charity. This has the effect of encouraging households to do their own saving for retirement or house purchase but it costs the government money in lost revenue. Economists call these flows tax *expenditures*.

Her Majesty's Treasury is the central government department responsible for advising the Cabinet how much the economy can afford to spend on public programmes and it masterminds the complex round of negotiations between the spending departments that determine how much is to be available to, for example, the health service or universities in the next year.

Gordon Brown, the Labour Chancellor, in 1997 changed this from an annual spending round to a biannual one. Major decisions about which service was to get what were taken as part of a Comprehensive Spending Review every two years and the totals were set for three years in advance. Small adjustments are made each year as the reserve fund that is held back is spent. These decisions, approved by Cabinet and parliament, determine how much the NHS and local authorities will receive.

Local councils get their largest income from a general or untied grant which they can spend on any of their services. They also receive some specific grants which are tied to particular smaller services. What they are permitted to raise additionally from the council tax is heavily constrained by government rules. Central government also allocates money to local health authorities and does so on the basis of a population-based formula which gives an area more money if it has more elderly or ill or poor people, because they use health services more. Once these local agencies receive

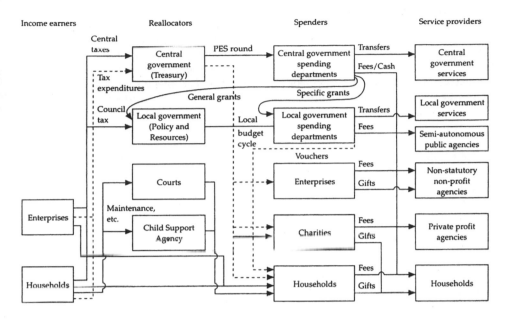

Figure III.10.3   The flow of funds

their money they then allocate it out to increasingly autonomous units such as schools or hospital trusts. Schools compete for students and are paid for each one they attract. Hospital trusts compete for patients and are paid for those they treat. Social services departments pay their own old people's homes or voluntary agencies or sometimes profit agencies to provide services for the old or the disabled.

Vouchers and Quasi-Vouchers

So far we have described the way grants are allocated to local authorities and then on to bodies like schools and hospitals. Some economists argue that these institutions will only work efficiently if they are forced to compete for custom and that public money for education should therefore be given, not to institutions like schools, but to individuals and families in the form of a voucher that can be cashed in at the school of their choice, public or private. I have reviewed the case for vouchers more widely

elsewhere (Glennerster, 1996). It is important to recognize that giving state schools, or GPs, money on the basis of the number of children or patients they attract is already a form of voucher – a 'quasi-voucher' system – and we have moved some way towards such a system in the UK in the 1990s.

Court-Based Welfare

Alongside the tax-based systems of welfare run other systems of redistribution to families in need. One of the most controversial is the system of court-based support for divorced or separated wives provided in theory by ex-husbands. This operates alongside the social security system, which has to come into play when this court-enforced system fails. As the Finer Committee pointed out two decades ago, this dual system of support works very poorly. Government has changed its attitude to such cases over the years (as discussed in chapter IV.5) and the Child Support Agency now seeks to recover money from fathers who are deemed responsible for the children they have fathered.

Giving

Individuals give large sums of money and time to voluntary organizations, and statutory ones too, helping to visit old people or run youth clubs. Giving cash attracts tax relief but giving time does not. In his classic study of blood doning, Titmuss (1970) showed how giving blood to the National Blood Transfusion Service without compensation was not only a tangible example of individuals contributing to a larger social whole and enriching that society in the process, but also turned out to be a more efficient process because donors had no incentive to lie about their medical history. This might make them carriers of infected blood, and where poor people were paid to give their blood they had an incentive to lie about their medical history. Feminist writers (discussed in chapters II.11 and III.4) have made us much more aware of the scale of giving that takes place within the family when women, and to a lesser extent men, undertake caring tasks. The personal social services budget would need to double if we were to pay women for these duties, represented by the line in figure III.10.3 that runs from households to households.

Rationing

We have seen that the Treasury essentially sets the limits to public spending on the social services, under political direction of course! The result is that the supply of these services is fixed by political decisions. Yet these services are free, or at least partly free. Price cannot rise to levels that will equate demand with supply. The result is that service providers have to take some action to set priorities and ration care. As is also discussed in chapter III.11, this may take the form of rules and entitlement to benefit, or judgements made by professional staff working to fixed budgets. The budgets they get may be the result of an explicit priority decision that a particular part of the service receive a given sum for that year, but exactly which patient or class of patient gets the service will usually depend on judgements made by professional staff in the front line. Rationing of scarce social policy resources thus takes place in a whole range of decisions, which descend from fairly explicit judgements made by Cabinet about what each service shall receive, through more explicit allocations on a formula basis to areas and, indeed, to institutions like schools. But these are followed by front-line and less explicit judgements about which child in a class or which social work client gets most of the worker's attention. You might like to discuss how we should make decisions to limit what we spend on health and who should be given priority. Should those who smoke and endanger their own health be supported by the rest of us when they become ill? Should we leave all these difficult decisions to doctors? You could also discuss the fundamental question addressed by John Hills (1993): can we afford the welfare state? These are some of the most difficult questions we face as a society. The responses to them are equally complex and varied, as the rest of this volume shows.

Guide to further reading

Burchardt, T., Hills, J. and Propper, C., 1999. *Private Welfare and Public Policy* (York: Joseph Rowntree Foundation) covers some of the key issues addressed in this chapter in more detail.

Falkingham, J. and Hills, J., 1995. *The Dynamics of Welfare* (Hemel Hempstead: Harvester Wheatsheaf) shows how and why the welfare state redistributes income through the lifetime.

Foster, P., 1983. *Access to Welfare* (London: Macmillan) summarizes the work on rationing, especially at the front line, well and simply.

Friedman, M., 1962. *Capitalism and Freedom* (Chicago: University of Chicago Press). A hugely influential book in which can be found most of the ideas of the Thatcher period in social policy. Makes the case for minimal government intervention, vouchers and student loans.

Glennerster, H., 1997. *Paying for Welfare: Towards 2000* (Hemel Hempstead: Harvester Wheatsheaf). Written because there was nothing else to teach from, this text summarizes in simple terms the economic theoretical literature about market and government failure and quasi-markets. It then describes the process of Treasury control and the finance of local government, with a separate chapter on the finance of each of the main services. It ends by asking: can we afford the welfare state?

Glennerster, H., 2003. *Understanding the Finance of Social Policy* (Bristol: Policy Press) is a text covering all aspects of the finance of social policy. It summarizes the theoretical economic literature on the subject and describes the practical ways in which each of the social services receives its funding in the UK and the policy issues that arise.

Glennerster, H., 1996. 'Vouchers and quasi-vouchers in education', in M. May, E. Brunsdon and G. Craig (eds) *Social Policy Review 8* (London: Social Policy Association).

Hills, J., 1993. *The Future of Welfare* (York: Joseph Rowntree Foundation). This colourful volume, with charts and diagrams, presents the range of arguments about whether we can or cannot afford to sustain the present levels of spending and how to pay for it in a very readable way.

Thain, C. and Wright, M. (1995) *Treasury and Whitehall: the Planning and Control of Public Expenditure 1973–1993*. Oxford: Oxford University Press. For those who need a detailed account of the way the Treasury controlled public spending in the Thatcher period.

Titmuss, R. M. T., 1970. *The Gift Relationship* (London: Allen & Unwin). Titmuss's last work, in which he takes the doning of blood as a parable for the virtues of giving in modern societies.

Many of these general issues can also be traced in the HM Treasury Report (2001), *Securing Our Future Health: Taking the Long Term View* at: www.hm-treasury.gov.uk

III.11
Principles of Welfare

Ruth Lister

Introduction

Definitions of social policy tend to centre on human welfare and on the societal institutions designed to promote it. A critical question both for social policy and for individuals and groups is how resources, limited by economic and political constraints, are allocated so as best to promote welfare and meet human needs. In other words, social policy is partly about how resources are rationed. This chapter discusses the key competing principles which govern this rationing process and thereby the rules determining the access of individuals and groups to welfare.

It begins by introducing some of the principal concepts upon which the chapter will draw, within the framework of different approaches to meeting need. The second section focuses more explicitly on the key principles governing access to welfare and their implications, drawing mainly on social security benefits as illustration. These principles are set out in diagrammatic form in figure III.11.1. The chapter concludes by exploring some of the ways in which welfare might be enhanced through the promotion of citizenship and welfare rights.

Different Approaches to Meeting Need

A primary criterion for assessing the different principles governing access to welfare is whether the rules derived from them are successful in ensuring that people's needs are met. The concept of *need* was discussed in chapter II.1. It is by no means straightforward when applied to the question of access to welfare.

On the one hand it is invoked to justify an approach to social welfare which is *rights*-based and which is founded on the principle of *social citizenship*. As is further discussed in chapter II.2, in this formulation the principle of need is counterposed to that of the market. The principle of social citizenship overrides (at least in theory, even if not always in practice) that of the market, in that it is argued that every member of society has a right to be able to participate fully in that society. This right has to be underwritten by the state so as to ensure that people are not totally reliant on the labour market to meet their needs. Social rights are necessary to enable people to exercise their political and legal rights. For example, without a home, it is very difficult to get on the electoral register, never mind receive a polling card. And although in theory we are all equal before the law, in practice some are more equal than others, so that without assistance from, for instance, the Community Legal Service, poor people's access to the law is effectively blocked. Nor, arguably, can people be expected to fulfil their responsibilities to the wider community as citizens if that wider community is not

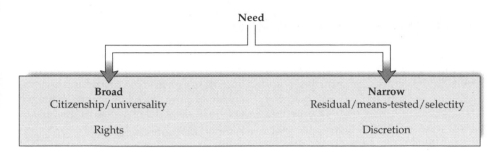

Figure III.11.1. Access to welfare: Interpretations of need

prepared to ensure that their needs are met.

The principle of citizenship is also about equality of status. Consequently, those subscribing to it argue that everyone should have access to the same set of rights, the principle of *universality*, instead of dividing off the poor from the rest of society through the application of *selective* mechanisms, such as means-testing, which promote *residual* welfare.

Yet proponents of such selective mechanisms also appeal to the concept of need to justify their position. When resources are limited, the argument goes, they should be targeted upon those who really need them. Means-testing, whereby assistance is limited to those whose resources fall below a certain level, is the most common means of *targeting*, particularly in social security schemes. The use of *discretion*, whereby officials or professionals decide what an applicant needs and what she can have instead of the applicant being able to claim on the basis of predetermined rights, is another approach, more common in the provision of services such as housing and community care. This individualized approach, it is contended, is more likely to ensure that the individual's 'true' needs will be met than one based on rigid rules. The disadvantages of such selective approaches are explored below.

In practice, the distinction between rights and discretion in meeting needs is not as clear-cut as this discussion might imply. On the one hand, officials often have to exercise judgement or discretion in applying the rules governing rights; on the other, discretion is frequently exercised on the basis of (non-legally binding) guidelines set down by central or local government. Nevertheless, as the basis for organizing access to welfare they represent two very different approaches. Together with the citizenship versus residual welfare models (discussed in chapter I.3), these distinctions have implications for the welfare achieved by individuals and social groups, which are explored in the next section.

Access To Welfare

Immigration and residence status

First, we need to take a step back and consider what for newcomers to a country is the first gateway to access to welfare: rules which include or exclude people on the basis of their immigration or residence status. As chapters II.12, II.16 and IV.6 also show, one way in which nation states can limit the resources devoted to welfare is to limit the access of non-nationals both through restrictive immigration and asylum laws and through circumscribing access to welfare for those immigrants and asylum-seekers allowed into the country. Here citizenship is being used as a tool of exclusion rather than inclusion, overriding rather than underpinning the basic principle of meeting need.

Many Western countries are now using both immigration and welfare laws to exclude 'outsiders' from their welfare benefits and services. Behind the ramparts of 'Fortress Europe', tougher laws have been enacted to exclude immigrants and asylum-seekers. In the UK, access to welfare has been tied more tightly to immigration or residence status, thereby making it more difficult for immigrants and asylum-seekers to receive financial or housing assistance from the state. This then has consequences for minority ethnic group 'insiders', who are frequently subjected to passport-checking when claiming welfare; some can be deterred from claiming altogether for fear that their own immigration status might be jeopardized or to avoid such racist practices.

Discretion

The potential for racist or other prejudiced attitudes leading to discriminatory decision-making by those controlling access to welfare is one of the chief arguments against the discretionary approach. Its roots lie in charity, where access to welfare was as likely to be governed as much by considerations of merit or 'deservingness' as of need. It was partly in reaction to this that a number of rights to welfare were enshrined in the post-war welfare state. Nevertheless, discretion continued to play a role.

In the British social security system, the extent of this role in the safety-net social assistance scheme was a major focus of debate in the 1960s and 1970s. Much of the criticism of the scheme was directed to its continued heavy reliance on discretion, which was seen as acting as a rationing system which put too much power in the hands of individual officials, leaving claimants uncertain as to what they might get and without any rights to back up a claim for help. Gradually, the scope of discretion was reduced, but one of the most controversial aspects of the reform of social security in the mid-1980s was its revival in the form of

the social fund – a cash-limited fund paying out mainly loans to meet one-off needs such as furniture and bedding. Discretion was reintroduced explicitly as a rationing mechanism to reduce expenditure on such one-off payments. The social fund is an example of how discretion can be managed on the basis of detailed official guidelines, without giving claimants themselves clear rights.

Discretion plays a more prominent role in the social assistance schemes of many other European countries and in the UK in the service sector. Even if a right to a service exists, it is harder to specify how that right should be met by the statutory authorities and professional interpretations of need come to the fore, again in the context of the rationing of limited resources. Thus, for example, the right to health care, enshrined in the British National Health Service, does not constitute a right to any treatment a user might demand; her right to treatment will be interpreted according to health professionals' assessment of her need.

In the field of community care, local authorities have a duty to assess the needs of disabled people, but they can then exercise their discretion as to whether and how they meet any needs that may have been identified. The exact boundaries between discretion and rights are, however, rather hazy here, as in a few cases the legislation has been used to require a local authority to provide a service once a need has been established. The problem is that, as long as local authorities' own resources are so limited, the temptation will be not to identify the need in the first place, so that discretion again comes into play as a rationing device (see too chapter III.10). The same applies to a more recent duty on local authorities to meet the separately assessed needs of carers. The power that the discretionary approach gives to professionals has been challenged by the disabled people's movement, a development addressed in more detail in chapter IV.4. Instead of having to rely on professional assessments of their needs, some disabled people are framing their demands in the language of citizenship rights.

Rights

The advantage of the rights-based approach to welfare is that it gives greater power to users by providing them with (more or less) clear, enforceable entitlements. Provided she meets the criteria of entitlement, the claimant can refer to legal rules in support of her claim. Not all rights claims are, however, rooted in the principle of citizenship. As figure III.11.2 indicates, rights too can be selective and the citizenship principle itself can be interpreted to embrace both unconditional and conditional forms of welfare.

Residual Selectivity

The case for selective means-tested welfare – that it targets help on those in greatest need – has long been the subject of controversy. (It should be noted here that, in the UK, some means-tested benefits have been transformed into tax credits, going further up the income scale than traditional means-tested benefits.) Critics point to the signifi-

cant minorities who fail to claim the means-tested benefits for which they are eligible: in 1999/2000, it is officially estimated that in the UK between £1.96 and £4.07 billion was unclaimed. The reasons are varied but include the sheer complexity of the benefits and the claiming process. Minority ethnic groups are particularly likely to underclaim. Similarly, there is evidence that as local authorities apply charges and means tests to more services, some people prefer to do without.

Means tests are also criticized for trapping people in poverty, as an increase in income reduces their benefit, and for penalizing savings. They do not necessarily provide people with genuine security, as changes in circumstances can affect entitlement. They also tend to disadvantage women in couples and to reinforce their economic dependence on male partners. Entitlement is calculated on the basis of a couple's joint income. This means that where, as is frequently the case, income is not shared fairly within a family, means tests may be failing to target help on women within families who need it, with potential consequences for the welfare of children. Moreover, because of the strict rules limiting earnings while one is claiming social

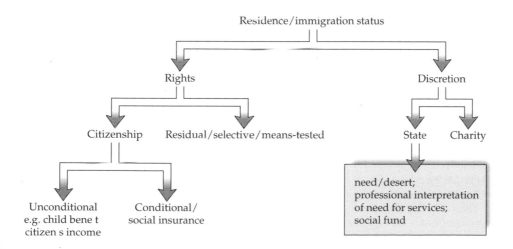

Figure III.11.2 Principles of access to welfare

assistance, it is not generally worth the partners of unemployed claimants doing paid work.

Claiming a means-tested benefit all too often means admitting to the label of poverty, which can still be experienced as stigmatizing. One of the dangers of a residual welfare system, it is argued, is that benefits and services confined to the poor can all too easily become poor benefits and services, as the rest of society no longer has an interest in ensuring their adequacy and quality. The United States is cited as an example. Thus, when access to welfare is confined to the poor or nearly poor, it contravenes the principle of common citizenship.

Citizenship: Conditional and Unconditional

In the British social security system, social insurance is often held up as exemplifying the principle of common citizenship. Here, access to welfare depends primarily on having paid contributions of a specified value while in work and, in the case of the unemployed, on being available for and actively seeking work. However, it is, some would maintain, a conditional and limited form of citizenship which is promoted by the current social insurance scheme. Instead of overriding the market as a mechanism for distributing income, it mirrors market principles by confining entitlement to those with an adequate labour market record and, through earnings-related pensions, perpetuating inequalities in earning power. Because the rules governing access to social insurance are based on male employment patterns, women, in particular, are the losers. Over 1.5 million women are excluded from the system altogether because their earnings are too low to bring them into the social insurance system. Immigrants too are disadvantaged.

The conditional nature of the social insurance (and social assistance) system is being intensified through increasingly tough rules enforcing the obligation to seek and take work, which is promoted as the best form of welfare. In addition, in certain circumstances entitlement to benefit is being made conditional on other forms of behaviour, for example entitlement to (a much enhanced) maternity grant is now conditional on attendance at child health checkups. This reflects a central tenet of New Labour's 'third way' philosophy: that with rights and opportunities come responsibilities. The whole issue of the proper balance between rights and obligations has thus become an increasingly central one in debates about welfare (see chapter II.10).

Totally universal, unconditional, citizenship benefits are rare. The closest approximation in the British social security system is child benefit, which is paid for virtually every child in the country. There are a number of other benefits which are paid to people in specific categories, such as carers and disabled people, without either contribution or means test. However, they tend to be less generous than their contributory equivalents.

The social security systems of different countries combine the principles of access to welfare in different combinations, although generally with one predominating. Thus, for instance, as noted in chapter I.3, the citizenship approach is associated with Scandinavia; the residual with the United States; and the conditional social insurance with Germany. The UK more than most is a hybrid but with an increased tilt towards a more residual model. The citizenship principle does, though, still operate in the National Health Service. However, as discussed above, it is difficult to operationalize in specific terms what is a generalized right to health care, free at the point of use.

The Enhancement of Welfare

The weaknesses in current welfare arrangements have prompted a range of proposals for improvement. These can be divided into substantive and procedural or process reforms.

Substantive reforms

One area of substantive reform proposals aims at shifting the balance of social security entitlement from residual to citizenship-based principles of access. One example is the recasting of social insurance so that it excludes fewer people and in particular better reflects women's employment patterns. Another is the idea of a citizen's income under which every individual would receive a tax-free benefit without any conditions attached. Access would be on the basis of citizenship rights alone. More narrowly, the replacement of the social fund with a system of clear rights to extra help, underpinned by a discretionary fall-back system, would enhance claimants' rights without losing the advantages of an element of discretion in the meeting of unusual needs.

The development of substantive rights to services is more difficult. One approach has been to suggest, as a first step, a framework of broad constitutional rights, partly building on the existing European Social Charter of the Council of Europe. This would provide rights to services at a generalized level, expressed as duties pertaining to government. Specific legislation would then need to develop more specific enforceable rights within such a framework.

Procedural or process reforms

It is easier to envisage how procedural reforms might improve access to welfare services. The Conservative government under John Major adopted such an approach in its Citizen's Charter. However, this was criticized as representing the principles of consumerism rather than citizenship, as the individual citizen's *qua* customer's rights were limited to the provision of information, the expression of choice and compensation claims for public services failing to meet Charter standards.

A more citizenship-oriented notion of procedural rights has been promoted by the Institute for Public Policy Research (see Coote, 1992). Procedural rights to welfare focus on the processes through which substantive rights can be secured, on how people are treated and the manner in which decisions are taken. An important element of procedural rights is enforceability. To access and enforce rights people must have information about them and often need advice and assistance in negotiating with welfare institutions and taking cases to tribunals or, less frequently, the courts. Access to such information, advice and advocacy has itself been referred to as a right of citizenship by the National Consumer Council. This right is promoted by a range of agencies, such as law and advice centres and local authority and voluntary sector welfare rights specialists.

This right is also promoted by self-help groups, where users help each other without having to rely on professionals. The principle of citizenship is taken still further in the growing demands for user or citizen involvement in service development. The case is made on the grounds that welfare will be enhanced both by the greater democratic accountability of welfare institutions and by the empowerment of users. Thus, in incorporating a more dynamic and active conception of citizenship, which treats people as active agents rather than as simply passive recipients of rights, the principle of citizenship is promoted in terms of both outcomes and process. The principle of user involvement is now recognized in community care law, although in practice it still has some way to go to avoid criticisms of tokenism.

Whereas initially user involvement was developed at the level of local service delivery, more recently there have been demands for its extension to national policy-making. An independent Citizens' Commission on the Future of the Welfare State, made of up of welfare service users, recommended that 'all future plans for welfare state reform should include a programme of effective and broad-based consultation with service users'. Likewise, the independent Commission on Poverty,

Participation and Power (2000), half of whose members had direct experience of poverty, called for greater involvement of people in poverty in decision-making that affects their lives, at both local and national level. Increasingly, it is being argued that the opportunity to participate in decision-making about welfare should be treated as a right.

Conclusion

This chapter has emphasized the importance of the principles which govern access to welfare resources, highlighting the processes of rationing involved and the ways in which different principles affect marginalized groups such as women, members of minority ethnic communities and disabled people. In considering approaches to the enhancement of welfare, it has focused on those which promote citizenship as opposed to residual selectivity. It has also underlined the significance of issues of process: procedural rights which assist people in claiming and enforcing substantive rights to welfare and user involvement in the development of welfare.

Guide to further reading

Coote, A. (ed.), 1992. *The Welfare of Citizens* (London: IPPR/Rivers Oram Press). An exploration of the ways in which substantive and procedural social citizenship rights can be developed, particularly in relation to service provision.

Commission on Poverty, Participation and Power, 2000. *Listen Hear. The Right to Be Heard* (Bristol: Policy Press). An exposition of the case for treating the involvement of people in poverty in welfare decision-making as a right.

Croft, S. and Beresford, P., 1992. 'The politics of participation', *Critical Social Policy*, 35. An introduction to ideas about user involvement.

Dean, H., 2002. *Welfare Rights and Social Policy* (Harlow: Pearson Education). A discussion of many of the ideas raised in this chapter through a critical exploration of welfare rights, social citizenship and social legislation in historical and comparative context.

Ditch, J. (ed.), 1999. *Introduction to Social Security* (London: Routledge). This edited collection provides an overview of social security issues including the ways in which women and black and minority ethnic groups are often disadvantaged by the principles governing access.

Dwyer, P., 2000. *Welfare Rights and Responsibilities. Contesting Social Citizenship* (Bristol: Policy Press). A discussion of the principles of social citizenship, which also includes the views of welfare users in relation to health, social security and housing.

Langan, M. (ed.), 1998. *Welfare: Needs, Rights and Risks* (London: Routledge/Open University). A critical discussion of 'how people get access to social welfare in the UK today', focusing on the social construction of concepts such as needs, rights and membership.

Oliver, M., 1996. *Understanding Disability. From Theory to Practice* (Basingstoke: Macmillan Press). A discussion of a number of the principles discussed in this chapter from the perspective of disabled people.

III.12
The Distribution of Welfare

John Hills

Introduction

Distribution is a central issue in the appraisal of social policies; for some, it is *the* central issue. Much of the justification advanced for social policy is in terms of distribution: 'without a National Health Service providing free medical care, the poor could not afford treatment'; or 'the primary aim of social security is preventing poverty'.

Most of this chapter is about the distributional effects of government spending on welfare services. However, redistribution – and its measurement – are not only issues for government. A major social policy development in the 1990s was the Child Support Act. Under this, the state attempts to enforce payments by absent parents (generally fathers) to parents 'with care' (usually mothers). These payments are important distributionally, but outside the 'welfare state'.

Whether redistribution is occurring can depend on the point of analysis. Under private insurance for, say, burglaries, a large number of people make annual payments (insurance premiums) to an insurance company, but only a small number receive payouts from the company. After the event (*ex post*) there is redistribution from the (fortunate) many to the (unfortunate) few. But, looking at the position in advance (*ex ante*), not knowing who is going to be burgled, all pay in a premium equalling their risk of being burgled, multiplied by the size of the payout if this happens (plus the insurance company's costs and profits). In 'actuarial' terms there is no redistribution – people have arranged a certain small loss (the premium) rather than the risk of a much larger loss (being burgled without insurance).

If you look at pension schemes over a single year, some people pay in contributions, while others receive pensions. On this 'snapshot', there is apparently redistribution from the former to the latter. But with a longer time horizon, today's pensioners may simply get back what they paid in earlier. Redistribution is across their own life cycles, rather than between different people.

Assessing redistribution depends on the aims against which you want to measure services, and the picture obtained depends on decisions like the time period used. The next section discusses the first of these issues, the aims of welfare services. The subsequent sections discuss the conceptual issues raised in trying to measure distributional effects, illustrate some of the empirical findings on different bases and discuss their implications.

Aims of Welfare Services

As previous chapters have shown, there is little consensus on the aims of social policy or of government intervention to provide or finance welfare services. For some, the primary aim of welfare services is redistribution from rich to poor. Whether the welfare state is successful therefore depends on which income groups benefit: do the rich use the NHS more than the poor, and are social security benefits 'targeted' on those with the lowest incomes?

For others, this is only a part of the welfare state's rationale. Depending on political perspective, other aims will be more important. Some of the main aims advanced and their implications for assessing distributional effects are as follows:

1 *Vertical redistribution.* If the aim is redistribution from rich to poor, the crucial question is which income groups benefit. Since welfare services do not come from thin air, the important question may be which are the *net gainers* and *net losers*, after taking account of who pays the taxes that finance welfare provision. Allowing for both benefits and taxes in understanding distribution has become even more important since the Government started using 'tax credits' (which count as reduced tax liabilities) instead of some cash benefits in the late 1990s.
2 *Horizontal redistribution on the basis of needs.* For many, relative incomes are not the only reason for receiving services. The NHS is there for people with particular medical needs: it should achieve 'horizontal redistribution' between people with similar incomes, but different medical needs.
3 *Redistribution between different groups.* An aim might be redistribution between social groups defined other than by income; for instance, favouring particular groups to offset disadvantages elsewhere in the economy. Or the system might be intended to be non-discriminatory between groups. Either way, we may need to analyse distribution by dimensions such as social class, gender, ethnicity, age or age cohort (generation), rather than just income. An important issue since the establishment of the Social Exclusion Unit in 1997 has been the

distribution of public spending between areas, particularly rich and poor neighbourhoods (Bramley and Evans, 2000).
4 *Insurance.* Much of the welfare state is insurance against adversity. People 'pay in' through tax or national insurance contributions, but in return, if they are the ones who become ill or unemployed, the system is there to protect them. It does not make sense just to look at which individual happens to receive an expensive heart bypass operation this year and present him or her as the main 'gainer' from the system. All benefit to the extent that they face a risk of needing such an operation. The system is best appraised in actuarial terms; that is, in terms of the extent someone would expect to benefit on average.
5 *Efficiency justifications.* An extensive literature discusses how universal, compulsory and possibly state-provided systems can be cheaper or more efficient than the market left to itself for some activities, particularly core welfare services like health care, unemployment insurance and education. Where this is the motivation for state provision one might not expect to see any redistribution between income or other groups. Services might be appraised according to the 'benefit principle' – how much do people receive in relation to what they pay? – and the absence of net redistribution would not be a sign of failure.
6 *Life cycle smoothing.* Most welfare services are unevenly spread over the life cycle. Education goes disproportionately to the young; health care and pensions to the old; while the taxes that finance them come mostly from the working generation. A snapshot picture of redistribution may be misleading – it would be better to compare how much people get out of the system over their whole lives, and how much they pay in.
7 *Compensating for 'family failure'.* Many parents do, of course, meet their children's needs, and many higher-earning husbands share their cash incomes

equally with their lower-earning wives. But in other families this is not so – family members may not share equally in its income. Where policies are aimed at countering this kind of problem it may not be enough to evaluate simply in terms of distribution between families, we may also need to look at distribution between individuals; that is, within families as well.

8 *External benefits.* Finally some, services may be justified by 'external' or 'spillover' benefits beyond those to the direct beneficiary. Promoting the education of even the relatively affluent may be in society's interests, if this produces a more dynamic economy for all. Appraisal of who gains ought to take account of such benefits (although in practice this is hard).

The relative importance given to each aim thus affects not only the interpretation placed on particular findings, but also the appropriate kind of analysis.

Conceptual Issues

As will already be clear, there is no single measure of how welfare services are distributed. It depends on precisely what is measured, and apparently technical choices can make a great difference to the findings.

The counter-factual

To answer 'how are welfare services distributed?', you have to add 'compared to what?' What is the 'counter-factual' situation with which you are comparing reality? A particular group may receive state medical services worth £500 per year. In one sense, this is the amount they benefit by. But if the medical services did not exist, what else would be different? Government spending might be lower, and hence tax bills, including their own. The net benefit, allowing for taxes, might be much less than £500 per year.

Knock-on effects may go further. In an economy with lower taxes, many other things might be different. At the same time, without the NHS, people would make other arrangements: private medical insurance, for instance. The money paid for that would not be available for other spending, with further knock-on effects through the economy. Britain without the NHS would differ in all sorts of ways from Britain with it, and strictly it is this hypothetical alternative country we ought to compare with to measure the impact of the NHS. In practice, this is very difficult – which limits the conclusiveness of most empirical studies.

Incidence

Closely related is the question of 'incidence': who *really* benefits from a service? Do children benefit from free education, or is it their parents, who would otherwise have paid school fees? Are tenants of subsidized housing the true beneficiaries of the subsidies, or can employers attract labour to the area at lower wages than they would otherwise have to pay? In each case different assumptions about who really gains may be plausible and affect the findings.

Valuation

To look at the combined effects of different services, their values have to be added up in some way, most conveniently by putting a money value on them. But to do this requires a price for the services received. This is fine for cash benefits, but not for benefits which come as services 'in kind', such as the NHS or education. To know how much someone benefits from a service, you want to know how much it is worth *to them* – but you cannot usually observe this. Most studies use the *cost* to the state of providing the service. But 'value' and 'cost' are not necessarily the same. It may *cost* a great deal to provide people with a particular service, but if offered the choice they might prefer a smaller cash sum to spend how they like: the cost is higher than its value to the recipients.

Distribution between which groups?

Comparing groups arranged according to some income measure is of obvious interest, but so may be looking at distribution between social classes, age groups, men and women or ethnic groups. A related issue is the 'unit of analysis': households, families or individuals? A larger unit makes some things easier: we do not have to worry about how income is shared within the family or household. But it may mask what we are interested in: for instance, distribution between men and women. It may also affect how we classify different beneficiaries. The official Office for National Statistics results described below examine the distribution of welfare benefits between *households*. In this analysis a family with four children 'scores' the same as a single pensioner living alone – the situation of six people is given the same weight as that of one person. Weighting each person equally may affect the picture.

Distribution of what?

Depending on the question, the definition of what is being examined will vary, for instance:

1   gross public spending;
2   net public spending after allowing for taxes financing services;
3   gross public spending in relation to need.

These can give apparently conflicting answers. NHS spending may be concentrated on the poor, but this may reflect their poor health. Allowing for differences in sickness rates, the distribution of NHS care in relation to need may not favour the poor after all.

Similarly, the gross benefits from a service may appear 'pro-rich'; that is, its absolute value to high-income households exceeds that to low-income households, say by 50 per cent. But if the tax which pays for the service is twice as much for rich households, the *combination* of the service and the tax may still be *redistributive*, in that the poorer households are net gainers and the richer ones net losers.

Time period

In a single week fewer people will receive a service than over a year. As services vary across the life cycle, a single year snapshot will differ from the picture across a whole lifetime. But available data relate to short time periods: there are no surveys tracking use of welfare services throughout people's whole lives. To answer questions about lifetime distribution requires hypothetical models – the results from which depend greatly on the assumptions fed into them.

Data problems

Finally, research in this area is based on sample surveys: whole population surveys like the census do not ask the questions about incomes and service use required. Even the sample surveys may not be very specific, asking, for instance, whether someone has visited a GP recently, but not how long the consultation lasted, whether any expensive tests were done and so on. Results assume that GP visits are worth the same to all patients. But this may gloss over the point at issue: if GPs spend longer on appointments with middle-class patients – and are more likely to send them for further treatment – the distribution of medical services may be 'pro-rich', even if the number of GP consultations is constant between income groups.

Some Empirical Results

This section illustrates some of these issues by considering findings from recent empirical analysis, contrasting the gross distribution of welfare services with that of the taxes required to pay for them, and showing the differences which result from switching from a 'snapshot' to a 'lifetime' perspective.

Cross-sectional redistribution

Figure III.12.1 shows official estimates of the average benefits in cash and kind from welfare services received by households in different income groups in 1999–2000 (Lakin, 2001). Households are arranged in order of 'equivalent disposable income' (that is, income including cash benefits but after direct taxes like income tax, and allowing for the greater needs of bigger households). The poorest 'decile group' (tenth) is on the left, the richest on the right.

On average, households with the bottom half of incomes received 2.4 times as much from cash benefits as those with the top half. Means-tested benefits like Income Support and Housing Benefit are most concentrated on the poorest, but even 'universal' benefits like the retirement pension are worth more to lower than to higher income households.

The figure also shows estimates of the combined value of benefits in kind from the NHS, state education and housing subsidies. Sefton (1997) suggests that such figures can be qualified on various grounds, such as the omission of the benefits of higher education for students living away from home (which tends to understate benefits to high-income households), or the way in which housing subsidies are calculated (which tends to understate benefits to low-income households). Also, the assumption that people of the same age and gender use the health service equally is not necessarily correct: other characteristics affect service use too. However, even with adjustments for such issues, the general picture is similar: benefits in kind are less concentrated on the poor than cash benefits, but households at the bottom of the distribution receive considerably more than those at the top. On the ONS's estimates, benefits in kind were worth an average of £4600 for the poorest tenth of households in 1999–2000 but only £2000 for the richest tenth. On these estimates, the absolute value of welfare benefits is greatest for low-income households, and much lower than average for high-income families. Taxation, by contrast, is greater in absolute terms for those with higher incomes (although it is not necessarily a greater proportion of income).

Most welfare spending is financed from general taxation, so it is hard to be precise about *which* taxes are paying for welfare: if state education was abolished, would it be income tax or VAT which would fall? Figure III.12.2 (Lakin, 2001) compares the total of welfare benefits given in the previous figure with the ONS's estimates of the impact of national insurance contributions and an equal proportion of each other tax to

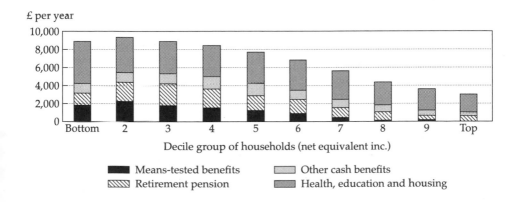

£ per year

Decile group of households (net equivalent inc.)

■ Means-tested benefits ▨ Retirement pension ▢ Other cash benefits ▨ Health, education and housing

Figure III.12.1 Welfare benefits by income group 1999/2000 (derived from Lakin, 2001)

cover the remainder of welfare spending. For the bottom five-tenths of the distribution, benefits are higher than taxes and the figures suggest a net gain; for those in the top four groups – particularly the top two-tenths – taxes are higher, suggesting a net loss. These results suggest that on a cross-sectional basis, the combination of welfare services and, on plausible assumptions, their financing is significantly redistributive from high- to low-income groups (although they say nothing about the scale of such gains in relation to 'need', such as for medical care).

Life cycle redistribution

The picture looks rather different over a lifetime. As discussed above, actually measuring 'lifetime' impacts of benefits and taxes is not straightforward. The findings in figure III.12.3 are drawn from a computer simulation model of 4000 hypothetical life histories (see Falkingham and Hills, 1995). The model builds up the effects of the tax and welfare systems on a wide range of individuals on the assumption that the systems remain in a 'steady state' for their whole lives. Its results therefore illustrate the lifetime effects of today's

systems, not a forecast of the combined effects of different systems which may apply in future.

The top panel gives a 'lifetime' analogue of the cross-sectional picture in figure III.12.1. The bars show total lifetime benefits from social security, education and the NHS going to each group of model individuals, ordered by their average *lifetime* living standards, with the 'lifetime poorest' on the left. The 'lifetime poorest' receive somewhat more than the 'lifetime richest', but the striking feature is that the overall distribution of gross benefits is much flatter than on an annual basis. Regardless of lifetime income, *gross* receipts look much the same.

Over their lives people both receive benefits and pay taxes. Those with higher lifetime incomes pay much more tax than those with low incomes. In effect, people finance some of the benefits they receive through their *own* lifetime tax payments. However, some people do not pay enough lifetime tax to pay for all of their benefits; they receive 'net lifetime benefits' from the system. These net lifetime benefits are paid for by others who pay more than enough tax to finance their own benefits; they pay 'net lifetime taxes' into the system.

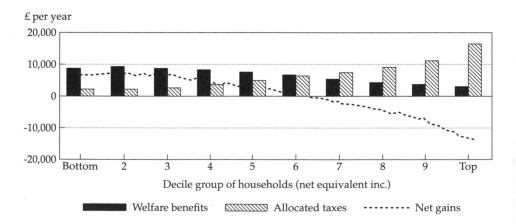

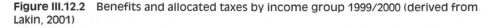

Figure III.12.2　Benefits and allocated taxes by income group 1999/2000 (derived from Lakin, 2001)

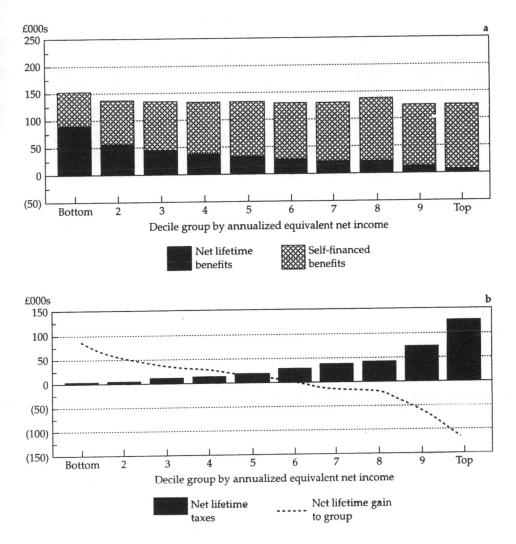

Figure III.12.3 Lifetime benefits and taxes by income group (1991 prices; finance from all taxes) a, gross benefits in cash and kind; b, net lifetime taxes and average net gain (after Falkingham and Hills, 1995, table 7.6)

The bars in the top panel of figure III.12.3 are therefore divided between 'net' and 'self-financed' benefits, the latter being a rising proportion moving up through the income groups. The bars in the lower panel show where the net lifetime taxes are coming from. Net lifetime taxes also rise moving up through the income groups. Finally, the line in the lower panel – analogous to

that in figure III.12.2 – shows the net gain or loss from the system to each lifetime income group as a whole. The bottom five groups are again net gainers on average; the sixth group breaks even; the top four groups are net losers. Thus, even on a lifetime perspective, the system does appear to redistribute from 'lifetime rich' to 'lifetime poor' (and also, importantly, from men to women, when the results are analysed by gender). However, the diagram suggests that *most* benefits are self-financed over people's lifetimes, rather than being paid for by others (see also chapter III.10). On these results, nearly three-quarters of what the welfare state does is like a 'savings bank', and only a quarter is 'Robin Hood' redistribution between different people (see Barr, 2000, for more discussion of this role of the welfare state).

Implications

In his book *The Strategy of Equality*, Julian Le Grand (1982) reaches the striking conclusion that 'Almost all public expenditure on the social services benefits the better off to a greater extent than the poor.' If so, a large part of social policy has failed in what many would see as one of its main aims. However, this conclusion needs careful interpretation (see Powell, 1995, for a discussion of some of the issues). It follows from an analysis which includes transport subsidies as a social service, but excludes social security (half of all welfare spending). It looks at gross benefits and their distribution between socio-economic and income

groups, but does not look at who pays for these services through taxation. For some services the analysis is in terms of the distribution of gross benefits between households unadjusted for need, but for others the conclusion only follows if one looks at the distribution of services in relation to need, notably of health care in relation to the reported health status of different groups (and analysis of more recent data than the 1972 figures used by Le Grand, such as that by O'Donnell and Propper, 1991, reaches different conclusions).

How welfare services are distributed has a major bearing on whether we judge them successful. But such judgements rest on a particular series of choices in the way in which distribution is analysed. Alternative ways of looking at the problem – including the kinds of results presented in the previous section – can give a very different impression, suggesting that it is highly unlikely that the poor would be better off and the rich worse off if welfare services were swept away. These are fundamental issues, but ones where care is needed in how they are analysed, and in defining exactly what question is being answered by that analysis.

Guide to further reading

Barr, N., 2000. *The Welfare State as Piggy Bank* (Oxford: Oxford University Press). This book examines, from an economics perspective, the way in which the welfare state distributes income across the life cycle, including detailed discussion of pensions, medical insurance, and student finance.

Bramley, G. and Evans, M., 2000. 'Getting the smaller picture', *Fiscal Studies*, 21, 2. This article looks at where public spending goes on an area basis, comparing use of public services in rich and poor electoral wards in three English local authorities. It provides the kind of analysis needed to examine whether spending is (and can be) 'targeted' on poor areas.

Lakin, C., 2001. 'The effects of taxes and benefits on household income, 1999–2000', *Economic Trends*, 56, 9 (April). This article (produced annually by ONS and available on their website, www.statistics.gov.uk) gives official estimates of the distributional effect of taxation and of a large part of public spending, including social security and welfare services.

Falkingham, J. and Hills, J. (eds), 1995. *The Dynamic of Welfare: The Welfare State and the Life Cycle* (Hemel Hempstead: Prentice Hall/ Harvester Wheatsheaf). This book looks at the impact of the welfare state taking a life cycle perspective using a variety of approaches, including presenting results from a computer simulation model, LIFEMOD.

Le Grand, J., 1982. *The Strategy of Equality* (London: George Allen & Unwin). This book advances the proposition that welfare services disproportionately benefit the 'middle class', examining health care, education, housing and transport.

O'Donnell, O. and Propper, C., 1991 'Equity and the distribution of NHS resources', *Journal of Health Economics*, 10. This study looks at more recent data than used in Le Grand's original study, and presents alternative ways of analysing the data, leading the authors to conclude that health spending in the UK is generally distributed in accordance with need.

Powell, M., 1995. 'The strategy of equality revisited', *Journal of Social Policy*, 24, 2. This article, followed by a reply by Le Grand, critically examines the evidence and conclusions presented in Le Grand's 1982 study.

Sefton, T., 1997. *The Changing Distribution of the Social Wage*, STICERD Occasional Paper 21, London School of Economics. This paper looks in detail at the distribution of government spending on health, education, housing subsidies and personal social services. It looks in particular at how they changed between 1979 and 1993, examining whether changes in the 'social wage' offset the growth in inequality of cash incomes.

The Centre for Analysis of Social Exclusion (CASE) at the London School of Economics places its discussion papers and other publications, some of which relate to distributional issues, on its website: http://sticerd.lse.ac.uk/case/publications/case.asp. The Department of Work and Pensions publishes an annual analysis of income distribution in the UK in its 'Households below Average Income', also available at: www.dwp.gov.uk/asd/index.htm. The Institute of Fiscal Studies presents analyses of the distributional effects of the annual Budget and other tax and benefit changes at: www.ifs.org.uk/publications/index.shtml. The Office for National Statistics produces an analysis of the distributional effects of government spending and taxation in an annual article in *Economic Trends*, also available at: www.statistics.gov.uk/themes/social_finances/key_reports.asp

III.13
Accountability for Welfare

Janet Newman

'Accountability' designates a set of values and institutions concerning the relationship between public services and the citizens or users they serve. Along with 'responsibility', 'transparency', 'responsiveness' and a host of other terms, accountability lies at the heart of a series of restructurings of the British state. During the post-war expansion of the welfare state the emphasis was on accountability for inputs – ensuring financial probity by checking that budgets had been spent on what they had been intended for, and that there were no financial irregularities. Accountability for what was delivered with the money spent – for the outputs or outcomes of public expenditure – was not a major concern. This period was also characterized by professional self regulation – the accountability of practitioners to their peers and ultimately to their professional body.

During the 1980s and 1990s there was a marked shift away from professional and towards managerial forms of accountability and control. The resulting 'audit explosion' shifted the focus of audit and inspection from monitoring financial probity and towards a much sharper emphasis on assessing the performance of organizations delivering public and welfare services. New Labour's processes of modernization can be viewed as further deepening and extending these processes, with the establishment of a plethora of new agencies concerned with setting and monitor-ing standards (the National Institute for Clinical Excellence, the Commission for Social Care Inspection, the National Care Standards Council, the Commission for Healthcare Audit and Inspection, and a host of others), the introduction of formal institutions of scrutiny in local government, and an increase in the importance of penalties experienced by service providers as a result of poor audit or inspection reports. These developments sit rather uncomfortably alongside current attempts to enhance accountability to users and communities through, for example, user involvement strategies or public consultation and involvement in decision-making. New Labour's emphasis on joined-up government, partnership working and public participation has also produced new challenges to traditional forms of accountability and the institutions of representative democracy from which they derive. But before discussing such shifts in more detail, it is necessary to clarify some basic concepts.

Unpacking Accountability

Definitions are problematic since accountability is a concept with highly normative overtones – everyone talks about it as a positive thing yet the concept carries widely different meanings and values. It is readily appropriated both by those seeking to resist change and those advocating change in the public policy system. In an attempt to

---

BOX III.13.1 Dimensions of accountability

Accountability *of whom?* – where does responsibility lie?

Possibilities include:

- Politicians – e.g. the relevant minister
- Designated senior officials – e.g. 'accounting officers' in the Civil Service
- Local managers – e.g. the chief executives of local authorities or hospital trusts
- Individual workers. – e.g. individual doctors, social workers

Accountability *for what?* – what criteria are used in making judgements?

Possibilities include:

- Probity of expenditure
- Upholding professional standards
- Value for money
- Organizational performance
- Delivery of policy goals

Accountability *to whom?*:

Possibilities include:

- Upwards to line manager, chief executive and elected representatives
- Downwards (to local communities, citizens or service users)
- Lateral (to peers, partners or colleagues)
- Outwards (to customers making choices through the market place)
- Inwards (to one's own sense of probity and ethics)

Accountability *through what means* – how are people to be held to account? What sanctions may be exercised?

Possibilities include:

- Reporting (e.g. 'rendering an account' through annual reports)
- Audit (e.g. examination of accounts, and/or of statistical measures of performance)
- Inspection (e.g. visits by Ofsted or the SSI)
- Democratic processes (e.g elections)

---

pin down a rather elusive and slippery concept, the literature has become littered with typologies of accountability. Some writers focus on analytical distinctions within the concept itself, setting out different dimensions of accountability (box III.13.1) while others highlight different forms and processes of accountability (box III.13.2).

Each of these different dimensions of accountability is the source of contested views. For example there is a long debate about where responsibility and accountability properly reside. Should it be the minis-ter, rendering an account to parliament and thus to the people, or does s/he have so little direct control over particular decisions made during the delivery process that responsibility should be seen to lie with the local chief executive or service manager? The tension between self-regulation and external scrutiny or intervention often lies at the heart of disputes about the accountability of public officials and public services, as well as debates about the control of the press, financial institutions, charities and political parties. There is also much debate about how to get the right balance between upward lines of accountability and those that emphasize accountability to users and communities. We can identify three different sets of assumptions about how public services should be delivered, each of which is based on a particular model of governance and raises particular accountability challenges (see box III.13.2).

Such typologies are always simpler than the phenomena they seek to categorize. Accountability is, in practice, a multi-layered and complex set of processes linking institutional rules with personal norms and values. It invokes ideas of morality and ethics as well as economy and efficiency. While there are many analyses of the institutional dimensions of accountability in the literature, there are very few studies of how individual or collective constructs of accountability are shaped within the dominant discourses and practices of any particular regime.

Accountability is also a *relational* concept: it rests on a range of assumptions about the relationship between the state and the public at large; between service providers and service users; between professionals and clients; and between central government and local managers. It is also a concept that involves conflicts over the proper distribution of power in a democratic society. Public bodies, from parliament to the police, from democratically elected institutions to the whole range of quangos that proliferated in the 1980s, have the capacity to make decisions over the use and allocation of resources. The disputes around how, and to

---

BOX III.13.2: Accountability and governance

- *Governance through hierarchy.* This is based on the traditional image of the welfare state, with services delivered through large bureaucratic organizations with long chains of command and formal rules and procedures. Accountability here is based on checking that administrative and financial responsibilities had been properly exercised. The challenge, however, is that there is little accountability for what was actually delivered.
- *Governance through markets.* This was the dominant model that emerged during the 1980s and 1990s and influenced a range of reforms based on the separation of purchasers and providers and the delivery of services through contract. Notions of accountability to consumers became much stronger in this period, with league tables, inspections and performance audits used to hold managers to account for the performance of their organizations. The challenge here concerns the difficulty of viewing public services as individual, rather than collective goods. There is little emphasis in this model of delivering effective outcomes for the communities and citizens as a whole.
- *Governance through networks.* Here accountability operates through influence and reciprocal relationships between actors in networks. This is a model that underpins the idea of professional accountability to one's peers. But it has become more important with the growth of partnership working and the increasing emphasis on delivering policy outcomes by working across traditional professional and organizational boundaries. The challenge here is that networks are diffuse and complex, with many reporting lines and relationships cutting across each other. The complexity of the emerging relationships produces a lack of transparency that makes it difficult for government, service users or citizens to hold actors to account.

whom, they should be accountable are therefore disputes about *power* – the limits of autonomy, the extent to which responsibility is delegated, the power of the state to inspect and to intervene where it judges that performance falls below a desired standard. At stake in the process of accountability, then, are struggles over power, over the boundaries of trust, over the meaning of democracy, and over the conception of the 'public' in whose name accountability is exercised.

Changing Notions of Accountability

Notions of accountability – both personal and financial – have long roots. Rulers, politicians, administrators and leaders have always had to render an account to those who appointed them or on whom their legitimacy depends. They have also often been held to account for some infringement of the norms and rules of behaviour in the office they hold. The penalties for such infringement have varied from losing one's head, to losing one's office, to suffering a loss of credibility and reputation. The notion of financial accountability grew alongside the growth of institutions and laws protecting commercial trading. Both forms of accountability – personal and financial – became institutionalized in the welfare state and public services. Personal accountability was enshrined in the idea of professional self-regulation and in the general ethos of public probity and public service expected of public sector workers. Financial accountability was institutionalized in the processes of financial audit and regulated by bodies such as the National Audit Office and Audit Commission. The probity of public expenditure was the overriding concern.

During the 1980s and 1990s public and welfare services went through profound transformations with the growth of managerialism and markets (see chapter III.5). This period saw the development of notions of accountability to users and citizens. There was increasing talk of public sector users as 'customers', the development of a host of quality assurance schemes, and the introduction, under John Major's government, of the Citizen's Charter. The managerial reforms were accompanied by, and indeed partly delivered through, changes in the focus, scope and power of audit bodies. Their focus shifted beyond the traditional focus on the probity of public expenditure to whether public resources were being used in a way that gave value for money, as measured by the three 'E's of economy, efficiency and effectiveness. The Audit Commission, responsible for auditing local authorities and health authorities in England and Wales, expanded its work to encompass questions of organizational design and management processes. It also produced a number of reports setting out good practice models for a range of activities from partnership working to the conduct of political business in local authorities.

This expansion was accompanied by a shift from the narrow focus on financial accountability towards what Pollitt et al (1999) term *performance* accountability. This was situated in the shift towards an increasingly dispersed and fragmented array of service delivery organizations that were hard to control from the centre. Performance audit emerged in the context of the search for ways of both giving autonomy – devolving power to local managers – while exercising some form of control. It is a strategy directed towards controlling and assessing the performance of multiple organizations in this dispersed field of provision created by processes of decentralization and the introduction of markets and contracts.

Audit, in this period, became much more than a question of 'checking the books' and ensuring that organizations had adequate systems of financial management. It also became concerned with assessing internal organizational arrangements and the organizational outputs that resulted from them. At the same time, it might be argued, notions of personal accountability – based on professional self-regulation and a commitment to public service values – became eroded as workers experienced traumatic shifts in their working lives and as the trust that had traditionally been placed in them, by both government and the wider public, was eroded. The increase in regulation, inspection and audit can be viewed as filling the resulting trust vacuum.

The 1997 Labour government's modernization programme was underpinned by a further audit explosion as the new administration sought to reform those parts of the public sector where, in their view, 'producer dominance' had survived the market and managerial reforms of the 1980s and early 1990s, notably health and social care services. There was a continued focus on organizational efficiency and performance alongside an attempt to sharpen accountability to users and local stakeholders. There was also a marked enlargement of the role of government as a regulator of services, setter of standards and guarantor of quality. Labour extended the regulatory role of government through its use of performance targets, standards, audit, inspection and quality assurance schemes.

The proliferation of targets and performance indicators has been linked to the requirement that organizations in most sectors 'render an account' by producing year on year plans reporting on past performance and outlining the way in which they intend to achieve improvements. Examples include Best Value performance plans, Health Improvement plans, School Development plans and a host of others. Many such planning processes are now mandatory and subject to audit and inspection processes. There has also been an attempt to regulate professional work by setting out a range of standards (e.g. those set out in National Service Frameworks) designed to overcome variations in standards in health, social services and other locally or regionally controlled services.

One of the most signficant development

under Labour was the introduction of a new system of clinical governance in health – a comprehensive approach covering clinical audit, evidence-based practice and standard setting. Such quality assurance processes are intended to shift the focus from external regulation by government or the professional body to the development of 'self-managing' organizational systems, procedures, guidelines and protocols, and 'self-regulating' practitioners.

But the 'belt and braces' approach to performance improvement meant that each of these instruments and strategies was reinforced by audit and inspection. Labour's approach to modernizing public services such as education, health, social services and probation was based on strengthening external oversight through expanding the range and powers of bodies involved in scrutiny, inspection and audit. It set up a number of quasi-state bodies concerned with inspecting and regulating the professional practice of doctors, teachers, social workers and others. It established a Commission for Care Standards in each region to regulate social care in domiciliary and residential settings. The role of the Audit Commission continued to expand, with new Housing and Best Value Inspectorates established under its aegis. A new body – Her Majesty's Inspector of Probation – was introduced. The multiplication of inspection regimes was accompanied by additional powers for Secretaries of State in education, social services and elsewhere to remove services from organizations receiving poor inspection reports. The Commission for Health Improvement was given authority to intervene in the running of Primary Care Trusts deemed to be performing poorly. OFSTED inspections were backed up by powers for the Secretary of State to remove functions from local education authorities (LEAs) or to close schools. The expansion of audit and inspection, then, was linked to a wider discourse of failure and the growth of threats and sanctions against organizations deemed to be performing poorly.

Representing the People: Accountability to Citizens and Users

Labour's approach to modernization is associated not only with attempts to sharpen upward accountability but also with efforts to make local authorities and service providers more accountable to their users and the communities they serve. As noted, a key theme in the market reforms of the 1980s and early 1990s had been the development of a consumer orientation in public services, with attempts to enhance the accountability of provider organizations direct to users and consumers. While consumers tended in practice to have little power to exercise choice of service provider or to influence the pattern of service delivery, a host of initiatives – from league tables to quality assurance schemes – flourished in the name of the customer. Public service providers also began to engage in more direct forms of communication with users, including satisfaction surveys, complaints schemes, and various forms of consultation exercises. Through the 1990s there was also a developing interest in involving citizens in decision-making through various forms of public participation and involvement: citizen's juries, citizen's panels, local area forums, tenant management groups and a host of community involvement strategies linked to urban renewal and regeneration programmes.

Labour built on these developments. The modernization agenda gave a high profile to public participation, for example with the requirement that local authorities consult with local people when drawing up plans for improving the performance of services under the Best Value framework. The zonal programmes and strategies for neighbourhood renewal emphasized the value of public involvement as a means of ensuring that such programmes were responsive to local needs and aspirations. The centrality of public participation in Labour's policy agenda is informed by twin sets of political goals. The first (and most public) are about

citizenship and the legitimacy of the political process. The rhetoric of public participation is peppered with notions such as 'reconnecting' citizens and government, or building an 'active' or 'responsible' citizenry. Such goals reflect dismay about the declining participation in formal elections and about the prevailing cynicism about the political process. The second set of political goals are more closely linked to the Labour government's drive to improve the performance of public services by creating challenges to 'producer power' from below.

This emphasis on the accountability of public service providers directly to their users and communities offers a form of accountability that is both more direct (i.e. not mediated by long hierarchies upward to an eventual body of elected representatives) and more differentiated (i.e. capable of ensuring that different interests and identities have some form of presence in the process of public participation). However the increasing emphasis on public participation sits uncomfortably with the traditional institutions of representative democracy and with the dominant patterns of upward, hierarchical patterns of accountability. Such tensions are exacerbated by the way in which the concept of accountability is being narrowed to a focus on accountability for organizational performance against government goals, targets and standards. This is an essentially managerial form of accountability – and one that may do little to redress the declining trust and confidence of the public in the government that is accountable to it.

Key issues and questions

Here I want to highlight four key questions that remain unresolved and that are likely to influence future debates and reform agendas.

1. Joined-up government
Measures of policy outcomes reflect the increasing political importance of cross

cutting policy agendas (e.g. preventing ill health, tackling social exclusion) that require 'joined up' government and partnership working. This can lead to problems of transparency (who is responsible for delivery) and accountability (who can be held to account for success or failure). It remains uncertain whether attempts to resolve such difficulties will result in the strengthening of hierarchical forms of governance that limit the dynamism and efficacy of network based action.

2. Central or local accountability?
Accountability is a site of major structural tensions in the increasingly multi-level governance of the UK. It is a site of tension between central and local government, with local politicians struggling to deliver services funded by government (with strong upwards lines of accountability) while at the same time delivering locally determined strategies formed out of their accountability to the local electorate. Local hospitals, schools and other providers, subject to increasingly stringent governmental audit and inspection regimes based on the delivery of central government targets, also seek to respond to locally determined goals and priorities, goals and priorities partly shaped by users and citizens involved in consultation exercises and decision making forums.

3. Outputs or outcomes?
How far will the current shift towards attempting to set goals and targets relating to broad policy outcomes, rather than organizational outputs, be sustained, and what are the implications for audit and evaluation? Public Service Agreements are also based on an attempt to introduce outcome-oriented performance indicators. A number of joint audits and inspection processes have been introduced. This partial shift towards auditing and inspecting outcomes is underpinned by an assumption of self-regulation: that is, that by specifying outcomes, local managers and professionals will be able to get on with

the job of finding the best means of delivering them. But the assessment and evaluation of broad outcomes, rather than organizational outputs, presents a number of challenges that currently remain unresolved. For example how might achievement against the goals of overcoming social exclusion or promoting good health be evaluated? And how could the contribution that a specific agency makes to such a goal be assessed?

4. User involvement and accountability
The current emphasis on user involvement in public and welfare services raises a number of questions about how accountability to users can be enhanced. First, should the focus simply be on accountability to the users of a particular service, or should there be a wider notion of accountability to communities and citizens on whom the service is likely to impact? Second, at what stage in the decision making process can user or citizen accountability best be exercised? Should it be at the stage of policy-making, of service-planning or service delivery or evaluation and research? Which – or what combination – is most likely to have an impact on the service itself? Thirdly, how might welfare services respond to the calls by many welfare users – and of welfare associations or movements – for a more inclusive and differentiated response to the production of social care?

The impact of the audit culture

The development of audit and inspection is linked to a wider discourse of failure and the growth of threats and sanctions against organizations deemed to be performing poorly. What are the implications of such threats and sanctions on organizations and the staff who work in them? What informal norms and practices – with beneficial or perverse effects – might result as organizations seek to position themselves as successful players in the eyes of audit and inspection bodies? How far will the audit culture produce the intended effect of enhanced self-regulation within public services? Will the current expansion of external regulation enhance or diminish the capacity of organizations to regulate themselves? What will be the consequences of the audit culture – and the way in which this is both mediated by and amplified in the media – on the motivation, morale and personal ethics of public service staff?

Guide to further reading

Barnes, M. and Bowl, R., 2001. *Taking Over the Asylum: Empowerment and Mental Health* (Basingstoke: Palgrave) is one example of ways in which accountability has been enhanced through the participation of, and collective action by, the users of mental health services.

Clarke, J. et al., 2000. 'Guarding the Public Interest? Auditing Public Services', in J. Clarke, S. Gewirtz and E. McLaughlin (eds), *New Managerialism, New Welfare?* (London: Sage/ Open University) offers a cogent analysis of the role of audit, inspection and other evaluative processes in the 'dispersed' state. It raises important questions about how the public and its interests are understood and represented in the practices of evaluation.

Newman, J., 2001. *Modernising Governance: New Labour, Policy and Society* (London: Sage), analyses key tensions within New Labour's approach to governance that are played out in both the modernization of services to enhance performance, and in the expansion of public participation in decision making. It explores questions of difference and diversity in both representative and participatory democracy.

Pollitt, C. et al., 1999. *Performance or Compliance? Performance Audit and Public Management in Five Countries* (Oxford: Oxford University Press) is a comparative study of the role of 'Supreme Audit Institutions' (e.g. the National Audit Office in the UK) across five European countries. It situates the audit process and the growth of SAIs in the trajectories of managerial reform in each nation and provides an excellent theoretical overview drawing on an extensive programme of research.

Power, M., 1997. *The Audit Society* (Oxford: Oxford University Press) provides a stringent critique of the audit explosion and its consequences.

Prior, D., Stewart, J. and Walsh, K., 1995. *Citizenship: Rights, Community and Participation* (London: Pitman), although pre-dating the current developments in public participation, gives a good overview of the shift from the focus on consumerist forms of accountability towards a focus on citizenship and citizen involvement.

Strathern, M. (ed.), 2000. *Audit Cultures: Anthropological Studies in Accountability, Ethics and the Academy* (London: Routledge). A collection of studies of the impact of the audit culture on people and institutions. The focus is on higher education but the relevance of the analysis is much broader. The anthropological approach brings fresh insights and enables a focus on the interaction between the financial and moral dimensions of accountability

The activities and reports of the Audit Commission and the National Audit Office can be tracked through: www.audit-commission.gov.uk; www.nao.gov.uk. Links to how accountability in the devolved parliament works are accessible at: www.scotland.gov.uk. www.service-first.gov.uk provides a library of performance indicator links and resources that can be used to find out how well services are performing in your area.

Part IV
Issues in Social Policy

Social Policy and Particular Groups

IV.1
Children

Malcolm Hill

The Scope of Children's Policy

It would be easy, but false, to assume that children's policy covers all social policies that relate to children. In fact, both policy analysts and governments have tended to adopt a narrower focus on public measures and services directed largely at vulnerable children.

There are several reasons for this. Firstly, the arena in which children usually spend the great majority of their time is the family home. Traditionally this has been seen as an area in which government should not intrude, but instead respect parental autonomy and privacy *unless* there are exceptional reasons. Children also spend much time in school, which has been dealt with separately as education policy. Arrangements for young children (such as nursery provision and parental leave) are usually part of family policy, while universal and selective financial support to parents to help cover the costs of bringing up children have been treated as part of social security or family policy. Hence children's policy and legislation has usually been concerned for the most part with *'child welfare'*, i.e. arrangements and services for children in difficulties, for example as a result of divorce, family separation, abuse and neglect by parents or criminal behaviour by the child.

In this sense, children's policy is concerned with personal social services for children, court services or their equivalent for children and families, voluntary children's agencies (NGOs) and the role of professionals and agencies working with children (e.g. health visitors, doctors, police). As in all spheres, formal agencies work within the context of informal welfare provided by kin, friends and others. For instance the care of young children typically involves combinations of informal care and usage of public nurseries, family centres or nursery schools. Increasingly, child welfare measures have been linked to wider policies affecting children. This is illustrated by government steps to assess the impact of any new policy on children (e.g. housing, transport). This chapter largely concentrates on the narrower definition of children's policy, but locates that within the broader conception.

The upper limit of childhood is ill-defined, recognizing the gradualness of the transition to adulthood via adolescence or youth (see chapter IV.2). The legal threshold varies according to the 'marker' of adulthood, such as school-leaving, entitlement to vote, drive or marry, legal capacity to give consent or being dealt with in an adult court for criminal activity. For general purposes and following the UN Convention (see page 291), children are regarded as those aged 18 or under. They make up just over one in five of the population.

The Changing Nature and Status of Childhood

Many writers have stressed that adult attitudes towards children and hence policy actions on their behalf are based on perceptions of children and childhood that differ according to time and place. For instance, over the centuries ideas have changed about the balance of nature and nurture in affecting children's personality and behaviour. Also ideas have varied about the extent to which children are typically inclined to be innocent or naughty, vulnerable or resilient, ignorant or knowing, and so on. Consequently it is always important to examine preconceptions about children and childhood. Recent theories stress that children are active participants in the worlds they inhabit and do not simply copy or react to actions by adults. It is suggested that, in the late or postmodern era, children are especially valued because they offer opportunities for close enduring relationships in a context of accelerating change and increased individualization (see chapter II.14). Nevertheless, children still have little power and low status in society, which makes them vulnerable to being ignored, exploited, demonized or ill-treated.

Children, Parents and the State

Children's policy is based on a fluid compromise between ideals and values concerning children, parents and the role of government. In the UK, strong values exist concerning family privacy and autonomy. On the whole it is accepted that parents are normally responsible for their children's upbringing and entitled to carry out their role without state interference. On the other hand, it has become increasingly accepted that in a complex, modern society, the government does have a role in supporting parents (or guardians). Thus, almost every Western society pays some form of family allowance or child benefit to all parents, though the amount per child, its duration and the taxation to be paid on it vary from country to country. All families with infants should have access to a health visitor and a child health centre. Although parents may educate children themselves or more commonly pay for private schooling, the majority of children aged five and upwards are educated in state schools. At different times and in different ways, both Conservative and Labour governments have committed themselves to making pre-school care and education widely available, at least from the age of three years.

Thus, provision of certain services for parents and children on a universal basis is now broadly accepted as a legitimate societal function, offering care and support. It has been argued that this is not an entirely benign or neutral matter, since certain expectations can be conveyed by the service providers and professionals concerned in order to alter parental attitudes and behaviour. Such health or social education is regarded by some commentators as a subtle form of social control to induce conformity to prevailing norms.

More overt social control may occur when it is thought that children are being seriously harmed by their parents or carers. This circumstance can warrant compulsory state intervention, resulting in formal supervision of the family or removal of the children, usually into a foster or residential children's home. In extreme circumstances, children can be looked after away from home or adopted against parental wishes.

Over the last 50 years, policy and legislation has oscillated in its emphases with regard to the state-parent-child triangle. A *laissez-faire approach* stresses non-intervention, on the basis that interference in family life is wrong (and usually unnecessary) except in very extreme situations. A *state paternalist or interventionist* approach concentrates on the duty of the state to promote and safeguard the welfare of children, overriding parental wishes and rights if need be for the sake of children. A *parentalist or birth family* perspective focuses on the state's responsibility to support families and reduce the pressures of poverty and other factors which prompt child-rearing problems, rather than remove the children. Legislation in place at the turn of the millennium sought to balance each of these three perspectives.

Needs, Risks and Rights

Public intervention with respect to children has usually been justified in terms of three overlapping approaches or discourses, associated with need, risk and rights. Most conceptions of social *need* (see chapter II.1) recognize that the fulfilment of human life across the life-span encompasses physical, social and autonomy needs and that the meeting these in childhood is fundamental for both current and later stages of life. Society as a whole is seen to have a duty to ensure that all children's needs (e.g. for education) are met, whether by direct or indirect actions. One justification for policy concentrating on vulnerable children is that their needs are greater than average or their families less capable than usual of meeting those needs, so special services are required. The legislative category of 'children in need' has been the basis for this more targeted provision. From the mid-1990s onwards the Department of Health in England and Wales developed an integrated framework for assessing children's needs, based largely on psychological and social work research and concepts.

One of the reasons why law-breaking by children is treated differently from adults' criminal activities is that experience and research evidence has shown that their 'deeds' reflect in part their 'needs'. In other words, deficiencies in care and upbringing are linked to criminal activity, so that the need for nurturing and education should be attended to alongside the young person's behaviour.

Since the 1970s, notions of *risk* have been increasingly influential, as a result of public and political concerns about child abuse. In particular, it is now widely recognized that considerable numbers of children are in danger as a result of neglect or ill-treatment within their families. In high profile cases when children have died or been severely abused, various professionals have been much criticized for not identifying high-risk cases and taking appropriate action to protect the children. As a result local authorities, police and health professionals have been encouraged to adopt a risk assessment approach, taking account of empirical evidence of the factors in the parents and children which indicate that abuse or re-abuse is probable. Despite efforts to make services more needs-based, evidence indicates that receipt of services is closely related to professionals' perceptions of the perceived risk to the child.

Both need and risk approaches depend on judgements being made about which children in what circumstances have needs or risks that require formal action or services. A *rights* approach (see chapter II.2) is regarded by many as based on fundamental entitlements and on equality. It was given major impetus with respect to children by the UN Convention on the Rights of the Child, approved in 1989 and subsequently ratified by nearly all nation states. The Convention contains 54 articles concerned with a wide range of civil, economic, social and cultural rights, which 'States Parties' commit themselves to respecting and furthering. These may be grouped as shown in table IV.1.1. Article 2 of the Convention states that the rights must apply to all children without discrimination, while later articles require special measures for certain categories of child (e.g. refugees, 'handicapped' children). Article 3 affirms that the best interests of the child must be the primary consideration in any decision or action concerning children. The Convention does not form part of the law in the UK but its principles are espoused in legislation and guidance, while forming a touchstone for assessing policy and practice.

Many children's organizations now go to considerable trouble to ensure that children's participatory rights are respected. They consult children and young people on

Table IV.1.1   United Nations Convention on the Rights of the Child: Key types of right

The right to . . .	Examples	Type of right
Survival and health	Life, survival and development	Protective rights
Safety	Protection from maltreatment	
Selfhood	Name, identity, privacy	Personal rights
Services	Highest attainable health services	Provision rights
	Education	
Serious consideration of the child's opinions	Express views and have them taken into account	Participation rights
	Freedom of expression and association	

important matters affecting them, both as individuals and as groups. Collective mechanisms for consulting children and young people (such as school and youth councils, day events, parliaments) help to ensure that adults are more aware of children's ideas. The danger exists that only the views of selected or self-selecting children or types of child are heard. Moreover, listening to children then taking no action can lead to disillusionment and cynicism.

Starting in Scandinavia, a number of countries have appointed an Ombudsman or Commissioner, independent of government, to act as an advocate and safeguarder with respect to children's rights. In the UK, Wales was the first nation to appoint a Children's Commissioner in 2000, a position also created by certain cities such as London.

The Welfare Mix in Child Welfare

Except in Northern Ireland, the prime responsibility for statutory children's services since the creation of the welfare state has been placed at local government level, unlike health and social security. Children's departments were created in 1948, but around 1970 these were merged in new Social Services Departments in England and Wales (Social Work Departments in Scotland) (see chapter IV.12). For some years these provided generic services for all age and client groups, but by the later stages of the twentieth century most departments had moved to a new separation of services for children and families at local area level. By contrast, in Northern Ireland (as in the Republic of Ireland), children's services have been part of the health service.

The three jurisdictions have always had separate legislation and organizational structures. From 1971 Scotland developed its own children's hearings system, with lay people making decisions about cases involving child abuse, young offenders or school non-attendance, in contrast to the court-based system of the rest of the UK. Fresh impetus to diversity was provided by the devolution measures introduced by the Labour government in the late 1990s. For example, the new Scottish Executive introduced its own child strategy, which requires all of its departments to consider in advance the impact of each of its policies on children. The Executive's Action Plan "For Scotland's Children" (2001) promoted inter-agency cooperation to create a single service system for children. While the Scottish parliament in Edinburgh passes its own statutes, the Welsh assembly is responsible for applying regulations for primary legislation framed at Westminster.

Statutory children's services have three main areas of responsibility:

- for *separated* children in foster and residential care or being placed for adoption;
- for *child protection*, i.e. actions and services with respect to children who have been abused or when abuse is suspected;
- to deliver *family support*, a range of practical and therapeutic interventions for families where there is a disabled member or where a child's health or development might otherwise be impaired.

The law, policy and guidance have stressed the importance of inter-agency cooperation for the sake of children. This began first in relation to child protection with requirements to establish joint planning and review mechanisms at strategic level and to share information and decision-making at case level. The 1990s saw moves towards various kinds of plan, including children's services plans, which were to be developed and implemented in a shared manner by social work, education, health and other relevant agencies.

Since before the origins of the modern welfare state, voluntary agencies have always played important roles, though the nature of their contributions has changed. Until the 1960s, for example, voluntary children's organizations ran many children's homes, but that aspect of their work diminished, often to be replaced by more specialist community-based services (e.g. dealing with the effects of child abuse or school-related difficulties). Increasingly, larger voluntaries have also taken on advocacy and policy-influence roles. Private for-profit organizations have not figured prominently in provision, but they have run certain residential establishments and specialist fostering programmes. In general, voluntary and private agencies provide their services to local authorities (health boards and trusts in Northern Ireland) for a charge. At different times and in different places, this has taken the form of a grant from the local authority for a global service or project, or charging of fees for individual children and families. The arrangement may take one of several forms including a contract, service agreement or partnership, with varying degrees of specificity and autonomy.

The Role of Inquiries

Perhaps more than any other policy area, children's legislation, policy and services have been driven by scandals and their associated inquiries and reports. Several of the most significant pieces of children's legislation in the late nineteenth and twentieth centuries were prompted or dominated by the deaths of children at the hands of a parent, step-parent or foster carer. After a period of quiescence, from 1973 onwards a series of inquiries came to dominate both political thinking and front-line practice. These highlighted the following issues in turn:

- physical injuries and neglect of children by parents;
- sexual abuse of children by family members;
- the ill-treatment of children in residential establishments;
- the sexual exploitation of children by strangers.

Inquiries criticized professionals and agencies for a variety or reasons, but perhaps the most repeated complaint was the failure to share information effectively and coordinate plans and actions. Inquiries themselves and their role in policy-making have been subject to criticism. For instance they are very costly and legalistic, generalize conclusions from exceptional cases and often ignore the impact of poverty and service resource constraints. Arguably this has contributed to a defensive and suspicious approach by children's services focused on the extremes, rather than the creation of collaborative and supportive relationships between agencies and communities.

As a result, the work of children's services became dominated by the objective of assessing accurately when abuse has occurred or is likely to occur. Inter-agency meetings have become a key means of seeking to ensure that the knowledge and actions of all those involved with a family were well coordinated. If abuse is established, then a common consequence has been formal supervision or removal of the child from home. The development of this mode of operation was linked to a wider trend in government towards managerialism (see chapter III.5), whereby staff were expected to adhere to detailed guidance and follow rules of practice, rather than use professional discretion and judgement.

From 1990 onwards, the prevailing approach was criticized on a number of grounds, but it has proved resistant to change. It has been argued that too much time and energy is devoted to investigating child abuse referrals, leaving many needy families without any positive help. The service has come to be seen with suspicion and has been stigmatized by the public. Wider societal and community factors in the generation of child abuse are neglected in the approach, which is predominantly reactive rather than proactive. On the other hand, it has also been claimed that errors are less common than formerly and that the system has reduced the number of non-accidental child deaths.

Children Looked After by Local Authorities

The Children Act 1989 introduced the term 'looked after children' into England and Wales to refer to children living away from home under local authority auspices as the official phrase to replace the term 'children in care', though the latter is still used informally. The Children (Scotland) Act 1995 and Children (Northern Ireland) Order 1995 followed suit, although with looked after children denoting a wider group in Scotland by including those subject to a formal supervision order. Most often children become looked after for multiple reasons, of which the most common include child abuse or neglect, family stress or conflict, parental illness or addiction and the child's behaviour. The vast majority of looked after children come from households who are poor and characterized by unstable membership. Children of mixed parentage are over-represented and there is evidence that the needs of black and ethnic minority children have often not been well met. The legislation requires that account should be taken of children's religious persuasion, racial origin, and linguistic and cultural background when making placement decisions.

The number of children looked after apart from their parents by local authorities at any one time is about 1 in every 200 children (about 52,000 in England on 31 March 2000). Since many are looked after for only short periods, the proportion who will be looked after at some point in their childhood is considerably higher however. As a result of the need to provide 24-hour care they account for a high proportion of children's services expenditure. The numbers of looked after children fell during the 1980s and 1990s, though began rising again in the late 1990s. At the same time, there was a significant shift to placing more children in foster care and fewer in residential care (mainly teenagers). Also increased numbers of children have been adopted from foster or residential care, while the numbers of infants adopted directly from their mothers has declined markedly since the 1960s.

Wider Children's Policies

Over many years a number of people have suggested that child welfare policy should adopt a more preventive approach. It is suggested that by intervening at an early stage and dealing with background rather than immediate factors, problems could be dealt with before they become too serious. This would also avert the need for the more expensive provision used when difficulties become severe. Early intervention was a key feature of the Labour government from 1997 onwards, exemplified by the Sure Start initiative directed at families in the early years.

Preventive approaches require action at societal and neighbourhood levels, in addition to those targeted at specific children and families *once problems have been identified* as in the conventional child welfare model. In this view measures to tackle poverty and social inclusion, promote child health and enhance educational and employment opportunities will not only improve those aspects of all children's and parents lives, but also contribute to the lowering of the stresses and vulnerabilities that result in child abuse, youth crime and family separation. Greater valuing of women and attempts to tackle male violence have also been stated as key requirements for reducing the incidence of harm to children.

Guide to further reading

An overview of the personal social services context across the constituent parts of the UK and Ireland is provided by contributors to the book edited by M. Payne and S. Shardlow *Social Work in the British Isles* (London. Jessica Kingsley, 2002). Lorraine Fox Harding has provided an insightful account of the differing value positions with regard to state policy relating to children in *Perspectives in Childcare Policy* (London: Longman, 1991). This is complemented by N. Parton's critical review of trends, with particular reference to child abuse and protection: *Governing the Family* (Basingstoke: Macmillan Press, 1991). *Children and Society* by M. Hill and K. Tisdall (London: Longman, 1997) places child welfare and related service developments within the context of children's lives, needs and rights.

Two more recent texts provide reviews of services and policies. J. Tunstill (ed.) *Children and the State: Whose Problem?* (London: Cassell, 2000) considers a range of relevant policy arenas, while N. Thomas provides a particular focus on looked after children, illuminated by the views of children from his own research: *Children, Family and the State* (Basingstoke: Macmillan Press, 2000). J. Horwath (ed.) *The Child's World* (London, Jessica Kingsley, 2001) presents some of the ideas underpinning the Department of Health's integrated framework for assessing children. Finally those interested in comparative material from elsewhere in Europe will find much interesting material in K. Pringle *Children and Social Welfare in Europe* (Buckingham: Open University Press, 1998), as well as the chapter by Cannan in Tunstill (2000).

IV.2
Young People

Bob Coles

The first edition of this book reported that 'youth' has been identified with 'social problems' throughout the centuries and that the late 1990s were no exception. The 'problems' identified then were issues of teenage pregnancy, educational disaffection (including truancy and school exclusion), drug misuse, youth homelessness, unemployment and crime. The chapter also used the plight of young people brought up in the public care as illustrative of the ways in which 'youth problems' were sometimes exacerbated by social policy intervention and that sometimes these were expensive, ineffective and disjointed. Five years on from the first edition, the 'problems' identified then are still with us but much has also changed in the intervening period, with youth policy issues receiving much more prominence on the government's social policy agenda. In the new century we have a Minister for Youth, a cross-ministerial working party on young people, a Children and Young People's Unit in Whitehall, a new 'Connexions Service' for all 13–19 year olds in England, new measures on youth crime and criminal justice, and a new and radical Act of Parliament designed to improve the welfare of care leavers. This revised chapter seeks to evaluate such social policies as they impact upon the welfare of young people. It also seeks to revise the picture of the social conditions of 'youth' in the light of recent social research.

Perspectives on Youth and Youth Transitions

'Youth' is often described as an interstitial phase in the life course between childhood and adulthood. Different social sciences emphasise different aspects of this. The term 'adolescence' is often used in psychology to describe biological and psychological aspects of physical, emotional and sexual maturation associated with the teenage years. Sociologists have more often defined youth as associated with institutional 'transitions', three of which predominate. The first involves completing education and entering the labour market – the school-to-work transition. The second involves attaining (relative) independence of families of origin (including partnering and family formations) – the domestic transition. The third involves moving from the parental home, sometimes initially into temporary 'transitional accommodation', but eventually achieving a 'home' independent of parents – the housing transition. Political scientists and others have focused on the ways in which different rights and responsibilities accrue to young people during their teenage years. Indeed some analysts have talked about youth citizenship as being distinctive from the full citizenship of adults. As an applied social science, social policy draws on all of these perspectives in order to provide a critical appreciation of how, to what degree, and in what ways the needs of young people are met.

The Polarization of Youth Transitions

The 'youth transition model' has proved especially useful in helping understand the 're-structuration' of youth that occurred in the last quarter of the twentieth century. It helps highlight the ways in which 'traditional transitions' have been replaced by 'extended' and 'fractured' transitions. 'Traditional transitions', commonplace until the mid-1970s, involved young people leaving school at minimum school leaving age and almost immediately and unproblematically obtaining employment. As young people worked, they continue to live in the parental home, they saved, formed partnerships, got engaged, then married, and on marriage, moved to their own home and started a family – usually, and unproblematically, in that order. In the twenty-first century, although significant numbers of young people still attempt some major transitions in their teenage years, traditional transitions have been largely replaced by 'extended transitions'. These involved longer periods spent in post-16 and higher education, longer periods of family dependency, later parenting, and more complex and extended periods in 'transitional housing'. 'Fractured transitions' refer to young people leaving school without securing a job or training, leaving home without attaining a stable home of their own, and so experiencing various forms of youth homelessness, even though homelessness does not always mean rooflessness.

The 1990s have seen a growing complexity in youth transitions with some marked regional variations. In the mid-1970s three in five young people left school at the age of 16 and moved straight into employment. Now, in most parts of the UK, only one in five young people leave education at the age of 16. Amongst those who do, on average, around 10 per cent will take part in government-supported training aimed towards the achievement of vocational qualifications, whilst about the same number will take up employment without training.

Regionally, many more take part in training in the Scotland, Wales and the North of England where employment at the age of 16 is more difficult. Drop-out rates from post-16 education, training and employment also remain high. The government estimates that around 160 thousand 16 and 17 year old young people (around 8 per cent of the age group), will spend significant periods of time not in any form of education, training or employment (NEET). This figure is also likely to be an underestimate and there are regional and spatial clusters where those NEET account for around one in five of the age group. The expectations of longer periods of family dependency for young people has also occurred at the very time when many families are unable to deal with the pressures and tensions involved. By the age of 16 only around a half of young people are living with both biological parents, many have experienced parental divorce or separation and significant numbers live with step-parents. 'Fractured transitions' often result from drop-out from families as well as drop-out from education, training or employment. 'Fractured' school-to-work transitions are also associated both with previous experiences of disadvantage (either in education, family life or both) and with other transition experiences – such as becoming a teenage parent, leaving home (often for negative reasons such as family disputes), or being involved in crime and the criminal justice system.

'Extended youth transitions' whilst increasing in popularity, are also complex. The youth labour market, which some commentators said had collapsed in the 1980s has re-emerged but in a different form. Many of the full-time jobs regarded in the 1970s and 1980s as low-skilled and dead-end, are now part-time jobs being done by school, college or university students. Extended transitions often do not imply a choice between education and employment but how to juggle both so as to minimise debt. But adding together those young people who cease full-time education at the age of 16 (20 per cent) and those who continue into higher education until age 21 or later (just over 30 per cent), still leaves around half of each cohort unaccounted for. Routes into work, partnerships and independent living of these 'ordinary kids' remains relatively under-researched. Some, predominantly housing-focused research indicates a worrying discongruence of housing and employment opportunities for young people. Where there are jobs, housing is scarce and prohibitively expensive. Where jobs are scarce, young people find it much easier to find places to live away from their parents but with poor or precarious job prospects. Most young people also delay becoming parents until their late twenties and routes into cohabitation and marriage are complex.

The Social Exclusion Agenda and the Emergence of UK Youth Policy

Much of the onus for the development of youth policy since 1997 has come through the activities of the Social Exclusion Unit set up shortly after the election. The Unit is part of the Cabinet Office, fulfils tasks set for it by the Prime Minister and reports directly to him. Its focus is 'social exclusion' – recognised as a complex, multi-faceted syndrome of disadvantage, the responsibilities for which span many different government departments. Many 'joined-up problems' require 'joined-up solutions' and much greater co-operation between government departments. Before the end of the century the SEU had produced five major reports on:

- truancy and school exclusion;
- rough sleeping;
- poor neighbourhoods;
- teenage pregnancy; and
- 16–18 year olds not in education, employment or training (NEET).

The topics chosen for these first studies are indicative of the intention of government to focus on early routes into, and forms of, social exclusion. The report on truancy and school exclusion pointed out that there had been huge rises in young people permanently excluded from school in England and Wales, of 450 per cent between 1990 and 1997 resulting in more than 13,000 young people permanently excluded from school – doing nothing and with little alternative educational provision. Fixed-term exclusions exceeded 100,000. Exclusions were also spatially clustered with some particular groups hugely over-represented. More than four out of five permanent exclusions from school were boys. Most were from secondary schools, with a quarter of all schools being responsible for two-thirds of all exclusions. African-Caribbean boys are five times more likely to be excluded than their white peers; those with special educational needs seven times more likely, and children 'looked after' (in care) ten times more likely, to be permanently excluded than their peers. Self-exclusion (truancy) was also reported to be widespread, but in this case as common amongst girls as boys. This was concentrated mainly (although not exclusively) in inner cities, and often related to the experience of bullying. Between 5 and 10 per cent of the mid-teenage population were 'hardcore non attenders'. The report also pointed to the links between truancy and school exclusion to poor (or no) qualification at the age of 16, later unemployment, and the involvement of young people in crime.

The SEU report contained a number of recommendations for policy and practice together with tough new targets to reduce both truancy and school exclusion by a third by 2003. It was closely followed by new circulars for schools and local education authorities issued by the (then) Department for Education and Employment (DfEE) giving new guidelines on how to try to tackle the problems. Local education authorities were given the responsibility of ensuring that all those excluded were reintegrated into full-time education within 15 days.

The fourth report of the SEU on teenage pregnancy was equally hard-hitting and the recommendations for policy and practice equally ambitious for change. The headline figures produced by the SEU were stark but already well-known. The rate for teenage pregnancy in the UK is twice that in Germany, three times that in France and six times that in Holland. By 1997 there were 90,000 conceptions to teenagers that we knew about, 7,700 to girls under the age of 16 and 2,200 to girls under the age of 14. Teenage pregnancy was also spatially clustered and much more likely to occur in particular groups. Young people whose parents were in unskilled manual jobs (or unemployed and previously in such jobs) were ten times more likely to become teenage parents than those whose parents had a professional background. Those living in social housing were three times more likely to be teen parents than those living in owner-occupied properties. Half of those young women 'looked after' (in care) would be a parent of at least one child by the age of 18. Also over-represented were the daughters of mothers who had been teen mothers themselves, those with poor (or no) school qualifications, those who truanted or had been excluded from school and those who disengaged from all forms of education, employment or training after compulsory schooling. Although the report emphasised the correlation of factors to do with the poverty associated with the neighbourhoods with high rates of teenage pregnancy, the SEU also drew attention to the links with being a victim of sexual abuse and having mental health problems. The recommendations included targets to reduce conceptions to young women under the age of 18 by a half by 2010. But although the report made radical suggestions about policy and practice to reduce pregnancies, it was also concerned to promote measures to help teenage parents continue with their education, prepare for work and employment, and give them support during pregnancy and their lives as young mothers, emphasising the SEU's concern with pregnancy as a route to social exclusion, rather than teenage pregnancy *per se*.

The fifth report was on young people not in any form of education, employment or training. Initially referred to 'status zero' because of not having a careers service record as either 1 (education), 2 (employment) or 3 (training), sociologists had also regarded it as a powerful metaphor for the fact that they 'counted for nothing and were going nowhere'. The SEU report confirmed that being disengaged at the ages of 16 and 17 was indeed highly correlated to later experiences of unemployment. It was also closely linked to educational disaffection and disadvantage prior to the age of 16 (truancy, school exclusion, and poor (or no) school qualifications), involvement in crime and teenage pregnancy. Once again the problem being addressed was 'joined-up' and as such required 'a joined-up solution'. The report, together with a government White Paper on Education *Learning to Succeed*, suggested the development of a new profession to help give guidance, advice and support for young people between the ages of 13 and 19 – the Connexions Service (see below).

Not all the SEU reports can be described in detail here. Clearly three out of the five had a youth policy focus. But a fourth report on 'poor neighbourhoods' also proved to be vital to the development of youth policy. Its main focus was on spatial clusters of disadvantage especially in some estates dominated by social housing and facing complex challenges of neighbourhood renewal. The SEU report was followed by the setting up of 18 separate Policy Action Teams (PATs) to develop policy in more detail. One of these (PAT 12) focussed on young people. Unusually, this was chaired by the Social Exclusion Unit and the agenda for change proved to be much wider than how to better develop provision for young people in poor neighbourhoods alone. PAT 12 produced a radical new vision for the better co-ordination of youth policy more generally. It recommended, amongst other things, the appointment of a Minister for Youth, a Cross Ministerial Working Group on Children and Young People, a Children and Young People's Unit and a Children's Fund to channel money into children's projects in some of the most deprived areas. These new structures, together with the new Connexions Service, have provided for the most radical shake up in the development of youth policy for a century or more.

Connexions

Writing in the Foreword to the Connexions Strategy Document, the prime minister declared it to be 'our frontline policy for young people'. The Connexions Service in England aims to offer a universal service to all young people between the ages of 13 and 19, through which all those who want or need it will be supported by a national network of personal advisers. The age span covers the years in which educational disaffection is most acute and disengagement and drop-out most likely. Yet one of the biggest challenges facing the new service is to provide intensive support to a minority of young people facing complex problems whilst not stigmaticizing them for being involved with the service. This is why Connexions is intended to be both a comprehensive, but targeted, service. The Connexions remit is also much broader than that of the old careers services in that it aims to provide (through Connexions Partnership Boards) the coordination of support and services across a range of different agencies. This will include health agencies (including the drug prevention and advisory service, and teenage pregnancy), education (including educational welfare and the youth service as well as schools and colleges), social services (including leaving care teams), youth justice (including the police and youth offending teams), those working with teenage pregnancy and teen mothers, housing departments, the voluntary sector (including youth homelessness projects) as well as careers advisers. It is recognised that most young people may only require information, advice or guidance on their education and learning, careers or personal develop-

ment. However, it is anticipated that others, at risk of disengaging, will need in-depth guidance and help in order to assess their needs and wants, to develop and support action plans, and to monitor progress. An even smaller group is expected to need even more intensive and sustained support and may require the Connexion personal adviser to act as a broker to more specialist assessment and support. This is likely to involve pioneering and new forms of multi-agency working. At the time of writing, there are 15 Connexions partnerships being piloted in England with the rest due to be rolled out in 2002–3. Whilst Scotland, Wales and Northern Ireland will not have a service badged as 'Connexions', similar multi-agency working is being developed in those countries too.

Beyond the Social Exclusion Unit

Two further developments in youth policy should also be noted, partly because they will be integral to the delivery of youth policy to two key groups of young people, and partly out of the curiosity that allowed development to be undertaken largely within Whitehall departments rather than under the intrusive gaze of the SEU. The first of these are developments in youth crime and criminal justice. The second is the reform of the 'care' and 'leaving care' systems.

The extent, the expense, and the ineffectiveness of responses to youth crime have been on the policy agenda for some time and were the subject of a hard-hitting analysis by the Audit Commission in 1996 – *Misspent Youth*. In opposition, New Labour spent a great deal of effort planning its proposals for change many of which were contained in the White Paper *No More Excuses* in 1997. This included a review of the bleak statistics of known youth offending:

- that it is primarily young men who offend;
- that most youth crime does not result in the offender being apprehended;

- that whilst some offending behaviour is widespread, a small number of persistent offenders are responsible for a large number of crimes;
- that young offenders often 'neutralise' their activity by beliefs about victims either not being much effected by the crime, or 'asking for it';
- that the youth justice system is very slow and ineffective taking as long as four months between initial arrest and the disposition of the police or courts.

The reforms of the youth justice system which followed the 1998 Crime and Disorder Act saw the creation of multi-agency Youth Offending Teams (YOTs) in all local authorities, drawing together police, probation, social services and others in community in a concerted attempt to address and reduce youth crime. The Act also introduced a whole range of new orders. These includes 'reparation orders' under which offenders meet with their victims under controlled conditions, listen to the impact their crime had had on the victim, apologise to them, and engage in some act of reparation in the community. 'Detention and training orders' involve sentences during which more serious offenders are given intensive forms of education and training with half the sentence being served in a young offenders institution and half in the community. Over both halves of the sentence there is continuity of support from a personal advisor who is part of the local youth offending team. Other orders include curfew orders and parenting orders. The monitoring of all issues concerning offending behaviour and the criminal justice system for 10–17 year olds is also now the responsibility of a new body – the Youth Justice Board.

The fortunes of 'looked after' children were reviewed in the equivalent chapter of the last edition of this volume. This review concluded that those brought up in care, while representing only a tiny (and declining) proportion of each cohort, were amongst the most highly vulnerable and most likely to experience 'fractured transitions'. Young people leaving care (usually at the age of 16 before 2001) were hugely over-represented amongst some groups: those truanting or excluded from school; those with no qualifications; the unemployed and benefit claimants; those suffering from mental illnesses; teenage mothers; young prisoners; and the young homeless. The care system was the subject of a thorough and far reaching review commissioned by the Conservative government in June 1996 and resulting in *The Report of the Review of the Safeguards for Children Living away from Home* in 1997. The government response came a year later and proposed new forms of inspection, quality assurance and standards of care under a *Quality Protects* initiative. Arrangements for young people leaving care were reviewed in a Green Paper *Me, Survive, Out There?* which formed the basis of the Children (Leaving Care) Act of 2000, implemented in October 2001. This makes it the responsibility of local authority social service departments to assess and meet the needs of all young people who have been 'looked after' for at least 13 weeks after the age of 14, until they reached the age of 21 or when they have completed their education, whichever is the later. Unaccompanied asylum-seekers are also to receive similar treatment. Importantly, young care leavers were involved in the consultation process and drawing up proposals for change. Indeed, being actively involved in the development of their own 'pathway plans' with a key worker named as responsible for helping them attain key milestones and giving support in their achievement of these, are also key elements to the reforms being implemented.

Conclusions

Much has changed in social policies affecting young people since the publication of the first edition of this book. Youth policy has received a much higher prominence in government policy and many far-reaching reforms have been set in train. Most pleasing of all is the adoption in government of the more holistic approach to youth policy academic researchers have been advocating for some time. Also of critical importance is the recognition that, to be successful, policy initiatives need to empower young people themselves rather than impose solutions on them. Yet much of this interest seems to have been fuelled by a recognition of the long-term expense of vulnerable or 'troublesome' groups of young people if issues concerned with disadvantage and disaffection are allowed to spiral out of control. Whether all young people will benefit from this attention is difficult to assess. Perhaps by the time of the third edition of the book we will be in a position to assess how far such developments have been successful.

Guide to further reading

The youth policy literature has expanded hand-in-hand with developments in youth policy. Two useful texts include B. Coles *Joining-Up Youth Research, Policy and Practice: A New Agenda for Change?* (Leicester: Youth Work Press-Barnardo's, 2000); J. C. Coleman and L. B. Hendry *The Nature of Adolescence*, 3rd edn (London: Routledge, 1999).

G. Jones and R. Bell *Balancing Acts: Youth Parenting and Public Policy* (York: Joseph Rowntree Foundation, 2000) is a recent review of the policy muddle on young people and a useful complement to this is a website with an even more comprehensive account the development of youth policy across a number of areas. See also R. Bell and G. Jones *Youth, Parenting and Public Policy: A Chronology of Policy and Legislative Provision* (2000), online at: http://www.keele.ac.uk/depts/so/research/youthchron.htm

The government's own review of youth policy can be found in: 'National Strategy for Neighbourhood Renewal', *Report of the Policy Action Team 12: Young People* (London: Stationery Office, 2000). There are also some useful statistical sources which draw together facts and figures about young people. These include J. Matheson and C. Summerfield *Social Focus on Young People* (London: Stationery Office, 2000).

There is also an annual publication from the Trust for the Study of Adolescence, the most recent being J. Coleman and J. Schofield *Key Data on Adolescence: 2001* (Brighton: Trust for the Study of Adolescence, 2001).

Finally, students may want to access recent research reports and policy development conducted both by government and by academics. A major ESRC programme on Youth, Citizenship and Social Change is being completed in 2001–2. Information about this is available via: http://www.tsa.uk.com/YCSC/index. The Joseph Rowntree Foundation has a continuing programme of research on young people. Findings from these are on the web and can be accessed via: http://www.jrf.org.uk. The Social Exclusion Unit has most of its reports available on the web (the cabinet-office/seu government site) and the Connexions Service and the Children and Young People's Unit can be accessed through the Department for Education and Skills.

Older people

Alan Walker and Tony Maltby

Older people have always been a major focus for social policy and, because the UK is an ageing society, their importance to the subject is likely to increase further. Like other modern welfare systems, the British welfare state originated in pension provision for older people and today this group are the main users of the health and social services and the main recipients of social security spending. Compared with unemployed people and lone parents, older people are often viewed as a group that is 'deserving' of social policy and, especially, social security. Indeed, it is sometimes said that the true test of a civilized society is how it treats its older and vulnerable groups. Despite this group's position as one of the most deserving of welfare, students of social policy will be aware that there are many negative images of old age. In common with other Western societies, Britain is a country in which age discrimination, or ageism, is widespread. Many cultural images of older people emphasize passivity and decrepitude; for example, W. B. Yeats, 'When you are old and grey and full of sleep, and nodding by the fire ..'. Television stereotypes older people in a variety of ways – kindly grandparents, mad aunts, burdensome parents and grumpy old men – many of which suggest detachment from mainstream society and, often, an association between old age and ill health. This age discrimination, both visible and invisible, has important policy implications and these

have not received the same sustained attention as those arising from sex and 'race' discrimination. Therefore, in this brief overview of key social policy issues affecting older people, we will focus on age discrimination, particularly its impact on the labour market. The two other key issues dealt with here are pensions and social care. Unfortunately, there is not space to pursue the many other important policy issues surrounding older people, but the guide at the end of this chapter provides the basis for further reading. We start with an outline of the population in question.

Who Are 'Older People'?

Before the advent of public pension systems, workers relied on the benevolence of their employers to provide occupational pensions and, in the late nineteenth century, it was common for people to work until their health failed rather than there being a fixed retirement age. (This is a situation that pertains today in much of the underdeveloped world.) As in most Western countries, it was the civil service that was the first major occupational group in Britain to secure the provision of pensions from their employers, and they adopted a retirement age of 70. This was the age used, for both men and women, when the first state pension was introduced in 1908, and it was reduced to 65 in 1925. In 1940, the pension age for women was cut to 60. The universalization of public pensions, following the recommendations of the Beveridge Report, maintained differential pension ages (65 for men and 60 for women). These were quickly adopted by employers as retirement ages – even though Beveridge had intended that people would work beyond the designated ages and earn additional pensions for doing so – and, in effect, they became the basic thresholds of old age for men and women. Thus, for much of the post-war period old age in Britain has been defined statistically as those over the state pension ages or those aged 65 and over. In 1993 the government announced that the state pension age will be equalized at 65 and that, to protect the expectations of women aged 44 and over, this will be phased in over ten years commencing in 2010.

Table IV.3.1 shows the proportion of the total population made up by different age groups, and the expected expansion in the numbers of older people over the next seven decades. As can be seen, population ageing consists of a shrinkage in the proportion of younger people coupled with a rise in the proportion of older ones. The two socio-demographic factors underlying this development are falling fertility rates and increasing longevity. The trend is a long-term one: at the turn of the twentieth century those aged 65 and over comprised just 4.7 per cent of the population and those aged 80 and over a tiny 0.3 per cent. Presently, there are some 10.8 million people over state pension age and this figure is projected to rise by 11 per cent to 11.9 million by 2011, to 12.3 million by 2021 and to 16 million by 2040 when the median age of the population is anticipated to be 44.5 years. Without the change of women's state pension age to 65 this figure would have been 18 million.

Hidden within the figures shown in table IV.3.1 is one of the most important features of the older population – its gender distribution. At successively older ages the proportion of women increasingly outstrips that of men. Currently, 49 per cent of those aged 0–24 are women, for the 25–64 age group it is 50 per cent, for the 65–74 group the figure is 53 per cent, for the 75 to 84 group it is 61 per cent and for those aged 85 and over it is 72 per cent. The main reason for this is that female life expectancy (at birth) exceeds the male rate by 4.9 years and, although male life expectancy is projected to improve over the next 45 years, so will women's. Therefore, by the year 2040 the differential will still be around five years (78.6 years for men and 83.6 years for women, compared with 75.1 and 80.0 respectively today). Largely because of different life expectancies, the majority of men aged 75 and over are married (62 per cent) whereas the majority of women of that age are widowed (64 per cent). Among black and minority ethnic groups the proportion of older people currently is much smaller

Table IV.3.1   Age groups as a proportion of total UK population (percentages)

Ages	2000	2010	2020	2031	2041	2051	2061	2070
0–14	18.9	16.8	16.2	16.0	15.3	15.3	15.5	15.4
15–29	19.1	19.6	18.1	16.8	17.2	16.9	16.7	16.9
30–44	23.0	20.9	19.3	19.5	18.1	18.4	18.7	18.3
45–59	18.5	20.3	21.3	18.3	19.4	18.6	18.2	18.8
60–74	13.1	14.9	16.4	18.7	17.1	17.2	17.7	16.8
75+	7.4	7.6	8.6	10.7	13.0	13.6	13.2	13.8
All ages	100.0	100.0	100.0	100.0	100.0	100.0	100.0	100.0

Source: Government Actuary's mid-2000-based principal projections.

than that of the white population – only 6 per cent aged 60 and over – though the figure for all minority ethnic groups mirrors that of the white group. A sure sign of population ageing is that there are three times as many people aged over 90 in 2000 as there were in 1971, and mirroring the gender differentials in lower age cohorts, women account for 78 per cent of this group.

Of course, population ageing is a sign of social and economic development, including the role of social policies in combating many of the diseases that cut short people's lives in previous centuries. However, the growing numbers of older people has not always been viewed in such a positive light. For example, it was common, particularly throughout the 1980s and early 1990s, for economists, international economic agencies (such as the IMF and World Bank) and some politicians to refer to the growing 'burden' that this represents. They would go on to suggest that the pension and health care costs associated with population ageing was unsustainable. In the USA, this pessimistic perspective took an extreme form in the 1980s, when war between the generations was predicted (Walker, 1996). What is lacking from most of these gloomy accounts is any evidence: they usually consist of projections and predictions which assume that policies remain stable while demography advances. What is overlooked is that 'old age' was defined (or in sociological terms 'socially constructed') in precise age categories by social policy (i.e. pension policy) and, therefore, it can be redefined as circumstances change. Indeed, this is happening in Britain to some extent, by the raising of the female pension age, and in several other European Union (EU) countries such as Germany and Italy. It is worth noting, though, that even without this change and assuming that pensions are raised along with overall living standards (which goes beyond current policy), the net effect of population ageing on the public finance over the next fifty years would be around 5 per cent of GDP – 'no more than the recent increase related to recession over the past *three* years' (Hills, 1993, p.14).

Older people themselves do not readily conform to their caricature as passive burdens. Surveys in Britain and other EU countries show a very different picture: the majority remain active, often making important contributions within families (for example, to childcare), and reject discriminatory labels such as 'the elderly' in favour of more active ones such as older people or senior citizens (Walker and Maltby, 1996). Older people favour inclusion in society rather than the exclusion that sometimes afflicts them.

Age Discrimination in the Labour Market

One of the main sources of exclusion is the labour market. We have already noted the conflation of retirement with pension ages and it has been argued by some that pensions policies were implemented as a labour market device to encourage the exit of older workers. In practice, older people, particularly older men, have been used as a kind of reserve army of labour – encouraged to stay in employment at times of labour shortage (as in the late 1940s and early 1950s) and quickly jettisoned when demand contracts (as in the mid-1970s). Mindful of the decline in the numbers of young people entering employment and the cost of pensions, the government is currently running campaigns to try to persuade employers to recruit or retain older workers through the New Deal 50+ and other similar programmes. This is an uphill task because, as table IV.3.2 shows, the horses have bolted. It is now only a minority of men that 're-tire' in the conventional sense of leaving work on or close to their sixty-fifth birthday. The majority leave employment at earlier ages and reach the statutory pension age in a variety of non-employed statuses, such as unemployment, long-term sickness or disability and early retirement.

Table IV.3.2   Labour force participation of older men and women in Britain
1951–98

	1951	1961	1971	1981	1985	1990	1995	1998
Men								
55–59	95.0	97.1	95.3	89.4	82.0	81.0	73.7	74.5
60–64	87.7	91.0	86.6	69.3	54.4	54.4	50.1	49.5
65+	31.1	25.0	23.5	10.3	8.2	8.6	8.2	7.6
Women								
55–59	29.1	39.2	50.9	53.4	52.1	54.9	55.7	54.6
60–64	14.1	19.7	28.8	23.3	18.9	22.7	25.0	23.7
65+	4.1	4.6	6.3	3.7	3.0	3.3	3.2	3.4

Sources: 1951–71, Census of Population for England and Wales and for Scotland; 1975–94, Department of Employment, *Gazette* (various); UK Labour Force Survey.

The dramatic growth of early retirement, or early labour force exit, since the mid-1970s has contributed to a redefinition of older people into two groups instead of one. The 'third age' covers those aged 50–74 and the 'fourth age' comprises those aged 75 and over. This distinction is sometimes used to imply that the former 'young old' are active while the latter 'old old' are passive but, as indicated later in this chapter, this is grossly misleading.

The main factors explaining the growth of early exit among British men are demand-related, particularly the recessions of the mid-1970s and early 1980s (Phillipson and Walker, 1986; Laczko and Phillipson, 1991). For many older workers the loss of a job in their fifties or even late forties means that they may never re-enter employment. This can have severe consequences for the individuals concerned and their families, including, most importantly, the necessity of living on a low income or in poverty for a long period before receiving a pension. It also means that the skills possessed by many older workers are lost forever. For the government it means not only lost revenue but also increased benefit payments.

Recent research has shown that people aged 50 to 60 face considerable discrimina-tion from employers. For example, age restrictions in job advertisements are a common barrier to employment. Employers often restrict access to training programmes to workers under the age of 50. Yet when employers are asked to rank the most important factors discouraging the recruitment of older workers, 'lack of appropriate skills' comes top. There is, it seems, a sort of self-fulfilling prophecy at work here. Many employers have been shown to hold stereotypical attitudes towards older workers; for example, that they are hard to train, are too cautious, cannot adapt to new technology and are inflexible. Such prejudices are not supported by research evidence, but they continue to exert a powerful influence over the life chances of people in their third age. Such discriminatory attitudes not only offend social justice but are increasingly at odds with Britain's ageing society and ageing workforce (by the year 2005 the majority of people in the labour market will be over 40). Historically, British governments have chosen to try to combat them by educating employers, most recently via a voluntary code of practice, about the value of recruiting and retaining older workers. In contrast to the passive, non-interventionist, approach of the UK government the USA has had anti-age discrimination legislation for more than a decade. However, the recent implementation of a European Directive has meant that the present government is required to enact anti-age-discrimination legislation by 2006.

Pensions and Poverty in Old Age

Pensions are one of the central social policy issues, but they are also one of the most contentious because of their sheer scale and their escalating cost in an ageing society. Social security is by far the largest single expenditure programme, and over half of it is devoted to older people.

Despite the scale of public spending there is still a close association between low incomes and poverty and old age. Beveridge had intended that the national insurance (NI) pension would overcome poverty in old age, or the giant of 'want' as he put it. However, older people formed the largest group among the poor for most of the post-war period, being exceeded by the unemployed in the early 1980s as unemployment spiralled and as the government began a long series of reductions in unemployment benefits (see Phillipson and Walker, 1986). When it came to establishing the level of the NI pension this was set below that of national assistance (now income support), which meant that receipt of the pension alone was not sufficient to lift older people above the official poverty line. Occupational pensions have raised the living standards of many pensioners, particularly couples, and the government has reduced the benefits of unemployed people more drastically than those of pensioners. Nonetheless, older people still form one of the largest groups living in poverty in the UK, and they are more likely to be poor than older people in other comparable EU countries (Walker and Maltby, 1996). In 1992/3 households where the head or spouse were aged 60 or over comprised 23 per cent of the poor (defined by the government as living below 50 per cent of average income after housing costs) and the unemployed

represented 22 per cent. One-third of older people, some 3.3 million people, live in poverty by this definition. Older people form a smaller proportion of the very poorest (the bottom 10 per cent) than do the unemployed (10 per cent compared with 33 per cent for the latter). Indeed, the impact of government policy on the unemployed and the relative rise in the living standards of older people can be seen by the fact that, in 1979, they comprised 16 per cent of the bottom 10 per cent, while pensioners made up 33 per cent.

The most recent Households Below Average Income Statistics (HBAI) show these trends continuing, with pensioners overall experiencing a higher rise in income (between 55–60 per cent) than those in work (who have seen rises of around 40 per cent). Other data, derived from the Pensioner Income Series shows that the incomes of the top 20 per cent of pensioners has increased by 70 per cent since 1979, whereas those of the lowest 20 per cent have risen by only 38 per cent. This is largely attributable to the increasing numbers of (mainly male) pensioners retiring with good occupational pensions. This is reflected in the average net income (after housing costs) figures. For couples aged below 75 their average income was £270 per week, for single people £125. Corresponding figures for those over 75 are for couples, £218 and for single people £109, a £52 and £16 difference.

The introduction of public pensions, which started in 1908 and were made universal forty years later following the recommendations of the Beveridge Report, served a number of functions. Most importantly, of course, they provided a secure income for those who did not have access to occupational pensions or whose employers had summarily dismissed them on grounds of age. At the same time, the introduction of state pensions was of crucial importance in the creation of mass retirement, which allowed employers to terminate working lives and to spread the cost of doing so over the whole population of working age. Although Beveridge had intended that a fund would be built up from the payments of contributions by employers and employees, the post-war Labour government decided to introduce the NI pension at once and the result is that the NI pension is financed on a pay-as-you-go (PAYG) basis. This means that the NI contributions of those in employment go to pay the pensions of those in retirement. In effect there is a social contract between the generations: those in retirement paid taxes and contributions to fund the pensions of the previous generation in the expectation that the succeeding generations would do the same for them. Other important elements of state welfare provision, such as the NHS and social services, are financed on a similar basis.

Unfortunately, the PAYG system is vulnerable to political interference and when the social contract was instigated those involved did not envisage that a future government would drastically rewrite the rules. This is what happened, in effect, in the 1980s. The Thatcher government was intent on cutting public expenditure and, because of the scale of pension spending, this was a prime target. Thus, in 1980, the government altered the uprating link for the NI pension from earnings to prices. The cumulative effect of this seemingly innocuous cut has been to reduce the value of the basic pension. The reductions represent more than one-third of the value of the existing pension levels. Then, in 1986, the government cut in half the value of the State Earnings Related Pension (SERP), which was introduced with all-party support in 1978 and was due to reach full maturity in 1988. The reduction in the SERP scheme affected women in particular because the relatively generous credits (called Home Responsibility Protection) for periods spent out of employment, (for example, in child-rearing) have been curtailed. These cuts had a deterrent effect on younger generations – undermining their confidence in the state pension system and encouraging them to invest in private pensions. It is a salutary fact that, if these trends continued, the NI pension would have been worth less than 10 per cent of average earnings in 2020. As well as deterrence, positive inducements were offered for people to opt out of the state sector and into the private one. These have taken the form of generous NI contribution rebates and tax relief, costing more than £16 billion. The result is that some six million contributors were enticed from the SERP scheme into personal pension plans leaving less than 17 per cent of the workforce in the SERP scheme. However, it is estimated that because of the mis-selling of personal pensions, as many as two million people would have been better off staying in the state scheme.

The Blair government, first elected in 1997 on a reformist agenda, has implemented a further change to the pensions system by enhancing the 'partnership' between the state and private sector, so that public expenditure by the state on pensions will shift towards the private sector, from 60 per cent at present to 40 per cent by 2050. Improvements in the position of the poorest pensioners was seen as a priority and this will be achieved through provision of the (means-tested) Minimum Income Guarantee (MIG); in reality Income Support for older people. Indeed, the policy towards improving the position of current pensioners is focused upon a means-tested route. In outline the new pensions structure is as follows. The Basic Pension will remain but shrink in real terms with the SERPS pension replaced from April 2002 by a new State Second Pension (SSP or S2P) in order to boost the pension of the lowest paid; those earning less than £9,000 per annum. Those earning above £9,000 per year and who are not members of an occupational pension scheme, have been encouraged to take out a funded Stakeholder pension available from April 2001. This is a low-cost, flexible savings device provided by the private sector, which upon retirement is used to buy an annuity.

At the time of writing, the government is introducing Pension Credit. It is made up of two components a guarantee and a savings credit. The former will replace MIG from 2003 but will work to raise the income of those pensioner couples whose pension and savings is less than £154 per week (and single pensioners with less than £100 per week) to these levels. Higher rates will apply to those with disabilities and all those 60 and over can claim. It will allow pensioners who are currently excluded or receive a lower amount of MIG because of savings to receive an income, as there will be no capital cut off. The other element, the savings credit, will be awarded for five years with no need to report minor changes and will provide all those who have savings and receive the guarantee a payment of 60 pence for every pound of second pension or other savings income they have, up to a maximum of £18.60 per week for couples and £13.80 a week for single people. Should the pensioner have no savings, the situation for many older pensioners, then this rises to £31 and £23 a week respectively.

Long-term Care

It is commonly assumed that older people, particularly those in their fourth age, are physically dependent. In fact, the vast majority of older people are active and able to look after themselves without assistance from others. Even among the very old the bulk of care is self-provided. Among people aged 80 and over only 15 per cent are resident in care homes, nursing homes or hospitals, and for those aged 90 and over the proportion is 36 per cent. However, as these figures suggest, there is an association between advanced old age and disability and, because women live longer than men, they are more likely than men to be disabled. The numbers of women aged 80 and over resident in homes and hospitals is nearly five times that of men.

For most of the post-war period the policy favoured by successive governments has been community care. In reality this has meant that families have been by far the main source of care for disabled older people and others needing support. Social

policy researchers have demonstrated that 'family' care usually means care by female kin, although in couples care by older male spouses is not uncommon. However, the socio-demographic changes referred to earlier are placing the family-based system of care under increasing strain. For example, smaller family size means fewer relatives to share care between. Greater longevity means that some caring relations across the generations are being extended, which may create strains on both sides. Increased female participation in the labour market imposes additional responsibilities on women. We do not yet have a clear picture of the impact of divorce on patterns of family care. Because of these changes and the growth in need associated with population ageing, there is a widening 'care gap' between the need for care among older people and the supply of both family care and formal care from the public, private and voluntary sectors.

The government's response in the 1980s to this growth in demand was to depart from the previous consensus on community care services being centred on local authority social services departments and to encourage the expansion of the private sector. This was achieved by means of social security subsidies for older people living on income support to enter private homes, while holding down expenditure on public services. The result was a huge rise in the numbers of older people entering private residential homes. The numbers nearly doubled between 1979 and 1984, and by 1994 had increased fivefold. Unfortunately, this policy conflicted with the government's desire to restrict public spending (the social security budget for board and lodging payments rose from £10 million in 1978 to over £2 billion in 1993). As a result measures were introduced, under the NHS and Community Care Act 1990, to curtail these escalating costs and to recast the role of local authorities as purchasers of services from the private and voluntary sectors instead of direct providers. At the same time, financial restrictions in the health service have led to a clearer line being drawn between health and social care, with the result that health authorities are reducing the numbers of long-stay beds for older people and expecting the social care system to take over responsibility for those former patients. Thus, although additional resources were allocated to local authorities for the implementation of the 1990 Act, they were insufficient to keep pace with rising needs and there was an urgent need for a radical reappraisal of long-term care policy. The Royal Commission on Long Term Care, promised by the present Labour government when in opposition, was set up as a policy response to this need and its report (*With Respect to Old Age*) was published in 1999. This was a very progressive document and was one of the first to banish the notion that there was a demographic time bomb and that older people were a 'burden'. It suggested in a nutshell that the costs of long-term care should be split between living costs, housing costs and personal care. Personal care should they suggested be provided from general taxation according to need and the other costs according to a means test. It also proposed the setting up of a National Care Commission to monitor the implementation of policy on long-term care. It was significant that the Commission went against the general trend of the time which suggested that provision for long-term care should be funded through private insurance or through a hypothecated tax and indeed, through a pre-funded insurance scheme. The government 'sat' on the report for a year and in 2000 produced a response within the NHS Plan. The Plan brought with it a distinction between nursing care which would be provided

free (and paid by general taxation) and personal care which would not. The exception to this was in Scotland where both would be provided free at the point of use. Further, in March 2001 the National Service Framework for Older People was outlined building upon a more positive treatment in policy of later life generally by the Labour government. It sets out eight 'standards' addressing the health care needs of older people and principle among these is the rooting out of age discrimination in the delivery of health care; the provision of person-centred care; promoting health and independence or older people and matching services to individual needs.

Conclusion

As will be apparent from this brief introduction, social policy towards older people in the UK is in a state of flux. This is partly because the foundations on which public support for old age were built in the immediate post-war period are being undermined by changes in the labour market and in the life course. However, although there was an institutional and ideological reluctance to come to terms with the reality of an ageing society up to the mid-1990s, since then a more positive outlook and policy orientation has increasingly been adopted by government. This is mirrored within some other EU countries and from the European Commission itself, for example the setting up of the AGE platform to represent the views of older people across the EU states. Indeed, the very meaning and nature of later life, old age and 'retirement' is changing as we embark on a new century.

Guide to further reading

Arber, S. and Ginn, J. (eds), 1995. *Connecting Gender and Ageing* (Buckingham: Open University Press). Readings on the important issue of the gendered nature of old age.

Bernard, M. and Phillips J., 1998. *Social Policy of Old Age* (London: CPA,). An extensive and wide ranging analysis by some of the major British social gerontologists providing both an historical overview and contemporary analysis of the major social policy issues. One of the best textbooks in this area available.

Bond, J., Coleman, P. and Peace, S. (eds), 1993. *Ageing in Society* (London: Sage). A general introduction to the field of social gerontology, soon to be updated and expanded and published as a third edition .

Bytheway, B., 1995. *Ageis* (Buckingham: Open University Press). A 'must read' for all students of social policy. Contains some challenging and thought provoking material.

Central Statistical Office (CSO), 1999. *Social Focus on Older People* (London: Stationery Office). A wide-ranging yet useful statistical summary.

Hills, J., 1993. *The Future of Welfare: A Guide to the Debate* (York: Joseph Rowntree Foundation). Very accessible account of the public expenditure and taxation issues surrounding the welfare state.

Laczko, F. and Phillipson, C., 1991. *Changing Work and Retirement* (Buckingham: Open University Press). Covers the main issues concerning employment.

Phillipson, C. and Walker, A. (eds), 1986. *Ageing and Social Policy* (Aldershot: Gower). A general introduction to the main policy issues related to older people and containing some classic chapters outlining the 'social construction of dependency' thesis.

Walker, A. (ed.), 1996. *The New Generational Contract* (London: UCL Press). Covers both macro and micro issues with regard to relations between the generations.

Walker, A. and Maltby, T., 1996. *Ageing Europe* (Buckingham: Open University Press). A general introductory comparative analysis of ageing and social policy in different EU countries.

IV.4
Disabled People

Mike Oliver

The evidence that disabled people experience severe economic deprivation and social disadvantage is overwhelming and no longer in dispute, whether it be from the government's own commissioned research, from research institutes and academics or from disabled people themselves. For example, after over a century of state-provided education, disabled children and young people are still not entitled to the same kind of schooling as their able-bodied peers, nor do they leave with equivalent qualifications. The majority of British schools, colleges and universities remain unprepared to accommodate disabled students within a mainstream setting. Thus, many young disabled people have little choice but to accept a particular form of segregated 'special' education which is both educationally and socially divisive, and fails to provide them with the necessary skills for adult living.

Similarly, since the end of the Second World War at least, disabled people have consistently experienced higher rates of unemployment than the rest of the population, not because they are unable to work but because of the discriminatory behaviour of employers in failing even to attempt to meet their legal obligations under the quota system and the lack of political will to insist upon its enforcement. As a result, currently, disabled people are more likely to be out of work than non-disabled people, they are out of work longer than other unemployed workers and when they do find work it is more often than not low-paid, low-status work with poor working conditions.

The majority of disabled people and their families, therefore, are forced into depending on welfare benefits in order to survive. Further, the present disability benefit system does not even cover impairment-related costs and effectively discourages many of those who struggle for autonomy and financial independence. Dependence is the inevitable result and this is compounded by the present system of health and welfare services, most of which are dominated by the interests of the professionals who run them and the traditional assumption that disabled people are incapable of running their own lives.

What is at issue is why this should be so, the role of welfare in compounding or alleviating this situation, and what can be done about it. I would argue that there can only be two possible explanations for the appalling economic and social circumstances under which the vast majority of disabled people are forced to live; one, that disability has such a traumatic physical and psychological effect on individuals that they cannot ensure a reasonable quality of life for themselves by their own efforts; the other, that the economic and social barriers that disabled people face are so pervasive that they are prevented from ensuring themselves a reasonable quality of life by their own efforts.

The former has become known as the individual model of disability and is underpinned by personal tragedy theory. It has been under severe attack in recent years from a variety of sources, to the point that it is now generally recognized that it is an inadequate basis for developing a proper understanding of disability. The latter has become known as the social model of disability, and has shifted the focus away from impaired individuals and on to restrictive environments and disabling barriers. This has received acceptance to such an extent that it has almost become the new orthodoxy.

The Classic Welfare State

The project to establish a welfare state which would provide 'cradle to grave' security for all its members has failed disabled people, as I have already suggested. This failure can be traced back almost to the foundations of the welfare state during the Second World War and the subsequent legislation that laid the foundations of the welfare state as we know it today.

The first Act of Parliament to treat disabled people as a single group was the Disabled Persons (Employment) Act 1944, which attempted to secure employment rights for disabled people. Further, the Education Act 1944, underpinned by an egalitarian ideology, specified that disabled children should be educated alongside their peers in primary and secondary education. The National Assistance Act 1948 laid a duty on local authorities to arrange a variety of services for disabled people, in both the community and institutions. The National Health Service Act 1948 also provided hospital-based treatment and long-term care for disabled people.

It soon became clear that implementation of the Disabled Persons (Employment) Act was more concerned with not upsetting employers than ensuring that disabled people seeking employment were treated fairly. The Education Act became the legal mechanism for the establishment of a huge infrastructure of segregated special education based around 11 medical categories. The National Assistance Act allowed, but did not require, local authorities to provide services and the choice for many disabled people was survive without assistance or go into residential care. The National Health Service Act offered little beyond acute treatment and long-term care usually meant living on a geriatric ward even if you weren't old.

Since the late 1950s there has been a concerted attempt by successive governments to reduce the numbers of people living in segregated institutions of one kind or another. The shift towards community-based services took a decisive turn in the early 1960s, when the government announced its intention to reduce the number of beds in mental hospitals by half. The rhetoric of community care continued to obscure the reality that for many previously incarcerated people, living in the community bestowed no more rights other than perhaps to starve, freeze or die alone.

By the late 1960s, attempts were being made to rationalize the chaos that was the reality of community care. The Chronically Sick and Disabled Persons Act 1970 was supposed to be the vehicle for this rationalization. It was even heralded at one point by two non-disabled commentators as a 'Charter (of rights) for the disabled', but the reality was that it was merely an extension of the needs-based welfare provision of the National Assistance Act.

The only two extra duties were to be imposed on local authorities: the duty to compile a register and the duty to publicize services. The former produced little information of value and the latter was widely ignored. The services listed under section 2 only needed to be provided where it was 'practical and reasonable' to do so, and for most local authorities it wasn't, so they didn't.

Despite the rhetoric of integration, community care and rights which emerged in the 1980s, neither the Education Act 1981 nor the Disabled Persons (Services,

Consultation and Representation) Act 1986 has significantly improved the quality of welfare services available to disabled people. The evidence for this continuing failure has been provided by:

- officially commissioned government research showing the extent of poverty and unemployment among disabled people;
- studies by independent research institutes showing that disabled people are 'last on the list' as far as welfare services are concerned;
- academics who show that services to enable disabled people to live in the community are inadequate;
- disabled people who condemn health authorities and social service departments that fail to provide them with a satisfactory quality of life.

What has become more contentious in recent years is the issue of statutory entitlements. It is certainly true that despite the establishment of a comprehensive legal framework for the provision of services to disabled people, these services somehow do not get delivered. The main reasons for this are: first, services have come to be provided on the basis of professional definitions of need; second, governments of all political persuasions have resisted pressure to force local authorities to meet their statutory obligations; third, those services that have been provided have locked disabled people into dependency upon them.

Rethinking Community Care

The problems with welfare services were not unique to disabled people and prompted a major review of the welfare state in the mid-1980s. Beginning with a damning report on community care from the Audit Commission (1986), the Griffiths Report (1988) followed in 1990 and, after much delay, this was incorporated into a White Paper, *Caring for People*. After a very short consultation period the White Paper was incorporated into the National Health Service and Community Care Act 1990 (see chapter IV.12).

Central to this legislation was a new managerial strategy for providing services which was to be supplemented by a market strategy that involved stimulating the private and voluntary sectors to act as providers of services, and the statutory authorities to act as enablers and purchasers of services rather than sole providers. By opting for this combination of market and managerial strategies, the government hoped that the problems of professional dominance and dependency creation would be addressed. However, such hopes were soon dashed, from the point of view of disabled people at least. Davis (in Swain et al. *Disabling Barriers - Enabling Environments*, London: Sage, 1993) comments on the continuing dominance of professionals over service delivery: 'At this juncture, our lives are substantially still in their hands. They still determine most decisions and their practical outcomes.'

It was clear by the time that New Labour came to power in 1997 that the reforms had not worked. There was little evidence that disabled people were being involved in the planning and delivery of services in the way that legislation had required. Nor was there much evidence that local authority assessment procedures adequately reflected the legal requirement to place individual needs at the centre of the reforms. Finally, studies began to show that the existing reforms were enough, and unless further changes were made, as far as disabled people were concerned, 'their opportunities to be independent citizens will disappear' (Morris, 1993).

These reforms did not change the balance of power between professional and service user. It was now the care manager who assessed the needs of the service user. Users did now have rights to see and even contribute to their care plans, but they had no greater rights to service and still no access to legally enforceable grievance procedures. Although the quote below was written before the recent legislation, the situation described by S. Cohen (*Visions of Social Control*, Cambridge: Polity Press, 1985) remained unchanged: 'much the same groups of experts are doing much the same business as usual. The basic rituals incorporated into the move to the mind - taking case histories, writing social enquiry reports, constructing files, organising case conferences - are still being enacted.' In the post-1990 world, the same people, albeit with different jobs titles and perhaps in plusher buildings, were doing the same things to disabled people although they were now to be called 'doing a needs led assessment' or 'producing a care plan'.

K. Davis ('Old medicine is still no cure', *Community Care,* 8 September 1990) is certain that the new profession of care management will not provide the necessary structural reforms (p.14): 'it is simply not enough for brokers, care managers or any other agent to potter about in the existing mish-mash of inappropriate and inadequate services, with a view to helping individual disabled people to piece together some kind of survival plan for existing in a hostile world. We have been there too long.'

So the welfare state, in both its classic and reformed guise, has not ensured the rights and entitlements of disabled people. A central commitment made by the New Labour government in 1997 was to further reform the welfare state in general and provision for disabled people in particular. The two main mechanisms for this were interrelated: the promotion of independence and an attempt to shift disabled people from welfare into work. To this end the Direct Payments Act (1996) was implemented, there was some tightening of access to Incapacity Benefit and some pilot projects were developed which aimed at getting disabled people back into work.

However some five years on less than 5000 disabled people are benefiting from the direct payments legislation and the unemployment rate amongst disabled people continues to remain unacceptably high. Welfare services as they are currently being provided are unlikely to satisfy dis-

abled people, and they fall short of the demands made by disabled people from all over Europe when they met at a conference in Strasbourg to discuss their own struggles for independent living.

> We demand social welfare systems that include personal assistance services that are consumer controlled and which allow various models of independent living for disabled people, regardless of their disability and income. We demand social welfare legislation which recognizes these services as basic civil rights and which provide necessary appeal procedures.
>
> (Press Release, European Network on Independent Living, 1989)

Reconceptualizing the Problem: From Needs to Rights

It is not denied any longer that the systematic deprivation and disadvantage that disabled people experience is caused by restrictive environments and disabling barriers. The point at issue here is what should be done about it. Until recently, successive governments have taken the view that the way to deal with this is through the provision of professional services aimed at meeting individual needs, coupled with a strategy aimed at persuading the rest of society to remove their disabling barriers, and to change their restrictive environments. In general the government's view has been that rather than legislating, the most constructive way forward is through raising awareness in the community as a whole.

As I have already argued, professionalized service provision within a needs based system of welfare has added to existing forms of discrimination and, in addition, has created new forms of its own, including the provision of stigmatized segregated services such as day care and the development of professional assessments and practices based upon invasions of privacy, as well as creating a language of paternalism which can only enhance discriminatory practices. On top of that, policies of persuasion have turned out to be bankrupt, as the cost of implementing them grows, while at the same time disabled children are still directed into segregated special schools, the number of disabled people who are unemployed increases and the number of disabled people living in poverty continues to expand. That this unacceptable situation is due to disabling barriers rather than personal limitations is now clear; it is also clear that previous attempts to dismantle these barriers have been based on incorrect understandings of the real nature of discrimination. Discrimination does not exist in the prejudiced attitudes of individuals but in the institutionalized practices of society.

This new understanding of the real nature of the problem involves the idea of institutional discrimination which can be described in the following ways. First, institutional discrimination is evident when the policies and activities of public or private organizations, social groups and all other organizational forms result in unequal treatment or unequal outcomes between disabled and nondisabled people. Second, institutional discrimination is embedded in the work of welfare institutions when they deny disabled people the right to live autonomously, through failure to meet their statutory obligations in terms of service provision, through their differential implementation of legislative and advisory codes, through interference in the privacy of disabled people and through the provision of inappropriate and segregative services.

Directly as a response to the demands from disabled people, the Disability Discrimination Act was passed in 1995 and has subsequently been modified by the New Labour government. Since its inception there have been three major criticisms of the Act. To begin with, its definition of disability relies upon the individual rather than social model. Additionally the Act is not comprehensive; it outlaws discrimination in some but not all areas of life and even allows for 'justifiable discrimination' where costs might be high, for example. Finally, the Act is difficult to enforce, as the newly formed Disability Rights Commission has

itself found. The recently incorporated European human rights legislation is likely to experience similar problems.

So while it could be argued that in Britain the first tentative steps to implementing a rights based approach to the welfare state have been taken, the kinds of demands that disabled people are making are still a long way from being met.

> disabled people themselves are demanding a new emphasis on civil rights, equal opportunities and citizenship. They see institutional discrimination as the main disability they face, and are lobbying for new equal rights legislation to outlaw discrimination on the grounds of disability. The first priority is equal access to basic essentials such as an adequate income, housing, access to employment, to public transport, to education and to the ordinary facilities of everyday life.
>
> (Doyle and Harding, in A. Coote (ed.) *The Welfare of Citizens: Developing New Social Rights,* London: Rivers Oram Press, 1992)

Conclusion

It is clear we have seen a significant shift in the discourses about disability, building upon the insights of the social model of disability. Issues of discrimination and civil rights are now on the political agenda and have become part of the welfare discourse. One commentator suggests that disabled people are 'seeking a model of welfare built not on need and philanthropy, but on equal citizenship as a means of self determination' (Coote, *The Welfare of Citizens*).

The government itself recognized that these shifting discourses needed a more appropriate political response and passed the Disability Discrimination Act 1995. Whether this represented a significant shifting from seeing disability as an issue of managed care to seeing it as one of civil rights is, however, open to doubt. Certainly its failure to make the Act comprehensive and the failure of the Disability Rights Commission to take an aggressive approach to enforcement leave this open to doubt.

Guide to further reading

Armstrong F. and Barton L. (eds), 1999. *Disability, Human Rights and Education: Cross-cultural Perspectives* (Buckingham: Open University Press). Focuses specifically on education and its relationship to human rights.

Barnes, C., 1991. *Discrimination and Disabled People in Britain* (London: Hurst and Co.). Develops the concept of institutional discrimination and uses published evidence to describe its nature and extent.

Barnes, C., Mercer, G. and Shakespeare, T., 1999. *Exploring Disability: A Sociological Introduction* (Cambridge: Polity Press). A comprehensive introduction to the issues.

Barton, L. (eds), 2001. *Disability Politics: The Struggle for Change* (London: David Fulton) . A series of essays written from international viewpoints.

Campbell, J. and Oliver, M., 1996. *Disability Politics: Understanding Our Past, Changing Our Future* (London: Routledge). Charts the rise of the disability movement and includes material on its relation to the welfare state..

Drake, R., 1999. *Understanding Disability Policies* (Basingstoke: Macmillan Press). A worthwhile attempt to provide a comparative account of disability policy.

Morris, J., 1993 *Independent Lives? Community Care and Disabled People* (Basingstoke: Macmillan Press). Good policy discussions on independent living and community care.

Oliver, M., 1990. *The Politics of Disablement* (Basingstoke: Macmillan Press). Describes the emergence of capitalism and the rise of the welfare state for disabled people.

Oliver, M., 1996. *Understanding Disability: From Theory to Practice* (Basingstoke: Macmillan Press). A series of essays, many of which are about social policy and disability.

Oliver, M. and Barnes, C., 1998. *Disabled People and Social Policy: From Exclusion to Inclusion* (Harlow: Longman Wesley). An introductory account and explanation of policy developments including useful source material.

Read, J., 1999. *Disability, the Family and Society: Listening to Mothers* (Buckingham: Open University Press). Important discussion of the relationship between policy issues and families with disabled members

Sayce, L., 2000. *From Psychiatric Patient to Citizen: Overcoming Discrimination and Social Exclusion* (Basingstoke: Macmillan Press). A useful discussion of the experiences of ADL in both Britain and America.

Thomas, C., 1999. *Female Forms* (Buckingham: Open University Press). Comprehensive coverage of disability issues from a feminist perspective.

Copies of the international journal *Disability and Society* (formerly *Disability, Handicap and Society*) are also useful.

IV.5
Lone Parents

Jonathan Bradshaw

Introduction

Changes taking place in family form pose new challenges to social policy. One of the most dramatic of these changes has been the increase in the prevalence of lone parent families during the past three decades. (The words single parent families and one parent families are also widely used to describe these families, but lone parents and lone parent families are preferred, despite their slightly emotive ring, in order to avoid confusion with one category of lone parents – single lone parents – and the difficulties of using 'one parenthood' and 'one parents'.) The rapid increase in the proportion of families with children headed by a lone parent has in recent years been evinced as evidence of:

- a breakdown of traditional family form;
- the collapse of the role of husband and father;
- an example of the underclass;
- a cause of a culture of dependency;
- a reason for the UK no longer being able to afford the welfare state;
- an example of how the welfare state has undermined the social structure;
- an important reason for youth crime, indiscipline, poor educational attainment and many other ills of modern society.

Indeed, for the student of social policy the vilification, indeed sometimes moral panic,

shown about lone parents by politicians, some academic commentators, the media and others has come so thick and fast that it has been hard to keep pace. It has to be admitted that many of the claims made about lone parents have yet to be investigated adequately empirically. Nevertheless, the subject of social policy has made a substantial contribution to what we do know. The purpose of this chapter is to show how social policy approaches the topic and what we have discovered.

A change as rapid as this presents the institutions of the welfare state with remarkable challenges, and there are fascinating opportunities to observe, and, indeed, to influence how those institutions adapt or fail to adapt to demographic change, how policy is made and the extent to which the state can or should attempt to influence or engineer changes in family form or in the behaviour of lone parent families. So though we may be concerned with the plight of lone parents, as students of social policy we recognize that the social policy context of lone parenthood is a rich arena for understanding the subject as a whole.

The Demography of Lone Parents

In the UK a lone parent is now commonly defined as: 'a parent who is not living as a married or cohabiting couple, may or may not be living with others (friends or parents), living with at least one of her or his children under 16 years or under 19 years and in full-time education.' However, definitions will vary according to purpose – benefit assessment, taxation, research surveys, the census and so on. It is important to be sensitive to these, particularly when making comparisons between countries.

Although they are lumped together in popular discussion, lone parent families are far from being a homogeneous group. At the moment less than 10 per cent of lone parent families are headed by men. Lone fathers tend to be older, have older children, are more likely than lone mothers to be in employment and about a third of them are widowers. The largest group of lone mothers is the previously married; that is, women who are divorced, separated or widowed. They tend to be older than other lone mother families and have older and more children. The most rapidly growing group of lone mother families is single, never married, lone mothers but increasingly there are two rather distinct groups among them. There are those who have never had a living together relationship with the father of their child. These tend to be younger and their children are young. The other half of single lone mothers are in fact more like divorced mothers, in that they became lone mothers as a result of cohabitation breakdown – they and often their child or children have lived together with the father. Official statistics do not always distinguish between these two groups of single lone mothers, but we know from birth registration data that about half of all births outside marriage are registered by both parents at the same address.

These differences in the characteristics of lone parents are important in thinking about social policy in relation to them. But there are also other important factors to take into account. These are summarized in box IV.5.1.

The Problems of Lone Parents

Why are lone parents the focus of social or collective concern rather than just a private matter? There are three main reasons.

> **Box IV. 5.1   Lone parenthood**
>
> - Being a lone parent is, for most, only a temporary experience. Most lone mothers and fathers repartner – creating step families
> - Some lone parents experience more than one episode of lone parenthood and experience more than one type of lone parenthood
> - Lone parents have become increasingly spatially segregated, concentrated in urban and inner city areas. But lone parents in rural areas may also have special problems
> - There is a much higher prevalence of lone parent families among Afro-Caribbean families but also a lower prevalence among Asian families
> - Lone mother families are concentrated in social housing – indeed, one of the consequences of relationship breakdowns is for lone mothers and their children to move down the housing ladder and at worst to experience homelessness

Dependency

Lone parenthood almost invariably results in a period of dependency on state benefits. Just over half of lone parent families are dependent on Income Support and over 80 per cent are supported by Income Support, Housing Benefit or Working Families Tax Credit (WFTC). This dependency on benefits costs a great deal of money: in 1994/5 benefit expenditure on lone parents was expected to be £9.1 billion, compared to £4 billion in 1989/90. Cash benefits are not the only resource costs of lone parenthood. For example, it has been estimated that an extra 800,000 dwellings are needed at any one time as a result of lone parenthood, and most of these are needed in the social sector.

Poverty

A corollary of dependence on means-tested benefits, but also associated with low earnings power and inadequate childcare, is the high prevalence of poverty among lone parents. There is evidence from the work of Millar (1989) that lone parents on social assistance (Income Support) are particularly hard pressed, not least because they are dependent for longer periods than married couples with children. Lone parents and their children make up a substantial proportion of the poor. In 1999/00, 58 per cent of lone parent families were living in poverty (with incomes below 60 per cent of median after housing costs), and although they represent only 9 per cent of the population as a whole, they formed 21 per cent of the poor after housing costs (DWP, 2001). The prevalence of poverty among lone parent families in Britain is high compared with other countries (Bradshaw et al., 1996).

The impact on children

Associated with this poverty is a general belief that divorce, and living in a lone parent family, is bad for children. Evidence on this needs to be interpreted with great care, not least because quite a lot of it is not very soundly based. The better evidence also relies to a considerable extent on the outcomes for children experiencing lone parenthood in the 1960s and 1970s, when it was much more unusual and therefore possibly more stigmatizing. Much of the evidence quoted uses American sources, where lone parenthood is more closely associated with race than it is in the UK. It is also very difficult to separate the influences of living in a lone parent family (and the associated deprivations) from the affects of unhappy family life prior to breakdown. The evidence has been reviewed by Burghes (1994).

The Objectives of Policy for Lone Parents

What might the objectives of social policy be for lone parent families? Box IV.5.2 presents a selection of possible objectives in no particular order. Of course many of these objectives either compete or are not easy to reconcile in practice.

Box IV.5.2   Possible objectives of policy for lone parents

- Maintain an adequate living standard for lone parents and their children
- Enable lone parents to support their children and to do so without work if they want to
- Meet lone parents' special and extra needs
- Reduce dependence on benefits
- Enable lone parents to work outside the home if they want to
- Discourage the breakdown of marriage and cohabitation and births outside marriage
- Make sure that absent parents contribute to the costs of their families
- Maintain equity with married/cohabiting couples
- Reinforce the institutions of marriage
- Encourage repartnering

Until 1997 there was a good deal of ambivalence about the primary objective of public policy in relation to lone parents. There has been a tendency in official pronouncements to emphasize that policy is neutral – neutral with respect to the treatment of different family forms and neutral with respect to the employment of lone parents. Policy was inevitably preoccupied with cost. A Cabinet Briefing Paper on lone parents leaked to the *Guardian* in September 1993 stated:

We have assumed that the primary objective of any measures taken will be to reduce the burden on public expenditure caused by lone parent families, and that measures should therefore be directed towards discouraging lone parenthood and other ways of reducing public expenditure which do not harm the interests of the children of lone parents.

However there has now been a shift in the emphasis given to the different objectives of policy in respect of lone parents.

Meeting the Extra Costs of Lone Parents

To take one example, following the report of the Finer Committee on one parent families in 1970, a number of changes were made to the tax and benefit system which sought to recognize the extra costs of bringing up a child alone. Thus, One Parent Benefit was introduced as an addition to Child Benefit for the first child in a lone parent family. A Tapered Earnings Disregard (a proportion of part-time earnings not taken into account in the means test) was introduced into Supplementary Benefit to encourage and enable lone parents to supplement their benefit income with part-time earnings. When Income Support was introduced in 1988, there was a lone parent premium in the scales of benefit, which also had its equivalent in Housing Benefit. In the income tax system, lone parents were treated no less generously than couples, in that they were entitled to an allowance equivalent to the married couples allowance. In the Family Credit means test, the income of lone parents was assessed in exactly the same way as that of couples.

Now it appears that this recognition of the extra needs of lone parents may be changing. The Tapered Earnings Disregard was abolished when Income Support started in 1988. In the 1996 uprating of benefits, One Parent Benefit and the Lone Parent Premium in Income Support were frozen, and in 1998 the Labour government abolished both these benefits altogether.

The Employment of Lone Parents

The main example of a less neutral stance in policy towards lone parents concerns employment. In many other countries, lone parents are expected to seek employment when their youngest child is three years old (Bradshaw and Finch 2002). In the UK, lone parents are entitled to Income Support until their youngest child is 16. This rule exists because of the strongly held view of some that it is in the interests of lone parent families, at least for a time after the birth of a child outside marriage, or after the breakdown of a marriage or cohabitation, that the lone parent should not be encouraged or made to take paid work. At other times it might be in the interests of the lone parent, her children and the community that she is not required to combine paid work and caring responsibilities. Further, it may be better for children for their mother to be at home, especially following a period of disruption in their lives. Yet the influence of these ideas on policy has been losing ground. This is partly due to the fact that while the proportion of married women in employment continued to increase rapidly, the proportion of lone mothers in employment had been static. Further, compared to other countries the proportion of lone mothers in employment in the UK is low (50 per cent in 2000 compared, for example, with 66 per cent in France, 68 per cent in Sweden and 79 per cent in the USA). Further, in most other countries most lone mothers working tend to work full-time, while in the UK they tend to work part-time. There is also evidence that, although employment is not a guarantee against poverty, in all countries including the UK the prevalence of poverty among lone mothers is much lower if they are in employment (Bradshaw and Finch, 2002).

While lone parents are not yet required to seek employment, there have been a number of changes in recent times, which indicate a less neutral position towards lone mothers employment. These, summarised as 'push' factors and 'pull factors', are presented in box IV.5.3. There is evidence that, together with improvements in the labour market, these changes have had an impact. The number of lone parents receiving Income Support has declined from over a million in 1995/96 to just over 800,000 in 2002. The proportion of lone parents in employment has increased from 41 per cent in 1990/91 to 50 per cent in 2000.

In addition to these measures there have been changes with a more ambiguous impact. In pursuit of its child poverty strategy (and to make good the losses from the abolition of the Lone Parent Premium in Income Support) there have been substantial improvements in the real level of Income Support. Also a small disregard of child support has been introduced from April 2002 for lone mothers on Income Support. Both these measures could reduce financial incentives to work, though they both raise the living standards of lone parents who are not in employment.

There are other measures that the government might consider to encourage and enable lone parents to enter employment:

1. One of the main financial disincentives to entering employment is the treatment of housing costs in the benefit system. While on Income Support rents and council tax are paid in full, as is mortgage interest after six months. When in employment, tenants are in principle eligible for Housing Benefit, though in practice most of those receiving WFTC are lifted out of eligibility. Mortgagees, who are increasingly prevalent among lone parents, receive no help at all. Thus, there are very sharp increases in housing costs for both tenants and owner occupiers when moving off Income Support into employment. The solutions to this include the lowering of real rents by increasing subsidies to enable lower rents in social housing, a lowering of the taper in Housing Benefit and the introduction of a mortgage benefit scheme.

Box IV.5.3   Lone parents and employment

Push factors:

• Lone Parent Premium in Income Support abolished in 1998
• New Deal for Lone Parents (now) requires lone parents on Income Support to attend an interview with a benefits advisor to discuss employment and training when the youngest child reaches school age
• Until 2002 there was no disregard of child support payments on Income Support

Pull factors:

• Introduction of a Statutory Minimum Wage
• Family Credit replaced by more generous Working Families Tax Credit, Child Tax Credit and Childcare Tax Credit in October 1999 and Integrated Child Credit in 2002
• Real improvements in Child Benefits
• A bonus (in WFTC) for working full-time
• The Childcare Strategy including the Neighbourhood Childcare Initiative which is an ambition to provide every lone parent in the 20 per cent most deprived Wards in England with a childcare place if they enter employment
• The whole of any Child Support Payment disregarded in assessing eligibility to WFTC

2. Introduce an effective child maintenance regime. The Child Support Act
1991 has failed to deliver on its objectives and caused major disruptions to
people's lives (Clarke et al., 1996). It is
widely considered to have been a major disaster in policy-making, and therefore it is a lesson for future attempts by
central government to intervene in this
sensitive area of people's lives. A new
scheme is being implemented which
may be an improvement. However, for
child support to be a solid support for
employment it needs, as already happens in many European countries, to be
guaranteed or underwritten by the
state; that is, paid to the lone parent
whether or not the absent parent makes
payments.
3. Childcare is probably at the heart of this
matter. Without good quality, flexible
and affordable childcare, including
holiday and after-school care, it is unlikely to be possible to make a big impact on lone parents' employment.
Compared with most other countries,
the provision of pre-school childcare in
the UK has been abysmal. Those lone
mothers who do work in the UK either
work full-time and for a wage that enables them to employ a child-minder, or
part-time, relying entirely on family or
other informal support. The most
prevalent patterns of childcare in other
countries are heavily subsidized provision in nurseries or, increasingly, subsidized and supervised family day care.
About half of three and four year olds
are already in nursery classes in the UK
(though with wide geographical variations) but at the moment this provision
is mainly part-time, motivated by educational objectives for the child rather
than the childcare needs of mothers.

The most prevalent form of full-time
childcare for the under-threes is child
minders – unsubsidized (except via the
Childcare Tax Credit), under-regulated
and with cause for serious anxieties
about quality. The Childcare Strategy
is having an impact, but to improve
childcare provision requires a major investment of public resources in direct
and indirect subsidies and the expansion of day nursery facilities.

The government may decide to make the
New Deal compulsory and require lone
mothers to seek work. However at the end
of the day there will be lone mothers who
do not want to and/or are unable to obtain
employment – because of the needs of their
children, their own lack of skills or ill health
or the lack of jobs in the areas they are living in.

Conclusion

In only a very short period, social policy
for lone parents has moved from the dol-
drums to the forefront of the political
agenda. Policy-making has been tentative
and incremental, seemingly bewildered
by the speed and nature of the changes.
Balancing the needs of lone parents, and
particularly their children, with other objectives of policy has not proven easy. The
result is high levels of poverty and dependence on benefits, certainly compared to
other countries grappling with the same
changes. It appears that policies are just
beginning to move in the right direction but
how far should policy enforce an employment obligation on lone mothers is a matter for debate. This is an arena where the
balance between individual and collective
solutions to social problems is still to be
settled.

Guide to further reading

The best source on the demography of lone parents is the quarterly journal, *Population Trends* which publishes regular articles summarizing the most recent data on family patterns: see, for example, J. Haskey 'One-parent families and their dependent children in Great Britain', *Population Trends*, 91 (1998).The most comprehensive studies of lone parent families in the UK have been a series of studies funded by the DWP: see R. Ford et al. *The British Lone Parent Cohort, 1991 to 1998*, DSS Research Report 80 (Leeds: Corporate Document Services, 2000) and A. Marsh 'Helping British lone parents to get and keep paid work', in Millar, J and Rowlingson, K. *Lone Parents, Employment and Social Policy: Cross-national Comparisons* (Bristol: Policy Press, 2001). Other chapters in that book are also well worth reading particularly on lone parents and employment. J. Bradshaw, and N. Finch *A Comparison of Child Benefit Packages in 22 Countries* (London: Department of Work and Pensions, 2002), also contains comparative data on policy and the employment of lone parents.

The best study of the living standards of lone parents is J. Millar, *Poverty and the Lone Parent Family: The Challenge to Social Policy* (Aldershot: Avebury, 1989). In Department for Work and Pensions (annual) *Households below Average Incomes: A Statistical Analysis*. (London: Stationery Office), there are up-to-date data on poverty among lone parents.

Until it sadly closed in 2001, the publications of the Family Policy Studies Centre in London were a good source of up-to-date research and policy commentary on lone parents, including L. Burghes and M. Brown *Single Lone Mothers: Problems, Prospects and Policies* (1995); J. Bradshaw et al. *The Employment of Lone Parents: A Comparison of Policy in 20 Countries* (1996); K. Clarke et al. *Small Change: The Impact of the Child Support Act on Lone Mothers and Children* (1996). L. Burghes *Lone Parenthood and Family Disruption: The Outcomes for Children* (1994).

Thanks to a generous donation by JK Rowling the National Council for One Parent Families has become much more active recently, publishing a Newsletter, Factsheets and guides on policies for lone parents. It also has an excellent website www.oneparentfamilies.org.uk..

IV.6
Migrants

Gail Lewis

Migrants are among the most demonized groups of people living in the developed world. Commonly constructed as a drain on welfare and other social resources and as posing a problem for social cohesion, they are presented as needing tight control on their freedom of movement both across and within international borders. This construction prevails in both official and popular discourse. In the context of Britain and the European Union more generally the group of migrants who have become most visible in public discussion are refugees and asylum seekers. In some senses they have been the most visible and tangible illustration of economic and political realignment in the context of regional and global forces. But migrants – and processes of migration – are not new phenomena, even if the numbers involved has increased enormously over the last twenty to thirty years. Connections between migrants and welfare have long been made and policies to control the flow and rights of migrants are part of the general domain of social policy. That this is so raises interesting and important questions for social policy.

As with other areas of social policy, one of the difficulties of exploring the relation between migrants and social policy is the rapidly changing policy environment. To gain a full picture of the relation between migrants and social policy at any one time it is important to be informed about the contemporary policy environment. At a more general and analytical level, however, it is possible to delineate lines of enquiry. These include definitional issues; migrants' access to welfare services and benefits; links between migrants and employment in welfare agencies; and the links between immigration, nationality and asylum policy, the treatment of migrants and national identity.

Definitions: Some Clarifications

The term 'migrants' is something of a catch-all phrase. It obscures important distinctions among those encompassed within it and conflates some of the factors that combine to influence the experiences of those who might be termed migrants. If we think about this last point first. Being a migrant is simultaneously a personal experience, a social and cultural experience and position, and a legal status. These combine to affect the lived reality and outcomes of the process of migration. There are though different categories of migrant: categories determined by the geography of migration, historical links between sending and receiving states, differential legal position, and the causes of the migration. Thus, although at its most general the term 'migrant' refers to individuals and groups who have moved from one place to another to live and work, it is a more complex term than this simple definition suggests.

First, there are those people who move within the borders of a state, often seeking paid employment and sometimes moving for the purposes of family formation or other emotional reasons. This kind of migration has been a continuous feature in Britain for at least four centuries and *internal migrants* such as these were subject to early forms of social policy control. In 1598 and 1601 two Acts of Parliament were passed that imposed conditions on access to parish relief by 'strangers' – i.e. non-parishioners. During the nineteenth century there were also large numbers of migrants from Ireland who came to Britain as workers, often in the developing canal and railways industries. At this time these migrants were legally internal because they were moving within the boundaries of the nation-state. Waves of migration from Ireland continued over the twentieth century with peaks in the 1950s, 1980s and to a lesser extent the early 1990s.

Unlike migrants from elsewhere, including from 1962 onwards those coming from the New Commonwealth and Pakistan, migrants from Ireland have never been subject to direct immigration control, although anti-terrorism legislation has been used to control movement. This can be partly explained by the historical link between Britain and Ireland and the complexities of policing the border between the Republic of Ireland and Northern Ireland, which remains part of the United Kingdom.

In the contemporary British and European Union context the term migrant refers to those who have crossed international borders. '*Immigrant*' is the term used to refer to such a person from the perspective of the country receiving the person. '*Emigrant*' is the term used for the same person from the perspective of the 'sending' country. Officially immigrants are those who have full legal entitlement to live and work in the receiving country, as in the case of EU citizens moving between member states. From the late 1940s until the early 1970s people moving from the New Commonwealth formed a substantial number of immigrants. However, by the end of this period primary immigration, i.e. first person immigration for the purposes of employment had mostly ceased, and family reunification became the main motivation for migrants from these countries. Similarly by the mid-1960s there were always more people leaving the UK than entering it and the number of white migrants from numerous sources was increasing. The introduction of successive immigration and nationality legislation from 1962 to 1988 was aimed at limiting migration from the New Commonwealth (see table IV.6.1).

There is also a category of people called '*temporary migrants*', including those on student visas. Temporary migrants often face various restrictions on their freedom of movement, their choice of occupation or industry, the rights of family reunification, and access to forms of social service or benefit such as housing, health or income maintenance systems.

Since the 1990s the category of migrants that has attracted official and popular attention are refugees and asylum seekers. In international law a *refugee* is a person who has been forced to leave their country of origin and has lost the protection of that state when outside its borders. The internationally accepted definition is that laid down by the 1951 United Nations Convention on the Status of the Refugee. Despite its international remit, this Convention developed in response to the specific conditions prevailing in Europe at the end of the Second World War. The Convention links refugee status to a 'well founded fear of being persecuted for reasons of race, religion, nationality, membership of a particular social group or political opinion . . .'. From the mid-1980s onwards, persecution, or fear of persecution on grounds of gender, became increasingly recognized within the terms afforded by the inclusion of the category 'social group' in the UN Declaration. For example, in 1985 the UNHCR Executive Committee accepted that refugee women and girls constituted the majority of the world's refugees. This was followed by the same organization issuing guidelines on the Protection of Refugee Women in

1991 and in 1993 the Canadian government issued guidelines for its own officials on the treatment of women claiming refugee status on the grounds of gender-related persecution. In relation to social policy, recognition of an individual's refugee status by the receiving state means that this individual has the same rights as citizens of that state. This means that recognized refugees have access to the full range of welfare services and benefits.

An *asylum seeker* is a person who has claimed refugee status but is still awaiting a decision as to whether the claim has been recognized. Even if the claim to refugee status fails, deportation is not always the result since they can be granted leave to remain on humanitarian grounds. People granted leave to remain may have some restrictions on their social rights and therefore their ability to access the full range of welfare services and benefits. Compared to refugees or those granted leave to remain, asylum seekers have the least rights and may be excluded from a wide range of welfare services, benefits and employment opportunities, and have restrictions on their movement.

Definitions: Some Problems

The atmosphere of hostility and suspicion that has surrounded those seeking to move from the underdeveloped South of the world to the over-developed North has led to many of them being labelled *'economic migrants'*. However, distinguishing between a refugee and an economic migrant is not as easy as it might seem. There are a number of overlapping reasons for this difficulty. The first relates to the limitations of the UN definition that has provided the basis of international law. This Declaration only applies to civil and political rights not social and economic ones and therefore it does not accommodate those people who are forced to leave their country of origin because of economic and/or social disruption caused by environmental, political or economic turmoil or war. These are pre-

cisely the reasons that propel most refugees from the underdeveloped South. Indeed there have been other declarations on refugees and refugee status that do recognize a wider range of causes of population movement. Two examples are the 1969 Organization of African Unity Convention Governing the Specific Aspects of Refugee Problems in Africa and the 1984 Cartegena Declaration on Refugees that emerge in the context of the specific conditions of South America. Both of these declarations went beyond the UN Declaration and recognized that generalized violence, internal conflicts and large scale human rights violation both created refugees and should be recognized as grounds for awarding refugee status.

Despite these attempts to extend the definition of a refugee there has been no fundamental change in the definition enshrined in international law. The consequence of this narrow construction of a refugee and its causes is that anyone who does not meet the terms laid out in the UN Declaration can then be defined as an economic migrant or 'bogus' asylum seeker.

A second and related area that both limits the claims to refugee status and yet illustrates the difficulties in distinguishing between a 'real' or 'bogus' refugee is in the field of policy. British government policy toward migrants attempts to steer a path through a number of competing, and at times antagonistic demands. On the one hand, as a signatory to the UN Convention, the government has to be seen to be acting in an internationally responsible way by receiving a 'fair' share of refugees. Government also has to be seen to welcome and recognize the rights to settlement of any potential immigrants who has freedom of movement or who can claim citizenship or nationality. For example, those who have a claim to citizenship or nationality because of family heritage or historical connection, as was the case of most migrants from the New Commonwealth until this was gradually eroded in successive pieces of immigration legislation after 1962. On the other hand, government also states a need to

Table IV.6.1   Development of principal British Aliens, Nationality and Immigration Acts in twentieth century

Legislation	Effect
1905 Aliens Act	Implemented in response to Jewish refugee migration from Eastern Europe. It established an immigration control bureau with the power of expulsion.
1914 Aliens Restriction Act	Established Home Office control over the internal movement of those defined as Aliens. Aliens required to register with the police.
1914 British Nationality and Status of Aliens Act	Affirmed that all inhabitants of the UK, the dominions and the colonies were 'British Subjects' owing allegiance to the crown. Did not allow for freedom of movement by all such inhabitants to all parts of the empire. Women were denied the ability to transmit British Nationality to children; they also lost this nationality on marriage to an 'alien' man; not the case for British men.
1919 Aliens Restriction (Amendment) Act	Extended the terms of the 1914 Aliens Act to peacetime. Removed right of former 'enemy aliens' to sit on juries or work for the government even if naturalized.
1948 British Nationality Act	Established two main categories of citizenship: a) citizens of the United Kingdom and Colonies (UKC); b) citizens of Commonwealth countries. Both of these had the imperial status of 'British subject' with the entitlement to settle in Britain. There was also a third category for citizens of Eire – who were deemed neither aliens nor subjects but had all the rights and duties of UKC subjects.
1957 British Nationality Act	Allowed people defined as of 'pure European descent' despite neither themselves nor their fathers being born in the UK to register as UKC citizens within five years.
1962 Commonwealth Immigrants Act	Represented the first major modification in the rights of entry attached to imperial nationality. Applicable only to those UKC subjects not born in the UK and not holding a British passport, it introduced a three-tiered work voucher system for would be Commonwealth migrants. They could also enter for the purposes of study. The work voucher system was modified further in 1965.
1968 Commonwealth Immigrants Act	Passed in response to the 'Africanization' process in Kenya and in the context of a formal right of entry for UKC subjects. The act denied automatic right of entry and settlement to those defined as 'Kenyan Asians'. Entry of UKC subjects was now only possible if they, or a parent or grandparent was born, adopted, registered, or naturalized in the UK. This situation contrasted to that of Kenyans of European descent who had had their right of entry protected in a special Nationality Act passed in 1964.

recognize the fears and protect the interests of their citizens who may not welcome the presence of migrants. In particular, the government states a need to limit the claims on public resources, including welfare services and benefits. Finally, government might also recognize the vital contribution that migrants might make to the economic, social and cultural life of the country. There are several ways that these competing pressures are negotiated.

- by de-legitimating the claims of would-be migrants;
- by restricting their access to employment, their freedom of movement, their social rights, including access to welfare services, and their ability to effect family reunification;
- more generally by denying them the opportunity to be socially included in the receiving country.

Different configurations of restrictions such as these emerge at different times and in relation to the different categories of migrants. In detailed social policy analysis therefore it is important to be clear about which of these is being referred to or analysed at any time.

British Policy: Past and Present

Table IV.6.1 shows a potted history of the development of immigration, nationality and asylum policy since the early twentieth century. What is less evident is the way in which state control on migration flows can also be controls on access to welfare services and benefits. Such a link can be seen as early as the 1905 Aliens Act, which included a clause that prohibited landing in the UK if the person could not prove the means to support themselves in 'decent sanitary conditions', if he or she was 'insane' or if he or she was likely to become a charge on the rates. Such clauses link permission to enter the country to a requirement not to have recourse to public goods or funds and they have become a feature of immigration legislation in the UK since the

latter part of the twentieth century. Despite this the term 'public funds' has not been defined in immigration or nationality law but immigration authorities have defined them as income support, family credit, housing benefit and housing provided by registered social landlords and other public bodies. It is also the case that since the late 1970s people whose immigration status has been deemed suspect have been asked for documentation to prove their eligibility to welfare services and benefits even if they do not have a statutory obligation to do so. In this sense, some agencies in for example the NHS have been operating a kind of racial profiling before delivering welfare services.

Since the late 1980s and early 1990s the main migration to the UK has been that of asylum-seekers requiring refuge from parts of the world ravaged by forms of political and/or social turmoil including war and 'ethnic cleansing'. The 1990s have also been characterized by the increasing use of welfare measures to control, monitor and marginalize asylum-seekers. Three pieces of legislation have been key: the 1993 Asylum and Immigration Appeals Act, the 1996 Asylum and Immigration Act and the 1999 Immigration and Asylum Act.

The 1993 Act introduced a provision for fingerprinting asylum-seekers. The 1996 Act removed access to welfare benefits for those claiming asylum once in the country rather than at the port of entry. The 1999 Act introduced measures to disperse asylum-seekers around the UK and to replace cash benefits with a voucher system. All of these measures were premised upon the idea that most asylum-seekers are 'bogus' and simply trying to abuse the British welfare state. There have been three further consequences of this legislation. The first has been to extend the control of migrants to other legislative areas, especially social policy, and administrative measures. This takes scrutiny of immigration and asylum policy away from parliamentary debate about these issues allowing measures to be enacted with less scrutiny. For example, the

1995 Social Security Act contains clauses limiting asylum-seekers' access to support and the 1999 Act opens up numerous channels for restricting asylum-seekers' rights via secondary legislation. Moreover, the use of administrative measures has a long history, reaching back to attempts to limit the numbers of people entering the UK from the black Commonwealth in the late 1940s and 1950s. A second effect has been to shift responsibility for the provision of welfare support away from centrally funded services to already under-resourced local authorities. In its turn this has led to the systematic marginalization of asylum-seekers within the social relations of welfare and increased hostility toward them, especially in those areas with higher numbers and limited local authority resources.

In 2002 the government introduced a new Bill into parliament that aimed to resolve the inadequacies of the voucher and dispersal system. This proposes a system whereby asylum-seekers will be held in reception centres until their application has been processed. It is unclear how successful this system will be but it is clear that it will do nothing to alter the process of marginalization and exclusion of asylum-seekers.

Employment in State Welfare

Migrants have been a major source of labour for British welfare organizations since the inception of the welfare state. Migrants from Ireland, the Caribbean, the Indian subcontinent, the Philippines, Singapore and Malaysia, and parts of the Arab world have predominated in this supply. The importance of migrants as a source of labour for welfare agencies has at times been recognized in immigration, nationality and asylum policy. For example, the voucher system introduced in the 1962 Immigration Act specifically included doctors and nurses and under the work permit system in operation in 2000 23 per cent were issued

for employment in health and medical services. Similarly, attempts to recruit general practitioners was an explicit feature of the 'Highly Skilled Migrants' scheme introduced in 2001. Migrants are also seen as a resolution for other welfare occupations that face serious shortages of personnel, for example, school teachers. There is, then, a tension between attempts to limit the flow of migrants into the country and recognition that they might provide a solution to a widespread problem.

Migrants, National Identity and Social Policy

Social policy is concerned with the promotion of well-being among a given population. As a field of study social policy is also concerned with exploring how this objective is achieved. In this context looking at policies towards different categories of migrants reveals some of the ways in which welfare systems reflect and construct ideas about the boundaries of national belonging and inclusion and ideas about the limits and extent of collective responsibility for individuals and groups defined as foreigners.

To the extent that nationality and immigration law constructs constituencies of belonging they are *cultural* processes and artefacts. This is so because they constantly produce and remake images of who 'the people' are and the obverse of this category the 'alien' or 'stranger'. In this sense policies toward and about migrants also say something about national identity in terms of ideas about the nations' ethnic character, its moral values and its social practices. However the degree to which laws of nationality and immigration actually facilitate a broadly *inclusive* understanding of national identity is open to challenge and change; and struggles over reception and treatment of various categories of migrants are often also struggles over the national identity.

Guide to further reading

Some key recent texts on migration, refugees and social policy in Britain and the EU are: M. Bommes and A. Geddes (eds) *Immigration and Welfare: Challenging the Borders of the Welfare State* (London: Routledge, 2000); A. Bloch and C. Levy (eds) *Refugees, Citizenship and Social Policy in Europe* (London: Routledge, 1999); M. Dummett *On Immigration and Refugees* (London: Routledge, 2001). For more detailed historical analyses, see: V. Bevan *The Development of British Immigration Law* (London: Croom Helm, 1986), which includes a detailed analysis of the 1905 Aliens Act; M. J. Hickman *Religion, Class and Identity* (Aldershot: Avebury, 1995) analyses the development of separate educational facilities for Irish Catholics in Britain; P. Gordon and F. Klug *British Immigration Control: A Brief Guide* (London: Runnymede Trust, 1985). Government websites, especially for the Home Office, also contain lots of relevant policy documents. Organizations such as the Joint Council for the Welfare of Immigrants and the Refugee Council also produce regular summaries, commentaries and analyses of British and EU policy toward migrants, refugees and asylum seekers.

Service-Based Issues

IV.7
Income Protection and Social Security

Stephen McKay and Karen Rowlingson

The incomes of individuals and families come from several sources – from the private sector through wages/salaries, from support from other family members, and often from the state in the form of cash benefits. The discussion of income maintenance and social security takes this as its starting point, sometimes looking broadly at the range of income sources, usually looking more narrowly at the role the state plays in maintaining incomes. Different welfare states play very different roles in income maintenance, from minimalist schemes existing only for the poor (if then), to comprehensive systems covering an extensive range of risks to income security, and involved in significant redistribution.

The Importance Of Social Security

This chapter provides an overview of social security in Britain. We will all spend most of our lives either receiving or paying for social security – frequently both at the same time. However, the system itself is far from simple and most of us understand very little about what it aims to do, how it operates and what its effects are. A number of facts illustrate the importance of the social security system in Britain:

- Government spending on social security benefits in the UK in 2001 is around £100 billion per year – about one-third of all

government spending and more than is spent on health, education and social services combined. This represents about £2,000 each year for every man, woman and child in the country, and in many years exceeds the total raised through income tax.
- Three-quarters of British households now receive at least one social security benefit, with one fifth of working age households receiving one or more means-tested benefits (cash benefits dependent on a family's level of income).
- One in three dependent children live in households receiving the main safety net benefit, Income Support, which is regarded by many as an income insufficient for 'normal' participation in society.

In fact, the benefits responsible for the greatest spending are the Retirement Pension, Income Support, Housing Benefit, Child Benefit, Incapacity Benefit and Disability Living Allowance – in that order. Social security benefits are paid mostly from general taxes and from specific contributions for social security – which we know as National Insurance.

Since the Second World War, spending on social security has risen continuously (see figure IV.7.1). These figures have been adjusted for inflation, and hence show the 'real' growth in total spending in this area. There has been a tenfold increase over the

£ billion
(real terms)

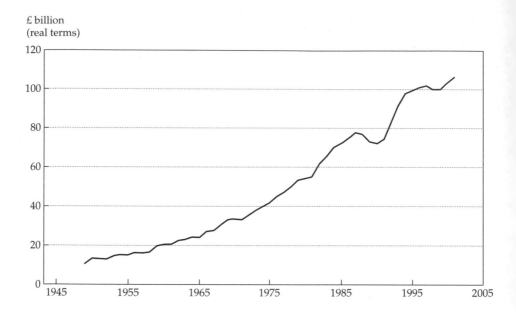

Figure IV.7.1 Spending on UK social security (in real terms)

period, with only occasional dips generally associated with times of falling unemployment.

What Is 'Social Security'?

Social security clearly plays a central role in people's lives. But what is meant by social security? There is no universally accepted neat definition of 'social security', and it may be defined in a number of ways.

Starting with the very widest definition, it is sometimes used to refer to all the ways by which people organize their lives in order to ensure access to an adequate income. This wide concept includes securing income from all sources such as earnings from employers and self-employment, financial help from charities, money from a family member and cash benefits from the state. So in the area of welfare related to maintaining income there are different means by which this may be achieved. Of foremost importance is the private sector, for exam-

ple earnings from employment and profits from self-employment are the chief source of income for most people of working age, and pensions in retirement are often based on such earnings.

A slightly narrower definition of social security would include all types of financial support, except those provided by the market system. In this way, reliance on the immediate or extended family would still be classed as helping to achieve social security. However, it is increasingly usual to adopt an even narrower definition, and to regard social security as those sources of immediate financial support provided by the state.

This debate about definition is, of course, important across the range of services studied within social policy. The study of health is broader than the activities of the National Health Service, for example, and the provision of care extends well beyond the social services.

The definition of 'social security' as the

system of cash benefits paid by the government to different individuals appears to be fairly simple and unproblematic. But it is inadequate or, at least, does not include the same range of activities that most people would regard as being social security. This is because some 'benefits' are not paid for by the state, or need not be. Statutory sick pay used to be paid by government but, whilst it remains a legal entitlement, it is now mostly a cost met by employers. There are also occupational schemes for sickness, widowhood and retirement that are similar to state benefits, and which have a similar function, but which are organized by employers. One could also envisage the government finding ways to 'privatize' what are currently state benefits, or instigating new compulsory private provision, perhaps for pensions. So, both voluntary employer schemes, and some programmes mandated by government, may also be classed as social security – neither of which neatly fit the above definition.

Another rather grey area is the distinction between cash benefits and systems of tax allowances and, increasingly, 'tax credits' which are the responsibility of the Inland Revenue. Tax credits have become an increasingly important part of the 'social security' system. The government generally prefers to see them as standing apart from social security benefits – in particular, that they are received by those in work, rather than those not in work. There are, however, good reasons for seeing tax credits as very similar to social security benefits as there are important areas where tax credits and benefits perform similar roles. The new Integrated Child Credit will, from 2003, be aimed at main carers who will often not be in work. And when Working Families Tax Credit replaced the social security benefit – Family Credit, in 1999, the new tax credit performed a very similar function to the previous benefit.

For the reasons mentioned above, it is difficult to give a precise definition of social security, and different people/organizations will prefer different definitions. In this chapter, we take a fairly pragmatic approach focusing on state systems of income maintenance – largely benefits (administered by the Department for Work and Pensions) and tax credits (administered by the Inland Revenue) but we also put social security within the context of other related forms of government and employer financial provision.

The Aims of Social Security

Having defined social security we now ask what are the aims of the system? The answer is complex. Like elsewhere, the system in Britain has evolved over time and so is not necessarily what would be designed if policy-makers were now starting from scratch. Furthermore, different parts of the system have different aims and so it is not possible to identify one aim and it is even arguable as to what the main aim of the system is. With these reservations in mind, box IV.7.1 lists some of the possible objectives of social security.

Within these general aims, the British social security system has been designed to achieve the following:

- maintain incentives for self-provision (such as through earning and saving);
- keep non-take-up of benefits low;
- counter possible fraud;
- ensure that administrative costs are low.

The aims of the British system have traditionally been more limited than those of systems in Europe, if wider than in some parts of the rest of the English-speaking world. The importance of relieving poverty in the British system explains the considerable reliance on means-testing in Britain. Receipt of means-tested benefits depends on a person or family having resources (typically income, and perhaps savings) below a certain level in order to receive benefits. Means-testing is also common in America, New Zealand and Australia but much less common elsewhere, especially in Continental Europe where social security tends to be less centralized and more

---

Box IV.7.1   Possible aims of social security

- Insuring against the risks of particular events in life, such as unemployment and short-term sickness
- Relieving poverty or low income
- Redistributing resources across people's life-cycles, especially from working age to retirement
- Redistributing resources from rich to poor
- 'Compensating' for some types of extra cost (such as children, disability)
- Providing financial support when 'traditional' families break down

---

concerned with income maintenance and compensation.

An Overview of the Current System

The social security system today is a highly complex organism which has evolved over time and which very few people understand in all its detail. For every possible generalization about the system there are myriad caveats which need to be made. It is therefore difficult to give a brief overview without over-simplifying the system and therefore possibly giving misleading information. Nevertheless, this chapter attempts to provide such an overview. There are various ways of classifying the different benefits in the UK system. For example, benefits can be categorized into two dichotomies: universal versus means-tested; contributory versus non-contributory. If we use the rules of entitlement as our yardstick, social security can be divided into three main components: contributory benefits (benefits which rely upon having paid contributions); means-tested benefits and tax credits (benefits which depend upon income); and contingent benefits (benefits which depend upon your position or category), as follows:

Contributory benefits

The root for the current social security system lies in the Beveridge Report published in the early 1940s, although insurance-based and other benefits had been introduced well before this time. At the heart of the Beveridge approach – of contributory benefits or 'social insurance' – is the idea that people face a range of risks that might lead to severe reductions in living standards. These include the risk of unemployment, or being incapacitated and unable to work, or retiring, or losing the main income-earner in a family. Some risks are rather uncommon, and relatively unrelated to economic circumstances, such as widowhood. Other risks, such as retirement, are much more widespread and predictable.

The main issues that arise with social insurance include:

- why should the state provide this service, rather than private insurance? What relationship should there then be between state and private insurance?
- what risks should be covered?
- on what basis should contributions be made, or be deemed to be made?

Social insurance benefits have entitlement based on having paid National Insurance contributions, and being in a risk covered by these benefits (such as unemployment or retirement). These benefits are individualized in that the earnings of a partner do not generally affect entitlement. The main benefit in this group is the State Retirement Pension. Other benefits are the contributory parts of Incapacity Benefit and contribution-based Jobseeker's Allowance.

Means-tested benefits/tax credits

Entitlement to means-tested benefits depends on the level of 'family' resources, particularly income and savings. The four main examples in the British system are Income Support, Working Families Tax Credit, Housing Benefit and Council Tax Benefit.

The system of benefits based on means-testing, particularly for those on low incomes, is sometimes known as 'social assistance'. In Britain, social assistance is almost synonymous with the benefit Income Support, and income-based Jobseeker's Allowance for unemployed people. These benefits are paid to those whose income and savings are below defined levels, taking into account the size and type of family.

Countries differ a great deal in the extent of this type of provision. In Australia and New Zealand, almost all benefits include an element of 'means-testing'. This does not mean that only the poorest may receive benefits – in some instances the aim is to exclude the richest rather than to include only the poorest. In much of Northern Europe, social assistance plays a much smaller role, picking up those not covered by the main social insurance system. In addition they are often administered locally, with local organizations having some discretion about the precise rules of entitlement.

Additional conditions are often attached to receiving social assistance. People of working age, without sole responsibility for caring for children or disabled adults, must be able to work, available for work and actively seeking work. In past times, they may have had to enter a workhouse to qualify.

Contingent benefits

These are sometimes referred to as categorical benefits or as non-means-tested and non-contributory. Entitlement depends on the existence of certain circumstances (or contingencies) such as having a child (Child Benefit) being disabled (Disability Living Allowance, Severe Disablement Allowance) or, at least until recent changes, being a lone parent (One Parent Benefit).

In the British social security system, some benefits effectively recognize that certain groups of people face extra costs which the state will share. The clearest example is benefits for dependent children and Child Ben-

efit. There is no test of contributions, and the family's level of income is not taken into consideration (at the present time). There are, however, certain tests of residence that must be satisfied. Disability benefits provide another example, where some elements are purely contingent and reflect neither means nor previous contributions

It is worth emphasizing that this division into three groups is something of a simplification of differences between benefits. Means-tested benefits do not just depend on financial resources; they tend to rely also on some combination of being in a particular situation or belonging to a particular family type. For example, able-bodied single people may only claim Income Support if they meet conditions relating to being unemployed. And it is possible for certain sources of income to affect contributory benefits, for example Jobseeker's Allowance and Incapacity Benefit (both contribution-based) can be reduced if a person receives income from a personal or occupational pension.

Who receives social security benefits and tax credits?

The government provides breakdowns based on the ages of recipients, and those whom benefits are intended to support. Based on such a classification, and various assumptions, benefit expenditure is split:

- 13 per cent may be attributed to the needs of children (with the money going generally via their parents);
- 31 per cent is spent on people of working age;
- 56 per cent is spent on people over working age;

It is also possible to look at the number of recipients. According to government figures, Winter Fuel Payments are the 'benefit' with the largest number of recipients, followed very closely by the Retirement Pension – both with over 11 million recipients. Child Benefit comes next with seven million families, followed by the key means-tested benefits. Disability benefits of various kinds also have very large numbers of recipients. The benefits with the most recipients are shown in Table IV.7.2.

Alongside benefits for different groups, there are also benefits to help people meet specific extra costs of living. Housing Benefit exists to help people pay their rent if they are on a low income. The cost of this benefit has increased dramatically in the last three decades because there has been a deliberate policy shift from subsidizing 'bricks and mortar' (in terms of low council rents) to subsidizing individuals (by raising rents and paying benefit to those on low incomes). While low-paid renters can receive help, those with mortgages are mostly denied assistance with their housing costs. Those on low income can also receive help with their council taxes. The other major benefit to help meet extra costs is the Social Fund. This is another distinctive feature of the British system although social workers in some other countries can give out money to people in need. The Social Fund is a much-criticized part of the system, particularly as claimants are mostly given loans rather than grants.

How Social Security Is Delivered

The Department for Work and Pensions (DWP) employs 125,000 staff, one quarter of the Civil Service, in over 2,000 locations. It is currently merging benefit and jobsearch services for working age people in a new outlet called 'Jobcentre Plus'. The service dealing with pensions and older people is the Pension Service. The Disability and Carers Service provides compensation for disabled people and their carers. The DWP is also responsible for the Child Support Agency.

The new 'tax credits' are the responsibility of the Inland Revenue, who administer them. Local authorities remain responsible for dealing with Housing Benefit and Council Tax Benefit.

Benefit levels, poverty and adequacy

In the last 20 years, expenditure on benefits has risen in both absolute and real terms. But increasing expenditure on benefits has not been fuelled by rises in the real levels of benefit and indeed there is widespread evidence that benefit levels are not adequate to meet people's basic requirements. Beveridge initially aimed to set benefits at subsistence levels according to budget studies in the 1930s but there is disagreement about whether he achieved this. The existence of price inflation means that benefit levels have to be raised every year ('uprated') otherwise they would be worth increasingly less in real terms. There is some evidence that both the initial levels of benefits and the uprating to prices in the 1940s

Table IV.7.2   Recipients of benefits in 2001/2

Benefit	Number of recipients (millions)
Winter fuel payments	11.1 million
Retirement pension	11.0 million
Child Benefit	7 million families with children
Council Tax Benefit	4.9 million
Housing Benefit	4 million
Income Support	4 million
Concessionary TV licences	3.6 million
Disability Living Allowance	2.3 million
Incapacity Benefit	1.5 million

were not performed correctly. In more recent years, some benefits have been frozen and others have been linked to price inflation rather than to wage inflation (if it was higher). This means that benefit recipients have become increasingly worse off, relative to workers. Moreover since the early 1980s more benefits have been brought within the scope of income tax, such as state retirement pensions, JSA and Incapacity Benefit, and this has affected the relative generosity of these benefits.

Benefits in cash and in kind

In most cases the aims of the social security system are achieved by paying out cash benefits. However this need not be the case. Benefits could be provided 'in-kind', either through providing services or vouchers that may only be spent on certain types of good. In the USA, an important method of providing for poor families is through the Food Stamps programme. This pays out vouchers that must be exchanged for food. In Britain receipt of Income Support and some other benefits carries with it rights to a passport to some services at no charge, such as dental treatment, eye examinations and legal aid.

The British system developed along two lines: the national social security system generally provided cash benefits to cover some needs such as the need for food, clothes and money for bills whereas other needs, such as the need for social care, was covered by local social services departments who provided in-kind services.

A Look Ahead

Social security, today as much as ever, is in a period of change. The government is seeking to differentiate those above and below working age, and to differentiate between those of working age who are in paid employment, and those who are not.

Two directions of reform are towards greater use of 'tax credits' provided by the Inland Revenue, and hints at 'asset-based welfare'. From 2003 in the UK, tax credits will separate out support for children, from support for workers. Many of the benefits currently directed at children's needs will be brought together in the form of a tax credit (payable to the main carer). The precise distinction between benefits and tax credits depends whether they are administered through the Inland Revenue rather than the DWP.

Guide to further reading

The main textbooks on social security are:

Alcock, P. (1987) *Poverty and State Support*. London: Longman.

Ditch, J. (ed.), 1999. *Introduction to Social Security*. London: Routledge (a collection of chapters on poverty and social security by different authors).

Hill, M., 1990. *Social Security Policy in Britain*. London: Edward Elgar.

McKay, S. and Rowlingson, K., 1999. *Social Security in Britain*. London: Macmillan Press.

Those wanting to keep up to date should read the journal 'Benefits', details on-line at www.benefits.org.uk. The Department for Work and Pensions publishes regular research reports, and press releases, at www.dwp.gov.uk. Figures on tax credits may be found at www.inlandrevenue.gov.uk. The Institute for Fiscal Studies (www.ifs.org.uk) produces timely commentaries on reform, from an economic perspective.

IV.8
Employment

Alan Deacon

Employment policies are central to the concerns of social policy. For millions of people work is not only their major – or sole – source of income, but it is also the basis of their social standing and of their self-respect. Those who are excluded from paid employment may experience not only poverty but demoralization and a loss of self-worth. Such exclusion, of course, is much more likely to be experienced by some groups in the population than by others. Unemployment is also linked to a range of other social problems. Whatever the precise patterns of causality, it is undeniable that communities in which unemployment is high are also disproportionately affected by ill-health, crime and family breakdown.

Unemployment is also very costly for governments. It increases expenditure on social security benefits and reduces the income from taxes and national insurance contributions. Indeed, those who planned and introduced the classic welfare state of the 1940s were adamant that it could only be afforded if unemployment remained low.

For all their significance, however, employment policies were long neglected in most social policy courses. Much attention was paid to the problems generated by a high rate of unemployment, but less to the policies and measures which could be adopted to reduce that rate in the first place. The obvious reason for this was that unemployment was seen as a problem of economics rather than of social policy, and employment measures and services were generally regarded as instruments of economic policy rather than as social services. This is still the case in respect of so-called comprehensive manpower policies which are concerned with the skills and capacities of the labour force as a whole. In recent years, however, far more attention has been paid to employment measures and services that are targeted at people in receipt of social security benefits. Indeed these so-called welfare to work programmes are now the cornerstone of New Labour's attempt to restructure Britain's welfare state.

The government's Green Paper on welfare reform claimed that its aim was to 're-build the welfare state around work' (DSS, 1998, p. 23). 'Our comprehensive welfare to work programme,' it claimed, would 'break the mould of the old passive benefit system' and would form the basis of a new contract between government and those claimants who were capable of work. 'It is the Government's responsibility to promote work opportunities and to help people take advantage of them. It is the responsibility of those who can take them up to do so' (p. 31).

The purpose of this chapter is to explain why welfare to work programmes have become so important, to outline briefly the main features of New Labour's New Deals, and to identify some of the most important policy issues.

The Nature of Welfare to Work Programmes

In broad terms, 'welfare to work' programmes have three interrelated objectives.

1. to increase the job opportunities available to welfare claimants. This can be done through the payment of subsidies to employers who take people directly off the unemployment register, through job creation schemes that provide temporary work for various groups amongst the unemployed, and through training and work experience schemes;
2. to improve the motivation and skills of particularly the young and the long-term unemployed, through an expansion of personal counselling and advice services along with educational and training initiatives;
3. to reform the structure of social security benefits so as to give claimants a greater financial incentive to take advantage of the opportunities created. This third objective can be achieved by enhancing the benefits paid to those in work, by imposing stiffer sanctions on those who fail to participate in the schemes, or by a combination of both of these approaches.

Before we discuss the policy issues that arise in respect of employment measures, there are two points that should be made about the context in which they operate.

The two roles of welfare to work programmes

The first point is that measures such as New Labour's New Deal programmes (discussed below) or the Restart schemes introduced by the previous Conservative government are trying to achieve two broad aims which may not be compatible. They are seeking to be of benefit to the substantial majority of the unemployed who are anxious to find work while at the same trying to prevent the abuse of the social security system by a minority who are not looking for a job or who are working while claiming benefit. This ambiguity was reflected in a memorandum submitted in 1994 to the Employment Committee of the House of Commons by the Department of Employment. This said that the requirement that the long-term unemployed attend a Restart course 'acts as a deterrent to those who are claiming fraudulently, or who are not genuinely seeking work. For genuine claimants – the majority – participation in the courses is of benefit in looking for work' (Employment Committee, 1994, p. 5).

This ambiguity, however, is only one manifestation of a broader and long-standing tension between the objectives of any employment service as a placing agency and its role in the administration of unemployment benefits. It has a clear responsibility to submit to employers those best qualified for the jobs available, but these are unlikely to be the people whose attitudes to work it is most anxious to test. More broadly, it would meet the immediate needs of employers most effectively by focusing its activities upon those who have just become unemployed and are more likely to be 'job ready' than the long-term unemployed. It is the latter group, however, who need more assistance in finding work. Hence the dilemma: giving priority to the short-term unemployed risks being accused of abandoning those who most need help; giving priority to the long-term unemployed risks alienating the employers upon whose cooperation it depends.

Unemployment: Stocks and Flows

The second point to make about the context in which employment measures operate concerns the difficult but very important distinction between the *flow* of people on to and off the unemployment register and the *stock* of people who are unemployed at any one time. There is not a static, standing army of unemployed. This is true even when unemployment is relatively high. In the twelve months to October 1994, for example, 3.9 million people came on to the register and

4.2 million people moved off it. The net reduction of 300,000 was thus the relatively small difference between two very large flows. What this means is that the majority of people who become unemployed find another job quite quickly. Using data for 1993/4, for example, the Department of Employment estimated that 50 per cent will return to work within three months, 67 per cent within six months and 84 per cent within a year. It is true, of course, that some of those who move off benefit quickly may be moving to temporary or very insecure jobs, and so are likely to become unemployed again. Nevertheless, the important point here is that only 16 per cent of those becoming unemployed are likely to remain out of work a year later. Those who do become long-term unemployed, however, find it increasingly difficult to get back into work. This is partly because the experience of unemployment erodes people's skills and motivation and partly because employers are reluctant to engage someone who does not have a recent work record. The outcome, then, is a division between a group who may remain on benefit for several years and a larger group who are moving on and off benefit. This will be the case even when unemployment is relatively low. By 2001, for example, overall unemployment had dropped to its lowest level for 25 years, but there were still 143,000 people over the age of 25 who had been unemployed for more than 18 months. Moreover, because the long-term unemployed remain on benefit for longer periods they form a higher proportion of those unemployed at any one time – the *stock* – than they do of those who become unemployed during a year– the *flow*.

The Growth of Welfare to Work Programmes

There are three main reasons why so much importance is now attached to welfare to work programmes.

1. The first is the widespread belief that globalization and the pressures of world-wide competition now preclude the national fiscal and monetary policies that were pursued in the past. In the eyes of many policy-makers and analysts, employment measures now offer the only practicable means of reducing unemployment.

2. A second reason is that New Labour in particular has become convinced that the key to reducing poverty lies not in raising the rates of benefits, but in extending the opportunity – and the requirement – to take paid employment. Back in 1988 the American analyst David Ellwood published a book entitled *Poor Support* (1988) in which he argued that cash benefits could never alleviate poverty. This was because of what he termed the 'helping conundrums'. The more adequate the level of benefit, for example, the more likely it was that people would reduce their efforts to find a job or would chose to become or remain single parents. The only way to avoid this 'catch 22' was to assume that anyone who was able to work should do so. Welfare for those who were capable of paid work should be redefined as transistional assistance. The aim should be to equip recipients with the capacities and skills they need to find a job, and then require them to do so. Once in work they should receive enough support through the tax and benefits systems to ensure that they escaped from poverty. Remaining on benefit, however, would not be an option; the 'long-term support system' would be 'jobs' (p. 181). This argument has proved to be enormously influential. As Howard Glennerster has recently pointed out, the Blair government had adopted all of the main proposals in *Poor Support* within two years of taking office (2000, p. 17).

3. A third reason why welfare to work programmes are attractive to New Labour is that the emphasis upon the mutual obligations of governments and claimants represents a practical expres-

sion of communitarian thinking. The New Deals outlined below can thus be presented as an example of the 'Third Way' in action (see chapter II.10).

New Labour's New Deals

It was in November 1995 that the Labour Party, then in opposition, announced plans for what was to become the first of six New Deal programmes. This first programme was targeted at young people (aged 18 to 24 years) who had been on benefit for six months. They were to be required to take one of four options: full time education, a job in the private sector for which the employer would receive a subsidy of £60 a week, work with a voluntary agency, or a placement on an enviromental task force. The most striking feature of the programme was that it was compulsory. Anyone who failed to take any of the options would face benefits sanctions. In the words of Gordon Brown, then Shadow Chancellor, 'simply remaining unemployed and on benefit' would no longer be condoned. This message has since become so familiar that it is easy to forget that the introduction of compulsion marked a radical shift in Labour policy.

The original programme is now known as the New Deal for Young People (NDYP). It now includes a self-employment option and also what is termed the 'gateway': a period of intensive advice and preparation prior to any job placement. This is intended to enhance the job readiness of young people and to make them more attractive to employers. It is also designed to reduce the problem of 'deadweight' (discussed below) by helping those who are already 'job ready' to move straight into work.

Two other New Deals are targeted at the long-term unemployed, and at unemployed people aged over 50 years. A further three programmes, however, cover groups who are not required to register for work as a condition of receiving benefits; lone parents, disabled people, and the partners of unemployed people. Indeed, a central difference between the approach of New Labour and

that adopted by previous Conservative governments is that the former has widened the scope of welfare to work. David Price, a former senior official in the Employment Agency, has recently written that the 'philosophy' of the New Deals is 'broadly consistent' with that of the Conservatives, but 'the concept of welfare has been broadened to include groups such as single parents and those on incapacity benefit' (2000, p. 311). The stated objective is no longer to reduce the rate of unemployment, but to reduce the total number of workless households. (It should be noted that this shift in the focus of employment measures is not without its critics. Some, for example, have argued that New Labour's preoccupation with paid employment devalues caring and other forms of unpaid work.)

These newer programmes are broadly voluntary, but in 1999 the Employment Service began to pilot a new service entitled ONE. This provides a single point of entry to both employment services and benefits for all claimants, and from April 2000 it became compulsory for all claimants in the pilot areas to attend an initial work-focused interview with a personal adviser. These first interviews are now compulsory for all those out of work for more than two years and for all lone parents.

Policy Issues

There are two questions that arise immediately regarding schemes such as the New Deals. Are they effective, and are they fair?

Are welfare to work programmes effective?

Critics of the New Deals argue that they will not create jobs on anything like the scale envisaged by the government, and that the jobs which are created will prove to be extremely costly for the taxpayer. This is because some of the people employed would have found a job anyway – the problem of *deadweight* – and because in many cases workers who benefit from the subsidy will get jobs at the expense of others who are thereby made unemployed in their place – the problem of *substitution*. This second criticism was also levelled at Restart, which was often accused of simply 'shuffling the pack' rather than reducing the overall level of unemployment. In response, advocates of welfare to work programmes argue that they give the long-term unemployed some work experience and thereby make them much more attractive to employers. This in turn will increase the effective supply of labour within the economy and thereby improve the trade-off between unemployment and inflation. An early book by Layard and Philpott (1991, p. 13) insisted that there 'is not a predetermined pool of jobs. If we can improve the supply of labour we can have new jobs without inflation rising.'

Are welfare to work programmes fair?

At the core of New Labour's approach to welfare to work is the principle of conditionality -the idea that an individual's entitlement to benefit should depend upon whether or not he or she is willing to take part in the programme.

The case *against* conditional benefits rests on the proposition that unemployment is a structural problem, beyond the control of the individual. Making benefits conditional upon behaviour, however, suggests that the claimant would have found work if he or she had tried harder, and this is manifestly unjust when the jobs are simply not there. If good jobs or training schemes are available, then the unemployed will take them anyway. Conversely, it is often counterproductive to force someone to attend a course which he or she considers to be unsuitable or even pointless – a view that has in the past been expressed strongly by some who have experience of providing courses (Employment Committee, 1995, p. 97).

The case *for* conditional benefits is usually advanced on three grounds. The first is deterrence: that it prevents the abuse of benefits. The second is a more moralistic argument:

that because the effect of prolonged joblessness is to demotivate claimants, it is reasonable to require them to take steps which are to their long-term benefit but which they would not otherwise take. The third argument is a more pragmatic one: that the electorate will be prepared to pay for employment measures only if they are sure that the unemployed are also required to do their bit. Indeed this approach is central to New Labour's attempt to rebuild popular support for welfare. Tony Blair told an audience in South Africa in 1996 that 'matching opportunity and responsibility is the only way in the modern world to obtain consent from the public to fund the welfare state'.

Conclusion

The debate about the effectiveness and fairness of the New Deals remains unresolved. This is because of the buoyancy of the economy throughout Labour's first term in office. It is difficult to tell how far the welfare work programmes contributed to this buoyancy or simply benefited from it. That said, it is true that over 280,000 young people had left the NDYP for sustained unsubsidised jobs (lasting 13 weeks or more) by the time of the election in 2001 (DfEE, 2001). A recent review of the operation of the New Deals by Jane Millar concluded that they had had a positive impact and that the introduction of personal advisors to provide claimants with counselling and encouragement had been a success. She added, however, the programmes had worked best for those who were most jobready and that they would have to work harder to reach those with multiple disadvantages and special needs (2000, p. vii). Indeed New Labour's welfare to work strategy faced two central challenges as it began its second term in office. First, how effective will the programmes be in a period of slower economic growth or even recession? Second, how can those programmes be adapted to cope with a clientele that includes an increasing proportion of people who are 'hard to help'?

Guide to further reading

Deacon, A., 2002. *Perspectives on Welfare: Ideas, Ideologies and Policy Debates* (Buckingham: Open University Press). Discusses welfare to work programmes within the context of broader perspectives on welfare reform, and examines the thinking behind New Labour's New Deals.

Department for Education and Employment (DfEE), 2001. *Towards Full Employment* (Cm 5084, London: Stationery Office). Outlines employment measures in operation in mid-2001.

Department of Social Security (DSS), 1998. *A New Contract for Welfare* (Cm 3805, London: Stationery Office).

Ellwood, D., 1988. *Poor Support* (New York: Basic Books). Argues that welfare for those capable of work should be subject to time limits and seen as a form of temporary assistance. A massively influential book in both Britain and the United States.

Employment Committee, 1994, 1995, 1996. *Second Report: The Right to Work/Workfare* (Report and Minutes of Evidence HC 31 Session 1994-5 and HC 82 Session 1995–6). A valuable source for the debate about the feasibility of job guarantee schemes and about conditionality. Also provides a summary of the measures in operation under the Conservatives in the mid-1990s.

Glennerster, H., 2000. *US Poverty Studies and Poverty Measurement: The Past Twenty Five Years* (CASE Paper 42, London: London School of Economics; www.lse.ac.uk/CASE). Discusses the influence of American ideas about welfare to work strategies upon New Labour.

Layard, R. and Philpott, J., 1991. *Stopping Unemployment* (London: Employment Policy Institute). An early statement of the argument that long-term unemployment could be virtually eliminated by an extension of employment measures and that entitlement to benefit should be conditional upon participation in such measures.

Millar, J., 2000. *Keeping Track of Welfare Reform: The New Deal Programmes* (York: Joseph Rowntree Foundation). Authoritative review of the early operation of the various New Deal programmes.

Price, D., 2000. *Office of Hope* (London: Policy Studies Institute). Insider account of the history of the employment services since 1945. Provides balanced assessment of the continuities and differences between Thatcherism and New Labour.

IV.9
Health Care

Judith Allsop

Why Do Health Services Matter?

A World Bank report, *Investing in Health* (1993) reviewed health policies world-wide and commented that governments were concerned with health policy for both individual and collective benefit. The report said (p. 17):

> Good health, as people know from their own experience, is a crucial part of well-being, but spending on health can also be justified on purely economic grounds. Improved health contributes to economic growth in four ways: it reduces production losses caused by worker illness; it permits the use of natural resources [hitherto] inaccessible because of disease; it increases the enrolment of children in school and makes them better able to learn; and it frees for alternative uses resources that would otherwise have been spent on treating illness.

Different countries, whether developed or developing, face similar problems in relation to health policy. They must decide how much they should spend on health care as opposed to other services that may have an impact of health. A wide spectrum of factors can affect health: the environment and the state of housing stock; income levels and the level of employment; access to and the level of education, particularly for women. So health policies should be seen in relation to other social policies. Yet governments must also provide services for the sick. Governments must strike a balance between maintaining health, preventing ill health and curing illness. Demand for health care tends to outstrip ability to pay irrespective of the method of funding, so mechanisms are required to contain costs. Health systems are strongly affected by history: by past capital investment as well as current spending. Moreover, they have proved resistant to change as there are vested interests in existing arrangements as shown by recent struggles over health policy reforms in France, Holland, Sweden, UK and the USA. Powerful political interests can skew the way policies are implemented and may even block policy change altogether.

In this chapter, the focus is on the contribution of social policy to the study of health care in the UK. Two broad approaches can be identified. The first concentrates on analysing issues that contribute to policies *for* health and can guide health service development. Here, the main focus is on identifying trends and planning for the future. Issues such as the health status of the population, the patterns of ill health and how effectively health needs are being met through the services provided are critical issues. A second approach focuses more directly on a critical analysis and evaluation of policy and the assessment of alternative strategies.

Analysis For Policy

Establishing health care needs

To assess what health services are needed, the demographic structure of the population and patterns of health and illness must be understood as these affect the demand for health services. Social policy analysts have made a major contribution to the investigation of the incidence of illness (morbidity) and death (mortality); how these vary between different social groups and in different regions of the country. Inequalities in health status have been identified using social divisions (see Chapter II.5) such as age, class, ethnicity and gender as well as between different regions. A number of empirical studies have shown that there is a strong association between poverty and ill health and that people from the lowest social group have mortality rates about three times higher than the highest social group on a range of indicators with a class-related gradient in between. Morbidity from a large number of conditions is also class-related, with a higher incidence of illness among poorer people. Thus, the better-off live longer and enjoy better health. During the 1990s, inequalities in health in the UK have widened rather than reduced. This trend reflects the increasing income differences between rich and poor. Indeed, it has been demonstrated that countries with narrow income differentials tend to have better health status.

While the findings of these studies have been unequivocal in demonstrating the link between poverty, low income and health, there are four number of explanations as to why some individuals are healthy and others are not. First, it has been demonstrated that poor health leads to poverty as learning and earning power may be affected. Second, there tend to be riskier environmental and material conditions in the areas that poorer people live. Third, some argue that the life style of the worse off contributes to illness. Smoking, excessive alcohol consumption, poor diet and a lack of exercise have a class gradient. However,

geneticists point out that family history also plays a part in increasing susceptibility to certain diseases. Indeed, not all poor people have bad health. In reality for individuals, health risks accumulate over time and the linkage between various causal factors may be cumulative over time.

Differences in views over the causes of ill health have led to different policy prescriptions. For example, Conservative governments have tended to support policies that encourage people to take personal responsibility for their health. They have favoured the provision of information and health education campaigns to alter people's behaviour. Labour governments have placed more emphasis on reducing inequalities in living conditions. However, there remain difficult policy choices about how to maintain health. Raising the income of the poor and improving environments is a long term goal that may not produce tangible benefit for decades. With limited resources, there is an argument for focusing on children's health as they have more life years left, and on community development to reduce exclusion. In practice, a variety of strategies have been adopted. These require evaluation to demonstrate those which are effective.

Who provides health care?

Health care can be divided into acute, caring and preventive services and there is a further division of labour between those who provide health care. Social policy researchers have drawn attention to the important role played by unpaid health workers in the informal sector. Most day-to-day health work is carried out within families, particularly by women acting as health educators and giving care and support to those who are ill or frail. Indeed, the NHS could not function without such unpaid labour. There is therefore an argument for supporting carers.

Within the formal sector, the NHS is a major employer and trainer of health professionals. It employs 1.25 million workers with a complex division of labour between various health workers. Although not the largest group, (there are well over half a million nurses), medical professionals have traditionally played a dominant role in health work. In the UK, doctors themselves can be divided into a number of specialties; however, the most important divisions are between general practitioners (GPs), hospital doctors and public health doctors. This division has its origin in the nineteenth century and affects the delivery of NHS services today. Most people are registered with the GP who provides first line care and acts as a gatekeeper to the more expensive and specialist hospital services. The only other way in which people can access care is through an Accident and Emergency department. This gatekeeping role is a rationing mechanism and helps to explain lower UK health care costs.

The Analysis of Health Policy

In the UK the study of health policy has tended to be a study of the National Health Service (NHS). Nevertheless, much can be learnt from looking at other health systems, particularly those within the European Union (EU) where societies are similar to our own. Comparisons have revealed both similarities and differences. Like other EU countries, the UK has an ageing population and elderly people are heavy users of health services. Indeed most health care expenditure is generated by the very young and the very old. A consequence of the demographic structure has been the continuing pressure to increase spending on health care: a pressure that has been increased by advances in medical knowledge, techniques and therapies as well as by people's rising expectations.

Cross-country comparisons have shown that the UK lags behind other countries in the amount that it spends on health care. For example, in 1998 it spent 6.8 per cent of Gross Domestic Product on health compared to an EU average of 8.4 per cent. It also lags behind in terms of health status. The UK has higher infant mortality rates and higher death rates from heart and circulatory disease and certain cancers than her European neighbours. Such comparisons have led to a sharper and more critical focus on a number of aspects of UK health policy such as the funding levels, the role of the private sector, how to achieve better outcomes for patients, the organization of the NHS and the adequacy of the supply, training and deployment of the NHS workforce.

Funding health care

Health care may be funded through direct payments, private insurance, a social insurance scheme, directly from taxation or through a combination of these. In the UK, since the 1946 National Health Act, health care has been provided virtually free at the point of service for the whole population and funded mainly from direct taxation (74 per cent). Some other European countries have social insurance systems although they also have higher levels of private spending via private insurance or direct payments. The UK tax-based system has certain advantages. UK governments have been able to maintain stricter cost control as a global sum is allocated to the NHS each year by the Treasury and the administrative costs are lower than social insurance, thus leaving more money for patient care. There is therefore more money available for patient care. Furthermore, a health service controlled from the centre means that priorities can be determined and in theory at least, applied across the country. The distribution of resources to different regions of the country has also been more equitable than in many other countries and access to health care is based on need rather than ability to pay.

The disadvantage of the UK funding system is that governments, particularly in the 1980s and 1990s, have not allocated sufficient resources to health to maintain standards and to meet people's expectations. The shortfall has not been made up by private spending. Only about 13 per cent of the population are privately insured. The NHS Plan published in 2000, while maintaining a commitment to a tax-based service, outlines proposals to improve the quality of health care through increasing the amount invested, managing performance better, giving a greater focus to primary and preventive care and, more controversially, bringing in more private investment to achieve a public/private partnership.

Organizational and management reform

Almost since its inception, governments irrespective of their political persuasion have tinkered with the structure of the NHS to improve performance. The most significant organizational and management changes were the 1990 health services reforms introduced by Conservative governments and the yet to be completed modernization programme begun by the 1997 Labour government. Both these reforms aimed to change the incentives for those working within the NHS to encourage the delivery of higher quality care within the budgets allocated. However, the strategies adopted have differed in emphasis.

The 1990 NHS and Community Care Act devolved responsibility from the central Department of Health to lower-level health authorities and introduced a split in functions between the budget holders (purchasers) who estimated need, determined priorities and commissioned services and the health care trusts that provide care in the hospital and community. There was an element of competition built into these arrangements as trusts could compete with each other or with private sector suppliers. The financial viability of trusts depended upon their ability to gain contracts. The theory is that these changes would encourage trusts to be more business-like. For the first time, health care was costed. The arrangements were referred to as 'managed' competition as the market was controlled

through government rules and regulations. Conservative governments also created incentives for private finance to enter the NHS and for older people to take out private insurance.

These arrangements strengthened the management function within the NHS. Trusts now had to develop business plans, put prices to health care interventions and produce costed contracts. Subsequent clinical activity had to remain at the levels planned. At the same time, directives from the Department of Health set a range of performance targets that were monitored through different forms of review. A variety of output and outcome measures have developed so that the performance of hospitals can be compared, and the results publicized. Thus, it is now possible for government and the public to compare length of waiting times for operations, and the mortality rates for different procedures.

Service priorities

The 1990 Act also took a further step towards promoting primary care – an area of relative policy neglect. Perhaps not surprisingly given an ageing population and the effectiveness of clinical medicine, there had been a drift towards hospital-based treatment. Not only was this more expensive, but it also encouraged the development of medical interventions and played down the critical role of maintaining health and preventing illness within the community. The reforms strengthened the position of the GP in relation to the hospital by encouraging them to develop their facilities at practice level and undertake more preventive health checks; and some GPs were able to purchase secondary care from hospitals and community nursing services for their patients. Pilot schemes were developed to evaluate locality-based purchasing where groups of GPs combined to contract for a range of services. In some areas, these schemes have been extended to cover the social care provided by local authorities. Collaboration between the authorities providing health and social care has proved difficult to achieve, yet is crucial for the proper care and support of those with health needs living in the community such as older people and people with mental illnesses or disabilities.

Under Labour governments, previous policies have been maintained and in some cases developed further. For example, the purchaser/provider split remains although there is now less emphasis on competition between trusts and more on building longer-term stable relationships between purchasers and providers. The private sector is also seen as having a role in developing capital projects as well as in providing services. Management has been strengthened further through clinical governance – the chief executive of each trust is now responsible for all aspects of care including clinical performance. This puts doctors on a similar footing to other employees. The 2000 NHS Plan sets the scene for further change. In future, primary care trusts will play a pivotal role in health care. Not only will they ensure that a good standard of preventive and diagnostic care is provided by family practitioners, they will also purchase health care from trusts and work collaboratively with local authorities.

Labour governments have placed an emphasis on providing high quality health care. This has been defined on the basis of six principles. It is care that is safe, effective, patient-centred, timely, efficient and equitable. One of the major weaknesses of the NHS has been the variations in how people are treated for the same condition and the failure to identify and disseminate best practice. Methods to establish best practice on the basis of evidence have developed and a number of new national bodies have been established to carry out the tasks of assessment, dissemination and inspection. It has been acknowledged that the delivery of health care is a multi-professional and often high risk activity where patient safety is the paramount concern.

The politics of the NHS

The health policy reforms and the concern to learn from policy failures as well as successes, has provided a role for social policy analysts in evaluating the impact of change, the factors associated with good and poor practice and the barriers to implementing new health policies. A major barrier to change in the past has been the configuration of political interests within the NHS and the discipline of social policy has made a major contribution to conceptualizing and studying those interests. A major shift in the configuration of those interests is now occurring and is being encouraged by government policies.

It has already been argued that providing health care is a people-intensive process. Indeed, two-thirds of health care costs go to paying the wages and salaries of staff. Political analyses of the NHS have identified a number of structured interests with different degrees of power and influence on the policy process. Governments and their agents, health service managers, make up one group. They are concerned with issues of funding, value for money and strategies for health care. The health professions constitute a second interest group. The professions have a monopoly of expertise. Ideally, their concern is to give the best possible care to each patient; however, they also seek to maintain clinical control over their own work in a way that has not always been in the public interest. The third structured interest is the community and the individuals that consume health care. Their concern is the treatment of their own ill health, that of their family and the services available to the community in which they live. It has been argued that the first two groups have dominated health care. Governments hold the purse strings and initiate policy while managers are responsible for implementation. Professionals are the holders of expertise. Doctors in particular have tended to dominate other professionals, they determine what health and disease is, the content of medical work and how medicine should be practised. By comparison, the user and community interest has been weak and because the NHS itself is a centralized monopoly provider, there have been few opportunities for those who use health care to make their voices heard. Nor, unless they happen to have a high income, can they opt out of the NHS.

Currently, a major shift is taking place in the configuration of interests. The health reforms, evidence-based medicine, and the closer scrutiny of clinical practice have changed the context of medical work and, in the wake of a number of highly publicized cases where individual doctors have been found to put patients as risk, measures have been put in place to ensure that the medical and other professions are more accountable both to other professionals and to the public. Changes in the division of tasks between health professionals have also meant that there must be a greater degree of partnership and less hierarchy.

However, the most radical change in health care is the rise of consumerism. Public expectations have risen along with educational levels, media coverage of health issues and the internet. There is more knowledge of what to expect. Also, there are increasing numbers of patient and carer groups with expertise in specific illnesses or conditions, and a particular knowledge the NHS who are concerned to influence policy. Increasingly, governments and indeed professional associations, are consulting with health consumer organizations and appointing their representatives to decision-making bodies. Plans for modernizing the NHS include proposals to establish a national body for patient and public involvement as well as local-level patients' forums. The rights of patients are also being strengthened as well as the means for redress should people be dissatisfied.

Conclusion

There is greater political consensus about health care than in other areas of social policy. This is because a tax-funded NHS is popular with an electorate. Governments have also calculated that a centralized health service provides benefits in terms of value for money. However, it is now acknowledged that additional resources will be needed to make up for the shortfall of under investment in the past and to bring the NHS up to EU standards. It is likely therefore, that taxes will rise to pay for health care. There may be more direct payments for certain services. Governments are also likely to seek private investment to supplement public funds.

The most important policy challenges will be both to meet people's expectations for prompt and effective treatment and at the same time to reduce existing inequities in the distribution of health services. The training of sufficient health professionals and the renewal of outdated facilities will be critical to meeting this challenge. However, these objectives take some time to achieve. It is likely that despite devolution of responsibilities for the delivery of health services to the local level, the degree and scope of regulatory control from the centre and the surveillance of everyday practice will continue to increase. This may affect the morale of those who work in the NHS.

In terms of broader aims, policies to maintain health and reduce health inequalities will take time to achieve their objectives. Many of the mechanisms to do so lie outside health care policy itself and depend upon income levels and community renewal. The success of many of the policies at present being developed rely on a stronger partnership between health professional, between communities and health professionals and on more equal relationships between patients and health professionals. There is a challenge for those studying social policy both to interpret how society and health needs are changing and to evaluate the effectiveness of policies in achieving their objectives. Social policy like clinical medicine should be evidence-based.

354 of JUDITH ALLSOP

Guide to further reading

Students of social policy should be aware that present policy is strongly influenced by the past. P. Thane provides a history of health and welfare in Britain in *The Foundations of the Welfare State*, 2nd edn (Harlow: Longman, 1996). The patterns of inequalities in health are reviewed by M. Drever and M. Whitehead *Health Inequalities* (London: Stationery Office, 1997), while D. Blane, E. Brunner and R. Wilkinson *Health and Social Organization: Towards a Health Policy for the Twenty-first century* (London: Routledge, 1996) provide a series of essays on recent research on the causes of ill health. Policies for public health in relation to risky behaviour are discussed by R. Baggott *Public Health: Policy and Politics* (Basingstoke: Macmillan Press, 2000).

There is a wide range of primary sources, such as government reports, White Papers and circulars. These should be read alongside critical commentaries. Of particular importance in understanding contemporary health policy is *The NHS Plan* (Secretary of State for Health, London: Stationery Office, 2000). The specially commissioned reports on policy options for the future provide a straightforward and clear account of the strengths and weaknesses of the NHS: *Securing our Future Health: Taking a Long-Term View* (London: Public Inquiry Unit, 2001 and 2002). Selected official statistics on government expenditure on health services and the activity of service providers, such as hospitals and general practitioners, as well as on mortality and morbidity rates are published annually in *Social Trends* (Central Statistical Office, London: HMSO and Stationery Office).

J. Allsop *Health Policy and the NHS: Towards 2000*, 2nd edn (Harlow: Longman, 1995); C. Ham *Health Policy in Britain*, 4th edn (Basingstoke: Macmillan Press, 1999); and R. Klein *The New Politics of the NHS*, 4th edn (Harlow: Longman, 2001), provide general overviews of health policy.

Priorities for health policy in an international context are discussed in World Bank *Investing in Health* (Geneva: World Bank, 1993). R. Saltman, J. Figueras and C. Sakellarides, (eds) *Critical Challenges for Health Reform in Europe* (Buckingham, Open University Press, 1998), provides an account of how different countries deal with similar problems.

Education

Miriam David

This chapter is about continuities and changes in policies on education in Britain, mainly in England and Wales, since the Scottish system is somewhat different in both policy development and administration. The continuities and changes in the political concepts about global economic contexts on markets both for parental choice and consumerism and also for skills for work or jobs, and the complementary arguments about standards and quality assurance, are the setting for the discussion. The main focus is on compulsory schooling, or rather education for five to sixteen year olds, but reference is also made to what is now known as lifelong learning. This includes what was traditionally known as further and higher education, and early childhood education, particularly that for children below five, the age of compulsory schooling.

The key characteristic of education policy under Conservative administrations for two decades was that of *diversity* to be achieved through markets, private enterprise and choice policies. Since they came to power in 1997, New Labour has continued to develop this as a key characteristic, but instead through policies on excellence. But New Labour has also introduced the notions of social exclusion and inclusion and identified policies specifically to tackle issues of poverty through education. These policies on social exclusion build upon developments made by the Conservatives but

modify the effects of social diversity aiming to provide opportunities for all. Michael Barber, in his capacity as Special Adviser to the first New Labour Secretary of State for Education, argued that: 'the case for public education needs to be restated for the new century [as] . . . a radically new conception. . . a good education system is increasingly important not only to the success of a modern economy but also to the creation of a socially just society.'

However, it is difficult at the present juncture to describe what used to be called the education 'system'. Another essential characteristic of education policy is that of central control of standards, defined broadly as raising educational achievement and/or reducing under-achievement. Previously Conservatives developed this approach alongside allowing markets to flourish. New Labour has elaborated control of standards into a fine art, with a plethora of organizations and initiatives.

Contextual Issues

All countries now have an education system and policies for educational developments, especially on training for particular forms of employment. In the advanced industrial societies, such as Britain, the educational system is highly developed and complex, and subject to regular changes in order to maintain competitiveness. Indeed the global 'knowledge economy' has become a key facet of international competitiveness and the need to enhance it has been one of the main reasons for educational policy developments in all industrial societies in the past three decades. Given globalization, defined as economic, cultural and ICT convergence, there have been similar developments to those in Britain in countries such as the USA, Canada, Australia and New Zealand, and many of the European nations. However, the form and content of the changes have differed in terms of the political complexion of the government and its values. In the 1980s and 1990s this was associated largely with Conservative or what have been called neo-liberal administrations.

Since the late 1990s in the UK New Labour's political values have shared many of the characteristics of neo-liberalism, especially in the ways in which they deal with, and move towards, what has been called a post-welfare society. They have continued an emphasis on moral values, individuality and a strong role for religion in the construction and implementation of educational policies. However, New Labour has re-introduced concerns with limited forms of equity and opportunity, seeing education and the knowledge economy as central to these. They have redefined such notions on an individual basis rather than on the basis of social groups, such as social class or those economically disadvantaged on the basis of family circumstances. The language and discourse of New Labour has shifted to issues of social exclusion. They aim, however, to tackle these diverse forms of poverty through education and individual measures to develop knowledge and skills for jobs and work, regardless of gender.

Few of the policy developments in Britain over the previous twenty years had issues of equality of opportunity, in terms of class, disability, gender, race/ethnicity or sexuality, uppermost or explicitly on the agenda. The concern had been more with efficiency, value for money, the development of performance standards and qual-

ity assurance rather than questions in particular of class, race/ethnicity or gender equity. However, given the interests of many social and educational researchers, it is possible to trace continuities and changes with respect to such issues as equality of opportunity.

On the other hand, the explicit goal of education policy, as with other areas of social provision, has continued to be to put the consumer or user of education centre stage. Thus, with respect to compulsory education and lifelong learning, especially early childhood education, parents have assumed a far greater prominence than hitherto, particularly with respect to school choice and power over educational decision-making. This has actually increased under New Labour with their many measures to provide parents with opportunities for involvement and control. In addition, there is evidence to suggest that children themselves have also assumed greater involvement in educational practices. This chapter will also consider how policies on education have increased the role of parent as the consumer in a range of contexts, from the marketing of educational institutions to various forms of involvement in educational processes and standards. New Labour has built upon Conservative policies and legislated for these developments in a number of contexts. Indeed, the very first piece of educational policy under New Labour, mandated both greater parental involvement through 'home-school agreements' and also required this in maintaining school standards, such as through involvement in supervising homework, checking on league tables and in the processes of education (Tomlinson, 2001, p. 93).

This then extended the period of policy development which had been called that of the 'ideology of parentocracy' to signal the pre-eminent position of parents afforded by the Conservative government, by contrast with previous Labour and Conservative administrations, who were committed to the 'ideology of meritocracy'. In this latter notion academic ability and merit rather than parental backgrounds of privilege or poverty were the determining factor in educational decisions. The term 'meritocracy' was originally coined by the late Michael, Lord Young of Dartington in 1956 in his book entitled *The Rise of the Meritocracy*, in which he satirized attempts to transform our education system from one based upon social and economic advantage to one based entirely upon academic merit. Nevertheless, the enduring feature of the post-war period to 1980 was the bipartisan consensus around equality of educational opportunity as a goal and principle. To some extent the ideology and goal of a meritocracy has re-emerged under New Labour.

Thus New Labour's commitment to what has been called the 'third way' (see chapter II.10) represents both continuities with the Conservatives and Old Labour and also changes. This chapter will now look at how the Conservatives developed their policies and how these have been continued and modified by New Labour. In particular, the shift towards markets and skills for a global labour market is one of the emblematic changes under New Labour. This chapter will consider them in the context of changing forms of analysis of policy discourse and how New Labour has developed a discourse about policies which relies more on a social research perspective.

Beyond the ERA 1988: A Return to a New Era?

The defining policy on compulsory education in England and Wales at present is the 1998 School Standards & Framework Act, which increased measures of parental involvement and control, within a framework of setting standards for educational achievement. Introduced by the first Secretary of State for Education and Employment under New Labour, David Blunkett, in a White Paper entitled 'Excellence in Schools' it also revised the various types of 'state' school that had been introduced by the Conservatives. Alongside the Act, a series

of policies were introduced to set and raise standards of literacy and numeracy, and also to provide resources for specifically defined issues of social exclusion, through *inter alia* Education Action Zones (EAZs).

This Act revised and modified but did not fully reverse the 1988 Education Reform Act, which was the defining piece of legislation introduced under the Conservatives and which had been known as the ERA. The then Conservative Secretary of State for Education, Kenneth Baker, deliberately chose to put in the term 'reform' in order that the initials would signal a new era. He had borrowed the idea of education reform from the USA, where it had already entered into common usage as a substitute for education policy. In the USA there was also a commitment to re-establish notions of educational excellence, and the Conservative government in Britain aimed to emulate the American example.

The first key feature of the ERA was that it was innovative in legislating on both compulsory and further and higher education, which no single piece of British educational legislation had captured before. Second, it sought to create a variety of essentially autonomous educational institutions, separate from and independent of local government and run largely as business concerns. Third, however, the Act also set in place, also as a unique landmark, a national curriculum, with associated schemes of testing and assessment, for compulsory education. In this respect, the ERA differentiated between compulsory and post-compulsory education, since with respect to the latter no national curriculum was developed, although new forms of vocational qualifications were developed for parts of further education. Many commentators on the ERA have mentioned, with respect to schooling, the balance between central control, particularly through the National Curriculum, and market forces, through the creation of a range of different types of school with the freedom to develop their own budgets.

However, the system created by the ERA was not as robust as had been anticipated and further measures were needed to strengthen particular objectives and parts of the system. Indeed, the balance between central control and market forces remained in place for three years until after Margaret Thatcher left office. John Major, as prime minister from 1991–7, was more committed to the user perspective and signalled this through the Citizen's Charter published in 1991. One of the first documents to take this forward was the Parent's Charter, entitled *You and Your Child's Education*, first published in 1991 and revised in 1994. In particular, this afforded parents rights to choose and to complain about the service they received for their child. In addition, further legislation was introduced to strengthen aspects of 'choice and diversity' rather than central control, tilting the balance towards consumerism rather than central direction. At the same time, however, national performance standards were developed and a new system of quality control introduced to ensure minimum standards. For example, the 1992 Education (Schools) Act, having abolished Her Majesty's Inspectors of Schools (HMI), created the Office for Standards in Education (OFSTED) and a system of regular and routine statutory reviews of school practice, and legislated for the publication of annual performance league tables, particularly of school examination results. This latter was largely with the aim of providing the information on which parents could make informed choices of their child's education.

Measures to enlarge upon the provisions of the 1988 ERA were incorporated into the 1993 Education Act, which established a Funding Agency for Schools (FAS) for the funding of grant-maintained schools and those local education authorities where the majority of schools had opted out of local authority control. From 1993 to 1997, when New Labour came to power, further accretions to educational policy were developed such that it could be argued that education had become fully marketized, although there was no one general education market in operation in England but a range of different types of school in any one area. In the case of secondary schooling a diversity had developed with respect to single sex and coeducation and forms of academic selection, and the balance between private and specialist schools.

Initiative Overload? New Labour's Policies On Schooling

Whilst it is possible to argue that the New Labour policies on compulsory education continued the policies of the previous Conservative administrations and are defined by the 1998 Act that is certainly not the sum total of their approach. It is also not the sum total of their approach to further and higher education, which they have now named lifelong learning, and this will be addressed below. In the five years since coming to office, there has been a plethora of strategies and initiatives, mainly building upon Conservative approaches of marketization and privatization and moving away from a traditional social democratic approach to equality of opportunity. This has been called post-welfarism where individuals are encouraged to compete for education, skills and jobs for themselves and the future of the national economy. On the one hand, there has been what Prime Minister Tony Blair called a 'one-size fits all approach' which aimed to ensure family, children and community involvement in all aspects of educational provision to develop educational effectiveness, through an emphasis on educational standards. The setting up of a Standards and Effectiveness Unit in the then Department for Education and Employment was also characterized by a relatively new approach to considering 'what works' through assembling 'evidence' about how to develop policies (see chapter II.10). Thus, a whole raft of policies and strategies have been proposed and implemented to try to develop new educational benchmarks and standards through examinations, assessment and performance, including new forms of managerial control of teachers. This has become known as the new public management or rather 'managerialism' (see chapter III.5). The culmination of these developments has been continuous change and initiatives to transform schools to 'achieve success' as the 2001 White Paper put it. Here the reinvigoration of faith schools was a defining moment.

On the other hand, New Labour has also been concerned with issues of inequality and poverty, identifying these as about social exclusion from forms of employment and citizenship rather than traditional concepts of social disadvantage and social welfare. The main thrust of policies here was economic and about training and skills for work. Many of these policies were developed and coordinated by a newly created inter-departmental administration to provide joined-up policies on social exclusion – the Social Exclusion Unit – attached to his Cabinet Office. Thus, traditional approaches to social welfare have also been transformed through education and economic policies, such that work has become a predominant focus.

The Social Exclusion Unit (SEU) has initiated and developed specific policies for education with paid work rather than social welfare being the key emphasis. Whilst arguing for changes to the welfare state to provide opportunities for all, the first annual report of the SEU identified young people, but specifically women as mothers, as a key social problem. A key shift has been about how girls and young women should be treated through policy measures, particularly if they become young mothers. One of the SEU's first policy recommendations was on teenage pregnancy and parenthood, since Britain was identified as having the highest rates in Europe throughout the 1980s and 1990s (SEU, *Teenage Pregnancy*). A strategy to reduce these rates to European levels (and those which prevailed in Britain in the early 1980s) was through education, and guidance on Sex and Relationship Education was developed to build

upon programmes of personal, social and health education which had developed in schools from the 1980s (SEU, *Schools Achieving Success*).

Initiative Overload? New Labour's Policies on Lifelong Learning

It is important also to note that these changes are not only pertinent to schools but have been affecting other levels of the education system. The Conservative administrations in the 1980s developed market policies and privatization for further and higher education as well as for schools, in particular through the 1988 Education Reform Act and the 1993 Further and Higher Education Act. These created new forms of further and higher education, a whole new set of higher education institutions, subject to new forms of management and quality assurance mechanisms. Similarly they introduced the market mechanism into early childhood education, such as through pilot schemes of education vouchers.

The New Labour administrations have gone much further than the Conservatives in developing private enterprise and choice mechanisms within all of these areas. First they have renamed education outside of compulsory schooling as 'lifelong learning' and developed a whole raft of policies for those deemed to be socially excluded. Whilst abolishing voucher schemes for nursery education, their strategies include Sure Start for mothers with young children, linked with area-based strategies such as EAZs and those for inner cities such as Excellence in Cities. Secondly, they have built upon but modified the findings of the 1997 Kennedy Report on further education and created, through the Learning and Skills Act of 2000, a range of forms of post-16 lifelong learning in various types of institution, subject to central control, inspection and quality assurance. Thirdly and perhaps most importantly, higher education has been subject to major reforms and transformations. In particular, in 1997, in response to the Dearing Committee's report entitled *Higher Education in the Learning Society* they abolished student financial support and inaugurated a system of fees for attendance in higher education. The Teaching and Higher Education Act of 1998 was the basis for further forms of privatization of higher education, and the extension of more detailed forms of quality assurance and enhancement. This went much further than the previous Conservative administration in transforming higher education towards a business model.

Education and Social Changes: Evidence About Equity

As the Social Exclusion Unit's first annual report noted, there have been profound education, family and social changes over the last fifty years. One of the key purposes of education policy and social reforms has been to direct these changes and monitor the developments through research evidence. For the first 35 years after the Second World War there was a bipartisan commitment to economic growth and equality of opportunity through the welfare state. Most of the accumulated social research evidence would suggest only limited achievements in reducing social class divisions and differences through education particularly on the basis of parental privilege or parental poverty. Subsequently, there has been a bipartisan commitment to economic competitiveness in a global and international market through education and training for jobs and paid work, rather than social welfare. The accumulating social evidence here is that social divisions and distinctions on the basis of economic, ethnic and cultural differences in family circumstances has indeed grown.

However, a key transformation has been in the education, economic and familial fates of women compared to men. A major study by Arnot, David and Weiner in 1999 attempted to elaborate and account for these changes in men and women's education and family lives and what has been called 'the closing of the gender gap'. It attributed the changes to social movements

such as the women's movement and feminism from the 1970s as well as to education and social policies. It concluded that:

The break with the principles of gender differentiation which were embedded in the development of mass schooling came about through a complexity of social forces. The tensions between the various value messages were augmented by complex social changes later inscribed in social democratic and New right reforms of the education system…The risk of dissolving the conventional family form for the maintenance of social order is great. Retaining a sense of continuity with the past is the function of school systems, since schooling contributes to the moral order as well as catering to the vicissitudes of the occupational structure. But in the UK, schooling appears to have broken with the traditions of the gender order. It is this decisive break with the social and educational past that lies behind the closing of the gender gap.

In conclusion, it can be argued that diversity remains the hallmark of education policies, albeit that the rougher edges of choice strategies in global markets have been modified by strategies to deal with social exclusion through new forms of education for paid work for men and women alike whatever their social, cultural, economic and familial circumstances. However, even these post-welfare policies for the new knowledge economy may not succeed in providing 'opportunities for all' because of massive social changes and global economic transformations. Most importantly transformations in education and knowledge have contributed to social, familial and gender changes and the ways in which we now study and understand these shifts. The recent evidence from a diversity of studies has demonstrated enduring social divisions despite the fact that policy developments have allowed for the growth of a mass system of early childhood, further and higher education and new forms of knowledge and learning. Yet these are no longer the concerns of policy-makers in the global knowledge economy.

Guide to further reading

The subject of education policy is of concern not only to social policy analysts but also to students of sociology and educational studies. There are several texts which explore research on particular policy changes in an international context, some key ones here being:

Apple, M. W., 2001. *Educating the 'Right' Way: Markets, Standards, God and Inequality.* (London: Routledge/Falmer).

Arnot, M., David, M.E. and Weiner, G., 1999. *Closing the Gender Gap: Post War Education and Social Change* (Cambridge: Polity Press).

Ball, S.J.. Maguire, M. and Macrae, S., 2000. *Choice, Pathways and Transitions Post-16: New Youth, New Economies in the Global City* (London: Routledge/Falmer).

Mortimore, P., 1998. *The Road to Improvement: Reflections on School Effectiveness* (Lisse, the Netherlands: Swets & Zeitlinger).

An excellent book which explores education changes in their political, social and economic contexts is S. Tomlinson *Education in a Post-welfare Society* (Buckingham: Open University Press, 2001).

There are also government publications which provide useful reading, in particular here the reports of the Social Exclusion Unit, namely *The Changing Welfare State: Opportunity for All: Tackling Poverty and Social Exclusion* (first annual report, Cm 4445, London: Stationery Office, September 1999); *Teenage Pregnancy* (Cm 4342. London: Stationery Office June 1999); and the White Paper *Schools Achieving Success* (Cm 5230, London: Stationery Office, 1999).

Numerous journals may be looked at for commentaries on education, the key ones being the *Journal of Educational Policy, British Educational Research Journal, British Journal of Sociology of Education, Education and Social Justice, Gender and Education* and *Journal of Social Policy*.

IV.11
Housing

Alan Murie

Introduction

Housing has formed a central part in debates about social problems and social policy. Images of affluence and deprivation, status and social standing, and issues of segregation and stigmatization, social exclusion and community integration are all strongly associated with housing. At the same time, housing forms the focus for family life. It is the place of residence, the home and place for homemaking, and can represent a significant source and store of wealth.

Housing involves the market, the state and the voluntary sector and processes of production, exchange, ownership and control. Unlike some areas of social policy, housing has never been a state monopoly, but there have been dramatic shifts in policy and the role of the state. Private ownership and provision has remained dominant throughout, but the form of provision has changed. The private sector has been involved in the production of state and state subsidized housing and the state is involved in the regulation and financing of private housing.

In Britain responses to the housing problems of the present century involved a significant role for the state. Council housing has been important in the general improvement of housing conditions and has had a marked impact on cities and towns. As policy has changed in recent years, the role of local government and local control over housing has declined. There has been significant centralization of policy. At the same time privatization has reduced the direct influence of the state over the housing sector.

The Historical Legacy

Accounts of the development of modern housing policy in Britain refer to the problems of nineteenth-century industrialization. They refer to reforms designed to control threats to the health of the whole population. Public health measures introduced in a market dominated by private landlordism had an impact upon the poor quality of the built environment but also made private investment in housing less attractive than in other sectors of the economy. The attempts to meet housing needs through philanthropic effort were insufficient, and before the outbreak of the First World War there was pressure to develop a new housing policy. There were proposals to introduce subsidies to enable local authorities to build affordable housing for working-class families. The effects of the First World War, including rent controls introduced to prevent exploitation of the wartime situation, and the post-war pledge to provide homes fit for heroes to live in, added to the case for a new policy. Against this background the key development in state housing policy was the introduction, in 1919, of Exchequer subsidies for council housing. From this date, and for the next sixty years, local authorities developed a key role in the provision of council housing. At the same time the private rented sector declined and private provision switched towards individual home ownership – initially among the more affluent sections of the community. The long-term decline of private renting was speeded by the reintroduction of rent control during the Second World War and by the process of slum clearance. Furthermore, as more affluent groups (influenced by a favourable financial environment) moved into home ownership, and as a high quality council rented sector developed, the rent levels that people were able and prepared to pay for properties which were not subject to rent control were not sufficient to make investment in rented housing an attractive option.

In the period 1919–79 local authority housing and owner occupation grew alongside one another. Following 1979, the restrictions on local authority house building combined with policies to sell council housing meant that the owner-occupied sector alone was a sector of expansion. The modernization of housing tenure led to a significant improvement in house conditions. New building, slum clearance and house improvement, combined with changes in household composition and affluence, created a very different housing environment.

Key Phases of Policy

In the period since 1919 there have been a number of different periods of policy. Continuities in policy were broken by the Second World War, with limited new building and the destruction of housing. In the period immediately following 1945 the emphasis upon the production of state housing was greater than at any other stage. Leaving aside this period, governments consistently encouraged home ownership and largely neglected private renting. Policies towards council housing were less consistent. In both the inter-war years and the post-war period policy shifted between general needs building and slum clearance rehousing. The high-quality, high-cost council housing built immediately after 1945 was associated with meeting general needs. The subsequent phases of policy included periods with an emphasis upon slum clearance rehousing and periods in which the council house building programme had a more limited role alongside house improvement programmes. In the period since 1979, the government's view has not favoured significant new building by local authorities and in the period after 1988 housing associations were the preferred vehicle for new social rented housing. The council housing stock declined in size as a result of the sale of properties, both to individual tenants and to alternative landlords in the form of housing associations. Some local authorities have transferred the whole of their housing stock to new housing associations and the fragmentation of control has increased, with the strategic or enabling role of local government replacing its role as direct provider.

In the more recent phases of policy, attitudes have been influenced by the view that the housing problem had largely been solved. The key agenda was no longer about providing housing and improving the quality of the housing stock but was on meeting aspirations about ownership and control. This focus fitted strongly with the Conservative Party's adoption of the idea of a property owning democracy and with the dominant concerns about reducing taxation and public expenditure in the period after 1976. Housing proved a valuable resource to Chancellors of the Exchequer. Not only could public expenditure on the formal housing programme be cut and the housing programme contribute in this way to Treasury objectives but the privatization of council housing could actually yield cash receipts which more actively helped in achieving these objectives. In terms of the generation of capital receipts, the sale of council houses has proved the single most significant part of government's privatization programme since 1979.

Tenure Changes

The policy developments described above have been associated with significant changes in tenure (table IV.10.1). Britain has moved from a nation of private tenants to a nation of home owners, with a transitional period in between in which a much more mixed tenure structure existed. These national figures obscure enormous local differences, with some localities dominated by public provision and others with little alternative to home ownership.

As tenures have grown or declined, so their nature and characteristics have changed. The private rented sector became a dilapidated sector housing a residual population of elderly long-term tenants and a more mixed, transient population using other parts of the stock. The home ownership sector and the council housing sector, which both developed in the 1920s catering for young families, have changed and diverged. The home ownership sector remains one which caters significantly for the most affluent sections of the population but has become differentiated. It also includes groups of very poor households, including the elderly and those who have experienced unemployment or other crises. It is also a sector marked by enormous differences in value and desirability – from luxurious rural and suburban mansions to inner-city housing, ill maintained before transfer from private landlords and ill maintained subsequently. The council housing sector now caters more exclusively for low-income groups. However, they are no longer predominantly families with children as they were in the early years of the tenure. Instead they include elderly persons, young lone parent households and those with long-term illnesses and disabilities. This pattern of change has been referred to as the residualization of council housing – the tendency for the poorest sections of the population to become more concentrated in council housing. It applies to the council sector as a whole but is most marked in certain parts of it. The pattern of tenure change and social change, the exercise of choice, the rationing of access and the allocation of council housing have tended to leave those

Table IV.11.1 Housing tenure in Great Britain, 1914–94 (percentages of all households)

	Public rented	Owner-occupied	Private rented[a]
1914	–	10	90
1945	12	26	62
1951	18	29	53
1961	27	43	31
1969	30	49	21
1971	31	53	17
1979	32	54	14
1984	27	60	13
1989	23	65	12
1994	20	67	14

[a] Including housing associations. Before 1988 housing associations were regarded as part of the public sector but a new financial regime involving greater use of private finance was introduced in 1988, and following that associations have been regarded as part of the private sector. They currently provide 4 per cent of the dwelling stock.
Sources: Malpass and Murie (1994) and Housing and Construction Statistics.

with least bargaining power in the worst or the least desirable housing.

The home ownership sector, in the post-war years until 1990, was increasingly associated with accumulation. Rising property prices meant that some owner occupiers' wealth increased significantly. This situation has changed since 1990. House prices fell in real terms and a considerable number of households were left with negative equity – the value of their property had fallen and was not sufficient to cover the outstanding mortgage. Although the market generally recovered after 1995 it continued to operate with much higher levels of arrears and repossessions and problems among home owners than had been the case previously.

For council tenants the right to buy introduced in 1980 enabled transfer of some two million dwellings out of a total of 6.5 million to home ownership on favourable terms. This transferred the advantages of home ownership but also exposed former council tenants to the risks associated with home ownership.

Homelessness

Debates about changes in tenure and the tenure structure focus upon households in housing. However, a key element of the debate about housing policy has always related to those who are not in housing or are in inadequate housing. In Britain the term 'homelessness' is usually associated with a legislative category which does not include all of those who are inadequately housed and in that sense are without an adequate home. At the same time it includes more than simply those who are without a roof over their heads. Research on homelessness in Britain has always identified the key role of the housing market in determining homelessness and the risks faced by ordinary families of becoming homeless because of the operation of that market.

The statistics on homelessness which relate to the legislative category 'the home-less' showed a considerable increase in homelessness since the late 1970s. It is generally accepted that this is associated with changes in the housing market and shortages of both social rented housing and affordable private rented housing. At the same time the pattern has been exacerbated by demographic trends, changes in the benefit system and changes in employment. Greater social inequality has resulted in a greater number of people being exposed to homelessness in Britain. More recent action to address homelessness has reduced the level of official homelessness and targeted rough sleeping with some success.

Housing in the Welfare State

Tenure restructuring in Britain has been associated with changes in the system of housing finance, taxation and subsidy. Rent control represented a form of subsidy to private tenants, protecting them from market prices. Subsidized council housing has involved a redistributive transfer in favour of the council tenant. The various fiscal and other supports to home ownership have involved transfers favouring the home owner. These have included tax reliefs for mortgage interest payments and capital gains. Mortgage interest tax relief involved very large sums of money, especially in periods of high house prices and high interest rates, and in general these benefited better-off households paying higher rates of tax and with larger mortgages. Only in the 1990s did changes in the system of tax relief moderate this regressive pattern.

The social division of welfare in relation to housing has not only benefited affluent groups, and the pattern of benefit in kind which council tenants have received in the form of subsidized high-quality housing has been a significant part of the redistributive structure of the welfare state. Through the 1980s the financing of council housing has changed, rents have been increased towards market levels and the system of finance has shifted from the general Exchequer subsidy system, which originated in 1919 and applied to the tenure as a whole, towards individual means-tested housing benefit. Assistance with housing costs in the council housing, housing association and private rented sectors is now provided through the social security system. Council tenants as a group no longer receive subsidy. Indeed, their rents are such as to enable a cross-subsidy towards those who are on housing benefit. The poorest tenants are subsidized by fellow tenants. Some owner-occupiers who are on income support also qualify for social security assistance, but through a different regime. Housing finance remains partitioned, with different arrangements for different tenures, and a unified system of housing finance that is tenure-neutral has not been developed.

Regeneration and Management

Council housing, when it was built, represented high-standard, desirable housing which was in great demand from households. This was particularly true of the majority of council housing, which was traditionally built houses with gardens. In some cases estates had a poor reputation from the outset and in some phases of building, especially associated with slum clearance, the quality of housing was not so high and the reputation of areas was damaged. The short-lived period in which high-rise flats were favoured as a result of government subsidy structures and the enthusiasm of professionals in local government also left an undesirable legacy in many areas. These parts of the council housing stock (and some areas outside the council sector) have increasingly become places of last resort. The concentrations of deprived households in these areas have become more apparent and problems of crime, drug abuse, unemployment and low social esteem have increased. Difficult to let, difficult to manage and difficult to live in, these estates have been the subject of important policy initiatives. These have involved local management, attempts to involve tenants in the management of areas and increased investment in dwellings, services and infrastructure. These interventions have generally had at least a short-lived positive effect but do not solve problems of deprivation, segregation and stigmatization. As social inequality has increased in Britain, so the pressures on these areas have become greater and management initiatives have been overwhelmed by changes in the economy and housing finance. The poverty trap and rising unemployment have made it more difficult for lower-income households to change their circumstances and to escape from these areas.

The response to this situation has resulted in higher rates of clearance and the emphasis in policy has shifted from management initiatives towards more holistic local regeneration policies with a strong emphasis on employment, education and training. Housing problems have become inextricably bound up with problems in the economy. The problems of lower-income households are not just housing problems but are affected by limited access to jobs and other services. Housing activity is a significant part of economic activity and has a major role in regeneration.

The Contemporary Housing Situation

In the mid-1970s it was widely argued that housing problems had been generally solved and what remained were specific, local problems which needed targeted interventions. By the mid-1990s it was difficult to retain this view of housing problems. Issues of homelessness and deprived council estates figured prominently in general images of social malaise. Social segregation and differentiation in cities was more striking than in the past and there was increasing reference to problems of racial segregation, urban crime, an underclass and patterns of inequality which are dysfunctional socially and economically. New problems were apparent in the owner-occupied sector. These were associated with the larger number of older and low-income households in the sector unable to maintain their dwellings adequately. Although the home ownership sector regained its buoyancy after the mid-1990s it can no longer be regarded as one which solves housing problems, but rather it contains its own share of them.

House condition problems have become more apparent in the local authority and the owner-occupied sectors as these age and as problems of under-investment become marked. With the continuing high level of dilapidation in the private rented sector, it is arguable that the need for clearance and replacement has re-emerged in Britain. With increased social inequality, shortages of affordable rented housing became more apparent. New concerns about the interaction between housing and health, housing and crime and housing and family life fed into emerging agendas to address social exclusion. Problems which were assumed to have been dealt with by the 1960s had been acknowleged still to exist in the late 1990s.

The deregulation of private renting and changes in the housing association sector have resulted in higher rents and fewer rights for tenants. Rooflessness and rough sleeping in British cities remained more evident than before the 1980s. Nevertheless rising employment through the 1990s and the portability of housing benefit meant that some groups had more choice especially within the rented sector. Choices between tenures exist for some households but for others there is no choice between dwellings, let alone tenures. While the housing situation has improved for the majority of households, problems within the sector have changed. Problems of the quality of housing in all tenures are evident and low demand is a major feature affecting all tenures in some regions. At the same time, housing policy has moved from a dominant and prominent position in the welfare state to a peripheral one. The emphasis in policy continues to be to dismantle the legacy of state

intervention through transfers of ownership and control. There is no longer a major programme of direct intervention in the housing sector designed to build high-quality housing for general household needs or for lower-income households, and the governance of housing is increasingly fragmented. The actions designed to raise council housing to a modern standard involve a new wave of major investment but the emphasis in policy has shifted towards relying upon the private market to make provision and providing means-tested social security support to enable people to meet the costs of housing. This recipe has not been working effectively and generates significant problems in relation to the poverty trap and work incentives.

The challenge for policy-makers is to reconstruct housing policy in a different social, economic and political context. Global issues and the competitiveness of economies prohibit the level of public sector borrowing or taxation which would be required to go back to large-scale public investment. The option favoured by successive governments has been to transfer the ownership of public housing to new organizations (local housing companies with some local authority involvement) outside the public sector and public expenditure definitions. A ten-year programme of this type and a programme to raise the standard of all social rented housing over the same period promises to further transform the housing sector by 2010. These approaches are linked to new strategies to address social exclusion and to achieve neighbourhood renewal. The search for effective housing and regeneration strategies is made more difficult by a housing finance system dependent on means testing. A return to some element of bricks and mortar subsidy in order to reduce the severity of the poverty trap would seem to be one component in a framework which could enable regeneration to be achieved.

The economic and other factors which are increasing social exclusion and segregation and affecting housing should not be underestimated. Policies which will avoid a continuing residualization and differentiation require new thinking about organizational structures, tenure relationships and systems of subsidy. Most of all they will need to be developed in conjunction with changes in the wider welfare state. The view that housing policy alone can remedy problems in the housing sector is now asserted by few people but the implications of this for what would make a difference is not so clear and it remains the case that review and reform of housing policy is an essential ingredient in strategies to reduce social problems relating to incomes, employment, health, social order and the family.

Guide to further reading

Contemporary housing policy issues are fully discussed in the journals *Housing, Housing Today, Inside Housing* and *Roof*. These provide journalistic articles, facts and figures and short critical articles on key issues. The leading academic journal in the field is *Housing Studies*. Key texts include:

Burnett, J., 1985. *A Social History of Housing 1815–1985*, 2nd edn (Newton Abbott: David and Charles). An introduction to the history of housing and the social context for changes in housing provision.

Cole, I. and Furbey, R., 1993. *The Eclipse of Council Housing* (London: Routledge). Wide-ranging discussion of the growth and decline of council housing and key policy issues related to that tenure.

Forrest, R., Murie, A. and Williams, P., 1990. *Home Ownership: Differentiation and Fragmentation* (London: Unwin Hyman). A broad discussion of the development of the home ownership sector and policies to encourage home ownership but emphasizing increasing variation within the sector.

Forrest, R. and Murie, A., 1990. *Selling the Welfare State*, 2nd edn (London: Croom Helm). Research-based account of the origins, details and consequences of policies for the sale of council housing in the UK.

Gibb, K., Munro, M. and Satsangi, M., 1999. *Housing Finance in the UK: An Introduction*, 2nd edn (Basingstoke: Macmillan Press). A clearly written description of the key policies and mechanisms of housing finance in the UK.

Hamnett, C., 1999. *Winners and Losers: Home Ownership in Modern Britain* (London: UCL Press). A discussion of key issues and inequalities associated with home ownership.

Hills, J., 1990. *Unravelling Housing Finance* (Oxford: Clarendon Press). A critical and analytic discussion of housing finance focusing on issues of efficiency and equity and with an important discussion of policy implications.

Malpass, P., 1990. *Reshaping Housing Policy* (London: Routledge). An account of the development of housing policy with a particular emphasis on the key issues of rents and central-local relations.

Malpass, P. and Means, R., 1993. *Implementing Housing Policy*. (Buckingham: Open University Press). A collection of papers on different aspects of the implementation of housing policy, focusing on implementation issues following new housing legislation in 1988.

Malpass, P. and Murie, A., 1999. *Housing Policy and Practice*, 5th edn (Basingstoke: Macmillan Press). A general introduction to housing policy in the UK with chapters on the historical development, the administrative and financial frameworks, the context for policy and key issues affecting the making, implementation and evaluation of housing policy.

Mullins, D. and Murie, A., forthcoming. *Housing Policy in Britain* (Basingstoke: Palgrave

Macmillan). The successor text to Malpass and Murie providing a wider treatment of contemporary issues and developments.

Up-to-date statistics are found in *Housing and Construction Statistics* (London: the Stationery Office) and in the annual reports and websites of the key government departments: the Department of the Environment, the Northern Ireland Office, and the Scottish and the Welsh Offices.

IV.12

The Personal Social Services and Community Care

John Baldock

The personal social services are one of the oldest but also usually one of the smallest parts of modern welfare systems. They can trace their origins to pre-industrial forms of alms- and care-giving, often organized by the church and religious orders. In the United Kingdom, by the end of the Second World War a substantial proportion of these activities had been taken over by the state. None the less, even at the start of the twenty-first century, public expenditure on what are called the personal social services is only a fraction of that spent on other major areas of state welfare. In the financial year April 2000 to March 2001, for the whole of the United Kingdom, some £12.9 billion was spent by government on these services, mainly by local authorities. While this is a great deal of money, about £198 per head of population, it is small compared with expenditure on education (£905), health (£879) or social security (£1,953).

There is a residual quality to the personal social services. Their responsibilities can sometimes appear to be a ragbag of disparate social rescue activities left over from the other parts of the welfare system. They have been called 'the fifth social service': seen as last not only in terms of size but also in terms of resort; the service people turn to when all else has failed. Yet it is this residual quality that makes them perhaps the most complex and fascinating of the social services. In order to understand the personal social services one has to come to

grips with many of the key issues of social policy: technical problems to do with organization, effectiveness and efficiency; and moral and political dilemmas to do with need and entitlement, rationing and fairness, dependency and autonomy. These are also essentially the most human of the public services; concerned with how individuals cope with a great variety of difficulties that life can throw at them. They may sometimes have to function as the nearest thing to a public substitute for the family. For example, local authorities are having to deal with a growing number of asylum seekers, including amongst them 'unaccompanied children', effectively waifs and orphans, a social need as old as humanity itself. The personal social services lie at the heart of what we, as citizens, can do and are prepared to do to help each other, and ourselves, in adversity.

Responsibilities and Organization

In industrial societies the main functions associated with the personal social services are: the care and protection of children who are at risk of harm or neglect or whose behaviour is beyond the sole control of their families; helping to organize and sometimes provide care and support for elderly people and others whose disabilities or illnesses mean they cannot manage on their own (these can include the younger physically disabled, people suffering from a mental illness, people with learning difficulties and people with chronic illness such as AIDS/HIV); supporting those who have been excluded by the wider society, such as the homeless, travellers, migrants and refugees; and assisting drug users and alcoholics. The help that is offered to these people is often called social work, and social workers are at the centre of the public image of the personal social services. However, in the United Kingdom, for example, in 2000 social workers accounted for only 20 per cent of the employees of the local authority social services; there is much other work carried out by residential and daycare staff (40 per cent) and by domiciliary workers (25 per cent) who provide help in people's homes.

The particular ways in which these functions are financed, organized and delivered vary considerably between even quite similar industrial nations, such as those of the European Union. There are also wide regional and local variations within countries. For example, in Britain levels of expenditure vary substantially between authorities, as do the mix of services they provide. One's chances of obtaining social services help can depend very much upon where one lives and whether the local authority has developed the sort of service one wants. Central government allocates money for social services to local authorities on the basis of standard spending assessments (SSAs) which are designed to reflect the relative costs of their providing equivalent provision while also taking account of the age structure of local populations and levels of deprivation. Local authorities are free to allocate the money according to political priorities and to supplement it from local taxes. In 2000–2001 Haringey spent 23 per cent less than its assessed budget of £184 per head while Kingston upon Thames spent 30 per cent more than its allocation of £156. The authority with the highest assessed expenditure was Tower Hamlets in London at £407 per head, which was in fact what it spent.

This chapter concentrates on the personal social services in the United Kingdom. While the details may be different in other industrial societies, the essential choices and problems are fairly universal. In Britain the term 'the personal social services' is generally used to refer to the work of local authority social services departments in England and Wales, of social work departments in Scotland and, in Northern Ireland, of social services staff within the health and social service boards. However, when the term first came into common usage in the second half of the 1960s, it was commonly extended to include a much wider range of provision by voluntary, charitable and private organizations that in some way sought to help people at the level of the individual or family, such as the work of the clergy, of the NSPCC (National Society for the Prevention of Cruelty to Children), of probation officers, of Relate (marriage guidance counsellors), to name a few of the huge variety of occupations and organizations providing personal help.

A Marginal and Residual Service

In principle the personal social services might become involved in almost any aspect of our lives from birth to death; in practice most people, even those with substantial social needs, will go through life with little or no contact with their local social services authority. This is because a key characteristic that marks out the public personal social services and makes them essentially different to the education or the health services, for example, is that they provide or are responsible for only a small part of personal social care in our society. Whereas the vast majority of people will turn to the NHS when they are ill and to state education for their children's schooling, it is not the case that most children with special social or physical needs, or most elderly people who need care, will receive help from their local social services. For example, in Britain at any one time a local social services department will be working with: a third of those over 85; less than 4 per cent of children in families living on benefit; less than 2 per cent of children with physical disabilities; and less than 10 per cent of those who are mentally ill and living in the community. This is not necessarily to say that the others either want help or are not getting it, but simply to emphasize that the public social services provide only a fraction of the social care needed or given. Most social care is provided by the family and, to a lesser extent, by friends and neighbours. Much of the most intensive caring, of frail elderly people, for example, is done by women.

This fact, that the state-funded personal social services provide for only a fraction of each of the wide variety of need groups they are charged with helping, is central to most of the key debates and issues which surround their work. It has meant that the services have always been open to criticism that what they are doing is partial, arbitrary, ineffective and ripe for review and change. Academic research into the effectiveness of social work interventions has rarely been able to show clear-cut benefits for those people who do receive services. This is mainly due to due a lack of clarity about social service objectives and the great variety of social and economic factors involved in achieving them. The British government now funds the Social Care Institute for Excellence (www.scie.org.uk) with the object of collecting and disseminating evidence of those interventions that work best. The marginal character of the local social services also means that in almost all their work success does not depend entirely or even mostly on what they achieve. In order to succeed in their goals they must work with a wide range of other services and agencies: statutory services such as general practitioners, hospital specialists, community nurses, housing and education departments as well as other members of families, neighbours, volunteers and voluntary organizations, the churches and, increasingly, private, profit-seeking care agencies.

Over more than the last half-century the greatest public attention has been paid to local social services when young children for whom they were legally responsible have come to harm (see chapter IV.1). Almost always the inquiries that follow these tragedies show that where children have been hurt or even killed by their parents or guardians, local social workers have failed adequately to monitor and co-ordinate the work and knowledge of all the many agencies and professionals who had some contact with the child.

A History of Frequent Reorganizations but Steady Growth

The British local authority social services have been subject to frequent and radical reorganizations. This does not reflect a high political profile and public interest but rather that users of social services are a transient sample of the poorest and least powerful and that politicians feel relatively free to impose new structures or models of working which reflect their particular perceptions of the problems and their solutions.

The public personal social services emerged from the whirlwind of post-1945 welfare legislation largely in the form of two distinct local authority departments: the specialist children's departments and the health and welfare departments, which dealt with adult users. In 1971 these were amalgamated, following recommendations of the Seebohm Report, within a single, generic social services department whose object was initially to provide one source of help – 'a single door' – to which all citizens in social need could turn. This was to be a bold and ambitious solution to the residual quality of the services, gradually turning them into a source of help that would be used by all classes – the social service equivalent of the NHS.

Only three years later, the 1974 reorganization of local government created a fresh round of new, often larger social services departments. In the late 1970s and early

1980s some departments further restructured themselves, devolving as much responsibility as possible to neighbourhood teams which would seek to redress their marginality by integrating their work into the life of local communities. In the mid-1990s social services departments experienced yet another round of reorganization with the creation of new unitary local government authorities following the work of the Local Government Commission in England and the even more radical changes legislated for Scotland and Wales. On 1 April 1996 Scotland replaced its 12 regional councils, each of which had a social work department, with 32 new unitary authorities. In Wales the eight counties together with their social services departments were abolished to create 22 new unitary authorities. In England the reorganization was less comprehensive, most of the counties surviving and losing only parts of their territory to the 47 unitary authorities created between 1996 and 1998, mainly in highly urbanized areas.

Many local authorities took the opportunity of the boundary changes to review the structure of their services and in more than a third of English authorities the traditional social services department no longer exists. Social services have often been merged with housing responsibilities and sometimes provision for children has been separated from that for adults by linking it with education.

The Health Act 1999, which came into effect on 1 April 2000, places a duty on local authorities and the health service to deliver relevant services in partnership and provided the legal basis for one side to take a lead in organizing both social and health care for a particular group, such as older people or those with mental illnesses. By 2001 the Department of Health had reported 61 projects, spending over £800 million through pooled funding arrangements. In a few cases health and social care budgets have been merged into single health and social care trusts. However, a key problem that still remains, particularly in England

and less so in Scotland, Wales and Northern Ireland, is that local authority boundaries are not coterminous with those of the health services. General practitioner services are generally organized into Primary Care Trusts with quite different territories based on practice populations. The NHS Regions overlap local authorities; Cumbria, for example, having to deal with two separate regional NHS offices and their distinct policies.

In the first five years after 1971 the new Seebohm departments grew fast, sometimes by more than 10 per cent a year. However, over the longer term, constraints on public expenditure from the mid-1970s have meant that service provision have never able to do more than match the growth of numbers in the relevant user groups, particularly of elderly and disabled people living in the community rather than in institutions. These numbers have been further increased as the NHS has run down its long-term care provision. None the less, the overall picture of the post-war growth of the personal social services, measured in both money and staff numbers, has been of steady increases averaging some 3–4 per cent a year in real terms. While there have been exceptions in some years and in some authorities (sharp cuts in real expenditure are not unknown), this is a record unmatched by any other of the major social services.

The Community Care Revolution

After 1979 the Conservative governments of Mrs Thatcher and John Major enacted more than fifty pieces of legislation that greatly changed and added to the responsibilities of the local authority personal social services. The most important were the National Health Service and Community Care Act 1990 and the Children Act 1989. Many of these new policies and systems came into effect in the five years from April 1991 and even in official documents they are frequently described as amounting to 'a revolution' or 'a sea change in the planning and delivery of services'.

The policies driving these changes were often portrayed as distinctly a product of the Conservative Right and its preference for private provision and market mechanisms. However, at the core of the reforms were two ideas as old as social work itself: that care in the community is to be preferred to care in institutions; and that prevention is better social work than rescuing social casualties.

The idea of community care has been a central post-war theme, to be found, irrespective of the government in power, in almost all the major inquiries and reports of the past fifty years. It essentially means that public support should not take place in institutions such as children's homes, special schools and communities, or in residential and nursing homes and long-stay hospitals, but rather that, whenever possible, care should be encouraged in people's own homes, or in foster homes, and that support should be family- and community-based. Similarly, the principle of prevention, particularly in social work with children and their families, is to be found at the heart of all the key post-war legislation, in particular the Children's and Young Persons' Acts of the 1960s, which emphasized preventing the need for children to come into local authority care (see chapter IV.1 for more discussion of this).

What was radical about the new community care policies was that local authorities were required to focus less on direct service provision and more on the enablement of social care by the private, voluntary and informal sectors. Over the last ten years social services departments have become 'minority providers within a mixed economy of independent care agencies'. In 2002 only a third of staff providing publicly funded social care were directly employed by local authorities. The remainder worked either for the for-profit or the voluntary sectors.

Most social care is now provided on the basis of a means test. Whereas in the 1960s the goal of the social work profession, set out in the Seebohm Report, was that the personal social services should become a system of universal, tax-funded provision, today only the very poorest are likely to have their care paid for. In 2002, 25 per cent of expenditure on home care support for older people was recouped through charges. Issues to do with the organization and fairness of fees and charges have become important.

Modernization and Regulation

The activities of local social services are monitored by the Department of Health's Social Service Inspectorate and its equivalents within the Welsh and Scottish Offices and in Northern Ireland. Many of their publications are free and report on inspections by teams that include lay members of the public and service users. The inspections tackle and report on consumer issues that have traditionally received little more than lip service, such as equal opportunities and sensitivity to issues of gender and ethnicity. In 1996 the Inspectorate began a series of reviews, conducted jointly with the Audit Commission, to discover and measure outcomes for users. The reviews have revealed considerable variations in the quality of services funded and supplied by local authorities and wide differences in the costs which are not reflected in outcomes. For example, the overall summary of the reviews of children's services in England and Wales up to 1998 observed that 'variation in performance within and between councils is marked and some aspects are not safe'. The report concluded that services 'not only have to improve, . . . they have to be transformed' (Social Services Inspectorate/Audit Commission, *Getting the Best from Children's Services: Findings from Joint Reviews of Social Services, 1998/9*, Abingdon: Audit Commission Publications, 1999).

As a result, the main focus of the New Labour governments since 1997 has been on what is called its 'modernization agenda' for the personal social services. In a series of white papers and other initiatives the government has set in place a tight regulatory framework that requires local authorities to define targets for their social services and to produce performance data that measure how far they are meeting them in comparison with other councils. The main components of the modernization agenda are:

- the five yearly reviews of councils' social care provision conducted by the Social Services Inspectorate (www.doh.gov.uk/scg/socinsp) and the Audit Commission(www.audit-commission.gov.uk/itc/) which can and do lead to aspects of provision being subject to 'special measures' requiring them to demonstrate improvements or risk having their provision taken over by external managers;
- the 'Best Value Process' (www.local-regions.detr.gov.uk/bestvalue/bvindex.htm) which from April 2000 has required councils to show, through published plans, that services are delivered to clear standards of cost and quality and by the most effective economic and efficient means;
- the Performance Assessment Framework (PAF) which requires councils to publish results against 50 performance indictors (see www.doh.gov.uk/scg/pssperform);
- the 'Quality Protects' circulars which require councils to submit action plans indicting how they will achieve eight national objectives for children's services (www.doh.gov.uk/qualityprotects/index.htm). These must be submitted before substantial ring-fenced funds are received by local authorities;
- the National Services Framework for Older People (http://www.doh.gov.uk/nsf/older people.htm) published in 2001 which sets out a ten year plan of service targets to be achieved by local authorities and the health service in the provision of coordinated services for older people. This will include a 'single assessment process' from April 2002 which will mean older people are not repeatedly and separately assessed by different parts of the health and social care services;
- the National Care Standards Commission (www.doh.gov.uk/ncsc/) which from April 2002 has registered, regulated and inspected care in private hospitals, children's and other care homes, monitored fostering and social care provided to people in their own homes as well as maintaining lists of people unsuitable for work with children and adults;
- the General Social Care Council (www.doh.gov.uk/gscc/) which registers qualified social workers and regulates training for the social care workforce. In 2002 the council issued codes of conduct for social care workers and employers and from 2003 it will oversee the replacement of the Diploma in Social Work with degree-level qualifications in social work;
- the Long Term Care Charters, 'Better Care, Higher Standards' which require local authorities and health services to agree and make public standards they will fulfill in key areas such as the provision of information to users and carers and the meeting of needs (http://www.doh.gov.uk/longtermcare/);
- the Disability Rights Commission (www.drc.org.uk/drc/default.asp) which from April 2000 has monitored and encouraged non-discriminatory good practice in the delivery of services;
- a substantial body of legislation passed between 1998 and 2002 (The Children Leaving Care Act, The Carers and Disabled Children Act, The Protection of Children Act, The Health Act and the Human Rights Act) which provide specific rights to users of services that local councils and others must abide by

Together these aspects of the modernization agenda amount to a revolution in the way the personal social services are managed. They are transforming a social care system that for most of the post-war period was governed by trust and unregulated professional standards and which provided only discretionary entitlements to users. What is now in place is a system of specific duties and targets for social care providers and, to a degree, explicit rights and obligations for users and carers.

The Consumer Experience of Community Care

In the case of children and younger adults who have physical disabilities or learning difficulties, or who suffer from mental illness, community care has become a reality in the limited sense that hardly any of these groups are now living in the large, impersonal and often isolated institutions that could still be found well into the 1970s. What is less clear is that the families and informal carers who now provide most care are getting adequate support. For example, services for children and families consume more than half of social worker time and nearly 26 per cent of departmental resources. This is very expensive work, since the number of children involved at any one time in the United Kingdom is less than 100,000, about 65 per cent of whom will be in foster homes, 10 per cent in children's homes (run by the local authorities or by voluntary bodies or profit-seeking firms) and the remainder at home. In 2001 the average cost of caring for children in all forms of placement was £350 a week.

However, the second core goal, that of prevention, remains elusive. The central aim of the Children Act 1989 was that social workers should work in partnership with families, proactively providing preventive services on the basis of needs and individual care plans, rather than responding mainly when some emergency or risk arises. The Social Services Inspectorate has published a series of reports which show that while progress has been made, most resources are still going on children on Child Protection Registers (about 50 per cent of cases), and cases where no immediate risk is expected are rarely, and usually inadequately, reviewed.

For the elderly, who are the fastest-growing category of people who need care, deinstitutionalization has been less successful. The longstay geriatric wards in NHS hospitals have all but disappeared, but the proportion of people over 75 who are in residential care or nursing homes has not fallen during the past three decades. However, the withdrawal of the social services departments from direct provision is taking place quickly. Fewer than 13 per cent of the 600,000 institutional places in the UK in 2000 were publicly provided; private and voluntary provision now predominates. The same is happening in the case of domiciliary services. By 1998 the independent sector (voluntary and for-profit organizations) provided 46 per cent of local authority purchases of homecare help and government policy intends this figure to rise to over 80 per cent.

Services are also more tightly targeted on those elderly people judged to have the greatest needs. The 1990 Community Care Act requires authorities to carry out needs-based assessments and these, though very time-consuming, have led to sharp reductions in the numbers of people who are then defined as eligible for local authority funded help. The number of households receiving homecare fell by over 13 per cent between 1994 and 1999. However, those receiving help are getting more hours. This is part of a trend that has led, in some parts of the country, to the withdrawal of domiciliary services from people who had got used to receiving them.

As in the case of children's services, the Social Service Inspectorate has been monitoring the effects on users of the changes in community care. While most users are reasonably satisfied, many of the problems the new assessment-based system was designed to remedy continue: users do not feel involved in their assessments; there is insufficient monitoring of provision by private suppliers; and coordination between social services and the NHS, particularly over hospital discharges, remains haphazard and continues to be a source of 'bed-blocking' by older people in acute hospital wards.

Conclusion

The publicly funded personal social services consume only slightly more than 1 per cent of the national product. At any one time they impinge little on the lives of the vast majority of the population. Yet they are utterly relevant to the lives of the poorest and most disadvantaged in our society: vulnerable children, disabled adults and frail old people. During the 1990s the financing and delivery of these services was radically transformed, with most provision transferred to the independent and voluntary sectors. In the first years of the twenty first century the 'modernization agenda' is leading to the disappearance of the Seebohm social services departments and their replacement with a greater variety of structures for the delivery of social care.

Guide to further reading

The pace of change means that textbooks are quickly out of date. The best currently available are Michael Hill (ed.) *Local Authority Social Services* (Oxford: Blackwell, 2000); Lester Parrott *Social Work and Social Care* 2nd edition (London: Routledge, 2002); David Denney *Social Policy and Social Work* (Oxford: Oxford University Press, 1998); Robert Adams *The Personal Social Services, Clients, Consumers or Citizens?* (Harlow: Longman, 1996). The most important sources for students are now available online and the best starting point is the web page of the Social Care Group (http://www.doh.gov.uk/scg/grpinfo.htm). A regular reading of the weekly professional journal *Community Care* is the best way of keeping up issues that affect social workers. The annual reports of the Chief Inspector of Social Services (available online at http://www.doh.gov.uk/scg/ssi.htm) provide comprehensive reviews and a rich source of references, but beware of the failure ever to mention poverty. Eileen Younghusband *The Newest Profession: A Short History of Social Work* (London: IPC Business Press, 1981), remains a classic history; and Maureen Oswin *The Empty Hours: A Study of the Week-end Life of Handicapped Children in Institutions* (London: Allen Lane Penguin Press, 1971) is a moving account of an institutional world that is fortunately gone. Margaret Forster *The Battle for Christabel* (Harmondsworth: Penguin,1992), and *Have the Men Had Enough?* (Harmondsworth: Penguin, 1990), are moving and beautifully written accounts of what care in the community mostly amounts to.

IV.13
Criminal Justice

Dee Cook

Introduction

The very abstract concept of 'justice' is often portrayed, in physical and sculptured form, as a blindfolded woman. This signifies the truly objective quality of justice which is meant to apply equally to all people, regardless of their age, gender, ethnicity and 'race', (dis)ability, wealth, employment status (or its lack) and home address. But there is much evidence that criminal justice in Britain is very far from 'blind' to these kinds of individualized factors, and that social inequalities along these lines permeate the workings of our criminal justice system. Put very simply, some criminologists argue that, in contemporary Britain, the criminal law is still predominantly imposed by the advantaged classes on the disadvantaged; by the old on the young; by whites on those from minority ethnic groups; and by men on women.

The purposes of this chapter are, firstly, to offer an introduction to the criminal justice system and its operation in twenty-first century Britain; secondly, to show how criminal justice and social policies have increasingly become entwined since the election of the Blair 'New Labour' government in 1997; and thirdly, to argue that the concepts of *social justice* and *criminal justice* are inextricably linked – as are the range of policies which are geared towards making them real.

What is 'the criminal justice system' and how does it operate?

The criminal justice system consists of:

- police;
- prosecutors;
- courts;
- prison;
- probation and social work services for offenders;
- compensation, victim and witness services.

The criminal justice system in England and Wales differs from that in Scotland, reflecting long-standing historical and legal differences. Taken together, these bodies share common aims and objectives, summarized as:

- reducing crime and the fear and costs of crime;
- dispensing justice fairly, thereby enhancing confidence in the rule of law.

(See www.homeoffice.gov.uk/rds/cjschap1.html.)

But the extent to which the criminal justice system can meet these overarching aims is limited by the extent and shape of broader structural and social inequalities. Crime and victimization has long been associated with a range of other negative social indicators including poor housing and transport, ill-health, lack of educational achievement, environmental decay and unemployment. In this respect, crime is often represented as both a *symptom* and a *cause* of many of these negative features – it is part and parcel of a limited 'quality of life' in poorer neighbourhoods, and at the same time represented as part of the cause of their spiralling decline.

The criminal justice system's aim of 'dispensing justice fairly' is similarly problematic because of the social factors that influence *who is policed, criminalized and punished*. The ways in which criminal justice system agencies (directly and indirectly) deploy stereotypes of crime-prone individuals, families, localities and ethnic groups can lead to patterns of policing and punishment which may undermine confidence in the fairness of the rule of law itself. For example, if policing resources are targeted on individuals, groups and localities which the police define as 'a problem' then a self-fulfilling prophecy will result. While such targeting may well yield arrests,

it may also damage relations between police and communities which feel they are, in some respects, 'over policed'.

Recent surveys on the extent of confidence in the criminal justice system indicate a falling off of public confidence, particularly in the police, and this is particularly so in the case of black and minority ethnic communities. This may be partly due to bad experiences of contact with the police, particularly in relation to stop and searches (which are often seen as too frequent and intrusive) and police responses to reports of racial harassment (which are often perceived as inadequate). Lack of confidence may also be partly due to low recruitment of minority ethnic officers: of the 125,000 police officers in post in England and Wales in 2001, only 2.5 per cent were from minority ethnic groups, although they constitute around 7 per cent of the general population. (However, black and minority ethnic groups were more than three times over-represented in prison, constituting 22

Table IV.13.1 Issues shaping criminal justice decisions (for 'white-collar' and 'traditional' offenders)

Sphere of decision making	*Decisive issues*
Policing and regulation	• Visibility of the crime • Perceived seriousness of the crime • Availability and targeting of investigation
Resources	• The 'letter of the law', evidence and proof • Extent of police/regulators' powers • Policing/regulation strategy: compliance or prosecution policy?
Prosecution and sentencing	• Crime seriousness • Ability to 'pay' for crime (or private justice?) • Access to legal advice and representation • Cautioning, bail and remand decisions • Positive or negative economic, social and family indicators • Previous convictions (or 'good character') • Judgements about the offender's 'threat' to society.

Source: adapted from D. Cook, *Poverty, Crime and Punishment*, London: CPAG, 1997.

per cent of the 66,000 prison population in 2001).

If the criminal justice system is visualized as a huge filter, then the ways in which it operates may serve to *filter in* certain individuals and groups, while it *filters out* others. 'White collar' offences can be defined as those committed by people of relatively high status in the course of their occupation and so include, for instance, fraud, embezzlement, tax evasion and corporate crimes involving health and safety violations and pollution. If we compare the ways in which these offences are treated with 'traditional' offenders (including 'street crime', assaults, theft and handling stolen goods, burglaries etc), there are a range of factors which prove decisive in filtering *the traditional offender in*, and the *white-collar offender out*, of the criminal justice system. These are summarized in Table IV.13.1 above.

Policing and regulating crime depends upon what is, and what is not, defined as criminal ('the letter of the law'); what is and what is not seen as a serious offence; how heavy the burden of proof is in a criminal case; how easy (or not) it is to obtain evidence and secure a conviction; and the investigatory resources available. Laws regulating business conduct (which often determine the basis of white-collar offences) tend to be complex and demanding. Getting sufficient evidence and proof to proceed into the criminal justice system arena is extremely difficult and, even if they were to come to court, trials are lengthy and costly and jurors may fail to understand all the evidence.

As a result, regulators often opt for securing the 'compliance' of offenders in future rather than seeking to prosecute them. White-collar offences are largely 'invisible', are committed in private business settings and are (wrongly) seen as 'victimless' and therefore less threatening. In any event, most non-police agencies regulating such offences – for instance, the Inland Revenue, Health and Safety Executive, Customs and Excise, Serious Fraud Office – are poorly resourced and over-stretched. Also, when

businesses themselves detect white-collar offences, they often seek redress from the offender through 'private justice' and the criminal justice system is not involved at all. (In extreme cases, as in the case of some banking frauds, the offender has been re-hired as a security consultant.)

By contrast, poorer 'traditional' offenders are filtered in to the criminal justice system through a parallel range of decisions, with very different outcomes: they are less likely to be able to pay for their crimes privately; they do not have access to the best legal counsel; where middle-class offenders are often seen to have 'suffered enough' through the stigma of being taken to court, the unemployed, uneducated, homeless and vulnerable are seen to have 'nothing to lose' and are disproportionately likely to be refused bail, remanded in custody and sentenced to imprisonment.

Where sentencing is concerned, negative factors affecting sentencers' decisions may also be gendered and racialized, with unemployed single mothers and black and minority ethnic young men disproportionately likely to end up in the 'hard' end of the criminal justice system more quickly then their employed, married and white counterparts – and the hard end is, ultimately, imprisonment. At the same time, wide variations between the practices of different courts may lead to 'justice by geography'.

But there is much that can be improved and reformed in the criminal justice sphere. Some recent positive examples include:

- the recommendations made in the Macpherson Report into the death of Stephen Lawrence, which marked an important shift towards acknowledging institutional racism within the Metropolitan police;
- recent government-driven strategies to prioritize and address domestic violence more effectively;
- a 'restorative justice' approach being adopted to provide innovative ways of working with young offenders and their

victims (for instance, through restorative justices conferences in which offenders are encouraged to confront the consequences of their crimes by meeting victims face to face).

Nonetheless, in summary, it must be said that the cumulative results of many of the routine decisions taken within the criminal justice process (described above) is that the overall aim of the criminal justice system to 'dispense justice fairly' is far from secured in contemporary Britain.

Linkages between Criminal Justice and Social Policies

Since the election of the 'New Labour' government in 1997, the spheres of criminal justice and social policy have been brought more closely together, most notably through initiatives in challenging social exclusion and through community safety. For example, the remit of the Social Exclusion Unit in England and Wales is to:

develop integrated and sustainable approaches to the problems of the worst housing estates, including crime, drugs, unemployment, community breakdown and bad schools etc . . . [by] 'setting in motion a virtuous circle of regeneration, with improvements in jobs, crime, education, health and housing all reinforcing each other.

(SEU, *Bringing Britain Together: A National Strategy for Neighbourhood Renewal*, CM4045, London: Stationery Office, 1998)

This remit clearly locates tackling crime in the context of the broader problem of *social exclusion* and so the policy goals of crime reduction, regeneration and neighbourhood renewal strategies are all inextricably linked. According to both the Home Office and the Social Exclusion Unit the 'fight against crime' is part and parcel of making Britain 'a better place to live'. This fight against crime is waged principally at the level of local neighbourhoods and through the operation of community safety strategies.

The 1998 Crime and Disorder Act requires all local authorities to work in partnership with local criminal justice, social services and health agencies and voluntary and community sector groups to identify and audit the problems of crime and disorder in their area. The crime audit provides the *targets* for these locally based community safety partnerships to develop strategies and monitor community progress towards them, thereby providing 'local solutions' to their identified crime and disorder problems. But there is clearly a huge variation in the scale and nature of problems faced by community safety partnerships in affluent areas and those located in the most deprived boroughs.

Within the current policy framework, then, tackling crime and its causes is seen as part of the broader aim of tackling social exclusion (while enhancing quality of life through community safety). This is in itself an important acknowledgement that the causes of crime lie beyond the boundaries of the criminal justice system itself. In a similar vein, multi-agency approaches to tackling youth offending (for example, through the work of Youth Offending Teams in England and Wales) seek to adopt a more holistic view of offenders and offending. The problem remains, how to be holistic *in practice* and to 'join up' policy where the solutions lie across departmental/resource/spatial boundaries. For example, while there is ample evidence that being 'looked after' (formerly described as being 'in care') is associated with the likelihood of offending, local authority resource constraints often mean they are unable to offer a suitable and stable environment and continuity of care and education services for looked after children to *prevent* offending effectively.

In policy terms, the crime problem is being defined by, and responses to it led by, the term *'crime and disorder'*, which is largely conceptualized as a problem of youth and social exclusion. While poverty and exclusion undoubtedly provide an important source of crime, they are by no means its only cause: moral, social, economic, individual and reflexive factors all play a part, as do calculations about risk (of detection and punishment). But without a clearer grasp of the diverse and multiple causes and forms of crime and the nature of their links (or not) with social exclusion, we cannot assume that the scattergun of anti-exclusion policies will inevitably 'hit' the causes of crime. At the same time, because community safety and social exclusion policies are driven by a very particular notion of what constitutes the problem of 'crime and disorder', they do not offer an effective means of addressing a range of other 'hidden' crimes – such as racially motivated crime, domestic violence and white-collar crimes such as fraud, pollution and tax evasion.

In addition, there are questions about the extent to which locally based community safety partnerships actually enable communities to define their own priorities for crime reduction and to enhance safety. While they aim to be inclusive and empowering for all members of local communities, critics argue that many community safety partnerships are merely 'clubs' or 'paper partnerships' which serve existing police, local authority and self-appointed 'community leaders' vested interests. In any event, there remains the central issue of how *local partnerships* (without core resources) can address the *structural factors* which underlie many of the anxieties and risks experienced by residents of the poorest neighbourhoods.

In summary, many argue that community safety strategies operate on the basis of a limited conception of the 'crime and disorder' problem; fail to address the complex root causes of crime; and instead stress the importance of *managing crime in its place* – within neighbourhoods. But place-based policies – including community safety and neighbourhood renewal strategies – are, by definition restricted in focus and are unable to address the wider structural inequalities which underlie the spatial ones.

Criminal Justice and Social Justice?

In 1993, while in opposition, Tony Blair (prime minister from 1997) pledged that a future Labour government would be 'tough on crime; and tough on the causes of crime'. In relation to punishment, they have exceeded their Conservative counterparts and presided over a record prison population (which has increased by over 200 per cent in the last decade). But what about being tough on the causes of crime? The Home Office blueprint for the next decade (entitled *'Criminal Justice: The Way Ahead'*) provides a diagram of ways in which the causes of crime are being tackled through a range of government agencies and initiatives, namely: the National Strategy for Neighbourhood Renewal; the SureStart programme (improving life chances for pre-school children); OFSTED (school inspectorate); New Deal programme; and the UK Anti-Drugs Co-ordination Unit.

This representation of the ways in which the causes of crime are to be addressed once again stresses a managerial and process driven approach. Crucially, it also demonstrates an *apparent* fusion of criminal justice and social policies – across the fields of health, education, welfare and neighbourhood renewal. While all of these dimensions of policy may well have some part to play in reducing crime over the long-term, one key aspect is missing.

Although research on the causes of crime is complex and contradictory, one message that remains fairly constant is that levels of crime in a society are related to its levels of social and economic inequality. And so while the extent of *unemployment and poverty* cannot explain levels of crime, the *gap* between the rich and the poor certainly is an important factor. A wide gap does seem to be associated with crime, which may be committed by the rich and the poor – the former because it is fostered by the ethic of wealth creation (by illicit as well as legal means) and the latter because crime may arise out of both need and a sense of frustration, injustice and having 'nothing to lose'. The implications for policy – criminal justice and social policy – seem clear, and would point to the need to reduce inequalities in income and wealth.

The political shifts marked by Thatcherism in the 1970s and Third Way politics in the 1990s signalled a profound move away from the former (socialist) goal of greater social equality and its key policy mechanism – income redistribution. The term poverty has largely been replaced by the softer focus on 'social exclusion', and the meaning of the term social justice has shifted too, as Tony Blair stated a fairly minimalist view in the wake of the 2001 election that 'public services are social justice made real'.

But in 1993 the Social Justice Commission had offered a more thorough definition of what social justice may involve. It identified the following principles.

- The foundation is the equal worth of all citizens.
- All are entitled to have their basic needs met.
- Self-respect and autonomy should be fulfilled through the widest possible spread of opportunities and life chances.
- Unjustified inequalities should be reduced and where possible eliminated.

If we return to the basic aims of the criminal justice system (outlined at the beginning of this chapter), they too depend on very similar foundations, as both have their roots in the concepts of *citizenship and legitimacy*. Without ensuring the equal worth of all citizens, mutual and self-respect and the meeting of basic needs, we cannot ensure that all have an equal stake in abiding by the law and so cannot 'dispense justice fairly' and enhance confidence in the law. In this respect criminal and social justice are inseparable.

Guide to further reading

Crawford, A., 1998. *Crime Prevention and Community Safety: Politics, Policies and Practices*. London: Longman.
Croall, H., 2001. *Understanding White-Collar Crime*. Buckingham: Open University Press.
Garland, D., 2001. *The Culture of Control: Crime and Social Order in Contemporary Society*. Oxford: Oxford University Press.
Hudson, B., 1993. *Penal Policy and Social Justice*. Basingstoke: Macmillan Press.
Matthews, R. and Pitts, J. (eds), 2001. *Crime, Disorder and Community Safety*. London: Routledge.

Part V
Resources

Studying Social Policy

V.1
Doing Projects in Social Policy

Hartley Dean

'Project' is an overworked word. It can be used to describe the simplest learning exercise or as a metaphor for the greatest of human achievements. Yet whenever the word is used, it refers to some kind of active process; to something that is performed or 'done'. This chapter is about the kind of projects which social policy students might be expected to do in order to develop and demonstrate their investigative skills; in order that they should be not the passive recipients of other people's knowledge, but the active creators of their own.

As a social policy student you might be asked to prepare and present a case study as part of the assessment within a particular module or unit; to undertake a systematic literature review as the basis for an extended essay; or to research and write a substantial dissertation as part of your degree. In this chapter we shall first discuss the essential activity – research – that is involved in doing all kinds of project. We shall then be concerned with choosing project topics, with the kind of approaches (or 'methodologies') you might use, the kind of techniques (or 'methods') that might be appropriate and the special ethical considerations that sometimes apply when you are investigating matters of social policy. Finally, we shall consider issues to do with writing up and presenting project findings.

What Is Research?

Some of the projects undertaken by social policy students involve observations, questionnaires, interviews, statistical analysis: these are the sort of technical processes which are often associated with the term 'research'. Certainly, most social policy students will at some point in their studies receive some formal training in technical research methods, and this chapter is partly intended to give you some idea of what to expect in this connection. However, it is important to emphasize that doing projects can also involve modes of inquiry and independent study which will carry you no further than the library and your own desk. Although distinctions may be drawn between 'theorizing' and 'research', any theorist of social policy must first find out about the origins, the substance and the impact of social policy, even if to do so he or she has to draw on and interpret work done by other people.

The research that is required for doing projects in social policy involves finding things out and then drawing conclusions. It entails some kind of synthesis by the student between information or 'facts' on the one hand and ideas or 'theory' on the other – that is how knowledge is produced. There is no reason why students, through their projects, should not only find out things for themselves but also make their own original contributions to knowledge, or their own recommendations for changes in policy. Box V.1.1 gives some examples of the sorts of inquiry students might typically undertake as projects. However, it illustrates no more than a tiny selection of the topics that might be appropriate, depending on your particular programme of study.

Choosing Project Topics

For some sorts of small-scale project you may be assigned a specific subject for investigation, but for most substantial project assignments or dissertations the first thing you will have to decide is what you want to study. Three things are important.

1. Choose a topic which interests you. Your project may involve many hours of work and you will need to sustain your commitment to it.

2. Your topic must be clearly focused. You will note from the selection of topics in box V.1.1 that they are all quite specific: they are addressed not to a general subject area, but to a particular question or

---

Box V.1.1

Type of project	*Examples*
Illustrative case study	a presentation to demonstrate how the concept of 'marketization' might help to understand recent developments in:

- (a) the health service;
- (b) the personal social services;
- (c) education;
- (d) housing; or
- (e) the social security system.

Extended essay	An assignment that investigates the likely outcome for a particular social group of some current legislative proposal, such as:

- altered arrangements for charging for 'personal care' in residential homes for frail elderly and disabled people;
- the introduction of the second state pension for women in part-time and/or temporary employment;
- the promotion of 'family-friendly' employment for low-income working families;
- new arrangements for regulating houses in multiple occupation for young homeless people.

Dissertation project	A project based on a small scale local investigation, but which might address the social policy implications of:

- the provision of housing for disabled people in a particular local ward;
- the physical security of women in a particular block of flats;
- the accessibility of leisure facilities to a particular minority ethnic community;
- the career destinations of 'middle' and 'working' class children from a particular local school.

problem. Some projects may be designed specifically to test a hypothesis or proposition. Others may set out to evaluate or explore the outcomes or the likely outcomes of specific policies or policy proposals. Students often start by saying, for example, 'I'd like to do something around homelessness', but they must then frame the particular question about homelessness and housing policy that they will set out to answer.

3. The topic must be 'do-able'. Although a project, especially a dissertation, may represent a substantial piece of work for you as a student, it will necessarily be conducted on a relatively small scale. It must be realistically planned and take account of the time, the resources and the opportunities which are available to you.

Additionally, you will need to take account of any specific guidelines that your institution provides and the advice of your project supervisor.

Methodology

When you choose your topic, you will also have to decide upon the conceptual approach, or 'methodology', which you will adopt. Methodology concerns the relationship between your theoretical stance and the manner in which you carry out your investigation. Students of social policy are introduced to questions of methodology in a variety of ways: sometimes formally as part of a 'research methods' module or unit; sometimes in the course of studying the philosophy of social science. Most projects in social policy do not fit neatly into any one methodological category or 'paradigm', but generally speaking you will need to be aware of three broad schools of thought.

- *'Hard' or empiricist approaches.* All project work involves the use of empirical evidence, but what is called empiric*ism* is an approach to evidence that is aligned to the conventions associated with the natural sciences. It is concerned to explain external realities from an objective standpoint. It tends to deal in processes of quantitative measurement.

- *'Soft' or interpretive approaches.* In fact, these are no less rigorous in their use of evidence than empiricist approaches, but interpretivism is a stance that characterizes a major strand within the *social* sciences. It is concerned to understand the nature or meaning of the social world from the subjective standpoint of the people involved. It tends to deal in processes of qualitative observation.

- *Critical approaches.* Any theoretical stance can result in criticism of social policy, but a critical approach to the use of evidence is one that is grounded in the analysis of social conflict or relationships of power (for example, Marxism, feminism, anti-racism or such movements as post-structuralism). A critical approach may draw on elements of either or both the other approaches insofar as they help to explain or understand social policy, but it is sceptical of empiricism and interpretivism because they do not *necessarily* question the underlying basis of the status quo.

Many projects in social policy are 'applied' rather than 'theoretical', and you may find it difficult to be explicit about the nature of your chosen methodology. It is none the less important that you should understand that no research activity can be free from the conceptual assumptions and values which you yourself bring to the project.

Methods and Project Design

Having determined what you will investigate and from what kind of perspective you will need to design your project. You may be required before you start to submit a formal research proposal that describes your project design. Writing research proposals is an important skill in itself and may be needed in your future career.

If your project is an assessed case study or extended essay then your principal method is likely to be a literature review. All social policy students will learn the skills required for undertaking literature reviews, including, for example, the use of computerized literature searches and citation indices. Reviewing and interpreting the existing literature on a subject is an essential form of research activity in its own right. In fact, almost any project is likely to incorporate a literature review as part of an investigation: this is necessary not only to familiarize yourself with the conceptual, historical and factual background to a subject, but because projects similar or identical to your own may already have been undertaken and the findings published.

If your project extends beyond a literature review, you will need to choose methods for gathering and analysing 'data'. The term data can apply to any kind of information resulting from counting, measuring or observing. Data can exist or be recorded in quantitative or numerical form on the one hand, or qualitative or discursive (i.e. written or spoken) form on the other. Box V.1.2 lists the principal means by which data might be gathered for a project. A project may employ data gathered using several different methods. If you are able to gather some primary data of your own – for example, by administering a questionnaire or conducting some interviews – this will bring added originality to your project. However, data gathering or 'fieldwork' can be very time-consuming and there are likely to be limits to how much you will be able to do.

Once gathered, data must be analysed. The patterns and relationships within quantitative data may be analysed using statistical techniques, ranging from the simple to the highly complex. The handling of quantitative data has been revolutionized by the development of specialized computer software that makes even quite sophisticated statistical manipulation relatively straightforward, and all social policy students will have an opportunity to learn about this. Qualitative data may be analysed either by coding them in ways which make it possible to apply quantitative techniques, or by a variety of inductive techniques for interpreting the content and the themes which occur within discursive material. There has been an upsurge of interest in qualitative data analysis in recent

---

Box V. 1.2

Data gathering method	*Examples*
Secondary source methods	• documentary/archive research • secondary data-set analysis
Survey methods	• questionnaires • structured interviews • telephone surveys
Discursive methods	• in-depth interviews • focus group discussions • life histories • diaries
Observational methods	• non-participant observation • participative/ethnographic observation • action research

years, including the use not only of conventional interview transcripts and observational reports, but of audio- and video-recordings and the development of computer software packages that aid the analysis of textual material.

Ethics

Projects in social policy are ultimately concerned with people and the things that affect their lives. Social policy itself is often concerned with especially vulnerable people. All social research involves ethical considerations and the sort of projects which social policy students undertake will sometimes raise particular issues, especially if you should seek direct access to the users or potential users of welfare services.

Many academic institutions have ethical guidelines or codes of practice that staff and students are required to follow, and some even have ethics committees to which project proposals must be submitted for approval. Some kinds of project may in any event require ethical clearance from other bodies: for example, any project which involves the collection of data from or about patients of the National Health Service must be considered by a local research ethics committee. Whether or not they are directly constrained, all students undertaking projects should take account of their ethical responsibilities. They are responsible to their fellow students and the institution at which they study – whose interests could be damaged if, for example, insensitive inquiries of local welfare agencies should sour future relations. Students must also be responsible for their own welfare and should not place themselves in dangerous situations. However, the most important area of responsibility lies in relation to research 'subjects': the people that your project is about.

This particularly applies if your research subjects participate directly by answering questionnaires, taking part in interviews or allowing themselves to be observed. It is essential, except in the most exceptional circumstances, that their participation should be on the basis of their informed consent. Not only should they agree to take part, but you should ensure that they understand the nature and purposes of your project. It will often be important in such circumstances to undertake to protect the confidentiality of people or organizations taking part; and to make sure that you do not (even inadvertently) pass on information about them that they would wish to be kept confidential, or disclose their identity in any report or publication if they should wish to remain anonymous.

At a more general level, you should be prepared to reflect on the nature of your responsibilities as a student/investigator to the people or group you are studying. For example, could the way in which you interact with, investigate or report on disabled people, asylum-seekers or 'the poor' have any adverse consequences, even at the level of perpetuating or reinforcing pejorative stereotypes? Projects that adopt an explicitly critical approach (in the sense outlined above) might imply a very particular ethical agenda. For example, some feminist methodologies seek as a matter of principle to eschew the traditional hierarchical relationship between researcher and researched in favour of a democratic and participatory relationship between the researcher and the women in whose lives she seeks to share.

The Presentation of Findings

The purpose of any project is fulfilled by writing it up or presenting it. There is no point in undertaking any sort of research activity unless you disseminate the findings. What is more, the skills involved in presenting findings are among the most important you will learn. They are skills required well beyond the boundaries of academia. At both a national and a local level the politicians who make social policy, the officials who interpret it and the agencies (public, voluntary and private) who deliver welfare services all require clear, concise and relevant information and commentary.

Students are likely to receive specific guidelines from their institutions and/or detailed advice from their tutors/supervisors about the writing of project reports. But in general, the report (whether it is presented orally or in writing) should be structured so as to provide a narrative. It should:

- explain how you first identified and defined the question or problem which the project addresses;
- set out the conceptual or theoretical framework you decided to use and why;
- outline the background provided by your literature review, the issues raised and any conclusions you may have drawn from the literature or from other secondary sources.

If your project entailed an original empirical investigation, it should:

- describe the research design and method(s) used, and the way you analysed the resulting data;
- explain any limitations or constraints to

which the project was subject, and the implications these might have for the reliability or validity of the findings;
- set out and discuss your findings;
- provide conclusions and, if appropriate, recommendations for action.

You will normally be expected to add a summary of the key points.

Conclusion

The opportunity to undertake projects represents an important part of a social policy degree. The value of doing projects in social policy lies in the experience it offers in independent study, the application of theory to 'real world' situations, the use of research methods, the development of skills of analysis, presentation and report writing. Projects put the student 'in the driving seat'. Social policy is full of controversies – about oppression, disadvantage and who gets what in a 'welfare state'. It is through projects that you may be able to explore the issues that excite or matter most to you, and in the manner best suited to your own aptitudes.

Guide to further reading

There is a vast and ever-expanding literature on research methods, although little of it is aimed specifically at social policy students. Nonetheless, an appropriate introductory guide is J. Bell *Doing Your Research Project: A Guide for First-time Researchers in Education and Social Science*, 3rd edn (Buckingham: Open University Press, 1999).

Another useful introductory text of relevance for social policy students is N. Gilbert *Researching Social Life*, 2nd edn (London: Sage, 2001).

For an accessible introduction to wider issues in social research see T. May *Social Research: Issues, Methods and Process* (Buckingham: Open University Press, 1993). Alternatively, for a comprehensive 'one-stop' textbook see, for example: W. Neuman, *Social Research Methods: Qualitative and Quantitative Approaches*, 4th edn (Boston: Allyn and Bacon, 2000).

A discussion of research ethics that is focused on social policy can be found in: H. Dean (ed.) *Ethics and Social Policy Research* (Luton: University of Luton Press/Social Policy Association, 1996).

Finally, two books that ostensibly examine different kinds of data analysis: D. Silverman *Interpreting Qualitative Data*, 2nd edn (London: Sage, 2001); D. Byrne *Interpreting Quantitative Data* (London: Sage, 2002). Both address key contemporary debates and in fact provide a critical discussion of the relationship between qualitative and quantitative research methods.

V.2

Fieldwork Placements and the Social Policy Curriculum

Duncan Scott

Students who have undertaken field-work placements as an integral part of their undergraduate social policy degree typically conclude that: 'I have learned more than I ever dreamed was possible in such a short period' and 'The fieldwork experience was a life-changing one for me. It put all my values and assumptions into question'. Yet, even while such positive experiences can be duplicated across a wide range of higher education institutions, there are signs that the commitment of social policy courses to fieldwork, as a central part of the undergraduate curriculum, is at best uneven and at worst in retreat.

This chapter will identify the changing nature of fieldwork placements, why students should be encouraged to undertake them, and will conclude by briefly considering the prospects for the further development of social policy fieldwork approaches in higher education.

What Is Fieldwork?

Popular perceptions

A quick look through the pages of university undergraduate handbooks provides a number of very common pictures. We see geography students sitting on the cliffs at Charmouth in Dorset (Oxford University), on boulders half way up a mountain in North Wales (Nottingham) or on a lava flow in Hawaii (Leeds). Similar pictures on the same theme portray archaeology students at an Iron Age burial site in Hampshire or human sciences students finding out about traditional medicine in Kenya (both Oxford).

Most of these pictures are about organized visits to study the physical environment – and they are popular with the editors of handbooks because the images convey a sense of the exciting possibilities awaiting the hopeful sixth former. More careful examination of the handbook might reveal a wide range of 'visiting' – from the language student who may spend up to a year in France, Germany or Spain, to the anthropologist off to Western Ireland or Africa, or the planning student fresh from a project in a suburban housing estate. In different ways all these forms of outreach demonstrate a belief in the importance of direct contact between the student and what he or she is studying. It is argued that greater closeness, even in some cases the development of social relationships, can lead to a deeper form of learning. The textbook is helpful up to a point; things become 'real' when they are observed, touched and related to.

Social Policy Fieldwork

Social policy fieldwork takes place within a 'family' of academic disciplines or areas of study (e.g. sociology, anthropology), often in collaboration with 'cousins' involved in professional training (e.g. social work). Figure V.2.1 attempts to illustrate this and to connect the departmental 'sponsor' of fieldwork with the intermediary agencies or clearing houses and the actual organizational placements. The broken lines indicate different routeways to a placement, i.e. a student may be placed directly with an agency, or be helped to locate one through the students' union or university settlement. Some students use previous experience either of a voluntary 'GAP' period between their secondary education and university (e.g. environmental or education projects) or of paid employment instead of undertaking a new, formally arranged placement. These alternative, 'unsponsored' placements are becoming more common, even during the

university course as the pressures of student finance lead to a situation where up to two-thirds of undergraduates have substantial term-time employment. The section on the right hand side of figure V.2.1, marked 'Continuing Work Experience', reflects this trend.

The early development of social policy fieldwork often took place via university settlements; in 1901 the Manchester settlement's annual report celebrated the fact that 'the Settlement is slowly if surely acquiring the character of a bureau of social information' (Rose and Woods, 1995, p. 77). A typical example of how students used the strategic location of the settlement to improve their own academic skills while producing something of use to local people is illustrated in figure V.2.2.

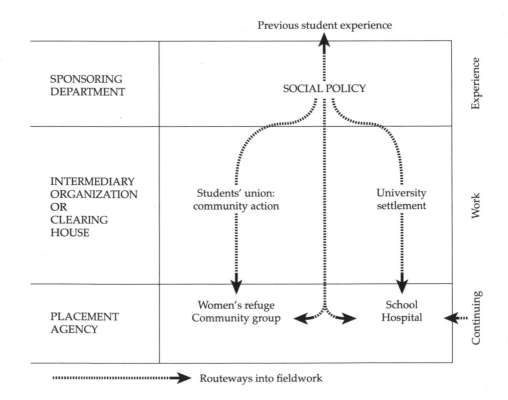

Figure V.2.1 The organization of fieldwork

Figure V.2.2 Manchester University Settlement Survey (Rose and Woods, 1995, p.78)

Reports by social policy fieldworkers were, however, not greeted with universal enthusiasm, as some people resented the 'snoopers' from the university; a Manchester councillor pleaded with his colleagues, in a 1935 housing debate, 'for God's sake, not to give room to those self-appointed investigators who went about dissecting and vivisecting the lives of the working class' (Rose and Woods, 1995, p. 82). These are continuing ethical and political concerns; if social policy fieldwork placements are constructed so as to allow students greater experiences of social needs and responses, a number of questions are raised. A social policy student summed up her experiences of a four-week placement in the

1990s: 'What justification was there for "letting loose" naive and green students like me in welfare settings where there are people whose permission is not even sought? What are the benefits to placement agencies who allow students to go in?' (Bridget, 17 November 1995).

Why Do Social Policy Fieldwork?

There are three overlapping *educational* arguments in favour of doing social policy fieldwork, and these are summarized in table V.2.1. All social policy fieldwork placements emphasize the centrality of finding out about social policy issues in society (level III), very often simultaneously reflecting on the processes whereby this finding out (or research) takes place. In some instances, there is also an emphasis on what are called 'transferable skills'; for example, a student may learn from participation in a group how to make decisions, work in a team and communicate. These skills are not specific to the particular social policy context, they can be transferred into settings such as a bank, factory or town hall (see level II in table V.2.1).

Inevitably, the process of entering what is often a completely new social world leads to new relationships. Although these are rarely more than temporary and superficial they can be the means through which a student learns to cope in a crisis, handle a conflict or work through personal uncertainties, fears and prejudices (e.g. about working with people with learning disabilities, ex-offenders, drug addicts, the mentally ill and so on). (See level I in table V.2.1.)

How a particular individual student combines these three purposes will depend on the circumstances of the placement and on his or her overall career direction. For example, he or she may intend to use the fieldwork as preparation either for further professional training or as the first piece of in-depth academic work which could, eventually, lead to more intensive postgraduate study. In the first example social work is a common career destination, but there are

Table V.2.1   Educational purposes in social policy

Purpose: 'knowledge about . . .'	Learning focus	Learning outcome
I Self	*through* relationships	personal growth
II Group	*from* relationships	team-building
		communication skills
III Society	*about* relationships	policy/practice
		knowledge

also parallel moves into teaching, housing, planning, youth work, welfare rights and paid work in voluntary agencies (e.g. work with the elderly, children and families).

A second response may involve a dissertation which grows out of the initial fieldwork placement. A student may revisit a women's refuge or a special school, and gather information about its policies and practices; this will usually form the basis of several linked chapters containing between 10,000 and 15,000 words. For undergraduates this is often the largest piece of written work they produce, and may give them confidence to undertake more advanced and intensive fieldwork at postgraduate level, as part of masters and doctoral programmes.

Since the Dearing Report on Higher Education was published in the late 1990s, there have been increasing calls to make the curriculum more directly relevant to the world of work. Within the social policy and broader social science communities there have been a number of pedagogic responses. These include:

1   a critical examination of the different ways in which the concept of 'Employability' has become integrated within the undergraduate experience (see A. Clark et al, 2002);
2   the production of audio-visual materials supporting community-based learning (Cobalt and Hall, 2002) and different work experience models (www.unn.ac.uk/academic/lss/sip).

What Is Involved In a Fieldwork Placement?

Practical matters

A placement may take place at the same time as coursework (e.g. every Wednesday for one or two terms) or in a block of time (e.g. four weeks in the vacation). When students are involved in exchange schemes with European universities they may spend a term or more away from their 'home base'. In a few cases a fieldwork placement may occupy 30 weeks and therefore constitute an extra year in the undergraduate degree programme.

Students may be placed within walking distance of their parental home, close to their termtime address or half the way around the world. Most are in Britain – popular examples include community centres, luncheon clubs for older people, schools for children with disabilities, residential units for ex-offenders, the homeless, refugees, the mentally ill, etc. Exotic examples include a kibbutz in Israel, orphanages in Romania, summer camps in Lithuania and the USA as well as development projects in the Third World.

The most common placements outside Britain are within the European Union Erasmus/Socrates programme. Students (individually or in small groups) exchange with their peers in EU member states; the period of study in the new institution replaces, for assessment purposes, the comparable time in their home university. While away from Britain the social policy student need not undertake a specific fieldwork placement, although visits to social policy institutions (schools, hospitals, prisons, hostels for refugees etc.) are often arranged. In a sense the whole exchange is like a 'giant' piece of fieldwork in which an individual can learn more about himself or herself and her or his skills in group situations, and deepen a comparative understanding of different policy environments.

The 'official' reasons for Socrates are that it will encourage the development of intellectual, cultural and linguistic skills and provide students with a valuable enhancement of their employability. It is becoming clear that some prospective employers consider time spent on exchanges as an indicator of individual initiative and of someone likely to be more enthusiastic and knowledgeable about Europe.

Students talk of the 'hassles' involved in preparing for all fieldwork and particularly the EU exchanges: extra costs, covering for accommodation left behind, learning enough of a new language, settling in, a different social life, administrative confusions and so on. A consistent majority come back with a greater understanding of themselves and of a wide spectrum of new knowledge about other countries. They talk incessantly of their experiences and show off their souvenir T-shirts. All in all they tend to support the idea of being 'somewhere else' long enough to notice and understand difference.

Academic matters

The location, status and significance of fieldwork in the undergraduate curriculum varies in three main respects:

1 Is it integrated or marginal? Do the weeks of fieldwork really connect in a direct way with substantial blocks of classroom teaching, or are they handled briefly and separately in the 'cracks' between the basic building bricks of the courses?
2 Is the fieldwork assessed or not? Do the reports really count towards the final degree classification?

3 Is the fieldwork compulsory or voluntary? Does the department expect you to make all the effort, or leave it to individual enthusiasms?

Whatever the departmental significance of fieldwork, its essential characteristics remain the same; it is about processes of individual (sometimes small group) interaction whereby the student seeks to understand the everyday life of individuals, groups and organizations by entering their social worlds or 'fields', and trying as much as is possible to see things from their point of view. Figure V.2.3 represents two related dimensions of this process: the fieldwork student is 'climbing into the picture', but the drawing alerts us to possible ways in which the social characteristics (e.g. age, gender, class, race), first of the student and second of those already in the field, will interrupt or shape subsequent relationships. Just how far the figure in the suit will really learn to see things from the perspective of the young workers in overalls is uncertain. All that is clear is that some social differences are likely to play a crucial role in the placement process.

Students who are asked to undertake 'projects', usually of a research-based kind, are less likely to engage in such social interactions; their task is primarily to observe, interview and record information. In some contrast, the fieldwork placement often hinges on the fact that it is through the varied relationships developed in the placement or work setting that particular experiences and insights are obtained. The student will negotiate formal roles and establish informal links with some of the people in the particular setting. For example, one student worked as a temporary security guard at a large international airport in the year prior to the dramatic events of 11 September 2001 in New York. He wrote about the patterns of 'occupational delinquency' among the permanent staff and attempted to explain why these arose; the human and policy implications of such an experience are clear.

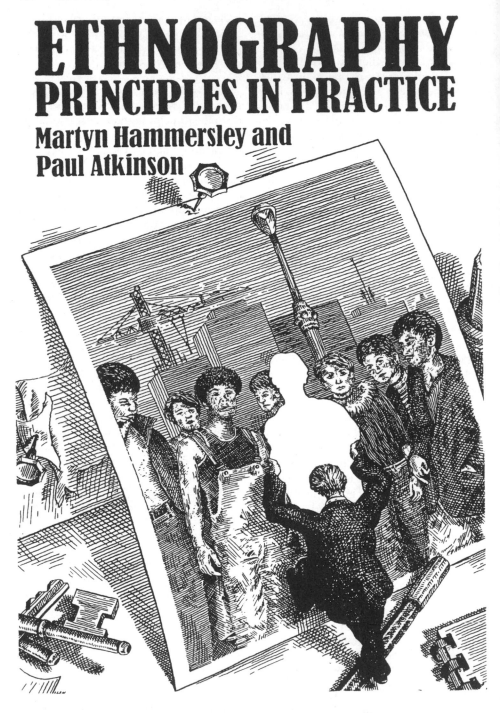

Figure V.2.3 'Climbing into the picture' by Andrew Robey (cover of M. Hammersley and P. Atkinson, *Ethnography: Principles in Practice* (London: Tavistock, 1983)

Some university departments view fieldwork placements in a fairly narrow way; they take the view that a young, inexperienced student 'should try to fit in with whatever they do' (Social Policy Placement Guidelines, 1995-6, X University). At the level of being polite they are absolutely right – the student is a guest and should not consciously create disturbances in her or his host agency. On the other hand, fitting in need not preclude other emotional and intellectual experiences. For a variety of reasons – the personal character of the student, the key individuals in the placement agency and the events which unfold during the fieldwork – an individual may react to the social field in more complex ways. For example, a trio of female students in an orphanage found the behaviour of key people 'irritating', 'puzzling', even 'objectionable'. They found themselves getting frustrated and angry and subsequently (back at university) reflected on different possible explanations for these responses. They concluded that some of the difficulties had been triggered by clashes of personalities (including theirs), but that others reflected on the way the orphanages were organized, and the level of social policy provision for children in the society as a whole. Instead of fitting in mentally and intellectually (to match their general and necessary politeness), they had learnt how to explore both their feelings and their analytic abilities. In short, they had learnt from their experiences about themselves, groups and institutions.

Fieldwork as art?

Because the student can't prepare for all eventualities, she or he must accept and creatively explore uncertainties when they arise. The report which emerges from such experiences can be more than a cold recitation of data gathering. Indeed, there are some commentators who argue that fieldwork accounts must be more than 'efficient', 'systematic' or 'scientific'. They would argue that fieldwork touches 'art' to the extent that the student can discover in 'personal experience an account that offers to a discerning audience a level of insight and understanding into human social life that exceeds whatever might be achieved through attention solely to gathering and reporting data' (Wolcott, 1995, p. 251).

If the student who interviews a young single mother in depressing circumstances is moved to anger and tears, she or he may search for ways to provide a degree of detail about the physical and emotional context – to convey the depth of the experience, to treat the person as more than another specimen to be put into a glass case. All of this raises ethical and political questions which must always be thought through. For example, what should one do if the woman appears to be an inconsistently competent mother, even when all her circumstances are considered? Again, what should be done if it is clear that a local authority social worker makes half-hearted attempts to contact the mother, or deliberately overlooks the complex family dynamics in order to 'manage' her or his case-load?

Finally, the novelist can reveal to us that fieldwork need not be all earnest soul-searching, that there may be moments, even whole periods of days and weeks, of enjoyment and fun. Dr Robyn Penrose, temporary lecturer in English at 'Rummidge' university, provides more than a wry smile for the reader as she struggles to make sense of her fieldwork placement at Pringle's engineering works (Lodge, 1989). We are presented with page after page of comic episodes neatly interwoven with more serious asides about the social distance between the ivory tower and the factory. Robyn's journey – from very reluctant fieldworker to defender of greater connections between the two institutions – can be ours; and we can laugh along the way!

Fieldwork in Higher Education: Continuities and Contradictions

Most social policy departments do not regard a compulsory formally assessed fieldwork placement as a necessary and integral part of their core curriculum. Yet, at the same time, they encourage the development of project work, organize European exchanges and practise an everyday, anecdotal form of fieldwork in the various ways in which lecturers intersperse 'tales from their domestic and neighbourhood lives' in their lectures. In other parts of the university, a wide range of departments will be sending out nurses to learn about localities, trainee teachers into classrooms, geographers to map housing estates and hillsides, planners to build models of new towns and so on. Over in the students' union, various societies will be organizing community action projects, helping in literacy schemes, environmental work and a multitude more.

Universities clearly encourage a loose form of fieldwork right across the campus. The big question is whether the processes of fieldwork are sufficiently anchored in the intellectual heartland of the curriculum, and not just mere decorations around its edge. Where the emphasis is on training, e.g. education and social work, integration is strongest.

Social policy academics have not yet developed a strong consensus for or against fieldwork. Individual departments seem to be more or less committed because of significant 'champions', i.e. individual staff who are strongly committed to the idea and have been around long enough to obtain and safeguard a place for fieldwork in the curriculum. Those who have abandoned fieldwork frequently talk about 'dwindling resources' without revealing how little placements actually cost, and with negligible attention to its academic benefits.

Meanwhile, across higher education, governments through the 1980s and 1990s have cried out for 'relevance'. This is a code word for making what students learn more exactly what commerce and industry require – a giant kind of 'fitting-in'. At least two processes may be taking place at more or less the same time, but for very different reasons. First, some social policy departments may be abandoning a strong commitment to fieldwork, because they perceive this to be a vital resource saving move, and because it will allegedly allow students to spend more time with more theoretical material. Second, other social policy departments may be promoting narrow forms of 'relevance', whereby students complete practical tasks for placement institutions ranging from businesses to hospitals to community centres.

Both tendencies have put forward strong arguments for their positions. The worry remains that if 'theory' is held to lie outside fieldwork then placements will become increasingly practical; 'relevance' will be similarly defined. Social policy can rediscover fieldwork as an intellectually legitimate activity and thereby guard against narrowness. It can redefine relevance and argue that fieldwork is one way in which students can be encouraged to develop a more confident self-knowledge and critical non-conformity. There are still examples upon which it can draw for sustenance. One of these has been termed 'critical adult education' – a tradition that seems to link personal growth with analyses of contemporary social problems. This tradition goes back to the beginning of the industrial revolution, when welfare explorers raised questions about inequality and poverty, violence and unaccountable economic and political systems, and suggested new possibilities of a more just kind.

No doubt personal growth and a critical engagement with social need can be developed in the library. The challenge from fieldwork is to make connections, to help students to learn how social policy isn't just observing and writing about the world, but trying to change it, and themselves in the same process; they have to begin somewhere.

Guide to further reading

The foundations of social policy fieldwork were laid down by those men and women in the nineteenth century who set out to record the size and shape of human need. They charted the living conditions of poor factory workers huddled together in sub-standard housing, and pressured politicians for reform. Towards the end of the nineteenth century many universities established 'settlements' from which fieldwork was undertaken. M. E. Rose and A. Woods *The Round House: A Hundred Years of the Manchester University Settlement* (Manchester: University of Manchester, 1995), provides a well-illustrated introduction to the fieldwork tradition from the 1890s to the present day.

A student interested in social policy fieldwork and its place in the curriculum could begin with A. Clark, S. Emmett, C. Middleton, D. Scott, T. Wengraf and N. Miller, *Making Connections: Work-based Learning, Employability and the Professional, Academic and Personal Development of Students* (Birmingham University, Centre for Sociology, Anthropology and Politics [C-SAP], 2002). Then, for an insight into the student perspective on fieldwork, they should read I. Cobalt and D. Hall, 'Incorporating change through reflection, Community-based learning', in R. Macdonald and J. Wisdom (eds) *Academic and Educational Development: Research, Evaluation and Changing Practice in Higher Education* (London, Kogan Page, 2002). The audio-visual materials connected to community-based learning developed by the 'Cobalt' (Community Based Learning Teamwork) project, can be accessed via <c-sap.bham.ac.uk> or www.hope.ac.uk/cobalt.

When a wider view is needed, books seem to operate on two, often disconnected, levels. Firstly, there are the sociological texts exploring the social dimensions of fieldwork; one of the most popular is M. Hammersley and P. Atkinson, *Ethnography: Principles in Practice,* 2nd edition (London: Routledge, 1995). The cover of their first edition is reproduced in this chapter, as figure V.2.3.

A more detailed collection of sociological essays on fieldwork is A. Coffey and P. Atkinson (eds) *Occupational Socialization and Working Lives* (Cardiff Papers in Qualitative Research, Aldershot: Avebury, 1994). Another 'how to do it', but at a more sophisticated and literary level, is Harry F. Wolcott *The Art of Fieldwork* (Walnut Creek, CA: Altamira,1995). Wolcott is an American anthropologist who sets out to show how fieldwork is more than a narrow mechanistic activity.

The second level of writing attempts to identify how the fieldwork tradition in social policy is more than the choices made by its teachers in specific departments: there are sets of wider structural influences derived from the interests of governments and industrialists. A good example of a short chapter that pulls together the historical legacy of fieldwork, and contemporary developments in the way it is being developed, is provided by Katherine Hughes, 'Really useful knowledge: adult learning and the Ruskin Learning Project' in Marjorie Mayo and Jane Thompson (eds), *Adult Learning Critical Intelligence and Social Change* (Washington, DC: National Institute of Adult and Continuing Education, 1995), pp. 97-110.

Finally, when students are even half-persuaded that fieldwork can and should be both creative and fun, they could read David Lodge *Nice Work* (Harmondsworth: Penguin, 1989).

Learning Resources

V.3
Guide to the Literature

Robert M. Page

As can be seen from the other chapters in this volume, the literature in social policy is both rich and diverse. In addition to books, articles and reviews the student of social policy will also find it rewarding to examine official government reports and research findings as well as material emanating from think tanks and non-governmental organizations. The importance of a number of government reports cannot be emphasized too strongly. For example, the Beveridge Report (on Social Insurance and Allied Services, 1942) continues to be one of the most widely cited documents in British social policy. While the reports of think tanks may resonate for shorter periods of time their impact should also be noted. For example, the report of the Commission on Social Justice (1994) has influenced the welfare agenda of New Labour.

As in the previous edition of the *Companion* this chapter will, for reasons of space, focus on books relating to social policy rather than articles or research reports. The social policy literature continues to grow at a rapid rate not least because of the emergence of publishers such as Ashgate and Policy Press who have been prepared to publish specialist monographs. This chapter is divided into three sections; *key texts*, *subject introductions* and *recent specialist titles*.

Key Texts

It is difficult to provide a list of key texts that will meet with anything like universal approval. However it is useful to reflect on some of the books that have had a significant influence on the development of the subject. As with other exercises of this kind, such as selecting the greatest players who have represented one's favourite football team, the main purpose is to provide an opportunity for further discussion and debate.

Richard H.Tawney (1931) *Equality*

Equality has proved to be one of the most influential texts for successive generations of social policy scholars and Labour politicians such as Crosland and Gaitskell. Tawney is highly critical of capitalism, which he believes lacks an ethical sense of social purpose and function. He argues for a redistribution of economic and social power towards working people and the creation of remoralized, cooperative, solidaristic communities in which the equal worth of all citizens can be upheld. *Equality* is underpinned by Tawney's Christian socialist beliefs. His stress on the importance of responsibilities as well as rights has contemporary resonance in the light of New Labour's attempt to restore the link between these two principles.

Richard Titmuss (1950) *Problems of Social Policy*

Problems of Social Policy was one of the officially commissioned civilian wartime histories. It is arguably Titmuss's finest work. Avoiding the danger of a dry factual overview of wartime developments, Titmuss captured the social impact of total war on the civilian population by means of 'selective illustration' (p.ix). By focusing on a limited range of issues, namely, evacuation, hospital services and care afforded to homeless people, Titmuss vividly illustrated the complexities of policy making, the adaptability and generous spirit of the civilian population and the positive role of collective action.

Thomas.H.Marshall (1950) *Citizenship and Social Class and Other Essays*

The work of T. H. Marshall remains important for students of social policy not least because of his innovative work on the notion of citizenship. In *Citizenship and Social Class*, Marshall charts the evolution of citizenship rights. Legal rights developed in the eighteenth century, political rights in the nineteenth century and social rights in the twentieth century. *Citizenship and Social Class* provides the reader with an opportunity to chart the development of Marshall's ideas concerning the possibility of establishing a society in which a modified capitalism and collectivist welfare can coexist. This perspective has been classified as a 'middle way' approach to social policy (Pinker, 1995).

Brian Abel-Smith and Peter Townsend (1965) *The Poor and the Poorest*

The publication of *The Poor and the Poorest* reopened the debate about poverty in post-war Britain. Abel-Smith and Townsend challenged the assumption that poverty had been banished as a result of the coming of the post-war welfare state. A key feature of this work was the idea that poverty should be examined in relative rather than absolute terms. This relative approach is developed at greater length in Townsend's (1979) later work, which attempted to measure poverty in an objective way (see Piachaud, 1987). *The Poor and the Poorest* was one of a number of

highly influential occasional papers on social administration that were published by Bell in the post-war period.

Richard Titmuss (1970) *The Gift Relationship*

In *The Gift Relationship*, Titmuss sought through a case study of blood donation to demonstrate that collectivist welfare could 'help to actualize the social and moral potentialities of all citizens' (p. 238). Whilst not wishing to make exaggerated claims about the altruistic sentiments of the British policy, Titmuss nonetheless wanted to show how the establishment of an institution such as the National Health Service could create the social cohesion necessary for displays of selflessness. One early critic of the book, Ward (1996), has recounted how he gradually came to appreciate the quality of this volume not least because it highlighted the rapidity with which 'market ideology has been transferred from economic theory to social policy' (p. 35). Titmuss's contribution to the study of social policy is usefully reviewed in recent publications by Alcock et al. (eds) (2001) and Reisman (2001).

Robert Pinker (1971) *Social Theory and Social Policy*

One of the major criticisms of the academic study of social policy and administration in the 1950s and 60s was its lack of theoretical rigour (see Mishra, 1981). In *Social Theory and Social Policy* Pinker reviews the historic roots of social administration and explores how the insights of sociology can enrich the subject. The book also contains valuable insights into concepts such as stigma, social exchange, selectivity, universalism, egoism and altruism.

Vic George and Paul Wilding (1976) *Ideology and Social Welfare*

Ideology and Social Welfare played a major role in expanding the focus of the subject from the 'bread and butter' issues of policy formation and service delivery to broader ideological debates about the role and purpose of social policy in a capitalist society. In the first edition of this highly readable book, the authors compared and contrasted the values, approach to society, attitudes to government and the welfare state of the anti-collectivists, the reluctant collectivists, the Fabian socialists and the Marxists. The book stimulated lively debate and criticism (see Williams, 1989). It has been reprinted and rewritten on a number of occasions, most recently as *Welfare and Ideology* (George and Wilding, 1994) in which six perspectives are featured; the New Right, Middle Way, democratic socialist, Marxist, feminist and Green.

Ian Gough (1979) *The Political Economy of the Welfare State*

Using insights from economics, sociology and political science, Gough examines the contradictory role of state welfare within capitalist societies. He demonstrates that the welfare state can simultaneously aid capital accumulation as well as provide important social benefits for the disadvantaged. Gough explores how this contradictory unity makes the welfare state prone to crisis. One of the great strengths of this book is the encouragement it gives students to consider the inter-relationship between economic and social policy.

Julian Le Grand (1982) *The Strategy of Equality*

In *The Strategy of Equality*, Le Grand casts doubt on the notion that the post-1945 welfare state primarily benefits the poor. Using examples from health care, education, housing and transport, Le Grand contends that the middle classes gained more from publicly funded welfare services than their working class counterparts. Although Le Grand's thesis has been challenged (Powell, 1995), it has served to stimulate much-needed debate about the precise role which

state welfare can play in bringing about a more equal society.

Charles Murray (1984) *Losing Ground*

The resurgence of neo-liberal ideas in the 1980s and 90s has had a dramatic impact on the subject of social policy. The American commentator Murray has proved to be one of the most influential contemporary advocates of these. In *Losing Ground* Murray contends that far from improving the position of the disadvantaged, government intervention has actually intensified their plight. His views on the corrosive effect of welfare dependency and lone parenthood continue to influence welfare debates on both sides of the Atlantic (Murray, 1990; Lister [ed.], 1996).

Gillian Pascall (1986) *Social Policy: A Feminist Analysis*

The way in which feminist ideas have moved from the periphery into the mainstream of social policy debates has been one of the most significant developments over the past thirty years (Wilson, 1977; Finch and Groves, 1983.) In this wide-ranging book, Pascall draws attention to the systematic disadvantages which women face in and outside the labour market. She highlights the various ways in which women have been denied equitable access to vital forms of welfare provision such as social security, health care and education. A revised edition of this book was published in 1997 (Pascall, 1997).

Fiona Williams (1989) *Social Policy: A Critical Introduction*

In this book Williams draws attention to the way in which the academic study of social policy with its emphasis on empiricism, pragmatism and idealism has for a large part of the post-1945 period failed to give sufficient attention to the inter-relationship between class, gender and race. She explores diverse feminist approaches and develops an anti-racist critique of the welfare state. This book has ensured that the issues of race/nation and gender are now given greater consideration in accounts of the development and current operation of state welfare.

Gosta Esping-Andersen (1990) *The Three Worlds of Welfare Capitalism*

While there have been a number of previous attempts to provide broad categorizations of welfare regimes (e.g. Titmuss, 1974), *The Three Worlds of Welfare Capitalism* has established itself as the most influential text in this sphere. Esping-Andersen has focused on the extent to which state welfare policies support or challenge market relations. He contends that capitalist welfare states can be divided into three ideal types – liberal, conservative/corporatist and social democratic. His work has led to renewed questioning about the extent to which the development of state welfare can be linked to such factors as industrialization, democracy and working-class pressure. It has also encouraged other writers to suggest modified or radically different formulations of welfare regimes (see Castles and Mitchell, 1992; Lewis, 1992; Liebfried, 1993).

Subject Introductions and Overviews

There is a wide range of introductory textbooks that are suitable for students embarking on a social policy degree course.

Cliff Alcock, Sarah Payne and Michael Sullivan (2000) *Introducing Social Policy*

Themes covered include:

- the welfare state in crisis;
- paying for welfare;
- theoretical principles and concepts;
- poverty and social security;
- education and training;

- family policy;
- the international perspective.

Number of chapters: 19.

Pete Alcock (1996) *Social Policy in Britain: Themes and Issues*

Themes covered include:

- the discipline of social policy;
- the state;
- ideologies of welfare;
- Europe and the European Union;
- local control of welfare services;
- paying for welfare.

Number of chapters: 14. The second edition is being published by Palgrave in 2003.

John Baldock, Nick Manning, Stewart Miller and Sarah Vickerstaff (eds) (1999) *Social Policy*

Themes covered include:

- welfare, ideology and social theory;
- economics and social policy;
- social need and patterns of inequality and difference ;
- the family and the production of welfare;
- professions;
- health and health policy;
- the care and protection of children.

Number of chapters: 21.

Ken Blakemore (1998) *Social Policy: An Introduction*

Themes covered include:

- ideas and concepts in social policy;
- the development of social policy in Britain;
- social policy and social control;
- policy making in education;
- health policy and health professionals;
- community and care;
- the future of social policy.

Number of chapters:10.

Nick Ellison and Chris Pierson (eds) (1998) *Developments in British Social Policy*

Themes covered include:

- theory in social policy;
- the changing politics of social policy;
- social security policy in Britain;
- housing policy;
- gender and social policy;
- race, racism and social policies;
- UK social policy in European union context.

Number of chapters: 17.

Michael Lavalette and Alan Pratt (eds) (2001) *Social Policy: A Conceptual and Theoretical Introduction*

Themes covered include:

- towards a new social democracy
- Marxism and social welfare
- racism and social policy
- social policy and homosexuality
- poverty, the underclass and social policy
- ageing, population and pensions
- children, social policy and the state

Number of chapters: 14.

Students approaching the subject of social policy for the first time may want to familiarize themselves with key developments in the history of social policy. Gladstone's (1999) *The Twentieth-Century Welfare State* provides a concise overview of the evolution of social policy throughout the twentieth century. More lengthy expositions on this period are provided by Thane (1996) and Fraser (2002). There are some equally impressive texts that focus on the post-1945 period. These include Timmins's (2001) magisterial review of the period entitled *The Five Giants*, which McCarthy (on the back cover of the book) praises for its 'wonders of narrative clarity, anecdote and human detail.' Other authoritative studies of the period include Lowe 's (1999) *The Welfare*

State in Britain Since 1945 and Glennerster's (2000) *British Social Policy Since 1945*.

Students of social policy will also find much of interest in some of the biographies and autobiographies of influential politicians such as Bevan (Foot, 1997; Campbell. 1987), Callaghan (Morgan, 1997), Wilson (Pimlott, 1993), Crosland (Jeffreys, 1999), Thatcher (Young, 1993; Campbell, 2000) and Major (Major, 1999).

Recent Specialist Titles

There is now a wide range of specialist texts in the field of social policy. Clearly in a short review of this kind it is not possible to do justice to such a vast literature. The following selections are intended to provide a flavour of some of the issues currently being debated.

Polly Toynbee and David Walker (2001) *Did Things Get Better?*

This text, published by two leading journalists writing for the *Guardian* around the time of the 2001 general election, provides a review of the first term of the New Labour government from 1997 to 2001. The book contains useful assessments of New Labour's approach to education, health care and the creation of a fairer society. They conclude that things did get better under New Labour but that there remains considerable room for improvement.

Anthony Giddens (2002) *Where Now for New Labour?*

The sociologist Giddens (1994, 1998, 2000) has played a key role in developing the so-called 'third way' approach of New Labour. In this short and highly readable book, he responds to some of the criticisms of New Labour, outlines his views on the revival of public services and globalization and explores what he terms the second phase of the Third Way. He concludes that New Labour 'stands firmly in the traditions of social democracy – it is social democracy, brought up to date and made relevant to a rapidly changing world' (p.78).

Nicola Yeates (2001) *Globalization and Social Policy*

The issue of globalization now features prominently in social policy courses. Nicola Yeates provides a useful guide to the various debates about globalization and its impact on state welfare. The book provides an in-depth review of the relationship between international government organizations and social policy as well as the global dimensions of social conflict and political struggle.

Mark Kleinman (2002) *A European Welfare State?*

In this book Kleinman provides a very clear guide to some of the key developments in European social policy. The first part of the book focuses on broad developments in European welfare, regime theory and globalization. Subsequent chapters are devoted to the development of EU social policy, the possibility of a European welfare state and European citizenship, the impact of economic integration, unemployment and social exclusion. The author concludes that although there are continuous pressures for greater integration of welfare at a European level, this will not lead to the development of uniform national welfare systems.

Rebecca Blank and Ron Haskins (eds) (2001) *The New World of Welfare*

This edited book provides an excellent overview of the direction of contemporary welfare policy in the United States. The book examines the background to the Personal Responsibility and Work Opportunity Reconciliation Act of 1996 and its subsequent impact on the level of welfare dependency. Detailed consideration is given to the question of how the key federal 'poverty' programme, Temporary As-

sistance for Needy Families, established under this act might be reformed when it comes up for 'reauthorization' in the autumn of 2002. The book contains contributions from a number of influential commentators including Murray, Mead, Heclo and Garfinkel.

Peter Taylor-Gooby (ed.) (2001) *Welfare States Under Pressure*

This volume reviews how the welfare states of Finland, Sweden, France, Germany, Spain, Switzerland and the UK are adapting to economic and social change. While there remain important differences in the welfare arrangements of these countries, the contributors highlight how each of these nations has devoted attention to welfare reform, pro-active labour market policies, cost containment and more diverse forms of welfare delivery.

Michael Lavalette and Gerry Mooney (eds) (2000) *Class Struggle and Social Welfare*

In recent decades social divisions such as gender, race, sexuality and disability have tended to receive greater attention than social class in the social policy literature. This lively collection of essays attempts to redress this balance. The topics covered include self-help and popular welfare, the Clydebank rent strike of the 1920s, abortion rights, riots and urban unrest in the 1980s and 1990s, the Poll Tax rebellion and the mental health users' movement.

Tony Fitzpatrick (2001) *Welfare Theory: An Introduction*

Fitzpatrick provides a useful guide to some of the key concepts that have traditionally been studied in social policy courses such as welfare, equality, liberty, citizenship, power and class. The author also explores some of the more recent theoretical developments in the subject. Amongst the topics covered are post-modernism and post-structuralism, environmentalism, risk society, the body and the new genetics.

Alan Deacon (2002) *Perspectives on Welfare*

In the first part of this volume Deacon examines five different approaches to welfare based on equality, self-interest, paternalism, obligation and 'time-limited' support. In the process Deacon explores the ideas of key thinkers such as Tawney, Titmuss, Murray, Field, Mead, Etzioni and Ellwood. In Part 2 Deacon provides a thoughtful overview of recent welfare reforms in the United States and Britain.

Marilyn Howard, Alison Garnham, Geoff Fimister and John Veit-Wilson (2001) *Poverty: The Facts*

Now in its fourth edition, this publication provides a concise introduction to a range of issues. It looks at concepts and measures of poverty, current poverty data, the impact of unemployment and changing family structures on poverty, the impact of poverty and deprivation with particular reference to children, the link between ethnicity and poverty, the distribution of income and wealth, the spatial dimensions of poverty and international trends.

Allson Park, John Curtice, Katarina Thomson, Lindsay Jones and Catherine Bromley (eds) (2001) *British Social Attitudes: The Eighteenth Report*

The annual *British Social Attitudes* reports always provide some fascinating information about social policy. By comparing findings over time it helps to chart the development of public attitudes to a range of issues. In the current volume John Hills explores the extent to which the public supports New Labour's approach to poverty and poverty reduction. Other chapters explore public views on such topics as marriage and cohabitation, teenage moth-

erhood and the National Health Service.

Other Sources

The *Social Policy Review*, published annually by Policy Press on behalf of the Social Policy Association, contains a broad cross-section of essays covering topical issues in social policy. In addition students should consult specialist journals, newspapers and periodicals.

Journals

There are a vast number of journals that are of use to social policy students. Many of these are now accessible in electronic versions to registered subscribers. Here is a selection: -

Critical Social Policy
Global Social Policy
Journal of European Social Policy
Journal of Social Policy
Policy and Politics
Politics
Social Policy and Society
Social Policy and Administration
The Political Quarterly

Newspapers and magazines

Newspapers
The various broadsheet newspapers provide details and commentary on social policy topics.

The Guardian
The Observer
The Independent
The Independent on Sunday
The Times
The Sunday Times
The Financial Times

It is also informative to examine the way in which social policy issues are covered in the tabloid press.

Magazines

A number of weekly or monthly magazines devote space to social policy issues. These include:-

New Statesman www.newstatesman.co.uk
The Spectator www. spectator.co.uk
The Economist www.economist.com
Prospect www.prospect-magazine.co.uk

Parties

It is worthwhile to look at the websites of the main political parties.

The Conservative Party www.conservatives.com
The Labour Party www.labour.org.uk
The Liberal Democrats www.libdems.org.uk

Government departments and the various think-tanks often provide information about social policy developments and details of relevant pamphlets and reports (see chapters V.4 to V.7).

Bibliography

Abel-Smith, B. and Townsend, P., 1965. *The Poor and the Poorest*. Occasional Papers on Social Administration, no.17. London: Bell.

Alcock, C. Payne, S. and Sullivan, M., 2000. *Introducing Social Policy*. Harlow: Pearson.

Alcock, P. (1996), *Social Policy in Britain: Themes and Issues*. Basingstoke: Macmillan Press.

Alcock, P. Glennerster, H., Oakley, A., and Sinfield, A. (eds), 2001. *Welfare and Wellbeing: Richard Titmuss's Contribution to Social Policy*. Bristol: Policy Press.

Baldock, J., Manning, N. Miller, S. and Vickerstaff, S. (eds), 1999. *Social Policy*. Oxford: Oxford University Press.

Blakemore, K., 1998. *Social Policy: An Introduction*, Buckingham: Open University Press.

Blank, R. and Haskins, R. (eds), 2001. *The New World of Welfare*. Washington DC: Brookings Institution Press.

Campbell, J., 1987. *Nye Bevan: A Biography*. London: Hodder & Stoughton.

Campbell, J., 2000. *Margaret Thatcher. Volume One: The Grocer's Daughter*. London: Jonathan Cape.

Castles, F. and Mitchell, D., 1992. 'Identifying welfare state regimes'. *Governance* 5, 1, pp.1–26.

Commission on Social Justice, 1994. *Social Justice*. London: Vintage.

Deacon, A., 2002. *Perspectives on Welfare*. Buckingham: Open University Press.

Ellison, N. and Pierson, C. (eds), 1998. *Developments in British Social Policy*. Basingstoke: Macmillan Press.

Esping-Andersen, 1990. *The Three Worlds of Welfare Capitalism*. Cambridge: Polity Press.

Finch, J. and Groves, D. (eds), 1983. *A Labour of Love: Women, Work and Caring*. London: Routledge & Kegan Paul.

Fitzpatrick, T., 2001. *Welfare Theory: An Introduction*. Basingstoke, Palgrave.

Foot, M., 1997. *Aneurin Bevan*. London: Victor Gollanz.

Fraser, D., 2002. *The Evolution of the British Welfare State*, 3rd edn, first published 1973. Basingstoke: Palgrave Macmillan.

George, V. and Wilding, P., 1976, *Ideology and Social Welfare*. London: Routledge & Kegan Paul.

George, V. and Wilding, P., 1994. *Welfare and Ideology*. Hemel Hempstead: Prentice-Hall/ Harvester Wheatsheaf.

Giddens, A., 1994. *Beyond Left and Right*. Cambridge, Polity Press.

Giddens, A., 1998. *The Third Way*. Cambridge: Polity Press.

Giddens, A., 2000. *The Third Way and its Critics*. Cambridge: Polity Press.

Giddens, A., 2002. *Where Now for New Labour?* Cambridge: Polity Press.

Gladstone, D., 1999. *The Twentieth-Century Welfare State*, Basingstoke: Macmillan Press.

Glennerster, H., 2000. *British Social Policy Since 1945*, 2nd edn, first published 1995. Oxford: Blackwell.

Gough, I., 1979. *The Political Economy of the Welfare State*. London: Macmillan.

Howard, M. Garnham, A., Fimister, G. and Veit-Wilson, J., 2001. *Poverty: The Facts*, 4th edn, first published 1990. London: Child Poverty Action Group.

Jefferys, K., 1999. *Anthony Crosland*. London: Richard Cohen.

Kleinman, M., 2002. *A European Welfare State?* Basingstoke: Palgrave Macmillan.

Lavalette, M. and Mooney, G. (eds), 2000. *Class Struggle and Social Welfare*. London: Routledge.

Lavalette, M. and Pratt, A. (eds), 2001. *Social Policy: A Conceptual and Theoretical Introduction*, 2nd edn, London: Sage.

Le Grand, J., 1982. *The Strategy of Equality*. London: Allen & Unwin.

Lewis, J., 1992. 'Gender and the development of welfare regimes', *Journal of European Social Policy*, 2, 3, pp.159-73.

Liebfried, S., 1993. 'Towards a European welfare state', in C. Jones (ed.), 1993. *New Perspectives on the Welfare State in Europe*. London: Routledge, ch.7.

Lister, R. (ed.), 1996. *Charles Murray and the Underclass: The Developing Debate*. London: IEA.

Lowe, R., 1999. *The Welfare State in Britain Since 1945*. 2nd edition, first published 1993. Basingstoke:Macmillan Press.

Major, J., 1999. *John Major: The Autobiography*. London: HarperCollins.

Marshall, T.H., 1950. *Citizenship and Social Class and Other Essays*. Cambridge: Cambridge University Press.

Mishra, R., 1981. *Society and Social Policy*. 2nd edition, first published 1977. London: Macmillan.

Morgan, K., 1997. *Callaghan: A Life*. Oxford: Oxford University Press.

Murray, C., 1984. *Losing Ground*. New York: Basic Books.

Murray, C., 1990. *The Emerging British Underclass*. London: IEA.

Park, A., Curtice, J., Thomson, K. Jarvis, L. and Bromley, C. (eds), *British Social Attitudes: The Eighteenth Report*. London: Sage.

Pascall, G., 1986. *Social Policy: A Feminist Analysis*. London: Tavistock.

Pascall, G., 1997. *Social Policy: A New Feminist Analysis*, London: Routledge.

Piachaud, D., 1987. 'Problems in the definition and measurement of poverty', *Journal of Social Policy*, 16, 2 (April), pp. 147–64.

Pimlott, B., 1993. *Harold Wilson*. London: HarperCollins.

Pinker, R., 1971. *Social Theory and Social Policy*. London: Heinemann.

Pinker, R., 1995. 'T. H. Marshall', in V. George and R. Page (eds), *Modern Thinkers on Welfare*, Hemel Hempstead: Prentice-Hall/Harvester Wheatsheaf, ch. 6.

Powell, M., 1995. 'The strategy of equality revisited', *Journal of Social Policy*, 24, 2 (April), pp.163–85.

Reisman, D., 2001. *Richard Titmuss: Welfare and Society*. 2nd edn. Basingstoke: Palgrave.

Report of the Commission on Social Justice, 1994. *Social Justice: Strategies for National Renewal*. London: Vintage.

Report of the Committee on Social Insurance and Allied Services (The Beveridge Report), 1942. Cmd 6404, London: HMSO.

Taylor-Gooby, P. (ed.), 2001. *Welfare States Under Pressure*, London: Sage.

Tawney, R. H., 1931. *Equality*. London: Allen & Unwin.

Thane, P., 1996. *The Foundations of the British Welfare State*. 2nd edn, first published 1982. London: Longman.

Timmins, N., 2001. *The Five Giants*. Rev. edn, first published 1995. London: HarperCollins.

Titmuss, R. M., 1950. *Problems of Social Policy*. London: HMSO and Longman, Green and Co.

Titmuss, R. M., 1970. *The Gift Relationship*. London: Allen & Unwin.

Titmuss, R. M., 1974 *Social Policy: An Introduction*. London: George Allen & Unwin.

Townsend, P., 1979. *Poverty in the United Kingdom*, Harmondsworth: Penguin.

Toynbee, P. and Walker. D., 2001. *Did Things Get Better?* Harmondsworth: Penguin.

Ward, C., 1996. 'Fringe benefits', *New Statesman & Society*, 8 March.

Williams, F., 1989. *Social Policy: A Critical Introduction*. Cambridge: Polity Press.

Wilson, E., 1977. *Women and the Welfare State*. London: Tavistock.

Yeates, N., 2001. *Globalization and Social Policy*. London: Sage.

Young, H., 1993. *One of Us*. Final edn, first published 1989. London: Pan.

V.4
Data sources in the UK: National, Central and Local Government

Fran Wasoff

Evidence, and the critical use of evidence, is central to the study of social policy. As a student of social policy you need to know how evidence informs social policy and be able to use and draw on evidence yourself to develop your own critical appraisal of social policies. Government, because of its responsibilities and resources, is one of the most important sources of empirical data for the study and practice of social policy. In addition, there are other sources of data at a national level which are important resources for understanding social policy and its effects. This chapter is an introduction to the main sources of empirical data produced by central government and other producers of data at a national level on social policy issues in the UK. In this chapter we look at:

- what are the main sources of data from government for the study of social policy?
- what is their nature, scope, advantages and limitations?
- how can you get access to data sources in print and electronically?
- pointers to further information about these data sources.

The main sources of data at a national level are national data-sets and statistical publications of government departments.

National Data Sources: Data-sets
What is a data-set?

A data-set is a collection of observations, measurements or variables from a study of a set of individuals (people or other units, such as households or houses), called *cases*, and contains all the variables measured for those cases. The most typical data-set has data collected from a survey. A data-set consists not only of the set of measurements for variables for each case, but also a list of the names and definitions of the variables and the values they can take (this is called a *code book*), so that the measurements can be understood and interpreted. National data-sets are important for the study of social policy since they typically contain information about a very large number of cases that, as a group, are representative of the nation as a whole, because the cases that are studied (the sample) are chosen by random sampling methods that ensure the sample closely approximates, or is similar to, the entire population from which it was chosen (Robson, 2001).

Who produces national data-sets?

Government surveys produce most of the significant national data-sets. Surveys are used by government to help inform policy making, implementation and evaluation. They are also important sources of evidence for the social policy academic community.

Box V.4.1   National data-sets used in social policy

- Census-based data-sets

Census of Population
Census Samples of Anonymised Records (SARs)
Longitudinal Study (LS)

- Continuous or recurrent cross-sectional surveys

General Household Survey (GHS)
Family Expenditure Survey (FES) / Expenditure and Food Survey (EFS)
Quarterly Labour Force Survey (LFS)
New Earnings Survey (NES)
Family Resources Survey
Census of Employment/ Annual Employment Survey
Scottish Household Survey

- Longitudinal surveys or panel studies

Longitudinal Study (LS)
British Household Panel Survey (BHPS)
National Child Development Study (NCDS)
Millennium Cohort Study
Quarterly Labour Force Survey (panel study element)

- Other surveys of government departments and non-government bodies

Households Below Average Income Data-set, 1961-1991 (HBAI)
British Social Attitudes Survey (BSAS)
National Child Development Study (NCDS)
British Household Panel Survey (BHPS)
Scottish Household Survey (SHS)

Many government surveys are conducted by the Office for National Statistics (ONS) which is the main central government body responsible for official statistics. The ONS is a government agency that is independent of other government departments. It was formed in 1996 by merging the OPCS (Office of Population Censuses and Surveys) and the CSO (Central Statistical Office). It is headed by the National Statistician, who is accountable to the Chancellor of the Exchequer. ONS is responsible for collecting and disseminating UK statistics, and coordinates a wide range of economic and social statistics collected by government. In 2000, National Statistics, the brandname or logo for statistics produced by the government statistical service, was created. Its website (http://www.statistics.gov.uk/) is the web gateway to official government statistics. National Statistics is advised by an independent organization, the Statistics Commission, consisting of a chairman and members appointed by the Chancellor of the Exchequer.

National data-sets commonly used in social policy are also produced by other, non-governmental, bodies, often with government support, such as the Economic and Social Research Council (ESRC), the National Centre for Social Research, the Institute for Fiscal Studies (IFS) and in universities, such as the Centre for Longitudinal Studies, Institute of Education, University of London and the Institute for

---

Box V.4.2   Statistical publications of other central government departments

- Education

Education and Training Statistics for the United Kingdom (www.dfes.gov.uk/statistics/)
Schools in England

- Employment

Labour Market Trends

- Health

Health and Personal Social Services Statistics for England
Health and Personal Social Services Statistics for Wales
Scottish Health Statistics

- Housing

Survey of English Housing
English House Condition Survey (Dept for Transport, Local Government and the Regions)
Scottish Executive Statistical Bulletin (Housing Series)

- Justice

Criminal Statistics England and Wales
Judicial Statistics England and Wales
Civil Judicial Statistics Scotland
British Crime Survey

- Social security

Work and Pensions Statistics (formerly Social Security Statistics) (Dept for Work and Pensions)

Social and Economic Research (ISER), University of Essex.

What are the most commonly used national data-sets?

Since social policy is a broad-based and multidisciplinary area of study, it draws on a wide range of data sources. In this chapter, we will look at some that are commonly used. National data-sets have several research designs: census, continuous or recurrent cross-sectional surveys (a 'snap-shot' in which each set of respondents are studied once at about the same time), one-off national surveys, and longitudinal surveys or panel studies (where data are collected from the same group of people more than once in order to study changes over time).

Census of Population

The British Census of Population is conducted every ten years. It is a cross-sectional 'snapshot' that contains information about every household and every individual in Great Britain. There is no sampling for the census, since it attempts to collect information from *every* household; each household is legally obliged to fill in a census return. The census contains information about household characteristics, such as housing tenure, house type and number of rooms, and family composition. It also has information about each person in the household, such as their ages, sex, social class, marital status, economic activity, ethnic origin (as the respondent defines it), occupation and educational qualifications. (It does not have information about household or individuals' incomes). It gives the most accurate count of population size (of people and households) for national and local areas. Like most government statistics, the results are published as tables of aggregate data, i.e. the individual cases are grouped together, and reported as a group; it is not possible to recover the individual observation or case. Census information is available not only at national level, but also at sub-national levels, such as regions, or even smaller geographic units. Small Area Statistics or Local Base Statistics can be used for local analyses, e.g. for local government areas. (For more information about the census, go to its website: www.census.ac.uk.) Census statistics are published as printed reports and as statistical abstracts, both available from reference libraries. A feature of census data is that the non-specialist user has access only to those tables that National Statistics has chosen to publish. But this may not meet all needs. In the 1991 census, a further important resource became available that goes a long way to dealing with this limitation.

1991 and 2001 Census Samples of Anonymized Records (SARs)

Census data can now be used for data analysis tailored to a researcher's individual requirements and objectives. Samples of Anonymized Records (SARs), also called census microdata, are subsets of census data available on a 'case by case' basis in an 'anonymized' form, that is, cases contain no names, addresses or any other information that would allow individuals or households to be identified. (This ensures that the census requirement for confidentiality and security of data is respected.) There are two types of SARs: household and individual. The household SAR is a 1 per cent sample

of households and the individuals in each of these households. It has information about household characteristics, such as housing tenure and number of rooms, as well as information about each person in the household and how they are related to the head of the household. The individual SARs are a 2 per cent sample of individuals in households and communal establishments, containing over 1 million cases and information about age, sex, social class, ethnicity, economic activity and housing circumstances. SARs are useful not only for studying patterns at a national level, but also at subnational level, e.g. regional levels. At the time of writing, SARs from the 2001 census were being developed. SARs are available as a resource to the academic community. Further information can be obtained from the Centre for Census and Survey Research (CCSR), University of Manchester, Manchester M13 9PL (www.ccsr.ac.uk/cmu/index.htm).

Recurrent or continuous surveys

The Office for National Statistics conducts a number of recurrent or continuous surveys which are cross-sectional surveys, repeated in approximately similar form annually or at other intervals. (They are called *continuous* surveys because, as they are so large, the work on them is carried out continuously, like the proverbial painting of the Forth Bridge in the past – it is not now painted continuously. When work on one survey is completed, the next one begins.) Two important surveys of this type for students of social policy are the General Household Survey and the Family Expenditure Survey.

General Household Survey (GHS)

The General Household Survey (GHS) is an annual multi-purpose survey, providing national (Great Britain) information on, for example, housing and consumer durables, household composition, social class, employment, income (individual and household), education, health and social services, transport, population and social security. It is a nationally-representative continuous survey based on a sample of the general population resident in private, non-institutional households (it does not collect information from people living in institutions or in Northern Ireland). Information is collected by face to face interviews with all household members for about 16,000 individuals and about 9,000 households, chosen as a stratified random sample; thus it cannot be used for analysis of sub-national areas. Most questions recur from year to year, but surveys in individual years may also contain special topics.

Family Expenditure Survey (FES)/Expenditure and Food Survey (EFS)

The Family Expenditure Survey (FES) was an annual UK multi-purpose survey of about 7000 households from 1957 to 2001. From 2001, it was combined with the National Food Survey and became the Expenditure and Food Survey (EFS). It is nationally representative, but not appropriate for sub-national analyses. Data is collected by face to face interviews and from expenditure diaries kept by adult respondents for 2 weeks. Children aged 7 to 15 also keep a simplified expenditure diary. It has information about household and individuals' incomes, expenditure, including some recurrent payments (such as rent, fuel bills, telephone bills, and hire purchase payments). Since 2001, information on diet and nutrition is included. The survey is used to calculate the UK Retail Price Index (RPI), but is also used more generally by government and academic researchers where detailed data is needed about income, expenditure and food consumption at the household, tax unit and individual levels.

Labour Force Survey

The Quarterly Labour Force Survey is conducted by the Office for National Sta-

tistics. Since it began in1973 (when it was known as the Labour Force Survey), its scope has expanded steadily. It became an annual survey in 1983 and in 1992 when the sample size was boosted, coverage was extended to Northern Ireland, residents in NHS hospital accommodation and students in halls of residences; at the same time the results were published quarterly. It is a national survey with individual and household level data about the labour market and is used by government (e.g. the Department for Education and Skills and the Department of Trade and Industry) in the making of social and economic policy, for example, to decide on the allocation of the EU Social Fund. It contains information about household and family structure, basic housing information, education and economic activity. Data from the survey are available for national and local government areas. It has cross-sectional and panel study elements and consists of a quarterly survey conducted in Great Britain throughout the year, in which each individual sampled is interviewed (personally and by telephone) five times at quarterly intervals, producing about 15,000 responding households in every quarter, 'boosted' by a larger survey for the spring quarter. As a result, there is interview data from over 44,000 households in Great Britain and over 4,000 households in Northern Ireland.

New Earnings Survey

The New Earnings Survey is an annual survey conducted by the Office for National Statistics of earnings of employees in Great Britain. There is a similar survey carried out for Northern Ireland. Information about earnings is collected from employers in a 1 per cent random sample of employees in PAYE. There is information about earnings by industry, occupation and national collective agreement. The survey has been conducted since 1970; since 1996, sub-national data also became available.

Family Resources Survey

The Family Resources Survey is a nearly national survey (of private households in Great Britain south of the Caledonian Canal) of about 24,000 households, carried out since 1992 by the Office for National Statistics and the National Centre for Social Research for the Department for Work and Pensions. Data is collected by personal interview and there is information about household characteristics, household income (including welfare benefits and unearned income), assets, pensions and savings, housing costs, consumer durables and information on childcare arrangements and costs, carers and disability. Information about individuals includes employment status and ethnic origin. The purpose of this survey is to provide the DWP with data to monitor and evaluate policy, to forecast benefit expenditure, and to contribute to other analyses such as Households Below Average Income.

Census of Employment/ Annual Employment Survey

This bi-annual census, carried out from 1971 to 1995, and supplemented by smaller monthly and quarterly surveys, describes the level and distribution of employment in Great Britain. It contains data on the number of jobs by local area, sex, and full and part-time work. A separate Census of Employment is conducted for Northern Ireland, and these data are combined with the Census of Employment to produce UK figures. This survey has a large sample size; it is either a full census of about 1.25 million businesses or a sample survey of about 300,000 businesses. In 1995, it was replaced by the Annual Employment Survey (AES) of about 130,000 businesses.

The Scottish Household Survey

The Scottish Household Survey is a multipurpose continuous survey carried out by the Scottish Executive since 1999, to run until at least 2003, to inform its work and that of the Scottish parliament, and as a resource for the policy and academic community (www.scotland.gov.uk/shs/). It provides regular statistical snapshots at both Scottish and local authority levels through interviews with members of over 30,000 households. Information is collected at a household and individual level about topics such as household composition, housing, transport, children, health, disability and care, employment, household income and expenditure, education, safety and social networks.

Longitudinal studies

The Longitudinal Study (LS)

The Longitudinal Study is based on census data and traces individuals from one census to subsequent ones. A 1 per cent sample of individuals (about 500,000 people) chosen from the 1971 census was followed to the 1981 and 1991 censuses. A similar sample was chosen from the 1981 census and traced forward. The Longitudinal Study links the returns of those individuals across censuses; this allows for comparison of snap-shots at ten year intervals. (For further information, see http://www.cls.ioe.ac.uk/Ls/lshomepage.html.)

British Household Panel Survey

The British Household Panel Survey is a nationally representative (Great Britain), large-scale (over 5,500 households and 10,000 individuals) longitudinal study funded by the ESRC, and managed by the Institute for Social and Economic Research. It aims to enhance our understanding of social and economic change at the individual and household level. It consists of annual surveys, beginning in 1991, following the *same* respondents over time, with data from personal and telephone interviews and self-completed questionnaires, and is expected to continue to at least 2004.

The Survey includes individual and household-level information about social structure and social and political attitudes, household organization, labour market behaviour, income and wealth, housing, health and education. It has been used to study how households change, for example, housing mobility and the distribution of resources within households (Berthoud and Gershuny 2000; http://www.iser.essex.ac.uk/bhps/index.php).

The National Child Development Study (NCDS)

The National Child Development Study is a large, nationally representative longitudinal study of all the children born in Great Britain during one week in March 1958. It has charted the lives of about 17,000 people from early childhood to the age of 33 in order to enhance our knowledge of the influences on human physical, educational and social development over the whole lifecourse. This birth cohort has been studied on five occasions, or 'sweeps': at ages 7, 11, 16, 23 and 33. For the first three NCDS surveys, information was obtained from parents (who were interviewed by health visitors), head teachers and class teachers (who completed questionnaires), the schools health service (who carried out medical examinations) and the children themselves (who completed tests of ability and, latterly, questionnaires). In the 1981 and 1991 surveys information was obtained from the cohort members by interviewers and self-completion questionnaires. The 1991 survey also collected information from husbands, wives, cohabitees, and some children of cohort members.

The study was conducted by the Social Statistics Research Unit, City University (now the Centre for Longitudinal Studies, Institute of Education), with support from other bodies, including the Economic and Social Research Council, the Departments of Health, Social Security, Employment, Education and Science, Environment, the Training Agency, Health and Safety Execu-

tive, and voluntary organizations, such as the National Children's Bureau. (For further information, see Ferri 1993 and http://www.cls.ioe.ac.uk/Ncds/nhome.htm.)

Millennium Cohort Study

The Millennium Cohort Study (MCS) began its first sweep in May 2001. It will collect information for a sample of 15,000 babies born in the UK for the 12 month period beginning on 1 September 2000. The study is funded by the Economic and Social Research Council, directed by a consortium headed by the Centre for Longitudinal Studies, Institute of Education, University of London and fieldwork carried out by the National Centre for Social Research. It is a multi-purpose study that will be based on structured interviews with both mothers and (where resident) fathers or father figures.

Other surveys of government departments and non-government bodies

British Social Attitudes Survey

This is an annual survey conducted by the National Centre for Social Research since 1983. It is based on a nationally representative sample of about 3,500 adults who are interviewed and complete a questionnaire about their attitudes, behaviour, and household and employment circumstances. It includes such topics as housing, employment, health, care, education, social security and tax, the welfare state, transport, environment and social inequality. Since 1999 it has been complemented by a similar Scottish Social Attitudes Survey.

Households Below Average Income 1994/5–1999/2000 (HBAI)

This data is obtained from the Family Expenditure Survey from which a secondary analysis (Dale, Arber and Proctor, 1988) of a subset of data is carried out, and from the

British Household Panel Survey. It describes household incomes and characteristics of nationally representative samples for the period 1994/5 to 1999/2000. Data for the period 1961–1991 is also available as the Households Below Average Income Data-set 1961–1991. These can be used as the basis for analysing trends in poverty, inequality and real living standards in the UK over nearly forty years. It is sponsored by the Department for Work and Pensions. There is information about household income, (before and after housing costs, and by source of income), household and benefit unit characteristics (e.g. region and housing tenure, economic status, number of children, type of benefit received), and includes analyses by gender, region, age and family type (Department for Work and Pensions 2001; http://www.dss.gov.uk/publications/dss/2001/hbai/index.htm).

Ad hoc and other cross-sectional surveys

There are many other important sources of national data for social policy from *ad hoc* surveys, which are single, one-off surveys carried out for a particular purpose, though they are often valuable for secondary analysis. They are carried out by a government department or by a non-government organization, with support coming from both public and private sources.

Getting Access to Survey Data

Data are available from printed sources and increasingly, from electronic sources.

Print access

Information derived from data-sets is typically published as tables of aggregate data; and in the case of continuous surveys, publication is periodic (e. g. every year or every quarter). Check the Reference Library in your university or college. A particularly useful source of data in social policy is the annual periodical *Social Trends,* (see below).

Electronic access

Data is increasingly available electronically, either as aggegrated data in tables and charts or as the data-set itself. Some data is available on the World Wide Web; see the National Statistics website and Chapter V.7.

Doing your own secondary data analysis with national data-sets

You may wish to have access to the data-set itself in order to learn research methods or to carry out your own research or in-depth project. Data is increasingly available in computer-readable form, in a variety of formats, to conform to different software packages. Access to national data-sets, while a valuable development for the research community, nevertheless requires a considerable level of computer literacy, since users may need to be familiar with various statistical and data management software, different computer operating systems and a variety of file transfer techniques across a network. A considerable investment of time and money may be required to learn the various software packages and to obtain the code books and questionnaires in order to use a data-set intelligently. Registration and an undertaking to use the data responsibly are normally conditions for obtaining access to a data-set. Some data-sets have been adapted as teaching data-sets; these also require registration, but this is usually integral to the course in which they are used.

How to find out more about data-sets

There is a great deal more to learn about national data-sets. There are a few references at the end of this chapter where you can start. In addition, some of the producers of national data-sets also produce newletters and bulletins to keep users up to date, such as the ESRC Data Archive Newletter, the General Household Survey Newsletter (published by the ESRC Data Archive) and the MIDAS newletter. If you have access to the internet or World Wide Web you can find out more if you visit appropriate websites. For more information about connecting to websites using the internet, see chapter V.7.

Central Government Statistical Data Sources

There are numerous statistical data sources collected and published by government bodies, available from many reference and university libraries, that inform the study of social policy. These are produced by government primarily to meet the needs of its own policy makers and those who monitor social policies, but they are also rich sources of evidence for students and the academic community. The data is usually presented as tables or graphically. The range is extensive; below some commonly used publications are listed.

Publications of the Office for National Statistics

The National Statistics website (www. statistics.gov.uk) is a web gateway to a very wide range of government statistical publications, often available for free downloading. The Office for National Statistics publishes a comprehensive reference, *Guide to Official Statistics* (2000) with information about where to find more. It is organized by subject area and includes population, education, labour market, health and social care, income and living standards, crime and justice, housing, environment and the economy.

- *Social Trends*. This is an annual publication of the Office for National Statistics which is a particularly useful multi-purpose source that draws together statistics collected by many government departments to give a statistical snapshot of society today, and how it is changing. Information is presented in user-friendly form variously as text, tables, charts and graphs. It is also avail-able electronically for free on the National Statistics website. Each chapter focuses on a different social policy area, such as population, households and families, education, employment, income and wealth, health, social protection, crime and justice, housing, environment, transport and leisure.

- *Key Data: UK Social and Economic Statistics* is another annual multi-purpose statistical publication of National Statistics that contains basic statistics in the main economic and social areas. Tables are taken from other publications.

- *Regional Trends* (National Statistics; annual) provides a wide range of regional demographic, social and economic statistics, presented by regional profile, topic, areas, counties and districts.

- *Population Trends* (National Statistics; quarterly) publishes articles on a wide range of population and health subjects and contains vital statistics summaries.

- *Annual Abstract of Statistics* (National Statistics; annual) publishes in a single volume statistics on population, vital statistics (births, marriages, deaths), social services, social security, National Health Service, law enforcement, education, employment, national income and expenditure, personal income and wealth and central and local government finance.

Public and tax expenditure

Every year the government produces a series of publications about its expenditure plans for the following few years. At the time of writing, the most recent was entitled *The Government's Expenditure Plans 2001 to 2004*. These are annual departmental reports published as parliamentary papers referenced with command numbers. There are separate publications from each government department, published as a series in March, with each report containing the department's own expenditure plans as well as useful information about users, programmes, plans for the future and operations. Relevant for social policy are the reports of Inland Revenue, the Department for Work and Pensions, the Department of Health, the Department for Environment, Food and Rural Affairs, the Home Office and the Charity Commission and the Lord Chancellor's Department. Another public expenditure data source is *Public Expenditure Statistical Analyses*, an annual overview of central and local government expenditure and trends in public expenditure, published by the Treasury, and available from National Statistics.

Statistical Information About Local Government

Some statistical information about local government is collected by local authorities but compiled and published centrally, such as:

- local government trends (Institute of Public Finance, www.ipf.co.uk);
- local government financial statistics (England) (Office of the Deputy Prime Minister);
- Scottish local government financial statistics (Scottish Executive).

There is also information about individual local authorities in publications on housing and education.

Local authorities collect information about performance indicators in social service, education and housing, which is collated and published in December by the Audit Commission for England and Wales and the Accounts Commission for Scotland. In addition, local authorities themselves collect and publish statistics about their own areas in relation to particular local authority operations, such as services for children; housing plans with statistical information; and plans for care in the community. These publications vary; sometimes they form part of authorities' annual reports to local government committees. Check with the individual authority to see what is available. Further information about local government can be obtained from the Convention of Scottish Local Authorities (COSLA), Rosebery Terrace, 9 Haymarket Terrace, Edinburgh EH12 5XZ, the Local Government Association (for English and Welsh local authorities), Smith Square, London; and the Scottish Local Government Information Unit (SLGIU), 50 Wellington Street, Glasgow G2 6HJ.

Guide to further reading

Berthoud, Richard and Gershuny, Jonathan (eds), 2000. *Seven Years in the Lives of British Families: Evidence on the Dynamics of Social Change from the British Household Panel Survey.* Bristol: Policy Press.

Dale, Angela and Marsh, Catherine, 1993. *The 1991 Census User's Guide.* London: HMSO (for further information about the Census, SARs, the Longitudinal Study).

Dale, Angela, Arber, Sara, and Proctor, Michael, 1988. *Doing Secondary Analysis.* London: Unwin Hyman. (A user-friendly handbook for carrying out data analysis on large government survey data.)

Department for Work and Pensions, 2001. *Family Resources Survey Great Britain 1999-2000.* London: Stationery Office. (A full guide to the survey [http://www.dss.gov.uk/publications/dss/2001/frs/index.htm].)

Department for Work and Pensions , 2001. *Households Below Average Income 1994/95 to 1999/00/* London: Stationery Office.

Ferri, Elsa (ed.), 1993. *Life at 33: The Fifth Follow-up of the National Child Development Study.* London: National Children's Bureau. (This volume describes the Fifth NCDS carried out in 1991 and its preliminary findings.)

Office for National Statistics (ONS), *Labour Market Trends* (a monthly magazine with labour market information and statistics, on line at www.statistics.gov.uk).

Office for National Statistics, 2000. *Guide to Official Statistics: 2000 Edition*. London: Stationery Office; also on the ONS website. (This is a easy-to-use and comprehensive reference to statistical publications and electronic data sources produced by government departments and agencies.)

Office for National Statistics, 2002a. *Family Spending – A report on the Family Expenditure Survey* London: Stationery Office; also on the ONS website.

Office for National Statistics, 2002b. *Living in Britain 2000: Results from the 2000/01 General Household Survey*. London: ONS; also on the ONS website.

Robson, Colin, 2001. *Real World Research*. 2nd edn, Oxford: Blackwell (a clear and comprehensive textbook of research methods for social scientists).

V.5
Other Sources of UK Data

Fran Bennett

Introduction

This chapter provides an introduction to the main sources of information on social policy issues produced by organizations in the UK other than central and local government, universities and other academic institutions, and commercial publishers. Its main focus is on publications from voluntary organizations, although 'think-tanks' and research institutes, foundations and some private sector sources are also mentioned. It refers primarily to organizations themselves, rather than particular books or reports, since many such publications quickly go out of date and/or out of print. Certain key texts are noted, however, as well as some annually updated guides and regular journals.

This introduction outlines problems in gaining access to publications from such sources. The next section gives an overview of the information which *is* available, reviewing some of its strengths and weaknesses and indicating how to use it. There is then a round-up of sources of information which crosses different social policy areas. The final section describes the main sources of information in specific subject areas.

There are several reasons why social policy students may be unaware of the information produced by non-academic, non-governmental sources, in particular voluntary organizations. Unless individual academics have personal links with such organizations, their publications may not appear on reading lists or in academic libraries. Some voluntary organizations who see themselves primarily as pressure groups may claim that 'spreading the message' is a high priority, but may focus more on policy-makers and the media than on students. Other organizations who see themselves primarily as service providers have only recently begun to put priority on reporting on their work for a wider audience, and may still have underdeveloped marketing and distribution systems.

All these factors mean that advance planning is essential. Public libraries or bookshops are likely to stock only the major texts from bigger organizations, and even then probably only those published in book format. However, voluntary organizations will often willingly send out their publications lists, and the academic library can then order the relevant books or subscribe to a journal.

Another useful source of information on recent reports from non-governmental (as well as official) sources in 12 areas of social policy is the 'Social Policy Digest' in the *Journal of Social Policy*, the quarterly journal published by Cambridge University Press and associated with the Social Policy Association. Institutional subscribers to the *Journal*, such as academic libraries, also have access to the electronic version, which students may therefore be able to use.

Students can write to voluntary organizations themselves. But these groups are usually very hard-pressed, and may receive hundreds of such requests. The more specific a request is, the more likely it is to get a quick reply – perhaps a summary of a publication, sent out free of charge. Orders for books may take several weeks, and payment may have to be sent with the order. It is possible to visit some organizations' headquarters to buy their publications; but most are located in central London. Finally, voluntary organizations are slowly exploiting the potential of the internet; but many have not progressed far enough for people to access their publications in this way, and some do not keep their websites sufficiently up to date. Website addresses are given below where these are known. (Remember that some foundations and voluntary organizations may have separate sections based in Scotland, Wales and/or Northern Ireland, and that some reports may cover one or two countries rather than the whole UK.)

Overview of Available Information

Material from sources outside academia and government has a crucial contribution to make to the social policy debate. But it has both strengths and weaknesses. Compared with academic publications, it is likely to be much more up-to-date, and so can take account of recent policy shifts. But most voluntary organizations' resources do not stretch to funding large quantitative studies – though a critique of existing data is common. Their material will be particularly valuable for its in-depth policy analysis, qualitative research findings and communication of the 'user's' perspective. It may not display much awareness of ongoing academic debates, however, even within its own policy area.

Most information from voluntary organizations or the private sector will be practical rather than theoretical in orientation. It is likely to focus on specific policy issues, rather than giving an overview of current developments or a historical or comparative perspective.

A publication will also have been written with a particular purpose. A pressure group, or a think-tank with a political affiliation, may want to make the case for or against a certain policy. A private sector organization may want to sell more of a particular product, such as a type of insurance policy. It could be argued, however, that any written product always contains its own agenda; some are merely more open about this.

Sources of Information which Crosses Different Policy Areas

Think-tanks

'Think-tanks' are usually small, policy-oriented organizations which hope to influence governments, opinion-formers, the media and the public. They are often overtly or covertly linked to particular political parties or ideologies. Their main method of communication is usually the written word – via journals, pamphlets and books – although some may also organize seminars or conferences and other activities.

The think-tanks which probably contribute most to current social policy debates include:

- *Demos* (The Mezzanine, Elizabeth House, 39 York Road, London SE1 7NQ; www.demos.co.uk), originally founded by a group associated with the radical journal *Marxism Today*;
- the *Fabian Society* (11 Dartmouth Street, London SW1H 9BN; www.fabiansociety.org.uk), set up in 1884, and linked to the Labour Party; it serviced the Commission on Taxation and Citizenship, which reported in 2000;
- the *Institute for Public Policy Research* (30/32 Southampton Street, London WC2E 7RA; www.ippr.org.uk), which is seen as left of centre; it serviced the Commission on Social Justice in the mid-1990s, and the Commission on Public Private Partnerships in 2000/1;

- the *Institute for the Study of Civil Society* (*'Civitas'*), formerly the Health and Welfare Unit of the Institute of Economic Affairs (The Mezzanine, Elizabeth House, 39 York Road, London SE1 7NQ; www.civitas.org.uk), which proclaims its political independence, but which many commentators would place on the right, with an emphasis on market solutions to welfare problems and a 'liberal' ideology;
- the *New Policy Institute* (109 Coppergate House, 16 Brune Street, London E1 7NJ; www.npi.org.uk) – left of centre, but difficult to classify in terms of a fixed political position;
- the *Social Market Foundation* (11 Tufton Street, London SW1P 3QB; http://www.smf.co.uk), interested in exploring a 'social market' approach to policy issues.

Several other think-tanks, including the Adam Smith Institute, the Social Affairs Unit and the Centre for Policy Studies – also usually placed on the Right of the political spectrum – have published many social policy reports in the past. Two other relatively new think-tanks on the Left are Catalyst (33 Bury Street, London SW1Y 6AX; www.catalyst-trust.co.uk) and the Smith Institute, set up in memory of the late John Smith MP (Victoria Station House, 191 Victoria Street, London SW1E 5NE; www.smith-institute.org.uk). A new think-tank on the Right is Politeia (22 Charing Cross Road, London WC2H 0HR; www.politeia.co.uk).

Think-tanks vary in size and the strength of their support; but some may consist only of a group of research associates loosely connected with the organization, and a part-time administrator to send out publications. They also vary in the quality and depth of their analysis; but their publications will usually contain strong views and policy prescriptions.

- The *Radical Statistics* group (c/o 3 Hazelhurst Road, Heaton, Bradford BD9 6BJ; www.radstats.org.uk for up-to-date information) is a group of statisticians and researchers committed to demystifying statistics and concerned about the lack of community control over their use. Articles in its journal have examined, for example, census figures, unemployment statistics and health/education data.

Two other important organizations that work as research institutes rather than think-tanks are:

- the *Institute for Fiscal Studies* (7 Ridgmount Street, London WC1E 7AE; www.ifs.org.uk), which concentrates on economic, public finance and tax issues, and is known in particular for quantitative, often secondary, research;
- the *Policy Studies Institute* (100 Park Village East, London NW1 3SR; www.psi.org.uk), which conducts primary research on a wide variety of social policy issues, supported by government departments, other government bodies and charitable funders.

Foundations

Foundations are usually grant-giving bodies. They commission research or policy analysis directly, or respond to requests for research funding, or do both. They may decide to fund a programme of work in a specific area, or set up an inquiry to investigate an issue.

Two of the best known foundations in the social policy area are:

- the *Nuffield Foundation* (28 Bedford Square, London WC1B 3JS; www.nuffieldfoundation.org), whose interests include education (in its broadest sense) and medicine;
- the *Joseph Rowntree Foundation* (The Homestead, 40 Water End, York YO30 6WP; www.jrf.org.uk), whose main area of interest is in the underlying causes of poverty, but which works on housing, disability and community care, the family and parenthood, volunteering, and

income and wealth distribution, among other issues.

The Joseph Rowntree Foundation publishes useful summaries (often called 'Findings', or 'Foundations') of the results from many of the research projects it funds. Individual copies are available free of charge, and on the website. The full reports are published by the Foundation itself or by another publisher. A key social policy text from the Foundation is: J. Hills with Karen Gardiner and the LSE Welfare State Programme (1997) *The Future of Welfare: a Guide to the Debate (Revised edition)*. York: Joseph Rowntree Foundation. This analysis examines critically the assertion that the welfare state is in crisis, and looks at options for change in social security, health, education and social services.

- The *Carnegie (UK) Trust* (Comely Park House, Dunfermline, Fife KY12 7EJ; www.carnegieuktrust.org.uk) is another grant-giving foundation, which also carries out inquiries of its own. It has recently investigated the issues facing both older people and young people in the UK.

Government-funded bodies

Some of the key government-funded bodies with broad-ranging responsibilities in the social policy field are:

- the *National Consumer Council* (20 Grosvenor Gardens, London SW1W 0DH; www.ncc.org.uk), which describes itself as 'the independent voice of the consumer', and has a special focus on low-income consumers;
- the *Equal Opportunities Commission* (Arndale House, Arndale Centre, Manchester M4 3EQ; www.eoc.org.uk), which examines inequality between men and women, and can support legal test cases and undertake investigations into particular organizations' practices;
- the *Commission for Racial Equality* (Elliot House, 10/12 Allington Street, London

SW1E 5EH; www.cre.gov.uk), which monitors racial discrimination and the position of minority ethnic groups in UK society; and
- the *Disability Rights Commission* (DRC, Freepost MID 02164, Stratford-upon-Avon, CV37 9BR; www.drc.gb.org), which is an independent body set up to secure civil rights for disabled people.

Most have their own publications programme. The EOC, for example, usually publishes annual editions of *Facts about Women and Men in Britain*.

- The *National Association of Citizens Advice Bureaux* (115-123 Pentonville Road, London N1 9LZ; www.nacab.org.uk) is also largely government-funded. There is a Citizens Advice Bureau in most towns, providing free advice and information on a wide range of topics. NACAB publishes 'evidence reports', and a quarterly journal, covering a variety of social policy issues based on bureaux' individual cases.

Sources of Information on Specific Social Policy Issues

Poverty and income distribution

Probably the most comprehensive source of information on the growth of poverty and inequality in the UK over the 1980s in particular is the report of the Joseph Rowntree Foundation's *Inquiry into Income and Wealth*, which drew together and analysed findings from specially commissioned research and other evidence (a summary is available). The first volume gives an overview and policy recommendations; the second gives more details of the research:

Barclay, P., 1995. *Joseph Rowntree Foundation Inquiry into Income and Wealth*, Volume 1. York: JRF.

Hills, J., 1995. *Joseph Rowntree Foundation Inquiry into Income and Wealth*, Volume 2. York: JRF.

A more recent report, by Gordon, D. et

al. *Poverty and Social Exclusion in Britain* (York: JRF, 2000) updates and adds to the 'Breadline Britain' survey of poverty originally developed in the 1980s.

Relevant research findings, summaries of current debates and an analysis of the impact of poverty on different groups are drawn together by the Child Poverty Action Group in M. Howard, et al. *Poverty: the Facts*, 4th edition (London: CPAG, 2001). (CPAG: 94 White Lion Street, London N1 9PF; www.cpag.org.uk.) This key text covers a much broader field than child poverty, and is updated every few years. CPAG also publishes a journal, *Poverty*, three times a year, containing new data, as well as news and feature articles.

A summary of the report of the Commission on Social Justice and a series of pamphlets are available from the Institute for Public Policy Research/Central Books. The full report was published in 1994: *Social Justice: Strategies for National Renewal*. (London: Vintage). Distributional issues, and the politics of taxation, are discussed in another useful publication, the report of the Commission on Taxation and Citizenship: *Paying for Progress: A New Politics of Tax for Public Spending* (London: Fabian Society, 2000).

'Empowerment', User Involvement and Participation

Community 'empowerment' often forms part of strategies to combat poverty and disadvantage, and many voluntary/community organizations are involved in promoting it. The *Community Development Foundation* (60 Highbury Grove, London N5 2AG; www.cdf.org.uk) produces many reports about community development work, and the *New Economics Foundation* (Cinnamon House, 6-8 Cole Street, London SE1 4YH; www.neweconomics.org) also publishes relevant reports. The *Urban Forum* (4 Dean's Court, St Paul's Churchyard, London EC4V 5AA; www.urbanforum.org.uk) brings together groups involved in area regeneration.

There is a strong movement towards or-

ganizations *of*, rather than *for*, service users, especially disabled people. One such body is the *British Council of Organisations of Disabled People* (Litchurch Plaza, Litchurch Lane, Derby DE24 8AA; www.bcodp.org.uk), which brings together many organizations run by disabled people. A commission to 'offer welfare state service users a real opportunity to say what kind of welfare state they would like to see' produced a report about its findings in 1997: P. Beresford and M. Turner *It's Our Welfare: Report of the Citizens' Commission on the Future of the Welfare State* (London: National Institute for Social Work).

The *UK Coalition against Poverty* (c/o OBAC, 1st Floor, Gloucester House, Camberwell New Road, London SE5 0RZ) groups organizations committed to participation by people living in poverty in policy debates and decision-making processes; in 2000, it supported a Commission which produced a report on this issue: *Listen, Hear! The Right to be Heard*. (Bristol: Policy Press/UKCAP).

Social Security and Income Protection

Several voluntary organizations publish annually updated handbooks on the social security benefits system:

- the *Welfare Benefits Handbook*, published by CPAG, covers the whole benefits system, and tax credits;
- the *Disability Rights Handbook*, covering benefits for disabled people, is published by the Disability Alliance Educational and Research Association (1st Floor East, Universal House, 88-94 Wentworth Street, London E1 7SA; www.disabilityalliance.org);
- *Your Rights* is published by Age Concern England (Astral House, 1268 London Road, London SW16 4EJ; www.ace.org.uk), and covers benefits for older people. These books are usually published each April. Changes in the benefits system during the year are

covered in articles in the organizations' journals (such as the *Welfare Rights Bulletin*, published by CPAG).

The same organizations often publish reports on proposed or actual policy changes in the social security system. Private sector bodies publishing documents on pensions and insurance provision include the Association of British Insurers (www.abi.org.uk), the National Association of Pension Funds (www.napf.co.uk), which brings together occupational pension scheme providers, and the Institute of Actuaries (www.actuaries.org.uk).

Health and health care

A useful source of information and views on services can often be obtained from service providers, the trade unions and professional associations. The *British Medical Association* (BMA House, Tavistock Square, London WC1H 9JP; www.bma.org.uk) and the *British Medical Journal* (www.bmj.com) have regularly commented on both public health issues and government health policies – see, for example, BMA (2001) *Leading Change*. The Association of Community Health Councils often publishes reports about issues of concern to patients: 30 Drayton Park, London N5 1PB (www.achew.org.uk).

A key foundation in the health field is the *King's Fund*, whose publications can be obtained from King's Fund Publishing, 11-13 Cavendish Square, London W1M 0AN (www.kingsfund.org.uk). The *UK Public Health Association* brings together individuals and groups interested in public health issues and commissions research and produces publications (Trevelyan House, 30 Great Peter Street, London SW1P 2HW; www.ukpha.org.uk).

Education

It is more difficult to point to key texts in education, since it spans such a broad area. *The Advisory Centre for Education* (1b Aber-

deen Studios, 22-24 Highbury Grove, London N5 2DQ; www.ace-ed.org.uk) produces handbooks about the current education system for parents, governors and schools.

The *Education Network* (c/o Local Government Information Unit, 22 Upper Woburn Place, London WC1H 0TB; www.ten.info) produces research and information relevant to local education authorities. The *Campaign for State Education* (158 Durham Road, London SW20 0DG; www.casenet.org.uk) produces briefings on current concerns in education, as well as information leaflets, booklets and a bulletin. The teaching unions, such as the National Union of Teachers (www.teachers.org.uk) and the National Association of Headteachers (www.naht.org.uk) also produce their own reports. Chapters in books published by CPAG deal with educational disadvantage and low income.

Housing

An annual publication, the *Housing Finance Review*, is produced by the Joseph Rowntree Foundation and the Chartered Institute of Housing (Octavia House, Westwood Way, Coventry CV4 8JP; www.cih.org); between them, the JRF and CIH also publish much other valuable source material on housing issues.

The major pressure group working on housing issues is *Shelter* (88 Old Street, London EC1V 9HU; www.shelter.org.uk), which produces regular publications analysing homelessness figures and commenting on policy proposals. *Homeless Link* (www.homeless.org.uk) brings together providers in the homelessness field.

Various organizations produce reports analysing issues relevant to their sector of the housing market. The publications of the *National Housing Federation* (175 Gray's Inn Road, London WC1 8UP; www.housing.org.uk), for example, cover issues relevant to social housing.

Personal social services

Organizations representing the interests of particular groups, such as *Age Concern England* (www.ace.org.uk) or *Help the Aged* (www.helptheaged.org.uk), and the *Disability Alliance*, which brings together many different disability organizations, often deal with issues about service provision as well as income. There are also many organizations that focus on specific disabilities. *Carers UK* (20-25 Glasshouse Yard, London EC1A 4JT; www.carersonline.org.uk) produces reports about informal care and the situation of carers. (For children and social services, see 'Children and the family' below.) The Association of Directors of Social Services (www.adss.org.uk) sometimes produces its own reports.

Law and the offender

There is a plethora of groups working on criminal justice and penal affairs issues, such as

- the *National Association for the Care and Resettlement of Offenders* (NACRO, 169 Clapham Road, London SW9 0PU; www. nacro.org.uk);
- the *Howard League for Penal Reform* (1 Ardleigh Road, London N1 4HS; http://www.ukonline.co.uk/howardleague.org.uk); and
- the *Prison Reform Trust* (2nd Floor, The Old Trading House, 15 Northburgh Street, London EC1V 0AH; www.prisonreformtrust.org.uk).

Many reports on these topics are published under a joint imprint: the *Penal Affairs Consortium* (Room A1024a, The Law Department, University of East London, Longbridge Road, Dagenham, Essex RM8 2AS; www.penalaffairs.co.uk). The *National Association of Probation Officers* and the *Association of Chief Probation Officers* also have a tradition of commissioning research and publishing policy analysis.

If the law itself is regarded as a social policy issue, the *Legal Action Group* (242 Pentonville Road, London N1 9UN; www.lag.org.uk) is a key organization. It publishes policy comment on issues such as proposals to reform legal aid.

Unemployment and the labour market

Key organizations in this field include:

- the *Centre for Economic and Social Inclusion* (PO Box 30069, 89 Albert Embankment, London SE1 7WR; www.cesi.org.uk), which is expert in government training and work schemes. Its journal is *Working Brief*, and it also publishes guides to benefits and training for unemployed people;
- the *Work Foundation* (3 Carlton Terrace, London SW1Y 5DG; www.theworkfoundation.com) produces policy reports on employment issues;
- the *Low Pay Unit* (9 Arkwright Road, London NW3 6AB; www.lowpayunit.org.uk), which has a journal, *The New Review*, and produces policy publications.

The *Trades Union Congress* (Congress House, Great Russell Street, London WC1B 3LS; www.tuc.org.uk) and the *Confederation of British Industry* (Centre Point, 103 New Oxford Street, London WC1A 1DU; www.cbi.org.uk) also produce regular reports on employment issues. The Joseph Rowntree Foundation organized a research programme on the future of work, which reported in 1997.

'Race' and gender

As mentioned above, the Commission for Racial Equality and the Equal Opportunities Commission publish material on 'race' and gender respectively.

Material on refugee/asylum issues is published by the *British Refugee Council* (3-9 Bondway House, Bondway, London SW8 1SJ; www.refugeecouncil.org.uk). The *Runnymede Trust* (133 Aldersgate Street, London EC1A 4JA; www.runnymedetrust.org) publishes reports on race and minority ethnic issues, and supported a Commission which produced in 2000 *The Future of Multi-ethnic Britain: The Parekh Report* (London: Profile Books).

The *Fawcett Society* (45 Beech Street, London EC2P 2LX; www.fawcettsociety.org.uk) has a brief to look at all aspects of gender inequality, although many groups also exist which publish material on the impact of specific policies on women. *Stonewall* is a pressure group for gay men and lesbians (46 Grosvenor Gardens, London SW1W 0EB; www.stonewall.org.uk).

Children and the family

The *National Family and Parenting Institute* is a voluntary organization producing briefings on families and family policy (430 Highgate Studios, 53-79 Highgate Road, London NW5 1TL; www.nfpi.org.uk). Publications from the *Family Policy Studies Centre*, which has now closed, may also still be useful, and are stored at the Department of Social Policy and Social Work, University of Oxford; some are available to buy via the Joseph Rowntree Foundation.

More specialist organizations publish material about specific types of family or issues – such as the *National Council for One Parent Families* (255 Kentish Town Road, London NW5 2LX; www.oneparentfamilies.org.uk), or the *Daycare Trust* (21 St. George's Road, London SE1 6ES; www.daycaretrust.org.uk).

Most children's charities produce some publications – on family centres, juvenile justice, child abuse, child poverty and other social policies affecting children. The rel-

evant umbrella organization is the *National Council of Voluntary Child Care Organisations* (Unit 4, Pride Court, 80-82 White Lion Street, London N1 9PF; www.ncvcco.org). The key research organization is the *National Children's Bureau* (8 Wakley Street, London EC1V 7QE; www.ncb.org.uk). The *National Youth Agency* publishes reports about young people and youth work (17-23 Albion Street, Leicester LE1 6GD; www.nya.org.uk).

The voluntary sector

The central texts on issues relating to voluntary organizations themselves are probably published by the umbrella body, the *National Council for Voluntary Organisations* (NCVO, Regent's Wharf, 8 All Saints Street, London N1 9RL; www.ncvo-vol.org.uk). It has equivalent bodies in Northern Ireland and Scotland. NCVO may also be a good starting point to find out what voluntary organizations are operating in the policy area of interest.

Conclusion

Publications from outside the academic and government mainstream are usually up-to-date and user-friendly. They are often written by people grappling with practical policy issues. They can contribute significantly to the study of social policy. If this chapter has helped to overcome their main drawback – that they are too often ignored as a source of added value for students – it will have performed a useful function.

V.6
European and International Data Sources

Deborah Mabbett

Introduction

This chapter reviews data sources which give information on more than one country. A number of resources have been developed to facilitate international comparative analysis. Some areas of social policy have proved more susceptible to comparison than others, and this is reflected in the data available. Generally, the sources discussed here should be used for comparative work rather than for extracting data for a single country. International data sources facilitate comparison by overriding the specific institutional features of each country; if undertaking a single country study, the researcher should usually grapple with these institutional specifics. National data are more fruitful for a researcher wanting to understand the peculiarities of one country's social policy environment.

Areas covered by European and international data sources

An important issue in the comparison of social policies is whether the comparison is to be confined to the welfare state, which means focusing on government expenditure, mandatory measures and the administration of programmes by public institutions. The idea of a 'mixed economy of welfare' has propelled some researchers towards a broader approach, in which the analysis extends to non-state provision of goods and services and their impact on welfare (see Higgins, 1986). The choice depends on the questions the researcher wants to answer. There are reasons to focus on the measures that governments have taken, while acknowledging that these measures will not provide a complete explanation of welfare outcomes. From the perspective of data availability, there is a wide range of material on welfare outcomes (poverty, health etc), a certain amount on government measures and rather little on non-state structures and provision. To some extent, this bias towards state action is deliberate. For example, the International Labour Organisation (ILO) definition of social security acknowledges explicitly that it is concerned with state activity, stating that 'the system must have been set up by legislation which attributes specified individual rights to, or which imposes specified obligations on, a public, semi-public or autonomous body'. One consequence is that legal obligations imposed upon employers (e.g. to pay sick pay in the early weeks of illness) are not included if they are met by direct relationship between the employer and the beneficiary and there is no 'mediating' public or autonomous institution taking contributions and paying benefits. The bias towards information on state activity is partly for a very practical reason: many data-sets rely on reports provided by government officials and information generated by government reporting structures.

The absence of a mediating institution also means the absence of a data collection point. One implication of this is that privatization of provision can mean that data are also privatized. For example, accounting and consultancy firms collect information on legislation on employee benefits (including sick pay, pension contributions, etc.) which they sell to multinational employers (e.g. the Europe Benefits Report produced by Watson Wyatt Data Services). The cost of these reports is prohibitive for most researchers. However, the OECD has recently turned its attention to improving the free availability of data on private welfare (see below).

European and International Organizations and Their Outlook

International organizations collect data for reasons which reflect their underlying concerns and motivations. They may be concerned to highlight inequality between rich and poor nations, to promote the values of a liberal market economy, or (in the case of the European Union) to promote the perception that a group of countries is similar and 'converging'.

The United Nations

Organizations of the United Nations have endeavoured to establish 'social indicators' which provide systematic and comparable measures of welfare outcomes, on a par with well established economic indicators. With a few exceptions (notably in social security), UN publications do not provide much insight into the detail of government programmes and social policy interventions. Often the data collected by UN organizations are intended to publicize the extent of social inequality between First and Third World countries, and to help to justify expenditure on UN projects and programmes to improve health, education and welfare outcomes. The UN organizations aim to present data on all member countries, but the researcher soon finds that the comprehensive coverage of the table formats is marred by a large number of missing observations. None the less, UN organizations are the best sources for readily accessible information outside the European Union (EU) and Organization for Economic Co-operation and Development (OECD) countries (see box V.6.1).

The Organisation for Economic Cooperation and Development

The OECD comprises all the EU member states and other developed European countries, along with several of the central European states, Turkey, the USA, Canada, Mexico, Japan, South Korea, Australia and New Zealand.

The OECD exists to promote 'economic cooperation', and its offices in Paris originally provided a forum for ministerial-level discussion on trade and economic policy. Social policy appeared on the agenda largely because of its macroeconomic implications: there is a lot of emphasis in OECD publications on the pressures for growth in health expenditure and pension costs, and on the fiscal effects of unemployment. Other social concerns common to member states have also been the subject of OECD research in recent years; for example, the OECD publishes extensively in the areas of transport and environmental policy.

As is shown in box V.6.2, the OECD is a repository for vast amounts of data. While some statistics are published regularly, in other cases the OECD's collection effort is related to the production of major reports, often for high-level government meetings and conferences. The fact that the OECD's work is very much oriented towards the production of policy advice for member countries is both a strength and a weakness for its use in comparative research. It is a strength insofar as a lot of information is reported about policy initiatives in member states, and statistics are often presented in a way which serves to highlight their policy implications. However, it is a weak-

---

Box V.6.1   Organizations of the United Nations and associated international bodies

1. The website of the United Nations Statistical Division (www.un.org/Depts/unsd) provides a good starting point for finding UN statistics. The social statistics available online include a link called 'The World's Women' which provides data on marriage, childbearing, literacy and health. The major publication on population is the Demographic Yearbook; it is not currently available online.

2. The 'global statistics' link to 'international statistics' includes links to the specialised UN agencies, including the following.

- The United Nations Educational, Scientific and Cultural Organization (UNESCO): UNESCO's statistical yearbook includes measures of education expenditure and government expenditure, numbers of teachers and pupils and illiteracy rates. Much of the data is available online

- The World Health Organization (WHO): WHO maintains a data-set on a range of socio-economic and health indicators from life expectancy, fertility and infant mortality to information on health care provision and health institutions. These data are published in the World Health Statistics Annual, and are also available online

- The International Labour Organisation (ILO): As well as providing quantitative information in reports such as The Cost of Social Security and The Yearbook of Labour Statistics, the ILO also maintains documentary databases covering labour law instruments, health and safety provisions and other material related to ILO conventions

- The World Bank publishes a Social Indicators of Development yearbook, which includes some social data from other UN organizations, along with Bank material from national reports. A particular focus of World Bank work on social indicators has been the measurement of poverty

---

ness in that the OECD's world view is imposed on the information in a somewhat relentless, and at times tedious, way. A key part of this world view is that countries can import and export policies with very little modification for country-specific conditions.

The European Union

The EU has been an important actor in increasing the amount of comparative information available for social research. The EU collects such information partly for the purpose of allocating funds (the Structural Funds are allocated partly on the basis of social indicators), but more generally in order to promote the development of social policy in the Union and encourage cross-national learning and exchanges of best practice. Social indicators are included in the accession monitoring process, and increasingly data are available on the applicant countries (Poland, Hungary etc) as well as the member states.

The main agency involved in this process is *Eurostat*. Its work is often shrouded in controversy, as its findings can have considerable political and financial significance. Member states frequently question Eurostat data and try to have them revised. One result is that the timeliness of the data is often poor. There is a great deal of emphasis on methodological consistency in Eurostat's work, reflecting the importance of being 'fair' to all the states. One result is that it is often difficult to relate the Eurostat data to national source data. For example,

Box V.6.2   The OECD

- The 'Statistics Portal' on the OECD website (www.oecd.org) provides a good access point for OECD statistics. The Social Expenditure (SOCX) database provides information on expenditure on pensions, health care, education, housing, employment programmes, sickness and maternity benefits and other programmes. Information on variables other than expenditure (numbers of beneficiaries, levels of benefits) is less complete. An interesting development in the 1990s was the inclusion of information on private social expenditure (primarily mandatory and voluntary expenditure on health insurance and pensions).

- SOCX is available on CD-Rom but is not online (at time of writing), but the link to 'Society at a glance' provides Excel datafiles on a wide range of subjects, including lone parent families, taxes, poverty and income distribution, low pay and earnings, strikes, drug addiction and crime. The data are sometimes rather roughly presented and are not always thoroughly documented or explained, but sources are given.

- The OECD has participated very actively in debates about health policy and health service reform, and its interventions are supported by the collection of an extensive array of health statistics, gathered together in the regular publication of *OECD Health Data* (a good introduction to this data is Poullier, 1993). As with SOCX, the main database is on CD-Rom but extracts can be found in OECD reports on the web. Areas covered include health status and demographic data, resources (expenditure, personnel), service utilisation, drug use and expenditure, and data on non-medical determinants of health.

- Other regularly published OECD statistical bulletins include *Employment Outlook, Labour Force Statistics, National Accounts* and *The Tax/Benefit Position of Production Workers*. These are good sources for data on economic growth rates, unemployment, labour force participation, wage levels, taxation and disposable income, birthrates and population projections, dependency ratios, and government expenditure and its components (health, pensions etc.). Data from *The Tax/Benefit Position of Production Workers* are often used in studies comparing replacement ratios (ratios of benefit levels to in-work income).

- National accounts are an important source of economic data (data on GDP, consumption, investment etc.). International comparability is achieved by common use of the UN System of National Accounts (UN SNA). However, the usefulness of national accounts for social policy research is rather limited. Social policy interventions are defined in very particular ways for compatibility with the overall SNA context. Thus, a variety of pension arrangements are separately accounted for under 'pension funds and other financial institutions', while some sick pay comes under 'wages and salaries' and social security benefits not provided on an insurance basis may find their way into 'general public services'.

the figures in the regular Eurostat publication *Social Protection Expenditure and Receipts* differ substantially from those in national publications, and from those reported in the ILO study, *The Cost of Social Security*. The introduction to the ILO's publication discusses the reasons for the discrepancies against Eurostat. The divergences in the estimates mean that only data from the same source can be compared; furthermore, a diligent researcher will have to spend some time uncovering the basis of the figures and ensuring that it is appropriate to the research objectives.

A major area for European statistical work has been the development of indicators of poverty and social exclusion. Studies have used the Household Budget Surveys of member states, along with the European Community Household Panel (ECHP). The social indicators gathered for the 2001-6 social exclusion programme included key aspects of monetary poverty, such as level, persistence, depth, and changes through time, as well as breakdowns by gender, age, household type and occupation.

Directorates-General of the European Commission also collect data related to their aims and concerns. *DG V: Employment and Social Affairs* (europa.eu.int/comm/employment_social) has initiated a number of projects to report on developments in social protection in member states and present data about them. MISSOC (Mutual Information System on Social Protection in the Community) is an information system based on rapporteurs from the member countries. MISSOC publishes quarterly information updates (MISSOC-Info), and an annual report on Social Protection in the Member States of the European Union, which is summarized in table V.6.1.

DG X: Information, Communication, Culture and Audiovisual Media is home to *Eurobarometer* (europa.eu.int/comm/dg10/epo/eb.html), which provides an abundance of survey-based attitudinal data, much of it of questionable quality and meaningfulness, e.g. about how satisfied people are with their lives in general, whether they think that there is too much inequality, whether they trust their central governments, etc. Surveys may seem to be an attractive source of data for international comparisons, as they are not affected by national differences in institutional structures. However, surveys have their own limitations which should not be underestimated. Problems which particularly affect international comparison include differences between countries in the way surveys are administered (whether the interview is by telephone or in person, and who is invited to respond to the questions), translation of questions, and cultural conventions affecting responses.

Other Official Data Sources

A number of regional international associations publish data relevant to social policy (for example, there are associations of the Nordic countries and the Latin American countries). The United States also puts resources into international data collection. For example, the Center for International Research at the US Bureau of the Census maintains a database on the ageing of the world's population. A major and well established exercise in describing social security schemes is the US Social Security Administration's (SSA's) publication *Social Security Programs Throughout the World*. The SSA's publication follows a strict format, presenting an identical matrix for each country, in which the columns are types of benefit (old age/invalidity/death, sickness and maternity, work injury, unemployment, family allowances) and each row describes specified characteristics of the benefit (first law, current law, coverage (residents, employed etc.), source of funds, qualifying conditions, benefit level etc.).

Data Held by Academic Institutions

The past three decades have seen a number of major comparative projects on the welfare state established, and the host institutions have established data-sets to support these projects. For example, the data for *State, Economy, and Society in Western Europe 1815-1975* (assembled by a team led by Peter Flora, published in Chicago by St. James's Press, 1983) are held at the Mannheim Centre for European Social Research (MZES), along with the data for a subsequent project on the Western European welfare states since the Second World War. Similarly, the data used by Esping-Andersen in *The Three Worlds of*

Table V.6.1   MISSOC comparative tables

Organization of social protection	Charts giving an overview of government administration of social security, health, family affairs, housing and labour
Financing of social protection	Financing principle, contribution rates and public authorities' contributions by ESSPROS[a] functional classification
Health care	Law (name and date), beneficiaries covered, conditions, organization of doctors and hospitals, benefits provided, charges levied
Cash benefits ESSPROS functional classification: 　Sickness 　Maternity 　Invalidity 　Old age 　Survivors Employment injuries and occupational diseases Family benefits Unemployment Guaranteeing sufficient resources	Law, coverage, conditions, duration and amount of benefits, taxation of benefits for each functional classification Additional information on particular benefits where relevant, including: ● accumulation (other benefits payable in conjunction, particularly with invalidity benefits); ● risks covered, prevention and rehabilitation (invalidity and employment injury); ● adjustment (indexation), early retirement, deferment (old age); ● single parent allowances (family benefits).

[a] ESSPROS: European system of integrated social protection statistics.

Welfare Capitalism (Cambridge: Polity Press, 1990) were drawn from a larger project based around a comparative data-set at the Swedish National Institute for Social Research. Access to these 'project' data-sets usually involves establishing a collaborative working relationship with a partner at the host institution, or attending the institution as a research student.

One important data-set which has more flexible access arrangements is the Luxembourg Income Study (LIS). LIS is an international cooperative venture to assemble micro-data files from participating countries' household surveys, achieve some consistency between the coding of the surveys, and make the data available to interested researchers. LIS has expanded steadily since its establishment in 1983 and now includes surveys from 25 countries. Since 1994, labour force surveys have been assembled on the same cooperative basis in the Luxembourg Employment Study (LES). Introductory user packages are available, and there is an abundance of research literature based on LIS data (see www.lisproject.org for working papers and publications). Note also that the 'publications' link gives access to other databases created by cross-national researchers, which are particularly valuable in providing qualitative information on institutions and policy parameters.

The availability of micro-data has facilitated new comparative work on the distribution of income, poverty and the impact of benefits on inequality. Familiarity with handling survey micro-data is necessary to use LIS and LES. Problems of setting up and coding, familiar to users of national micro-data-sets, mean that the data are at least five years old by the time they become available. None the less, LIS and LES offer great opportunities to apply sophisticated statistical techniques to international comparative work.

Conclusion

International comparative analysis of social policy is an expanding field. There are several motives behind this expansion: increased social integration in the case of the EU, the possibilities for transferring policy innovations between countries, a desire to understand the social policies of economic competitors or the search for evidence for critiques of national social policy. In the abundance of international comparative data is the basis for much interesting and insightful research, but there are also plenty of possibilities for meaningless comparison, and many traps for the unwary.

Guide to further reading

Butare, T., 1994. *Social Security Quantitative Data: an Inventory of Existing Databases*, Occasional Papers on Social Security (Geneva: International Social Security Association). A survey with contact addresses encompassing social security data-sets held at academic research institutes as well as those maintained by national public authorities and international organizations.

Higgins, J., 1986. Comparative social policy. *Quarterly Journal of Social Affairs*, 2, 3, 21-42. An overview and critique of different methodological approaches to comparative social policy.

Poullier, J.-P., 1993. *OECD Health Systems*, 2 vols, Health Policy Studies no. 3 (Paris: OECD). A comprehensive presentation of OECD health data, with commentary.

Smeeding, T., Rainwater, L. and O'Higgins, M., 1990. *Poverty, Inequality and Income Distribution in a Comparative Perspective* (Hemel Hempstead: Harvester Wheatsheaf). A compilation of studies using LIS which gives insights into the research questions which can be examined using micro-data and the methodological issues which arise.

V.7
The Internet and Web-Based Sources

Melanie Ashford and Pat Young

A Revolution in Learning and in Social Policy

The technical advances which have enabled computers to become items of everyday equipment and have created the possibilities for electronic forms of communication are far reaching in their effects. In both education and social policy, traditional power relationships have the potential to be transformed by the democratization of control and access to information, and the scope for global communication. As a student of social policy, you are participating in a revolution in learning. Technological advances provide the means for new ways of learning, which accompany wider changes in attitudes to knowledge and relationships between knowledge, the economy and the rest of society. The changes are sometimes conceptualized in terms of 'modernity' and 'post-modernity', or through the idea of a 'knowledge economy' or society. This kind of social transformation is itself of interest to students of social policy. New opportunities for innovative research and applications of theories are presented as novel forms of communication impact on the wider world of policy development and service provision.

This chapter looks at the various ways you can use information and communication technology to aid and enhance your learning. Computers allow direct, independent and usually free access to a vast range of information – from government documents, hot off the press, to personal web pages of service users. To get you started, we recommend websites particularly useful for the study of social policy, but new websites are opening all the time, whilst others close or sometimes change location. We also introduce you to a range of electronic databases, including indexing and abstracting services. Some of these require a username and password, usually available from university libraries. As well as new ways to access information, computers offer new forms of communication. Through e-mail, chatrooms, and computer conferencing, you can communicate with your tutors, with fellow students, with students in other universities and colleges across the country and the world. Virtual Learning Environments (VLEs) are being purchased by universities to provide a framework for online learning and teaching, and academic discussion lists are organized and moderated to allow communication in a wider community. All of these services allow access any time, and from any place you have the means to connect a computer to a phone line.

This democratization of knowledge creates new demands. You need access to equipment and some basic level of competence in using it. The technical skills are probably the most easily learned, and programmes and sites are becoming increasingly user-friendly. If you use a computer to word process assignments (and many higher education institutions now demand that you do so), you already have the basic skills needed for the applications described here. The more significant demands created by today's 'knowledge society' require an understanding of the nature and origins of knowledge and, crucially, the capability to assess the value of information and degree of data pollution. Anyone can post information on the web: learning to discriminate amongst the vast range of information is essential for producing quality work to academic standards.

Communicating with others through electronic means also demands new skills. Teachers and students alike are exploring effective ways of organizing and participating in online discussion groups and electronic group projects.

Policy in the making

Documents from the government (www.ukonline.gov.uk) and other publicly accountable bodies are available for public scrutiny. Documents which were previously only available to those who were 'in the know', and who had time to offer their views within a given time-frame, are now more easily and widely accessible. The government's commitment to 'open government' and targets for internet access (themselves an interesting topic for social policy analysis) create the potential for a more collaborative approach to governmental and organizational policy-making.

At the time of writing (2002), local health authorities are engaging users and local communities in a debate on plans for the modernization of the health service. This can be accessed through the websites of the health authorities. At the national level, the Department of Health website (www.doh.gov.uk) has detailed reports of the consultations to develop National Service Frameworks affecting all aspects of provision. Looking, for example, at the Children's National Service Frameworks, the site allows you access to information on the organizations and individuals involved in the various levels of the consultation, as well as the views being expressed. In addition to providing new means of studying the process of the development of social policy, you can of course use your understanding to make informed contributions to the debate. Through the discipline of Social Policy, you can also research and analyse the gaps between rhetoric and reality in these shifts in power over the policy-making process.

Information Through the Internet

What is the internet?

The internet is a global network of computers, enabling an exchange of data, news and opinions. It is a rich resource of information, although there is also much misinformation (and propaganda). Care must be taken in validating sources. Government departments, universities, voluntary organizations and commercial interests all have their own sites, which can be accessed freely with a computer linked to a server to phone line, and installed with appropriate software. Access is simple, becoming relatively cheap, and browsers – the software necessary to allow people to read text and images – are now free. Websites usually include hyperlinks, which enabled further branched information to be accessed with a click of a button.

The internet, with its fast connections to the World Wide Web (usually shortened to 'web'), email, chatrooms and other forms of communication, offers students the opportunity to find information from different sources all over the world. The Web is easy to use, is growing daily and many forms of information are available for electronic retrieval.

Searching the internet

There are a range of different ways to search the web, appropriate to different purposes and kinds of information. The search engines listed below all provide options for limiting the search to the UK, which is one way of narrowing the focus of a search (more on this below).

- Search engines, for example Alta Vista (www.altavista.co.uk) or Infoseek (www.infoseek.co.uk) are useful for finding specific information. Google (www.google.co.uk) is popular with students for its speed and ease of use.
- 'Meta search engines' will search a group of single search engines to give a higher number of results, for example, infospace (www.infospace.com/uk/). ixquick (www.ixquick.com/uk) also ranks results based on the number of 'top ten' rankings a site receives from the various search engines.
- Directories or subject indexes are usually human-compiled web guides that list sites by category, eg. Yahoo! (www.yahoo.co.uk), Lycos (www.lycos.co.uk).
- Gateways offer access to selected information and are particularly appropriate for academic work. The Social Science Information Gateway (www.sosig.ac.uk) is a freely available site which provides selected, high quality, internet information for students and academics.

Specific collections of resources are available to social policy students. The Policy Library (www.policylibrary.com) is a not-for-profit organization aiming to place public policy knowledge in the public domain. This contains a database of online policy and research papers and literature reviews which provide a context for research. The Social Policy Association (www.social-policy.com) have a developing list of social policy related websites. SWAPltsn (www.swap.ac.uk) is the learning and teaching resource network for social policy and contains a powerful searchable database. Many social policy departments in higher education institutions offer their own listings of useful websites, and some have gateways connected to their library web pages. Further information on online databases is provided below.

Search strategies

The most common headache when using a search engine is the search which produces thousands of sites. At the opposite end of the scale, there are times when you find nothing. The strategies listed below enable you to target your search more effectively and hopefully will produce a more appropriate list of sources.

- Use precise terms or phrases to limit and focus the search, avoiding very general terms such as 'policy'.
- Much of the information on the web is American, so if you only want UK material, ensure you use a UK version of the search engine (as listed above).
- Use wildcards (usually the symbol *) where allowed (for example, social* for social and socialize). This can be used at the beginning and end of words.
- Ensure that the search engine finds pages that have all the words you enter, not just some of them. The + symbol lets you do this, so it may be helpful to type into the query box when looking for, for example, social policy in housing, + social + policy + housing. Only pages containing all three words will appear. Using the terms 'and' or 'not' can also be useful.
- Alternatively, you may want a search engine to find pages that have one word in them but not another word. The − symbol lets you do this, for example housing − Shelter.
- Most search engines allow a phrase search. This is where you specify the term exactly by using quotation marks, for example "housing associations". The three simple strategies listed here can also be combined.
- Enter multiple spellings where appropriate eg. colour and color if wanting results from other than the UK.

- Use gateway thesauri – the list offered by the gateway – to aid your searching.

Another strategy is to restrict use of a search engine to occasions when you have a very specific subject. Databases (see below), government sites, quality newspapers or electronic journals are generally better sources for writing essays or dissertations, as they screen out much of the non-academic information from the web.

The web can be very seductive in taking you in different directions through a trail of hyperlinks. You need to be disciplined and stay focused on your particular search. Going from one site to another at the click of the mouse, you will find some sites or pages which are more useful than others, and may ultimately reach a dead end. To go back over your journey one step at a time, use the 'back' button on your browser. Browsers also provide various means of retracing the whole journey. Don't forget to bookmark (or add to your favorites folder) useful sites to which you may want to return.

Popular social policy websites:

- Paul Spicker provides introductory material on social policy at www2.rgu.ac.uk/publicpolicy/introduction/index.htm
- The government website (www.ukonline.gov.uk) offers government information online
- You can also access individual government departments for example the Department of Health (www.doh.gov.uk)
- Care and Health (www.careandhealth.co.uk) provides useful information for keeping up-to-date on new legislation
- The Joseph Rowntree Foundation (www.jrf.org.uk) publish summaries of research on poverty, housing and other social issues online
- A number of national voluntary organizations have developed informative websites, for example Shelter on hous-

ing (www.shelter.org.uk), MIND on mental health issues (www.mind.org.uk) or Age Concern on ageing (www.ace.org.uk).

Quality control

How can you judge the reliability of information found on the web? Information on the web is not vetted in any way. Anyone can download an authoring software package, and publish electronically. Excellent resources reside alongside the most questionable.

Authorship

It is important to think about who wrote and provided the information, and for what purpose. Do they have some authority on the subject? Are they providing academically respectable information? Do they have a political or other motive? The address, or Uniform Resources Locator (URL) provides some clues. Addresses are made up of the following parts: transferprotocol://servername.domain/directory/subdirectory/filename.filetype.

The first part of the URL indicates what type of information is being transferred and, usually, the 'door' to the server is being entered. The standard format for the Web is http, indicating hypertext. The second part is the allocated area where the pages are located. The domain indicates the institution, organization or company, for example:

edu = American educational institution
ac = UK educational institution
gov = government
org – used by non profit organizations
mil = American military
mod = UK ministry of defence
co or com = a company

These letters are usually followed by the country (but note that this is not always applicable to America) as in www.doh.gov.uk. You can feel more confident of the quality of information within sites carrying with ac, gov or org domains – although of course the government and voluntary organizations are presenting information with their own particular slant, and you still need to think critically about what you read (see below).

Using a gateway such as SOSIG (described above) limits you to sites which are considered academically useful sources of information. Using the hyperlinks within a trustworthy sites can also give you more confidence. You may recognize the author from your study of Social Policy. Otherwise look for biographical information from which authority of the author can be assessed. If there is no email address, or telephone number given, you need to question the motives of the author(s) of the site.

Critical evaluation

As with all sources of information, websites rarely provide a completely neutral perspective in the information they choose to present, and the way in which it is presented. The popularity of the internet makes it the perfect arena for commercial, religious and socio-political publishing. You need to be aware of particular biases in the information you are accessing.

Ask yourself the following questions about a website:

- What is the purpose of the site?
- How does the author refer to other sources?
- Is there an explanation of any research methods used?
- Do other websites refer to this site?
- Does this site offer further sites for reference?
- Is there a date on the website indicating when it was posted to the Web? This helps to see if it has been updated recently.

Referencing

Remember that you need to reference web pages in your work, providing the full URL,

page references and the date you accessed the information. For more detail on all these aspects of using the web, access internet for social policy at www.sosig.ac.uk/vts/social-policy/. This site has been specifically designed for social policy students and provides a useful tutorial on internet information skills and more starting points for searching the web.

Online discussion groups

Electronic discussion groups have been set up in most disciplines. Access www.jiscmail.ac.uk for simple steps to join Social Policy discussion lists. You will receive e-mails of contributions made by others and can participate in a discussion by sending an e-mail, which will then go to everyone on the list. Mailings often includes information on conferences and jobs, as well as discussions of particular issues.

Electronic databases

More and more of the resources which used to occupy the reference and indexes sections of academic libraries are available electronically. Initially, databases were made available in the form of CD-ROMS, which can be borrowed and used in a library, or accessed through university networked PCs. Increasingly, databases are accessible through the internet. The major advantage for students of electronic databases is the facility for speedy electronic searching. (Note that the advice on focused searching techniques offered above applies to databases as well as to search engines.) Some databases require you to register and use a password; in other cases the databases are purchased by libraries and accessed in the library or elsewhere after issue of an 'ATHENS' username and password.

There are various kinds of databases available. Some are indexes, providing bibliographic references to articles and books, which you will then need to follow up. Others provide the full text of articles. Particularly useful for research projects in social policy, there are also databases of statistical and other research material. Here we indicate some of the relevant databases; you will be able to obtain more information from your library.

- *The UK Data Archive (UKDA)* (www.data-archive.c.uk) is a resource centre that acquires, disseminates and preserves the largest collection of digital data for social sciences and humanities in the UK. Its primary aim is to support secondary use of quantitative and qualitative data for research and learning.
- *MIMAS* (www.mimas.ac.uk) is a national data centre to provide the UK academic community with flexible online access to socio-economic, spatial and scientific data, and to bibliographic and electronic journal data services. It also offers statistical analysis packages and visualization tools, computing resources for storage and manipulation of data, together with data sharing and gateway services.
- *ASSIA (Applied Social Sciences Index and Abstracts)* provides an index and abstracting service covering over 650 journals relevant to the social sciences. Subjects include: crime, economics, education, employment, health, politics, race relations and social issues. You will need an 'ATHENS' password to access ASSIA outside of a library.
- *Caredata* (www.elsc.org.uk bases_floor/ caredata.htm) is a database of abstracts of social care literature. It contains over 50,000 abstracts of books, central and local government reports, research papers, publications of voluntary organizations, and articles from a wide range of journals. The database covers UK, North American and other English-language resources. It is freely available through the internet.
- *Social Trends* may be available in your library, allowing you to download the latest statistics on population, education, labour market, income and wealth, expenditure, housing, environment and transport.
- *UK Official Publications* covers 20 years of government information, with many documents archived in full text form. Again this is available through academic libraries.

Virtual Learning Environments (VLEs), or Managed Learning Environments (MLEs)

A VLE provides a framework for online course materials and course-related activities. Seeking to encourage electronic forms of learning and teaching, higher education institutions are investing in VLEs, some using commercial companies such as Blackboard or WebCT. These are usually browser-based systems, which work over the internet or an Intranet. The VLE is accessed internally or externally through the university or college website.

Most VLEs are student-centred in that they are:

- fully browser-based with no extra software being required;
- work within a secure environment that it is private to students and staff on a module;
- able to be updated directly and easily by lecturers; and most importantly,
- easy to use.

Modules or courses created within a VLE will contain relevant materials such as handbooks, assignment information, reading lists and lecture notes. VLEs are password protected, so that only recognized users have access.

As with other forms of online learning, VLEs allow you to access course materials at a pace and time which suits you, and from a location of your choosing. Students with disabilities or health problems which make physical access to the classroom difficult, those who work full-time or who have caring responsibilities can study from home or work. The information presented is interactive and individualized to the needs of each student, for example, incorporating feature such as large print for a visually-impaired student. Well-designed online materials are layered, with hyperlinks to additional pages containing further information. In some cases, self-assessment quizzes allow you to test your own learning.

A VLE will also allow for a range of different forms of communication between students. These may include online discussions or projects, sometimes forming part of the formal assessment for the course. The tutor will take the role of a moderator, encouraging participation and ensuring basic rules are not broken, and perhaps summarizing key points, but control of the form of the discussion and the directions in which it goes lies with the participants. Online discussions allow greater time for thought and reflection than verbal interaction and some students who are shy in the presence of others are more confident in virtual communication. VLEs also commonly provide space for more informal peer-group communication. Here students can interact with one another in a secure environment and work together within a learning community, as the emerging conversation is stored for every participant to read.

VLEs allow course tutors and administrators access to information about student time spent online. Tutors can record whether students have accessed materials, how often and for how long, and log into student discussions. As with other uses of technology, the liberating potential of the technology is counter-balanced with new forms of increasing surveillance and control.

Software to Support Research Activities

Information technology provides a number of tools to help you organize and analyse primary and secondary research. These are purchased in the form of CD-ROMs, for installation on personal computers. Postgraduate students may be able to access these programs through a faculty or institutional site licence.

Endnote is an example of a program which is available for storing references from your reading and producing bibliographies as you write. Endnote (www.endnote.com) offers a trial version of the database and an online interactive tutorial to introduce the features of the system.

For analysing quantitative data, the most popular software packages are the Statistical Package for the Social Sciences (SPSS) and MINITAB. These programs allow you to process data without detailed knowledge of statistics, although you do need to understand the strengths and limitations of the various procedures. SPSS is a powerful tool for summarizing frequencies, exploring relationships between variables and carrying out statistical analyses in large data sets. MINITAB is designed more specifically for students and encourages the development of research skills and knowledge. Training in the use of these statistical packages may be offered in your college or university.

Several packages are available to help in storing, cross-referencing and analysing qualitative data. Ethnograph is probably the simplest to learn, but least sophisticated. More complex programs are provided by NUD*IST, Nvivo, QuestionMark and Atlas ti. All the packages come with electronic and written instructions. There are trial versions available through the websites of the companies and also websites offering advice on choosing software and supporting users.

Conclusion

The rate of change in information and communication technologies has been rapid. Through the internet, you have almost immediate access to resources, which ten years ago would have taken hours, days or weeks to track down. Personal computers provide easy storage and retrieval for large quantities of information. From word processing to qualitative and quantitative data analysis, software packages allow increasingly sophisticated means of organizing, transforming and analysing information. E-mail and the internet make worldwide communication between individuals and communities quick and cheap.

Innovations in ICT continue and the pace of change is more likely to increase than slow down. This chapter has provided some starting points for using ICT in social policy, but learning how to best use information technology is a lifelong task. Throughout your education, and into employment, you will improve your skills incrementally as the technology and its applications continue to develop and change. The transferable skills you develop in your social policy course will support your entry into a labour market where knowledge and communication skills are increasingly important.

Guide to further information

The Internet for Social Policy – www.sosig.ac.uk/vts/social-policy/ – covers all aspects of searching and using electronic sources for studying social policy. Within the site there are links to many further sources of information including databases, documents and particular sites specific to social policy as well as sources of detailed guidance on aspects of using online resources such as referencing.

A wide range of books, articles and websites are available to support the use of software packages for analysing research data. Online resources include:

Christine A. Barry (1998) *Choosing Qualitative Data Analysis Software: Atlas/ti and Nudist Compared Sociological Research Online*, vol. 3, no. 3, [online] available from:

www.socresonline.org.uk/socresonline/3/3/4.html (accessed 04.02.02)
www.spss.com/software/spss for SPSS
www.minitab.com/ for MINITAB
www.qualisresearch.com for Ethnograph
www.atlasti.com

Both NUD*IST and NVivo can be explored at www.qsr-software.co.uk/software.

Part VI
Careers in Social Policy

VI.1

Careers and Postgraduate Study in Social Policy

Margaret May and Catherine Bochel

Social Policy and the Graduate Labour Market

Whatever the product or service being provided, the context or size of an enterprise, effective policy evaluation is central to decision-making and organizational success. In consequence there is a high demand for graduates skilled in policy analysis and appraisal, aware of resource and implementation issues and the complexities of meeting the needs of varying stakeholders. This chapter can only provide a brief indication of the consequent range of options open to social policy graduates. Exploring and evaluating these is in itself a form of policy analysis, drawing on a knowledge of current social trends and the skills intrinsic to the subject. It raises many questions about the direction and implications of current labour market developments that you may wish to investigate further and which impinge directly on the issues addressed in the rest of this *Companion*. One aim of this chapter therefore is to provide you with further insights into the scope and nature of social policy enquiry. More immediately it is designed to enable you to make the most of the competitive edge acquired through studying the subject and reflect on how it equips you to meet prospective employers' requirements.

Increasingly these include the expectation that graduate employees will at some stage undertake further study. This may be to deepen their knowledge or gain specific training. Large organizations in particular place great stress on recruiting staff committed to continuous forms of learning and personal-professional development. Equally significantly many social policy graduates wish to maintain and extend their cognisance of the subject. Their interests as well as those of employers have been met by a proliferation of graduate programmes and widening opportunities for studying and working overseas.

Our main aim therefore is to support your career planning and the advice available from your careers service by:

- briefly surveying the changing nature of the UK graduate labour market, the prospects of social policy graduates within it and the range of opportunities open to them;
- helping you to identify the attributes your studies enable you to bring to the labour market and how you might deploy them to best effect in the recruitment process; and
- outlining the main routes into and possibilities presented by postgraduate study.

The UK Graduate Labour Market: Prospects for Social Policy Graduates

Over the last quarter of the twentieth century the UK moved from a selective higher education system catering for a minority of

18-year-old school-leavers to a mass service providing for individuals of varying ages and backgrounds entering through diverse routes. In the late 1960s less than 10 per cent of young people went into higher education, with only some 30,000 gaining places on undergraduate courses. By the beginning of this century 35 per cent of 18-year-olds were entering university, some 250,000 people annually graduated with a first degree and a further 400,000 were studying at postgraduate level. These numbers are set to rise again as the Blair government pursues its target of enabling 50 per cent of 18 to 30 year olds to experience higher education by 2010. Agencies such as the Institute for Employment Studies (IES), the Association of Graduate Careers Advisory Services (AGCAS) and the Association of Graduate Recruiters, as well as governmental bodies and Higher Education Institutions (HEIs) point to a parallel surge in postgraduates, with one in four graduates likely to undertake advanced study.

In promoting this expansion successive governments have been driven by the pressures of an increasingly competitive, global economy and the related on-going restructuring of the UK's productive base. Over the last half century it has shifted from the comparative stability offered by an economy centred on manufacturing, the utilities and other industries to a more fluid, consumer-powered one based on services and, increasingly, the trading of knowledge. Forms of employment and ways of working have changed in line with this transformation, the associated spread of new technologies and the premium attached to developing and sustaining customer-centred organizational strategies. In a process that has accelerated since the 1980s, employment patterns have become more diverse with fewer people working for large companies or in mass forms of production and the majority employed in small and medium-size enterprises (SMEs). Growing numbers have also moved into self-employment. Many large organizations have developed flatter, less hierarchical structures demanding both greater teamworking and autonomous decision-making from their staff. On the other hand these include a significant number of UK conglomerates and multinational corporations whose workforce planning is geared to an international market.

With many small firms also tied into the wider economy, the UK labour market has been marked by a progressive upward shift in staffing profiles, towards higher-level occupations and within these to higher order skills and competences. This has been reflected in growing demand for graduates in many areas of employment which traditionally relied on less qualified labour. It has also led to a greater emphasis in job specifications and related advertising on applicants' skills and their ability to slot quickly into their role ('to hit the ground running', 'think on their feet', 'learn as they work'). These developments have not been confined to the private sector. Similar reconfigurations have taken place in public and voluntary agencies, where the many changes associated with 'new managerialism' (see chapters III.5 and III.13) have (whatever one's views on their merits) opened up new areas of employment and altered the competences required.

It is in this expanding, but diverse and highly competitive, skills-oriented graduate labour market that you are likely to find yourself. So what are the prospects for social policy graduates? These can be gauged from several sources: the annual First Destination Statistics compiled by University Careers Services, more general 'snapshot' and longitudinal surveys conducted by other agencies and data collected by social policy degree providers. Unfortunately the first only provides information in broad subject groupings. Contrary to the known pattern of graduate transitions into work, it also only captures 'career destinations' six months after graduation. Together with other studies, however, recent First Destination Statistics suggest that the relatively low levels of unemployment in the labour market as a whole have been reflected in the employment prospects of graduates. They also point to considerable demand for social science students which compares favourably to that of other subjects. For example in the early 1990s, the unemployment rate for social science graduates six months after qualifying was 10.5 per cent. By 2000 the equivalent unemployment rate was 4.9 per cent (as opposed to 5.5 per cent for graduates as a whole). Salaries followed a similar pattern with social scientists receiving at least the average starting salary (of £18,000 in 2001) and continuing to earn a salary in line with graduates in general in their first years of employment. Moreover, like graduates in general, they were likely not only to have higher starting salaries than non-graduates (at least 30 per cent), but higher lifelong earnings (Elias et al, 2000; HCSU, 2002).

Comparable national surveys of social policy graduates' employment are not currently available. But it can be gleaned from the raw data held by university careers services and departments, studies conducted by the latter for audit purposes and more general surveys of graduate vacancies. Though these too have their methodological limitations, they confirm earlier findings (in the first edition of this *Companion*) that those who have studied social policy fare better in the labour market than other social science graduates and are more likely to enter areas with fast- track career opportunities. A preliminary exploration of departmental data from English universities undertaken for this chapter revealed a similar picture, indicating that social policy graduates are highly likely to gain employment in their chosen areas.

What also emerges from such studies is the diverse range of employers who now seek the knowledge and skills gained through studying social policy. Before looking at these, however, a number of other features of the graduate labour market are worth noting. One, obscured by the First Destination Statistics, but evident from other sources, is the extended nature of the transition into employment. Many graduates now take up to three years before settling into a clear occupational pathway. Most move initially into one of three types of 'starter posts':

- *entry level posts* which offer the experiential base to progress into 'second step' positions with greater responsibility;
- *taster jobs*, often on short-term contracts, taken to test the feasibility and appropriateness of one/more possible careers;
- *interim work* of a temporary, casual, or part-time nature, frequently in 'non-graduate' occupations stemming from earlier part-time or vacation work which allows individuals to 'shop around', firm up their career interests, and support themselves whilst applying for permanent positions or undertaking further study.

Recent analyses suggest that the last is an increasingly prominent feature of the graduate experience and one that should not be seen as a sign of 'failure' but an inevitable concomitant of the growth in the graduate workforce. They also, however, reveal the increasing diversification of the graduate labour market and the extent to which it is subject to wider fluctuations in the economy. Though the signs for social policy graduates are currently positive, it is as well to be aware of this potential volatility and the competition posed as more graduates enter the market. You may well need to be flexible and consider employment in areas and organizations that have not traditionally relied on graduates or been viewed as 'social policy recruiters'. In these circumstances an understanding of how the market operates, the qualities sought by employers and, above all, your personal priorities are essential. The key lies in investing in career planning from the outset of your studies rather than deferring it until late in your final year (Purcell, et al, 1999). These are all issues on which your social policy training has an immediate bearing and to which we now turn.

What Are Graduate Employers Looking For?

While the ongoing restructuring of the UK economy has opened up a multiplicity of new or re-styled occupations for graduates, it is still useful to distinguish between two main career streams:

1. functional and professional careers, which demand particular forms of knowledge and expertise; and
2. management and administrative careers in a host of settings which often require a broader knowledge base and generic competences.

The experience of recent social policy graduates suggests their studies equipped them for posts in both domains, a pattern that also emerges from studies of employers' recruitment literature and procedures. What these also reveal is the extent to which many areas of employment are not subject bounded and employers' expectations that applicants for both subject-related and generalist posts possess graduate-level skills.

Soft skills

Looking at the headline requirements in adverts, the types of questions asked in application forms, interviews and assessments (box VI.1.1), it should be clear that employers are as concerned with applicants' attributes as their academic qualifications. The possession of a degree is taken as an indicator of a level of intellectual attainment and, equally importantly, of a range of essential 'soft' skills of value in any area of employment (box VI.1.2). Though the tenor for these is set by 'blue chip' companies, they are also central to the recruitment strategies of other businesses and public and voluntary agencies. Two thirds of organizations routinely include such skills in their job specifications, particularly for managerial and other team leader roles. Three-quarters also seek evidence of 'soft' skills at interview stage and this contrib-

utes substantially to the final selection (AKR, 1999). They also constitute a key element in reference requests, both from employers and employment agencies.

Beyond these employers frequently also ask for less tangible personal qualities, featured in their advertising as well as their selection measures (box VI.1.3). Developing these skills and qualities is integral to the process of studying social policy as should quickly become apparent if you map the skills acquired during your studies on to the inventory in box VI.1.2. Alongside these general graduate skills, however, social policy equips you with a range of subject specific competences. These are set out, along with the soft skills built into your degree in the *Social Policy and Administration Benchmark Statement* (www.qaa.ac.uk/crntwork/benchmark/socialpolicy) and, increasingly in the 'programme specifications' published by HEIs. In addition to the analytical and evaluative skills intrin-

Sample advert VI.1.1 *(Voluntary Organisation)*

Childcare Development Officer

To assist in the development of 'wrap around services' for 0–14s and the recruitment, training and support of childcare workers.

Requirements: good honours degree; uptodate knowledge of social policies affecting children and childcare; understanding of issues affecting excluded groups; good organisational, communication and interpersonal skills, ability to 'self-service' and take decisions, to work independently and in a team, to build links and network with community groups and work with partner organisations.

Box V1.1.1.   Sample application form/ Interview questions

How did you arrive at your career choice?

Describe three factors which you consider to be instrumental in shaping your career choice.

What have you gained from your degree studies that has equipped you for this post?

What skills and attributes make you a suitable candidate for this post?

What led you to apply for this post?

What do you consider to be the main challenges faced by this (organisation/business/service)?

Describe how you plan your work to meet targets and objectives.

Describe a situation in which you worked as part of a group. What was your contribution?

Think of a situation where you were part of a successful team. Describe your role in achieving the team's goals.

Give an example of a situation when you developed effective working relationships with people of different backgrounds or views to accomplish an important task.

Describe a situation where you met resistance to your opinion. What course of action did you take and what was the outcome?

Describe a situation where you found your views on achieving a gaol differed to that of others. What did you do? Why? With what outcome?

What positions of responsibility/leadership have you held? Describe your involvement and what you achieved.

Describe a situation that you consider to be a good example of using your initiative. What did you do? Why?

Describe a situation in which you successfully influenced others to complete a task the way you thought best. What was your role? How did you achieve the result you felt best?

Give an example of when, as leader of a group, you set directions for them, gained their commitment and led them to achieve the set target.

Describe a challenging project that you had to undertake, how, why and to what effect you dealt with it.

Describe a situation where you generated a new idea or process that led to improved results.

---

sic to the subject, these include high-level problem-solving skills and proficiencies in organizational and user analyses, assessment of the effectiveness of different interventions and research techniques. As critically studying social policy engenders sensitivity to the values and interests of others and awareness of the complex, contested, negotiable nature of decision-making. These characteristics are sought by many organizations and help account for the extensive demand for social policy graduates.

Work experience

Much of the evidential base for demonstrating the transferable skills prized by employers will come from your academic studies. But increasingly employers also seek evidence that you have been able to apply and enhance these in the workplace. To support you many social policy programmes include work-placements or work-based forms of learning. You can also, however, draw on part-time employment undertaken alongside your studies or the skills gained

Box VI.1.2   Soft skills commonly specified by graduate recruiters

- Commercial/policy/organisational awareness
- Analytical and problem-solving skills
- Self-management: self-starter; time management; ability to prioritise, work to deadlines, under pressure and independently
- Project management and organisational skills
- Inter-personal skills: team working, listening, facilitation, negotiation, networking; management of others; leadership
- Communication and presentation skills (oral-face to face and telephone - and written fluency/ ability to deal with varied audiences)
- Numeracy/data interpretation
- IT skills
- Research skills
- Capacity to learn/self-develop/ manage own learning

Box V1.1.3   Personal qualities

- Highly-motivated/enthusiastic
- Proactive
- Self-starter
- Focused
- Flexible/adaptable
- Culturally sensitive
- Customer-oriented
- Change/results-oriented
- Strategic thinker/visionary

through voluntary work. Employers view the latter in particular as indicative of 'management potential' and you may find it worthwhile looking at the options available and becoming involved in the work of a local group or the many activities within or linked to your institution.

Sample advert VI.1.2 *(Local Authority)*

Trainee Regeneration Officer

Working with the Community Regeneration Coordinator you will be responsible for assisting in project development and promoting community activity.

Requirements: good honours degree; knowledge of current policy developments, good communication and inter-personal skills, ability to work under pressure and willingness to undertake further training.

Social Policy Graduates in the Market Place: Employment Options and Opportunities

As we have already indicated social policy feeds into a wide range of careers, so much so that looking at the experience of recent graduates and the current graduate labour market it is easier to summarize what you cannot do! (mostly occupations and positions demanding highly specialist scientific, technical or professional expertise, though this can often be gained by further training). Traditionally most social policy graduates sought careers in the public services.

Box VI.1.4

'It is a myth that social work provides the main career outlet for social policy graduates. Public and welfare services generally are clearly key areas of employment, particularly since it is a concern with social issues that attracts many students in the first place. But the qualities they bring with them are also widely sought after in other human services' (University Careers Adviser).

Sample advert VI.1.3(*LA/Voluntary Organisation Partnership*)

Sample advert VI.1.4 (*Health Care Market Research Company*)

Project Officer: Supporting People

To join a team responsible for developing, funding and monitoring housing related support and assist in the promotion of effective consultation processes with key stakeholders.

Requirements: a highly motivated and customer focused graduate with a good working knowledge of current housing and related policies, an understanding of research methods and strong communication and team skills.

Market Researcher

The position involves helping to: design/manage research projects on healthcare related issues, analyse the findings and make recommendations that will influence marketing strategy and promotional campaigns.

Requirements: self-motivated graduate with good honours degree, preferably with a knowledge of current social and health policies, and strong research, interpersonal, analytical and written communication skills.

This is still a popular choice and one that offers considerable opportunities for fast career progression. It also secures extensive training, benefits such as funded pensions and pay schemes often based on incremental scales. Public sector employers are also in the vanguard of work-life balance and family-friendly initiatives. It is a misconception, however, to equate this area simply with social work or direct service provision. Though social policy as a subject originated in social work training, it has long diverged from its roots (see chapter I.1) and graduates have found their subject a basis for a whole range of options outside both the traditional 'caring' type occupations and the public services (box VI.1.4). As should already be clear these include the increasing number of management and administrative positions in a welter of non-statutory services. Bearing this in mind we will first look at those areas where an understanding of social policy is of direct relevance and highly regarded by recruiters.

'Social policy' career pathways

The subject knowledge of social policy underpins and informs an array of 'entry-level' and subsequent occupations. The many changes instituted by recent governments mean that many of the openings on which it has a direct bearing may well be offered by voluntary and community or commercial organizations as well as public agencies. The types of public service employment too have expanded in ways that are increasingly difficult to encapsulate and can only be tracked through keeping up to date with the subject itself!

For instance, the emergence of new structures (Health Trusts: PCTs), initiatives (the New Deals; Sure Start; Urban Regeneration, Neighbourhood Renewal; Action Zones; Community Safety), benefits (Stakeholder Pensions; Baby Bonds), services (Connexions; Learn Direct; the Single Gateway), and partnership working in its myriad forms entail a host of new 'front-line' and project management starter posts with opportunities for fast progression. The advent of the 'evaluative state 'and the increasing emphasis on user-involvement and consumer-oriented provision have been reflected in a parallel raft of new opportunities. These include the increasingly important areas of policy research and development and consumer information, advice and protection as well as general management. Similarly the A/AS level in social policy, vocational GCSEs in Health and Social Care and the inclusion of citizenship in the national curriculum are opening up opportunities in teaching (where traditionally social policy graduates were unable to teach their subject directly). With further public service changes in the pipeline, the current decade is likely to see a continuing growth in demand for staff with a knowledge of social policy. Though pay for many occupational groups has not matched that in the private sector and public service employment has suffered from highly negative media coverage, if current government policies take off you may find yourself working in a very different climate.

In broad terms, therefore, you will find it helpful to consider the varying positions (summarized in job titles and specifications), career trajectories and rewards characteristic both of 'traditional' and 'newer' public services. Detailed reviews can be found in specialist career guides (obtainable through your careers service), but the main areas are summarized in box V1.1.5.

Co-relatedly, you should also explore the relative merits of working for different levels of government and also the parallel avenues available in non-statutory agencies

Sample advert VI.1.5 *(Central Government)*

***

Graduate Trainee: Housing Inspection

To assist in shaping policy on housing-related issues, project management and inspection with the opportunity to study for appropriate professional qualifications

Requirements: good honours degree in an analytically-based subject, the ability to solve problems, good communication skills and a high level of IT literacy.

***

(see part III of this *Companion*). Voluntary and community organizations and social enterprises have become significant economic players. They employ increasing numbers of paid staff in fund-raising and resource management, marketing, training, research, lobbying and project management as well as overseeing and delivering welfare, housing and advisory services, community and recreational schemes. A background in social policy is also of direct utility to commercial organizations trading in welfare, particularly care services and the many financial services businesses involved in selling pensions and other financial products.

'Generalist' career pathways

Many social policy graduates opt to work not only in these fields, but in other settings where their people-centred background offers particular value. This applies espe-

***

Box V1.1.5 'Social policy' career opportunities

- Adult care services
- Childcare and family services
- Community development
- Connexions
- Criminal justice services
- Early years services
- Economic development
- Education and training /lifelong learning
- Employment services
- The health service
- Housing
- Immigration services
- Income maintenance services
- Information and advice services
- Legal services
- Leisure services
- The police
- Research and policy development
- Urban regeneration
- Youth and/or youth justice services

***

cially to areas such as human resource management, counselling, and public and customer relations with their affinities to many of the issues addressed on social policy programmes (for which there is also considerable demand in the public sector). But it also applies to the broad field of marketing where social policy graduates can draw on their skills in research and needs analysis. Information from careers advisers shows that in practice social policy graduates are recruited to a wide spectrum of occupations in a variety of services, working both 'in-house' for large companies and for smaller firms and agencies (box V1.1.6). More broadly, surveys of employer recruitment show that over 40 per cent of vacancies for graduates advertised in the UK do not ask for specific degree subjects (IES, *Annual Graduate Review*, 2001). Rather they are looking for graduates with a span of skills and, above all, the potential to develop them further.

Successful Career Planning

The wealth of subject-related and generalist opportunities and the skills they require are

Sample advert VI.1.6 (*Local Authority*)

Policy Officer (Community Safety)

To support the implementation and monitoring of the of the authority's community safety strategy, undertake research and support funding bids.

Requirements: knowledge of issues relating to crime and disorder, experience of and the ability to undertake research and analyse the policy implications, effective written and oral communication skills, ability to work individually and as part of a team and to deadlines.

---

indicated in the boxed sample advertisements in this chapter. Given the possibilities and the patterning of employer expectations, forward planning is essential. This involves more than researching the opportunities available, though this is clearly crucial. Knowledge and understanding of yourself and your competences are also vital. Many graduates underestimate the skills they have, including those gained from paid or voluntary work. It is therefore vital to start by looking at yourself, reviewing your abilities and interests, how they relate to the choices available and how you might 'market' yourself to best advantage. Ideally, this should be an iterative process in which you capitalize on your social policy skills and invest in the tasks summarized below.

Produce a self-profile

- Sort out your motivations and priorities. (What is important to you? What expectations do you have from your career? What drives you? Is it money, security, new challenges, service to society –'giving something back', 'making a difference'?);

Box V1.1.6   Typical 'generalist' areas of employment

- Financial services
- Retail services
- Leisure services
- Employment services
- Communication and media services
- Legal services

- Recruitment
- Human resource management
- Counselling
- Research
- Policy analysis and development
- Marketing, market research, public relations, advertising
- Customer relations
- Project management

- Identify any constraints you face (geographical location, family or other commitments);
- Review your skills/ personal qualities (What knowledge and abilities do you have? How might these relate to employer expectations? What sort of work environment are you likely to perform best in? Do you need to boost your skills portfolio in any way?)

Use your research skills to develop a job search strategy

- Draw on this chapter to extend your knowledge of the social policy graduate labour market. (What have previous graduates done? What are the current trends? What remuneration packages and other rewards do different organizations/occupations offer?)
- Establish where the positions you are most interested in are likely to be advertised. (Surf the net, relevant newspapers and journals, make use of careers workshops and recruitment fairs, read the guides produced by AGCAS and other bodies.)
- Research your preferred organizations and their application processes. (Are there particular entry routes? How should you apply for the post you are interested in – directly/online/form-based for? What specific skills are being sought?)

Use your careers service

Your institution's careers service should be able to offer advice and information on possible areas of employment, skills analyses, job search techniques and ways of preparing for the various selection procedures used by graduate employers. If you are uncertain as to which direction to take they can also offer you a range of computer-based and personal forms of guidance.

Market yourself

- Familiarize yourself with graduate employers' selection procedures (box VI.1.7.);

Box VI.1.7   Graduate employers' selection procedures

- *The Application* may consist of an EAF (an employer's pre-set form, increasingly supplied electronically as well as in hardcopy), an SAF (standard application form) or the submission of a CV and a personal statement/covering letter. Application forms usually provide space for these, though as with 'direct' applications it is helpful to add a brief covering letter.

- *(First) Interview/Assessment* may take the form of a one-to one interview (usually based on the application) but increasingly candidates are also expected to provide a short presentation to a small panel. Many large organizations utilize telephone interviews at this stage, and/or psychometric tests. These may include one or more of the following: verbal, numerical, diagrammatic/critical reasoning and intelligence tests; personality profiling; aptitude tests (taken in Assessment Centres or other venues).

- *(Second) Interview/Assessment* may consist of a short 'follow-up' to the first, but more usually consists of a mix of assessments often over one to two days, involving both group sessions (discussions/role play exercises/projects) and individual tasks (prioritising or 'in-tray' exercises/documentary analysis/report writing/scenario exercises and, if not used earlier, psychometric tests).

- *(Final) Interview* – the follow up to any of the above.

- Map your skills and qualities against those commonly required (boxes VI.1.2 and 3); Review how you can use them to answer the questions you are likely to encounter on application forms and at interviews (box VI.1.1);

Sample advert V1.1.7 (Voluntary Organisation)

Advice and Information Officer (Carers)

To provide advice and information to carers

Requirements: in-depth uptodate knowledge of social security benefits ands an understanding of the range of issues facing carers; good communication, organisational and IT skills

---

- Keep your CV in order and up-date it regularly;
- Ensure that you tailor personal statements and covering letters to specific posts;
- Network: talk to people working in areas that appeal to you, use your workplace and other contacts.

Keep your referees informed

Almost all employers seek references and this often requires considerable extra support from your tutors. The type of information requested commonly includes opinion on applicants' attitudes and character, their ability to fulfil the person specification, and information on reliability and commitment. Your tutors will expect you to ask permission to use them in this process and will be better placed to support you if they are kept informed of your applications and progress.

Postgraduate Study and Further Training Opportunities

In considering your career options you might also need to explore the possibilities of further study. It may be that you wish to enrich your understanding of social policy and contribute to its development by undertaking your own research or studying abroad. Alternatively your chosen career may demand that you develop more specific knowledge or skills or you may feel that you need to enhance your employability by gaining an additional qualification. As with career planning, it is therefore vital to research the costs and benefits as well as the range of options available before committing yourself. Though the returns are often high, postgraduate study is an expensive process. State funding is limited. Most students find it necessary to fund themselves. In consequence over half study part-time. Nevertheless the available evidence suggests that many social policy graduates find this a worthwhile venture and one which enables them to continue to capitalize on their subject knowledge and skills whatever form of postgraduate training they follow.

Broadly speaking this can be divided into three alternatives:

- *Vocational courses* leading to professional qualifications;
- *Taught courses* leading to: a postgraduate certificate (PG Cert.), postgraduate diploma (PG Dip.), or masters degree (MSc, MA, MBA, MPA);
- *Research courses* leading to an MPhil or PhD.

A professional qualification is compulsory in many of the areas (such as social work, teaching, the law) which social policy graduates traditionally entered. But it is also increasingly a prerequisite for moving from 'starter' to 'second step' posts in many fields. Career progression in human resource managment (HRM) and marketing, for instance, is contingent on successfully completing a course recognized by the relevant professional bodies. In other areas too you may find it worthwhile extending your subject knowledge through a vocationally oriented postgraduate course. These range from specialist programmes equipping you for particular areas of employment such as housing or health-promotion or specific organizational settings such as the voluntary sector, through to broader-based courses in management. Many institutions

Sample advert VI.1.8 (Local Authority)

Assistant Policy Research Officer

To support the development and evaluation of corporate strategies and policies and partnership working

Requirements: thorough understanding of national and local policy context, strong analytical and research skills, good communicator, research or relevant experience desirable.

---

run programmes that offer both professional accreditation and a masters degree, and, increasingly, for those with managerial work experience an MBA or MPA (Masters of Business/Public Administration) geared either to specific services (such as the NHS or local government) or more general senior management posts.

Many graduates, however, prefer the flexibility afforded by less overly vocational courses. Here too there is an ever-expanding range of programmes, enabling you to take your study of social policy further or move into cognate areas such as evaluative research or urban regeneration. Many taught programmes are offered on a credit-accumulation basis and can be studied in a variety of modes, institutionally, work and web-based. They usually have to be completed within a set time, normally between one and two years. Postgraduate study by research demands a more extensive time commitment, particularly for a PhD, which usually requires three to four years' full-time study (more than five on a part-time basis). It involves the submission of a thesis based on a major piece of independent research advancing current knowledge. Many students register for an MPhil initially, transferring to a PhD after their first year if their progress is deemed satisfactory. An MPhil is similar to a PhD, but shorter in terms of time-scale and word

length with less emphasis placed on the originality of the research undertaken. Both require advanced methodological skills, gained through completing a postgraduate course in research methods during the first year of study.

Determining where to study

As with other career decisions, determining where to study hinges on a range of factors. Some prefer the familiarity of the institution where they took their first degree; others seek to broaden their experience. For research degrees the potential supervisor is the prime determinant, for taught and vocational programmes it is the content. Funding too is a major consideration and one that often necessitates part-time study close to home. Whatever your interests you will find it helpful to adopt the same strategies as you would apply to job searching, clarifying your motivation and suitability for further study, particularly on a part-time basis, and the provision which most 'matches' your needs.

Your careers service will again hold a range of publications and be able to advise you on the processes involved. In addition to providers' prospectuses, postgraduate courses are regularly advertised in the quality press (particularly the *Guardian*, *Independent* and *Times Higher Education Supplement)*. A wealth of information is also readily available on the net and in guides such as *WHAT?* You should also consult your tutors who are well-placed to advise you of the options available and the institutions or potential supervisors most appropriate for your areas of interest.

The application process

Unlike undergraduate study there is no central application or clearing system for most forms of postgraduate study. Instead you have to apply directly to each provider (the exceptions include teaching and social work training). Again starting early in your final year if you want to progress straight into

Sample advert VI.1.9 (Voluntary Organisation)

Funding Adviser

To be responsible for researching and providing information, advice and practical support in seeking appropriate funding sources for voluntary and community groups and supporting them in making bids

Requirements: A policy-related degree, sound knowledge of the voluntary and community sectors, strong research, communication and networking and organisational skills.

---

postgraduate studies is essential. Admissions tutors for vocational and taught masters courses will want to assure themselves (through the application form and subsequent interview) that you have not only an appropriate background, but the ability and commitment to undertake more advanced study. For an MPhil or PhD selection hinges on the quality of the research proposal which forms the core of the application process. This may be open-ended or it may involve you applying to undertake research in a pre-designated area. Either way, as with other postgraduate applications, it is vital to seek your tutors' advice in designing this and ensuring in advance that they are willing to provide references.

Sources of funding

Though various forms of sponsorship and support are available, they tend to be highly competitive and geared to particular forms of training. Most postgraduates rely fully or in part on their own sources. Nevertheless it is worth considering the options available and bidding for one or a mix of them. At the time of writing these fell into five main groups:

1. *Public funding* through Research Council Awards (primarily for M Phil and PhD studies – applications for which should be made through the Department where you intend to study) and traineeships (for teaching, social work).

2. *Institutional funding.* This comprises bursaries, scholarships, studentships, teaching and research assistantships (again bid for directly). Most social policy research grants are awarded by the ESRC (www.esrc.ac.uk) whose studentships are confined to those studying for research degrees in 'outlets' approved in the 2001 Research Assessment Exercise. Such studentships are available either on a three year basis for those who have completed an approved postgraduate social research course or four years (called One plus 3) for those who have not, with the first year being devoted to completing such a programme successfully. To be considered you will need a good upper-second and often a first-class honours degree as well as a viable research proposal. To widen opportunities for postgraduate study many higher education institutions (HEIs) also offer graduate teaching or research assistantships whereby postgraduates gain free tuition and can partly fund their studies through undergraduate teaching or working on specified projects. Competition for these, as for universities' own scholarship schemes and PhD study generally, is intense, but not frighteningly so and the demand for well-qualified researchers means that this form of postgraduate study is worth exploring.

3. *Employment-based support.* Many, particularly large employers, provide considerable support for staff development and training. The most wide-ranging but most competitive form of support is provided through *Graduate Traineeships,* aimed at those with man-

agement potential. These offer a package of benefits, including a well-paid post with prospects for fast progression, in-house training often linked to postgraduate or professional courses, and assistance with paying off undergraduate loans. Such schemes are now offered by statutory as well as private sector organizations and include several initiatives to recruit graduates from traditionally disadvantaged groups or with special needs. Though traineeship schemes are inevitably limited, many employers also provide other forms of support, contributing to the cost of fees, books or other costs and/or offering paid study leave (elements of remuneration packages worth bearing in mind in job searching).

4. *Loans.* Career Development Loans are sponsored by the government and available from certain banks, covering fees for full-time courses, living expenses and other costs. Professional Study Loans are offered by many high street banks, usually for specified professional courses.

5. *Assistance from charities,* of varying amounts and based on varying criteria.

Negotiating these options is a time-consuming process but is eased by making full use of the two key directories (*Prospects Postgraduate Funding Guide* and *The Grants Register,* Waterlows Specialist Information Publishing). Reports from HEIs suggest that social policy graduates are particularly well-placed to apply for both private and public service schemes. But the general picture, as for all graduates, is one in which most are self-funding. Nevertheless they report favourably on the experience and its employment outcomes.

Studying, Working and Volunteering Abroad

Though the discussion here has focused on opportunities in the UK, there is a growing trend for social policy gradu-

ates, like others, either on graduating or later to seek employment or study abroad. In terms of the latter social policy in many countries is commonly taught within broad-based social or political science departments (see chapter I.3). These offer numerous opportunities for postgraduate study, but are subject to varied application processes and stiff competition for funds. The options, including the availability of programmes taught in English, are best explored through specialist guides and directories (*Commonwealth University Yearbook, Hobsons' Study Europe* and *Peterson's Graduate Programs* – on the USA). In terms of employment, linguistic skills permitting, the range of subject-related and general options is, if anything, even wider than in the UK, as is the scope for volunteering. Many positions will, however, demand professional qualifications and these again should be tracked through the specialist literature.

Conclusions

The evidence suggests prospects for social policy graduates are healthy. Whether you want to become a journalist, enter the legal or teaching professions, be a welfare or financial services manager, join the police or community safety service, become a civil servant or work in local government, a social or political researcher, a Citizens Advice Bureau worker or a human resources manager, an understanding of how welfare institutions operate to meet human need is vital. A knowledge of policy processes, the way in which policies are formulated and implemented, who they impact on and why and how organizations work and interact is equally essential in many occupations. This is particularly the case if you seek to promote change, as is an appreciation of the problems that may be experienced by individuals and groups and the effects of exclusion, poverty, disability, ethnicity, gender and social class.

It is this subject knowledge and the skills

it embodies which give social policy graduates an 'edge' when applying for employment. Though success is also contingent on
obtaining a good degree and learning how
to develop and present oneself, it should
not be measured solely in economistic
terms: '. . . .Social Policy skills are often

highly transferable and valued by many
potential employers. They also provide a
foundation for continuing and lifelong
learning and for active engagement as citizens in the wider life of a society' (*Social
Policy and Administration Benchmark Statement:* www.qaaa.ac.uk).

Guide to further reading

Trends in the graduate labour market are best tracked through the *Annual Graduate Reviews* produced by the IES, the surveys of AGCAS, the Higher Education Careers Serv-
ices Unit (2002), the IDS' annual studies on *Pay and Progression for Graduates* and the
publications of organizations such as Austin Knight Research (AKR, 1999) and the CIPD.
Useful longer-term analyses can be found in P. Elias, A. McKnight, K. Pilcher and C.
Simm *Moving On: Graduate Careers Three Years after Graduation* (London: DfEE, 2000); and
K. Purcell, J. Pitcher and C. Simm *Working Out? Graduates Early Experience of the Labour
Market* (London: DfEE, 1999).

Information and advice on employment and postgraduate opportunities can be accessed
through a multiplicity of sources, the best starting points being: the *Prospects Series* published by the CSU, www.prospects.ac.uk (which also lists AGCAS publications);
www.hobsons.com/career/shtml; www.doctorjob.com; www.jobsearch.co.uk;
www.jobworld.co.uk; www.sosig.ac.uk; Association of Commonwealth Universities
www.acu.ac.uk; *Hobsons Guide to International Programmes in Europe* sites.hobsons.com/
studyeurope. These will often provide links to or advice on more specific, specialist sources
such as *Opportunity* (a careers journal aimed at Black and Asian students) and
jobability.com (an online recruitment service for disabled people).

Appendix: The Social Policy Association (SPA)

The SPA is the professional association for academics, researchers and students in social policy and administration. As an academic association in the social science field, it is a member of the Association of Learned Societies in the Social Sciences (ALSISS), and it has close collaborative links with other professional associations in cognate fields, such as the British Sociological Association (BSA) and the Political Studies Association (PSA).

The SPA is a membership organization and membership is open to all students, teachers and others working in the social policy field. All members pay an annual fee and in return receive a range of membership services including:

- a regular and popular newsletter;
- free subscription to the leading social policy journals, the *Journal of Social Policy* and *Social Policy and Society*;
- a small grants scheme to support the setting up of seminars and conferences for members;
- subgroups for postgraduate students, women members and comparative policy analysis;
- an annual conference held in July each year at an academic institution in the UK;

The cost of membership varies with income across a number of broad bands, and membership is also open to corporate bodies such as research institutes. The majority of members of the SPA live and work in the United Kingdom, but the Association also has active members all over the world, including in particular Europe, North America, the Far East and Australia. The Association is also developing formal links with partner organizations in other European countries in order to develop further comparative work within the discipline.

The Association is managed by an Executive Committee comprised of members elected at the Annual Conference, with members serving on the committee for periods of three years at a time. In addition there are officers – a Chair, Secretary and Treasurer – also elected and serving on a three-year basis. Students of social policy are encouraged to join the Association and to contact staff members in their departments, schools or faculties. The SPA can be contacted through its web page www.social-policy.com

Index